The Evolution of
Modern Humans
in Africa

African Archaeology Series

Series Editor
Joseph O. Vogel

The **African Archaeology Series** is a series of volumes intended to present comprehensive and up-to-date summaries of current research on the African cultural past. The authors, who range from palaeoanthropologists to historical archaeologists, work in Africa and detail the results of their ongoing research interests. Though the essential subject matter of each volume is drawn from archaeology, they are equally dependent upon investigation of the historical and anthropological records as well. The authors understand the diversity and depth of African culture and history, and endeavor to explore the many sources of the African experience and the place of the African past and lifeways in the broader world. At the same time, the series permits Africanist scholars the opportunity to transform their field results into more general syntheses, giving context and meaning to a bare bones archaeological record, exploring and utilizing new techniques for explaining, as well as comprehending, the past.

Books in the Series:

Chapurukha M. Kusimba, *The Rise and Fall of Swahili States* (1999)

Michael Bisson, S. Terry Childs, Philip de Barros, Augustin F. C. Holl, *Ancient African Metallurgy: The Socio-Cultural Context* (2000)

Innocent Pikirayi, *The Zimbabwe Culture: Origins and Decline of Southern Zambezian States* (2001)

Sibel Barut Kusimba, *African Foragers: Environment, Technology, Interactions* (2002)

Augustin F. C. Holl, *Saharan Rock Art: Archaeology of Tassilian Pastoralist Iconography* (2004)

J. D. Lewis-Williams, D. G. Pearce, *San Spirituality: Roots, Expression, and Social Consequences* (2004)

Peter Mitchell, *African Connections: Archaeological Perspectives on Africa and the Wider World* (2005)

Andrew B. Smith, *African Herders: Emergence of Pastoral Traditions* (2005)

Colleen E. Kriger, *Cloth in West African History* (2006)

Roger Blench, *Archaeology, Language, and the African Past* (2006)

Peter R. Schmidt, *Historical Archaeology in Africa: Representation, Social Memory, and Oral Traditions* (2006)

Pamela R. Willoughby, *The Evolution of Modern Humans in Africa: A Comprehensive Guide* (2007)

Submission Guidelines:
Prospective authors of single or co-authored books and editors of anthologies should submit a letter of introduction, the manuscript, or a four to ten page proposal, a book outline, and a curriculum vitae. Please send your book manuscript or proposal packet to:

African Archaeology Series
AltaMira Press, 4501 Forbes Boulevard, Suite 200, Lanham, MD 20706 USA

The Evolution of Modern Humans in Africa

A Comprehensive Guide

PAMELA R. WILLOUGHBY

ALTAMIRA
PRESS

A Division of
ROWMAN & LITTLEFIELD PUBLISHERS, INC.
Lanham • New York • Toronto • Plymouth, UK

AltaMira Press
A Division of Rowman & Littlefield Publishers, Inc.
A wholly owned subsidiary of The Rowman & Littlefield Publishing Group, Inc.
4501 Forbes Boulevard, Suite 200
Lanham, MD 20706
www.altamirapress.com

Estover Road, Plymouth PL6 7PY, United Kingdom

British Library Cataloguing in Publication Information Available

Library of Congress Cataloging-in-Publication Data

Willoughby, Pamela R.
The evolution of modern humans in Africa : a comprehensive guide / Pamela R. Willoughby.
    p. cm. — (The African archaeology series)
Includes bibliographical references and index.

ISBN-13: 978-0-7591-0118-0 (cloth : alk. paper)
ISBN-10: 0-7591-0118-3 (cloth : alk. paper)
ISBN-13: 978-0-7591-0119-7 (pbk. : alk. paper)
ISBN-10: 0-7591-0119-1 (pbk. : alk. paper)

1. Human evolution—Africa. 2. Human evolution—Tanzania. 3. Paleolithic period—Africa. 4. Paleolithic period—Tanzania. 5. Fossil hominids—Africa. 6. Fossil hominids—Tanzania. 7. Africa—Antiquities. 8. Tanzania—Antiquities. I. Title.

GN281.W55 2007
599.93'8096—dc22
                        2006024336

Printed in the United States of America

∞ ™ The paper used in this publication meets the minimum requirements of American National Standard for Information Sciences—Permanence of Paper for Printed Library Materials, ANSI/NISO Z39.48-1992.

The question of questions for mankind—the problem which underlies all others, and is more deeply interesting than any other—is the ascertainment of the place which Man occupies in nature and of his relations to the universe of things.

T. H. Huxley 1959:71 (1863)

Contents

Figures, Maps, and Tables

MAPS

TABLES

Foreword

The investigations of early artifact-strewn and other hominid sites in the Omo Valley of southern Ethiopia that unearthed collections of crude utilized flakes shaped on small quartz nodules stimulated the debate among archaeologists, and others, over the beginnings of humankind's career and events leading to the physical, cultural, and psychological evolution as well as the forerunners of later forms of humanity. Discoveries elsewhere in eastern Africa, as well, attested to the fact that someone was making tools to prescribed cultural formats at least a million and a half years ago. At the same time, the bones of different animals garnered from a variety of environments near these sites suggest that the toolmakers consistently ventured far and wide to bring meat and other provisions home to their bases. The refuse littering the surfaces of these living sites even suggests that some were used intermittently, or that they were occupied for only part of the year. These indications suggest repetitive kinds of activity from which we can posit a basic kind of transhumance foraging, scheduling an annual round of activities, in order to exploit seasonally available foods. The geographical distribution of similar kinds of tools and subsistence strategies suggests that the earliest humans participated in interaction spheres, sharing information with others of their kind. That is, it seems that they communicated intelligence relating to the cycles of nature, the opportunities to exploit them, and the technical means of enhancing productivity by improved technology. Some millions of years ago, humanity invented culture to successfully fit it into desirable eastern African landscapes, where humans prospered and multiplied. In this book, Pamela Willoughby describes a later, equally critical, episode of human endeavor. A time associated with the coming of a newer, more modern kind of humanity equipped with even more adept cultures.

Some years ago, the archaeologist V. Gordon Childe posited a theory of culture-history predicated upon climactic "revolutionary" transformations. Now we can suggest a different scenario postulating the archaeological history of humanity as, generally, a more cautious affair. That it is a process of accumulating small accretions to the cultural repertoire, none in themselves posing a serious challenge to an existent status quo, but each, nonetheless, capable of giving birth, eventually, to major changes in orientation. This process does not necessarily encompass the dramatic adoption of new technologies or other radical shifts in emphasis that some models of culture change often assume. Nevertheless, perceptible evolutionary shifts in orientation do seem to occur from time to time. From our point of view, the past 200,000 years contained such an episode. Whether we subscribe to a dynamic view of culture-history or one of more cumulative kinds of change, we will agree that in this book Dr. Willoughby addresses one of the more consequential episodes in humanity's résumé; one replete with portents, novel opportunities, more refined technologies, and full-fledged behaviors—the African Middle Stone.

It was an episode we identify with the kinds of human that replaced earlier physical types and generalized industries, while enhancing the generalized format of foraging behavior devised at the dawn of time. Dr. Willoughby offers us the picture of a world of increasingly effective hunter-gatherers, maturing a range of acquired social behaviors, while embracing innovative manufacturing techniques and implements. However, for all its novelty, it is not a "revolutionary" transformation. These efforts in the late Pleistocene were preceded by a long period of human adaptation and experimentation encompassing the cultural achievements of earlier types of *Homo* in East Africa.

The time described by Dr. Willoughby was the culmination of a long evolutionary process. However, the earlier episode was more than a prelude to modern enterprises and the earliest humans were more than our crude forebears. Their first living sites scattered throughout eastern Africa represent more than transient groups of rudimentary foragers and toolmakers. Our cultural ancestors emerged out of the range of clever, facile and upright walking hominids in eastern Africa, establishing social groupings that affected the varied behaviors ancestral to those of more modern humans. That is, they behaved in ways that we can comprehend as human; behaviors culturally determined rather than genetically proscribed. They possessed more than a capability to manufacture, use, and reproduce tools and an ability to make and control fire. They possessed other learned traits as well; such as co-operative well-versed social interaction, scheduled subsistence routines touring familiar domains, and the gathering and communication of vital information, along with other patterned cultural programs. These behaviors, though honed to a fine edge by later foragers, were clearly part of the repertoire of our oldest relatives alive in eastern Africa more than a million and a half years ago.

From the earliest time, a talent for organizing into societies characterized humans, shaping recurrent daily activities within closely knit cohorts, collaborating with similarly organized neighbors, sharing advantageous technological and environmental information. At this time, humans devised an adaptable transhumant lifeway, reaping a succession of natural harvests as part of their annual round. This acquired way of life served them well, bringing forth our earliest and most long-lived social and economic organization, the family band. Eventually it would adjust to the diverse environments of the Earth. This social universe perpetuated the notion of learning passed from generation to generation, honing faculties derived from experience and human ingenuity, introducing novelty from time to time. It even circumscribed a worldview beyond tools and subsistence, though we are not yet privy to how they viewed themselves within their universe.

We can only speculate how the very earliest societies organized themselves. We can only suggest they successfully coordinated activities within and among the different neighboring bands; that their social behaviors were ones we would recognize. Though the principles reinforcing their conduct as interactive communities may now be beyond our ability to fully understand, it is obvious that long ago the use of intelligence to an evolutionary advantage separated flourishing bands of hominids from their less attentive cousins. Consequently, human evolution became a tale of the attractiveness of exploring new cultural skills. Over time, humans perfected an extensive repertoire of extra-somatic behaviors crafted from refined industrial abilities, amassed knowledge, social adroitness, and increasingly, the ability to communicate technical as well as more abstract concepts.

Soon, bands of *Homo erectus*, using an economical stone-working technique based on the reduction of cores into a number of pre-formed blanks, dominated African landscapes for nearly half a million years, moving humanity out of Africa, in large numbers, for the first time. This trend to flake-based tools, maximizing the quantity of edge available from a given piece of stone, offered these transhumant foragers the capability of easily moving from place to place bearing lightweight composite tools and replacement materials. Though *Homo erectus* was, apparently, successful, their days were numbered by the increasingly modern populations who extended their own numbers and range, settling onto a variety of environments, adapting, culturally, to a diversity of economic opportunities. As groups of more modern *sapiens* types became more adept at exploiting specific segments of the environmental mosaic, they devised specialized tool inventories crafted to meet unique needs. As described here by Dr. Willoughby, these adaptations of the basic forager format gave impetus to a growing facility to exploit territorially specific economic opportunities. Consequently, we detect the rise of a kind of "ethnicity" as local interaction spheres gave rise to regionally specific cultures, the varied cultures of the African Middle Stone Age. The earliest stages of humanity's deployment were complete.

Given the early importance of Africa in the many stages of human biological and cultural evolution, it is fitting that we review the evidence associated with the emergence of our kind there. It is particularly worthwhile to review what is often referred to as the African Middle Stone Age, since it is more usual to discuss equivalent data from better-known regions in Europe and the Middle East, or to limit description to the African skeletal evidence. However, the discussion is more acutely textured than one of relating, solely, the categorical identity of human remains or the appearance of novel tool types and stone-working methods. Dr. Willoughby's focus encompasses the development of a distinctive physical type and regionally specific cultural detritus, as well as the refining of a range of uniquely human behaviors associated with the early forms of *Homo sapiens*. She clarifies this interlude of physical development, as well as cultural diversity, with great authority. Due to its overall importance, as well as to evaluating the broad picture of the origins of the forager lifeway in Africa, we are pleased to offer this thorough examination of the origins of modern humanity.

Joseph O. Vogel

Preface

In 1987, three geneticists, Rebecca Cann, Mark Stoneking, and the late Allan Wilson, published a revolutionary paper. Using mitochondrial DNA taken from living people from different parts of the world, they argued that all of us were descended from a population, or possibly even a single woman, who lived in Africa over 100,000 years ago (Cann et al. 1987). Within a year, it was suggested that these people were actually anatomically modern *Homo sapiens* like us today, and African prehistory was revolutionized. Until then, our concepts of modern human origins were totally based on archaeological and fossil material from Western Europe. Here, an archaic population with one kind of archaeology, the Neanderthals of the Middle Palaeolithic, appeared to be replaced by a new population or species between 40,000 and 30,000 years ago. These newcomers, referred to as Cro-Magnons, had a much more elaborate material culture, which is assigned to one or more industries of the Upper Palaeolithic. It included some of the earliest organic (bone, antler, and ivory) tools, jewelry, portable art, more elaborate burials, and a number of other significant cultural innovations. The appearance of these items with the first people who were skeletally similar to us became the basis for the idea of an Upper Palaeolithic creative revolution that separated our direct ancestors from all other early human species.

Since the first mitochondrial DNA paper, new chronometric dating techniques and more detailed genetic studies of living people all point to a pre–Upper Palaeolithic appearance of anatomically modern *Homo sapiens* in Africa.

There is no question that Africans who lived at the same time as the European Neanderthals were anatomically (or skeletally) modern. But their archaeological sites seemed remarkably similar to those of their European cousins, quite different from those of their Cro-Magnon descendants. So it was suggested that they must have undergone some marked behavioral transition that made this new technology and adaptation possible, if not inevitable. It might also explain the rapid dispersal of people out of the continent after 50,000 years ago, and their ultimate success in populating the globe. It did offer an explanation of why these people did not migrate out of Africa earlier, but it leaves a number of new problems. Many researchers feel that, since these early Africans had a Middle Palaeolithic adaptation, they had to be more Neanderthal-like in their behavior. Obviously, this makes both groups significantly different from us. But rather than proposing an earlier appearance of modern humans, Middle Palaeolithic people in both Africa and Europe have been denied their humanity, and are presented as people without true culture. Somehow the Africans prevailed, and became the ancestors of all of us today. This book offers a reassessment of the ideas about the earliest modern humans, and shows that models created for Europe do not always work elsewhere.

ACKNOWLEDGMENTS

I would first of all like to thank Joseph O. Vogel, my editor, for his mentorship and patience. Rosalie Robertson, Jehanne Schweitzer, Sarah Walker, and the production staff of AltaMira Press have also been of great assistance, as was Mitch Allen, the founder of AltaMira, who encouraged me to write this book. Moira Calder prepared the index and Ellen Henderson served as copy editor. I would also like to thank Dr. David Lubell, my MA supervisor at the University of Alberta, who introduced me to African archaeology. Dr. James Sackett, my PhD supervisor at UCLA, taught me much about Palaeolithic archaeology, the history of archaeological thought, and about style, ethnicity, and the Upper Palaeolithic revolution. When I chose to work on Early Stone Age material from Africa rather than on the material culture of early modern people in Western Europe, he made it possible. This was done in collaboration with the late Dr. Glynn Isaac of the University of California at Berkeley. It is quite ironic that, in my later focus on the Middle Stone Age in East Africa, I have returned to the questions of modern human origins that James Sackett drilled into my head, albeit from a Western European perspective.

As is the case for many other North Americans who became specialists on the Africa Stone Age, I also owe a special debt to the late professor John Desmond Clark of the University of California at Berkeley. Desmond Clark pioneered the study of Upper Pleistocene Africa, and concluded decades ago that the continent had a major role in our recent origins. He lived to see his ideas confirmed by molecular and archaeological research he could only have dreamed about. Among other things, he assisted me in the development of my field project on the Upper Pleistocene and Holocene archaeological record of Mbeya and Iringa regions in southern Tanzania. For permission to conduct this field research, I would like to thank the Department of Antiquities, Ministry of Natural Resources and Tourism, Government of Tanzania, as well as COSTECH, the Tanzania Commission on Science and Technology.

I would like to thank the community of scholars working on the Upper Pleistocene archaeology of Africa whose research is discussed in this book. They were, and continue to be, pioneers in the collection of the empirical data now of such critical importance for evaluating the questions associated with the emergence of modern humans. Additionally, some of the South African site photographs in chapter 10 are the result of an unforgettable 1998 archaeological tour of the Cape region led by Professor Hilary Deacon of Stellenbosch University.

The genetic evidence for modern human origins continues to change the research focus of prehistorians and palaeontologists. For an introduction to this data, I would like to thank Professor Luca Cavalli-Sforza and other organizers of the four Cold Spring Harbor conferences on human evolution held between 1997 and 2002. They, and other speakers, were quite tolerant of an archaeologist trying to understand the implications of this emerging, but critical, science.

I would also like to thank my parents, Stuart and Iola Willoughby, who supported me when I decided that Palaeolithic archaeology was a possible career. Finally, I would like to thank my numerous students who have borne with me while this book was developed. In various courses and discussions, they helped me hone the ideas which are presented here.

A work that describes the research of many people from different fields needs to use many different sources. A number of the figures and maps reproduced here are taken from previously published sources. I would like to thank the following people and institutions for permission to reprint these illustra-

tions. Figure 2.2, which illustrates the origins of the multiregional theory, is
reprinted with permission of the University of California Press. Figure 2.3,
the African pluvial sequence, comes from Basil Cooke's (1957) paper in the
Proceedings of the Third Pan-African Congress of Prehistory, which was held in
Livingstone, Zambia in 1955. This is reprinted with permission from the Livingstone Museum. Random House in the United Kingdom is now the owner
of the original publisher, Chatto and Windus. According to their records, they
assigned all rights back to the Livingstone Museum in 1971 (Catherine Trip-
pett, personal communication).

Figure 3.2, the oxygen isotope sequence for the last 300,000 years, is used
with the permission of the Royal Society and Dr. Christopher Stringer. Figure
6.1, a mitochondrial DNA molecule, and figure 6.5, a human Y chromosome,
are both used with permission of John Wiley and Sons, Inc. Figure 6.2, Cann,
Stoneking, and Wilson's famous mitochondrial DNA chart, is reprinted with
permission of Dr. Rebecca Cann, Dr. Mark Stoneking, and the Nature Publishing Group. Figure 6.3, great ape and human mitochondrial DNA diversity,
is used by permission of the *Proceedings of the National Academy of Sciences* as
well as Dr. Pascal Gagneux. Figure 6.4, illustrating Neanderthal mitochondrial
DNA genealogy, is reprinted with permission of Dr. Svante Pääbo and the
Nature Publishing Group. Figure 8.1, Nubian 1 and 2 production methods, as
well as map 3.2, Africa showing features of general circulation and rain belts
in January and July, are both reprinted with permission of Elsevier. Figures
8.2, 8.3, and 8.4, photographs of Dakhleh Oasis and its archaeological contents, are published with permission of the original researcher, Dr. Maxine
R. Kleindienst. Figure 8.5, the north face of the Haua Fteah stratigraphic
sequence, and figure 8.6, Libyan Pre-Aurignacian artifacts from Haua Fteah,
are both published with permission of Cambridge University Press. Figure 8.7,
Levallois and Aterian artifacts from northwest Africa, is used with permission
of *Sahara* and Dr. André Débénath. Figure 10.4, flake-blades from the MSA
1 levels of Klasies River, and figure 10.5, crescents from the Howieson's Poort
levels at the same site, are used with permission of the University of Chicago
Press.

Map 3.1, contemporary African vegetation zones; map 3.3, Africa during the last glacial maximum; and map 3.4, Africa in the early Holocene, are
all taken from Jonathan Adams's pioneering palaeoenvironmental website
("Review and Atlas of Paleovegetation: Preliminary land ecosystem maps of

the world since the Last Glacial Maximum," Oak Ridge National Laboratory, Tennessee (http://www.esd.ornl.gov/projects/qen/adams1.html). They are reprinted with the permission of Dr. Jonathan Adams. Maps 8.1, 8.2, 9.1, 9.2, and 10.1 were prepared using the free Online Map Creation website developed by Martin Weinelt. It is available at http://www.aquarius.geomar.de/omc/. Finally, quotations from A. J. H. Goodwin and C. Van Riet Lowe's seminal 1929 publication, "The Stone Age Cultures of South Africa" (*Annals of the South African Museum* 27), are included with the permission of the Iziko Museums of Cape Town, South Africa. I am deeply grateful to all these researchers and institutions for their assistance.

1

Modern Human Origins: A People without History

Admittedly, they [Middle Stone Age Africans] *had much more than an elementary grasp of stone flaking; they often collected naturally occurring iron and manganese compounds which they could have used as pigments; they apparently built fires at will; they buried their dead, at least on occasion; and they routinely acquired large mammals as food. In all these respects and perhaps others, they may have been relatively advanced over earlier archaic people. However, in common with earlier people and with their Neandertal contemporaries, they manufactured a relatively small range of recognizable stone artifact types; their artifact assemblages varied remarkably little through time and space (in spite of notable environmental variation); they obtained stone raw materials overwhelmingly from local (versus far distant) sources (suggesting small home ranges or very simple social networks); they rarely if ever utilized bone, ivory or shell to produce formal artifacts; they left little or no evidence for structures or for any other formal modification of their campsites; they were relatively ineffectual hunter-gatherers, who lacked, for example, the ability to fish; their populations were apparently very sparse, even by historic hunter-gatherer standards; and they left no indisputable evidence for art or decoration.* (Klein 1995:181–182)

There was no "human revolution" in Africa. Rather . . . novel features accrued stepwise. Distinct elements of the social, economic, and subsistence bases changed at different rates and appeared at different times and places. We describe evidence from the African MSA to support the contention that both human anatomy and human behavior were intermittently transformed from an archaic to a more modern pattern over a period of more than 200,000 years. (McBrearty and Brooks 2000:458)

Palaeoanthropology, the inter- and multi-disciplinary study of human origins and evolution, has a history of vocal debate centered on contested ideas about our past. Often this is played out in the public sphere. New fossil discoveries are announced in press conferences and presented as if they totally change our understanding of our own remote history. The pace of such finds has increased in recent years, but their meaning is still subject to interpretation. At one time or another, various genera and species of fossil humans have been proposed as the ultimate ancestor, just to be supplanted by others (Lewin 1987; Willoughby 2005). This is nothing new. There is a long history of speculation about human origins; it has even been suggested (Stoczkowski 2002) that key ideas can be traced back to classical times (contrast with Corbey 2005; Corbey and Roebroeks 2001a, 2001b). However, as a scientific discipline, the study of human evolution is in a class by itself. It sometime seems that no one lets the facts get in the way of a good theory, and there are many more theories than facts to support them. In a revealing article that preceded the overthrow of the general consensus about Miocene ape and early human evolution, David Pilbeam (1980:262) suggested that many theories were "fossil proof," so could not be tested at all. In reality, fossil remains, their morphology, and their place in time and space are the only objective facts; everything else is someone's opinion. In order to increase the data base, one either has to find a new fossil specimen, or offer a different interpretation. Until recently, this vocal debate was restricted to the question of the origins of the earliest humans. But since the late 1980s, the beginnings and early history of our own species, *Homo sapiens*, has become a focus of rapidly expanding attention. Somewhat predictably, conclusions drawn from new finds and reinterpretations have also created heated arguments.

Over the last few years, a vast number of fossil human species and genera have been proposed, separated from our closest living relatives the African apes at the Linnaean level of Family Hominidae or only at the Tribe Hominini. In common language, they become "hominids" or "hominins." This book will use the latter, tribal designation, to refer to fossil (and modern) humans, as opposed to the great apes and their fossil ancestors (Marks 2002). We are in an era of splitting fossil forms into more and more categories, seemingly aided and abetted by cladistics or phylogenetic systematics (Hennig 1966). Cladistics is a system of classification that only requires a single new shared derived character or synapomorphy to identify a new clade or group of related organisms with a common descent. Individual taxa or morphological types are organized into nesting clades or branches in order of appearance of these synapomorphies. The resulting cladogram provides an evolutionary picture of relationships between these forms.

Whatever is responsible for the explosion in names, there are now at least seven genera (*Sahelanthropus, Orrorin, Ardipithecus, Kenyanthropus, Australopithecus, Paranthropus,* and *Homo*) and over twenty human species (Brunet 2001; Brunet et al. 1995, 1996, 2002, 2005; Haile-Selassie 2001; Johanson and White 1979; Johanson et al. 1978; M. Leakey et al. 1995, 2001; Pickford and Senut 2001; Senut et al. 2001; White et al. 1993; WoldeGabriel et al. 2001; Zollikofer et al. 2005). Most of the newest discoveries date to the earliest periods of our existence in Africa, the Pliocene (from 5 to 1.8 million years ago) or even the late Miocene (from 8 to 5 million years ago). This is the theoretical limit for early hominins using molecular estimates of how far back in time we shared a common ancestor with African apes (Sarich and Wilson 1967; Ruvolo 1997). By the 1960s, the paramount role of Africa in early human origins had also been demonstrated by the application of new chronometric or "time measure" dating methods, such as potassium-argon and fission track (Leakey et al. 1961). However, it was assumed that once hominins dispersed out of Africa, Western Europe became the focus for subsequent biological and cultural innovation and change. It was here that fossil hominins had first been discovered, and where archaeological or cultural sequences were initially established. It would take almost three more decades before this framework would begin to be dismantled.

THE ORIGIN OF MODERN HUMANS IN AFRICA

As recently as the late 1980s, the standard model for the emergence of modern humans remained unchallenged (Bordes 1971; Smith and Spencer 1984). It was assumed that members of our own species, *Homo sapiens*, appeared simultaneously throughout Eurasia and Africa around 40,000 years ago, evolving wherever earlier hominin groups had lived. This became known as the continuity, candelabra, or multiregional model since it emphasized gradual, parallel change from a common root or stem, but with some cross-regional gene flow (Howells 1976; Thorne and Wolpoff 1981, 1992; Wolpoff 1989a, 1989b; Wolpoff et al. 2004). The development of modern skeletal anatomy at this time apparently coincided in Europe with the appearance of the Upper Palaeolithic. This archaeological period is associated with the earliest evidence of organic tool production (bone, antler, ivory), personal adornment (jewelry), art, and many other innovations in material culture and behavior (Bar-Yosef 2002; Klein 1992; Mellars 1991, 2004, 2005). Even the method of stone artifact production changes, as tools are now produced from long, parallel-sided blades removed from cylindrical or prismatic cores. All of these changes have been explained as part of a new behavioral package, a creative explosion (Pfeiffer 1982) that produced hunter-gatherer adaptations similar to those observable in the ethnographic present (Binford 1989). Since the first people who were anatomically indistinguishable from people today produced it, it seemed logical that all aspects of their material culture should be different from those of other hominins. As a result, the Upper Palaeolithic became the yardstick by which behavioral or cultural modernity was measured, a role it maintains today. However, in the late 1980s, new chronometric dating techniques (Wintle 1996), along with methods for analyzing the evolution of aspects of the human genome (Cann et al. 1987), suggested that *Homo sapiens* had a much longer history, one that was largely African. The oldest anatomically modern human fossils in North Africa are associated with Middle Palaeolithic artifacts, while their counterparts south of the Sahara made Middle Stone Age or MSA artifacts. Both relied on the production of flake tools from radial, circular, or Levallois cores rather than on Upper Palaeolithic prismatic blades. While Middle Palaeolithic/Middle Stone Age sites date back to at least 200,000 years before present, the technology they exhibit was developed in the Late Acheulian, by 500,000 years ago. There was little sign of Upper Palaeolithic innovations when the first anatomically modern Africans were living.

For the first time in the Old Stone Age or Palaeolithic, there was a disjunction between the pace of biological and cultural evolution. It was anatomically non-modern European Neanderthals and coeval modern African Middle Palaeolithic (or MSA) people who now shared a technology, and perhaps a basic cultural system. But these two populations varied significantly in physical appearance, possibly enough to represent separate species. On the other hand, there did not seem to be any behavioral revolution that produced anatomical modernity in Africa. Were these people really modern in the sense of their descendants, the European Cro-Magnons of the Upper Palaeolithic, or were they behaviorally more like Neanderthals?

Sociocultural anthropologists dealing with living societies define culture as learned behavior, values, beliefs, and attitudes shared by people as members of a society. While archaeologists deal with past societies through their material culture and refuse, they are also trying to describe and to explain the cultural system in which these items were produced, utilized, and ultimately discarded. This requires a basic assumption: individuals who share the same rules of artifact production probably belong to the same cultural system and learned to manufacture artifacts from the same teachers. Shared material culture can also have symbolic meaning, and acts as a proxy for measuring social relationships between individuals in the same social group, and between related social groups. These cultural systems are the result of symbolically based language and culture. When, how, and why did such cultural systems develop? It is generally assumed that earlier hominins lack symbolically based culture; this achievement is supposed to be restricted to Upper Palaeolithic and later populations. African Middle Palaeolithic/Middle Stone Age people are almost identical to us in their anatomy, but their material culture and social organization was different from that of their presumed descendants. They are anatomically modern, but could be behaviorally non-modern, whatever this is supposed to represent.

Over the last two to three decades, archaeologists and palaeoanthropologists have written about early modern Africans in the same way that Europeans initially wrote about non-Western people. Both are treated as distinct, as "others," outside the range of what it means to be cultured or civilized. Early European explorers were fascinated by the cultural and biological diversity of people they encountered worldwide. But there was little attempt to link non-Western history and culture with Western technology and achievements. Just as indigenous groups became people without history (Wolf 1982, 1997), early modern Africans and their Neanderthal cousins in Eurasia have become people without behavior or true culture (Willoughby 2000; Speth 2004). This book evaluates the claim that the earliest modern humans were not truly modern by examining recent archaeological, paleontological, palaeoenvironmental, and genetic evidence about the origin and dispersal of *Homo sapiens*. There is a vast literature on modern human origins, most of which has appeared in the last two decades (Aitken et al. 1993; Akazawa et al. 1998; Bräuer and Smith 1992; Clark and Willermet 1997; Crow 2002; Dibble and Mellars 1992; Gamble 1986, 1994, 1999; Kaufman 1999; Kusimba 2005; Lewin 1993;

Marean and Assefa 2005; Mellars 1990; Mellars and Stringer 1989; Nitecki and Nitecki 1994; Omoto and Tobias 1998; Orscheidt and Weniger 2001; Smith and Spencer 1984; Stringer and Gamble 1993; Stringer and McKie 1996; Trinkaus 1983, 1989; Trinkaus and Shipman 1993; Van Andel and Davies 2003; Willoughby 1994; Wolpoff and Caspari 1997). But African evidence remains surprisingly peripheral to the central debate. A couple of recent review articles address the issue by stating that African Middle Palaeolithic/Middle Stone Age people could have been behaviorally modern. There are more than occasional examples of artifacts that fit the trait list of the European Upper Palaeolithic (McBrearty and Brooks 2000; Henshilwood and Marean 2003; Wong 2005). A similar possibility has been proposed for the European Neanderthals (D'Errico 2003; D'Errico et al. 2003). Aspects of behavioral modernity could have gradually appeared over the course of the Upper Pleistocene in Africa, and were not the product of sudden change. Notwithstanding these attempts, most researchers rely on European data to assess the fundamental differences between the Middle and Upper Palaeolithic, and supplement it with conclusions drawn from the South African research of Richard Klein (1992, 1994, 1995, 2000, 2001b). Klein maintains the traditional picture, and believes that until Africans developed Upper Palaeolithic–like adaptations, they could not become modern in any way. This book was conceived as an attempt to reassess and to challenge this overly simplistic perspective.

THE PEOPLE WITHOUT HISTORY

The debate about behavioral modernity and human evolution has remarkable similarities to the ways anthropologists and others have traditionally looked at non-Western people. While it is now common to challenge the role of the researcher in preparing ethnographic accounts (Clifford and Marcus 1986), one of the first reflexive treatments of anthropology was presented by Eric Wolf. In his famous book, *Europe and the People without History*, Wolf (1997; orig. pub. 1982) discusses the study of aboriginal or indigenous people in disparate parts of the world who only enter the historical record when explorers and others from literate societies observed and recorded their behavior. He argued that these people had their own history, which could be understood through the study of oral tradition, life experience, and material culture, as well as through documents written by outsiders. In reviewing what is known about aboriginal history worldwide, Wolf addressed some fundamental questions in anthropology. What is the place of the (non-Western) people studied by anthropologists in a larger world? How are the others different from us, and how did these differences arise? How does the perception of difference influence how people are treated or studied? How did aboriginal people interact with Europeans and how were both groups transformed by this process? Wolf says that he wrote the book as an anthropologist, in order to show his colleagues that history matters. The reverse was also true; historians in turn could benefit from an anthropological perspective. He stresses that the "people without history" was not his phrase; it actually goes back to Marx and Engels in the nineteenth century (Wolf 1997:x). It was meant to be ironic:

> my intent was to challenge those who think that Europeans were the only ones who made history. I took AD 1400 as the initial dateline for the presentation precisely because I hoped to make clear that European expansion everywhere encountered human societies and cultures characterized by long and complex histories. (Wolf 1997:x)

Everyone had a history, but only some groups had it recorded for posterity. Alternately, this history was unrecognized, or at worst was ignored or dismissed as irrelevant for understanding the general human past. Sometimes it depended on cultural complexity. It was hard to ignore monumental art and architecture. But hunter-gatherers in Australia and southern Africa were treated almost as part of the fauna, as part of nature rather than as fellow humans. Wolf also stressed the need for inter-disciplinary studies. For historians, anthropology provided a way to write pre-colonial history. This is why Iron Age archaeology became so popular in the 1950s in sub-Saharan Africa when newly independent countries wanted their own history (Shepherd 2003; Trigger 1984). In turn, for anthropologists, it was necessary to reveal how their methods and conclusions had a history. In this way, he was presenting a postmodern perspective well before postmodernism was developed as a specific framework or methodology.

As Wolf illustrated, anthropology as a discipline has its origins in the expansion of Europe. It became the way to record and to evaluate information about the numerous human groups and cultures found throughout the globe, both in the present and in the past (Gamble 1994). By the nineteenth century, many accounts of the lifeways and habits of disparate groups existed, painstakingly recorded by explorers, traders, and missionaries, among others.

These accounts covered all aspects of behavior, both biological and cultural. People varied greatly in physical appearance, attitudes, beliefs, lifeways, and cultural systems. Some rational way was needed to catalog, to describe, and then to explain this variation. Just as plants and animals were being sorted and classified, human societies could be studied scientifically. This information became the raw material for an integrated study of all people, what we now know as anthropology. The recognition of modern human biological and cultural variation was a product of the eighteenth century, the great age of exploration and natural philosophy. Naval officers such as Captain James Cook had mapped the Pacific (Thomas 2003); all the continents had been discovered, including Australia and Antarctica. Almost everywhere Europeans went, they encountered people with different physical features who exhibited a bewildering variety of cultures. Who were these people and how did they relate to Europeans? What was the source of this variation in appearance and culture, and had it changed or developed over time?

The expansion of Europe and early descriptions of non-Western peoples eventually overlapped with the discovery of the remote past of Europeans. Over time, a number of people had collected intriguing items from what appeared to be ancient contexts in northwestern Europe. Many appeared to be manufactured by people and a relative order of their appearance was established by researchers such as Danish museum curator C. J. Thomsen (1836). By the early nineteenth century, there was a geological framework in which to place the oldest of these discoveries (Hallam 1989; Hutton 1795; Lyell 1830–1833). But there was another obvious frame of reference, since some of these items were superficially like the artifacts still in use by people in different parts of the world. Given that many social theorists held to a concept of psychic unity of people worldwide, it was logical to use non-Western technology and behavior in order to reconstruct the historical stages that Europeans must have passed through in remote times. Generally referred to as "the establishment of human antiquity" (Grayson 1983; Van Riper 1993; Bowler 1989), this process is further discussed in chapter 2.

Once there was an evolutionary framework for them, fossil remains of early humans were also soon identified, but these were much more controversial. The first European fossils that relate to the issue of modern origins were reported in 1859 from the Feldhofer Cave in the Neander Valley in Germany (Klein 2003; Schmitz et al 2002). Although members of the same group had already been discovered in Engis, Belgium, and the British colony of Gibraltar (Stringer et al. 2000; Trinkaus and Shipman 1993), these fossils became known as Neanderthals or Neandertals (figure 1.1), depending on which form of German orthography is used (Neanderthal will be used here). They were the first members of a widespread pre-modern European population, one with its own distinctive archaeological associations, those that became referred to as Middle Palaeolithic or Mousterian. By 1868, skeletal remains of anatomically modern people had been uncovered from an ancient context at the Abri Cro-Magnon in the Vézère River Valley of central France (Henry-Gambier 2004). "Cro-Magnon" soon became synonymous with Upper Palaeolithic humans, Pleistocene people who were anatomically and culturally like us, and who postdated the Neanderthals. As soon as it became clear that Neanderthals were genuine fossil humans, the great debate began. How are they related to us, and what does a study of Neanderthals tell us about the evolution of human anatomy and behavior?

Figure 1.1 The Neanderthal statue at the entrance to the Musée National de la Préhistoire, Les Eyzies de Tayac, Dordogne, France. Close-up of the statue at right

In no small way, the study of human origins has parallels with the expansion of Europe and the European discovery of the wider human world. Both led to the development of speculative theories about human history and ultimately to the development of academic disciplines that tried to determine our relationship to others using scientific methods. But when it comes to studying our own species, there are additional questions. What was unique about us, and how did it develop? At what point in history did people leave a natural life and develop material culture, then ultimately the complex cultural systems observable at present? While early research centered on what made humans different from other animals, with additional fossil finds the question has become what makes *Homo sapiens* unique? In other terms, when did hominins really become human? Was this a sudden process, and what was responsible for it? For William Howells (1967), *Homo sapiens* are "entirely like ourselves" (in Ingold 1995:242). For Chazan (1995b:234), they are members of groups who could trace their ancestry back to the event or events that produced "us." What makes living humans different from apes and other hominins could be anatomical, behavioral, moral, or even spiritual.

In the century and a half since the first Neanderthal was identified, the same issues keep reoccurring. Was there a relationship between the ancestors of living people and the Neanderthals? Did the late Pleistocene around 40,000 years ago see the replacement of one kind of human by another? Were Neanderthals behaviorally clueless, randomly wandering across periglacial Eurasia? What about coeval human populations that are anatomically more modern than Neanderthals? Did symbolically based language and culture only begin 30,000 to 40,000 years ago with the prismatic blade tool technology of the European Upper Palaeolithic, giving modern *Homo sapiens* an unbeatable advantage? In the last two decades, the appearance and spread of anatomically modern *Homo sapiens* has once again become a central research focus.

WHAT IS AN ANATOMICALLY MODERN HUMAN?

Ever since scientists began to recognize a fossil record of human evolution, they have emphasized its diversity. Just as there are many different human populations today, erroneously referred to as separate races rather than cultures or ethnic groups, ancient human history is rife with candidates for relationship to us. But what continues today is the firm belief that, no matter how many fossil hominin species can be recognized, there is something unique and special about us, *Homo sapiens*. Look around the room or around any public place; all the people you see are anatomically modern humans. It should be simple enough to describe what we have in common biologically, culturally, or in evolutionary terms, but this has been quite difficult. Generally, the only thing that palaeoanthropologists can agree on is that the processes that produced modern humans were complex and multifaceted, but also confusing. Consider the following statements:

> The last two decades have witnessed the rise of a concept and a key character in palaeoanthropology whose impact is matched only by its vagueness: the anatomically modern human. (Roebroeks and Corbey 2001:72)
> The only taxon that everybody currently agrees upon as being in some sense essentially human is our own species, commonly referred to as "anatomically modern" *Homo sapiens* (AMHS). This is not a taxon with any formal definition—the phrase "anatomically modern" has no clear or established meaning—but simply a scientific-sounding way of evading the fact that there is no agreement on the list and distribution of the defining autapomorphies of the human species. (Cartmill 2001:104)
> The fundamental problem of diagnosing ancient examples of "modern" humans, morphologically and behaviorally nevertheless persists because there is no agreement on how this should be carried out. (Stringer 2002b:574)

As is shown in chapter 2, the species *Homo sapiens* was defined by the great systematist Carolus Linnaeus (1758) in the eighteenth century. No type specimen was assigned, but various geographic sub-species were defined using physical appearance, dress, and culture as criteria. The first fossil representatives of our species were discovered at the Abri Cro-Magnon in Les Eyzies, France, in 1868. Workmen building a railway uncovered the site that ultimately yielded the remains of four adults and four young children. These skeletons possessed modern anatomy but were associated with extinct fauna and stone tools belonging to the early phases of the Upper Palaeolithic (Tattersall 1995:25; Gambier 1989:197; Henry-Gambier 2004). The first two adult skulls were well preserved and shared a number of characteristics with living humans: a long, high cranial vault, a vertical forehead, and a well-marked canine fossa or depression above the canine in the maxilla. Other features were a broad, short face, with a supraorbital region that was small and divided into superciliary and supraorbital arches (Gambier 1989:197).

Living people share all of these traits, so that Cro-Magnon soon became a synonym for modern people.

When other kinds of fossil humans were identified, palaeontologists and anatomists attempted to differentiate *Homo sapiens* morphologically (Kennedy 1984, 1992; Kidder et al. 1992; Lahr 1996; Lieberman 1995, 1998; Pearson 2000a, 2000b; Relethford 1994, 2002). But since they were us, a little ethnocentrism persisted. Marcellin Boule felt that the Neanderthals presented "a contrast with the . . . Cro-Magnons [who with their more elegant] bodies, finer heads, large and upright foreheads . . . manual dexterity . . . inventive spirit . . . artistic and religious sensibilities . . . [and] capacities for abstract thought were the first to deserve the glorious title of *Homo sapiens*" (Boule 1913 in Tattersall 1995:46). For Grahame Clark in the 1940s, anatomically modern humans "possessed a finely chiseled head poised on a well balanced vertebral column" (in Gamble 1994:157). This is eerily reminiscent of Charles White's statement about Caucasians in his *An Account of the Regular Gradation of Man* (1799): where else shall we find, "that nobly arched head, containing such a quantity of brain" (White in Gould 1981:73)? The difference is that Boule and Clark were comparing modern humans with fossil ones, while White was contrasting his fellow Europeans with other "races" of people.

Chapter 2 will show how the concept of anatomical modernity has developed since the original Cro-Magnon finds. In this introduction, I will briefly review recent attempts to define the species. Most researchers would take a report by Day and Stringer (1982; Stringer et al. 1984) as the starting point. Discussing the Omo Kibish specimens from southern Ethiopia (see chapter 7), they attempted to define *Homo sapiens* morphologically, using seven anatomical characters. These include rounded parietals and occipital bones, as well as decreasing brow ridges (Balter 2002:1221). But as Lieberman and colleagues point out (Lieberman et al. 2002:1134), the cranial features were not independent variables; most related to a general globular shape of the skull. For the supporters of the multiregional model, *Homo sapiens* is "a morphologically diverse species with archaic and anatomically modern 'grades'" (Lieberman et al. 2002:1134). In this sense, it is not a true palaeospecies, so multiple taxa could be sunk into it, including *Homo heidelbergensis* (or "archaic *Homo sapiens*"), as well as the Neanderthals.

Lieberman et al. (2002; Lieberman 1998) offer an alternative, focusing on changes in growth and development. For them, two processes can define what is unique about modern human anatomy: reduction of the face and increasing globularity of the skull. Through statistical analysis, they conclude that the unique features of the modern human skull involve changes in the cranial base angle (flexion), length and width of the cranial fossae, as well as facial height and length. These defining traits show up early in child development, but may have involved only minor morphological changes (Lieberman et al. 2002:1138–1139). But they produced a true palaeospecies, qualitatively different from all of its ancestors.

THE ARCHAEOLOGICAL CONTEXT

There is an archaeological record in Africa that spans the last 2.5 million years, overlapping with the appearance and biological evolution of the genus *Homo* (Toth and Schick 1986) (table 1.1). When compared to earlier bipedal hominins, the most notable difference in *Homo* relates to encephalization, the process of increasing brain size relative to overall body size (Wood 1992). Some researchers also see material culture as our invention or adaptive niche (Wood and Collard 1999; Foley 1987b). After the beginnings of flaked stone technology, the pattern is normally whenever new hominin species appeared, their artifacts also changed. For example, the earliest members of the genus *Homo* are associated with Oldowan artifacts, pebble (or core) tools, and flakes, what Grahame Clark (1977:23) labeled Mode 1 technologies. Others refer to cores and flakes as flaked pieces and detached pieces respectively (Isaac and Harris 1997), stressing that it is not possible to be sure which are the tools and which the refuse of manufacture. Flakes were removed from pebbles through hard hammer percussion (stone on stone) and bipolar methods (where the core is placed between a hammer stone and anvil, then struck). Once flaked, the raw material is classified as a core, while the detached pieces include flakes, blades, chips, and chunks. All detached pieces are classified as debitage (from the French word *débitage* meaning "garbage" or "waste"), unless they are shaped further; if so, they become "retouched pieces" or "tools." Groups of artifacts from the same stratigraphic unit or location are grouped together into assemblages. Sets of assemblages of similar age that contain the same artifact and tool types are lumped into the same industry, culture, or industrial complex. Examples of Mode 1 industries are the Oldowan and Developed Oldowan of Olduvai Gorge (Leakey 1971; Stiles 1979a, 1979b) which could have been produced by early *Homo* as well as coeval hominins (*Paranthropus boisei*). The Eurasian chopper-chopping tool tradition (Movius 1944) also fits into this category, even though it was produced much later, and by *Homo erectus*. Here a series of flaked pebbles of varying form (choppers, chopping tools, polyhedrons, and spheroids) are associated with flakes and some unifacially (one side) retouched flake tools or scrapers.

Table 1.1. The Palaeolithic sequence

Palaeomagnetic Chrons and Subchrons	Geological Time Scale	Dates (in years before present)	Archaeological Periods	Hominins
Bruhnes Normal Chron (C1n)	Holocene		Later Prehistory	
		10,000 BP	Epipalaeolithic	
	Upper Pleistocene	30,000 to 40,000 BP	Upper Palaeolithic / Later Stone Age	Homo sapiens worldwide
	Middle Pleistocene	128,000 BP	Middle Palaeolithic / Middle Stone Age	Homo sapiens in Africa; Homo neanderthalensis in Europe
		780,000 BP	Acheulian with Levallois flake tools	Homo heidelbergensis
Matuyama Reversed Chron (C1r)	Lower Pleistocene		Acheulian	Homo ergaster, Homo erectus
Jaramillo Normal Subchron (C1r.1r)				
Matuyama Reversed Chron (C1r.1r)		1,600,000 BP	Oldowan	Earliest Homo (Homo habilis, Homo rudolfensis)
Olduvai Normal Subchron (C2n)		1,800,000 BP		
Matuyama Reversed Chron (C2r)	Pliocene			
Reunion Subchron (C2r.1n)			Start of archaeological record	
Matuyama Reversed Chron (C2r.1r)		2,600,000 BP		
Gauss Normal Chron (C2An.1n)				

Mode 2 is usually defined in relation to Acheulian assemblages, which are associated with *Homo erectus* (or *Homo ergaster* in Africa) and *Homo heidelbergensis*. Here large bifacial retouched tools were shaped on cores or flakes using hard and/or soft hammer percussion to produce a long, sinuous edge. Characteristic tools are hand axes and cleavers; hand axes are large triangular tools, while cleavers have a straight, unretouched edge or bit perpendicular to the long axis of the piece. Cleavers can only be manufactured on flakes, and are more common in African Acheulian sites where flakes were the preferred preform. Outside of Africa, they are usually found only in southwestern Europe (France and the Iberian Peninsula), as well as in South Asia. The approximately 780,000-year-old Acheulian site of Gesher Benot Ya'acov in northern Israel also has cleavers, leading its excavators to suggest that, unlike other Eastern Mediterranean sites, it was colonized directly from Africa (Goren-Inbar and Saragusti 1996). Similar arguments could be made for the presence of cleavers in southwestern Europe. At the Burg-Wartenstein "After the Australopithecines" conference in 1973, participants mounted a skit where two *Homo erectus* swim the Strait of Gibraltar bringing the African Acheulian to Europe (Butzer and Isaac 1975). The type site for the Acheulian is St. Acheul in the Somme River valley of northwestern France. This was where such artifacts were first studied in detail early in the nineteenth century (Grayson 1983; Van Riper 1993). The various kinds of bifaces have received a great deal of attention from archaeologists. They show evidence of shaping to a preferred form or standardized proportions, but there is an active debate about whether or not this represents stylistic input (Ambrose 2001a; Isaac 1977; Roe 1994, 2001a, 2001b). The earliest Acheulian sites are around 1.5 million years old in Africa. Outside of Africa, the earliest assemblages tend to have Mode 1 technologies—Dmanisi in Georgia (Gabunia et al. 2001), the Gran Dolina in Spain (around 800,000 years old) (Carbonell et al. 1995), and most if not all sites in the Far East. It is possible that the first people who dispersed out of Africa had Mode 1 technologies, and left well before the Acheulian began.

Acheulian sites show increasing evidence of technological change starting around 500,000 years ago. New methods of tool manufacture are applied, and attention shifts to producing standardized flaked tools from prepared (Levallois) or radial/circular cores. Levallois techniques involve the production of a core so that flakes of predetermined shape can be removed. Classical Levallois methods involved radial flaking of cores, then the preparation of a new striking platform at one end through faceting or notching, and the subsequent removal of a finished tool (Bar-Yosef and Kuhn 1999:323). The tool was not modified further, except through use and resharpening. Levallois methods were used to produce flake, blade, and/or pointed tools. Standard flake tool methods were also employed. These involve removing flakes from similar radial cores, then retouching them into finished items. Typical retouched tools in Mode 3 industries include a variety of side scrapers, points, notches, and

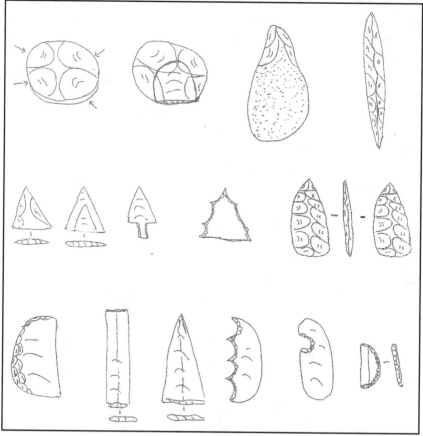

Figure 1.2 Typical Middle Palaeolithic/Middle Stone Age/Mode 3 stone artifacts. Top from left to right: radial and classical Levallois cores, Sangoan core axe, and Lupemban lanceolate. Middle: two Levallois points, an Aterian point, a convergent scraper, and a bifacial point. Bottom: side scraper, parallel and convergent flake-blades, denticulate, notch and crescent

denticulates (Bordes 1961, 1972, 1981; Shea 2006) (figure 1.2). These tool types first appear in the late Acheulian, then become the main classes of tools in assemblages dated younger than 200,000 and 300,000 years ago. They are associated with *Homo heidelbergensis* and Neanderthals throughout Europe and the Levant, as well as with early modern humans in Africa (Foley and Lahr 1997). Researchers such as Desmond Clark see the beginnings of Mode 3 and the disappearance of large bifaces as a sign of a "very significant behavior-technological change" (Clark 1993a:152) from handheld tools to hafted ones (Ambrose 2001a:1751; Tryon and McBrearty 2002:214). As a result, it is assumed that these tools required more complex planning and foresight for their manufacture than seen earlier. Such industries can be classified as Middle Palaeolithic, Mousterian, after Le Moustier, a famous French Neanderthal site, or Levalloiso-Mousterian if they contain a high percentage of Levallois products. In sub-Saharan Africa, they are part of the Middle Stone Age, after terminology first proposed in 1929 for South African archaeological sites by Goodwin and Van Riet Lowe (Goodwin 1929d; Thackeray 1992).

The exact steps involved in production of Levallois tools are of continuing concern to Palaeolithic archaeologists (Boëda 1994; Chazan 1997; Dibble and Bar-Yosef 1995; Mellars 1996; Van Peer 1992). Boëda divides Levallois methods into two categories, lineal and recurrent, and then subdivides these further (Chazan 1997:725; Mellars 1996:62). Lineal methods involve removing a single flake as a finished tool. More flakes can be removed, but each time, the core preparation methods have to be repeated (Mellars 1996:64). Recurrent techniques produce a series of flakes from the same upper core face, and can be unipolar, bipolar, or centripetal (involving radial flake removal) (Mellars 1996:71). Others, such as Van Peer (1991, 1992) rely on refitting cores and flakes in order to understand the production process or *chaine operatoire*.

While early African modern humans manufactured Mode 3 industries, with or without Levallois methods, the earliest modern humans in Europe are associated with Mode 4 (figure 1.3), prismatic blade tools belonging to the Upper Palaeolithic (de Sonneville-Bordes 1963, 1974/75, 1975; de Sonneville-Bordes and Perrot 1953–1956). These are manufactured on conical or cylindrical cores, and parallel-sided blades are removed through soft hammer percussion or an indirect punch technique. In the latter case, an antler tine or other pointed object is placed next to a ridge on the core. Force is applied by striking the tine with a hammer in order to remove a parallel-sided blade.

It is not the beginning of blade tool manufacture, but the association of such blades with a variety of new technologists that marks the Upper Palaeolithic cultural "explosion."

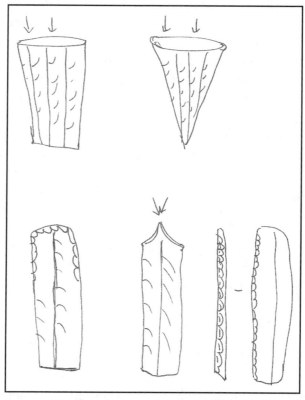

Figure 1.3 Typical Upper Palaeolithic/Mode 4 stone artifacts. Top: cylindrical and conical single platform blade cores. Bottom from left to right: end scraper on blade, dihedral burin, backed blade

At the same time Mode 4 industries were used in Europe, people in sub-Saharan Africa were manufacturing some blades, but more often microblades or bladelets. Bladelets are small blades with a maximum width of 1 to 1.5 cm (Bar-Yosef and Kuhn 1999:323). Elsewhere, these appear late in the Pleistocene or in the postglacial and are referred to as Epipalaeolithic and Mesolithic respectively. They are associated with small geometric microliths, used for the creation of composite tools, as well as with backed bladelets (with 90° retouch extending along most of an edge). In sub-Saharan Africa, such industries are

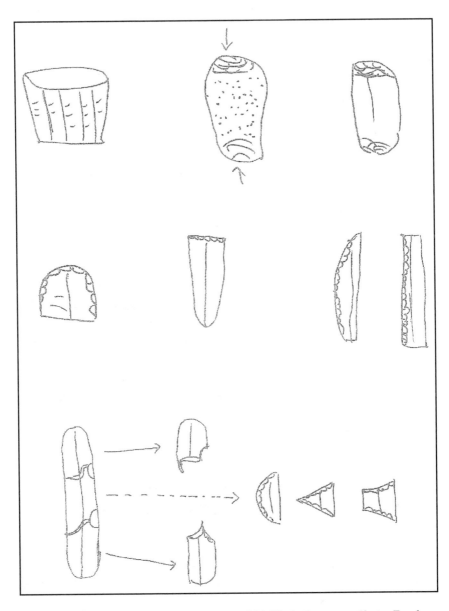

Figure 1.4 Typical Later Stone Age/Epipalaeolithic/Mode 5 stone artifacts. Top from left to right: prismatic bladelet core, bipolar core, and an *outil écaillé* (scalar piece). Middle: end scraper on flake, truncation, curved backed and straight backed piece. Bottom: microburin technology and its products: a proximal and distal microburin and geometric microliths—a crescent, a triangle, and a trapeze

classified as belonging to the Later Stone Age or LSA (Van Riet Lowe 1929a) (figure 1.4). Blade technologies are often described as laminar or lamellar, from the French *lame* for blade or *lamelle* for bladelet. Sometimes the word Leptolithic is also used, from Laplace's (1966) terminology emphasizing the technological continuity between the Upper Palaeolithic and subsequent industries.

While Clark's modes have an evolutionary sequence, it is possible to have more than one method in use at the same time. All lithic or stone tool production methods involve removing flakes from cores. Both bifaces and Levallois flakes tools were manufactured at the same time by the same people. Tryon and McBrearty (2002:211) point out that the same African Acheulian assemblages can have pieces characteristic of Modes 2 (bifaces), 3 (Levallois debitage), and 4 (blades), while Middle Stone Age ones can have all of these plus Mode 5. There are also different ways to produce what look like the same kinds of tools. Some archaeologists distinguish between prismatic blades and other parallel-sided flakes. For the former, one or more ridges are created by bifacial flaking. These produce a crested blade or *lame à crête*. After its removal, the ridges from prior blades are used to remove all subsequent blades. There is no modification or preparation of the striking platform (Bar-Yosef and Kuhn 1999:323) as there would be for Levallois blades. In South Africa, blades form the bulk of debitage in Middle Stone Age assemblages. However, researchers have traditionally classified them as "flake-blades" (Singer and Wymer 1982), as their striking platforms are facetted rather than plain.

WHEN DID PEOPLE BECOME BEHAVIORALLY MODERN?

Until the late 1980s, it was generally believed that behavioral modernity emerged when the first anatomically modern humans appeared, sometime around 40,000 years ago. In Europe, there was a clear break in human populations and their cultural achievements. However, it is now clear that the first anatomically modern people were African and manufactured Mode 3 flake tools rather than Upper Palaeolithic blades. But the earlier appearance in Africa of modern anatomy has had little impact on debates about how behavioral modernity was achieved. This continues to be centered on Western European evidence. Many archaeologists (Bar-Yosef 2002; Henshilwood and Marean 2003; McBrearty and Brooks 2000; Mellars 1991, 2002, 2004, 2005) have used a trait list or laundry list approach to describe the innovations at this time. They include: (1) blade (Mode 4) or bladelet (Mode 5) technology; (2) more evidence of curation of tools, saving them for repeated and future use; (3) tools manufactured using organic raw materials—bone, ivory, and antler; (4) appearance of composite tools, taking separate elements and combining them together; (5) evidence of personal adornment or jewelry; (6) portable art, such as female ("Venus") and animal figurines; (7) parietal art (cave painting and engraving); (8) long-distance transport of raw materials and/or finished tools; (9) development of trade, exchange, and information networks; (10) regional variation in stone tool assemblages, reflecting stylistic or isochrestic patterns (functionally equivalent choices); this may be the first sign of ethnic self-identity (Sackett 1977, 1982); (11) specialization in hunting one or two species; (12) use of fish or shellfish; (13) increasing size of residential groups; (14) more structured settlements; (15) collector/radiating rather than forager/circulating pattern of mobility (Binford 1980; Lieberman and Shea 1994); (16) burial sites with grave goods appear or become more complex (Gargett 1989, 1999); (17) there is an increasing tempo of change; (18) groups expand into new territories such as Siberia, the Americas, and Australia; (19) all of these innovations are associated with anatomically modern *Homo sapiens* (Mellars 1991, 1993, 2005; Bar-Yosef 2002).

Taken together, these changes are supposed to be part of a behavioral package associated with the earliest Upper Palaeolithic industry in Europe, the Aurignacian. Aurignacian sites are dated to between 45,000 and 27,000 years ago, and are widely distributed throughout Europe (Davies 2001:198). They are also found in the Levant (Gilead 1991), but tend to be younger than those from central and Eastern Europe. The place of origin of the Aurignacian remains unknown, but the Balkans remain the leading candidate (Bolus and Conard 2001; Conard and Bolus 2003; Davies 2001:195, 212). Davies (2001:195) suggests that, while it probably developed from early blade industries in the Middle East, the true Aurignacian might have only emerged in Europe.

Aurignacian sites contain a number of distinctive tool types, and many researchers see them as representing the dispersal (or migration) of the first truly modern people (Klein 1992:8; Davies 2001:195; Gravina et al. 2005; Mellars 1991, 2005, 2006). Characteristic stone tools are carinated, keeled, and nosed scrapers, busked burins, and bladelets with semi-abrupt retouch. Many assemblages also contain Mousterian tools such as side scrapers and denticulates (Davies 2001:198; Laville et al. 1980:41; Straus 1995:9). There are also a range of bone tools including split-based bone points as well as biconical and simple lozenge points (Davies 2001:198). While there are many Aurignacian sites, few are associated with skeletal remains.

The Aurignacian has taken on an almost mythic role for those who support an extreme replacement model. It is said to mark the abrupt transition from acultural Neanderthals to fully modern humans. Klein (1992:8) states that "its remarkable uniformity and synchroneity over a vast area clearly suggest that it was the product of a rapidly expanding population." It represents the start of the Upper Paleolithic creative explosion (Pfeiffer 1982), a great leap forward (Diamond 1997: Proctor 2003:216), a big surprise (Binford 1985; Proctor 2003:216) or a symbolic and cerebral Rubicon (Schepartz 1993:93). It represents both a qualitative and quantitative leap over all earlier achievements. For Ingold (1994:311, 1995:243), "from the moment when 'modern human' capacities were established, technology 'took off,' following a historical trajectory of its own thenceforth effectively decoupled from the process of evolution." For Tattersall (2002:126), the first Cro-Magnons "led lives that were drenched in symbol." Those who study the transition in Europe are now emphasizing more gradual changes (Straus 1995:7; Gamble 1994) and the mosaic or mixed nature involved in the appearance of the Upper Palaeolithic. But these arguments seem lost in the general debates about what made some people really human.

New information about the early appearance of anatomically modern humans in Africa has not led to a reassessment of Upper Palaeolithic achievements. In fact, many researchers now see all hominins prior to 40,000 to 30,000 years ago as non-modern, people without culture, regardless of which species is involved. Both Neanderthals and African early moderns are relegated to an "almost, but not quite there" category, somehow lacking key aspects of humanity (Haidle 2000; Willoughby 2000; Speth 2004). In their review of Neanderthal biology and culture, Stringer and Gamble (1993) contrasted "ancients" with "moderns," the people without culture versus our direct ancestors. For them, Neanderthal stone tools were only "versions of the unmodified pebbles that wild chimpanzees have been observed using to crack open nuts in the forests of West Africa" (Stringer and Gamble 1993:177). In recent years, Gamble has modified this position slightly. He argues that traditional models see Lower and Middle Palaeolithic people as "the stomach-led and the brain-dead" (Gamble 1999:xx; Proctor 2003:228). Stomach-led refers to the role of hunting in models of early human development while the latter "attributes change to a gradual awakening of the hominid grey matter as though they had trouble for many long millennia not only in tying their shoelaces, but also in finding their feet" (Gamble 1999:xx). Ancients such as Neanderthals are described as behaviorally clueless, randomly wandering the glacial world of Eurasia in search of shelter, a meal, and a mate. So how are archaeologists supposed to explain African anatomically modern humans who were archaeologically similar to these benighted folk? In order to examine this issue more clearly, the focus of attention must shift from Europe to Africa, as this is the one continent in which there undoubtedly were anatomically modern humans before the appearance of the Upper Palaeolithic. How could any of them have possibly become the ancestors of all of us today?

THE PEOPLE WITHOUT CULTURE

Human cultural modernity is distinguished from human anatomical modernity only because there seems to have been a time when creatures with skeletons virtually identical to ours were living without many of the cultural capacities displayed by later humans. (Proctor 2003:234–235)

The earliest members of our own species are associated with Middle Palaeolithic assemblages in North Africa and with the coeval Middle Stone Age in sub-Saharan Africa. Many replacement advocates place Middle Palaeolithic/Middle Stone Age modern humans into a group along with the Neanderthals, and stress that both are missing something in their basic behavioral repertoires (Willoughby 2000). Since it cannot be biological, the difference must lie in the cultural realm. What they offer for an explanation is the notion of culture itself, the set of rules and standards by which societies operate. On very flimsy evidence, it is concluded that there was an absence of symbolically based language and culture in all humans prior to 30,000 to 40,000 years ago, regardless of which species is involved (Chase and Dibble 1987; Clark 1981; Hayden 1993; Klein 1992, 1995, 1998, 1999, 2001a; Noble and Davidson 1996; Speth 2004). This also offers an explanation for why no modern humans are found outside of Africa until after 40,000 years ago. They needed this cognitive reorganization to develop new technologies and adaptations, ways of living that allowed the Out of Africa II migration to occur. Indirectly, this idea maintains the traditional perspective of an Upper Palaeolithic revolution. One is forced to conclude that, despite the early appearance of anatomically modern humans in Africa, their cultural achievements remain marginal or irrelevant for world prehistory.

Up until the late 1980s, researchers saw the African Middle Palaeolithic/ Middle Stone Age as static and unchanging, falsely describing the continent as a "region of cultural stagnation and genetic isolation" (Clark 1974a:187). Since these assemblages were associated with fossils of anatomically modern people, it was assumed that they must be very recent. This perspective only started to change with the development of new chronometric dating techniques, discussed in chapter 4. It soon became clear that European and African Middle Palaeolithic industries spanned the same time range; the oldest dated between 200,000 and 300,000 years ago while the youngest were between 30,000 and 40,000 years old. Africa was the birthplace of our own species, and "we" had appeared much earlier than previously thought.

Specialists in African prehistory are divided about whether Middle Stone Age Africans were behaviorally modern or culturally challenged like their Neanderthal cousins. Some search for Upper Palaeolithic traits in earlier African sites (Clark 1974a; Deacon and Wurz 2001; Henshilwood and Marean 2003; Henshilwood et al. 2001; McBrearty and Brooks 2000; Potts 2001; Tryon and McBrearty 2002; Willoughby 2001a) and argue that if there was a cultural revolution, it accompanied the appearance of modern skeletal anatomy. Others recognize that there is something not quite right with Middle Stone Age people. Ambrose and Lorenz (1990:28) have suggested that "perhaps early Upper Pleistocene man [in Africa] had modern biological hardware, but simply lacked the software—the cumulative body of knowledge and tradition—required to make effective use of a technology not yet invented." But the most visible critique is that presented by Richard Klein (1992, 1995, 1998, 1999, 2000). For him, Upper Palaeolithic Europeans were "remarkably innovative and inventive" (Klein 1992:7), but African Middle Stone Age and Middle Palaeolithic people were not. An expert in the study of faunal remains from South African sites, he notes a large difference between the Middle and Later Stone Age people in terms of what animals they utilized and how they went about acquiring resources. He attributes these differences to their

separate adaptive strategies, as well as to differences in their human population densities. Klein accepts that the archaeological record shows a major
transition around 50,000 to 40,000 years ago, both in Europe and Africa; "this
transformation represents the most dramatic behavioral shift that archaeologists will ever detect" (Klein 1992:5) except for the origins of hominins
themselves. In Europe, the transition occurred because one kind of hominin,
Homo sapiens, replaced another, the Neanderthals. But in Africa, Middle
Palaeolithic/Middle Stone Age people were already anatomically modern,
or the closest to it of any of their contemporaries (Klein 1999:401), so the
change must be due to some other cause. For Klein, more complex culture is
a result of a neurological reorganization; something changed in the brain that
allowed the development of "the fully modern ability to manipulate culture"
(Klein 1992:5).

Since the brain was already modern over 200,000 years ago, we may never
know what the change was. But it is clearly represented in the African archaeological record (Klein and Cruz-Uribe 1996). Klein has more recently
recognized that his model is based on studying assemblages that are widely
separated in time. South African coastal Middle Stone Age sites are, on average, more than 50,000 years old, while Later Stone Age ones from the same
area are less than 20,000 years old (Klein and Cruz-Uribe 2000:170–171). In
fact, at famous Middle Stone Age sites like Die Kelders 1 (Marean 2000; Marean, Goldberg et al. 2000) and Blombos Caves (Henshilwood et al. 2001), the
Later Stone Age occupation is no more than 2,000 years old. There are very
few places where there are any archaeological sites documenting the transition between the Middle and Later Stone Age. The interior of southern Africa
may have some (Wadley 2001a, 2001b; Wadley et al. 1997), but the most likely
place to find them may be in East Africa (Klein 1992:12; Klein and Cruz-Uribe
2000:193). The transition is associated with the onset of a new glacial phase.
In much of Africa it became too dry, and deserts expanded at the expense of
grasslands and equatorial rainforests. Potts (1998, 2001) has argued that the
pace of glacial and interglacial cycling quickened in the later Pleistocene. It is
more than likely that populations were under stress due to changing environments. This may have promoted cultural innovation, but almost led to the extinction of our founding population, if the evidence of a mitochondrial DNA
bottleneck discussed in chapter 6 is supported (Gagneux et al. 1999; Rogers
and Harpending 1992).

SYMBOLISM—THE ROOT OF BEHAVIORAL MODERNITY?

Nobody will dispute that the Cro-Magnons must have possessed language more or less as we are familiar with it, whereas it's anyone's guess how the Neanderthals communicated. (Tattersall 2002:129)

What is it that actually changed during the transition? For many anthropologists, the key innovation in the evolution of modern humans was the development of symbolically based language and culture (Bar-Yosef 2002; Bickerton 1990, 2002; Chase 2001; Chase and Dibble 1987; Chazan 1995a; Coolidge and Wynn 2001, 2005; H. Deacon 2001; T. Deacon 1997; Dorus et al. 2004; Lieberman 1989, 1998; Lindley and Clark 1990; Mellars 1989, 1991, 2005; Milo and Quiatt 1993, 1994; Donald 1991; Schepartz 1993; Speth 2004; Wadley 2001a; Wynn and Coolidge 2004; Wurz 1999). Wadley (2001a:201) defines modern human behavior as the "symbolic use of space and material culture to define social relationships, including significant groupings based on attributes such as kinship, gender, age or skill. . . . Symbolism maintains, negotiates, legitimizes and transmits such relationships." All humans today have such abilities; the question is, when did they develop? Was it a slow process or a rapid, revolutionary one?

Anatomists have identified two speech centers in the left hemisphere of the human brain. Broca's area is the motor area that allows us to speak, while Wernicke's area allows the comprehension of spoken language (Falk 1992:69, 2004). By examining endocasts, molds of the inside of fossil skulls, anatomists believe that these speech centers had appeared with early *Homo* around 2.5 million years ago. Over the course of the evolution of our genus, brains became enlarged relative to overall body size. Various theories exist as to why this happened, such as the beginnings of a fully terrestrial life (Stanley 1992), the development of material culture, even the onset of global glaciations (Calvin 1998, 2002; Stanley 1995, 1996). Recent work has identified a myosin gene that maintains strong jaw muscles in living primates. Remarkably, a mutation in humans switched this protein off around 2.5 million years ago, possibly eliminating one constraint on brain size (Currie 2004; Stedman et al. 2004). Was brain expansion this simple?

The earliest modern humans have a brain case indistinguishable from ours. Somewhere in the course of the evolution of *Homo*, this brain could have taken on a new role. "The evolutionary process that formed the brain mechanisms that allowed us to talk produced the *human* brain, a brain adapted for thought and language that differentiates humans from all other living species" (Lieberman 1998:xiv; italics in original). When this happened is not clear, but there were fundamental structural adjustments in the mouth and throat, which made complex language possible. Humans possess a larynx, a structure in the neck that contains the vocal cords. Above it is the pharynx, a tube that opens up into both oral and nasal cavities (Laitman 1984, 1985; Tattersall 2002:165–166). In mammals, fossil humans, and newborn infants, the larynx is located high in the neck; this position makes it possible to breathe and swallow at the same time (P. Lieberman 1998:59; Lieberman et al. 1992; Tattersall 1995:212, 2002:116). After the age of three months, the larynx begins to descend down into the pharynx, reaching its final position at about age fifteen (P. Lieberman 1998:59). The low position lengthens the pharynx, increasing the potential for sound modulation in the supralaryngeal tract (Tattersall 2002:166), and the creation of complex sounds. But it comes with a cost that will be familiar to some of us; it is possible to choke on food if it goes down the wrong way (P. Lieberman 1998:48). Given the risk, why did this feature change? Obviously, because it increases the ability for complex speech, and looking back on this event, it had a profound adaptive role. At present, language and communication are fundamental to human existence, so understanding when this change occurred would help us understand the process of hominization. But was this language ability present in the first anatomically modern humans, or did it only appear with the Upper Palaeolithic or Later Stone Age? The linguist Philip Lieberman (1998:5) supports the former, and classifies early African modern people *Homo sapiens loquax*. But others see fundamental change only around 50,000 years ago. A group of geneticists are beginning to offer a possible answer. They identified a mutation in a FOXP2 gene that affects the ability of people to make complex sounds (Lai et al. 2001). The evolutionary geneticists sequenced this gene in humans and other mammals, and argued that it only changed fundamentally around the time of the emergence of *Homo sapiens* (Enard et al. 2002b). This could have occurred around 200,000 years ago, or as recently as 50,000 years ago, as Klein predicted. Other genetic changes point to the continued evolution of the human brain (Evans et al. 2005; Mekel-Bobrov et al. 2005; Voight et al. 2006).

As reviewed in chapter 6, molecular techniques for understanding human evolution have themselves evolved geometrically in the last two decades.

While non-coding or "junk" DNA was the focus of early work, proteins and genes are now being studied. For the former, only mutation produces change. For the latter, all forces of evolution could have a role, including gene flow, recombination, genetic drift, and natural selection. It is the role of selection that is of most interest to evolutionary biologists. Just as Charles Darwin (1859) proposed almost 150 years ago, within a population there is a great deal of variation. Natural selection acts on this variation, since individuals are competing for survival. Individuals possessing favorable mutations survive to adulthood to reproduce, at the expense of others. Over a long time, these favorable variations could lead to changes within the population, and within the species. Evolution is a process where costs and benefits are continually being weighed. An adaptation for complex language and symbolic culture is proposed as the prime mover underlying modern human behavioral origins. But it may have also come at a price, with the frequency of mental illnesses like schizophrenia and attention deficit hyperactivity disorder (ADHD) (Crow 2000; Horrobin 1998, 2001; Ding et al. 2002).

SUMMING UP

This book is organized into a number of thematic chapters. Chapter 1 introduces the research problems associated with the origin and early evolution of modern humans in Africa. How do we define an anatomically modern human? What does behavioral modernity mean, and what is the difference between biological and behavioral modernity? Why does one appear to precede the other? If not anatomy, then what changed to make these African people modern and secondarily, to allow the Out of Africa II migration that took their descendants on an unexpected global journey? Was the development of symbolically based language at the root of the cultural explosion that is inferred to have occurred prior to this dispersal? What does this say about the pattern of African cultural evolution over the span of the Upper Pleistocene?

Chapter 2 attempts to provide a historical perspective on this problem. It reviews the history of modern human origins research, and shows that, until recently, this has been a completely European issue. Neanderthals were not anatomically modern, nor did their Middle Palaeolithic tool kit have anything that could remotely be called behaviorally modern. Subsequent Cro-Magnons had skeletal structures similar to living people, and their appearance coincides with the development of a prismatic blade or Mode 4 technology supplemented by organic tools, art, personal adornment, and new ways of using resources and the landscape. This co-occurrence of modern anatomy and modern technology in Western Europe had been worked out by the late nineteenth century, and then became the model against which all other regions would be measured. In its simplest terms, Mode 3 people were lacking something that Mode 4 technology provided. History shows that African Stone Age research took another trajectory. Right from the start, it looked as if anatomically modern humans could be found with either the equivalent of Upper Palaeolithic artifacts or with earlier Middle Palaeolithic ones. But if anatomically modern humans were associated with Middle Palaeolithic tools, both had to be quite recent, leading to ideas that African peoples had failed to evolve in the Upper Pleistocene. This perspective only changed in the late 1980s with the development of the new chronometric dating techniques reviewed in chapter 4 and with increasing precision in the study of genetic variation in living people (chapter 6).

Chapter 3 reviews the palaeoenvironmental context in which *Homo sapiens* developed. This process took place during the Pleistocene epoch, a time when environments were fluctuating wildly between cold, dry glacial periods and warmer, wetter interglacial ones. What was responsible for these changes, and how are they reflected in African environmental history? What role may Pleistocene environmental shifts have had in the origin and dispersal of modern humans? Chapter 4 discusses the ways early modern human sites are dated, and how the development of newer chronometric dating techniques in the 1980s led to the recognition of the paramount role Africa played for the emergence of our own species. Finally, there were ways of determining the age of sites that were older than the radiocarbon limit of about 40,000 years ago. Chapter 5 reviews the alternative models proposed for the origin and initial dispersal of anatomically modern humans. This process involved one or more "Out of Africa" dispersals or migrations. How many of these events occurred, and when and why did they take place? What information is available about possible routes into Eurasia, and when did *Homo sapiens* arrive in other continents? Chapter 6 outlines the genetic evidence for our recent history as a species. Initially drawn from studies of phenotypic variation and mitochondrial DNA, genetic methods have become so sophisticated that any genetic locus can now be analyzed. These include the male sex or Y chromosome as well as genes. Some researchers have even been able to extract mitochondrial DNA from fossil Neanderthals in Europe, providing the first new line of evidence about our relationship with these people. Genetic data might point to the mechanisms behind behavioral modernity, and might be able to say something about our common humanity. The rest of the book deals with more traditional sources of information about later African human evolution: the fossil hominins (chapter 7) and associated archaeological evidence (chapters 8 through 10). This information is divided by geographical region, and illustrates that, while there is nothing that opposes the idea of an African origin of *Homo sapiens*, the process and pattern our ancestors took to become modern is still unclear. While some regions of Africa are well studied, others have seen little attention. The concluding chapter 11 reviews the evidence for the emergence of behavioral and biological modernity in Africa and tries to answer some of the questions raised at the beginning. What is behavioral modernity? What is biological modernity? Was Africa as central to later human evolution as it certainly was earlier in our history? In evolutionary terms, what does it mean to be a modern *Homo sapiens*? Were the earliest anatomically modern people more like their ancestors, or like their putative descendants, the Cro-Magnons of Europe? Were they really people without culture, only slightly better than apes? Or was there something special about them that eventually led to their global supremacy? Finally, if these people truly were the ancestors of all of us today, why are we reluctant to give them the status they deserve? Or do all of these questions take the wrong approach altogether?

> The entire project of searching for the genesis of some essential humanity is seriously misguided. We look in vain for the evolutionary origins of human capacities for the simple reason that these capacities are not fixed genetically but continue to evolve alongside the conditions of their development, in the course of history itself. (Ingold 2002:64)

2

Historical Perspectives: The Place of Humans in Nature

The archaeology of modern human origins is a challenging topic, but not a new one. (Deacon 2001:213)

Any theory of the origin of Homo sapiens *has to be based on paleontological facts and only on them.* (Weidenreich 1947:200)

The Swedish botanist Carolus Linnaeus (1707–1778) originally defined our own species as *Homo sapiens* in his monumental classification of life, *Systema Naturae*, or *The System of Nature*. The tenth edition, published in 1758 (Linnaeus 1758), is considered Year One, or the starting point for all modern biological classification. Linnaeus, or Carl von Linné, was a well-to-do natural philosopher, a member of a group who felt that all life on earth could be studied in a systematic way (Broberg 1975:287). He worked within a scientific tradition developed from a period when gentlemen scholars maintained cabinets of curiosities, their own private museums. These were composed of whatever someone wished and included coins, plants, animals, fossils, minerals, and ethnographic and archaeological specimens (Piggott 1981:21; Jenkins 1978). The keen motivation of such naturalists has been one of the major themes in Patrick O'Brian's (1980) novels about the early nineteenth century British Royal Navy. When his ship is captured by the American Navy during the War of 1812, O'Brian's naturalist and surgeon (and occasional spy), Dr. Stephen Maturin, explains that his journals are coded in cipher because "it is notorious that the natural philosopher is extremely jealous of his discoveries; he wishes to have the credit of first publication; and he would no more share the glory of a new-found species than a naval commander would wish to share his capture of a ship" (O'Brian 1980:112). While recording new life forms is sometimes little more than a hobby, Maturin and his genuine colleagues shared a passion for understanding the natural world.

LINNAEAN SYSTEMATICS AND THE PLACE OF HUMANS IN NATURE

The method of classification or systematics developed by Linnaeus is composed of a hierarchy of terms starting with "subspecies," "species," "genus," "family," "order," up to the level of "kingdom." The only levels that correspond to observable life forms are subspecies and species. For Linnaeus, groups of animals that share the same characteristics are species, while their separate geographic populations represent subspecies. Species are given two names, the first derived from the genus, while subspecies adds a third name. For example, *Homo sapiens* or "wise man" is a species, while *Homo sapiens sapiens* is a subspecies within it. Both belong to the genus *Homo*, which in turn is classified in the Order Primates and Kingdom Animalia, or animals, organisms that ingest food. The concept of species has evolved significantly since Linnaeus's time and now includes both living and extinct forms. The standard definition in use today is Ernst Mayr's (1942) biological species concept: groups of naturally occurring populations that are reproductively isolated from all other such groups. This reproductive ability is directly observable, and creates a fixed boundary for species membership. For fossil species or palaeospecies, the assumption is that their shared anatomical features imply membership in the equivalent of a biological species. Whether or not palaeospecies represent something real and finite has been the subject of recent debate in human evolution. For some, they represent clearly defined categories with a specific distribution in time and space (Rightmire 1990, 1998b). For others, they just represent stages in a continuous line of ancestors and descendants that is arbitrarily split into categories for heuristic purposes (Brace 1967, 1995; Frayer et al. 1993; Wolpoff et al. 1994).

As was the case for most natural philosophers of the eighteenth century, Linnaeus assumed that the diversity of life was the product of divine creation, of the events described in the biblical book of Genesis. There was no higher duty than the classification of life, as it served as a direct way to understand God's purpose in nature (Barber 1980). In a way, they were documenting the creation itself, as it was assumed that life forms had not changed in any significant way since their first appearance.

What was unique and innovative about Linnaeus was his eventual inclusion of humans into a single Order with monkeys, apes, and prosimians, first labeled Anthropomorpha, and then Primates (Marks 1995:49). It was a bold move to suggest that humans had a biological connection to other animals. But a little ethnocentric bias crept in regardless. The name Primates reflects the central place of humans in the natural world; any life form related to us had to belong to the most important group. Over the course of the thirteen editions of *Systema Naturae*, terminology changed. In the first edition (1735), *Homo* was placed in Anthropomorpha, one of four kinds of Quadrupedia or quadrupedal animals. Quadrupedia eventually becomes part of the Class Mammalia, and Anthropomorpha became the Order Primates (Chazan 1995b:230).

A number of researchers have pointed out that Linnaeus's only definition for the species *Homo sapiens* was the phrase *nosce te ipsum*, literally "know for yourself" (Ingold 1995:254) or "know thyself." This was borrowed from classical Greek philosophy. The maxim has been attributed to many Greek philosophers, including Socrates, but was also carved at the Temple of Apollo at Delphi (as *Gnothi se auton*) (Wilkins 1979). There was no type or reference specimen defined for this species, as is normally required. In order to remedy this, the famous American vertebrate palaeontologist Edward Drinker Cope (1840–1897) left his body to science with the express wish that he could be designated the type. This request was promoted, in the 1990s, by Robert Bakker, better known for his warm-blooded dinosaur theory (Bakker 1986). But Cope's skeletal pathologies, reportedly the result of syphilis, make him an unlikely candidate even if some modern committee on nomenclature could decide on such an important question.

For Linnaeus, reason is what differentiated humans from all other animals (Ingold 1995:253). He defined two species of humans, *Homo sapiens* for the diurnal type, and *Homo sylvestris* for the nocturnal form (Wood and Collard 1999, 2001:64; Chazan 1995b:230). Said to be based on an ape from Java, *Homo sylvestris* is now recognized as the "man of the forest" or the orangutan (*Pongo pygmaeus*). By the time the 10th or definitive edition of *Systema Naturae* was published in 1758, European naturalists were well aware of the biological and cultural diversity of human groups worldwide. As a result, Linnaeus separated

Homo sapiens into separate geographic groups including most of the "races" recognized during his lifetime. These included *Homo sapiens americanus* for aboriginal Americans: described as "red, ill tempered, subjugated. Hair black, straight, thick; nostrils wide; face harsh, beard scanty. Obstinate, contented, free. Paints himself with fine red lines. Ruled by custom." Europeans or *Homo sapiens europaeus* were defined as "white, serious, strong. Hair blond, flowing. Eyes blue. Active, very smart, inventive. Covered by tight clothing. Ruled by laws" (Linnaeus in Marks 1995:50). As a nod to what would later be called cryptozoology, Linnaeus included a fifth category, *Homo sapiens monstrosus* (Goodman 1995:218; Wood and Collard 1999, 2001:64). This would include wild and monstrous humans, unknown groups, and more or less abnormal people (Broberg 1975:291). From his writings, it seems that Linnaeus was a soft primitivist (Piggott 1976), someone who would see humans living in a state of nature as noble savages rather than as brutes. But he also felt that at least some human populations had degenerated from the perfect state of existence given to Adam and Eve. Created by God and given a tropical paradise to live in, the Garden of Eden, they had lost through their own sin the right to perfection, and their descendants were forced to disperse over the globe (Broberg 1975:292).

Linnaeus was but one of a number of natural philosophers who laid the foundation for a study of humans and their yet unrecognized past. "Before about 1859 most Western natural historians and philosophers were as certain that the advent of the human species was a fairly modern event as they are now quite certain that it was a fairly ancient one" (Grayson 1983:2). The Society of Antiquaries was founded in London in 1718 (Daniel 1975:20) and after Linnaeus's death, his collections were sold and shipped to England, where a Linnaean Society was founded in 1790 to promote his research methods. It remains one of the most important biological organizations today. The first hint of a human past earlier than recorded history came in 1797 with John Frere's (1800) report to the Society of Antiquaries on the discovery of some flint artifacts at Hoxne in Sussex, England (Grayson 1983:55–56; Trigger 1989:88). They came from a clay deposit twelve feet below the modern surface, along with "some extraordinary bones, particularly a jaw-bone of enormous size, of some unknown animal" (in Grayson 1983:57). He went on to state that these pieces were found under what appeared to be a marine layer, suggesting that at some later period, the sea had flooded the land. "The situation in which these weapons were found may tempt us to refer them to a very remote period indeed; even beyond that of the present world" (in Grayson 1983:57). Frere was a catastrophist, a supporter of the geological view that there had been many earths, yielding a succession of life over time (Rudwick 1976). However, he did think it was possible that people had lived in one or more of the previous stages, rather than just the most recent one.

As Europeans traveled the globe, they discovered a bewildering variety of life forms and human cultures. Eighteenth-century writers such as John Locke and Adam Smith speculated on the nature of human society, and, like many others, attempted to explain racial, ethnic, and cultural differences. They used a rank order of social development, with stages defined by economic changes from hunter/gatherer through farmers and pastoralists to city dwellers (Bowler 1989:17; Piggott 1976:153), not radically different from what is taught in world prehistory courses today. Their ideas were grouped by Piggott under the label of primitivism, and ranged from "hard" to "soft." Most writers believed in psychic unity, the possibility that all human groups had the same level of intelligence; all could therefore benefit from the new knowledge of the Enlightenment. (It was only in the later nineteenth century that the differences between people were explained as a product of biology, or inherent, unchangeable, unyielding, racial differences.) Cultural progress was seen as the dominant feature of history. But what had motivated people to change? They sought to improve their position, and might act out of selfish motives; but generally, these actions would benefit society as a whole (Bowler 1989:21). The stages that Europeans had passed through could be reconstructed by looking at the behavior of contemporary non-Western people (Piggott 1976:152–153), what became known as the comparative method. As one of the first Palaeolithic or Stone Age archaeologists, Sir John Lubbock, later wrote: "The Van Diemaner and South American are to the antiquary what the opossum and the sloth are to the geologist" (Lubbock 1865; also in Harris 1968:153).

The history of these non-Western people was explained as a result of separate or single creation, polygenesis or monogenesis. In the Book of Genesis, the Bible states that humanity was created by God in the Garden of Eden and spread to other parts of the world from there. While a literal reading of the Bible promoted a single origin from Adam and Eve, or monogenesis, many writers thought that the loss of the perfection of Eden led to the decline of all subsequent people. Some could have fallen further than others, becoming culturally inferior. Darwin (n.d. [1871]:537) himself might have been appealing to supporters of the biblical ideology when he stated that "those naturalists, on the other hand, who admit the principle of evolution, and this is now admitted by the majority of rising men, will feel no doubt that all the races of man are descended from a single primitive stock." However, this conclusion could also be rejected if one preferred the concept of separate origins or polygenesis. By the nineteenth century, many people were arguing that the biblical account only referred to the origins of Caucasians like themselves; in other continents, separate creations could have happened. For Charles Darwin, the differences between races were the product of long-term adaptation to specific environments (Darwin n.d. [1871]:552, 555; also Keith in Bowler 1987:96). The co-discoverer of natural selection, Alfred Russel Wallace (1823–1913), stated that evolutionary theory made the study of racial origins possible for the first time. "[We now have] the permission . . . to place the origin of man at an indefinitely remote epoch. . . . and we can now speculate more freely on the parentage of tribes and races" (Wallace 1865:209–210; in Jones 1999:37).

THE GENESIS OF THE EUROPEAN PALAEOLITHIC

The Palaeolithic, or Old Stone Age, is the first period in human prehistory. It extends from the earliest recognizable stone tool production around 2.5 million years ago in Africa up until the end of the Pleistocene Epoch around 10,000 years ago. In the 1830s, using museum collections that he organized by use, then raw material and shape, Christian Jurgesen Thomsen (1788–1865) described three stages of prehistory for Denmark: the Stone Age, Bronze Age, and Iron Age (Thomsen 1836; Trigger 1989:76; Daniel 1943; Graslund 1987). This idea was later tested by J. J. A. Worsaae (1821–1885) using the associations of artifacts in excavated prehistoric sites, as well as by studying the successive layers of archaeological sediments. Together, these methods, seriation and stratigraphy respectively, provided the first way of relative dating of prehistoric archaeological sites. Three decades later, the growing recognition of the human past led Sir John Lubbock, later ennobled as Lord Avebury, to split the first of Thomsen's three ages into two periods: the Palaeolithic or Old Stone Age, and the Neolithic or New Stone Age (Lubbock 1865, 1969). The former was the age of flaked stone tools, belonging to the drift and cave periods, while the latter was the age of polished stone tools. Drift referred to sediments associated with glacial episodes, whereas the cave period related to archaeological sites such as those in the Perigord region of southern France.

The final proof of the antiquity of humans came in 1858 with the excavation of fifteen or sixteen stone artifacts associated with bones of extinct fauna at Brixham or Windmill Hill Cave, near Torquay in southwestern England. William Pengelly, who directed the research, described the artifacts as coming from under "a sheet of stalagmite from 3 to 8" thick; and having within it and on it relics of lion, hyena, bear, mammoth, rhinoceros and reindeer" (in Daniel 1975:58). The key was the sealed occupation level; there was no way that later material could have penetrated the travertine or flowstone to become associated with the truly ancient fossils. Brixham Cave had been selected for excavation in the hope of finding such an association of stone artifacts and extinct (Pleistocene) fauna (Gruber 1965:385; Grayson 1983:179).

How geologists came to accept the existence of the Palaeolithic has been discussed in detail in several recent sources (Grayson 1983; Sackett 1981, 2000; Van Riper 1993). Nineteenth-century geologists were some of the first to accept the uniformitarian principle: processes that could be observed at present were responsible for creating the geological record (Hutton 1795; Lyell 1830–1833). Since most of these processes were slow, they implied that a great deal of time was involved. Another assumption of uniformitarianism was that the earth was a steady state system, continually renewing itself. As Hutton (1795) wrote in his *Theory of the Earth*, "there was no vestige of a beginning—no prospect of an end" (in Hallam 1989:33–34; Gould 1987:65). So there could be no directional change or progress, just continuous erosion, deposition, and uplift.

Many geologists had discovered what appeared to be human-produced items in apparently ancient geological strata. But most of these were open-air sites, where mixing of material of different ages could not be avoided. Jacques Boucher de Crevecoeur de Perthes (1788–1868), a customs officer at Abbeville, France, was notorious for his claims that extinct fauna and stone artifacts were associated in diluvial age terraces of the Somme River. Diluvial referred to periods of flooding, the most recent of which was supposed to be the Noachian flood recorded in the Bible. In one of his most famous statements, Boucher de Perthes declared "God is eternal, but man is very old" (in Grayson 1983:xi). The ever increasing evidence of this antiquity was presented in the multiple, successive volumes of his *Antiquités Celtiques et Antédiluviennes* (Boucher de Perthes 1847, 1857, 1864). When the first volume appeared, however, it did not have the desired effect. His sloppy field methods were well known. They had given French research such a bad name that the local scientific society, the Academy of Amiens, instructed a physician and respected local antiquarian, Dr. Marcel-Jerome Rigollot (1786–1854), to investigate Boucher de Perthes's seemingly outrageous claims. Rigollot chose to excavate similar deposits at the nearby site of Saint Acheul, and he became convinced that Boucher de Perthes was right. As all archaeologists know, Saint Acheul became the type-site for the Acheulian, or Acheulean, one of the earliest archaeological industries in Europe, if not the oldest (Roebroeks and van Kolfschoten 1996). Unfortunately, Rigollot died before he could spread the word. It was not until Brixham Cave was re-excavated that the question seemed to be answered. In 1859, also the year of publication of the *Origin of Species* (Darwin 1859), a group of British geologists and antiquarians traveled to Abbeville and Saint Acheul to see for themselves. Upon returning home, they all gave a series of presentations to British scientific societies confirming these astonishing finds (Grayson 1983; Van Riper 1993). John Evans, who became one of the first Palaeolithic specialists in England, concluded that "this much appears to be established beyond doubt. That in a period of antiquity remote beyond any of which we have hitherto found traces, this portion of the globe was peopled by man" (Evans 1859 in Daniel 1975:61).

Other sites that became famous for their Palaeolithic record were the limestone caves along the Dordogne and Vézère rivers in the Perigord in south central France. Here Edouard Lartet conducted excavations and initiated the use of Pleistocene faunal sequences for relative dating. By the time the Second World's Fair (the *Exposition Universelle*) was held in Paris in 1867, the Palaeolithic had been subdivided into a number of stages. Lartet was given the job of organizing prehistory exhibits, but it was really his assistant, Gabriel de Mortillet (1821–1898) who did the work. At the time, de Mortillet was the assistant curator at the Musée des Antiquités Nationales at Saint-Germain-en-Laye, a museum created in the former palace of King Louis XIII west of Paris. His exhibits, described in the guidebook *Promenades préhistoriques à L'Exposition Universelle*, included a gallery of the history of work. Palaeolithic artifacts were prominently displayed, and were organized into stages: the Lower, Middle (Mousterian), and Upper Palaeolithic (including the Aurignacian, Solutrean, and Magdalenian) (Bowler 1987:30; Daniel 1975:105–106; Trigger 1989:96). Typical Lower Palaeolithic artifacts were those from Abbeville and Saint Acheul. Mousterian or Middle Palaeolithic tools were those manufactured using flakes struck from radial or circular cores, then retouched into points, side scrapers, and denticulates. Alternately, they could have been removed from prepared Levallois cores as finished tools. On the other hand, Upper Palaeolithic ones were made on parallel blades removed from prismatic cores. Retouched tools included end scrapers, burins, points, and the first true organic items, manufactured from bone, antler, or ivory. It soon became apparent that the various kinds of Palaeolithic industries or cultures were associated with different kinds of humans, and only the Upper Palaeolithic was found with people who were anatomically modern.

THE BEGINNINGS OF A FOSSIL HUMAN RECORD FOR EUROPE

A fragmentary skull of a child found at Engis, Belgium, in 1829/1830 is the earliest example of what would later become recognized as the Neanderthals (Schmerling 1833–1834; Spencer 1984). A similar, but adult, skull was found in 1848 in the Forbes Quarry at Gibraltar (Stringer et al. 2000). But the first find that would be recognized as some kind of fossil human came from the Neander Valley in Germany, 13 km east of Dusseldorf. This valley had been named Neandertal or Neanderthal in 1850 in honor of Joachim Neumann (or Neander in Greek) (1650–1680), a minister, teacher, poet, and hymn composer who often visited the area (Schmitz et al. 2002:13342). There were many rock shelters and caves, including the Kleine Feldhofer Grotte or "Little Feldhofer Cave," near the Feldhof farm (Schmitz et al. 2002:13342; Janković 2005:379; Straus 2005). Miners discovered remains in August 1856 including a skull cap and fifteen postcranial bones (Schmitz et al. 2002:13342). The miners apparently only collected the larger, more easily identifiable bones, since no artifacts or fauna were ever recovered (Schmitz et al. 2002:13342). The first scientific reports were composed by a local schoolteacher, Johan Carl Fuhlrott (1803–1877), as well as by Herman Schaafhausen (1816–1893), the professor of anatomy at the University of Bonn (Schmitz et al. 2002:13342; Trinkaus and Shipman 1993:49). Schaafhausen (in Tattersall 1995:14) provided a detailed anatomical description and emphasized the unique features; for him, the remains were undoubtedly some kind of fossil human from the diluvial period. But one of Schaafhausen's colleagues, Friedrich Mayer, wrote in 1864 that the Neanderthal skeleton was more likely a modern individual suffering from skeletal pathologies (childhood rickets) or trauma. It was Mayer who concluded that the Neanderthal skeleton was probably that of a Cossack soldier on his way back home in the early nineteenth century after the end of the Napoleonic wars (Trinkaus and Shipman 1993:58).

There is little remaining at the Feldhofer site today, but in 1997, scientists discovered sediments that had been removed from the cave and thrown 20 m down the rock face (Schmitz et al. 2002:13342–13343). These were excavated and led to the recovery of stone artifacts belonging to either the Micoquian (late Acheulian or early Middle Palaeolithic) or Gravettian (Upper Palaeolithic) industries. Excavations in 1997 and 2000 produced sixty-two more hominin skeletal remains; all are Neanderthals, including some pieces that refit onto the original Neanderthal specimen (Schmitz et al. 2002:13343, 13346). Up to three individuals are represented: the original Neanderthal, another adult, and one sub-adult (identified by an isolated deciduous molar) (Schmitz et al. 2002:13344). Accelerator radiocarbon dates on three samples range between 39,000 and 40,000 years old (Schmitz et al. 2002:13345).

One of the first researchers to discuss the Neanderthal cranium, Thomas Henry Huxley (1825–1895), had mixed feelings about its significance. For him,

> though truly the most pithecoid of known human skulls, the Neanderthal cranium is by no means as isolated as it appears to be at first, but forms, in reality, the extreme term of a series leading gradually from it to the highest and most developed of human crania. (Huxley 1959:181–183; Orig. pub. 1863.)

Another researcher, the Irish anatomist William King, concluded in 1864 that the Neanderthal represented a new species, which he defined as *Homo neanderthalensis*. It was a backhanded compliment, as he put it at the bottom of the ladder of progress, even below the most "primitive" of contemporary humans (Trinkaus and Shipman 1993:88–89). The French anatomist Marcellin Boule (1861–1942) was the first to do a detailed anatomical study of a Neanderthal, the La-Chapelle-aux-Saints skeleton discovered in 1908 (Boule 1911–1913). He recognized that it was riddled with pathologies, but tried to reconstruct its morphology as if these problems did not exist. He concluded that Neanderthals would have been brutish and quite primitive, comparable to Australian aborigines, his idea of the lowest scale of human development. Boule also believed that the Neanderthals belonged to a separate species (Trinkaus and Shipman 1993:302). By this time, many Neanderthal sites had been identified. Also, the 1907 discovery of the Mauer or Heidelberg mandible led Otto Schoetensack (1908) to define *Homo heidelbergensis*, now felt to be the type specimen of the species who was the last common ancestor of Neanderthals and modern humans (Rightmire 1998b).

Anatomically modern humans had been found in ancient contexts such as the Abri Cro-Magnon at Les Eyzies de Tayac in the Dordogne River valley. In 1868, workmen clearing land for a railway uncovered anatomically modern human skeletal remains associated with extinct megafauna, marine shell beads, and distinctive stone artifacts (Henry-Gambier 2004). Further excavations by Louis Lartet, the son of Edouard Lartet, and his English colleague, Henry Christy, led to the recovery of five burials, including one infant (Daniel 1975:96–97; Lartet and Christy 1865–1875). They were associated with the same kinds of artifacts first identified in 1852 at L'Aurignac in the Haute Garonne (Henry-Gambier 2004:90). Here, a series of blade tools, organic tools, and portable art objects were associated with the remains of about seventeen early modern human skeletons (Alexander 1872:342). It became the type site for the Aurignacian, now interpreted as the earliest industry of the Upper Palaeolithic one associated with modern Cro-Magnons (Davies 2001). By 1867, the year of the Paris *Exposition Universelle*, it was generally accepted that there were at least two human groups in ice age Europe, the Neanderthals and Cro-Magnons, each with its own kind of archaeology, Middle and Upper Palaeolithic respectively. How the humans and their respective industries are related to one another remains one of the most significant problems in human palaeontology.

The British anatomist Sir Arthur Keith (1866–1955) had one possible answer. He believed that there was an early form of modern human in Europe, one that pre-dated the Neanderthals. For him, the earliest modern "pre-sapiens" form had lived during the Middle Pleistocene, hundreds of thousands of years in the past (Hawks and Wolpoff 2003:89). He thought that the differences between geographic populations were significant, and therefore had needed a lot of time to diversify (Dennell 2001:52–53). For Keith, the fossil hominins specimens from Piltdown provided a good example of what appeared to be a geologically ancient, but essentially modern, human. The Sussex, England, site had produced a hominin cranium, mandible, and isolated canine tooth. While the cranium was large and globular, as in living people, the mandible and tooth exhibited ape-like characteristics (Spencer 1990a, 1990b). English anatomists hailed the discovery of an ancient Briton; too long they had watched continental Europeans build a fossil human record. But as most people know, it was not to be. In the 1950s, the development of the "FUN" dating techniques, measuring change over time in fluorine, uranium, and/or nitrogen, exposed Piltdown as a hoax (Poirier 1977:33; Oakley 1970). It was composed of a relatively recent Romano-British skull and a modern orangutan jaw (Weiner 1955).

NINETEENTH-CENTURY EVOLUTIONARY IDEAS

Research on early humans, either Neanderthals or Cro-Magnons, was not done in a scientific vacuum. Biological change over time, or "descent with modification," became the framework for understanding the history of life, and Charles Darwin (1859) provides a mechanism for understanding how such changes occurred. In developing his natural selection theory in *The Origin of Species* (Darwin 1859), Darwin borrowed the ideas on population history developed by Thomas Malthus (1798). Malthus argues that the human population doubles every twenty-five years, but the amount of available food only increases arithmetically. Unchecked, this would lead to a struggle for existence and the survival of the fittest members of society. In nature, population increase is checked by the struggle for existence, while humans had to apply artificial restraints to reproduction. Through numerous examples, Darwin shows that animal breeders recognized individual variation within a species, and chose individuals with favorable characteristics for reproduction. Given enough time, these traits would show up in higher frequencies in future generations. Nature could also select individuals. Individuals within a species varied; most of these variations are neutral, but some give an advantage in the struggle for existence. Individuals with variations that allow their survival would pass the traits on to future generations. Given enough time, such gradual changes would be preserved and eventually lead to new species.

Darwin shared the perspective of the early naturalists such as Linnaeus. He believed that all life was linked in a great, continuous chain of being, constantly changing. "As natural selection works solely by and for the good of each being, all corporeal and mental endowments will tend to progress toward perfection" (Darwin n.d. [1859]:373). But this was the product of the interaction of individual organisms and species with their natural environment. While contemporary critics argue that Darwin removed God from creation, Darwin only addressed the issue of human evolution toward the end of *The Origin*. He predicted that "much light will be thrown on the origin of man and his history" (Darwin n.d. [1859]:373), and waited until 1871 to address the topic himself.

In *The Descent of Man*, Darwin (1871) said that he would address three questions: "to consider, firstly, whether man, like every other species, is descended from some pre-existing form; secondly, the manner of his development; and thirdly, the value of the differences between the so-called races of man" (Darwin n.d. [1871]:390). He cited the work of Boucher de Perthes as proof of a long human history in which many changes could have occurred (Darwin n.d. [1871]:390, 431). For him, the discovery of fire was one of the most important human inventions, next to language (Darwin n.d. [1871]:432). He proposed the now classic idea that early humans had adopted upright locomotion using the hind legs (bipedalism) in Africa in order to free the hands for toolmaking and tool using. In turn, this could have led to decreased canine and jaw size and to brain expansion (Darwin n.d. [1871]:435–436). He concluded that researchers have not yet found the proverbial missing link, since "those regions which are the most likely to afford remains connecting man with some extinct ape-like creature, have not as yet been searched by geologists" (Darwin n.d. [1871]:521). In terms of the race question, Darwin argued for monogenesis and continuity (Darwin n.d. [1871]:536).

Darwin was not alone in developing his theory of natural selection. There are many accounts of how the naturalist Alfred Russel Wallace (1823–1913) wrote out some ideas on the transmutation of species while conducting biogeographic research in South East Asia, and then mailed them to Darwin for his opinion (Ruse 1979; Young 1992). Darwin was shocked; he had been writing his big book on species for over twenty years. Now Wallace had produced the perfect summary for it, the same theory. As Darwin then wrote to Charles Lyell, "I never saw a more striking coincidence; if Wallace had my ms. sketch written out in 1842 (Darwin 1909), he could not have made a better short abstract. Even his terms now stand as heads of my chapters" (in Barber 1980:266). Darwin's colleagues decided to publish Wallace's paper along with Darwin's original 1844 sketch or outline, thereby establishing who had the priority in terms of coming up with the theory of natural selection (Barber 1980:267–268). Where Darwin and Wallace fundamentally disagreed was on the issue of human evolution; for Wallace, natural selection could account for many things, but not for the human mind (Bowler 1987:3; Camerini 2002:15, 154). It merely acted on things that affected survival: the evolution of speech, weapon making, and the sexual division of labor. But the human mind had to be special, the product of an unknown higher law or superior intelligence (Camerini 2002:153–154).

> Let us fearlessly admit that the mind of man (itself the living proof of a supreme mind) is able to trace and to a considerable extent has traced, the laws by means of which the organic no less than the inorganic world has been developed. But let us not shut our eyes to the evidence that as Overriding Intelligence has watched over the action of those laws so directing variations and so determining the accumulation, as finally to produce an organism sufficiently perfect to admit of, and even to aid in, the indefinite advancement of our mental and moral nature. (Wallace in Camerini 2002:163)

Here is the problem of the people without culture laid out clearly. Life forms could have arisen under natural selection, but humans are special, unique in creation. On the other hand, Wallace did not think that modern Europeans were any better than anyone else, in the present or past. He believed that humans had not advanced morally or intellectually since the earliest phase of their existence (Camerini 2002:156–157, 161).

At this time, the first cultural anthropologists were taking documentation of the variety of human societies and ranking them on a unilineal or single scale of progress or development (Morgan 1877; Tylor 1871; Stocking 1987; Bowler 1989). Others used the theory of natural selection to support a perspective relying on biological determinism. For them, societies were at the level they deserved because of inherited traits.

MORE RECENT IDEAS ABOUT NEANDERTHALS

In the early twentieth century, Franz Boas (1858–1942) argued that an academic anthropology had to separate culture, race, and language (Boas 1940). Each culture was now seen as unique, with its own history (Marks 1995:21). At the same time, specialists in human evolution began to take a more biological and palaeontological approach, one which would have profound effects on the interpretation of our past. Comparative anatomy continued, but it was recognized that researchers would need to understand early humans in terms of adaptation and selection, rather than in terms of racial stereotypes. But the position of Neanderthals only really started to be changed in the 1950s, when William Straus Jr. and A. J. E. Cave wrote one of the most famous statements about Neanderthals:

> Notwithstanding, if he could be reincarnated and placed in a New York subway—provided that he were bathed, shaved and dressed in modern clothing—it is doubtful whether he would attract any more attention than some of its other denizens. (Straus and Cave 1957:359)

F. Clark Howell (1952, 1957) also supported this view. He argued that classical Neanderthal traits emerged during the last full glacial (traditionally referred to as the Wurm), due to population isolation. But there were earlier forms with mixed or transitional morphology, his "generalized Neanderthals," who could have been the ancestors of both Neanderthals and moderns (Bowler 1987:76). The hominins of the Mugharet et Tabun and the Mugharet es Skhūl, side by side on Mount Carmel south of Haifa in what is now Israel (McCown and Keith 1937), were offered as proof of the morphological diversity of Upper Pleistocene people (figure 2.1).

Figure 2.1 Mount Carmel, northern Israel, showing, from left to right, the caves of el Wad, Skhūl, and Tabun

C. Loring Brace (1964) argued that Neanderthals just represented one stage in the continuous, gradual evolution of the genus *Homo*, that directly ancestral to modern Europeans. Fieldwork at Shanidar Cave in Iraq in the 1950s (Solecki 1971) clinched this new interpretation. A number of Neanderthal burials were excavated, including one which apparently contained some wildflower pollen (Shanidar 4). This was interpreted as a form of grave offering, as well as indirect evidence of some sort of social welfare policy. From the evidence of skeletal pathologies, especially of Shanidar 1 (head injuries, crushing of the right side of body, and the absence of the right forearm), it seemed possible that elderly and infirm members of a group were cared for on a regular basis. Now Neanderthals came across as warm and fuzzy, true humans who cared to bury their friends and relatives, "the first flower people" as Solecki (1971) christened them at the height of the North American hippie movement.

Others used this new evidence in order to identify significant morphological differences between Neanderthals and early moderns. Erik Trinkaus (1983, 1984) examined the rather fragmentary pelvic remains from Shanidar and concluded that female Neanderthals could have had an extended gestational length, possibly carrying children up to eleven or twelve months prior to birth. Their offspring could therefore have been born more mature, less dependent on parents for learning (Trinkaus 1984). Perhaps this could explain the lack of variability in their stone tools and material culture. This conclusion was later challenged by Yoel Rak (1990) who studied the pelvis from Kebara, Israel, discovered in 1983 (Bar-Yosef et al. 1992). The first relatively complete Neanderthal pelvis ever found, the Kebara individual had a birth canal similar to that of *Homo sapiens*. Rak concluded that no significant behavioral differences probably existed between the two groups. Trinkaus (1993) then shifted his attention to the angle of the femur neck to shaft, and argued that this was significantly different in Neanderthals and early moderns. Similar claims to that of Trinkaus have been made for the Neanderthal hyoid from Kebara. Some have argued that the position of the larynx was too high in the throat for real speech (Lieberman 1991:65–69), or the hyoid was really no different from that of pigs (Laitman et al. 1990). Others see it as anatomically and functionally equivalent to that of living humans.

In the 1990s, largely due to the increasing support for the Out of Africa II model, there was a return to a non-cultural view of Neanderthals (Speth

2004). Alternatively, anatomically modern humans were supposed to have some inbred advantage—a shorter birth span (Zubrow 1989) or more complex social systems, involving symbolic behavior and trade (Horan et al. 2005). However the transformation happened, Neanderthals once again became Boule's arthritic people without significant cultural achievements. But compared to earlier hominins, they still had to be given some credit, some level of technological competence (Stringer and Gamble 1993:95).

For Stringer and Gamble, even the evidence for intentional Neanderthal burial is suspect. Rather, they point to the density of carnivore bones in archaeological sites as a clue for explaining varying degrees of completeness of hominin skeletons. Where carnivores did not make great use of caves, more complete skeletons are found. In Central and Eastern Europe, hominin finds are very fragmentary, while carnivore remains are abundant. Carnivores were the likely agents of preservation of hominin skeletons, rather than any cultural practice (Stringer and Gamble 1993:160). At least this is more reasonable than other suggestions. For example, Andrew Sherratt (1997) suggests that Neanderthals might have had very different adaptations from more recent people,

> including hairiness, subcutaneous fat, and even (dare one speculate?) hibernation. (The latter habit, if it was associated with 'sleeping-hollows' filled with insulating vegetation, would mimic burials if their occupants did not survive the winter; and in some cases were deliberately covered by later inhabitants of the cave). (Sherratt 1997:282)

An alternative way to explain modern human origins was promoted by Franz Weidenreich (1873–1948), the German anatomist who took over the study of the "Peking Man" fossils, *Sinanthropus pekinensis*, after the untimely death in 1934 of the Canadian anatomist Davidson Black (Sigmon and Cybulski 1981; Weidenreich 1937). Weidenreich presented his model of human evolution to the American Anthropological Association in Chicago in 1938 (Hawks and Wolpoff 2003:90). He proposed a continuous line of evolution from earlier to modern humans with secondary divergences that led to modern races (Weidenreich 1943, 1947). By examining the fossils, he defined a series of anatomical traits that could be traced through time, and argued for regional continuity; "neither any gaps nor deviations are recognizable" (Weidenreich 1947:189; figure 2.2).

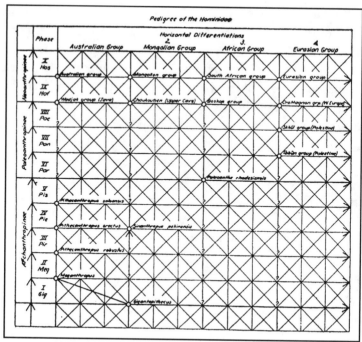

Figure 2.2 The origins of the multiregional theory. Weidenreich's
(1947:201) trellis view of human evolution. Reprinted with permission of
the University of California Press

Weidenreich and his successors, among them Brace (1964, 1995), Wolpoff,
Thorne, and others, have become categorized as the proponents of multiregionalism, or continuity from earlier to modern humans (Frayer et al. 1993;
Thorne and Wolpoff 1981, 1992; Wolpoff 1989a, 1989b, 1992; Wolpoff and
Caspari 1996; Wolpoff and Thorne 1991; Wolpoff et al. 1988, 1994, 2000).
They used the same methods as Weidenreich, attempting to define regional
skeletal traits that could be traced through time. Some proposed that early
humans became modern as they relied more and more on material culture; as
tools became more sophisticated, there was less need for strong jaw muscles
and associated structures (Brose and Wolpoff 1971; Hawks and Wolpoff
2003:92).

W. W. Howells (1942, 1976) was the leading proponent of the possibility
that Neanderthals were a separate species from modern humans. In 1976, he
wrote a provocative article summarizing the evidence for modern human
origins in much the same way as researchers continue to do today (Howells

1993; Orig. pub. 1976.). The question of modern human origins, he wrote, "continues to be surprisingly obscure" (Howells 1993:628). In order to understand it, he presents evidence from his own studies of modern human cranial variation (Howells 1973) as well as from available genetic and fossil data (Howells 1993:628; Lewontin 1972; Cavalli-Sforza et al. 1994). He outlines various models for modern human origins, and states his preference for a single center of origin and ultimate replacement of all non-modern people, what he calls the Noah's Ark hypothesis. Continuity (the "candelabra" model) was not rejected outright, but Howells thought that there is no evidence for it (Howells 1993:628–629). While this article is remarkably precocious, its author did err in one significant prediction. He concluded that only an intensive study of the European Neanderthals would offer a solution to the question of modern origins. Howells had no inkling about how soon this Eurocentric conclusion would be challenged. But the new lines of evidence, both molecular (chapter 6) and geochronological (chapter 4), would go far to demonstrate the validity of his original ideas.

SOUTH AFRICA: THE THREE STONE AGES

> Higher cultures can pass from south to north and survive, but lower cultures passing from south to north are immediately subdued and assimilated by the higher, better organised folk of the Mediterranean. As a result, although 'something new' is always expected out of Africa, these things are only 'new' from their very age. Africa is a pocket from which nothing tangible returns. (Goodwin and Van Riet Lowe 1929:3)

In this new postmodern world, the sociopolitical context in which African archaeology developed has become of interest to scholars (Robertshaw 1990a:4; Schlanger 2003; Shepherd 2002, 2003). Archaeological research soon followed the "scramble for Africa," when western European powers took control of most of the continent. By the late nineteenth century, there were clearly demarcated spheres of interest (Pakenham 1991; Robinson and Gallagher 1961), the boundaries of which were confirmed at an international conference in Berlin between 1884 and 1885.

The first people who conducted any kind of archaeological research were Europeans resident in the colonies as missionaries and political and/or military officials. For most of them, there was an African prehistoric past, but they only focused on the Stone Age. The Iron Age proto-historic and historic archaeology of sub-Saharan Africa only became a focus of interest after countries became independent, starting in the late 1950s (Robertshaw 1990a:4). It offered a source of information about the pre-colonial past, a historical period for which, outside of the regions of Islamic influence (Insoll 2003), there were few available written sources.

Sir Langham Dale wrote one of the first accounts of stone tools in 1866. He reported the discovery of stone artifacts along Maitland Road on the west side of Table Bay, near Cape Town (Goodwin 1928b, 1929d:119). Dale was one of the first South African archaeologists; he regularly corresponded with leading British prehistorians (Goodwin 1928b:425).

By the time A. J. H. Goodwin (1900–1959) arrived at the University of Cape Town in 1923 (Shepherd 2002:194; Gowlett 1990), there were numerous accounts of prehistoric tools. Trained in social anthropology at Cambridge University (Schlanger 2003:12), Goodwin was given the task of classifying the numerous prehistoric artifacts of the South African Museum (Deacon 1990a:42; Schlanger 2003:12). In collaboration with Pieter Van Riet Lowe (1894–1956), Goodwin created a new sequence for South African prehistory. As Van Riet Lowe had already discovered, Goodwin soon realized that the standard European Palaeolithic sequence did not provide an adequate model for this material. Their alternative classification involved the definition of three stages: Early Stone Age or ESA, Middle Stone Age or MSA, and Later Stone Age or LSA. Specific industries and "variations" were defined as subsets of these stages. The Early Stone Age included a number of already recognized units: the Stellenbosch, Fauresmith, and Victoria West industries (Goodwin 1928a:410; 1929d:95; Klein 1970). The Middle Stone Age included the Still Bay, Glen Grey, and "a variety of industries showing Mousterian origins" (Goodwin and Van Riet Lowe 1929:3). The Later Stone Age was composed of three phases of the Smithfield (A, B, and C) and then the Wilton, which could be directly connected to the "strandloopers" or coastal wanderers seen by early Dutch explorers (Goodwin 1929a, 1929b, 1929c, 1929d; Goodwin and Van Riet Lowe 1929; Hewitt 1921; Van Riet Lowe 1929a, 1929b).

Goodwin and Van Riet Lowe (1929:2) were acutely aware that, unlike Europe, in South Africa there did not seem to be a sequence of glacials and interglacials which would assist in chronological ordering. The only means of dating involved relative methods: stone artifact type (style or typology) and differential states of surface weathering (or patination). Occasionally, this was supplemented by the discovery of a site with a stratified sequence of cultural deposits (Deacon 1990a:43).

While they insisted on their own local sequence, Goodwin and Van Riet Lowe did subscribe to the common assumption that cultural change was due to human migration. They proposed successive waves of migrants from the north. For them, the Mediterranean Sea seemed to be less of a barrier than the Sahara desert (Goodwin and Van Riet Lowe 1929:3; Shepherd 2002:195). Stone Age people were seen as "helpless recipients of successive waves of innovation from Europe, the font of knowledge and invention" (Deacon 1990a:46; Shepherd 2002:195). The Stellenbosch culture was seen as the oldest evidence of human occupation. It was interpreted as an intrusive core industry, while its successors, the Victoria West and Fauresmith, were seen as local developments (Goodwin and Van Riet Lowe 1929:3). Defined by large core tools (choppers, bifaces), the Fauresmith was the first stage of the Early Stone Age to include substantial numbers of flake tools (Goodwin 1928a:411, 1929c:72). The variety of assemblages from this time period led them to define a Middle Stone Age (Goodwin 1928a:411).

> We are here faced for the first time with the appearance of a conventionalised flake technique in addition to the more normal coup-de-poing [hand ax] forms so typical of the Earlier Stone Age. The flake type represented shows a series of flake-implements, frequently with faceted butts, and showing a tendency to convergent rather than parallel flaking on the outer face of the flake. (Goodwin1929d:97, 1928c:411)

Goodwin and Van Riet Lowe (1929:7) recognized the similarity between the South African Middle Stone Age and the European Mousterian or Middle Palaeolithic. The flake elements of the Fauresmith and the Middle Stone Age both probably derived from "a 'Mousterian' influence or infiltration, not necessarily from Europe, but certainly from the north" (Goodwin 1929d:98). But it was just as possible that Middle Stone Age cultures evolved locally, directly from the Fauresmith (Goodwin 1928a:411).

The defining characteristics of the Middle Stone Age involved tool shape and production methods:

In the MSA the striking platform is not flat, but is distinctly faceted. The trimming flakes are not parallel (as they are in the LSA), but tend to be convergent; as a result of this preparation, the final flake removal is eminently suitable for use as a point, and, indeed, the typical implement throughout the MSA Industries is the worked point in a variety of forms. (Goodwin 1929d:98, 1928a:411)

There was not enough information to divide the Middle Stone Age into industries ("where a group is certain and definable"), so Goodwin (1929d:99–100, 1928a:411) also created a number of "variations." These could represent the products of cultural mixing, local evolution, or differences in raw materials (Goodwin 1928a:412). When he finished, Goodwin had recognized four Middle Stone Age types: the Glen Grey Falls Industry, the Pietersburg Variation, the Still Bay Industry, and the Howieson's Poort Variation. He suggested that this could be a time successive or evolutionary sequence, but was not at all certain (Goodwin 1929d:100).

Glen Grey Falls was defined by the presence of projectile points intermediate between the small handaxes of the Fauresmith and Still Bay lanceolates (Goodwin1929d:100, 1928a:413). The Pietersburg Variation included better quality tools than Glen Grey Falls; there were two kinds of lance heads, along with leaf shaped points similar to Still Bay ones (Goodwin 1929d:109; 1928a:414). The Still Bay was defined by the presence of a "lance head, worked evenly and neatly over both faces" (Goodwin 1929d:119). A variety of points could be present; these included laurel and willow leaf forms, typical triangular Middle Stone Age points, as well as oak leaf ones (wide and rounded with scalloping on edges) (Goodwin 1929d:119). In other words, they were serrated or denticulated.

In the South African Museum collections, there were also some rough side scrapers as well as a single lunate or crescentic scraper (Goodwin 1929d:120). At 30 mm in length, it was larger than those found in the Wilton, an early Holocene culture (Hewitt 1921), and had a curved edge retouched by backing (Goodwin 1929d:120). Both Goodwin and his former Cambridge professor, Miles Burkitt, concluded that the Still Bay Industry was a mix of local Middle Stone Age and immigrant, more progressive ("Neo-anthropic") influences; this was the same explanation given for the Howieson's Poort (see below) (Goodwin 1929d:129; Burkitt 1928:170). In a wonderfully vivid attempt at historical reconstruction, Goodwin and Burkitt proposed,

that the racial types represented by the two industries were not mutually abhor-
rent, but sufficiently alike physically to allow a mixture of some sort. From our
knowledge of modern races we may presume that such a mixture implied the
presence of two types of implement makers (i.e. the men), and not merely con-
cubinage resulting from wars, as in this latter case the two types of implements
could not both survive. (Goodwin 1929d:129)

Burkitt had visited Goodwin and had been introduced to the South African
Stone Age. In turn, he "scooped" his former student, rushing into print his
own analysis in *South Africa's Past in Stone and Paint* before Goodwin could
complete his own (Burkitt 1928; Schlanger 2003; Schrire et al. 1986; Shepherd
2002:194–195). This would easily be considered an ethical violation today,
but perhaps Burkitt compensated for it by the number of prominent Stone
Age archaeologists he trained, including Goodwin, Louis Leakey, J. Desmond
Clark, and J. G. D. (Grahame) Clark (Gowlett 1990:21).

The other Middle Stone Age culture that still persists today is the Howieson's Poort. The site of the same name is located three miles southwest of
Grahamstown. It was excavated in 1925 by J. Hewitt, the curator of the Albany
Museum, and his colleague, Father R. P. Stapleton, Rector of St. Aidan's Col-
lege (Hewitt and Stapleton 1925; Stapleton and Hewitt 1927, 1928; Burkitt
1928:47). In a single layer about four inches thick, located about eight feet
below the surface, they recovered Still Bay–like points, large crescents, pointed
blades with an oblique edge at their distal end, various scrapers, as well as
the "first true burins to be recognized in South Africa"(Goodwin 1929d:133–
134). Burkitt (1928:47), stated that "if found in Europe these artefacts would
unhesitatingly be classed as Upper Palaeolithic." Goodwin (1929d:143) concluded that "it would thus appear that we have in the MSA a number of more
or less allied groups" but suggested that they all had a common origin in the
Mousterian (Goodwin 1929d:143). But Van Riet Lowe (1929a:147) was convinced there was an evolutionary sequence.

Goodwin and Van Riet Lowe (1929:7) also defined a series of stages for the
subsequent Later Stone Age. With its focus on bladelets and microliths, it was
possibly derived from the late Mesolithic or early Neolithic of North Africa.
This stage was also defined on technological grounds, the "making of a flat
percussion or striking platform, and the removal of a series of longitudinal
and parallel trimming flakes struck from about the edge of the striking plat-

form, and running down one face of the stone to flute it at right angles to the platform" (Goodwin 1929d:98). In other words, flakes or blades were struck from conical or cylindrical cores.

By 1955, when the Third Pan-African Congress of Prehistory was held in Livingstone, Northern Rhodesia (now Zambia), there was growing support for applying the South African sequence in other parts of sub-Saharan Africa (but see Malan 1957 for an alternative opinion). A lot of research was taking place in North Africa, but the European Palaeolithic sequence seemed to work there (Clark 1957:xxxi; 1970:38). The congress recommended using the three stages (Early, Middle, and Later Stone Age) with "Intermediate" or transitional periods in between. The First Intermediate period, between the Acheulian and the Middle Stone Age, would include the Sangoan and Fauresmith, while the Second (between the Middle and Later Stone Age) was marked by industries such as the Magosian (Clark 1957:xxxiii). The Magosian was initially defined by E. J. Wayland for material from Magosi in the Karamoja region of Uganda, a "microlithic culture with a Stillbay flavour" (Leakey 1936a:66). It was later shown to be an artificial mix of two different periods. The Sangoan was an industry from central Africa, presently associated with forest or woodlands. It includes heavy duty or core tools such as picks and core axes, along with flake tools (Tryon and McBrearty 2002:212). But where associated palaeoenvironmental indicators could be found, past conditions appear to have been more open. For example, at the western Kenyan Sangoan site of Simbi (McBrearty 1992; Tryon and McBrearty 2002:212), bovid teeth and soil carbonates both point to grassland habitats at time of occupation.

Until the early 1970s, the Middle Stone Age was thought to be coeval with the European Upper Palaeolithic, because both were associated with what appeared to be anatomically modern humans (Klein and Cruz-Uribe 1996:315; Clark 1970:124; Butzer 1971:462). As Barham (2001b:67) states, for most researchers "the post-Acheulian archaeological sequence for central Africa as a whole appeared largely of Late Pleistocene phenomenon." However, new dates that began to appear suggested that it overlapped with the Middle Palaeolithic instead (Vogel and Beaumont 1972; Klein and Cruz-Uribe 1996:315). Similarities with Neanderthal archaeology suggested that African Middle Stone Age people had somehow failed to develop the new technologies associated with the European Upper Palaeolithic. It was not until the 1980s that researchers began to argue for an African origin of anatomically modern humans, or at least for an early appearance of moderns on the continent. But there remained a serious problem. How could early moderns be anatomically like us but culturally similar to Eurasian groups like the Neanderthals, who were obviously not modern in morphology or behavior? The whole issue would only get worse when new dating techniques confirmed the antiquity of anatomical modern people throughout the African continent.

EAST AFRICA: PREHISTORY AND PLUVIALS

In one of the few treatments of the history of East African prehistoric research, Robertshaw (1990b:78) shows that there were traditionally two periods of interest. One is early human origins, and East Africa (along with South Africa) has produced the oldest evidence of fossil humans and their material culture. On the other end of the time scale, Iron Age and proto-historic archaeology became important, because it offered a way to do pre-colonial history. The wealth of Medieval Swahili coastal cities also attracted immediate attention. The Middle and Later Stone Age, the periods in between these two extremes, somehow got lost in the shuffle. One of the earliest accounts of research in East Africa was written by the Scottish geologist J. W. Gregory (1896). Gregory defined the term "rift valley" (Cooke 1958:3) and recognized the tectonic origins (Kent 1978:2) of this major feature of the landscape. The Eastern branch is named the Gregory Rift Valley in his honor. He noted the existence of former lakes, now dry, and proposed that glacial phases might correlate to the time of their maximum extent (Cooke 1958:3–5; Hamilton 1982:24), unwittingly beginning the great debate about pluvials and prehistory. He was also the first to describe stone tools (Gregory 1896:322–325), and also discovered the Acheulian site of Olorgesailie near Lake Magadi in southern Kenya (Leakey 1936a:38; Gowlett 1990:17).

The most important place for understanding the Stone Age prehistory of East Africa is Olduvai Gorge, a massive feature cut into the Serengeti Plain of northern Tanzania. The gorge exposes a 2-million-year-long layered sequence of rocks and sediments, with occasional volcanic tuffs stratified in between. There are artifacts throughout the sequence. The first scientist to observe it was German entomologist Wilhelm Kattwinkel, who, as legend has it, almost fell into the gorge in 1911 while in hot pursuit of a butterfly for his collection (Leakey 1974:155; Morell 1995:57). Anyone who has been to Olduvai can sympathize; there is little sign of the gorge until one reaches the edge. When

Kattwinkel visited, the mainland of Tanganyika was part of German East Africa. Hans Reck of the University of Berlin also visited the gorge in 1913 and discovered an anatomically modern human skeleton in one of the lower units, Bed II (Tattersall 1995:81). The issue was whether this skeleton, classified as Olduvai Hominid 1 or OH 1, was intrusive from a later period or truly ancient (Leakey 1936a:173; Tattersall 1995:81). By 1931, when Louis Leakey (1903–1972) first visited the site, Tanganyika had been a British protectorate for over a decade, awarded to them by the League of Nations after the end of the First World War. Leakey was the child of British missionaries and had grown up in central Kenya (Cole 1975). He organized his first East African Archaeological Expedition in 1926 (Leakey 1931, 1936a, 1953; Robertshaw 1990a:7). This involved the investigation of sites mainly in the Kenyan central rift valley (around Lakes Nakuru and Naivasha). But he remained intrigued with the German accounts of Olduvai, so he organized an expedition to the site in 1931, accompanied by Hans Reck (Tattersall 1995:82). Among other achievements, they identified the presence of stone artifacts in situ in Bed I (at FLK I); this material led to the definition of the Oldowan culture (Leakey 1967:xi). They also tried to assess the context in which Reck's human skeleton was found, as Leakey felt that it was genuinely ancient. Leakey had a lifelong habit of making claims for ancient modernity (Bowler 1987:100). In the 1930s, he recovered hominin material in western Kenya at Kanjera (where skull fragments seemed to be associated with Acheulian hand axes) and Kanam (where what he thought was a *Homo sapiens* mandible was found in what seemed to be an ancient context) (Leakey 1936b; Tobias 1962). Neither proved to be ancient moderns, nor did the Olduvai skeleton.

For the rest of his life, Leakey made regular return visits to identify sites, collect artifacts, and work out the geological and archaeological sequence at Olduvai (Leakey 1967:xi). From the mid-1930s onward, this work was done in collaboration with his second wife, Mary D. Leakey (1913–1996). His initial work concentrated on the Acheulian, which was classified using Abbé Henri Breuil's re-interpretation of Boucher de Perthes's Somme River terrace sequence as a model (Leakey 1951). But Mary Leakey (1975, 1994) would reassess this evidence and state that there was no significant progressive change in the Olduvai Acheulian despite its duration of close to 1.3 million years. The pace of fieldwork picked up after the 1959 discovery of OH 5, the *Zinjanthropus boisei* skull (Leakey 1959) and the first *Homo habilis* (Leakey et al. 1964) a year later. Increased funding led to the excavation of old land surfaces with associated stone artifact and faunal remains. The Leakeys had pioneered the exposure of these "living floors" years before at Olorgesailie (Leakey 1952). The original surface was uncovered and all significant finds were plotted on spatial maps. Sometimes this would involve massive clearance of overburden, still visible decades later at sites such as FLK *Zinjanthropus*, the Bed I surface associated with this "robust" australopithecine. Their study of the archaeological remains in Beds I and II at Olduvai (M. Leakey 1971) would set the standards for all later East African Early Stone Age research, and would also provide a cultural historical yardstick.

At the same time as the Leakeys were initiating the study of the prehistory of Kenya and northern Tanganyika, E. J. Wayland was conducting similar research in Uganda. The first director of the Geological Survey of Uganda, Wayland lived in the country between 1919 and 1939. He returned in the 1950s to conduct research at the site of Nsongezi (Cormack 1999:8; Kent 1978:2; Wayland 1934). His first field experience had been in Ceylon (now Sri Lanka), where he examined the local geology as well as the Stone Age prehistoric record (Wayland 1934:335). As he would continue to do in Uganda, Wayland interpreted what he saw in the light of the model of glacial meteorology formulated by C. E. P. Brooks (Cooke 1958:7; O'Brien 1939:6). Brooks had proposed that ice sheets would be responsible for permanent anticyclones above them; precipitation would therefore be slight. The deficit in the balance of rainfall would be made up in non-glaciated regions, which would experience pluvials or wet periods (O'Brien 1939:6). Wayland himself argued that there was no way to account for his geological evidence without using such a glacial model (Van Riet Lowe 1952:9). The "vicissitudes of climate were so important and so pronounced in the higher latitudes that one is led to imagine some connection between them and such climatic changes of similar date as can be demonstrated elsewhere" (Wayland in Van Riet Lowe 1952:10). But he noted that correlation did not necessarily mean causation. Northern glaciations and tropical pluvials might both have been produced by some third agency (Wayland in Van Riet Lowe 1952:11). Twenty-four of Wayland's publications, from 1928 to 1958, deal with the "Pleistocene, Pluvial Periods, lake levels and climatic changes" (Langlands 1967:40). Clearly, it was central to all of his geological reconstructions. However, Wayland did recognize the role of tectonic activities in the creation of the rift valley and its lake basins. In one of his most famous papers, he admitted "that the effects of earth movement and of pluviation can be aggravatingly similar and often impossible to distinguish on individual sites. It became apparent that, in order to draw the necessary distinctions, regional research was necessary, and that correlation must be effected over very wide areas" (Wayland 1934:339, 346).

Later researchers would have mixed views on the quality of Wayland's archaeological research. For Van Riet Lowe (1952:13), "his attitude toward associated finds and correlations of events embodies the most balanced caution and patience of the true scientist." However, Merrick Posnansky (1967:10, 1970), who also played a major role in creating a Ugandan prehistoric record, had a different opinion: "Wayland the seeker of a climatological sequence ruined the work of Wayland the archaeologist." Among his achievements was the creation of a long culture historical sequence for Uganda, but only one of them, the Sangoan, is still in use today (Cooke 1958:8; Posnansky 1967:9; Wayland 1934:336). It was interpreted as "mainly a flake culture allied to the Levalloisian but influenced to some extent by elements of the hand-axe culture" (Leakey 1936a:48), and would eventually become part of the "First Intermediate" period.

Leakey himself defined a variety of post-Acheulian industries, on comparison with sites in Europe and South Africa (Leakey 1936a:49–54). Some were characterized by triangular bifacial hand axes (Pseudo Stillbay, Nanyukian), other by backed blades (early Aurignacian) (Leakey 1936a:52–54). While faunal correlation was possible, all of this research was limited by the lack of chronological control. Leakey's pioneering work on the climatic and human history of Lakes Nakuru, Elmenteita, and Naivasha offered a possibility (Leakey and Solomon 1929; Leakey 1936a:12; Hamilton 1982:2). The climate stratigraphic data was used to identify a series of pluvial or wet periods (Cole 1954:34). Erik Nilsson had found confirmation of Pleistocene climate change in the East African mountains (Ruwenzori, Elgon, Kenya, and Kilimanjaro), where there was evidence of repeated high-altitude glaciations (Wayland 1934:342; Livingstone 1975:256). These could be correlated with the glacial phases of the Northern Hemisphere.

The term "pluvial" was first defined by Frank Dixey as "a climate of long extent, consistently wetter (though allowing for minor fluctuations within the whole) than the climate pertaining today" (in Flint 1959b:346). An interpluvial was a period that had a similar environment to the present, but was drier (Flint 1959b:346). In Africa, it was assumed that glacials were represented by cool moist periods, while interglacials had climates similar to present (Leakey 1967:79; Hamilton 1982:2). The cause of a pluvial was temperature change; cooler environments would lower potential evapo-transpiration, and higher amounts of available water would then be available (Hamilton 1982:64). It did not have to mean increasing precipitation. Evidence for such climates could be seen in the geological record, and then could be correlated over long distances. Five pluvial stages were eventually recognized: three main and two less important wet phases. These include the Kamasian or second pluvial, Gamblian (third), Makalian (fourth), and Nakuran (fifth). A Kanjeran was eventually added as the first pluvial (Leakey 1936a:12, 1955:293, 1967:80; Bishop 1967:377) (figure 2.3). These were initially accepted as lithostratigraphic or rock stratigraphic units, rather than merely climatic ones (Cooke 1957:51). The system was accepted by the participants at the First Pan-African Congress of Prehistory in Nairobi in 1947 and was refined at the second congress held in Algiers in 1952 (Leakey 1955; Bishop 1967:377; Clark 1957:xxxi).

All along there were some criticisms of the pluvial chronology (Flint 1959a, 1959b; Bishop and Posnansky 1960; Cooke 1957, 1958; Solomon 1939). Those who objected were split between those who were not sure if the information was wrong, and those who thought that unequivocal proof had yet to be discovered (Flint 1959b:343). Alexander du Toit (1947), a South African researcher, returned from the first Pan-African congress and wrote a critique of the entire approach. It seems fitting that Basil Cooke, a vertebrate palaeontologist and geologist, used the Fifth Alexander du Toit lecture to assess the geological evidence (or lack of it) for pluvials. He argued that while local sequences were well defined, regional correlations were not (Cooke 1958). East African pluvials did not always seem to happen in sync with Northern Hemisphere glaciations (Cooke 1957:55). Quite remarkably, Cooke concluded by suggesting that archaeological evidence would provide a better method for dating and cross correlation (Cooke 1958; Flint 1959a:281, 1971). He felt that stone tools could be used "more or less as zone fossils, equating typological equivalents on the time scale and evaluating the climatic background accordingly" (Cooke 1957:53). At the same time, American geologist Richard Foster Flint (1959a, 1959b) conducted a study tour of East African sites. What he saw in the field also led him to express dissatisfaction with the pluvial sequence

60

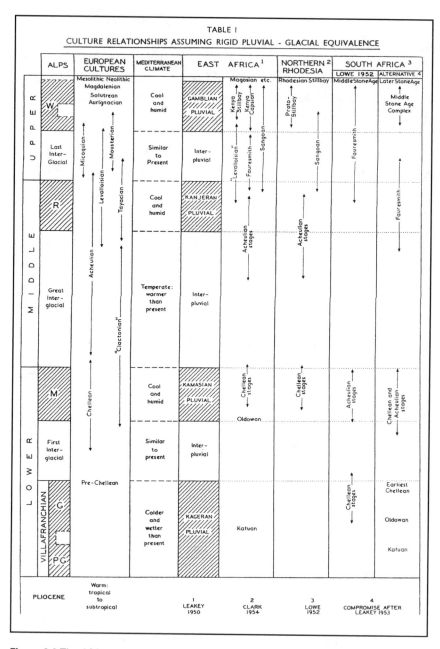

Figure 2.3 The African pluvial sequence (Cooke 1957:52). Reprinted with permission of the Livingstone Museum, Livingstone, Zambia

(Flint 1959b:343). Other causes, such as tectonic activity, had to be dismissed before a pluvial explanation could be accepted (Flint 1959b:356).

One of Wayland's geological successors in Uganda was W. W. Bishop (1931–1977). Bishop served from August 1956 to May 1959 as the Pleistocene geologist for the Geological Survey of Uganda and from 1962 to 1965 as curator of the Uganda Museum (Cormack 1999:7; Day and Banham 1999). His own fieldwork (Bishop 1969, 1978; Bishop and Posnansky 1960) was conducted at a time when the pluvial model was being replaced. He was one of the organizers of the 1965 Burg Wartenstein conference on the "Systematic Investigation of the African Later Tertiary and Quaternary" (Bishop and Clark 1967). Here Flint (1967) and Cooke (1967) repeated their call for a firm stratigraphic framework for any reconstruction of Pleistocene geology. By this time, the pluvial sequence was replaced due to detailed mapping and correlation of rock outcrops. In Bishop's immortal conclusion, "attractive though the idea may have seemed, human strength of character was neither tempered in the head of a Pliocene drought, nor quenched in the Pleistocene pluvials" (Bishop 1976:227). From now on, lithostratigraphy would be the basis for regional correlation (Bishop 1967, 1969; Hay 1976).

The development of radiocarbon dating in the 1950s also helped immeasurably. When applied to pluvial phases in lake deposits in the Omo River basin of Ethiopia as well as at East Turkana, Kenya, it became apparent that high water intervals belonged to the Holocene (Butzer 1975:867; Butzer et al. 1972; Hamilton 1982:2–3, 45; Livingstone 1975). In fact, it was wetter in interglacials, rather than full glacials. But what were palaeoclimatologists supposed to do about genuinely Pleistocene deposits? As recently as 1982, Hamilton (1982:45) reported that there was little progress in dating high lake stands which were beyond the radiocarbon limit; also, tectonic activity might account for changing water levels in East African lakes.

What does the pluvial model say about the African origins of *Homo sapiens*? It was mentioned earlier that Louis Leakey was convinced of the presence of modern humans in the remote past of East Africa. He did not let his failure to find genuinely ancient moderns at Kanjera and Kanam dissuade him; somewhere there should be incontrovertible proof. Since large African mammals had not changed much in the interval since the Middle Pleistocene, little time had passed (Leakey 1936a:163). Surely anatomically modern humans must have a similar antiquity.

"If this is true, then upon theoretical evidence we may conclude that man as we know him today, man of the species *Homo sapiens*, was probably also fully evolved *physically* by the beginning of the Middle Pleistocene" (Leakey 1936a:163–164; italics in original). He concluded that *Homo sapiens* might have been responsible for the Acheulian as well (Leakey 1936a:164). Noting that Upper Pleistocene deposits contained anatomically modern fossils in many parts of the world, their common ancestor must have evolved and dispersed much earlier (Leakey 1936a:164–165). Why could not Africa be the place where this occurred?

CHANGING PERSPECTIVES IN AFRICAN STONE AGE RESEARCH: NEW DATES, NEW MODELS

Just as one kind of chronometric dating, radiocarbon, eliminated the idea of wet glacial periods in Africa, new methods would change our concept of earlier phases of African prehistory. By the time the *Zinjanthropus* skull was discovered at Olduvai Gorge, there were many fossil hominins that had been blasted out of breccia in a series of dolomite caves in South Africa. These came from sites such as Taung (in 1924), Sterkfontein (starting in 1936), Kromdraai (starting in 1938), Swartkrans (starting in 1948), and Makapansgat (starting in 1946/1947) (Dart 1925; Broom and Robinson 1949; Brain 1993); similar sites are still being discovered in the Sterkfontein Valley (Keyser et al. 2000). When Piltdown was finally removed from the tree of human evolution, prominent anatomists such as Wilfrid Le Gros Clark (1947) traveled to South Africa and, for the first time, promoted the acceptance of these australopithecines as our human ancestors (Shepherd 2003:37; Tobias 1984). The first Middle Stone Age hominins were found by miners working at Broken Hill Mine in Northern Rhodesia (now Kabwe, Zambia) in 1921 (Woodward 1921). But since they were not really modern in appearance, they did not figure in the debate about the origin of the Cro-Magnons of Europe.

The pace of East African early hominin research increased in the 1960s with the discovery of the first ancient fossil hominins in Bed I at Olduvai Gorge, Tanzania: *Zinjanthropus boisei* in 1959 and *Homo habilis* in 1960 (Leakey 1959; Leakey et al. 1964). But it was the application of potassium-argon dating to the volcanic lavas and tuffs at Olduvai that would shock scientists. The initial dates for the Lower Pleistocene deposits of Bed I made these two hominins between 1.7 and 1.8 million years old (Leakey et al. 1961). This was quite unexpected; at the time it was generally felt that this period began only 600,000 years ago (Editors of *Life* 1961:29). As a result, Louis and Mary Leakey received sufficient funds to allow for the excavation of old land surfaces with scatters of stones and bones. These living floors became the focus of much debate about the nature of early hominin adaptations (Isaac 1978a, 1978b; Bunn 1991; Willoughby 1991). Were they hunters or gatherers? What was the role of meat use in early human evolution? How did the reliance on stone tools and material culture begin, and how did it affect our evolution?

The new dates and methods also led to an explosion of palaeoanthropological research in East Africa. A team investigated the Shungura Formation west of the Omo River in southern Ethiopia between 1967 and 1974, recording over 700 m of fossiliferous deposits (Coppens et al. 1976). The methods pioneered here became the basis for the multi-disciplinary approach to human origins work still practiced as palaeoanthropology today. Omo Shungura also produced some of the world's earliest stone tools, approximately 2.3 million years old (Merrick 1976; Merrick and Merrick 1976). Later deposits in the Kibish Formation at Omo yielded two skulls, one of which was considered modern, the other near modern; both were thought to be about 130,000 years old (Rightmire 1984:313–314; 1989:109; but see McDougall et al. 2004 for new dates). Research on the east side of Lake Turkana (until 1976 Lake Rudolf) began in 1969 (Isaac and Isaac 1997), while the west side was first studied in the 1980s. By then, palaeontologists had prospected in the Afar Rift Valley to the north in Ethiopia. Starting in the 1970s, the Hadar area yielded a wealth of hominins, between 3 and 4 million years old (Johanson and White 1979; Johanson et al. 1978). Subsequent work in the Middle Awash has produced hominins extending back over 5 million years ago (Haile-Selassie 2001; White et al. 1994), as well as new examples of most members of the genus *Homo* (Asfaw et al. 2002; White et al. 2003).

South of Olduvai in the 1970s, a volcanic ash layer at Laetoli (originally Laetolil) yielded the world's earliest human footprints (Leakey and Harris 1987; Leakey and Hay 1979); German palaeoanthropologist Ludwig Kohl-Larson identified the site in 1935 when he visited the Lake Eyasi area. Interestingly enough, the Leakeys visited the site in 1959 and decided against further work, since it did not have Oldowan artifacts (Leakey 1967:xii). However, the footprint tuff lies beneath a Middle Stone Age deposit, in which Mary Leakey's team later discovered a skull, labeled Ngaloba or LH 18 (Laetoli Hominid 18) (Leakey et al. 1976).

But the later stages of African Stone Age prehistory remained hampered by the lack of chronometric dates. If they were less than 40,000 years old, radiocarbon could be applied. If older, then only relative methods provided any estimation of their true age. The discovery of anatomically modern or near modern fossil remains with Middle Stone Age or Middle Palaeolithic artifacts was long used to argue that both were recent. This led to the assumption that African modern people had somehow failed to develop culturally. New dating techniques pioneered in the 1980s led to a substantial revision of age estimates (see chapter 4). Both the artifacts and the fossils were quite ancient, offering support to new genetic data and Out of Africa II model of modern human origins (Stringer and Andrews 1988a). Now Africa was seen as the place of origin of almost all hominin species, including us (Simons 1989).

Many archaeologists and human palaeontologists were reluctant to accept the primal importance of Africa in the later stages of human evolution. A new debate arose about what makes hominins human, a debate remarkably similar to that which first led to the rejection of the South African australopithecines. Prior to the Second World War, it was assumed that the brain led the way in early human evolution; in addition, it was felt that the oldest fossil hominins should be from East Asia (Dennell 2001:50). The australopithecines were in the wrong place with the wrong kind of anatomy since they had small brains, but they were bipedal. For anatomists such as Sir Arthur Keith, a brain size of around 900 cc divided living apes from living humans (Dennell 2001:50). For most early-twentieth-century palaeontologists, a similar boundary or "cerebral Rubicon" of about 700 to 900 cc split humans from non-humans. The Asian species, *Homo erectus*, was the first to pass this boundary (Wood and Collard 1999:68–69). Now with the revision of dates for early modern humans in Africa, a similar problem presents itself. There now appears to be a symbolic Rubicon, separating behaviorally modern humans from all others, including the *Homo sapiens* of the African Middle Palaeolithic and Middle Stone Age. Only the former are people with culture, with mental capacities like us today. What these earlier "others" in Africa represent is the subject of the debates at the heart of this book.

3

The Palaeoenvironmental Context: The Origin and Dispersal of Modern Humans

> *The distribution and density of the human population in Africa is regulated primarily by the availability of water to drive biological and human activities.* (Gasse 2000:189)
>
> *It may be worth suggesting that the archaeology of Pleistocene man might be subsumed within palaeontology, with the recognition that the archaeologist is studying one animal among a range of species, an animal which happened to make tools and leave them behind as an additional category of behavioural evidence. While for practical purposes it may be necessary to specialize in the analysis of artifacts, it would be short-sighted to interpret their patterning independent of palaeontological and palaeoecological evidence.* (Turner 1984:212)

In the twenty-first century, there is growing concern about climate change and global "warming." How many of the observed changes are due to anthropogenic (human) causes? Do greenhouse gases released into the atmosphere produce abnormal temperature increases worldwide? Or is what we are experiencing part of the natural cycle? What effect will these changes have on human adaptation and survival? Could human activity actually produce irreversible climate change? This debate must seem strange to a Quaternary geologist, someone whose interests lie in understanding the environmental context of the last 2.6 million years of earth history (Burroughs 2005; Clague 2005; Macdougall 2004; Pillans and Naish 2004). Comprising the Pleistocene and Holocene epochs, the Quaternary was a time of continuing climatic instability, shifting periodically from long cold glacial to warm interglacial conditions and back again (Hewitt 2000:907; table 1.1). As Alley (2000b:3) has stressed, "large rapid and widespread climatic changes were common on earth for most of the time for which we have good records, but were absent during the few critical millennia when humans developed agriculture and industry." So we may not know what is normal, expected, or predictable anyway. Environmental changes during the Quaternary are closely associated with key periods in human evolution, something that has long been recognized (Bobe and Behrensmeyer 2004; Calvin 2002; deMenocal 1995, 2004; Vrba 1993, 1995; Vrba et al. 1995). The onset of glacial conditions around 2.6 million years ago corresponds to the appearance of the genus *Homo*. These first hominins had enlarged brains relative to body size and an adaptive system involving some kind of material culture.

CAUSES AND CONSEQUENCES OF QUATERNARY ENVIRONMENTAL CHANGE

The environmental change defining the Quaternary epoch continues a pattern begun in the preceding Tertiary period. An ice cap centered in Antarctica started growing in the Oligocene epoch, around 35 million years ago, and in the Arctic around 2.4 million years ago (Hewitt 2000). In the mid-Tertiary, the tectonic uplift of central and East Africa began. This process, accompanied by rifting, faulting, and volcanism, continues intermittently to the present day (Hamilton 1982:8). These forces led to the creation of the two branches of the East African rift system, the Albertine or Western Rift, associated with the great lakes (Lakes Nyasa/Malawi, Rukwa, Tanganyika, Albert, and Edward), and the Gregory or Eastern Rift, named for the Scottish geologist who was one of the first to describe it (Gregory 1896). Tertiary uplift along the western margins of East Africa also led to the reversal of formerly west-flowing rivers, creating basins like that in which Lake Victoria lies. Drainage in the northwest was diverted northward and became part of the Nile system (Hamilton 1982:12). It disrupted the continuous band of equatorial rain forest in central Africa, the fossil remnants of which can be seen in the petrified forests near Sibilot Mountain east of Lake Turkana in northern Kenya. Additionally, it may have split the range of the last common ancestor of African apes and early hominins, leaving the apes in the western rain forest, but forcing hominins on to the drying woodlands and savannas to the east (Coppens 1994). The rift valleys became sediment traps receiving and preserving the phenomenal paleontological and geochronological record that allows us to understand the Plio-Pleistocene evolution of humans. The earliest bipedal hominins appeared in Africa during a long period of cooling in the late Miocene, 5 to 8 million years ago (Haile-Selassie 2001; Brunet et al. 2002; Senut et al. 2001). In Eurasia, grasslands replaced widespread tropical forests, and the Mediterranean evaporated 5 to 6 million years ago, an event which is labeled the "Messinian salinity crisis" (Hsu 1983; Duggen et al. 2003; Krijgsman et al. 1999). The inhabitants of these mid-latitude Eurasian tropical forests included an amazing variety of apes, almost all of which went extinct in the late Miocene (Kordos and Begun 2002; Begun 2003). But in Africa, according to most classical models (Dart 1953, 1957; Lovejoy 1981; Stanley 1992, 1995, 1996; Vrba 1993, 1995), the environmental change led to new opportunities for more terrestrial life, and the first bipedal hominins developed in response. Alternatively, Eurasian hominoids became more mobile, and, in a drying world, they might have returned to the home of their Early Miocene ancestors, to become the direct ancestors, not only of African hominins, but also of chimpanzees and gorillas as well (Heizmann and Begun 2001; Kordos and Begun 2002; Begun 2003).

Why did this cycling begin around 2.6 million years ago? This date has recently been chosen by the International Commission on Stratigraphy as the start of the Quaternary, even though the same committee favors retaining 1.8 million years ago for the beginning of the Pleistocene epoch (Clague 2005). Until around 3 million years ago, North and South America were separate continents. Warm water from the Pacific Ocean circulated freely into the North Atlantic through what is now the Isthmus of Panama. This Great American Seaway began to shrink around 4.6 million years ago and forced a detour of the conveyor belt of ocean currents. Today, the Gulf Stream is part of a conveyor belt that brings warmer water from the south to the North Atlantic, making Europe much warmer than North American locations at the same latitude. In the north, the water from this current cools and sinks, and then moves southward at great depths (Broecker 2000; Broecker and Denton 1990; Calvin 1998, 2002).

In the late Pliocene, continental drift created a land bridge where Panama is today (Cane and Molnar 2001); there is evidence for increasing circulation of this North Atlantic conveyor (including the Gulf Stream) (Wright 2001:142). This sudden change could have led to a significant temperature drop in the Northern Hemisphere, and to the onset of glacial conditions. Cane and Molnar (2001) have identified another possible cause, the closure of the Indonesian seaway 3 to 4 million years ago as New Guinea moved north. This led to more water flowing from the North Pacific into the Indian Ocean, which altered the precipitation pattern in East Africa and made it more arid. This continental displacement may also have decreased atmospheric heat transport from the tropics to higher latitudes, leading to the formation of northern ice sheets and the onset of global glaciation (Cane and Molnar 2001:157).

Whatever initiated this system, it has been a major component of earth climate ever since. Modeling past climate is not an easy task. For the Quaternary, the data consists of proxy records that must be linked to global circulation patterns. In the nineteenth century, geologists like Louis Agassiz (1840), working with terrestrial records in the Swiss Alps, identified deposits associated with four phases of ice advance subsequently named the Gunz, Mindel, Riss, and Wurm (Penck and Brückner 1909; Roberts 1984). Within these long cold periods or glacials were shorter periods of ice advance, stadials and retreat, and interstadials. Long periods of warmer conditions were defined as interglacials.

Various theories have been offered for why this cycling continued over the course of the Pleistocene (Bradley 1985; Imbrie and Imbrie 1979; Macdougall 2004). Most climatologists would agree that it is still underway. Milutin Milankovitch (1879–1958), a Serbian astronomer, proposed the most plausible hypothesis. Building upon the earlier work of James Croll, Milankovitch's "orbital theory" of the ice ages is based on variations in insolation or sunlight reaching the earth (Croll 1867, 1875; Milankovitch 1920, 1941, 1969). He proposed that three factors regulated the frequency of ice advance and retreat (Imbrie and Imbrie 1979). The first is obliquity, the tilt of earth's spin or rotation axis, the line connecting the north and south poles. It is currently 23.5° from vertical, but fluctuates from 21.5° to 24.5° and back again approximately every 41,000 years. The greater the tilt, the more intense the seasons in both hemispheres become. The second is the shape or eccentricity of earth's orbit around the sun. Over 100,000 years, it stretches into a more eccentric ellipse and then grows more nearly circular again. As orbital

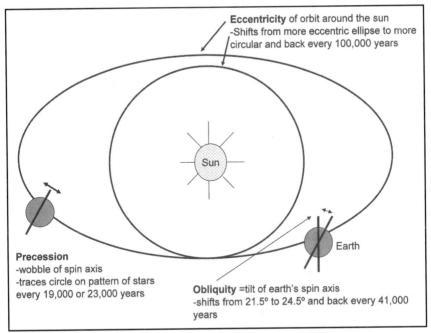

Figure 3.1 The Croll-Milankovitch astronomical theory of the Quaternary ice ages

intensity increases, the difference in the earth's distance from the sun at the orbit's nearest and farthest points grows, intensifying the seasons in one hemisphere and moderating them in the other (Alley 2000a, 2000b; Broecker and Denton 1990; Imbrie and Imbrie 1979; Macdougall 2004). The effect of the 100,000-year cycle is to determine how important the precession or third factor is (Alley 2000b:97) (figure 3.1).

While obliquity and orbital eccentricity change the intensity of the seasons, precession affects their interaction. The precession or wobble of the earth's spin axis traces out a complete circle on the background of stars every 19,000 or 23,000 years (Broecker and Denton 1990). It determines whether summer falls at a near or far point in the earth's orbit (Alley 2000b:97). At present, the Northern Hemisphere has summer and the Southern Hemisphere has winter when the earth is farthest from the sun. The Northern Hemisphere has winter and the Southern Hemisphere has summer when the earth is closest to the sun; about 10,000 years ago, this pattern reversed (Alley 2000b:97). Some threshold insolation value could control the development of glacial ice; all it would take would be a summer when not all snow or ice melts.

From the start of the Quaternary up to 900,000 years ago, ice sheets fluctuated in accordance with the 41,000-year cycle; afterwards, the 100,000-year cycle replaced it, and the scale of climate change becomes increasingly dramatic
(Hewitt 2000:907; Servant 2001:121; Crowley 2002:1474; deMenocal 1995,
2004; Trauth et al. 2005; EPICA 2004:623; McManus 2004:611). Whatever
caused this Middle Pleistocene revolution is not clear, but its impact could
have been catastrophic (EPICA 2004:625; Walker 2004:597; White 2004). The
newly dominant 100,000-year cycles,

> have also been the largest in magnitude of all the ice-age cycles, combining
> with a long term climatic trend towards more glacial conditions over mil-
> lions of years to produce several of the most extreme glaciations on record
> (the last glacial maximum of the last ice age, MIS 3, for instance). (McManus
> 2004:611)

Warm periods have a duration of around 10,000 years, while cold stages
last for about nine times as long (deMenocal 1995:53; Calvin 2002:212). If the
Holocene or current period represents an interstadial, another glacial is in our
near future. But studies of MIS, or marine isotope stage, 11, between approximately 430,000 and 402,000 years ago, reveal an interglacial that lasted about
28,000 years. Somehow it missed the trigger that would return the globe to
glacial conditions after about 10,000 years of warmth (McManus 2004:612).
MIS 11 exhibits similar atmospheric conditions to the present, not counting human impact on greenhouse gases (EPICA 2004:626; Walker 2004:596;
White 2004:1610).

In the deep-sea cores, there is a similar proxy record. Around 900,000 years
ago, there is an increase in the amplitude of oxygen isotope fluctuations in organisms extracted from deep-sea sediments. This is accompanied by 100,000,
23,000, and 19,000 frequencies. Before this date, there does not seem to be any
23,000-year cycle. It is possible that some terrestrial force produced a bulge
in the earth at the equator and subsequent flattening at the poles at this time,
so that this process may be responsible for the 23,000- and 19,000-year forcing. Precession may be a recent phenomenon (Servant 2001:121,126) and not
orbitally driven at all.

The evidence to confirm the Croll-Milankovitch theory was initially
recovered during the coring of deep-sea sediments in the world's oceans
beginning in the 1960s. These sediments are formed by remains of micro-

organisms, including foraminifera, radiolaria, and diatoms. Some of these are planktonic, living near the surface of the ocean, while others are benthic, living in deep water. Many secrete tests, external shell-like protective covers of $CaCO_3$ or silica. These tests contain oxygen extracted from seawater in relative isotopic amounts identical to those in the ocean at the time they are absorbed (Alley 2000b:92). After death, these organisms settle slowly but continuously from the water column, form ooze, and provide the bulk of marine sediments. Some of these taxa are also good index fossils for biostratigraphic purposes, and help determine the age of deposits. Others provide detailed information concerning ocean water temperature or volume. For example, in polar waters today, the foraminifera *Globorotalia pachyderma* coils its test to the left, while in temperate waters, the same species coils right. In tropical waters, another related species, *Globorotalia menardii*, is dominant.

Foraminifera absorb oxygen from the surrounding seawater in the isotopic ratios present during their life. Isotopes are forms of elements with identical chemical composition but a different number of neutrons; as a result, their atomic mass varies. Unstable or radioactive isotopes form the basis for radiometric dating (chapter 4), but stable isotopes of oxygen can be used for environmental reconstruction. Oxygen has eight protons, but eight to ten neutrons; so three isotopes are possible. In the atmosphere, 99.759% of oxygen is ^{16}O, 0.0374% is ^{17}O, and 0.2039% is ^{18}O (Bowen 1978:62). When removed from water, by evaporation or precipitation, isotopes are lost at different rates depending on temperature. As Emiliani (1955) determined, the ratio of ^{18}O to ^{16}O (recorded as $\delta^{18}O$) can be used to determine ocean water temperature or water volume, acting as markers of glacials and interglacials. During glacial events, sea levels dropped as more water was locked up on land as ice. Deep-sea cores should be ^{18}O enriched, because in colder conditions, less of the heavy isotope evaporates relative to the lighter ^{16}O. Similar patterns can be found in apparently annual or seasonal growth rings in ice in Greenland and Antarctica. But due to the global water cycle, the ice ratios should be the opposite of those in the deep-sea cores. Water evaporated from oceans eventually falls as precipitation and enriches ice. During glacials, ice cores should be ^{18}O depleted and ^{16}O enriched. In interglacials, as temperature increases and ice melts, ice should be ^{18}O enriched (^{16}O depleted), while deep-sea cores should be ^{18}O depleted. More of the heavier isotope can be evaporated out of oceans as atmospheric temperature increases; it is then deposited in ice due to precipitation.

During glacials, sea levels decrease, creating land bridges and new territory for colonization by plants, animals, and early humans. In interglacials, sea level increases, flooding coastal areas. There is less ice on land and ocean temperatures are warmer. Shackleton (2000; Hays et al. 1976) recognized that [18]O ratios reflect ocean volume rather than ocean temperature (Broecker and Denton 1990) and they serve as a history of Quaternary climate change. The recognition of these cycles in deep-sea cores led to the definition of a series of oxygen isotope stages (OIS) and sub-stages. These have recently been re-labeled as marine isotope stages (MIS), and are relatively well-defined chronological phases, identifiable in the marine record as well as in the ice cores of Greenland and Antarctica. Given consecutive numbers, they are counted from present (as MIS or OIS stage 1, the Holocene or the current interglacial) back in time. Odd numbers represent warm periods, even numbers cold ones; for example MIS 2 is the last glacial, and extends from approximately 32,000 to 13,000 years before present (figure 3.2; table 3.1). At the height of MIS 2, it is thought that much of Africa was abandoned, as conditions became too dry and cool to support life. MIS 3 dates between 64,000 and 32,000 years ago, and is the time in which modern humans entered Europe, interbreeding with or replacing the indigenous Neanderthals

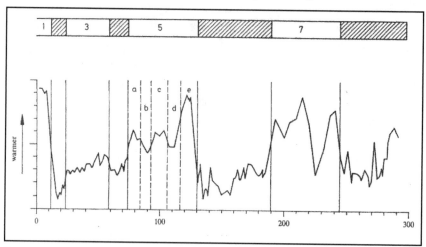

Figure 3.2 The oxygen isotope sequence for the last 300,000 years (Aitken et al. 1993:8). Reprinted with permission of the Royal Society and Dr. Christopher Stringer

Table 3.1. Marine Isotope Stages for the last 300,000 years

Marine Isotope Stages and Sub-stages	Approximate Time Range (in years BP= before present)	Environmental Context in Africa	Hominin Origins and Dispersals	Cultural Phases
1	13,000 BP to present	Holocene; warm conditions similar to present; sometimes wetter than present, producing large lakes, such as Mega Chad		Epipalaeolithic, Mesolithic, and all later cultural periods
2	32,000 to 13,000 BP	Last glacial maximum (LGM); extremely cold and dry; expansion of Sahara and Kalahari deserts; loss of rainforest; vegetation zones compressed toward the equator	Modern humans worldwide; last Neanderthals in Europe	Western Europe: Solutrean North Africa: no occupation? Sub-Saharan Africa: Middle/Later Stone Age transition in some localities?
3	64,000 to 32,000 BP	Interstadial; unstable climate that fluctuated on short time span; sea level about 70 m lower than present	Out of Africa II: modern humans enter Middle East, East and South Asia, and Europe; displace (replace?) Neanderthals	European Middle/Upper Palaeolithic transition Sub-Saharan Africa: Middle/Later Stone Age transition?
4	75,000 to 64,000 BP	Stadial; intense cold; vegetation in Africa similar to LGM; expanded North African desert; sea level about 75 m below present level	Neanderthals in Middle East, modern humans in Africa	Middle Palaeolithic in North Africa/Middle Stone Age in sub-Saharan Africa
5a	85,000 to 75,000 BP	Warmer		Middle Palaeolithic/Middle Stone Age
5b	95,000 to 85,000 BP	Cooler		Middle Palaeolithic/Middle Stone Age
5c	105,000 to 95,000 BP	Warmer		Middle Palaeolithic/Middle Stone Age

Table 3.1. Continued

Marine Isotope Stages and Sub-stages	Approximate Time Range (in years BP= before present)	Environmental Context in Africa	Hominin Origins and Dispersals	Cultural Phases
5d	116,000 to 105,000 BP	Cooler		Middle Palaeolithic/ Middle Stone Age
5e	130,000 to 116,000 BP	Last interglacial = Riss/Wurm or Eemian Interglacial in Europe; rainforest expanded; rainfall higher in North Africa; African environments spread into Middle East	Modern humans ("Proto-Cro-Magnons") at Skhūl and Qafzeh in Israel	Middle Palaeolithic/ Middle Stone Age
6	195,000 to 130,000 BP	Glacial; drier than now; extended North African desert	For Foley and Lahr (1997), development of moderns in Africa, Neanderthals in Europe; other models already present in OIS 7	Middle Palaeolithic/ Middle Stone Age
7	251,000 to 195,000 BP	Temperate or cool	Foley and Lahr (1997): Mode 3 expansion into Eurasia by Homo helmei; for others, time of first modern humans appearing in Africa, Neanderthals in Europe	Middle Palaeolithic/ Middle Stone Age
8	297,000 to 251,000 BP	Glacial	Homo heidelbergensis in Africa and Europe	End of the Acheulian; start of the Middle Palaeolithic/ Middle Stone Age

Source: Compiled from Bradley 1985; Stringer and Gamble 1993; Adams et al. 1997; Kukla et al. 2002.

(table 3.1; Boquet-Appel and Demars 2000; D'Errico and Goni 2003; D'Errico et al. 1998; Zubrow 1989). It also saw the Middle to Upper Palaeolithic archaeological transition in Europe, and in some parts of Africa, the Middle to Later Stone Age shift. MIS 4, extending from 75,000 to 64,000 years ago, is associated with cold, stadial conditions. It might have been cold and harsh enough for some cold-adapted European Neanderthals to migrate or retreat into the Middle East; whether they encountered *Homo sapiens* during this journey is still debatable. Stage 5 is subdivided into five sub-stages, from 5a (the most recent) to 5e (the earliest). Sub-stages 5a and 5c represent interstadials, while 5b and 5d were periods of returning cold conditions. MIS 5e represents the last interglacial, traditionally known in Europe as the Riss-Wurm or Eemian Interglacial (Shackleton et al. 2002; Kukla et al. 2002). Climate was as warm, if not warmer, than present. Warmth-loving species such as hippopotamus lived in Britain, and African flora and fauna spread into the Middle East, along with early modern humans, who left their remains at the Mugharet es Skhūl and Jebel Qafzeh in Israel. The first anatomically modern humans and Middle Palaeolithic or Middle Stone Age industries may have emerged in Africa during MIS 7, between 251,000 and 195,000 years before present, if not earlier.

In an important paper, Hays et al. (1976) provided evidence for Milankovitch forcing of global temperatures using two deep-sea cores drilled from sediments in the Southern Indian Ocean (Crowley 2002:1473). They measured three phenomena: (1) the ^{18}O composition of planktonic foraminifera, (2) T_s, an estimate of summer sea surface temperatures (from a statistical analysis of radiolarian assemblages), and (3) the frequency of occurrence of another radiolarian species, *Cycladrophora davisiana*, which serves as an independent proxy for water temperature (Hays et al. 1976:1122). One core (RC11-120) has a complete sequence back to MIS 9 while the other (E49-18) is only missing the Holocene record. They found that the T_s curve in both differs markedly from that produced using the oxygen isotope values. There is an abrupt increase in estimated temperature of up to 6°C in MIS stage 1 and at the bases of MIS stages 5, 7, 9, and 11 as temperatures begin to moderate. Otherwise, temperatures fluctuate less than 3°C (Hays et al. 1976:1124). The dominant climatic periodicity was the 100,000-year eccentricity cycle (Hays et al. 1976:1131).

Ice cores from Antarctica (Vostok, Byrd, and the new EBC core) (EPICA 2004) and Greenland (GRIP, GISP2, NGRIP, and others) offer a more precise record. Here there are annual, and often seasonal, layers with a record of trapped greenhouse gases (CO_2 or carbon dioxide and CH_4 or methane), oxygen isotopes comparable to the deep-sea record, as well as dust and pollen initially extending back 110,000 years before present (Alley 2000a:1332). In Greenland, winter snow is buried without being exposed to sunlight. Since snow deposited in summer is heated by sunlight, there is a change in texture, producing a seasonal signal (Alley 2000b:44). The Greenland Ice Core Project core was obtained by a European consortium from 1989 to 1992 and is over 1,200 m long (Johnsen et al. 2001:301). The Greenland Ice Sheet Project 2 core is the product of an American research team and was extracted from 1989 to 1993 just 20 m west of the Greenland Ice Core Project location (Alley 2000b:21). Both extend back in time to about 250,000 years ago (Calvin 2002:218; Johnsen et al. 2001:303). The Greenland Ice Core Project core recorded twenty-four interstadials during the last ice age (Hewitt 2000:907).

The Vostok core at one time had the record for the longest sequence; it extends back to around 420,000 years ago, so it includes part of MIS 11 (Walker 2004:596; EPICA 2004:623). This has recently been superseded by the EBC core investigated by EPICA, the European Project for Ice Coring in Antarctica (EPICA 2004; McManus 2004:611; Walker 2004; White 2004). Located at Dome C (75°06′S, 123°21′E), 560 km away from the Vostok core site, the researchers have drilled through slightly more than 3 km of ice (EPICA 2004:623; Brook 2005; Siegenthaler et al. 2005; Spahni et al. 2005). It covers at least the last 740,000 years, nearly doubling the time available for study (White 2004:1609). With continued drilling to bedrock, the EPICA team members hope that it may extend back to 960,000 ± 20,000 years (EPICA 2004:623, 627). The EBC core documents the second of the two major Quaternary shifts, the Mid-Bruhnes Event or Termination V, the change from MIS 12 to MIS 11, around 430,000 years ago. Since then, there have been four separate 100,000-year-long glacial-interglacial cycles (EPICA 2004:625). Before Termination V, there were fewer extremes in temperature between glacials and interglacials. But warm phases lasted longer than they do after Termination V, so balance the record (EPICA 2004:625; McManus 2004:612; Walker 2004:597).

Alley (2000b:4) describes the Greenland cycle as illustrating a long gradual process of temperature decrease to glaciation, a faster onset of warmer conditions, a few millennia of stability, then the pattern is repeated. For him, the Holocene has been the longest stable interval and is quite abnormal (Alley 2000b:82). Information from the ice cores shows that the climate could change quickly and abruptly, perhaps even within the lifetime of an individual person, even early humans that rarely made it to what we now consider middle age. One's ability to plan for the future could have been greatly affected. If humans used seasonal rounds to acquire resources, their success might be affected in drastic ways. Perhaps, as Potts (1998, 2001) argues, albeit for earlier stages in human evolution, it was the behavioral flexibility of early humans that led to their survival. But the link between environment and people could have been broken in the last few hundred thousand years. This could have produced changes in human adaptation, at or near the time of the emergence of anatomically modern people. The genetic evidence reviewed in chapter 6 implies that our survival as a species was no sure thing (Gagneux et al. 1999).

Wallace Broecker (2000) recognized another factor regulating the advance and retreat of glaciers. The path of ocean currents is determined by water temperature and salinity (Calvin 2002:311). Today, warm water flows north on the surface of the Atlantic (as the Gulf Stream and North Atlantic Current). It cools and sinks, then travels south through the deep ocean of the North Atlantic to Antarctica and then to the Indian and/or Pacific Ocean (Alley 2000b:145; Calvin 2002:302). It takes over a thousand years to complete a loop in this circulation system (Calvin 2002:239). Broecker's model explains how locations in Europe are warmer than equivalent latitudes in North America (Calvin 2002:6). He showed that ocean circulation depends on salinity as well as temperature (Alley 2000b:145), and simulated what would happen if the salt conveyor failed (Calvin 1998, 2002:217). There seems to be two alternative climatic conditions in the Pleistocene and Holocene. In interglacials, warm currents penetrate far north into the Atlantic, and help to melt sea ice that is reflecting sunlight back into space; this would produce a warmer earth. If the North Atlantic current fails, the north end of the conveyor is deflected south at lower latitude. Heat stops flowing to northern waters and the result is cool, dry, possibly glacial conditions (Calvin 2002:234).

In polar regions, sea ice caps the ocean surface during winter, preventing winds from evaporating surface water and leaving salt behind (Calvin 2002:237). In cold periods, sinking of northern waters slows or stops and salt is not removed (Alley 2000a, 2000b:153; Calvin 2002:238). Any additional influx of fresh water can decrease North Atlantic surface salinity and thermohaline circulation, leading to cooling of Western Europe (Marotzke 2000:1347). So there are a number of factors that could have led to the onset of glaciation. Broecker's original hypothesis was that changes in global circulation of currents could cause the onset of a glacial in the Northern Hemisphere. He became famous for his 1987 pronouncement that adding greenhouse gases to the atmosphere might trigger one of these changes. Global warming, he suggested, could lead to a sudden, unexpected glacial event, basically freezing Europe and leading to a worldwide catastrophe (Broecker 1987; Calvin 2002:260). He originally believed that the North Atlantic conveyor was stuck in the "on" position in interglacials, creating the same conditions that can be observed at present (Broecker 2000:18). But he now thinks that changes in the strength of conveyor circulation can increase or decrease northern sea ice cover. During glacials, sea ice greatly expands as ocean circulation flips. During interglacials, when sea ice cover decreases, there would be little ice cover when greenhouse warming induces ocean reorganization; global warming will then only have a minor impact on climate (Broecker 2000:19). This will no doubt reassure the global climate change community.

Until 1987, arguments about the causes of climate change focused on the waxing and waning of ice sheets within the Milankovitch model (Broecker 2000:14). But Hartmut Heinrich added a new element when he reported the discovery of six depositional layers occurring at 10,000-year intervals in a deep-sea core from west of the British Isles (Broecker 2000:15). During the last glacial, and probably earlier, expanded ice sheets in the Northern Hemisphere led to surges and releases of icebergs. In the coldest part of glacials, ice sheets extend onto the continental shelf off Labrador in northeastern Canada; these break off and melt, adding fresh water to the surface of the Atlantic and exotic rocks to the deep-sea record (Calvin 2002:217, 304). What were eventually termed Heinrich events could have led to abrupt oscillations in climate, identified as Dansgaard-Oeschger events or cycles (Johnsen et al. 2001:300). These are periods of abrupt temperature change of about 15°C (Calvin 2002:303; Johnsen et al. 2001:303). They might be caused by drifting continents, wiggles in the earth's orbit (precession), surges of ice sheets, and/or sudden reversals in ocean circulation (Alley 2000b:84). During the last ice age, there were several Dansgaard-Oeschger cycles, one every 750,000 years (Calvin 2002:218). The Quaternary Environment Network members report that these Heinrich events probably affected the northern monsoon, also influencing African climatic patterns (Adams et al. 1997).

Paleoclimatologists have tried to reconstruct the environments of the Pleistocene, the epoch in which the evolution of the genus *Homo* took place. In northern environments, glacials were a major factor in human existence. Even the general public sees the typical early human either as a caveman living in ice age Europe or as a hunter on the open African savanna. But it is becoming clear that the bulk of human evolution occurred during periods of instability or continuous climatic fluctuation, patterns that still may be operating at present. While about a tenth of the earth's land surface is now covered by ice, at the height of the last glacial around 20,000 years ago, the ice cover tripled (Alley 2000b:88, 91). If today's ice sheets melted, the global sea level would rise by over 200 feet (Alley 2000b:92).

The Pleistocene is subdivided into three stages (Lower, Middle, and Upper Pleistocene) using the global palaeomagnetic record, the random fluctuations of intensity, and direction of earth's magnetic field (figure 1.1; Fuller et al. 1996; Glatzmaier et al. 1999; Glatzmaier and Olson 2005; Hoffman 1988). Magnetic particles in sediments or rocks exhibit an alignment, either to the magnetic North Pole (as at present), or to the South Pole. Stages of one kind of polarity are "normal" when pointing to the north magnetic pole, and "reversed" when pointing south. Long periods of one direction of polarity are referred to as chrons (previously epochs), and are named for the geophysicists who first identified this phenomenon: the Bruhnes Normal Chron for the last 780,000 years, the Matuyama Reversed for the period from 2.6 million to 780,000 years ago (Baksi et al. 1992), and the Gauss Normal for the range from 3.6 to 2.6 million years ago (table 1.1). Shorter periods of opposite polarity within a chron are subchrons (formerly events) and are named for places where the sequences were first recognized (Fuller et al. 1996; Hoffman 1988). The Olduvai Subchron, a short period of normal or north polarity from 1.8 to 1.6 million years ago within the Matuyama Reversed Chron, marks the start of the Pleistocene. But it should probably be placed at the Gauss/Matuyama boundary at 2.6 million years, when global climatic cycling actually began (Suc et al. 1997). There are also biostratigraphic markers for the beginning of the Pleistocene, such as the appearance of the foraminifera *Globorotalia truncatulinoides* in deep-sea sediments (Roberts 1984:47). The last shift from reversed to normal, the Bruhnes/Matuyama approximately 780,000 years ago, defines the boundary between the Lower and Middle Pleistocene. The start of the Upper Pleistocene is conventionally placed around 128,000 to 130,000 years ago, and marks the onset of the last interglacial, MIS stage 5e. It ends around 13,000 uncalibrated years ago with the beginning of the Holocene,

MIS stage 1. There has been no change in polarity since the end of the Middle Pleistocene, but Hulot and his colleagues recently suggested that such a process might be beginning (Hulot et al. 2002; Olson 2002).

In summary, there is substantial evidence for global climatic change and regular cycling beginning around 2.6 million years ago, and possibly still operative today. While most past environmental research has taken place in middle to high latitudes in the Northern Hemisphere, there is evidence from Africa of significant changes in the past. But, as elsewhere, such data have to be interpreted. One cannot measure past climate directly, so indirect methods or proxy indicators are used. There are also problems in correlating this proxy evidence with environmental reconstructions and palaeoanthropological data.

MODERN AFRICAN CLIMATES AND VEGETATION

Africa straddles the equator, with about 80% of its land surface located within the tropics (Murdock 1959:1). Geologically, it is old, and is derived from the breakup of Gondwana during the Mesozoic era (Bechky 1990:2; Seyfert and Sirkin 1973). Ancient rocks are exposed on the surface in many places, and in others are covered with sedimentary rocks (Murdock 1959:1). The basic topography is made up of a series of plateaus that range down to a narrow coastal plain. These plateaus are higher in the south and east than in the north and west, except in East Africa (Murdock 1959:1). African vegetation zones (map 3.1) are distributed in relation to precipitation regimes (Gasse 2000:190). Moisture is much more important than temperature (Murdock 1959:5). At the two ends of the continent, there are Mediterranean zones with dry summers and winter rainfall; the dominant vegetation is a form of sclerophyllous scrub known as *fynbos* in South Africa and *maquis* in the Maghreb. These areas are affected by the equatorial displacement of mid-latitude westerly winds during winter (Gasse 2000:190), and are bordered by subtropical deserts, the Namib and the Sahara (Murdock 1959:4–5).

There are three main desert regions: the Sahara, the northeast Horn, and the coast of southwest Africa (Murdock 1959:6). The Sahara is the largest desert in the world and covers the northern third of the continent. With less than 5 in (approximately 125 mm) of precipitation per year, it is bordered by areas of higher rainfall: the Mediterranean coast to the north and the Sahel to the south (Bechky 1990:2, 4). The Sahel is a semi-desert transitional zone between the Sahara and the savannas to the south; it has an average of 16 to 20

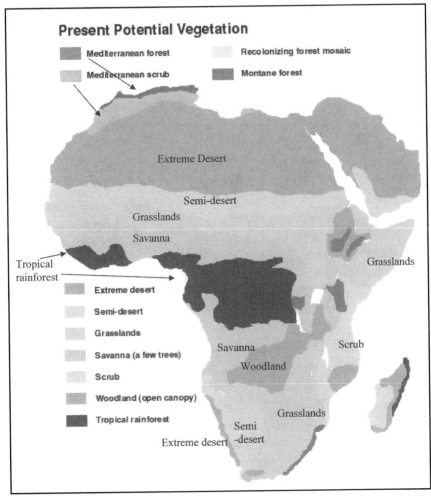

Present Potential Vegetation

Mediterranean forest

Mediterranean scrub

Recolonizing forest mosaic

Montane forest

Extreme Desert

Semi-desert

Grasslands

Savanna

Tropical rainforest

Grasslands

Extreme desert

Semi-desert

Grasslands

Savanna (a few trees)

Scrub

Woodland (open canopy)

Tropical rainforest

Savanna

Woodland

Scrub

Grasslands

Semi-desert

Extreme desert

Map 3.1 Contemporary African vegetation zones (modified from Adams et al. 1997). Reprinted by permission of Dr. Jonathan Adams

in (400 to 500 mm) of rainfall per year. South of the Sahel, rainfall increases markedly, supporting lightly wooded grasslands or tropical savannas, in an east-west zone (Bechky 1990:5). Savannas are grasslands with scattered trees; where there is sufficient water, baobab and *Acacia* are dominant; in drier areas, thorny shrubs are more frequent (Murdock 1959:6).

In West Africa, Guinea savanna merges into the zone of equatorial rain forest (Bechky 1990:5). Despite its popular image of unbroken jungle, most African regions get less than 40 in (1,000 mm) rainfall per year and this comes in distinct seasons. "By far the greatest part of Africa is covered by zones of vegetation adapted to varying degrees of aridity: savanna and desert" (Bechky 1990:2). Rain forest is found only in coastal strips along the Gulf of Guinea and in the Congo basin. The vegetation zones surrounding the rain forest are composed of grasslands as well as dry forest, with flat-topped deciduous trees which shed leaves during the hot and dry season (Murdock 1959:6). In West Africa, vegetation patterns are zoned by latitude from the Sahara desert in the north, to Sahelian vegetation, Sudanian, Guinea-Congolia/Sudanian transitional, Guinea-Congolian (the tropical rain forest), Guineo-Congolia/Zambezia transitional, Zambezian, Kalaharan, and to the Karoo-Namibian in the south. Afromontane vegetation occurs at elevations above 2,000 m, while there are mangrove swamps along the coast (Dupont et al. 2000:100; Hamilton 1982:16).

The equatorial region of Africa is part of a zone of low pressure enclosed between the high pressure belts of two hemispheres (Dupont et al. 2000:96). Within this area, trade winds meet at the surface. In West Africa, the Inter-Tropical Convergence Zone or Meteorological Equator ranges from the Gulf of Guinea to far over the continent, forming the boundary between the northwest trade winds and the southwest monsoon (the southeast trades change direction after passing the equator and become the southwest monsoon) (Dupont et al. 2000:96). Over the oceans and at high altitudes, the Inter-Tropical Convergence Zone remains near the geographic equator, but over land it forms an oblique northern dipping plane in the lower troposphere and migrates seasonally with the sun (Dupont et al. 2000:96). Its northernmost position is around 24°N in August, and its southernmost position is at 4°N in January and February (Dupont et al. 2000:96). Regions near the equator get water all year. In the semiarid desert fringe, it rains only at the height of summer, while in between there are double peaks of precipitation (Dupont et al. 2000:96). The bands of monsoonal climates that border the equatorial region experience summer rainfall and winter drought (Gasse 2000:190). Subtropical West, Central, and East Africa seem to become more arid when North Atlantic sea surface temperatures are colder, such as during full glacials (deMenocal 1995:55). Most regions north of the Gulf of Guinea are less than 500 m in elevation, but there are also mountainous regions. In contrast, the Congo basin averages around 100 m in elevation (Dupont et al. 2000:96).

In East Africa, savannas dominate the high plateau and extend well south. There are different types of savanna. Some are pure grasslands, while others contain various woodland communities. "When one adds desert steppe and dry forest to savanna and mountain grasslands, the proportion of the surface of Africa which can support herbivorous animals is really extraordinary" (Murdock 1959:6). Savannas have higher precipitation than drier regions to the north (500 to 1,000 mm per year) but rainfall is irregular and seasonal (Bechky 1990:5). Hydrological features include the large internal drainage basins occupied by the rift valley lakes, as well as large rivers fed by the humid equatorial belt (the Congo, Nile, and Niger) (Gasse 2000:190). East Africa experiences rainfall during the passage of the Inter-Tropical Convergence Zone, or ITCZ. In January, the dry, dusty, northeast trade winds flow over this region (Hamilton 1982:11; deMenocal 1995:53), while the southeast trades, off the Indian Ocean, dominate in July. April is wet, when the Inter-Tropical Convergence Zone is located between 3°N and 3°S; by June it shifts north and rainfall begins to decrease (September being driest). Some westerly winds from the South Atlantic cross the Congo basin and make the Western Rift area moist (Hamilton 1982:11; map 3.2). While East African summer rainfall is a result of the westerly flow of the African monsoon, the amount is variable due to a topographic rain shadow effect (deMenocal 1995:53). The Tropic of Capricorn marks the edge of a distinctly temperate southern African region;

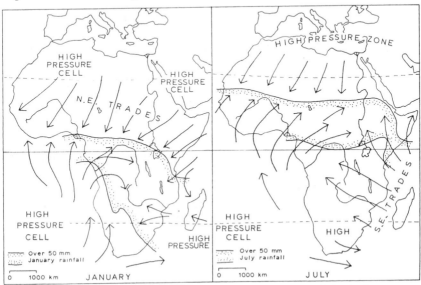

Map 3.2 Africa showing features of general circulation and rain belts in January and July (Hamilton 1982:12). Reprinted with permission of Elsevier

here tropical savannas are transformed into grasslands (Bechky 1990:6). The climate gets increasingly dry toward the South Atlantic coast as the semidesert Kalahari merges with the Namib Desert. On the east coast, the Indian Ocean warms the land; as a result, semitropical climate persists almost to the Cape (Bechky 1990:6).

Climatologists understand the basic modern rainfall regime of Africa quite well. But a recent guidebook to East Africa concludes that "Africa's equatorial forest is an ancient ecosystem, the product of ages of environmental stability" (Bechky 1990:6). Evidently this is not the case. The Quaternary history of Africa revolves around the global cycles of cold and warm conditions, which bring dry and wet conditions respectively. Both would have affected early human adaptations, as well as the distribution of flora and fauna.

THE PLEISTOCENE ENVIRONMENTAL HISTORY OF AFRICA

Quite early in the twentieth century, it was recognized that the great lakes of East Africa had been larger in the past (Butzer 1971, 1976; Butzer et al. 1972; Hamilton 1976, 1982; Johnson et al. 1993; Livingstone 1975). Freshwater lakes also existed in the Sahara desert in regions totally dry today (Sutton 1977). These observations were used to create a climato-stratigraphic sequence of wet stages or pluvials, such as the Kamasian, Gamblian, Makalian, and Nakuran (Leakey 1936a, 1955). Wet phases were thought to be synchronous with high-latitude glaciation (Leakey 1936a:10, 16), while interglacial conditions would be similar to present. More importantly, they provided a sequence for relative dating and correlation of fossil and archaeological sites. But more recent environmental research has shown that glacials in Africa were periods of heightened aridity, and lakes were only enlarged in warmer periods, notably the early Holocene (Cooke 1957, 1958; Flint 1959a, 1959b, 1967, 1971). Lake Victoria apparently dried up during the last glacial (Hamilton 1982:61; Johnson et al. 2002; Thomas 2000:27; Verheyen et al. 2003:325). Rivers such as the Nile either disappeared or did not have enough water to make it all the way to the Mediterranean. The equatorial rain forest appears to have been reduced to refuge areas. This has made it difficult for archaeologists to determine when the initial human settlement of the rain forest occurred. Later Stone Age people are present by the terminal Pleistocene (Barham 2001b; Mercader 2002, 2003a, 2003b; Mercader and Brooks 2001), but many older sites such as Matupi Cave in the Eastern Congo are associated with savannas rather than rain forest (Mercader et al. 2003; Van Noten 1977).

There is evidence of the onset of glacial/interglacial cycling in the earlier stages of human evolution or about 2.6 million years ago. This can be seen in the expansion of grasslands and concomitant decrease of rain forest, and in the change in large mammal faunas from browsers to grazers. From the middle Miocene (12 million years ago) until about 2.8 million years ago, subtropical African climate varied at precessional periodicities (at 19,000 to 23,000 intervals) (deMenocal 1995:53, 55). The first glacial cycles are associated with the increasing importance of the 41,000-year cycle. This lasts until about one million years ago, and then there is a shift to the 100,000-year pattern of eccentricity forcing (Behrensmeyer 2006; deMenocal 1995:55, 2004; ERICA 2004; McManus 2004; Trauth et al. 2005). After this, a change in intensity of seasonal winds carrying dust from Arabia and East Africa leads to increased drying in sub-Saharan Africa (Partridge 1997:9). In southern Africa, extensive dune fields develop and occasionally extend well into the Congo basin. One of these, labeled the Mega Kalahari, has been described as "the largest single body of windblown sand in the world" (Partridge 1997:9). At its largest extent, it covered 2.5 million square kilometers (Barham 2001b:74).

In the Middle Pleistocene, from 780,000 to 128,000 years ago, there is "recurrent and dramatic change" in African climates and landscape (Potts 2001:5). Potts has modeled responses to landscape changes and suggests that Middle Pleistocene African hominins, late *Homo erectus/Homo ergaster* or archaic *Homo sapiens/Homo heidelbergensis*, were able to cope with them quite successfully (Potts 2001:9–10, 15; Trauth et al. 2005). This behavioral flexibility is also seen in increasing archaeological variation and innovation in later periods, which contrast with the apparent stasis in technology seen in the Acheulian (Potts 2001:17). Since Acheulian sites are found in a wide variety of environmental settings, Middle Palaeolithic/Middle Stone Age variation may represent an adaptation to increasingly unpredictable climates (Potts 2001:17–18).

In the Upper Pleistocene, deMenocal (1995, 2004) proposes that there were two separate influences on climate, one in high latitudes (the glacial cycles), and the other in low latitudes (moisture). During glacials, it was drier and cooler in Africa. The intensity of the monsoons was controlled by the dominance of orbital precession (the 23,000 to 19,000 cycle) (deMenocal

1995:53). Monsoons and moisture were greatest when earth to sun distance was at a minimum, perihelion, during boreal summer (deMenocal 1995:53). A 900,000-year deep-sea core from West African site 663 shows that aeolian or windblown dust and savanna grass phytoliths are most frequent when the North Atlantic sea surface temperatures were coldest (up to a 12°C drop in temperature) (deMenocal et al. 1993). Pollen records show that West African vegetation zones were pushed southwards during glacials (deMenocal 1995:56). When high-latitude ice sheets were small, before 2.8 million years ago, they apparently did not affect Africa in any significant way. Afterward, when ice sheets increased in size, cold glacial North Atlantic sea surface temperatures produced cooler and drier conditions in Africa. East African vegetation became dominated by savanna as precipitation became more seasonal (deMenocal 1995:57). At the same time, the distinctive *fynbos* scrub vegetation of the South African Cape province emerged (Partridge 1997:9). During the Plio-Pleistocene, there were alternating wet and dry seasons in Africa, with significant peaks in windblown dust (deMenocal 1995:58; 2004; Trauth et al. 2005). These changes "may have established discrete opportunities for ecologic fragmentation and genetic isolation leading to the eventual rise of arid-adapted species" (deMenocal 1995:58). These could have included the first members of the genus *Homo* and *Homo sapiens* as well.

An attempt to reconstruct the late Pleistocene and Holocene environmental history of Africa and other continents has been made by the members of the Quaternary Environment Network led by Jonathan Adams (Adams et al. 1997). Their data come from lake and ocean pollen records, the dust record in deep-sea cores (as a proxy for aridity), as well as terrestrial evidence (grain size, sediment, and geomorphological analysis). An example of such a record is that from the Pretoria Saltpan in South Africa. An impact crater 40 km north of Pretoria, its central lake has accumulated 90 m of sediments for the last 200,000 years (Partridge 1997:10; Partridge et al. 1997). Another pollen record comes from off the West African coast, from five different cores. Together they give a vegetation history for the last 150,000 years (Dupont et al. 2000:96), showing that rain forest was widespread in interglacial times (MIS 1 and MIS 5), but reduced during glacials. However, it appears that some equatorial regions remained forested throughout even the coldest periods.

The Quaternary Environment Network (Adams et al. 1997) gives this general picture of African environmental history. MIS stage 6 dates between

195,000 and 128,000 years ago; it represents the next to last or "penulti-mate" glacial. Around 150,000 years ago, conditions were generally drier than present, and there was a large desert covering much of North Africa (Adams et al. 1997). From 150,000 to 130,000 years ago, Africa was colder and more arid than present, then there was a warm, wet phase which lasted until around 115,000 years ago, MIS 5e (Adams et al. 1997). During MIS 6, savanna grassland and open dry forest covered large areas on the northern coast of the Gulf of Guinea in West Africa. The southern Sahara reached far to the south (14°N) and the Namib Desert far to the north (Dupont et al. 2000:95). Pollen in deep-sea cores in the Gulf of Guinea shows that the rain forest decreases in extent, as do coastal mangrove swamps, both indicators of wet conditions. *Podocarpus*, the yellow wood, brown or black pine, is a montane tree genus. Its occurrence fluctuates over the course of the late Pleistocene as moisture regimes change (Dupont et al. 2000:95). The distri-bution of vegetation in West Africa at this time is similar to the conditions observed during MIS 2, the last glacial maximum. Toward the end of MIS 6, mangrove swamps decrease. Late Pleistocene West Africa was clearly more arid than earlier (Jahns et al. 1998:277).

MIS stage 5e represents the warmest and possibly wettest conditions prior to the Holocene. African forests are extensive, and modern deserts were al-most completely covered with vegetation. In West African ocean pollen cores, data from this period are limited. Available records show increasing rain for-est and mangroves and a drop in dry forest and savanna. Desert limits shift to higher latitudes, a condition seen again in the early Holocene (Dupont et al. 2000:113). After 115,000 years ago, rain forest decreases, but not as much as in full glacials; *Podocarpus* has its largest and most westward expansion (in sub-stages 5d, 5b, and 5a), then decreases (Dupont et al. 2000:116; Jahns et al. 1998:277). Its last occurrence in the Guinea mountains dates to MIS sub-stage 5a (Dupont et al. 2000:95). During sub-stages 5d to 5a, between 90,000 and 110,000 years ago, there is evidence of increasing aridity and dryness (Adams et al. 1997). In sub-stages 5c and 5a, the rain forest reclaims some of the ter-ritory lost during stadials 5d and 5b (Dupont et al. 2000:95). Further south, the *miombo* woodland of the Zambezian zone (characteristic of much of the modern vegetation in Tanzania, Zambia, and Zimbabwe), expands early in MIS 5 (Dupont et al. 2000:95). *Miombo* is a moist savanna dominated by tall, densely spaced leguminous trees such as *Brachystegia*, *Jubelnardia*, and *Iso-*

berlina (Hamilton 1982:19; Barham 2001b:71). At the Pretoria Saltpan, there is not a lot of evidence available between the last interglacial (MIS 5e) and around 40,000 years ago. But precession-driven fluctuations in precipitation decrease in amplitude around 80,000 years ago as temperature drops and ice sheets grow (Partridge 1997:12–13).

During MIS stage 4, from 75,000 to 58,000 years ago, sea level drops 75 m below present. Vegetation conditions are similar to those of the last glacial maximum, with desert greatly expanded in North Africa. Rain forests crash and recover only slightly during MIS stage 3. Mangrove swamps decrease in West Africa except along the Ivory Coast and the northwest Gulf of Guinea, and *Podocarpus* forests are found only in Angola and possibly in the Congo (Dupont et al. 2000:95). It is at the boundary between MIS stages 5a and 4 around 73,000 years ago that Mount Toba in northern Sumatra, Indonesia, exploded, leading to a sudden global cooling and perhaps to a nuclear winter scenario (Wintle 1996:131; Ambrose 2003:231). Ambrose (1998a, 2003) and others (Rampino and Ambrose 2000:71, Rampino and Self 1992; but see Gathorne-Hardy and Harcourt-Smith 2003) propose that this event would have led to cold conditions and extreme drought in rain forests and monsoonal regions. This in turn may have precipitated the transition to the Later Stone Age and the Out of Africa II movement of modern humans (Willoughby, forthcoming).

For MIS 3 and 4, there are apparently no terrestrial pollen records in West Africa. But offshore sediments imply dryness and increasing erosion along the Congo River (Dupont et al. 2000:116). Marine pollen records are similar to those from MIS 2 (Dupont et al. 2000:116). MIS stage 3, from around 57,000 to 24,000 years ago, is associated with an unstable climate that fluctuated on spans of a few thousand years; at other times, it was still cool but not as arid (Adams et al. 1997). Sea level was approximately 70 m below present and southern Africa became extremely dry around 43,000 to 40,000 years ago (Adams et al. 1997). Shortly before the last glacial maximum, between 28,000 and 22,000 years ago, North Africa and the Levant were wetter than now, and there is some evidence that the equatorial rain forest was reduced (Adams et al. 1997). Conditions were cooler and moister than present, but not as cold as in the last glacial maximum (Thomas 2000:28). At the Pretoria Saltpan, various lines of evidence show a drop in temperature of about 2°C to 3°C during MIS 3 and MIS 2 (Partridge 1997:15).

MIS 2 (map 3.3) includes one of the coldest periods ever, the last glacial maximum. At this time, the Sahara expanded as far south as 14°N (as it did in MIS 6), and the Namib Desert expanded as far north as 12°S (Dupont et al. 2000:119). Intermediate vegetation zones were compressed toward the equator, and tropical rain forests were reduced to small refuge areas. The last glacial forms the break between the Middle and Upper Palaeolithic in North Africa,

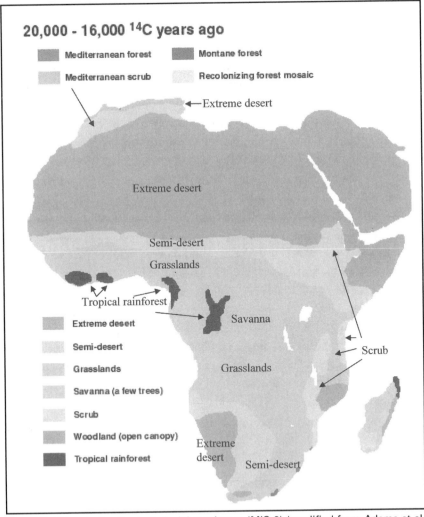

Map 3.3 Africa during the last glacial maximum (MIS 2) (modified from Adams et al. 1997). Reprinted by permission of Dr. Jonathan Adams

as conditions became so dry and arid that people may have abandoned the whole region (Close 1986). It may also explain the lack of Middle/Later Stone Age transitional sites in much of sub-Saharan Africa, and the absence of a late Pleistocene record at places which were intensively occupied earlier, such as Die Kelders Cave 1 (Marean 2000; Marean et al. 2000) and Klasies River in South Africa (Singer and Wymer 1982). MIS stage 2 is better known than any other period apart from the Holocene, possibly due to its recent age. Sea level was reduced from 120 to 140 m below present. But Adams et al. (1997) argue that in most places, the steepness of the continental shelf in Africa means that not much more land was exposed. The exception is the southern part of South Africa, where the coastline may have retreated by a distance of about 100 km. During MIS 2, tropical rain forest decreases, and savanna or grassland replaces it in most of equatorial West Africa (Dupont et al. 2000:95), but not everywhere. In five pollen records taken from Western Rift Valley lakes, Jolly et al. (1997) observe a major reduction in forest at this time. It is replaced by dry grassland and ericaceous scrub, rather than the moist forest observable today.

Two cores were also drilled into sediments at Lake Malawi and produce a record for the last 25,000 years (Johnson et al. 2002). Around 12,000 radiocarbon years before present, there is a shift in sedimentation rates from about 0.2 to 0.5 mm per year (Johnson et al. 2002:113). Diatoms are used to estimate lake biomass and productivity, and they show lower mean values for the Pleistocene than the Holocene. The transition between the two seems to have occurred around 13,000 years ago and again around 10,300 years ago (Johnson et al. 2002:113).

From pollen grains in deep-sea cores off of West Africa, there is evidence of decreasing rainfall, increasing windiness and evaporation rates, and greater seasonality (Thomas 2000:27; Dupont et al. 2000:117). Montane taxa descend to lower altitudes as temperatures cool and grasslands expand. One of the most important biogeographic questions is whether or not there were refugia, regions where the rain forest could survive even in the coldest, driest periods. Early research on plant and animal biogeography led Hamilton (1976, 1982) to suggest that the equatorial rain forest was broken up during the Pleistocene (Dupont et al. 2000:96), but that the forest had survived in isolated pockets. Hamilton proposed three refuge areas: west of the Congo basin in Equatorial Guinea, along the coasts of Cameroon and Gabon, east of the Congo basin, and several small areas along the coast of Liberia and the Ivory Coast (Dupont et al. 2000:96). Others proposed the eastern Congo (formerly Zaire); the western fringes of Uganda, Rwanda, and Burundi; the Indian Ocean coast of Tanzania; the west coast of Cameroon and Gabon; as well as northern Mozambique and parts of Ethiopia (Moore 1998:124–125). In West Africa, Dupont and his colleagues propose the existence of such refugia south or southwest of the Guinea mountains; southwest of the Cameroon mountains, in Gabon; the Congo; and in some patches on the north coast of the Gulf of Guinea (Dupont et al. 2000:117).

In the Western Rift, there is contradictory information. Pollen cores are used to suggest that savanna open woodland vegetation was prevalent from 30,000 to 11,000 years ago, while forest was present only along river edges (Adams et al. 1997). Six pollen cores have been extracted from five bogs: three in southern Uganda, one in Burundi, and another in Rwanda; this region is presently the catchment for the Congo and Nile rivers (Jolly et al. 1997:496). During the last glacial maximum, ericaceous scrub and grasslands with patches of open canopied montane forest surrounded this area. As a result, they (Jolly et al. 1997:495) argue that the "central African forest refuge . . . did not extend to the eastern flanks of the Albertine Rift" but gradually reappeared late in the Pleistocene. Either the forest was further west, or "we should be considering the survival of much smaller, dispersed patches of forest rather than a major refugial forest block" (Moore 1998:125). Other research in the same region suggests that between 30,000 and 15,000 years ago, there was 32% less precipitation than present (Bonnefille and Chalie 2000:25). Maximum precipitation values of 600 mm per year date to around 8,000 years ago, 42% more than now. At present, this area experiences a tropical humid climate with summer rains, with a mountain climate year-round at over 1,800 m elevation (Bonnefille and Chalie 2000:25–27). The oldest levels in the pollen core date to around 39,000 to 40,000 years ago, and represent a time of extensive forest development, similar to that of the Holocene. In glacial times, dry conifer forest was more widespread than now and reached central Africa (Bonnefille and Chalie 2000:35). During the last glacial maximum, when temperatures cooled, vegetation was more open, with minimum forest around 16,000 years ago (Bonnefille and Chalie 2000:35).

Rivers and lakes were also reduced during MIS 2. The Nile had a lower discharge than present, and there is fossil evidence of deposits formed by flash flooding in otherwise arid places. There were moister conditions in the northwest Sahara where some Mediterranean steppe vegetation existed. Woodland conditions existed in the Atlas Mountains and coastal region, and vegetation zones were lowered by more than 1,200 m (Adams et al. 1997). In river valleys in Sierra Leone there are no sediments dated between 20,500 and 12,700 years ago (Thomas 2000:29). Lake Bosumtwi (6°30´N, 1°25´W) lies in an approximately 1.07-million-year-old meteor impact crater in the forest zone of southwest Ghana (Brooks et al. 2005:237). While it is surrounded by rain forest today, in the last glacial maximum sediments, there is almost no tree pollen. Grasses dominate from around 28,000 to less than 12,500 years ago, producing conditions similar to those in the modern Sahel today (Talbot et al. 1984; Talbot and Johannessen 1992). Rain forest pollen reappears in the core around 9,500 years ago (Thomas 2000:27; Dupont et al. 2000:117). A more recent study of the seismic stratigraphy of Bosumtwi suggests that there were several periods of aridity in the Pleistocene, around 65,000, 86,000, and 108,000 years ago (Brooks et al. 2005:247). In eastern and southern Africa, there is evidence for greater aridity than present, and cooling amounting to several degrees centigrade; high mountain glaciers were lowered about 1,000 m in altitude. Some of the great lakes in East Africa were significantly reduced. Lake Victoria was almost empty from around 17,300 to 15,000 years ago and again from 14,000 to 13,000 years ago. Today its maximum depth is 67 m, but it is suggested that it dropped by 65 m during the last glacial maximum (Thomas 2000:27). Other figures suggest that the lake dried out completely around 20,500 years ago. Gasse (2000:195, 200) describes two paleosols (old soils) dating to between 20,500 and 17,900 years ago, and before 15,300 years ago. Lake Albert in the western rift also shows evidence of paleosols dating to 18,000 and 13,000 years ago; it is suggested that the lake dropped to 54 m below its present level (Thomas 2000:27). At Lake Tanganyika, the second deepest lake in the world today, water level dropped from 350 to 400 m between 21,700 and 12,700 years ago (Thomas 2000:27; Bonnefille and Chalie 2000:43; Gasse 2000:195).

In southern Africa, the evidence is mixed. The Cape was drier than present, and there were greatly expanded desert areas in Botswana and Namibia. The Pretoria Saltpan presently experiences about 630 mm precipitation per year (Partridge 1997:10). Here, when the summer insolation increased about 15%, rainfall increased 68% from a low of 535 mm to almost 900 mm (Partridge 1997:10). The lowest amount occurred near the end of MIS stage 7, while the last glacial maximum is estimated around 560 mm (Partridge 1997:10).

The last 13,000 radiocarbon years represents MIS stage 1 or the Holocene. At this time, temperature and moisture increased throughout most of Africa. In the early Holocene (map 3.4), the rain forest shows its greatest extent and the Sahara was completely vegetated; afterward, conditions became more arid, similar to present (Adams et al. 1997). In the Sahara, there is evidence of sudden changes from dry to wet conditions around 15,000 and 11,500 years ago (Gasse 2000:202). The early Holocene saw extremely wet conditions and savanna where desert is now (Gasse 2000:204). Freshwater lakes were common, with gigantic fish such as Nile perch. In West Africa, mangrove swamps and

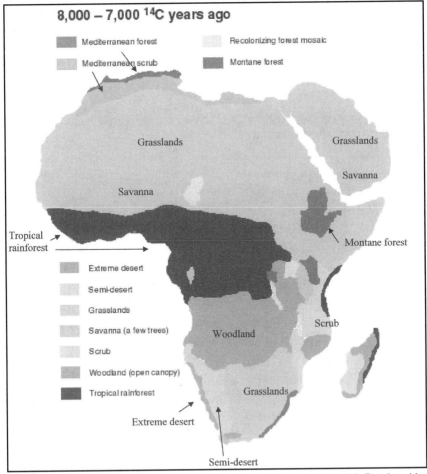

Map 3.4 Africa in the early Holocene (modified from Adams et al. 1997). Reprinted by permission of Dr. Jonathan Adams

rain forests were widely distributed and the savanna corridor now present in Togo and Benin did not divide the Guinea and Congolian rain forests (Dupont et al. 2000:95). But Goucher (1981) has proposed that the lack of rain forest in Togo is a result of tree cutting to produce charcoal to fuel the almost industrial level of production of iron during the pre-colonial period.

In general, there is no modern analogue for environmental conditions during any stage of the Pleistocene. Interglacials are cooler and drier than present, but also occasionally wetter and warmer, as in the early Holocene period in North Africa that Sutton (1977) aptly labeled the African "aqualithic." During glacials, sub-Saharan Africa was substantially drier than present, leading to fully desertic and semi-arid steppe conditions (Clark 1988:251) and the elimination of most of the forest (Foley 1989:306; Dupont et al. 2000:118). Such environmental cycling must have influenced the distribution of humans and the natural resources they relied upon.

THE RELATION OF ENVIRONMENT TO THE ORIGIN AND DISPERSAL OF MODERN HUMANS

What did the fluctuations in environments mean for the distribution of humans over the landscape? The appearance of modern humans in Africa probably took place sometime during MIS stages 6 to 8 between 200,000 and 100,000 years ago. This may be associated with the end of the Acheulian (Tryon and McBrearty 2002). At the same time, Neanderthals were developing in Europe. The first humans to live there during full glacials, their diagnostic anatomical features were possibly the result of long-term adaptation to cold and aridity (Smith 1991).

The first modern humans outside of Africa are those found at Mugharet es Skhūl and Jebel Qafzeh, and they date to MIS stage 5e (Bar-Yosef 1989a, 1989b; Tchernov 1988). Whether or not this represents the start of the Out of Africa II migration can be disputed, since all proxy indicators show that at this time the Levant was biogeographically part of Africa. Desmond Clark (1988:251) proposes that people began to produce local archaeological industries during MIS 5 (128,000 to 75,000 years ago). Foley and Lahr (1997; Lahr and Foley 1994, 1998, 2001) and Barham (2001b) propose a similar model. During stage 4, colder conditions returned. It is at this time that some Neanderthal populations moved south from Europe into the Levant, leaving their remains at sites such as the Mugharet et Tabun and Amud in Israel and Shanidar Cave in the Kurdistan region of Iraq (Akazawa et al. 1998). But it is extremely likely that Neanderthals and modern humans only encountered one another about 40,000 years ago.

Many archaeologists see the African Middle to Later Stone Age transition as the marker of the onset of behavioral modernity. This transition must have occurred well before MIS 3, when their descendants brought the Upper Palaeolithic into Europe (Mellars 1989, 1991, 1993, 2002, 2005). But how the Later Stone Age was initiated is hard to measure in Africa, as it is associated with dry and cool conditions (McBrearty 1993; Willoughby 1993b). Large areas of the continent may have been abandoned. The South African coast, with its phenomenal Middle Stone Age record, has few sites dating to the period after 50,000 years ago. The next oldest are Later Stone Age occupations which are less than two millennia old, and which often contain evidence of pastoralism (Die Kelders, Blombos Cave) (Wadley 1993). A Later Stone Age is said to exist by around 40,000 years ago at sites like Matupi Cave in the eastern Congo (Van Noten 1977), Enkapune ya Muto in central Kenya (Ambrose 1998b), and Border Cave in South Africa. In others, the Later Stone Age may only start around 20,000 years ago (such as Rose Cottage Cave) (Wadley 1997, 2000). On account of this gap, Klein (1999:492) argues that East Africa may be the only place where the Middle to Later Stone Age transitional record will ever be found. Those of us who conduct research in East Africa are attempting to test this idea.

For Klein, this transition is a behavioral one, made in response to a neurological change that made symbolic behavior, complex language, and modern hunter-gatherer existence possible. Others see a more geographic cause. Sherratt (1997:281) along with Foley and Lahr (1997; Lahr and Foley 2001) suggest that the Sahara desert acted as a pump, sucking in human populations, and then dispersing them as it waxed and waned in response to Quaternary orbital forcing. "Was it, perhaps, as a result of adjustment to desiccation that the final elements of the Human Revolution clicked into place?" (Sherratt 1997:281) Did this event, or process, bring the Upper Paleolithic or its sub-Saharan African counterpart, the Later Stone Age, into existence? When glacial conditions prevailed, the Sahara acted as a barrier between the regions to its north and south. In wetter phases, as monsoon rains extended north beyond their usual range, the desert was replaced by grassland. Such a region might have then acted as a corridor, enhancing the possibilities for long distance migration (Calvin 2002:201).

Robert Foley (1987a, 1989) was one of the first archaeologists to examine the issue of human origins and dispersal from a biogeographic perspective. He originally suggested that Africa might be the tropical region most affected by Pleistocene changes (Foley 1989:308; Roberts 1984). Humans and their ancestors lived where they did in response to both local and global environmental conditions. Along with Marta Lahr (Foley and Lahr 1997; Lahr and Foley 1994, 1998, 2001), Foley has since proposed that there was an additional migration of African hominins into Eurasia prior to that of modern *Homo sapiens*. The behavioral sign of this migration is the appearance and spread of Mode 3 (Levallois, Mousterian, Middle Stone Age) technologies. They argue that this mode, shared by Eurasian Neanderthals and modern humans, represents the appearance of abstract mental processes in both taxa (Foley and Lahr 1997:9). Their common ancestor is reclassified as *Homo helmei* after the cranium from Florisbad, South Africa (Lahr and Foley 2001:26). Foley has long proposed that new technologies accompanied hominin speciation events and change for much the same reasons (Foley 1987b), a sort of bio-cultural synchrony of the sort which accounts so well for the Oldowan and Acheulian. They suggest that behavioral change preceded biological change, and that the end of the Acheulian and the onset of the Middle Paleolithic/Middle Stone Age is the sign of something special yet to come (Lahr and Foley 2001:25, 27). They see multiple Out of Africa events, one for *Homo erectus/ Homo ergaster*, a second for *Homo helmei*, and ultimately, a third for the African descendants of *Homo helmei*, anatomically modern *Homo sapiens* (Foley and Lahr 1997:19). Glacial cycling drives these migrations and speciation events. They suggest that populations of *Homo helmei*, carrying a Mode 3 technology, entered Eurasia during MIS stage 7. As it became increasingly cool in MIS stage 6, Europe and Africa were isolated from each other, leading to the fragmentation of Mode 3 populations into regional groups; in Africa, their descendants became moderns, in Europe, Neanderthals (Foley and Lahr 1997:23). While one would assume that such a model would closely link Neanderthals and modern humans, Foley and Lahr see the African Middle Stone Age as technologically more advanced. Sites of this age are said to contain a "relatively high number of innovative elements" (Foley and Lahr 1997:25–26). This implies a basic split that is surprisingly similar to Klein's (1992, 2000, 2001a) model of instant, overnight, neurological change. In one of their latest research papers, Underhill's genetic research group joins forces with Foley and Lahr (1997; Lahr and Foley 1994, 1998, 2001) to try to link these proposed migrations to Y chromosome markers (Underhill et al. 2000, 2001) in modern men worldwide.

The Chronological Framework: Dating the Appearance and Spread of *Homo sapiens*

In fact, long before an archaeological frame has been fitted by cross-datings firmly on to Europe and the Near East . . . a more trustworthy chronology, independent of archaeology and of any historical assumption, may well have been provided by radiocarbon. . . . In other words, archaeologists will abandon responsibility for chronology or themselves become nuclear physicists. In any case every prehistorian must master enough mathematics, physics and chemistry to appreciate the limitation of the information the latter can provide.
(Childe 1981:167; orig. pub. 1957)

V. Gordon Childe, one of the few archaeologists of the mid-twentieth century who continued to be interested in social phenomena and cultural evolution, first published this statement in 1957, a time when archaeologists were provided with one of the first chronometric or "absolute" dating techniques, radiocarbon, ^{14}C, or carbon-14. Using ubiquitous material such as charcoal, shell, or bone, it offered a method of age estimation independent of artifact style, type, stratigraphy, and context and preconceived archaeological frameworks. But rather than accepting the new methods on their face value as many did, Childe reminds us that archaeologists must learn to understand their limitations. A number of case studies have confirmed the need to be cautious, such as the reassessment of the age of megalithic monuments in northwestern Europe (Renfrew 1973) and the problems in the 1970s with dating the Plio-Pleistocene KBS tuff at Koobi Fora, East Turkana in Kenya

(Hay 1980; Lewin 1987). They show that "absolute" dates are only as good as their context and correlation with results from other dating methods. It appears that archaeologists must either specialize in dating, or learn enough to become knowledgeable consumers of the information provided to them by geochronologists, as Childe proposed.

DATING THE APPEARANCE AND SPREAD OF *HOMO SAPIENS:* A BEGINNING

The development of radiocarbon dating techniques led to a transformation of prehistoric archaeology and all other historical sciences. Nineteenth-century archaeological chronologies had been constructed using changes in artifact style and stratigraphy, relying on the relative order of events. The materials chosen for artifacts, the manufacturing techniques employed, and especially their final shape could be studied, and the pattern(s) of change over time inferred if a culture-stratigraphic sequence existed. Archaeological types could function almost as index fossils if they were dated in at least one locality and were widespread over space but restricted in time. Excavation had demonstrated that in a series of sediment layers, the deeper the level, the older it was, and that became the basis for stratigraphy. Together, these methods provided the relative order of events at individual sites, and when cross-correlated, at other sites and regions. But with new chronometric techniques, age could be determined independent of archaeological context.

But only certain periods in our past benefited from these initial approaches. As recently as the late 1980s, research on much of Middle and Upper Pleistocene prehistory was hampered by the lack of dated archaeological sites or fossil localities. By this time, East Africa had become the main region for the study of the earliest stages in human evolution. Here fossil hominins were abundant and more easily collected than in South Africa dolomite caves (where they had to be blasted out of a limestone cemented breccia matrix). Their age could also be determined using potassium-argon (K-Ar). This method of dating volcanic lava and ash was developed in the early 1960s and was initially limited to volcanic localities older than 500,000 years. Radiocarbon, on the other hand, could be used for almost any organic material that was less than 40,000 years old. Palaeoanthropologists studying the intervening period in the Old World were out of luck. At the Burg Wartenstein conference on the Middle Pleistocene (Butzer and Isaac 1975), this chronological gap was what Glynn Isaac (1975) famously labeled "the muddle in the middle," and has only been recently readdressed (Barham and Robson-Brown 2001).

How do chronometric dating techniques work, and how is the gap in coverage narrowed? Literally meaning time measure, chronometric dating methods give precise age estimates (table 4.1). Many, such as radiocarbon, ^{39}argon/^{40}argon, and uranium disequilibrium series, are based on regular radioactive decay from a parent to a daughter isotope. Unlike the oxygen isotopes that provide a means of environmental reconstruction, those used for dating must be unstable or radioactive, changing over a known period of time. The rate of decay is geometric and is called a half-life; it represents the amount of time it takes for half of the parent isotope to change into the daughter form. If the rate of change covers the time period of interest, the half-life is known, and the amount of an isotope is measured, the age of a specimen (or associated material) can be calculated. Such an estimate is a measure of probability and is reported as an average with a range of error (one or two standard deviations). In radiocarbon dating, an estimate of 5,000 ± 50 before the present suggests that there is a 67% chance that the date falls within the range plus or minus one standard deviation, or, in this example, between 4,950 and 5,050 years ago. Doubling the standard deviation provides a 95% confidence interval, but the range is now wider, between 4,900 and 5,100 years ago. By convention, "present" is considered to be AD 1950.

Carbon-14 (^{14}C) is produced by cosmic ray bombardment in the upper atmosphere and is ultimately absorbed into all living organisms. After death, ^{14}C decays into ^{14}N and a beta particle over a half-life of 5,730 years (Taylor 1997). Conventional radiocarbon dating calculates the amount of residual ^{14}C in organic materials and is limited to the last 40,000 years, making it of limited value for palaeoanthropologists. It was used to date Upper Palaeolithic archaeological sites, as well as to estimate when humans first entered the Americas and Australia (Wintle 1996:124). But by the 1970s, it was becoming clear that the amount of ^{14}C in the atmosphere was not constant, and had fluctuated randomly over time. Radiocarbon dating of long-living trees, such as bristlecone pine (*Pinus longaeva*), whose actual age had been determined through the counting of annual growth rings (dendrochronology) showed that it was necessary to recalibrate or correct

Table 4.1. Dating techniques applicable to later Quaternary sites

Method	Material to Be Dated	Effective Time Range
CHRONOMETRIC		
Radiocarbon (^{14}C): Conventional and AMS (Accelerator Mass Spectrometry)	Organic material: charcoal, bone, shell, etc.	Recent to 40,000–45,000 years ago
Electron Spin Resonance (ESR)	Dental enamel, speleothems (stalagmites, stalactites, and flowstone)	10,000 to 1,000,000 years ago
Thermoluminescence (TL)	Burned flint tools, pottery, or bleached sediments such as loess (dating when heated or exposed to sunlight last); measure by exposing sample to heat	Recent to 100,000 BP —on flint, from 1,000 to over 500,000 years ago; on sediments, from 1,000 to 800,000 years ago
Optical stimulated luminescence (OSL) and IRSL (infrared stimulated luminescence)	Bleached sediments; similar to TL, but involves exposing sample to light	Recent to 150,000 BP
Uranium series ^{230}Th/ ^{234}U ^{231}Pa / ^{235}U	Materials containing calcium carbonate ($CaCo^3$); eg., travertines, speleothems (stalagmites, stalactites), corals	Recent to 350,000 years ago (^{230}Th/ ^{234}U); 10,000 to 150,000 years ago (^{231}Pa / ^{235}U)
Thermal ionization mass spectrometry (TIMS)	Bones, corals; combine with ESR to assess uranium uptake in teeth; increases precision of U-series dating	Only limit is sufficient material for dating (Wintle 1996:135)
^{39}Argon/^{40}Argon, including single crystal laser fusion methods (SCLF)	Volcanic rock and ash	50,000 years ago to origin of earth; new versions extend into historic range
Amino acid racemization	Ratite (ostrich) eggshells	Recent to 200,000 BP in tropics (Miller et al. 1993)
Obsidian hydration	Obsidian stone artifacts	Recent to around 40,000 BP?
RELATIVE		
Stratigraphy and lithostratigraphy	Sediment and rock sequences	No limit
Biostratigraphy	Fossiliferous sediment sequences	No limit
Paleomagnetism	Global sequence of north/ "normal" and south/"reversed" magnetic polarity	No limit
Marine (Oxygen) Isotope Stages	Foraminifera, radiolaria, and other organisms in deep-sea (ocean) sediment cores; gases trapped in glacial ice	Pleistocene and Holocene epochs (last 2.6 million years)
FUN (Fluorine, Uranium, Nitrogen)	Bones, teeth	Recent to last few hundred thousand years

Source: Compiled from Wintle 1996; Schwarcz 2001; Klein 1999.

all radiocarbon age estimates. The further back in time one went, the more the ^{14}C date diverged from the true age of a sample. These tree rings allow a correction to the radiocarbon curve as far back as 10,000 years ago. Beyond this, ages are calibrated using uranium series and thermal ionization mass spectrometry (TIMS) of corals. The 40,000-year effective boundary for radiocarbon has proven hard to penetrate. Newer methods, such as accelerator mass spectrometry (AMS), date the number of carbon isotopes directly, requiring smaller and smaller samples (Taylor 1997; Wintle 1996:127). It was originally thought that accelerator mass spectrometry would allow material as old as 100,000 years to be dated, but the range has not been extended any further back than using conventional radiocarbon. A date of 40,000 years ago corresponds with the beginnings of the Upper Palaeolithic, as well as the appearance of anatomically modern people throughout the Old World (Mellars 2005, 2006). It is not surprising that archaeologists linked the two phenomena. The impressive cultural achievements of the Upper Palaeolithic made for ancestors we could easily claim as our own. For the French, they even represented their earliest civilization, one supplanted by Mesolithic postglacial barbarians (Willoughby 1976). In the absence of any true age estimates, the African Middle Palaeolithic and Middle Stone Age were assumed to be the same age, since they were associated with the same kind of modern human skeletal remains.

This association was initially used to show how far Africa lagged behind the achievements of early modern Europeans. In his 1970 synthesis, *The Prehistory of Africa*, Clark (1970:124) agreed that Upper Pleistocene Africans were associated with flake tool assemblages and Levallois production methods little different from those of Middle Palaeolithic Neanderthals. A year later, Karl Butzer wrote that,

> equally intriguing is the more subtle, geographically significant appearance of new population centers in Eurasia, the continent which had eclipsed the African heartland by the late Pleistocene. If tool-workmanship be an index of cultural progressiveness, and site tool density an index of population size, then Africa would probably qualify as the major center of population and cultural innovation of early and middle Pleistocene times. But during the last interglacial, tool-craftsmanship found a new focus in Europe, at least judging by the artful hand-axes of the final Acheulian, or the fine flaking techniques of the Mousterian. And population density, insofar as can be inferred from the evidence,

achieved a new high during the European late Pleistocene. By this time Africa
may have become a cultural backwater. (Butzer 1971:462)

In other words, while in Europe modern humans expressed their cognitive
and behavioral prowess through the manufacture of standardized blade tool
assemblages, bone, ivory, and antler tools, portable and parietal art, and complex social systems, their African counterparts were continuing to wallow in
the Middle Palaeolithic Mode 3 doldrums (Willoughby 2000).

Another early dating method that was applied to East African sites was
obsidian hydration analysis. Obsidian is a volcanic glass and forms when lava
at the surface cools so quickly that crystals do not form. It is an important
raw material for flaked stone tool production, as it produces sharp, but brittle,
edges. Each lava flow has a unique chemical composition, so obsidian sources
can be readily identified. When an obsidian edge is broken, it begins to absorb
water from the surrounding environment. A hydration layer is created on the
surface and increases in thickness over time, giving a relative date (Renfrew
and Bahn 2000:156). However, hydration rates are dependent on local temperature and environment. Prior to the development of chronometric dating
methods that worked on Upper Pleistocene materials, obsidian hydration was
used to date Middle and Later Stone Age artifacts and their cultural context.
The time limit for obsidian hydration is not clearly established, and for most
sites, it has been supplanted by other dating techniques. But there are still
many archaeologists who are convinced that it represents a valid way of determining when artifacts were produced.

MORE RECENT CHRONOMETRIC DATING METHODS

New chronometric dating techniques first applied in the 1980s showed,
quite unexpectedly, that most Mode 3 industries were of similar age wherever they were found in the Old World. In addition, it has become clear
that African early modern human remains are associated with artifacts that
could be 100,000 or 200,000 years old or even older. The first reassessments
of site age using these methods were published within a year of the earliest
mitochondrial DNA results. Together, they combined to destroy the old,
Eurocentric model. It was apparent that anatomically modern humans had
lived well before the onset of the Upper Palaeolithic cultural "revolution,"
just not in Europe. It also put a focus on the Middle Palaeolithic/Middle

Stone Age of Africa, as this was the time and place in which our own species must have originated.

What are these dating techniques which overthrew conventional palaeo-anthropological wisdom? In a 1996 article, Wintle describes most of them as "small, hot and identified by acronyms" (table 4.1). Small refers to required sample size, hot to the need to preheat samples, and acronyms will become self-evident in the following discussion. Some are refinements of older techniques, while others are completely new. But they all have had a revolutionary role in revising our understanding of the African emergence of modern humans.

One dating technique is a refinement on potassium-argon (K-Ar), the method used to measure the radioactive decay from potassium (^{40}K) to argon (^{40}Ar) in volcanic rock samples (lava or ash). Heating drives out the remnant argon gas, so the amount in a sample is a function of time since its formation. ^{40}K is a long-lived isotope, with a half-life of about 1.3 billion years, so the method can be used to date volcanic material ranging from the formation of the earth until around 500,000 years ago. Its most notable contribution to palaeoanthropology came in 1961 with the publication of a date for the *Zinjanthropus boisei* skull (or OH-5), a *Paranthropus* or robust australopithecine associated with Oldowan artifacts from Bed I at Olduvai Gorge in Tanzania (Leakey et al. 1961; Tobias 1967a). Recognized as Lower Pleistocene, it was originally thought to be about 500,000 years old. But the potassium-argon estimate suggested that it was 1,750,000 ± 200,000 old (Leakey et al. 1961), effectively tripling its age.

Conventional potassium-argon dating is outside the range of time of interest here, but newer methods using a single mass spectrometer extend the range into the Upper Pleistocene and Holocene, and even into historical times. Here neutrons convert a portion of ^{39}K to ^{39}Ar, an artificial isotope. The amount of ^{39}Ar is compared to the amount of ^{40}Ar, producing an estimate of age; it is referred to as the ^{39}Ar/ ^{40}Ar or argon/argon method. Refinements include single crystal laser fusion (SCLF), where a high-powered laser fuses a single grain of the sample and drives off argon for measurement in a mass spectrometer, giving a more precise date calculated from a distribution in ages in individual grains (Schwarcz 2001:44). It has been used to clarify the exact age of the Bruhnes/Matuyama palaeomagnetic boundary at 783,000 ± 11,000 years ago (Wintle 1996:129), the onset of the Middle Pleistocene.

Most recently, it has been shown that one can even extend ^{39}argon/^{40}argon dating into the radiocarbon (and modern) range (Wintle 1996:130). Renne and colleagues dated volcanic material from the famous eruption of Mount Vesuvius near modern Naples, Italy, that buried the Roman cities of Pompeii and Herculaneum in AD 79 (Renne et al. 1997; Lamphere 2000). Their dates overlapped with this well-known, historically recorded event.

Uranium or uranium disequilibrium series (U-series) relies on the radioactive decay of three types of uranium isotopes: protactinium-uranium (^{231}Pa/^{235}U), uranium (^{234}U/^{238}U), and thorium-uranium (^{230}Th/^{234}U). The decay series from ^{230}Th to ^{234}U is the most widely used and has a range from recent to 350,000 years ago. Materials that can be dated include corals and stromatolites as well as calcretes, calcitic deposits formed in sediments in arid regions. Speleothems, calcite, or aragonite deposits formed in caves (stalactites, stalagmites, and flowstones) can also be dated, as well as travertines (layers of calcite precipitated from hot or cold spring waters that have circulated through limestone aquifers) (Schwarcz 1992:58). Uranium series does not require knowledge of environmental conditions since the sample was deposited. This is a requirement for optically stimulated luminescence (OSL), electron spin resonance (ESR), or thermoluminescence (TL) (Schwarcz 1993:13). Due to the way samples are reported, uranium-series dates always have asymmetrical error factors (Schwarcz 2001:50).

One assumes that the ratio of the two isotopes is zero at the time of formation and that the only changes have been due to radioactive decay (Schwarcz 1993:15). Over time, uranium radioactively decays into thorium, until secular equilibrium is reached, a state where the rate of growth of a daughter isotope equals its rate of decay (Schwarcz 1992:58, 2001:42). Uranium from surrounding sediments is absorbed by bones and teeth after burial, but thorium or protactinium is not. Therefore the amounts of these isotopes are a result of radioactive decay and markers estimating the time elapsed since deposition (Schwarcz 2001:42). Uranium series can be used on samples between a few hundred years old up to about 350,000 years ago; this range might be extended as far back as 500,000 years if thermal ionization mass spectrometry is employed (Schwarcz 1992:58, 1993:19).

Thermal ionization mass spectrometry is a method used to measure small quantities of heavy isotopes in bones and coral; it is similar to accelerator mass spectrometry ^{14}C (Schwarcz 1993:17). It increases the accuracy of uranium series, since one is counting atoms directly, and may be used directly to date hominin teeth (Schwarcz 1992:60, 2001:42). It can be combined with electron spin resonance to assess uranium uptake and has been used to date corals in an attempt to extend the calibration curve for radiocarbon dating back to around 30,000 years ago (Wintle 1996:134; Schwarcz 1993:20).

Some buried materials are able to trap electron charges freed from atoms as a result of bombardment by radioactive radiation. This property can also be exploited for dating purposes, as it provides an estimate of time elapsed since the traps were last emptied (Schwarcz 2001:46). Electron spin resonance is a method used to measure the accumulated dose and time since burial (Schwarcz and Grün 1992:145). As is the case for thermoluminescence (TL), electron charges are trapped at defects in crystalline materials (Schwarcz and Grün 1992:145). The source of radiation can be internal (due to traces of uranium, thorium, and potassium in the sample) or external (in surrounding sediment and from cosmic rays) (Schwarcz and Grün 1992:145). The measured signal must start with zero and increase over time; its intensity is a function of age since deposition of the sample (Schwarcz and Grün 1992:145; Schwarcz and Rink 2000). Tooth enamel is the material of choice. Speleothems, corals, and travertines can also be dated this way, but only within the uranium series time range, the last 450,000 years (Schwarcz 2001:47–48; Grün and Stringer 1991:155). Enamel is a well-crystallized hydroxyapatite mineral-like bone, but has an organic content of less than 1%. Both electron spin resonance and thermoluminescence require knowledge of environmental and burial history (Schwarcz 1992:56). At death, tooth enamel contains no uranium, thorium, or potassium. Soon after burial, uranium is absorbed into all parts of a tooth: the enamel, dentine, and cementum (Schwarcz and Grün 1992:146). The amount of uranium is a function of age. The intake of uranium into bones and teeth was one of a series of relative dating techniques developed in the middle of the twentieth century. Jointly known as the FUN techniques (Poirier 1977:33; Oakley 1970), for fluorine, uranium, and nitrogen, their most famous application was the revelation of the recent age of the Piltdown fraud (Weiner 1955). Buried bones absorb fluorine and uranium from the surrounding environment, but lose nitrogen over time. Although this process is temperature dependent, bones from the same place of the same age should have similar amounts of fluorine or uranium. This remains one of the few dating methods that can be used directly on bones.

Uranium uptake history lies between two limiting models, early uptake (EU) and linear uptake (LU) (Schwarcz and Rink 2000:122). In the early uptake model, results are calibrated using the assumption that uranium was absorbed into the tooth enamel soon after burial. It gives the lower possible age (Schwarcz and Grün 1992:146). In the linear uptake model, calculations are made assuming that uranium was absorbed at a continuous rate over time. If there is not a lot of uranium in a sample, the early uptake date will be similar to the linear uptake one. "Without further evidence one can only assume that the ESR ages calculated with the EU and LU models more or less bracket the true age" (Grün and Stringer 1991:162). Uranium-series and ESR can be used together in order to model the process of uptake (Schwarcz and Grün 1992:164). Some of the most recent attempts to date Pleistocene material rely on a combination uptake, or CU model (Porat et al. 2002). For dentine and cementum, uranium uptake is somewhere in between early and late uptake, while for enamel, uptake is slightly delayed (Porat et al. 2002:109).

ESR has been used to date many Middle Palaeolithic sites, especially those associated with early modern humans (throughout Africa and in the Middle East at the Mugharet es Skhūl and Jebel Qafzeh (Vandermeersch 1981). At Qafzeh, a minimum of twenty individual modern humans were excavated. Dates from associated animal teeth average around 115,000 ± 15,000 years ago through the linear uptake model, and 93,000 ± 13,000 years ago using the early uptake model (Aitken and Valladas 1992:143, 1993). At Skhūl, similar estimates were obtained: 81,000 ± 15,000 years old (EU) and 101,000 ± 12,000 years old (LU). The Kebara Neanderthal burial, on the other hand, was more recent, dated to 60,000 ± 6,000 (EU) and 64,000 ± 6,000 (LU) (Schwarcz and Grün 1992:147). This was the opposite of what was expected, based on evidence from Europe. It is not too much to conclude that, as have Schwarcz and Grün (1992:147), "these results set the stage for a revolution in the chronology of the evolution of modern humans."

ESR can also be used on travertines and speleothems, but only within the uranium-series time range (Schwarcz 2001:48). Schwarcz and Rink (2001) have modified ESR so it can be used on unburned flint artifacts. They argue that the outer 2 mm of stone is exposed to a dose of beta particles from the surrounding sediment that does not penetrate into the interior of the material. The difference in equivalent radiation dose between the skin and the interior can be used as a measure of time since burial, essentially since the sample was last zeroed (Schwarcz and Rink 2001; Schwarcz 2001:48).

Thermoluminescence has long been used to date pottery and gives the date a vessel was fired. It is also used on sediments such as sand and loess, to date when they were exposed to sunlight last, presumably at time of burial. Aeolian or windblown deposits are exposed to light during transport, or while exposed on the surface prior to burial (Aitken and Valladas 1992:139). Water borne sediments can also be dated using thermoluminescence and a related method, optically stimulated luminescence (Aitken and Valladas 1992:139). Exposure to heat (upward of 400°C) or sunlight zeroes radiation, effectively bleaching the samples (Aitken and Valladas 1992:139). Mineral grains then begin to trap electrons produced by radiation, and the amount of radiation becomes a function of age (Wintle 1996:125; Schwarcz 2001:46). In the laboratory, electrons are released by heating at a constant rate; a peak of light emission comes at a particular temperature range. Electron number is measured by the intensity of light emitted from a sample (Schwarcz and Grün 1992:145).The dating signal is stimulated by heat (or by light in the case of optically stimulated luminescence). This measurement is combined with a determination of the sample's radioactive context, as estimated from the burial environment (Wintle 1996:125). Thermoluminescence, optically stimulated luminescence, and electron spin resonance are jointly referred to as "trapped electron dating" methods (Aitken and Valladas 1992:139).

Thermoluminescence can be used to date any sediment exposed to sufficient sunlight; this includes African Middle Stone Age and Middle Palaeolithic archaeological and fossil sites (Feathers and Bush 2000:91). But Feathers and Bush (2000:91) note that many sites of this age are found in caves and rockshelters, whose complex depositional environment makes it difficult to identify whether samples were sufficiently heated ("bleached" or "zeroed") at time of formation (Feathers and Bush 2000:91). To get an accurate estimate of age at Die Kelders Cave 1 on the coast of South Africa, they dated samples using thermoluminescence and optically stimulated luminescence and then added dates obtained using infrared stimulated luminescence (IRSL) of feldspars to derive equivalent dose measurements (Feathers and Bush 2000:105).

But thermoluminescence was strikingly used at the Levantine Middle Palaeolithic sites that contain early moderns, "Proto-Cro-Magnons" in Vandermeersch's (1981) classification, as well as Neanderthals. Valladas and her

colleagues proposed that thermoluminescence could also be used to date siliceous rock (flint, chert, cryptocrystalline silica) artifacts that accidentally fell
into a fire or hearth or had been deliberately heat-treated (Aitken and Valladas
1992:139; Valladas et al. 1987, 1988). Possibly because this method was experimental, they published their 60,000-year-old date for the Kebara Neanderthal
first (Valladas et al. 1987). Since this fell into the expected range, it would
indicate that the method worked. A year later, the same group published dates
for the proto-Cro-Magnons of Jebel Qafzeh, averaging 92,000 ± 5,000 years
ago (Valladas et al. 1988). Six thermoluminescence dates for Skhūl averaged
around 119,000 years old, with a standard deviation around 18% (Aitken and
Valladas 1992:143). All of these dates were unexpected, as modern humans,
even those associated with the Middle Palaeolithic, were all supposed to be
younger than the radiocarbon limit of 40,000 years ago. Anatomically modern
humans must have preceded Neanderthals in the Middle East, or were contemporary with them (since the neighboring site of Mugharet et Tabun had
yielded a Neanderthal sample from deposits which could be the same age as
the Mugharet es Skhūl) (Garrod and Bate 1937; McCown and Keith 1937).

Optically stimulated luminescence (OSL) and infrared stimulated luminescence (IRSL) are used on sediments to measure the exposure of individual
grains of quartz or feldspar to light (Wintle 1996:131). The dating signal here
is stimulated by light rather than heat, and sediments from the last 150,000
years can be dated (Aitken and Valladas 1992:139).

Amino acid racemization (AAR) offered immediate potential to palaeontologists and archaeologists because it dated bone directly, not associated
material (Bada and Helfman 1975). Proteins are made up of combinations of
twenty amino acids; these occur in left and right isonomers or enantiomers or
mirror images. In life, only left (L) coiling enantiomers exist. After death, there
is a change in amino acid structure from L coiling to D (dextra or right) coiling
until there are equal amounts of both. The process of change is known as racemization, and if one knows the rate of racemization for a specific amino acid
and can calculate temperature and humidity of the burial environment, an age
(since death) can be estimated. It requires a reference specimen of a known date
in order to provide a baseline for calibrating results. One of the few methods
that would encompass the "muddle" of the Middle and Early Upper Pleistocene,
amino acid racemization fell out of favor when accelerator mass spectrometry
radiocarbon dating was applied to AAR-dated human bones from early, pos-

sibly pre-Clovis, archaeological and fossil sites in North America. Rather than being quite ancient (Bada 1985), most were less than 5,000 years old, a tenth of their estimated antiquity (Taylor et al. 1985). When the initial reference sample was re-dated, similar dates were obtained (Bada 1985).

Newer work using ratite or ostrich eggshell (Brooks et al. 1990; Miller et al. 1993) is said to compensate for some of these problems. Ostrich eggs were widely used prehistorically as a food source, and their shells were subsequently used as water bottles and decorative materials (for jewelry such as beads). The presence of ostrich eggshell beads in some African Middle Stone Age sites is used as proof of modern-like culture at least by 40,000 years ago (Ambrose 1998b; Robbins 1999). The structure of an ostrich shell is believed to protect the protein within it, so there should be no contamination during burial (Wintle 1996:133). Dating is based on the racemization or epimerization of the amino acid isoleucine in calcite crystals (Brooks et al. 1990; Miller et al. 1993). It is felt that the best samples come from stratified cave sites (Miller et al. 1993). At Border Cave in South Africa, there are 4 m of deposits of alternating brown sandy silts and white ash. Radiocarbon dates are used to calibrate the rate of racemization of the ostrich eggshell; one provided an age of 36,100 ± 900 years old (Miller et al. 1993:65). They estimate that the Howieson's Poort level at Border Cave lies between 69,000 ± 7,000 and 106,000 ± 11,000 years old, suggesting that the earliest Middle Stone Age is at least 100,000 years old (Miller et al. 1993:65). The Howieson's Poort Industry, found stratified between more typical Middle Stone Age levels at some coastal South African sites, is an unusually precocious industry, suggestive of the Later Stone Age (Thackeray 1992).

So amino acid racemization offers the potential of dating a material that is quite common in African archaeological sites. But its most important application has been its use to determine whether or not sufficient DNA is present in an ancient bone sample. This is part of the protocol of the researchers from the Max Planck Institute for Evolutionary Anthropology in Leipzig who have been successful in extracting mitochondrial DNA from European Neanderthals (Krings et al. 1997). This issue is treated in more depth in chapter 6.

RELATIVE DATING METHODS

It must not be assumed that chronometric dating techniques, despite their attractiveness, have replaced traditional methods of determining site age, as Childe warned us almost fifty years ago. Relative dating is still important as it allows for local sequences to be determined and then cross-correlated to other sites and regions. Lithostratigraphy involves recording a sequence of events in a series of rocks or sediments. The oldest deposits are on the bottom, with younger deposits superimposed. Some deposits can be chemically identified and traced over long distances. A series of lithostratigraphic units can be defined, including beds, members, and ultimately, formations. A formation is a regional sequence composed of a group of members and is named for the place where this rock sequence is present, for example, the Koobi Fora Formation at the east side of Lake Turkana, northern Kenya. Biostratigraphic units are defined and dated using their fossil contents. The most useful species are those with a wide geographic distribution, but with a short time of existence. The appearance or disappearance of such index fossils also help to date a stratigraphic unit, since much of the African record of Plio-Pleistocene human evolution is paralleled by splitting and diversification of large mammal species, including bovids, suids, and elephants. In more recent periods, one relies more directly on micromammals such as mice and voles (Cooke and Maglio 1971; Harris and White 1979; Vrba et al. 1995). For example, the appearance of *Arvicola terrestris cantiana* is used as a proxy marker of the initial human settlement of Europe around 500,000 years ago (Dennell and Roebroeks 1996). In deep-sea cores, certain foram species can be used as markers; for example, *Globorotalia truncatulinoides* marks the start of the Pleistocene epoch. Well before the invention of chronometric dating techniques and even before the antiquity of humans had been established, great chunks of earth history were divided into eras (such as the Cenozoic), periods (Tertiary, Quaternary), and epochs (Pleistocene, Holocene) on the basis of their lithostratigraphic and biostratigraphic contents. This system is still in use today, reflecting its continuing utility.

Palaeomagnetic stages can be identified in ancient sediments and rocks and used for relative ordering of archaeological and fossil materials, as long as they are at least 780,000 years old (the date of the last change from the Matuyama Reversed to the Bruhnes Normal Chron). The oxygen (or marine) isotope stages (OIS or MIS) created from understanding the environmental record from deep-sea and ice cores can also be used as a relative dating tool. But normally, they are used as a convention or rule to report the estimated age or context of a site.

These new chronometric dating methods have had the same kind of impact on the understanding of later human history as the growing molecular evidence discussed in chapter 6. Developed around the same time, investigations using these tools have fundamentally changed our perception of the origins and subsequent evolution of *Homo sapiens*. Africa, a continent that was felt to be marginal, is now central to this problem. Geneticists look to those working in the African Middle and Upper Pleistocene to provide the hard fossil and behavioral data to confirm their models of dispersal and migration. But the lack of substantial field research makes it almost impossible to propose even general models of cultural history: what occurred, where, and when? At the other extreme, the region where the most research has been done on early modern humans, Western Europe, is revealed as geographically marginal to the study of Pleistocene human evolution. Despite its role in the history of development of Palaeolithic systematics (Sackett 1981, 2000), Western Europe could have had only a peripheral role in the Palaeolithic world (Straus 1995:4; Kleindienst 2001:4). It was the end of the universe to early modern Africans and may have even been settled by them later than they reached Sahul, the ice age supercontinent composed of Australia, Tasmania, and New Guinea (Bowler et al. 2003).

One final comment remains to be made. The chronometric dates that are cited in the rest of this book are reported as published in the original sources. For example, radiocarbon dates should be assumed to be uncalibrated, unless explicitly stated in the text.

5

Out of Africa: When and How Many Times? Alternative Models of Modern Human Origins

Africa's supremacy in the development of Australopithecus, *of earliest* Homo *and of anatomically modern humans seems unlikely to be seriously challenged. We, ourselves, are likewise descended from the people of African descent who seem to have colonized Europe under the name of Cro-Magnons. Even so, to diminish our very own Neanderthals to a footnote of history seemed to smack of colonialism in reverse.* (Aldhouse-Green 2001:114)

It is not enough to claim that the "out of Africa" scenario happened; it is incumbent upon those archaeologists who postulate it to bring forth archaeological evidence to demonstrate their position or to explain why archaeological data, particularly lithic technology and typology, are not relevant. (Marks 1992:245–246)

According to Desmond Clark (1981:164), "the appearance of modern man is the most significant event in the whole long record of mankind's biological and cultural evolution." This rather chauvinistic statement was made long before the growing geochronological and genetic conclusion that *Homo sapiens* evolved solely in Africa. However, Peter Bowler, a historian of science, cautions us that "whatever the potential interest of the actual discoveries, it seems obvious that a comprehensive study of how understanding of human evolution was developed must focus on the theories, not on the fossils" (Bowler 1987:5–6). Bowler wrote this statement in relation to Piltdown, but it could easily have been written about the controversies concerning the African origin of *Homo sapiens*.

As described in chapter 2, the modern human origins debate repeats very old ideas that first surfaced as part of the race issue. Did humans have a single center of origin or many? Was the process of early history one of monogenesis or polygenesis? How many branches were there and did these correspond to living races and/or subspecies? Such models eventually were framed as debates over the relative roles of genetic drift and gene flow in our early history. Over the same time period, there has been a change in our understanding of the Middle Stone Age and its antiquity. New dating methods provide the hard evidence that anatomically modern humans were present in Africa well before they first appeared elsewhere. Smith (1992b:243–244, 1993) sees the dating methods in chapter 3 as just as important as genetic data for the delineation of the Out of Africa II model. But Smith (1992b:243) also believes that "there is nothing inherent in the pertinent African fossil record itself which identifies Africa as the source for all modern people."

Then what evidence do we have for the African origin of modern humans and how is it linked with models of earlier origins and migrations? The concept of "Out of Africa" goes back to classical antiquity (Feinberg and Solodow 2002). Most historians are familiar with the concept that the continent had the continuing capacity for creating novelties. "There is always something new coming out of Africa" is a phrase that Aristotle used in his *Historia Animaliam* in order to refer to the diversity of animals from Libya. He suggested that new forms developed from indiscriminate mating and hybridization at water holes in the North African desert (Feinberg and Solodow 2002:255, 257). For Aristotle, the saying was already a proverb, so he was not its ultimate source (Feinberg and Solodow 2002:257). Most antiquarians cite Pliny the Elder (AD 23–79), who perished while observing the eruption of Mount Vesuvius. He wrote that *unde etiam vulgare Graeciae dictum, semper aliquid novi Africanum adferre* or "that is the origin in fact of the saying common in Greece, that Africa is always producing something new" (in Feinberg and Solodow 2002:258). Erasmus in his *Adagia* quoted the commonly accepted version: *Ex Africa semper aliquid novi* (Feinberg and Solodow 2002:259). This was also Clark's (1970:15) opening quote in his pioneering *Prehistory of Africa*. While this idea was used in classical times to marvel at the wonders of Africa, by the nineteenth century, it was changed in order to emphasize the differences between Europeans and Africans and the inadequacies of the latter. But it gained currency again as the English title for Isak Dinesen/Karen Blixen's

1938 novel, *Den Afrikanske Farm* (Dinesen 1937, 1938). In it she discusses her life as a coffee farmer in highland Kenya before and during World War I. It is this connection, along with the 1985 Academy Award–winning movie of the same name starring Meryl Streep and Robert Redford, that popularized "Out of Africa" once again. It was soon adopted by palaeoanthropologists as the shorthand for various scenarios for early migrations in human evolution. Despite its current meaning, researchers are not sure if "Out of Africa" relates to a specific event or a long-term process.

> The rather glib titles "Out of Africa I" for the *erectus* migration, and "Out of Africa II" for the movement of the first *Homo sapiens sapiens* people into the Near East may be convenient for some purposes, but they tend to mask the fact that there must have been a continuous trickle of human migration along broadly the same routes during much of the Pleistocene. (Roe 2001b:642)

Others have complained that the models seem to argue more for "Out of Africa, thank God!" (Proctor 2003:225), the belief that once humans left the founder continent, things could really take off. As recently as the late 1980s, the majority opinion was that the earliest stages of human origins took place in Africa, but once early hominins dispersed into Eurasia, the focus of change and innovation shifted to Europe. Until very recently, most sources emphasized that, during the Upper Pleistocene, Africa lagged far behind Western Europe in cultural achievements (Butzer 1971:462; Clark 1970:124; Stringer 2002b:568). Even the recognition that our own species has an African origin has not been sufficient to change this perspective. For most researchers, the Cro-Magnon universe centered on the Dordogne and Vézère river valleys in southern France remains the yardstick by which true modernity is measured. For them, the people who produced the magnificent cave art at Lascaux and others who carved ivory and bone into representations of animals and humans are the first true people with culture.

OUT OF AFRICA I

One thing that is not disputed is that Africa was the continent in which the Family Hominidae (alternatively Tribe Hominini) first appeared. How many species this family contains is debatable (Willoughby 2005). Under the current classification, there is a surprising diversity of hominin genera and species. Along with the Late Miocene hominin recently described from Chad

(Brunet et al. 2002, 2005), there are presently about seven genera, and twenty-three or twenty-four valid species of (sometimes presumably) known bipedal humans (table 5.1). The first with modern body proportions was *Homo erectus* or *Homo ergaster*, a species which is found at Dmanisi in the Middle East 1.8 million years ago (Gabunia and Vekua 1995; Gabunia et al. 2001) and in Southeast Asia (Java) possibly a million years ago, if not earlier (Curtis et al. 2000; Swisher et al. 1994). They or their possible descendants, *Homo heidelbergensis*, who have cranial capacities within the modern range, represent the first Europeans. The oldest European site is around 800,000 years old (the Gran Dolina at Atapuerca, northern Spain) (Carbonell et al. 1995), and hominins are found further north only after 500,000 years ago. According to Roebroeks (2001:455), after this time "both demographical momentum and behavioral capacities enabled a substantial colonization of large parts of Europe, and a virtually continuous hominid presence of more than 400,000 years."

Table 5.1. Currently recognized genera and species of the Family Hominidae or Tribe Hominini (with year of definition)

Genus	*Sahelanthropus*
Species and Subspecies	*Sahelanthropus tchadensis* (2002)
Ardipithecus	*Australopithecus*
Ardipithecus ramidus ramidus (1994, 2001) *Ardipithecus ramidus kadabba* (2001)— reassigned to *Ardipithecus kadabba* (2004)	*Australopithecus anamensis* (1994) *Australopithecus afarensis* (1978) *Australopithecus bahrelghazali* (1995) *Australopithecus africanus* (1925) *Australopithecus garhi* (1999)
Kenyanthropus	
Kenyanthropus platyops (2001) *Kenyanthropus rudolfensis* (2001) = *Homo rudolfensis*	*Orrorin* *Orrorin tugenensis* (2000)
Paranthropus	*Homo*
Paranthropus boisei (1959) *Paranthropus aethiopicus* (1985) *Paranthropus robustus* (1938)	*Homo habilis* (1964) *Homo rudolfensis* (1976) *Homo erectus* (1891) *Homo ergaster* (1975) *Homo antecessor* (1997) *Homo heidelbergensis* (1908) *Homo neandertalensis* (1864) *Homo sapiens* (1758) *Homo sapiens idaltu* (2003) *Homo floresiensis* (2004)

Most researchers agree on this basic scenario; the debates range about how many out of Africa events occurred after the initial dispersal of *Homo erectus* (figure 5.1). For some (Foley and Lahr 1997), there were multiple migrations; each hominin species had an African origin and a subsequent dispersal. Every time the basic technological pattern changed, there is supposed to be another migration. For Foley and Lahr (1997), the maker of Mode 3 tools (radial flaking plus or minus Levallois techniques) was a species labeled *Homo helmei* (taken from the original name for the Florisbad skull from South Africa). Originally African, they later spread to Eurasia, becoming the last common ancestor of African moderns and European Neanderthals. For others, *Homo heidelbergensis* is the last common ancestor.

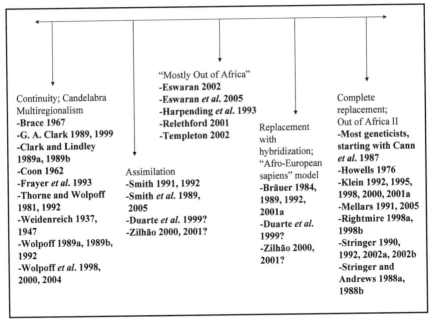

Figure 5.1 Models of modern human origins and their adherents

Recently, a number of skeletons have been reported from the island of Flores, east of Java in Indonesia (Lahr and Foley 2004; Brown et al. 2004; Morwood et al. 2004, 2005). They are remarkable in being tiny; the best preserved individual is approximately 18,000 years old and was only about a meter tall. Even more unexpected, its cranial capacity was only about 380 cc, making it smaller than some of the earliest australopithecines. About five years earlier,

Morwood's team reported pebble tools in association with around 800,000-year-old fauna on Flores (Morwood et al. 1998, 1999). Flores was apparently always an island separated from mainland Southeast Asia. It lies in Wallacea, the biogeographic province between the Pleistocene supercontinents of Sunda (mainland Southeast Asia as well as islands such as Java) and Sahul (Australia, Tasmania, and New Guinea) (Allen et al. 1977). Therefore the toolmakers must have crossed open water to get there. Now Morwood and his colleagues are proposing that this or other populations of *Homo erectus* evolved in place into *Homo floresiensis*, a separate species that became extremely small through the same process that led to pygmy elephants on the island.

The recognition of the association of anatomically modern humans and Mode 3 tools (Middle Palaeolithic or Middle Stone Age) led to a new controversy. It split the notion of anatomical modernity from that of cultural modernity for the first time. Cultural modernity meant being like European Upper Palaeolithic peoples with their prismatic blade Mode 4 technology, art, and personal adornment (Klein 1992; Mellars 1991, 2005). For Aldhouse-Green (2001:115), this discontinuity "freed archaeologists from the tyranny of the formula 'blades = brains.'" But did it? There are many Africanist archaeologists who think that behavioral modernity was only achieved there around 50,000 years ago or later, with the appearance of the Later Stone Age. It is supported by the fact that no anatomically modern humans are found outside of Africa until after 40,000 years ago, except at Skhūl and Qafzeh which are more correctly seen as African sites (Tchernov 1988). This is in addition to the alternate models of the origins of modern humans that are reviewed in the next few sections.

OUT OF AFRICA II OR REPLACEMENT

Out of Africa II is also known as the "replacement" or "recent African origin" model (Pearson 2004; Stringer 1989a, 1989b, 1990, 1992, 1993a, 1993b, 1994; 2002b; Stringer and Andrews 1988a, 1988b; Howells 1976). In this scenario, anatomically modern humans developed in Africa between 200,000 and 100,000 years ago. Sometime later they dispersed into Eurasia and replaced the indigenous people with little or no mixing or hybridization (Stringer and Andrews 1988a, 1988b; Stringer 2002a; 2002b:563). The strongest evidence for this model comes from mitochondrial DNA of living humans and Neanderthals (Cann et al. 1987; Krings et al. 1997, 2000; Ovchinnikov et al. 2000; Weaver and Rose-

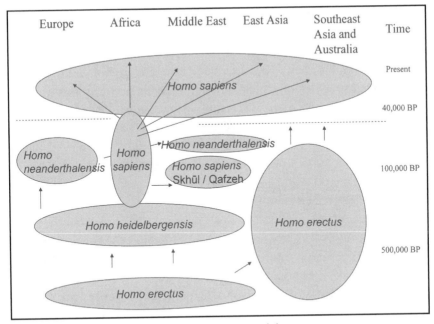

Europe   Africa   Middle East   East Asia   Southeast Asia and Australia   Time

Homo sapiens

Homo neanderthalensis

Homo neanderthalensis   *Homo sapiens*   *Homo neanderthalensis*

Homo sapiens Skhūl / Qafzeh

Homo heidelbergensis   *Homo erectus*

Homo erectus

Present

40,000 BP

100,000 BP

500,000 BP

Figure 5.2 Replacement model of modern human origins

man 2005) and studies of other genetic loci. This all suggests that only a small African group composed the founder population that became the ancestors of all of us today (figure 5.2). Other lines of support come from the anatomically modern fossils associated with Middle Palaeolithic or Middle Stone Age tools at a number of African sites. This fossil evidence is reviewed in chapter 7. One of the earliest supporters of the replacement model was Christopher Stringer (2002b:575). Within a year of publication of the first mitochondrial DNA tree in 1987, Stringer and his colleague, Peter Andrews, concluded that the problem of modern human origins had been solved and that "palaeoanthropologists who ignore the increasing wealth of genetic data on human population relationships will do so at their peril" (Stringer and Andrews 1998a:1268). But even for Stringer (2002b:576), "it is still unclear what drove the evolution of *Homo sapiens* in Africa." More recently, similar ideas have been presented using molecular data drawn from our fellow travelers, body lice (Kittler et al. 2003) and stomach bacteria (Falush et al. 2003; Spratt 2003).

A modified version of the replacement model is Harpending's "weak Garden of Eden" proposal (Harpending et al. 1993). For him, there was an African origin; then, after some period of time elapsed, there were one or more episodes of genetic bottlenecking that reduced human variation even more. Some geneticists propose that the population of early modern Africans dropped to around a thousand individuals. It was only when population sizes sufficiently recovered from this event that the Out of Africa II migration occurred. This model explains the lack of genetic variation in living people, something that is more remarkable when our mitochondrial and nuclear DNA loci are compared to those from the great apes (Gagneux et al. 1999; figure 6.3). In both versions, outward phenotypic traits that mark culturally defined racial differences between us today developed only in the last 50,000 years.

REPLACEMENT WITH HYBRIDIZATION

Gunter Bräuer (1984, 1989:133, 2001a) proposed a slight alternative to the "Out of Africa II" model. It is referred to as "replacement with hybridization," or the "Afro-European *sapiens* model." Basically, Bräuer suggests that, as modern humans entered Eurasia, they mixed with some local groups, producing hybrids. Examples of people of mixed heritage include the early Cro-Magnons from Mladeč in the Czech Republic (Smith 1982, 1984). These individuals have modern postcranial skeletons with tropical limb proportions, but some of the crania exhibit supraorbital tori and occipital features mimicking a Neanderthal bun (an occipital hemi-bun) (Smith 1984). There was also evidence of possible hybridization or continuity between the recent Neanderthals of Krapina and Vindija Caves in Croatia and early modern humans (Ahern et al. 2004). The Vindija Neanderthals show some traits in common with anatomically modern people, so they could just as easily represent an intermediate stage (Bräuer 1984; Smith 1984), as proposed by the supporters of the multiregional theory. At the other end of Europe, there is another possible hybrid, or possibly a descendant of one: the Gravettian child from Lagar Velho, Portugal (Duarte et al. 1999; Zilhão 2001).

MULTIREGIONAL AND CONTINUITY MODELS

The supporters of multiregional continuity propose that everywhere earlier hominins existed they evolved into *Homo sapiens* through a process of gradual adaptation (figure 5.3). Some degree of gene flow between neighboring groups led to the genetic and morphological similarities seen worldwide today. This model began with Franz Weidenreich (1937), who noted similarities between *Homo erectus* fossils from Java and China and later archaic and modern hu-

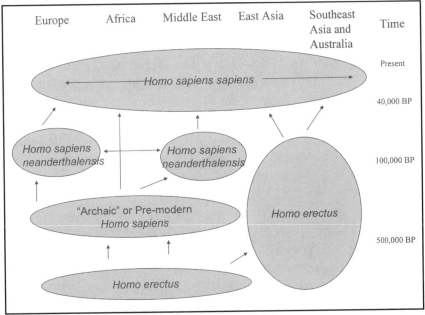

Figure 5.3 Multiregional model of modern human origins

mans in the same regions. He widened this to argue for four parallel lines of development to modernity (figure 2.2), what Howells (1976) would later call the candelabra theory (Tattersall 1995:213). Modern forms developed almost simultaneously throughout the Old World, but from different ancestors. C. Loring Brace felt that there could only have been one hominin species at a time, and that this form had gradually become modern, as material culture played an increasing role in development (Brace 1967; Brose and Wolpoff 1971; Hawks and Wolpoff 2003:92; Proctor 2003:221). Even the idea of hominin species was a mistake, as there could have been one form through time. *Homo sapiens* itself could be used to describe all members of the genus *Homo*, rather than just the recent species. A similar model was that of Coon (1962), but he saw separate development into moderns, with Caucasians leading the way, and Australian Aborigines bringing up the rear, still in the process today of becoming truly modern *Homo sapiens*. Few supported this idea when it was first published, and no multiregionalist today would accept it either.

The current version of the multiregional model is most associated with Brace, Thorne, and Wolpoff (Thorne and Wolpoff 1981, 1992; Wolpoff 1989a, 1989b, 1992; Wolpoff et al. 2004). They accept parallel development, but feel that enough gene flow took place between separate regions to enable the final product to remain a single species, *Homo sapiens*. The strict interpretation of multiregional continuity would be that there was only one "Out of Africa" event, that of *Homo erectus*. If so, phenotypic features observed today developed in parallel lines in each continent over the course of the next million years. Evidence cited as proof of this model includes anatomical traits, both metric and non-metric, that are supposed to show continuity over time from *Homo erectus* to modern humans in East Asia, from *Homo heidelbergensis* to Neanderthals to moderns in Europe, and from *Homo heidelbergensis* to moderns in Africa. What for Bräuer are hybrids are seen as proof of continuity for Thorne and Wolpoff (1992; Frayer et al. 1993).

There have been different versions of multiregionalism in the past and even at present. In his recent review, Stringer (2002b:565) points out that recently there has been a shift closer to the assimilationist perspective described in the next section on more intermediate perspectives. In this version, there are still parallel lines of evolution, but modern Africans show the most genetic diversity because their numbers were always much larger than coeval populations in Eurasia (Stringer 2002b:565).

MORE INTERMEDIATE POSITIONS

Ever since the Out of Africa II model was proposed as an alternative to multiregionalism, other researchers have presented positions that lie within the two extremes. One of these is Smith's (1992a; Smith et al. 1989, 2005) assimilation model. It proposes an African origin but no replacement (Stringer 2002b:564). Instead, it suggests that gene flow from Africa, along with hybridization and/or selection, could have made many people essentially modern (Stringer 2002b:564). There were probably always more Africans than non-Africans, leading to the false conclusion that Africans were the sole founder group. In a recent review article, Stringer describes this position as a modified multiregional perspective or "Multiregional II" (Stringer 2002b:565).

Relethford (2001) and Templeton (2002) support versions of this model and argue that modern human origins was a "mostly out of Africa" event, but not exclusively. Like Smith, they suggest that significant gene flow from Africans into Eurasian archaic humans could hide the true signs of regional continuity. Eswaran (2002; Eswaran et al. 2005) presents the most recent variant of this mode. He offers a mathematical model for the dispersal of modern genes out of Africa, using a diffusion wave based on Sewall Wright's shifting balance theory. This model too proposes a significant degree of assimilation of Eurasians to African genetic patterns. Along with two geneticists, Eswaran (et al. 2005) has refined this argument using nuclear DNA variation. They continue to support an intermediate theoretical position, somewhere between multiregionalism and complete replacement.

ROUTES OUT OF AFRICA

How did the dispersal or dispersals out of Africa happen? Direct evidence is limited to genetics and to biogeographic reconstructions of possible routes; however, fossil and archaeological data for them are extremely sparse. Desmond Clark (1989) hypothesized about three possible routes of migration: from the northwest coast across the Mediterranean Sea to Spain, from Ethiopia via the Red Sea to Yemen, or from Egypt through the Sinai to the Levant (Clark 1989:580; Marks 1992:239). The first is the least likely. While Morocco and Iberia are extremely close, Neanderthals persisted in the latter up to less than 30,000 years ago. The oldest Upper Palaeolithic sites appear to be in Cantabria (in northern Spain), but even their early radiocarbon dates are suspect (Zilhão 2001; Zilhão and D'Errico 1999; Straus 1995, 2001). There are no anatomically modern humans outside of Africa before 40,000 years ago except for Skhūl and Qafzeh. The time period associated with the first European Cro-Magnons also corresponds to the possible depopulation of North Africa and the Sahara, the early Upper Palaeolithic (Close 1986; Close and Wendorf 1990). The presence of Late Pleistocene Neanderthals in Iberia argues against the direct entry of modern humans into Europe across the Strait of Gibraltar. This is unexpected, as the earliest hominin sites in Europe are found in Iberia, and Acheulian people here made their bifacial tools on flakes, following the African method.

Clark's third most likely route was eastward along the Mediterranean coast, via Cyrenaica (coastal Libya) to the Egyptian delta to the Sinai. It is also possible that people spread north through the Western Desert of Egypt and along the Nile Valley to the Nile delta and northeast to the Sinai (Marks 1992:237), but there is little direct evidence. "An examination of the archaeological record of Egypt and Sudan indicates that at no point in this long period is there any convincing evidence for Northeast African/Levantine connections on more than the technocomplex level" (Marks 1992:229). In other words, there are broad archaeological similarities between the two regions, but little evidence of a real connection (Marks 1992:239).

There are few Early Upper Palaeolithic sites in the Nile Valley, and none between 38,000 and 25,000 years ago; after this date, what are described as true Upper Palaeolithic sites appear (Van Peer 1998:130). For Van Peer (1998; Vermeersch 2001:105), who has done extensive studies of Middle Palaeolithic sites in the Nile Valley, the appearance of the Nubian Complex (described in chapter 8) in the north is the sign of the "Out of Africa II" migration, but even he does not have any idea of when people moved from there into the Levant. He demonstrates that it is hard to compare Levantine and Egyptian Middle Palaeolithic industries because of the differences between archaeological materials and how they are studied. In the Levant, archaeologists with many occupation sites in caves concentrate on the finished tools (mainly Levallois products), while in Egypt, the sites are surface scatters of quarry debris, and lack these types (Vermeersch 2001:104–106).

A recent study of the oxygen isotope sequence in Red Sea sediments might shed some light on this problem (Sirocko 2003; Siddall et al. 2003). The Red Sea is an enclosed basin, connected to the Indian Ocean at the Strait of Bab el Mandeb, a feature that is presently only 18 km wide. There also is a sill or shelf of land 137 m below the modern surface. During the last glacial maximum (MIS 2), this feature would have been only 15 m underwater (Sirocko 2003:813), and might have provided a route for dispersal. The $\delta^{18}O$ measurement (the ratio of ^{18}O to ^{16}O) in the GEOTUE-KL 11 sediment core from the central Red Sea records several minimal and maximum values especially between 70,000 and 40,000 years ago when the southwestern monsoon did not reach this far north (Siddall et al. 2003:854–855; Sirocko 2003). There is no record at all for the last glacial or for the early postglacial. At this time, the water was either too cold or too salty for plankton to exist (Siddall et al. 2003:854). So precisely when Out of Africa II is predicted to occur, the environments in the Horn of Africa possibly became too cold and dry to support human populations. This corresponds to the period of depopulation at the Middle/Upper Palaeolithic boundary in North Africa, and also to the time proposed by the evolutionary geneticists for one or more major episodes of bottlenecking and near extinction.

All lines of evidence (genetic, archaeological, and fossil hominin) point to a time of extreme population stress in Africa at the time of the proposed great migration. As Marks (1992:239) suggests, using archaeological data, it is more likely that a population movement occurred between 150,000 and 50,000 years ago during the height of the Middle Palaeolithic rather than later. But there is no sign of anatomically modern humans outside of the continent until after this time, and the earliest Upper Palaeolithic ("modern") sites in North Africa date to after the last glacial maximum (around 18,000 years ago).

Some geneticists believe that there was an early migration following a coastal route from northeast Africa through the Arabian Peninsula to South and Southeast Asia, bringing people to Australia perhaps before they entered Europe. Evidence for this can be found in mitochondrial DNA distribution patterns (Quintana-Murci et al. 1999) as well as from Y chromosomes (Wells 2002:74; Wells et al. 2001; Underhill et al. 2001). One of the few coastal archaeological sites supporting this interpretation belongs to the Middle Stone Age. Artifacts are associated with an emerged coral terrace on the west coast of the Buri Peninsula, near the village of Abdur in Eritrea. They date to 118,000 to 126,000 years ago, using the TIMS (thermal ionization mass spectrometry) method of thorium/uranium dating (Bruggemann et al. 2004; Stringer 2000; Walter et al. 2000:66–67). This would put the occupation during oxygen isotope stage 5e, the same time as Skhūl and Qafzeh in Israel, the earliest anatomically modern people outside of Africa.

Recently, there has been an attempt to assess this idea from the southern Arabian Peninsula. Rose (2004a) has described a number of surface occurrences of undated but Middle Palaeolithic–looking stone artifacts in Oman. They are associated with ancient river channels and now dry lakes. The main retouched tools are small bifacial pieces, ranging in shape from foliates to ovates (Rose 2004a:552). Noting that there is little sign of bifacial technology in the Near East after MIS 6, Rose draws a connection with Middle Stone Age industries of East Africa and the Sudan (Rose 2004a:554). If it is confirmed that these are Middle Palaeolithic in age, these sites might help document the route of the "Out of Africa" migration or migrations. Also, recent reports on mitochondrial DNA and Y chromosome variation within aboriginal groups such as the Andaman Islanders and the Orang Asli or original people of the Malay Peninsula support the idea of an early arrival of modern humans here and in South and Southeast Asia (Forster and Matsumara 2005; Macaulay et al. 2005; Thangaraj et al. 2005). It is highly likely that this migration or these migrations occurred before what we people of Western European descent see as the main event, the arrival of anatomically modern humans in Europe.

What about the groups who stayed behind in Africa and became associated with the Later Stone Age? They seem to get overlooked by all researchers. One of the only comments comes from Derek Roe, looking at the archaeological record from Kalambo Falls, Zambia. This region continued to be occupied between the two Out of Africa migrations. "Human evolution did not stand still here, simply because the local population was not being exposed to the evolutionary hazards and stimuli of Out of Africa travel." (Roe 2001b:643). But even Roe (2001b:643) concludes that there are too few hominin remains known from Africa at this time to understand the local processes that led to anatomical modernity. A significant problem obviously remains. The period proposed for the transformation of anatomically modern people into Later Stone Age behaviorally modern ones is the least represented in the African archaeological record. If the processes of evolutionary modernization at this time were quick or slow, radical or gradual, they still remain for us to discover.

6

Mitochondrial Eve and the Middle Stone Age: Genetics and Human Variation

Generally it is difficult to find genetic markers that exist in one human population and not in others. Instead, human populations tend to differ in having varying proportions of the same allelic versions of genes; that is, most DNA variants are globally widespread and not unique to individual populations. (Ruvolo 1997:518)

What proteins did for evolutionary studies above the species level, mitochondrial DNA may be able to do for the study of evolution at and below the species level. (Wilson et al. 1985:377)

If there was no "human revolution" around 40,000 years ago, there has clearly been a revolution in the way we examine human origins. Geneticists studying variation in living human populations have plotted when and where key changes in our past occurred (Carroll 2003). The culmination of this research was the announcement in 2001 that two different research teams, one public (International Human Genome Sequencing Consortium 2001, 2004; Stein 2004) and one private (Venter et al. 2001), had mapped the entire human nuclear genome, 3 billion base pairs long. Attempts to determine the function of individual parts of the genome and how they interact with environmental factors have continued unabated. A portion of the funds for the original Human Genome Project was assigned to the examination of global genetic diversity (Cavalli-Sforza et al. 1991). Similar research is currently being funded by the National Geographic Society as the "Human Genographic Project" (Wells 2002). This Human Genome Diversity Project was an attempt to sample "remote" human populations in order to salvage information about genetic diversity before these groups mixed with outsiders. The ideal group was believed to be a population with few genetic founders (10 to 100 people) and who had been isolated from all other such groups for millennia (Cann 2001:1743). While the assumption of the existence of isolated populations can be questioned, this research has profound significance for the study of human history. These data have led to a number of models for the origin and dispersal of our species. Based on preliminary discussions of human genealogy, some geneticists have even proposed that their methods should replace traditional palaeoanthropological sources of data: fossils and artifacts (Wilson and Cann 1992).

THE GENETIC REVOLUTION

James D. Watson and Francis Crick (1953) demonstrated in the 1950s that the DNA (deoxyribonucleic acid) molecule, the basis of heredity, consists of two strands coiled in a double helix. DNA is composed of nucleotides: a sugar, a phosphate group, and one of four nitrogen-containing bases: adenine (A), thymine (T), guanine (G), and cytosine (C) (Relethford 2001:11). Adenine on one strand is always matched with thymine on the other, guanine with cytosine. A sequence of three bases or codon dictates the presence of a specific amino acid; the order of amino acids determines which protein is present. Nuclear DNA is inherited equally, one strand from each parent, through splitting and recombining at conception. DNA is found within chromosomes; in humans there are twenty-two pairs of chromosomes, numbered from largest (1) to smallest (22), and one pair of sex chromosomes (XX for females or XY for males). DNA is also found in mitochondria, organelles in cells outside the nucleus which convert sugar into energy. The mitochondrial DNA genome forms a circle of two DNA strands composed of about 16,569 base pairs, and includes thirty-seven genes (figure 6.1). Since segments of mitochondrial DNA mutate quickly, they can be used to examine recent human evolution (Relethford 2001:19).

Both nuclear and mitochondrial DNA contain genes that specify a functional polypeptide or RNA product (Strachan and Read 1996:592), ultimately dictating heredity. Coding and non-coding regions are present in both. Coding regions determine the order of amino acids and proteins, while non-coding or "junk" DNA lie in between, with no apparent function. But it does reveal

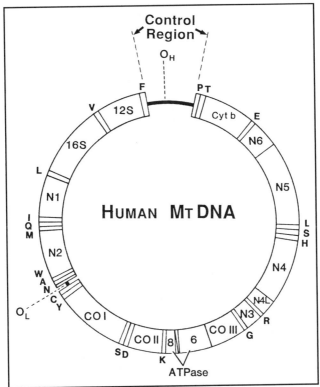

Figure 6.1 A mitochondrial DNA molecule (Stoneking 1993:61). Reprinted with permission of John Wiley and Sons, Inc.

significant historical information, since it only changes as a result of mutation. Kimura (1983) originally suggested that many mutations, chemical changes in DNA bases from one generation to the next, were evolutionarily neutral, so they did not affect the fitness or survivability of an organism. These neutral mutations seem to occur at a fixed rate over time from generation to generation. If the rate of change is known, as well as the degree of difference between two individuals at a particular locus or position, the date that they shared a last, or most recent, common ancestor can be determined. Examining mitochondrial DNA in this way, three human geneticists, Rebecca Cann, Mark Stoneking, and Allan Wilson (1987), proposed that all living humans worldwide could be traced back to one common ancestor or population who lived in Africa between 100,000 and 200,000 years ago, during the Middle Palaeolithic/Middle Stone Age (figure 6.2). Since mitochondrial DNA is passed exclusively through the female line, it

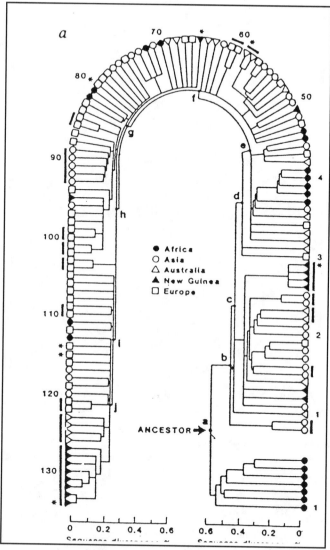

Figure 6.2 Cann, Stoneking, and Wilson's (1987:34) mitochondrial DNA results. Reprinted with permission of Dr. Rebecca Cann, Dr. Mark Stoneking, and the Nature Publishing Group

was no surprise that this ancestor was immediately nicknamed "Mitochondrial Eve." Given the degree of variation within living human populations, it was proposed that Mitochondrial Eve was African, but lived much more recently than *Homo erectus/Homo ergaster*, the species traditionally thought to be at the root of modern human diversity, according to the multiregional theory (Frayer et al. 1993; Thorne and Wolpoff 1992; Wolpoff 1989a, 1992; Wolpoff et al. 1988, 2000; Wolpoff and Thorne 1991). Along with the innovations in dating outlined in chapter 4, this mitochondrial DNA model led to increasing support for a relatively recent African origin for living people worldwide, what became known as the replacement model or Out of Africa II.

More recent work on great ape mitochondrial DNA has shown that living humans are the exception in the Superfamily Hominoidea for their lack of intra- or within species genetic variation (Gagneux et al. 1999; figure 6.3). Our closest living relatives, chimpanzees (*Pan*) and gorillas (*Gorilla*) have up to ten times as much within group variation as we do, suggesting that their recent evolutionary history was quite different from our own. Extinction as well as genetic drift (or founder effect) must have been important factors in all stages of human evolution.

The Mitochondrial Eve model offers an explanation for the lack of genetic differences in living humans worldwide. Since all of us share a recent common ancestor, there has not been enough time for selection and other evolutionary processes to affect the basic human genome in significant ways. Outwardly expressed phenotypic characters (skin and hair color, hair form, facial features, body structure, and so on) are not important at the level of the genome, but do reflect long-term processes of natural selection. Races, in the sense of biological subspecies, do not exist in humans. What we normally think of as racial variation is really composed of cultural, linguistic, historical, or ethnic differences, the products of learned, not innate, factors. This anthropological party line has become a rallying point, and one of the leading conclusions of the evolutionary aspects of the Human Genome and Genome Diversity Projects.

GENETICS AND HUMAN VARIATION: EARLY RESEARCH

As described in chapter 2, ever since Europeans began traveling the world, they noticed the physical and behavioral differences between people they met. There were long debates about how significant these differences were, and what they represented. It was not until the nineteenth century that human variation was explained as the product of inherited, biological traits, and not until the twentieth century that the basis of heredity began to be understood. Nineteenth-century researchers had developed sophisticated ways of measur-

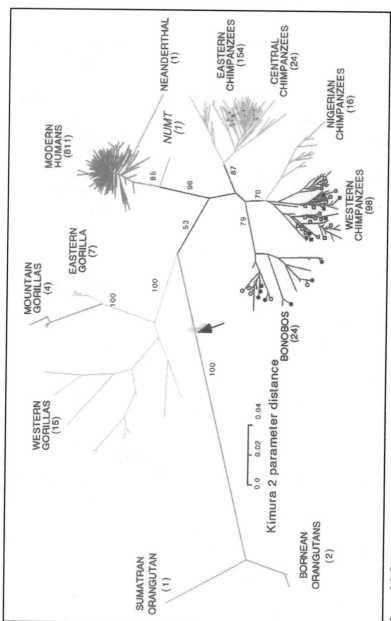

Figure 6.3 Great ape and human mitochondrial DNA diversity (Gagneux et al. 1999:5079). Reprinted with permission of the *Proceedings of the National Academy of Sciences* and Dr. Pascal Gagneux

ing and describing differences in human appearance or phenotype. Much of this work concentrated on craniometry, the measurement of the skull, its size, shape, and significant features (Gould 1981). The contents of the skull, the human brain, were also the focus of much attention, as it was assumed that they provided a way to understand individual differences in intelligence and cognitive capacity. Many early anthropologists attempted to define human types as belonging to geographically specific groups or "races," and there was a debate over whether or not these races had a common origin. Supporters of monogenesis believed in a descent from a single ancestor and supported a literal reading of the biblical book of Genesis, the descent from Adam and Eve. They could believe in the basic brotherhood of humanity. Or, like Johan Friedrich Blumenbach, they might argue that the differences between populations were a product of how much some groups had degenerated from the founders, in his case, Caucasians (Grayson 1983:144). Others, such as Charles White and Louis Agassiz, the founder of the Quaternary glacial theory, preferred polygenesis and did not have this dilemma; they could freely support a separate origin and development of geographically distinct populations. For Agassiz, the "assertion of the common descent of all races of men from a common stock is a mere human construction . . . what are called human races, down to their specialization in nations, are distinct primordial forms of the type of man" (in Grayson 1983:162).

With the adoption of Darwinian evolutionary theory in the late nineteenth century, there was increasing interest in variation within species. In the *Origin of Species*, published in 1859, Darwin (n.d.) proposed that some variations give an individual an advantage in a struggle for existence in a particular environment, allowing that individual to survive and reproduce at the expense of others. Over significant time, favorable variations are preserved in populations due to this differential survival. When an ancestral group was split into reproductively isolated subsets, the genetic differences that developed could ultimately lead to the origin of new species. This process of natural selection is only one of a number of factors that affect the evolution of populations. A population is a group of interbreeding individuals who share a common gene pool or genetic composition. They change over time due to mutation, natural selection, recombination, genetic drift, gene flow, and in humans, differential mating practices (Jurmain et al. 1997). Mutation is a chemical change in DNA. It may involve a substitution in a single base (point mutation), or the insertion or deletion (indels) of one or more bases. For example, Alu insertions are a kind of mutation unique to the Order Primates; a specific sequence about 300 base pairs long is occasionally inserted into the genome (Batzer et al. 1996; Knight et al. 1996). Alu insertions may represent up to 5% of the human genome (Relethford 2001:18). They allow a phylogenetic ordering of all primates, as one can easily define the ancestral state (which is the absence of an Alu insertion at a particular locus).

Recombination involves the splitting and reordering of nuclear DNA at conception, as half is inherited from each parent. Genetic drift or founder effect involves chance fluctuations of allele percentages in the gene pool. It is important where population size is small, as genetic variants present in an individual may be reproduced at a higher frequency than if the individual belonged to a large gene pool. Gene flow involves the introduction of new genes or alleles (variants of a gene present in at least 1% of a population) from nearby populations, due to contact or migration. In humans, social or cultural factors also influence the gene pool, so that mating is seldom random. Individuals or their families choose mates and marriage partners who share the same culture, ethnicity, religion, value system, and even appearance.

Physical anthropologists still use specific measurable morphological characters in cranial and post-cranial bones to examine "biological affinity" and evolutionary relatedness between individuals and populations. Today, these traits are interpreted within evolutionary theory, but similar questions were addressed with older methods well into the 1960s. Carleton Coon's *The Origin of Races* (1962) was one of the last attempts to look at racial origins using this type thinking or typological approach. It was written well after the "modern synthesis" of genetic and palaeontological data of the mid-twentieth century (Huxley 1942; Simpson 1944), which confirmed the uniformitarian principle that the forces of evolution observable today were the same as those that had produced the fossil record. Ignoring this approach, Coon used geographically specific human populations as subspecies and stressed that each had a separate line of evolution from *Homo erectus*. Not content with parallel development, he believed that these separate lineages had differential rates of evolution. The most evolved were Caucasians and had become *Homo sapiens* earliest, the least evolved Australian Aborigines were just on the verge of becoming human now (Coon 1962).

It is a fair inference that fossil men now extinct were less gifted than their descendants who have larger brains, that the subspecies which crossed the evolutionary threshold into the category of Homo sapiens the earliest have evolved the most, and that the obvious correlation between the length of time a sub-species has been in the sapiens state and the levels of civilization attained by some of its populations may be related phenomena. (Coon 1962: ix–x)

Since he observed a living Australian woman ("Topsy the Tiwi") with a cranial capacity of less than 1000 cc, Coon (1962:411) concluded that "the Australian aborigines are still in the act of sloughing off some of the genetic traits which distinguish Homo erectus from Homo sapiens" and represent the last subspecies to cross the line to modernity. Coon's book was the text for my first course in biological anthropology as an undergraduate in 1971. Although we were instructed to ignore the theory as unsound, this experience may have soured me for life on the study of racial variation and racial evolution. Supporters of the multiregional theory have often been tarred with the same brush, as opponents stress the similarity to Coon's model. But there are key differences between the two, since gene flow between groups did not occur, according to Coon, but is a major process for current multiregional concepts.

How do geneticists address biological relatedness? Until DNA base sequences could be measured directly, classical genetic markers were used. These are obtained from blood groups, serum proteins, and red blood cell enzymes (Ruvolo 1997:517). Some measure the reaction between antibodies and antigens (substances which produce a reaction to a given antibody) (Relethford 2001:15). An example is the ABO blood group system on chromosome 9 which represents antigens on the surface of red blood cells. Three alleles or variants are present: A, B, and O. A and B are co-dominant and O is recessive. This means that one has to inherit an O from each parent to have type (or more appropriately, phenotype) O blood. Either genotype AO or AA will express itself as phenotype A, since A is dominant over O. Most populations have all three alleles, but the percentage of occurrence varies continuously or clinally across space. There are many other blood group polymorphisms, including the Rhesus factor, MN, Duffy, and so on. But no discrete racial or population specific types can be found. Using such criteria, Frank Livingstone (1964) made the famous statement that, for humans, "there are no races, there are only clines."

Livingstone's assumption was tested by Richard Lewontin (1972). By 1972, there were over thirty-five known blood group types, fifteen of which had alternate alleles in frequencies of over 1% occurrence (meaning that they are fixed in the population). Of these, nine were well enough known to be used for comparative research. Lewontin calculated the amount of population differences in allele percentage occurrence for seventeen polymorphic traits. He divided his study population into seven geographic groups, with several populations in each, and calculated between and within population diversity. He was trying to determine "how much of human diversity between populations is accounted for by more or less conventional racial classification" (Lewontin 1972:386). He concluded that 86% of the variation he measured occurred within single populations, 8% between populations within races, and only 6% between geographically separated populations or races (Lewontin 1972:396). In other words, a person from one population or race has a better chance of being genetically different from a member of his own group than two people of widely separate ancestry. Having demonstrated that the notion of race as geographically discrete groups does not work for humans, he concludes that,

> human racial classification is of no social value and is positively destructive of social and human relations. Since such racial classification is now seen to be of virtually no genetic or taxonomic significance either, no justification can be offered for its continuance. (Lewontin 1972:397)

A number of geneticists, notably the Stanford University group led by Luca Cavalli-Sforza (Cavalli-Sforza et al. 1993, 1994; Cavalli-Sforza and Feldman 2003; Barbujani et al. 1997; Ramachandran et al. 2005), have spent their careers analyzing genetic diversity in and between human populations. By the late 1980s, they had produced a tree of relationship between forty-two human populations, examining the frequency of occurrence of 120 alleles associated with forty-four polymorphisms (Mountain et al. 1993:70). Their tree first split African and non-African groups, lending support to the Out of Africa theory of modern human origins. Their second branch split Southeast Asians and Pacific Islanders from northeast Asians, Caucasoids, and Amerindians, suggesting two main migrations into Asia (Mountain et al. 1993:72).

If such distributions reflect history, they have been produced by population contact and by the forces of evolution. But traits continue to occur clinally across space, but independent of one another. For example, in indigenous

Europeans, skin color varies from light in the north to dark in the south, while the frequency of type B blood increases from west to east. More recent work on "the apportionment of human diversity" is reviewed by Brown and Armelagos (2001). Lewontin's basic conclusion that there is more genetic variation between individuals within the same ethnic group than between individuals of different groups has been upheld in numerous subsequent studies (Feldman et al. 2003). The only thing missing was an explanation for why there is such little variation in humans. It is only in the last two decades that an answer was provided, and it is our relatively recent common origin as a species.

Starting in the 1980s, geneticists began looking for additional markers that might reflect evolutionary history. One way was through DNA-DNA hybridization, where a single DNA strand was taken from two separate species, artificially combined, and then the strength of the new bond was tested through heating. Degree of similarity is inferred from how long it took to sever the ties between the two strands. When applied to the great apes, this method suggested that humans and chimpanzees were closely related (Sibley and Ahlquist 1984; Bailey 1993). Restriction fragment length polymorphisms (RFLP) also measure the degree of genetic relatedness between individuals. Certain enzymes are used to cut DNA molecules at specific sequence locations. Fragments of different lengths can be placed in a gel, separated by electrophoresis, and ultimately assigned to different genotypes (Mountain et al. 1993:72; Relethford 2001:17; Wilson et al. 1985:385). This method produced similar results to those derived from classical genetic markers. There was a large difference between Africans and non-Africans (Mountain et al. 1993:75).

THE PLACE OF HUMANS IN RELATION TO THE GREAT APES

One of the first anthropological questions that early geneticists sought to answer was the relationship of humans to the living great apes: gorillas and chimpanzees in Africa and orangutans in Southeast Asia. Palaeontologists studying the evolutionary history of these hominoids traced their origins as far back as the Miocene epoch, between 25 and 5 million years ago. In a landmark reclassification, Simons and Pilbeam (1965) grouped all known Miocene apes from Europe, Asia, and Africa into two categories: dryopithecines and ramapithecines. Mainly known from teeth and jaw fragments, dryopithecines were supposed to be the ancestor of living apes, ramapithecines of bipedal hominins or humans. Their Middle Miocene age implied that their last common ancestor had lived even earlier. The first sign that something was wrong with this classification was the discovery of relatively complete jaws. Unlike the modern ape U-shaped or human parabolic dental arcade (tooth row), many of the new forms were V-shaped, constricted in the middle while diverging more posteriorly. By the early 1980s, two more or less complete faces had been described, one from Turkey (Andrews and Tekkaya 1980) and the other from the Siwalik Range in Pakistan (Pilbeam 1982). These *Sivapithecus* fossils were similar to ramapithecines and to modern orangutans, not to later humans. So it appeared that no Miocene hominoid was directly related to humans. The next oldest fossil which could be human was an African australopithecine, and was less than 5 million years old. There was (and remains) a gap in the African fossil record in the Late Miocene, between 5 and 8 million years ago, just when molecular studies say the split between African apes and humans occurred. This gap may be narrowing, as within the last few years three research teams have proposed Late Miocene candidates for the world's earliest hominin: *Sahelanthropus tchadensis* from Chad (Brunet et al. 2002; Vignaud et al. 2002), *Ardipithecus ramidus ramidus* and *Ardipithecus ramidus kadabba* from the Middle Awash in Ethiopia (Haile-Selassie 2001; White et al. 1994; WoldeGabriel et al. 2001), and *Orrorin tugenensis* from central Kenya (Pickford and Senut 2001; Senut et al. 2001).

The Late Miocene date for our last common ancestor with apes was estimated using Kimura's (1983) concept of neutral mutation. Underlying evolutionary history of a lineage is a constant clocklike rate of mutation in non-coding areas of the genome. If the rate of change can be determined, two or more individuals can be sampled for the same locus, and an estimate can be made about when they had a last (or most recent) common ancestor. Through analysis of primate blood proteins, Morris Goodman (1962, 1963) was the first to propose a date for the last common ancestor of living apes and humans. African apes and humans were genetically very close, with orangutans being more different. But he accepted the majority interpretation of the fossil record that placed ramapithecines on the human line. Since these fossils dated to the Middle Miocene, he concluded that the rate of molecular change must have slowed down in later hominoids. This was the only way that he could reconcile the fossil and genetic evidence (Goodman 1962, 1963, 1996).

A few years later, Vincent Sarich (1985; orig. pub. 1971) and Allan Wilson (Sarich and Wilson 1967) conducted similar studies and agreed that there was little difference between African apes and humans. But they were more than willing to reject the accepted interpretation of the fossil evidence. They developed methods to quantify immunological reactions more directly, as well as to quantify differences between species as an "immunological distance" (Sarich 1985; Pilbeam 1986). They used serum albumin, a protein composed of about 570 amino acids and compared reactions between different primate species (Sarich 1985). It showed that African apes and humans had a very recent common ancestor. Sarich answered critics of his molecular model with one of the most famous statements in the history of palaeoanthropology:

> To put it as bluntly as possible, I now feel that the body of molecular evidence on the *Homo-Pan* relationship is sufficiently extensive that one no longer has the option of considering a fossil hominid specimen older than about 8 million years as a hominid *no matter what it looks like*. (Sarich 1985:321, orig. pub. 1971; italics in original)

One of the palaeontologists whose interpretations Sarich rejected, David Pilbeam, was quite dismayed. If African apes and humans had a recent common ancestor it "meant that morphologists were not reading the morphology very well. And that upsets morphologists (it still does)" (Pilbeam 1986:299). He was forced to conclude that theories of human origins "are unconstrained by fossils: they are fossil-free or in some cases even fossil proof. . . .Yet we all thought the fossils were contributing a great deal" (Pilbeam 1980:267).

By 1982, it was clear that even elementary molecular studies were giving a clearer, but significantly different, picture of hominoid relationships than the fossil evidence. Some geneticists even concluded that fossil evidence was no longer necessary. But without it, we would not know of the tremendous variety of hominoid and hominin species. More recent studies of great ape genetic variation give us a better picture of our own evolution. There are three subspecies of common chimpanzees: *Pan troglodytes schweinfurthii* (Eastern long haired), *Pan troglodytes verus* (Western masked or pale-faced), and *Pan troglodytes troglodytes* (Central black faced) (Ruvolo 1997:519). Geographically separate, they exhibit from 21% to 37% of total species diversity in mitochondrial DNA and overlap with the amount of genetic diversity within a single population (38% at Gombe in Tanzania) (Ruvolo 1997:519). Both chimpanzees and gorillas show a tremendous amount of within-group mitochondrial diversity (Ruvolo 1997:520), much more than in living humans. This would support the replacement model of modern human origins. But Ruvolo (1997:522) reminds the reader that there may have been more differences in the past, but gene flow may have homogenized groups.

Also using mitochondrial DNA, Gagneux et al. (1999) demonstrate that African apes show much more intra-species variation than humans (figure 6.3). They conclude that the founder population for modern humans lived much more recently that thought, and went through a number of episodes of population reduction through bottlenecking. This was a startling conclusion, as our ancestral population may have almost gone extinct more than once. Kaessmann et al. (1999) examined a 10,154 base pair sequence on the X chromosome (Xq13.3). Chimpanzee diversity was found to be four times that of humans, and the age of the chimpanzee last common ancestor was calculated to be three times as far back in time as "Mitochondrial Eve." The lack of genetic diversity for humans was a product of either selection or drift (Kaessmann, Wiebe, and Pääbo 1999:1160).

MITOCHONDRIAL DNA AND MODERN HUMAN ORIGINS

Most of the recent studies of genetic history rely on mitochondrial DNA, which is inherited exclusively through the maternal line. It is present in cells in many copies (versus one for nuclear DNA) (Hagelberg 1996; Harpending et al. 1996). It has a high rate of change over time, so it can be used to measure recent evolutionary events (Relethford 2001:19; Ingman et al. 2000:708). The mitochondrial genome forms a circle with two strands (forward and reverse or heavy and light) (figure 6.1). These contain coding areas (for genes), non-coding DNA, and the control region, which regulates replication (Cann 1987, 1988, 1992; Relethford 2001:19). The latter comprises less than 7% of the mitochondrial genome (Ingman et al. 2000), but contains two hypervariable regions (referred to as HVR) or segments (HVS). These are labeled with Roman numerals I and II, producing units of analysis HVRI and HVRII (or HVSI and HVSII).

By the early 1980s, it was recognized that mitochondrial DNA underwent no recombination except perhaps in the displacement or D-loop (Wilson et al. 1985:384; Zischler et al. 1995). RFLP analysis was used to compare individual mtDNA genome sequences (Wilson et al. 1985), and it was concluded that, the human species has an anomalously low level of mtDNA variability, in spite of an apparent normal level of nuclear variability. . . . The idea that *Homo sapiens* is a younger species than is typical for other higher primates and that a transient bottleneck was involved in its formation merits continuing scrutiny. (Wilson et al. 1985:393)

In their initial 1987 paper, Cann et al. (1987) used information from the control region of 145 individuals and two cell lines (one an African American, the other a !Kung San). Some samples that were donated to Cann came from placentas of women having babies in San Francisco hospitals. (These days, a swab of the mouth or an individual hair provides a sufficient sample for DNA extraction.) Populations sampled came from Africa (20 individuals), Asia (34), and Europe (46), as well as Australian (21) and New Guinea (26) Aborigines (Cann et al. 1987, 1994; Stoneking 1993, 1994; Stoneking and Cann 1989; Stoneking et al. 1993; Wilson and Cann 1992; Wilson et al. 1991). Only two "Africans" were born in sub-Saharan Africa; the rest were African Americans. Mitochondrial sequences were divided by enzymes into restriction fragment length polymorphisms, leading to the identification of 467 different sites; 195 of these showed some kind of variation. The average number of sites was 370 per individual (Cann et al. 1987). It is not clear in the original paper how the rate of mutation was determined. But subsequent publications make it clear that the degree of difference within living New Guinea Aborigines was calculated using what Vigilant et al. (1991:1503) call a midpoint method. Archaeologists generally agree that New Guinea was first settled between 35,000 and 50,000 years ago, although this can be debated (Terrell 2001:200). This gives a mutation rate of 2% to 4% per million years, and a date between 143,000 to 285,000 years ago for our common mitochondrial DNA ancestor. Since living Africans are genetically more diverse than anyone else today, and there are Africans who can trace their ancestry to the founder without any non-African ancestors, it was assumed that this continent was our initial source. The date for the earliest departure from Africa would be the age of the branch of the tree without Africans. This occurs around 135,000 years ago (Cann et al. 1987). The hominin species represented here was not identified. It could still be archaic *Homo sapiens* (or *Homo heidelbergensis*) or anatomically modern *Homo sapiens*. But this study lent support to Howells's (1976) "Noah's Ark" model of modern human origins which soon became re-christened with a myriad of names, including Mitochondrial Eve, Out of Africa II, replacement, or the recent African origin hypothesis.

Since most of the Africans were American born, there was concern about how reliable these conclusions were. A restudy with additional samples was supposed to reassure the doubters (Vigilant et al. 1991). It included the analysis of two hypervariable mitochondrial DNA segments in 189 people, including 121 Africans, 20 Papua New Guineans, 1 Australian Aborigine, 15 Europeans, 24 Asians, and 8 African Americans. It also made use of the first chimpanzee mitochondrial sequence as the out group (Vigilant et al. 1991). A total of 1,122 base pairs of non-coding DNA in the control region were amplified with enzymes then counted directly. A total of 135 unique types were produced, many of which were specific to geographic region (Vigilant et al. 1991:1504). A tree was created using parsimony analysis, one requiring the fewest branches to account for the observed variation. It also produced two branches—one of exclusively African types and the other with all other people, including other Africans. The rate of mutation for these loci was estimated to be between 11.5% and 17.3% base substitutions per million years. This produces a date for Mitochondrial Eve between 166,000 and 249,000 years ago (Vigilant et al. 1991). Their results were also "consistent with an origin of anatomically modern humans in Africa within the last 200,000 years, with subsequent migrations out of Africa that established human populations in Eurasia" (Vigilant et al. 1991:1506).

Rogers and Harpending (1992) have used mismatch distributions, a statistical method where one measures the amount of genetic difference between all pairs of people for a segment of DNA. They plotted the percentage of individuals with no base pair differences, then one difference, then two, and so on. This produces a wavelike shaped bar chart if a population underwent a size increase or decrease (bottleneck), as well as an estimate of when this happened and initial population size. Their results support a "weak Garden of Eden" model where Mitochondrial Eve existed around 100,000 years ago, but the population expansion out of Africa took place much later (Rogers and Harpending 1992; Ruvolo 1997:531). This could support Klein's (1992) expansion of behaviorally modern people out of Africa after 50,000 years ago.

Ingman et al. (2000) were the first to sequence the entire mitochondrial genome. They sampled fifty-three individuals from fourteen different ethnic groups; all sequences are unique and vary in length from 16,558 to 16,576 base pairs (Ingman et al. 2000:712). They compared their results to those derived from Kaessmann et al.'s (1999) study of Xq13.3 from the same people.

They concluded that the sequences evolve at a constant rate, except for the D-loop (Ingman et al. 2000:708). They calculated a mutation rate for the rest of the mitochondrial DNA genome of 1.70×10^{-8} substitutions per site per year (Ingman et al. 2000:712). Then they produced a tree where the three deepest branches were exclusively sub-Saharan Africans, while the fourth was the first to link Africans and non-Africans. The amount of genetic variation in Africans was two times that for non-Africans. Their estimated date for the most recent common ancestor for all living people averaged at 171,500 ± 50,000 years ago (Ingman et al. 2000:711). The youngest branch with both African and non-Africans began about 52,000 ± 27,500 years ago (Ingman et al. 2000:712); shortly afterward there was a population expansion in non-Africans (Hedges 2000:653). The Out of Africa II expansion began around 38,500 years ago, which overlaps with the onset of the Eurasian Upper Palaeolithic (Ingman et al. 2000:711).

Mitochondrial DNA has also been used to plot the routes of subsequent human migrations (Forster 2004). In a recent review, Cann (2001) summarizes the current state of knowledge. An initial dispersal from Africa via north and East Africa is marked by the mitochondrial DNA haplogroup M. A haplogroup is a population sharing the same mitochondrial sequence at a particular locus. It is constructed from related haplotypes, "a group of linked nucleotide sequence variants that share common substitutions" (Cann 2001:1744). Once felt to be an East Asian marker, haplogroup M occurs in high frequencies today in India and Ethiopia (Quintana-Murci et al. 1999). Quintana-Murci et al. (1999:437) propose that this variant split from the East African ancestral form somewhere over 50,000 years ago. As it is almost absent in the Levant today but common in Saudi Arabia, they propose that populations moved from Ethiopia across the Red Sea into the Arabian Peninsula and eventually to South Asia. Their data produce a common ancestor in Eastern Africa around 60,000 years ago, and they propose that this region was the source of Mitochondrial Eve. In Asia, these founders underwent a demographic and geographic expansion; populations increased and the territory they occupied grew. Members of haplogroup M who remained in Africa were restricted geographically until 10,000 to 20,000 years ago, and then expanded (Quintana-Murci et al. 1999:439). Evidence for this migration comes from whole mitochondrial DNA genome sequencing as well as from the identification of the M168 mutation in the Y chromosome (Cann 2001:1744;

Quintana-Murci et al. 1999:439). As Cann (2001:1744) affirms, "Africa has apparently acted as a source population throughout the history of our species, where humans achieved high rates of reproductive success that allowed them to expand and fill an abundance of ecological niches." Within Africa, it was East Africa that was the source region for the expansions (Quintana-Murci et al. 1999:439) that ultimately peopled the Old World with anatomically modern humans.

Most studies of mitochondrial DNA give a consistent picture: a recent African origin and a subsequent dispersal around 50,000 years ago. But Templeton (2002) has reassessed the genetic evidence for modern human origins using mtDNA, Y chromosomes, and data from coding areas in the nuclear genome. He used a different statistical method, a nested clade phylogeography analysis of eleven trees using the GEODIS program. Nested clades are groups of haplotypes arranged by increasing numbers of mutations (Cann 2002:32); they can be used to analyze historical events without regard to a priori models. Long a critic of the replacement model (Templeton 1992, 1993, 1994), Templeton first tested a null hypothesis of no association between geography (location of individual and population sampled) and the haplotype tree (its place on the network of relationships). If the null hypothesis can be rejected at a 5% level of significance, one can then attempt to interpret pattern biologically (Templeton 2002:45).

Templeton used populations from different parts of the world whose haplotypes have already been determined. He used a number of genetic markers including mitochondrial DNA, Y chromosomes, and other nuclear markers and the results were combined with those from previously published studies (Cann 2002:33; Templeton 2002). He noted that the time to most recent common ancestor depends on locus, as mtDNA and Y chromosomes detect only recent events, while markers on the X chromosome and autosomes reveal more ancient ones (Templeton 2002:47). The tree Templeton produced has a number of surprises. He has an African origin, with initial spread out 1.7 million years ago; the 95% confidence interval is phenomenally large, between 8.5 and 0.61 million years ago. This would represent Out of Africa I, the migration of *Homo erectus/Homo ergaster*. There was a subsequent move out of Africa, one with a 95% confidence interval between 0.84 and 0.42 million years ago and again between 0.15 and 0.08 million years ago. The most recent one was not a replacement event, but a major population movement characterized by interbreeding. It is likely the earlier one was too (Templeton 2002:48–49). He concludes that there were at least two major expansions out of Africa after *Homo erectus*; one corresponding with the Acheulian, the other with the appearance of modern humans. "The hypothesis of a recent out of Africa replacement event is therefore strongly rejected" (Templeton 2002:49), but he does conclude that modern traits first appeared in Africa. "The genetic impact of Africa upon the entire human species is large" (Templeton 2002:50) but not exclusive. He recognizes that his model is similar to gene flow models, such as the assimilation model of Smith et al. (1989), the multiregional model with admixture (Wolpoff et al. 1994), and Relethford's (2001) conclusion of "mostly out of Africa" (see chapter 5 for a discussion of these models). While Templeton feels that the bulk of genetic data argues against strict replacement, other researchers say the issue is still open. Cann (2002:33) states that the evidence must continue to be tested against archaeological and linguistic data from specific regions of the world. Hammer and Zegura (2002:306–307) point out that the Y chromosome tree, mitochondrial tree, and trees based on other nuclear loci do not have to agree for one explanation to work. In general, most genetic studies propose that there was a recent African origin for living humans. The estimated date for a most recent common ancestor occurs much too late for it to be *Homo erectus/Homo ergaster*, the species predicted by traditional multiregional models. But whether or not this African "Mitochondrial Eve" population immediately expanded into Eurasia is unclear. Some recent mitochondrial DNA studies support the "weak Garden of Eden" perspective of Rogers and Harpending (1992; Harpending et al. 1993, 1998) where a founder population in existence over 100,000 years ago only expands out of Africa after 50,000 years ago. So the issue of why people did not move into Eurasia earlier than they did (Klein 1998) still remains to be answered.

NEANDERTHAL DNA

One way to combine paleontological and genetic research is through the retrieval and analysis of DNA from fossil remains (Willerslev and Cooper 2005). Polymerase chain reaction or PCR makes the extraction of ancient DNA possible, but only small fragments a few hundred base pairs long can be recovered. Samples must be less than 100,000 years old, making *Jurassic Park* (Crichton 1990) entertaining fiction rather than a future possibility (Krings et al. 1997:19; O'Rouke et al. 2000:218; Ovchinnikov et al. 2000:492; Willerslev and Cooper 2005). These individual fragments are cloned, sequenced, and overlapped, then compared to the modern or "Cambridge reference sample." The number of total base changes is counted and compared to the rate of substitution to get a date of split from a last or most recent common ancestor. So far, only mitochondrial DNA has been successfully extracted, as it is relatively abundant. Contamination of ancient hominin with modern human DNA remains a much more serious problem, as it is hard to determine whether one has a genuine sample. Preservation of ancient DNA depends on temperature (the lower and more constant the temperature, the better) and the acidity of the surrounding sediments (O'Rourke et al. 2000; Smith et al. 2001).

Before a geneticist tries to convince a curator or palaeoanthropologist to sacrifice a treasured piece of a fossil human, amino acid racemization (AAR) is used as a measure of how likely it is that ancient DNA is preserved. Once used solely as a dating technique, amino acid racemization is based on the principle that all amino acids in a living organism coil in a single direction, left. After the death of the organism, these amino acids racemize or change from left (L) enantiomers to right (D or dextra), the two optical forms or isomers of amino acids (Bada and Helfman 1975; O'Rourke et al. 2000:219) until there are equal amounts of both. Experimental work has shown that the rate of aspartic acid racemization is a good predictor of DNA preservation. As long as this D/L ratio is less than 0.11 to 0.12 (i.e. 11% to 12%), ancient DNA is likely to be present (Krings et al. 1997:20).

In a pioneering yet sophisticated study, Krings et al. (1997; Ward and Stringer 1997) reported the extraction of mitochondrial DNA from a humerus of the original Neanderthal skeleton recovered in 1859 from the Feldhofer Cave in Germany (figure 6.4). The D/L ratio in the Feldhofer Neanderthal was right at the limit predicted for DNA extraction. Krings and his colleagues used two separate primers and sequenced 105 base pairs in HVRI in the mitochondrial control region. This produced eighteen and twelve clones respectively (Krings et al. 1997:20). Three of the clones were quite similar to the human reference sequence, while the remaining twenty-seven were quite different. Those similar to living humans were dismissed as modern contamination, either in the laboratory or in the museum from which the sample was taken.

The average number of differences between living humans is 8.0 ± 3.1, while it is much larger, 25.6 ± 2.2, between the Neanderthal and living humans. The same human samples had an average of 55.0 ± 3.0 differences

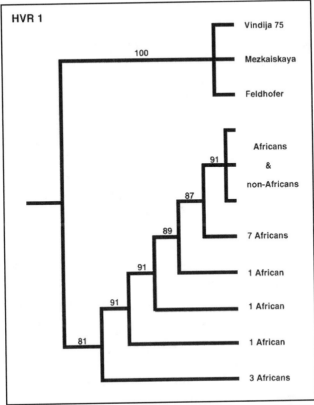

Figure 6.4 Neanderthal DNA genealogy (Krings et al. 2000).
Reprinted with permission of Dr. Svante Pääbo and the Nature
Publishing Group

from chimpanzee sequences (Krings et al. 1997). A date of divergence between chimpanzees and humans of around 4 to 5 million years ago produces a Neanderthal and modern split sometime between 550,000 and 690,000 years ago. This date corresponds to an estimate for the first settlement of Europe (Roebroeks and van Kolfschoten 1994), or alternatively, Europe north of the Mediterranean Sea (Dennell and Roebroeks 1996; Roebroecks 2001). In other words, if "Mitochondrial Eve" existed in Africa between 120,000 and 150,000 years ago, Neanderthals and modern humans last shared a common ancestor four times earlier than this (Krings et al. 1997:25).

Two years later, the same team reported sampling 304 base pairs from hypervariable region II of the Feldhofer Neanderthal (Krings, Giesert, et al.

1999). The average difference between living humans was 10.9 ± 5.1. The average difference between humans and chimps and/or bonobos (*n* = 9) was 93.4 ± 7.1. Living humans to the one Neanderthal produced an average of 35.3 ± 2.3 differences (Krings et al. 1999). When individuals from different human populations were compared to the Feldhofer Neanderthal, a total of 34.4 ± 2.7 differences were seen for Africans, 35.8 ± 2.1 for Europeans, and 33.8 ± 2.0 for Asians. The Neanderthal was no closer to modern Europeans than to any other group (Krings et al. 1999), lessening the likelihood of its contribution to the modern European mitochondrial genome. Creating a phylogenetic chart rooted with a chimpanzee and bonobo mitochondrial DNA sequence, a rate of change of 0.94×10^{-7} substitutions per site per year per lineage was produced. This gives an average date for the most recent common ancestor of the Neanderthal and modern humans at 465,000 years ago, with a range from 317,000 to 714,000 years ago. Mitochondrial Eve is dated to an average of 163,000 years ago, with a range from 111,000 to 260,000 years before present (Krings et al. 1999:5584).

In March 2000, there was a second report of Neanderthal DNA, in this case from Mezmaiskaya Cave in the northern Caucasus of Russia (Ovchinnikov et al. 2000:491). Here a Neanderthal infant skeleton had been recovered and radiocarbon dated to 29,195 ± 965 years ago (Ua-14512) (Ovchinnikov et al. 2000). Three hundred and forty-five based pairs were sequenced from two overlapping fragments of hypervariable region I (Ovchinnikov et al. 2000). There were twenty-two differences from the modern human sampled as a reference, and twelve differences from the Feldhofer Cave Neanderthal. However, the two Neanderthals share nineteen substitutions relative to the modern human reference sequence (Ovchinnikov et al. 2000). The two Neanderthals are quite similar to each other, despite the thousands of kilometers between their places of discovery, and they likely shared a common ancestor 150,000 to 352,000 years ago (Ovchinnikov et al. 2000:492). But neither was probably an ancestor of modern Europeans (Hoss 2000:454).

A third site, Vindija Cave in Croatia, has also yielded mitochondrial DNA samples (Krings et al. 2000). Seven out of fifteen Neanderthal bones from layer G3 contain enough DNA to examine further. One, dated by accelerator mass spectrometry radiocarbon methods to over 42,000 years ago, was sampled. Krings et al. (2000) used primers that allowed both modern human and Neanderthal DNA sequences to be amplified. A total of 357 base pairs of HVRI and 277 base pairs of HVRII were sequenced. When compared to the reference sample, it differed by nine substitutions and in the length of a stretch of C and T residues in HVRII. It also differed from a sample of modern humans ($n = 663$) by 34.9 ± 2.4 substitutions and by an insertion of an adenosine residue (also present in the Feldhofer specimen). Like earlier studies, this Neanderthal was deemed to be no closer to modern Europeans than to any other modern human population. In a further study, Krings et al. (2000) examined 345 base pairs of HVRI in 3 Neanderthals, 5,530 modern humans, 359 common chimpanzees, and 28 gorillas. Intra-group diversity was 3.73% for Neanderthals, $14.82\% \pm 5.70\%$ for the chimpanzees, $18.57\% \pm 5.26\%$ for gorillas, and $3.43\% \pm 1.22\%$ for modern humans. So like modern humans, the degree of genetic variation within the Neanderthals is quite small. In living humans, low genetic diversity in both mitochondrial and nuclear DNA probably represents rapid population expansion from a small founder population. A similar situation may have occurred in European Neanderthals (Krings et al. 2000:145–146).

In 2002, researchers reported the recovery of sixty-two additional Neanderthal bone fragments from the Feldhofer type site (Schmitz et al. 2002). These came from sediments thrown 20 m down a hill during the 1856 excavation of the site by miners. One of two bones sampled produced a 357 base pair sequence of HVRI. It has twenty-three differences from the Cambridge modern reference, and seventeen from the closest modern human recorded in GenBank (Schmitz et al. 2002:13, 346). Relative to the other Neanderthal mitochondrial DNA sequences, it has between one and four substitutions. In general, it clusters with them versus contemporary modern humans and is only one substitution different from the Vindija sample. Since it shows three differences from the first Neanderthal at Feldhofer, it must represent a second individual (Schmitz et al. 2002:13346).

Most recently, a group of Italian geneticists claim to have extracted a 260 base pair sequence of mitochondrial DNA from the HVRI from two Cro-Magnon fossils from Paglicci Cave in southern Italy. These fossils are radiocarbon dated to between 23,000 and 24,000 years ago (Caramelli et al. 2003:6593, 6595). The specimens have sequences within the range of modern Europeans, and are quite different from Neanderthals (Caramelli et al. 2003:6595).

The general conclusions from ancient DNA studies are also supported by a recent analysis of mitochondrial DNA variation using phylogenetic analysis or cladistics (Knight 2003). Another study compared Neanderthal and early modern European (Mladeč, Cro-Magnon, Abri Pataud, and La Madeleine) mitochondrial DNA, and found no sign of a link between the two (Serre et al. 2004). A Neanderthal femur shaft from the cave of Les Rochers-de-Ville-neuve in Vienne, France, dated to around 40,700 years ago (Beta-177765) by accelerator mass spectrometry, has also yielded a limited mitochondrial DNA sample (Beauval et al. 2005:7086).

Y CHROMOSOME STUDIES

The study of the male or Y sex chromosome (figure 6.5) began much later than mitochondrial DNA research. Except for a small piece at each end, most (95%) of Y is non-recombining and can be used to trace the male line of descent (Stumpf and Goldstein 2001; Relethford 2001:20). Referred to as the NRY or non-recombining Y, it is flanked by pseudo-autosomal regions (Hammer 1995; Hammer and Zegura 1996, 2002; Hammer et al. 1997, 2001; Shen et al. 2000:7354), tips of mammalian sex chromosomes involved in recombination during male meiosis (Strachan and Read 1996:594). It comprises the largest non-recombining block of nucleotides in the human genome, an estimated 50 million base pairs in length (Hammer and Zegura 2002). "Other than for its role in male sex determination, mediated by the SRY gene, the Y-chromosome has been perceived as functionally desolate" (Shen et al. 2000:7354) as it contains several dozen genes versus 2,000 to 3,000 on the X chromosome (Jegalian and Lahn 2001:56). No doubt this is reassuring to the male half of our species! The first Y chromosome RFLPs were identified in 1985 (Lucotte 1989, 1992); by 1990, SRY had been identified as the sex-determining region (Jegalian and Lahn 2001:57).

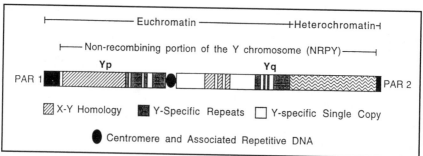

Figure 6.5 A human Y chromosome (Hammer and Zegura 1996:117). Reprinted with permission of John Wiley and Sons, Inc.

The noncoding part of Y has a lower level of variation than any other region of the chromosome. By late 1996, less than sixty NRY polymorphisms had been discovered, only eleven of which could be typed. In 1997, Underhill et al. reported nineteen new polymorphisms identified via DHPLC, denaturing high performance liquid chromatography (Hammer and Zegura 2002:304). Using this method, more than 250 SNPs and small indels (insertions or deletions) have been identified on NRY (Hammer and Zegura 2002:304). A SNP (pronounced "snip") is a single nucleotide polymorphism, where there is more than one alternative base in at least 1% of the population (Relethford 2001:18). Other markers on the NRY include microsatellites (short tandem repeats or STRs, 1 to 6 base pairs long) and minisatellites (10 to less than 100 base pairs, longer repeats) (Hammer and Zegura 2002:308). Single nucleotide polymorphisms and small insertions or deletions are preferred for evolutionary work since they have a low frequency of back and parallel mutation. One can also easily determine the ancestral state since there is likely to be only two alleles. They are referred to as binary or bi-allelic markers or unique event polymorphisms, UEPs (Hammer and Zegura 2002:308; Stumpf and Goldstein 2001:1738). The Y chromosome exhibits little variation in single nucleotide polymorphisms. There is an average of one difference per 10,000 base pairs, versus one per 1,000 to 2,000 base pairs elsewhere in the genome (Hammer and Zegura 2002:308).

Underhill et al. (2000) examined the non-recombining region of the human Y chromosome (NRY), and identified 160 bi-allelic and one tri-allelic sites. This produced a genealogy of 166 haplotypes. The 167 NRY polymorphisms included 91 transitions, 53 transversions, 22 small insertions or deletions (indels), and 1 Alu insertion. All were bi-allelic except for one double transversion, M116, that has three alleles (Underhill et al. 2000:358). A transition is a change from a purine to another purine (for example, A or G), or a change from pyramidine to pyramidine (C or T). A transversion is a nucleotide substitution from purine to pyramidine or vice versa (Strachan and Read 1996:243, 596).

They root their tree using great ape Y chromosomal data. This tree has 116 haplotypes in ten haplogroups. Haplogroups I and II are restricted to Africa and occur today all over the continent, in at least small frequencies (Underhill et al. 2001:46–47). These groups are now referred to as haplogroups A and B (Hammer and Zegura 2002). They are distinct from all other African and non-African Y chromosomes on the basis of the M168 mutation (Underhill et al. 2001:47). Members of group II have the M60 and M181 mutations and are found today throughout Africa and Pakistan (Underhill et al. 2001:47). Groups I and II represent an early diversification and dispersal of human populations in Africa (Underhill et al. 2001:49). Thomson et al. (2000) estimated the age of the last, or most recent, common ancestor at 59,000 years before present, with a 95% confidence interval ranging from 40,000 to 140,000 years ago. The M168 mutation is present in all non-African Y chromosomes and represents the date of the Out of Africa II migration or the maximum age for the first non-African Y chromosomes, about 40,000 years ago (Underhill et al. 2000:358; Thomson et al. 2000). There are four separate clusters of the M168 mutation; these represent a population division event prior to the main Out of Africa II migration, between 50,000 and 40,000 years ago (Underhill et al. 2001:50).

Underhill's group concluded that a small subpopulation of modern humans left Africa, separated into several isolated groups (giving rise to haplogroups III to X, now C to J), remained small through last glacial, then simultaneously went through expansion (Underhill et al. 2000:359). These dates are "considerably younger than the earliest evidence for dispersals of modern humans" (Underhill et al. 2001:46), but are consistent with Klein's idea of change around 50,000 years ago. In a more recent paper, Underhill et al. (2001:44–46) sampled 1,062 men from twenty-one populations for 205 NRY polymorphisms and thirteen more from published literature. This produced 131 unique haplotypes, which define ten groups, seven of which provide a single clade (Underhill et al. 2001:46). Then they used this information to reconstruct late Pleistocene population history.

In their scenario, early in marine oxygen isotope stage (MIS) 5, between 130,000 and 90,000 years ago, there was a human expansion throughout Africa, north and south of the Sahara, and into the Levant (marked by Skhūl and Qafzeh) (Underhill et al. 2001:49). From 130,000 to 70,000 years ago, there may have been several expansion events and the extinction of earlier human NRY variation (Underhill et al. 2001:49). Later African population history is less clear. The onset of the last glacial around 70,000 years ago (MIS 4) probably led to fragmentation of African environments and to the isolation of northwest and northeast Africa from each other and from regions south of the Sahara (Underhill et al. 2001:50). Lahr and Foley believe that African populations acquired variation that was exported out in multiple waves, a version of the "weak Garden of Eden" model (Underhill et al. 2001:50). They moved through the Horn of Africa into India as well as via the Levant (Underhill et al. 2001:50). Later on, there was evolution of NRY diversity within Africa; marked by the M180 mutation, this represents the Bantu Expansion recognized archaeologically by the spread of Iron Age farmers (Underhill et al. 2001:50).

Other studies reach similar time conclusions. Thomson et al. (2000) examined three genes (SMCY, DBY, DFFRY) in fifty-three to seventy human Y chromosomes, as well as in chimpanzees and other great apes. They estimate a Y chromosome most recent common ancestor around the same time as Underhill's group. The branch at the deepest point on their tree is likewise African, and diversity outside of Africa is derived from a small number of African ancestors (Thomson et al. 2000:7360–7361). Shen et al. (2000:7354) examined four Y chromosome genes (SMCY, UTY1, DBY, and DFFRY) in fifty-three to seventy-two people. Chimpanzees, gorillas, and orangutans were also sequenced for SMCY. In coding regions, humans differ in 125 positions from apes (Shen et al. 2000:7354). When results from the other three genes are added, eighteen major haplotypes are produced: 10 Asian, 5 African, and 3 other (Shen et al. 2000:7357). By 2001, two labs had independently produced similar global evolutionary trees for NRY (Underhill et al.2001, Hammer et al. 2001; Hammer and Zegura 2002:304). A Y chromosome consortium (YCC) has also been created in order to standardize terminology and to report research results (Hammer and Zegura 2002:304). A tree of relationships produced by this consortium uses 237 NRY polymorphisms and has eighteen major haplogroups (Hammer and Zegura 2002:303). The root of the tree is obtained by sequencing the great ape, and the time to a most recent common ancestor for human men is calculated using the Genetree program. The date obtained is 90,420 ± 20,090 BP (Hammer and Zegura 2002:314). Phylogenetic analysis of NRY haplogroups obtained from a sample of 2,007 men supports an African origin of modern NRY diversity. While Africans have the most diversity, Asia has the most major haplogroups (Hammer and Zegura 2002:303). Similar trees can be used to measure the degree of relatedness of modern African populations. Some rather surprising results are being produced. Most sub-Saharan Africans are closely related to one another, with Pygmies, Khoisan, and Eastern Africans the most differentiated (Semino et al. 2002). In a study of

Ethiopian and Senegalese Y chromosomes, a number of haplogroups were defined. Haplogroups I and II (now A and B) are African only, and are the most divergent. These are present in higher percentages in hunter-gatherers and in some Ethiopians and Sudanese (Semino et al. 2002; Cruciani et al. 2002). Only these groups belong to the deepest lineage. Most African Y chromosomes belong to haplogroup III (or C), which may represent Out of Africa II (Semino et al. 2002). Other haplogroups point to later migrations back to Africa.

Studies of non-African populations also exhibit similar results. Ke et al. (2001) studied three Y chromosome markers: YAP (an Alu insertion), M89, and M130/RPS4Y, a change from C to T. They also examined the T mutation at the M168 locus; this variant is shared by all non-Africans and has a date of origin averaging around 44,000 years ago (Ke et al. 2001:1151). All Asian men (n = 12,127 individuals) and populations (n = 163) they sampled have these three polymorphisms, and there are no ancient non-African Y chromosomes in extant East Asian populations (Ke et al. 2001:1151). Such results, they argue, support a recent African origin.

OTHER NUCLEAR DNA STUDIES

In a pioneering study, Wainscoat et al. (1986) studied a number of closely linked nuclear DNA polymorphisms in the beta-globin gene cluster in individuals from eight populations. Using RFLP analysis of five polymorphic loci, they identified thirty-two possible haplotypes (Jones and Rouhani 1986:449). Non-Africans shared a limited number of common haplotypes, and their genetic distance study "indicates a major division of human populations into an African and a Eurasian group" (Wainscoat et al. 1986:491). Since the earliest modern humans are African, the genetic data is consistent with an African origin for our species (Wainscoat et al. 1986:493, 1989).

Tishkoff et al. (1996) examined alleles from two linked markers about 9,800 bases apart, in a non-coding area of the CD4 gene, located on the short arm of chromosome 12. They identified a short tandem repeat, where the sequence of TTTTC re-occurs four to fifteen times. There is also a deletion of 256 base pairs of a 295 base pair Alu element in all chromosomes, which occurred after the split of humans and great apes (Tishkoff et al. 1996:1381). These two are co-related, an example of linkage disequilibrium. Both were typed in over 1,600 individuals from forty-two populations. This linkage is present in all non-Africans, but must have been lost in ancestral Africans due to mutation and recombination. The migration from Africa involved reduction in the number of Alu+ (positive) haplotypes, in other words, some sort of founder effect. An Alu– (negative) chromosome with a 90 base pair single tandem repeat allele was the only one left in populations that left Africa (Tishkoff et al. 1996:1383).

Human history can also be studied from the genetics of our fellow travelers, the bacterium *Helicobacter pylori* (Spratt 2003; Falush et al. 2003) and body and head lice (Kittler et al. 2003; Reed et al. 2004). *H. pylori* is a bacterium that colonizes the human gastric mucosa. Acquired orally, it causes gastric and duodenal ulcers. Falush and colleagues report the study of polymorphisms in eight genes in *H. pylori* from twenty-seven human populations from around the world (Falush et al. 2003). This species has greater sequence diversity than most other bacteria, approximately fifty times that of humans (Falush et al. 2003:1582). As a result, it might give a more precise measure of genetic diversity and history. Results are similar to those drawn from human genetic investigations. As for body lice, *Pediculus humanus*, Kittler and his colleagues suggest that their most recent common ancestor can help us determine when humans started wearing clothing (Kittler et al. 2003), since body lice live in clothing and only move on to the skin to feed once or twice a day (Reed et al. 2004:e340). Using both mitochondrial and nuclear DNA sequences, they put the start of clothing at around 72,000 ± 42,000 years ago, close to the time of the first dispersal of modern humans out of Africa. Reed and his coworkers take this a step further. They trace the evolutionary history of head lice and discover two lineages, one of which (with both body and head forms) went through a bottleneck precisely when early modern humans did in Africa (Reed et al. 2004:e340). The other is restricted to the New World at present, but has an evolutionary history back to around 1.8 million years ago. They raise the scenario of some sort of cultural or biological contact between populations of *Homo erectus* and early *Homo sapiens*, in which the archaic louse form gets passed to modern humans (Reed et al. 2004).

CAN GENETIC DATA POINT TO THE MECHANISMS BEHIND BEHAVIORAL MODERNITY?

Klein (1992) and other researchers see the Middle to Later Stone Age transition in Africa as a proxy for the beginnings of behavioral modernity. He suggests that some fundamental reorganization of the brain produced complex language and that new communication skills led to technological and cultural innovations that fueled the Out of Africa II juggernaut. Now there may be some genetic evidence that lends support for such a transformation. In 2001, a of team of geneticists and medical researchers (Lai et al. 2001) reported the discovery of a gene (FOXP2) which has a role in the ontogeny of centers of the brain as well as facial muscles involved in speech and language. FOXP2 is a forkhead box P2 gene which is found on chromosome 7 at position 7q31 (Enard et al. 2002a, 2002b; Lai et al. 2001:520; Marcus and Fisher 2003; Vargha-Khadem et al. 2005). Disruption of this gene has been identified in half the members of three generations of one family, and in one unrelated individual, all of whom have severe speech disorders (Lai et al. 2001:520; Enard et al. 2002b). This point mutation is absent in 365 Caucasian controls, and changes the codon for the amino acid arginine into one that codes for histidine (Lai et al. 2001:521). This single nucleotide change may disrupt the DNA binding properties of FOXP2, leading to significant problems in control over oral-facial muscles (Enard et al. 2002b:869). Mutations in FOX genes in humans are associated with many congenital diseases, including abnormalities in the neural structures associated with speech and language (Lai et al. 2001:522).

A year later, the same researchers teamed up with geneticists from the Max Planck Institute for Evolutionary Anthropology in Leipzig to trace the evolutionary history of the FOXP2 gene (Enard et al. 2002b:869). They sequenced its amino acids in a chimpanzee, gorilla, orangutan, rhesus macaque, mouse, and human, and also looked at differences between living humans (Enard et al. 2002b:869). The human FOXP2 protein only differs from that of the mouse in three amino acid positions. Non-human primates have only one difference to a mouse, but two differences to us (Enard et al. 2002b:869). The two mutations in humans, therefore, must have developed after the split from African apes (Enard et al. 2002b:869). In forty-four sampled humans, there was no sign of any variation (Enard et al. 2002b:869). The last common ancestor of mice and humans existed about 70 million years ago. In about 130 million years of separate evolution (two lineages, therefore double the time), there has been only one change (Enard et al. 2002b:869). But after the human–chimp split, two amino acid changes have become fixed in the human lineage (Enard et al. 2002b:869; Vargha-Khadem et al. 2005:137). Whatever it was that led to the human changes, it might have had a selective advantage. The appearance of this gene in its present form may date to between 10,000 and 100,000 years ago (Enard et al. 2002b:871). These estimates are "concomitant with or subsequent to the emergence of anatomically modern humans" (Enard et al. 2002b:871) and support Klein's hypothesis of the appearance of a brain for behavioral modernity at this time. But the dates overlap with the appearance of anatomically modern people, not just with the onset of the Later Stone Age or Upper Palaeolithic.

AFRICAN GENETIC HISTORY AFTER THE FOUNDERS

Most genetic studies have identified Africa as the continent of the founder(s) for all living human populations as well as the source of the earliest hominins. There may be more genetic diversity in living African populations, and all non-African populations may be merely a subset of this African variation (Chen et al. 1995, 2000; Watson et al. 1996, 1997). However, there has not been very much research on the genetic history of Africans after the founding group(s) migrated out to take on the indigenous Neanderthal and other archaic populations in Eurasia.

Watson et al. (1996, 1997) have examined the history of expansion events within Africa. They studied hypervariable region I in the mitochondrial DNA of 241 individuals from nine ethnic groups (Watson et al. 1996:437–438). They used pairwise differences between and within populations to create a neighbor-joining tree, with 232 different lineages (Watson et al. 1996:438). Mean pairwise differences range from a minimum of 8.46 ± 3.36 to a maximum of 21 differences (Watson et al. 1996:438). !Kung San, Mbuti, and Biaka ("Pygmies") hunter-gatherers show ten times more sequence differences than other groups (Watson et al. 1996:437). Watson's group argues that the three hunter-gatherer populations have remained constant in size, while other African groups, farmers, and herders, have expanded (Watson et al. 1996:437).

Examining 407 mitochondrial DNA sequences from the control region of thirteen African groups, they conclude that most variation is a result of one or more demographic expansions between 60,000 and 80,000 years ago. The earliest date represents the Out of Africa II event (Watson et al. 1997:691). Most (87%) of the mitochondrial sequences fall into four major clusters (haplogroups L1a, L1b, L2, and L3) (Watson et al. 1997:694). These clusters are geographically widespread and reflect demographic and territorial expansion (Watson et al. 1997:694). The rest (13%) are isolated and not shared between populations (Watson et al. 1997:694). In order to calculate a date for a most recent common ancestor, Watson's group uses a nuclear fragment of mitochondrial DNA that is believed to have integrated chromosomally before Mitochrondrial Eve came into existence. The average transition distance from this nuclear fragment gives an estimated date for our last common ancestor between 111,000 and 148,000 years ago (Watson et al. 1997:694).

The two largest African mitochondrial clusters, L2 and L3, represent about 70% of their sample. They choose East Africa as the source of the founder population, and date it to between 60,000 and 80,000 years ago (Watson et al. 1997:694, 697). The low mtDNA diversity of modern humans must be the result of a founder effect long after the origin of anatomically modern *Homo sapiens* (Watson et al. 1997:697). Looking at their tree, Watson's group proposes that only one mtDNA sequence, or very closely related ones, participated in the earliest expansion, around 100,000 years ago (Watson et al. 1997:697). A small sub-population carrying this lineage may have acquired some selective advantage and survived at the expense of others. This advantage, which is unspecified, may have allowed for increased reproductive success around the beginning of the last glacial (Watson et al. 1997:697).

> It seems reasonable to speculate that a behavioral innovation appeared some 60,000 to 80,000 years ago in a subpopulation of anatomically modern humans, containing the ancestors of L3 (and possible also L2), who have previously been living with a Middle Palaeolithic/MSA technology and that this small subpopulation subsequently expanded as a result. This change may well correspond with the evidence for the dramatic increase in communicative activity that is associated with either the LSA or an even earlier period in Africa . . . and the Upper Paleolithic in Eurasia. (Watson et al. 1997:697)

WHAT GENES SAY ABOUT OUR COMMON HUMANITY

As recently as the late 1980s, it was believed that Africa did not contribute much to later human evolution. The earliest people to enter Eurasia were assumed to be the ancestors of the Upper Palaeolithic modern humans, whose creative skills we still admire thousands of years later. The focus of most Upper Pleistocene prehistoric research was Europe, and we still know much more about this continent than all others. Generations of Palaeolithic archaeologists were trained to see Western Europe, especially France, as the standard against which all other regions in the Old World had to be measured. The presence of *Homo sapiens* fossil remains with non-Upper Palaeolithic technology at numerous sites in Africa was used to show how far behind Europe our original home continent had fallen.

Two things have changed this perspective. One is the focus of this chapter, the mitochondrial, nuclear, and Y chromosome studies which date the formation of our species and model its subsequent history. The other is the revolution in chronometric dating techniques discussed in chapter 2. New methods took us beyond the radiocarbon boundary of 40,000 years ago and confirmed the early appearance of modern humans in Africa as well as at the Mugharet es Skhūl and Jebel Qafzeh in the Levant. African Middle and Later Stone Age prehistory and human evolution have gone from marginal to central in the debate about our remote history (see the papers in Barham and Robson-Brown 2001 for an attempt to redress this omission). While the quality of genetic data is increasing exponentially, the fossil and archaeological evidence from Africa has not begun to match it. We know quite a bit about individual sites but have not sampled enough of them to see a general pattern. Geneticists are proposing where and when certain events occurred, but the hard evidence to test these ideas still awaits discovery.

While many archaeologists and human palaeontologists are willing to accept the Out of Africa II model wholesale, we are often not aware of the state of the debate among the geneticists who formulated it. Cann (2001:1743) recently asked whether or not "this information, gained from gene genealogies of hemoglobins, low-recombining portions of the X, mitochondria, and Y sequences, can ever generate a consistent picture when compared to frequency data. Can we map the rise and fall or particular alleles at a given locus and integrate this information across an entire chromosome?" In turn, until recently, geneticists talked in terms of the changes in individual loci and did not consider issues related to individuals or whole populations. It was as if genes moved, and the organisms that carried them were unimportant. An adequate assessment of human history may require "a multidisciplinary perspective embracing evolutionary ecology, genetics and palaeoanthropology" (Cann 2001:1744).

But there are profound conclusions to be drawn from our revised understanding of our origins. It reflects our common humanity, regardless of ethnicity, language, or culture. This research should have repercussions for our understanding of human population variation, the study of "race," and/or ethnicity. Ever since Lewontin (1972) attempted to quantify the role of race in human genetic variation, geneticists have agreed that there is a lack of significant population differences by geography or place of ancestry. Humans have no sub-species, as our extremely recent common origin of humans confirms that there has not been enough time for sub-specific or racial variation to develop. Anthropologists agree that human variation does not reflect significant biological differences within and between populations (Billinger 2006; Brace 2005). Most of our ideas about race really relate to ethnicity, religion, or culture. We inherit a biological makeup, but the bulk of our variation is learned, a product of socialization. This is why human cultural variation greatly outweighs physical differences between populations. We are not even certain how such outward physical traits are inherited, because even biology can be molded by environment.

So why do we continue to divide people into groups using meaningless criteria? As Lewontin (1972:385) wrote over thirty years ago, "despite the objective problems of classification of human populations into races," scientists and lay-people alike continue to use these categories. Perhaps it makes it easier to understand differences, but our world is framed by our history. It was Europeans who wrote the history of humanity, as Eric Wolf (1997) cogently analyzed. These days, genetic data may rewrite our folk conceptions of our past (for attempts to look at human variation from a modern anthropological perspective see Relethford 2002; Relethford and Harpending 1994). But how reliable will this new history be? Relethford (2001:3, italics in original) concludes that "genetic variation today is a *reflection of the past*" and needs to be interpreted appropriately. Other geneticists are blunter. At the first Cold Spring Harbor Laboratory conference on human evolution in 1997 (Cavalli-Sforza and Watson 1997), James Watson, the codiscoverer of the structure of DNA as well as the laboratory director, began his address by stating that all human groups have legends, stories about their history. But he went on to conclude that such stories were all wrong, as DNA offered the undisputable historical facts, the real truth (Watson, personal communication). In an increasingly fragmented world, anthropologists would do well to educate scientists, human geneticists, and the public about our common, shared past. As Svante Pääbo (2003:410) recently wrote, "from a genomic perspective, we are all Africans, either living in Africa or in quite recent exile outside Africa." While it was once thought that globalization would reduce cultural variation, people hang on to their culturally defined identities, often to some extreme level (Barber 1992, 1996). But the growing body of molecular data shows that unity must be the primary force for human history, not diversity, division, or conflict.

7

The Fossil Hominin Evidence

A key finding is that bones of essentially modern aspect are associated with early Late Pleistocene MSA artifacts. (Rightmire and Deacon 2001:536)
The African fossil record is largely mute on the evolutionary origins of anatomically modern humans. (Klein 2001b:6)
Not one [African] specimen thought to be an early modern has a defensible radiometric date. (Wolpoff 1989a:64–65)

What is the fossil evidence of early modern humans like in Africa and elsewhere? How is it used to argue for an earlier appearance of modern people here than in Eurasia? Is there any evidence of a sudden speciation event that produced the first *Homo sapiens*? Or was it a gradual process, much as the multiregional evolutionists suggest? In chapter 5, several models were reviewed. Which furnishes the most coherent explanation? And what are the implications of these models for understanding our origins and later human evolution?

It is surprising, in light of the intensity of the current debate about modern human origins, to see how limited the Middle and Upper Pleistocene African fossil evidence actually is (Bräuer 1992). It often consists of single bones from dubious contexts. Other specimens are surface finds, without any association whatsoever. Even those excavated from archaeological sites generally lack any reliable age estimate. Many were recovered long before modern methods of research were developed, so their associations were not always recorded. How useful then is this fossil record, beyond providing general anatomical details? The answer, once again, depends on whom you ask. The historian of science, Peter Bowler (1987:5), argues that for early researchers, the fossils had meaning only to the extent that they could be fit into theories of how human evolution occurred. Little has apparently changed, as the same evidence is used to argue different, often contradictory, models. The African fossils can be used to argue either continuity or a sudden appearance of modern anatomy sometime around 200,000 years ago. Alternatively, they may say nothing about the pattern or processes of human origins, as Klein (2001b:6) says in the introductory quote above. They also do not address the question of replacement directly, beyond showing that modern features were present here long before they appeared in Eurasia. What happened to these people if and when they left Africa is someone else's problem entirely.

Does the evidence fit expectations of the supporters of Mitochrondrial Eve? Generally, yes, as there is nothing about the fossil evidence that rejects conclusions from any of the recent DNA studies. While Cann and her colleagues propose that our last common mitochondrial ancestor could have been an "archaic" *Homo sapiens* (Cann et al. 1987:35), many palaeontologists immediately assume that she was already anatomically modern. The African hominin evidence shows such archaic humans, now generally referred to as *Homo heidelbergensis*, were followed by anatomically modern people. The transition between the two took place by 200,000 years ago. The great antiquity of *Homo sapiens* in Africa reinforces the major role the continent had in all phases of human evolution. But it also brings out the contrast between the beginnings of anatomical modernity and behavioral modernity (as measured by the achievements of the European Upper Palaeolithic).

AFRICAN HOMININS: AN INTRODUCTION

In 2003, the L. S. B. Leakey Foundation celebrated the centennial of the birth of Louis Leakey (1903–1972). Leakey was the public face of palaeoanthropology in North America for much of the mid-twentieth century, courtesy of many *National Geographic* articles, documentaries, and Leakey's own gregarious personality. Leakey was responsible for the investigation of Olduvai Gorge, where his second wife Mary's interpretation of the Stone Age record provided the yardstick for almost 2 million years of human history (M. Leakey 1971, 1994). As discussed in chapter 2, what is less known about Louis

Leakey is that he and his family have long promoted a radical view of human evolution that owes a lot to the Piltdown controversy: the idea that *Homo sapiens* had an extremely ancient history (Bowler 1987:101). In many species of animals, Leakey argued, there had been no marked anatomical changes since the Middle Pleistocene. "If this is true, then upon theoretical evidence we may conclude that man as we know him to-day, man of the species *Homo sapiens*, was probably also fully evolved *physically* by the beginning of the Middle Pleistocene period" (Leakey 1936a:163; italics in original). He noted that many Upper Pleistocene African sites contain modern human remains, so they must have dispersed even earlier (Leakey 1936a:164–165):

> The species *Homo sapiens* was probably evolved during the early part of the Pleistocene period, and that by Middle Pleistocene times, at latest, his physical evolution as a species was complete. . . .If we believe theoretically that the species *Homo sapiens* was in existence in Middle Pleistocene times, we are forced to the conclusion that *in all probability* men of the species *Homo sapiens* were responsible for the great hand-axe culture. (Leakey 1936a:163–164; italics in original)

Leakey had a history of finding modern skeletons in what were, or were thought to be, ancient deposits. The cranial fragments from Kanjera, the Kanam mandible (Leakey 1936b), and Reck's Olduvai skeleton or OH1 (Leakey 1932; Day 1986:177) all were proposed to be ancient moderns. He was upset when this conclusion was rejected by others, or put into the unknown or "suspense account" (Leakey 1936a:165). The Kanam mandible, basically the symphysis or midline area, is one of the few that is genuinely believed to be ancient. What made it modern looking was the possibility that it exhibited a mental eminence or chin. But Tobias (1962) demonstrated that the "chin" was actually a tumor. The OH1 skeleton was later dismissed as a modern burial intruding into the early Pleistocene deposits of Bed II (Day 1986:177), and, while Kanjera is a genuine site (Ditchfield et al. 1999; Plummer et al. 1999), Leakey's fossil is also recent. The Leakeys have long supported the idea of an ancient African *Homo*, an early large-brained hominin, the common ancestor of all later humans. It would be ironic if Louis Leakey's ideas turn out to have some validity, even if for the wrong reason. In fact, Omo-Kibish now dates back to almost 200,000 years ago (McDougall et al. 2004), just as Leakey originally proposed.

Before discussing the African Middle and Upper Pleistocene fossil evidence, it is necessary to review terminology. The first hominin to attain modern body size and also to leave Africa was *Homo erectus*, though African representatives of this species are often referred to as *Homo ergaster*. At a minimum, *Homo erectus* is an Asian species first defined in 1894 by the Dutch army doctor Eugene Dubois as *Pithecanthropus erectus*. His type specimen consisted of a femur and small, flat calotte or brain case recovered in 1891 from river gravels at Trinil, Java, as well as a mandible fragment from the nearby site of Kedung Brubus (Dubois 1894; Day 1986:337; Shipman 2001; Theunissen 1989; Klein 1999:259). The name was derived from Ernst Haeckel's hypothetical human ancestor in *The History of Creation* (1868), *Pithecanthropus alalus*, "ape man without speech." This form was proposed to be hairier than living humans, half erect, and descended from the anthropoid apes. Dubois and G. R. Von Koenigswald found similar remains in the 1930s, and other related fossils still occasionally surface today (Baba et al. 2003). The Canadian anatomist Davidson Black classified other fossils found at Zhoukoudian near Beijing, China, as *Sinanthropus pekinensis* (Sigmon and Cybulski 1981). By 1941, over forty individuals belonging to this "Peking Man" group had been recovered (Jia and Huang 1990). In 1939, Von Koenigswald and Franz Weidenreich (1937) suggested links between the Javanese and Chinese fossils. Eventually, they were grouped into the same species, *Homo erectus*. Its basic definition has not changed much in the intervening years. *Homo erectus* is a fossil species with a time range from around 1.5 million to around 600,000 years ago in Africa, and possibly as recent as 250,000 years ago in China (Wu 1985; but this idea is contested by recent TIMS uranium-series dates; see Shen et al. 2001).

Homo erectus has a long, low cranium, ranging in size from 775 to 1225 cc, with an average volume around 1000 cc (about 87% of modern *Homo sapiens*). From the rear, the skull seems to be pentagonal or gabled, as it exhibits strong angulation along the sagittal and metopic sutures, as well as in the occipital area (Rightmire 1990:175–178). Internally, the inner and outer tables are thickened. The face is robust, with significant alveolar prognathism, and a large continuous brow ridge or supraorbital torus (Rightmire 1990:175–176). There is a large mandible, with a receding symphysis; in other words, it lacks a chin, as do all pre-modern humans (Rightmire 1990:177). The postcranial skeleton is remarkably modern, but robust. In the long bones, the cortical bone is thick, and the medullary cavity (hollow area for marrow) is small. This condition is referred to as stenosis. The femur is platymeric or flattened when viewed in anterior-posterior aspect (Rightmire 1990:177).

Do coeval African hominins belong in *Homo erectus* or do they need their own specific designation as *Homo ergaster*? *Homo ergaster* is a species defined by Groves and Mazak (1975). In a review of early Pleistocene hominins, they divided specimens into three separate groups: *Homo africanus* (what generally was referred to as *Australopithecus africanus*), *Homo habilis*, and *Homo ergaster*. *Homo ergaster* is distinguished from the other two by smaller premolars and molars, a broad premolar often with a single root, small P_4 (second premolar) re P_3 (the first premolar), a thick, massive mandible, and a cranial capacity larger than *Homo africanus* (Wood 1991:83). In this group, Groves (1989) included two crania, KNM ER 1813 and ER 3733 (Wood 1991:92). The species name came into general use after Bernard Wood (1991) discussed it in his study of early *Homo* crania from East Turkana, northern Kenya. In his monograph, Wood classified the ER 3733 and 3883 skulls and mandibles ER 730, 820, and 992 as "*Homo* affinity *Homo erectus*" (Wood 1991:268). With Alan Bilsborough, Wood concluded that the difference between these specimens and *Homo erectus* was as great as that between *Homo erectus* and *Homo sapiens* (Bilsborough and Wood 1986). As a result, they might need their own species designation, and *Homo ergaster* was as good as any (Wood 1991:268–269). African forms have a rounder head and thinner cranial vault bones than *Homo erectus*; both these features are derived toward *Homo sapiens*. Shared with Asian *Homo erectus* are features such as a larger body and brain than in earlier hominins, within the range of modern humans (Klein 1999:281). In addition to the remains from East Turkana, specimens like the teenager from Nariokotome, Kenya (WT 15,000) (Walker and Leakey 1993), the mandibles from Tighenif, Algeria, and the numerous specimens from coastal Morocco fit into this group, whatever it is called.

For some, the African forms should be classified as *Homo ergaster* while Asian ones should be considered *Homo erectus* (Groves and Mazak 1975; Wood 1991). *Homo sapiens* would then be derived from *Homo ergaster* exclusively (Klein 1999:275). For others, Asian and African Middle Pleistocene hominins make up a variable population of the same species (Kramer 1993; Rightmire 1990; Asfaw et al. 2002; along with the supporters of the multiregional theory). This widely spread group would then be the ancestor of

Homo heidelbergensis, the last common ancestor of modern humans and the Eurasian Neanderthals (Rightmire 1998b:222).

Schoetensack (1908) described the first *Homo heidelbergensis* specimen, the Mauer mandible that had been found in a gravel quarry near Heidelberg, Germany, in 1907 (Rightmire 1998b:221). Fossils lumped into this category range in age from around 600,000 to between 300,000 and 200,000 years ago. This form, found in Africa as well as Europe, used to be called archaic *Homo sapiens*, and shows a mix of traits of both *Homo erectus* and *Homo sapiens*. It had a larger and rounder brain than *Homo erectus*, but a more massive, projecting face than seen in modern humans. This face exhibits a supraorbital torus that arches over the midline of the nose, forming an "M" that looks like the McDonald's fast-food chain logo. The postcranial skeleton is virtually identical to that of anatomically modern humans. Examples include the population from the Sima de los Huesos or "Pit of Bones" from Atapuerca, Spain, (Arsuaga et al. 1997) and most other early Europeans. In Africa, numerous finds fit into this species, such as the crania from Ndutu, Kabwe, and Bodo.

AFRICAN ORIGINS: THE EARLIER FOSSIL RECORD

This section reviews the African fossil evidence for *Homo erectus/Homo ergaster*, the species which arose in Africa prior to the first dispersal of humans into Eurasia, and that parallels Asian *Homo erectus* in time. The specimens are generally grouped geographically from north to south.

Some of the earliest fossil hominins were discovered in coastal Morocco as a result of the construction of a modern harbor at Casablanca before and during World War I (Biberson 1961a, 1961b; Hublin 1985, 1993, 2001; Raynal et al. 1995, 2001). Deposits were quarried, leading to the discovery of a series of Quaternary marine and terrestrial terraces. Each represents an ancient shore covered by dunes, increasing in age as one moves inland (Hublin 2001:100). Pierre Biberson (1961a) named these stages; marine ones include the Ouljian presently 5 to 8 m above sea level, the Harounian at 18 to 20 m, the Anfatian at 25 to 30 m, the Maarifian at 55 to 60 m, and the Messaoudian at 80 to 100 m (Hublin 2001:100). Paralleling this sequence were the terrestrial deposits: the Amirian, the Tensifitian, then the PreSoltanian, and the Soltanian (Hublin 2001:100). These provided a relative dating system that was matched by Biberson's artifact sequence of four pebble tool stages and eight Acheulian ones. More recent work (Raynal et al. 1995, 2001) shows that there is no clear evidence of human occupation until around the end of the Lower Pleistocene, about 800,000 years ago.

In the Grotte des Littorines in the Sidi Abderrahman quarry near Casablanca, two parts of a mandible were found in 1954. These came from a sandstone lens labeled level F, and are assumed to belong to the mid-Middle Pleistocene (Hublin 2001:107). The Thomas Quarries, a few hundred meters away, are a series of three caves (Hublin 2001:106). In the Thomas I Quarry, a single mandible was recovered in 1969 along with faunal remains and "archaic Acheulian" artifacts. These are estimated to be between 400,000 and 600,000 years old. The mandible consists of the left body and part of the ramus. The bone is described as gracile, but the teeth are quite large (Hublin 2001:106; Arambourg and Biberson 1956). This site has been the subject of a recent 65 m² excavation by Raynal.

In the Thomas III Quarry, facial fragments were discovered in 1977 (Hublin 2001:103,107). At the nearby site of Salé, most of a single skull was found in 1971. Despite some pathological remodeling on the back of the head, the skull is estimated to be around 880 cc in volume, well within the range of *Homo erectus/Homo ergaster*. It consists of a vault, endocast (a fossilized brain), and part of the left maxilla (with the lateral incisor to the M^2) and lower face (Conroy 1997:324). It is said to exhibit many *Homo erectus* features, including postorbital constriction and frontal keeling (Conroy 1997:324). Other traits are more like *Homo heidelbergensis*: the position of the parietal eminences (high on the skull) and a more rounded occipital than seen in earlier *Homo* (Conroy 1997:324; Hublin 2001:109). It is dated by electron spin resonance to 389,000 years ago (early uptake model) or 455,000 years ago (linear uptake) (Hublin 2001:107).

In 1933, twenty-three fragments of a cranium and a fragment of a left maxilla were found at the Kebibat quarry, near Rabat (Hublin 2001:109; Klein 1999:266). Blasted out by dynamite, it represents the first Middle Pleistocene hominin cranium from North Africa (Hublin 2001:109; Débénath 2000:132). Its stratigraphic location is uncertain and is best estimated to be between 250,000 and 350,000 years old. The bones come from an individual around fourteen to fifteen years old. The cranial bone is thin, and the occipital is rounded (without the torus or shelf of bone seen in classical *Homo erectus*) (Hublin 2001:110). This means it could be a *Homo ergaster* (as opposed to *Homo erectus*) or else it belongs in *Homo heidelbergensis*.

Another Moroccan find is from Ain Marouf or El Hajeb. Studied in the early 1950s, the site yielded a shaft of a femur, along with mammal fauna, and Acheulian artifacts. The site is described as early Middle Pleistocene on bio-stratigraphic grounds, and the femur is said to exhibit a mix of Neanderthal and modern features (Geraads et al. 1992; Hublin 2001:105; Klein 1999:265). Once again, this might be another way of saying it is similar to *Homo heidelbergensis.*

Tighenif (formerly Ternifine) is 20 km east of Mascara, Algeria. First examined in the 1870s, a 1954–1956 excavation produced hominin and faunal remains, as well as stone artifacts (Geraads et al. 1986). These included three mandibles, one isolated parietal (Tighenif 4), and several isolated teeth, possibly from another individual, from eight to ten years old (Hublin 2001:104; Conroy 1997:324). They were the first African finds similar to *Homo erectus* in Asia, but Camille Arambourg (1963) gave them their own name, *Atlanthropus mauritanicus* (Klein 1999:265). The site is placed near the Lower/Middle Pleistocene boundary, contemporary with the Thomas Quarries. Palaeomagnetic studies show normal polarity throughout, meaning the site is less than 780,000 years old (Geraads et al. 1986:386).

A number of sites in Ethiopia and Eritrea have yielded fossil hominins. This region is the northernmost (in Africa) extension of the Gregory Rift Valley system, long the source of Pliocene hominin remains. A relatively new area investigated is Buia in the Danakil (Afar) Depression of Eritrea (Abbate et al. 1998) (map 9.3). Buia is 100 km south-southeast of the capital of Massawa and is located within the Danakil Formation, which is 1,000 m thick (Abbate et al. 1998:458). Between 1995 and 2003, a joint Italian and Eritrean research team discovered a nearly complete hominin skull (UA 31), two lower incisors, and three pelvic fragments at Uadi Aalad (Abbate et al. 1998:458; Macchiarelli et al. 2004). They were associated with fauna and Acheulian artifacts thought to be around 1 million years old (Martini et al. 2004). The fauna is described as composed of typical African savanna species and includes *Elephas recki, Hipparion,* and *Equus* species, as well as many bovids (Abbate et al. 1998:458–459). Palaeomagnetic data suggest the presence of two reversed and two normal zones; the skull was recovered from near the top of the lower normal zone, which is interpreted as the Jaramillo Subchron (Abbate et al. 1998:348). This is also supported by fission track dates (Macchiarelli et al. 2004:134). The skull is missing the base, the mandible, and part of the face, but its cranial capacity can be estimated at between 750 and 800 cc (Abbate et al. 1998:459–460). The skull is described as very long relative to its breadth. Its face is short and narrow; the maxilla is present, but contains only tooth roots, not teeth. It exhibits substantial subnasal prognathism and has a heavily built, forward projecting supraorbital torus. It has the McDonald's arch of a classic *Homo heidelbergensis*. There is no sagittal keeling; in the occipital area there is a "slightly thickened angular torus" (Abbate et al. 1998:460). Like many other African specimens, it has a mix of *Homo erectus* and *Homo heidelbergensis* traits (Abbate et al. 1998; Macchiarelli et al. 2004:138). It is similar to *Homo erectus/Homo ergaster* in its long oval braincase, low cranial capacity, massive supraorbital torus, and the fact that its greatest breadth is low. But it is like *Homo heidelbergensis* in its high maximum biparietal breadth (Abbate et al. 1998:460).

Farther south, at Konso Gardula in the Middle Awash of central Ethiopia, researchers recovered a mandible with P_4 to M_2 as well as an isolated upper M_3. Associated with typical Acheulian artifacts, it is estimated to be between 1.9 and 1.3 million years old (Conroy 1997:33; Klein 1999:274). From Bouri, in the Dakanihylo Member of the Middle Awash, Tim White's research team recovered a cranium and other skeletal remains considered to be typical of *Homo erectus/Homo ergaster* (Asfaw et al. 2002; Clark et al. 2003:748). Generally referred to as "Daka," this formation is between 22 and 45 m thick and is older than the unit from which the Bodo skull is derived (Asfaw et al. 2002:317; Clark et al. 1994). ^{39}Argon/^{40}argon dates the base of the member at 1.042 ± 0.009 million years ago. All sediments show reversed polarity, confirming an age older than 780,000 years ago (Asfaw et al. 2002:317).

Early Acheulian artifacts are also present: hand axes and cleavers with fewer flake removals than found in the later phases of the Acheulian (Asfaw et al. 2002:317). Faunal remains include bovids representative of grassland and adjacent water margin habits; many exhibit stone tool cut marks (Asfaw et al. 2002:317). The skull, BOU-VP-2/66, includes a calvarium, the vault, and supraorbitals and is estimated to be about 995 cc in volume (Asfaw et al. 2002:317). There is some keeling on the frontal and parietals, but no true occipital torus. Both keeling and an occipital torus are characteristic of Asian *Homo erectus*. The face shows thick supraorbital tori that are strongly arched. The vault is shorter and smaller than OH 9 and is similar to the Buia cranium from Eritrea (Asfaw et al. 2002:317). Other hominin remains of similar age are three isolated femora and one proximal tibia. These show marked platy-meria and a thick midshaft cortex found in Asian *Homo erectus* (Asfaw et al. 2002:317). The remains are seen as intermediate between African *Homo ergaster* and Asian *Homo erectus*. They are interpreted as a stage in the evolution of a single African lineage. Alternately, they could represent an Asian *Homo erectus* returning home (Asfaw et al. 2002:318). But Manzi et al. (2003:731) argue that it is more like earlier African *Homo ergaster*, and is distinct from the Asian species. Another cranial fragment was discovered in 1973 at Gombore II, part of the complex of sites from Melka Kunturé, Ethiopia. It is estimated to be between 1.3 million and 780,000 years old (Klein 1999:265, 274; Rightmire 1984:302). In this group, here are also possibly cranial fragments from Member K of the Shungura Formation, on the west side of the Omo River in southern Ethiopia (Klein 1999:274).

The Omo River drains into Lake Turkana (formerly Lake Rudolf) in northern Kenya. Almost continuously since first investigated in 1969, the Lake Turkana basin has yielded hominin fossil and archaeological sites. The east side is referred to as Koobi Fora or East Turkana. Due to its previous name, the hominins are still catalogued as "KNM ER" or Kenya National Museum East Rudolf with their specimen numbers. Material from the west side of the lake was collected after the name change and is referred to as "KNM WT." Early Pleistocene *Homo* species from Lake Turkana could belong to *Homo habilis*, *Homo rudolfensis*, or *Homo erectus/Homo ergaster* (Wood 1991, 1992). In this section, only the latter are of concern.

The two crania, KNM ER 3733 and 3883, come from the Upper Member of the Koobi Fora Formation and are estimated to be around 1.8 to 1.7 million years old (Conroy 1997:329; Klein 1999:287). ER 3733 is composed of a skull and partial face, while ER 3883 is a partial face and braincase; both are estimated to have a volume of 800 to 850 cc (Conroy 1997:329). Both exhibit a maximum breadth low on the skull and have a round cranium (not an angled one as in *Homo erectus*). There is postorbital constriction and a variable supraorbital torus (Conroy 1997:329). In this group also belongs ER 1808, a partial skeleton interpreted as showing pathological features, possibly due to hypervitaminosis A (a disease obtained by eating carnivore liver or raw honey) (Walker et al. 1982; Conroy 1997:331). The most spectacular find is KNM WT 15,000, from the Nariokotome Member of the Nachukui Formation, West Turkana. This almost complete teenage skeleton was found in 1984 in sediments above a volcanic tuff potassium-argon dated to 1.65 million years ago. Using modern grown rates, it is estimated to have been ten to twelve years old. The cranium is around 880 cc in volume. It exhibits a long, narrow body, typical of tropical people who maximize surface exposure to lose body heat (as predicted by Bergmann's and Allen's laws). KNM WT 15,000 would have been about 5 ft 3 in tall; if he had lived until adulthood, he would have been over 6 ft (Conroy 1997:331; Walker and Leakey 1993).

South of Lake Turkana, still within the Eastern or Gregory Rift, is Lake Baringo. Here researchers discovered two mandibles and some postcranial remains, including an ulna. These are estimated to be between 700,000 and 250,000 years old (Leakey et al. 1969; Conroy 1997:334). Recently, a research team working at Olorgesailie, an extensive Acheulian site complex in southern Kenya, reported the discovery of fragmentary cranial bones dating to between 900,000 and 970,000 years ago (Potts et al. 2004; Schwartz 2004). While an adult, this individual was extremely small, and overlaps in size with crania from Dmanisi in Georgia, which are twice as old. On the other hand, it shares some morphological features with younger skulls such as Bodo and Kabwe, normally assigned to *Homo heidelbergensis* (Potts et al. 2004:76–77).

Just across the border is Olduvai Gorge, Tanzania, the famous site that exposes about 2 million years of geological and human history. The geological sequence is subdivided into seven members, starting with Bed I (at the bottom), Beds II to IV, then the Masek, Ndutu, and Naisiusiu Beds (Hay 1976; M. Leakey 1971, 1994). Individual localities are given letter names, with the bed number attached; for example, MNK II would be the Mary Nicol Korongo (gully) from Bed II. Bed II, where the first *Homo erectus/Homo ergaster* fossils are located, ranges in age from 1.71 to 1.2 million years old (Hay 1976:25–28, 1990:29). At Olduvai, a number of specimens are assigned to *Homo erectus/ Homo ergaster*. As is the case for Daka, the skulls, around 1 million years old, such as OH 9, resemble *Homo erectus*. OH 9 is a cranium without its face; it comes from LLK in Upper Bed II and is estimated to be around 1.2 million years old (Conroy 1997:326). OH 12, from VEK in Bed IV, could be between 620,000 and 830,000 years old or around 1.1 million. Including a partial face, the brain volume is between 700 and 800 cc (Klein 1999:274). Other specimens include three mandible fragments, OH 22, 23, and 51. OH 22 comes from VEK/MNK in Bed III/IV. OH 23 is from the Lower Masek Beds and is estimated to be between 970,000 and 780,000 years old (Klein 1999:274). OH 51 is also a partial mandible from the GTC locality in Bed III (Klein 1999:265). Another specimen, OH 28, is a hip and femoral shaft from WK IV, where it is associated with Acheulian artifacts (Conroy 1997:329).

Famous for their early hominin record, the South African limestone cave sites have yielded some specimens that might be included in *Homo erectus/ Homo ergaster*. It is also just as possible that these represent the earlier species, *Homo habilis* (Conroy 1997:335). These include SK 15 and SK 847 from Swartkrans, originally classified as *Telanthropus capensis* (Robinson 1953; Clarke 1977). There is also SK 45, a mandible fragment; the SK 80, a maxilla fragment; SK 18bm, a proximal radius; and SK 18, a lower P_3. On stratigraphic grounds, all of these specimens are estimated to be between 1.8 and 1.5 million years old (Klein 1999:274–275).

OUT OF AFRICA I

When and how did the first hominins disperse out of Africa? While there are quite early dates from some of the Java *Homo erectus* localities (Swisher et al 1994; Curtis et al. 2000), the first well-documented hominins in Eurasia come from Dmanisi, Georgia, 85 km southwest of the capital of Tbilisi (Gabunia and Vekua 1995; Gabunia et al. 2001). The site is on a cliff overlooking the confluence of the Masavera and Pinozouri rivers (Gabunia et al. 2001:159). During archaeological excavations at a medieval castle, fossiliferous deposits were discovered. The base of the geological sequence is the Masavera Basalt, which is ^{39}argon/^{40}argon dated to 2.0 ± 0.1 million years ago, and by conventional potassium-argon to 1.8 ± 0.1 million years ago. The basalt and overlying Unit A exhibit normal polarity, probably the Olduvai Subchron (between 1.78 and 1.95 million years ago) (Gabunia et al. 2001:162). The total thickness of the deposits is about 2.5 m (Gabunia et al. 2000:1022). Intrusive fills into level A2 contain most of the vertebrate and hominin remains, as well as a few stone artifacts. These sediments and the overlying Unit B show reversed magnetic polarity (Gabunia et al. 2001:162). Unit B1, composed of brown loamy sands cemented by carbonates, contains the bulk of the stone artifacts, and Unit B2, 1.2 m of yellow brown sand, is sterile (Gabunia et al. 2000:1022). Dmanisi's fauna is mainly Eurasian, rather than African (Gabunia et al. 2001:162, 169). Most of the artifacts are Mode 1 pebble tools, cores, and flakes of local quartzite and basalt. This makes it possible that hominins dispersed into this region before the Acheulian appeared around 1.5 million years ago.

Five hominin specimens have been recovered from Dmanisi: two mandibles and three crania (Gabunia et al. 2001:159; Vekua et al. 2002:85; Balter and Gibbons 2002). The crania are about 780, 650, and 600 cc, respectively. All show a mix of Asian *Homo erectus* and African *Homo ergaster* traits, but are more like Africans (Gabunia et al. 2001:166). The third skull is quite small and has been compared to *Homo habilis* (Vekua et al. 2002:85; Balter and Gibbons 2002). Similarities to *Homo ergaster* include the moderate size of the supraorbital tori, the tall, thin walled cranial vaults, small brain size, and some features of dentition (Gabunia et al. 2001:166–167). Asian *Homo erectus* features include well-developed supraorbital tori and an angled cranial vault along with large orbits (Gabunia et al. 2001:165–166; Vekua et al. 2002:88).

NEANDERTHALS AND EARLY MODERN HUMANS

On the surface, the later European fossil record seems to be quite clear. Neanderthals are associated with Middle Palaeolithic archaeological sites. Anatomically modern *Homo sapiens* with Upper Palaeolithic tool kits succeeded them between 40,000 and 30,000 years ago. In the Middle East, the situation is a little more complicated, since both Neanderthals and modern humans are found in Middle Palaeolithic sites, but never together.

In Europe, the earliest hominin and archaeological sites are located in the Mediterranean fringe, close to Africa. At least one, the TD 6 horizon at the Gran Dolina, Sierra de Atapuerca, Spain, is associated with reversed polarity. Here some fossil bones classified as *Homo antecessor* are associated with pebble tools and flakes; all are considered to be around 800,000 years old. Somewhat more problematic is the Ceprano skull from Italy; in morphology, it is intermediate between *Homo erectus* and *Homo heidelbergensis* (Ascenzi et al. 1996, 2000; Manzi et al. 2001). Both specimens cast doubt on the "short chronology" for peopling Europe, the belief that no one entered the continent until around 500,000 years ago (Roebroeks and Van Kolfschoten 1994; Dennell and Roebroeks 1996; Dennell 2003; Gamble 1986, 1999). But the dating of the Gran Dolina has led to a modification of this model: no one got further north in Europe than the Mediterranean until 500,000 years ago (Roebroeks 2001). Similarities in stone tool technology (production of bifaces on flakes rather than cores) suggest that hominins could have crossed directly from North Africa to Western Europe during Acheulian times (Alimen 1975;

Barton et al. 2001). This is not the case for modern humans, as Neanderthals persisted in Iberia until less than 30,000 years ago.

Most early European hominin sites are associated with (relatively) warm interglacial and interstadial phases. It is possible that more northern areas were entirely abandoned during full glacials (Klein 1999:326). For Klein (1999:326), the subsequent Neanderthals "did scarcely better," a sentiment shared by others (for example, Shea 2003). Outside of sites like the Sima de los Huesos at Atapuerca, recently re-dated to around 400,000 years old (Arsuaga et al. 1997; Bischoff et al. 2003), the hominin evidence of the earliest Europeans is limited. Many sites have a single specimen, such as the tibia shaft from Box-grove, England (Roberts et al. 1994), or the cranium from Petralona, Greece (Murrill 1981). From what we know, most crania are large and round enough to be classified as *Homo heidelbergensis*; this too suggests a relatively recent colonization of temperate Europe. When anatomical features are compared, it is clear that these early Europeans are already derived toward Neanderthals in their faces and crania. The most likely explanation is one of evolution in place from *Homo heidelbergensis* to Neanderthals at the same time that *Homo heidelbergensis* was changing into modern humans in Africa (Rightmire 1998b). There is no need to argue for the presence of another species, a Mode 3 using hominin, intermediate between *Homo heidelbergensis* and Neander-thals as Foley and Lahr (1997; Lahr and Foley 2001) do. Early Europeans are associated with either Acheulian or core and flake tool assemblages; the latter are referred to by a variety of names (such as Clactonian, Premousterian, or chopper-chopping tool tradition (White 2000; Rolland 1998, 2001).

The descendants of these early people are the Neanderthals. They are found in sites from Western Europe to the Middle East and east to Teshik Tash in Russia. Their distribution in time is less clear, as the answer depends on the definition of Neanderthal. Early Europeans shared some Neanderthal traits, and their incidence increases over time. "Classic" Neanderthals are those present from the last glacial (Howell 1957). All share a long, low braincase, with a large cranial volume ranging from 1,245 to 1,740 cc with an average of 1,520 cc (Klein 1999:377). Their skulls are generally oval ("en bombe") when viewed from the rear (Smith 1991:225). The frontal is low and receding with a continuous supraorbital torus forming a double arch, as found with *Homo heidelbergensis*. The back is in the form of an occipital bun or "chignon" with a depression above, called the suprainiac fossa. Neanderthal faces are long and prognathic, especially along the midline, giving them a beaked appearance (Klein 1999:377; Smith 1991:225). The nasal aperture and cavity are very large, with enormous sinuses and an inflated maxilla, without a canine fossa (Smith 1991:225). Teeth are generally large and worn, with a distinctive wear of incisors and canines that may be related to their use as tools. Back teeth show enlarged pulp cavities or taurodontism. Since the face is pulled so forward, there is a gap or retromolar space behind the wisdom tooth (M_3).

Neanderthals have short distal limb segments and their long bones are bowed (Klein 1999:380; Churchill 1998). Their average height is around 166 cm (5'4") as opposed to 178 cm (5'8") for early modern humans (Klein 1999:384). Their body plan, barrel chests, short distal limb segments, and sinus features have all been proposed as long-term adaptations for the cold, dry conditions of glacial Europe (Smith 1991:225–227). For Fred Smith, they "seem to represent the high-water mark for the genus *Homo* in favoring the brawn approach to environmental adaptation" (Smith 1991:225). Neanderthals are associated with Middle Palaeolithic artifacts and assemblages. These are generally referred to as Mousterian, after the site of Le Moustier, France. François Bordes (1961, 1972, and 1981) pioneered a way to study all retouched tools from Mousterian sites by plotting their percentage frequencies in cumulative graphs. He identified four basic patterns, and since they occurred randomly over time and space, he felt that each represented the tools of a particular people, their stylistic or ethnic signature (Bordes 1973; Bordes and de Sonneville-Bordes 1970). Others have suggested that they represent tool kits for specific tasks (Binford 1973; Binford and Binford 1966, 1969) or just the reduction stage at which tools were discarded (Dibble and Rolland 1992; Rolland and Dibble 1990).

In Europe, the earliest modern humans are referred to as Cro-Magnons, after the French site where they were originally discovered in 1868. The Abri Cro-Magnon (or Cro-Magnon rock-shelter) is located in Les Eyzies. Workmen clearing ground for a railway uncovered deposits with a number of human burials, with associated artifacts (Henry-Gambier 2004). The skeletons of these individuals were more rugged than today, but were virtually modern. They became the model for "anatomically modern" *Homo sapiens.* Their brain size is within the modern range of 1,000 to 2,000 cc, with an average of 1,350 cc. The vault is high and parallel sided (Klein 1999:498). They show a flat, vertical forehead, without a supraorbital torus. Instead, they exhibit superciliary and supraorbital arches and variably bulging lateral arches (Klein 1999:498–499; Gambier 1989:197). The face is tucked in underneath the braincase; there is a canine fossa in the maxilla, and the mandible has a mental eminence or chin (Klein 1999:499). Postcranial bones tend to be less robust than seen in earlier humans; researchers such as Klein (1999:500) suggest this implies more reliance on technology than physical strength. Modern humans tend to have long limbs relative to trunk length (Klein 1999:501). Fossil Cro-Magnons from France were reviewed by Gambier (1989). When compared to living humans, they are more robust and have longer cranial vaults. Some Neanderthal traits (occipital bun, posterior position of mental foramen, robusticity of skeleton) are variably expressed, but none "show the most diagnostic Neandertal apomorphies, nor are 'transitional' morphologies present" (Gambier 1989:204).

There is no evidence for an in situ transition from Neanderthals to moderns in Europe. But since there are so few early Upper Palaeolithic Western European fossils known, it is not clear what they should look like (Gambier 1989:206; Henry-Gambier 2004:104). It is possible that they first appeared in eastern and central Europe, and spread west from there (Bräuer 1989:138). However, recent chronometric dates at some famous Aurignacian sites such as Vogelherd, Germany, and the Cro-Magnon site itself show that the fossil hominins are not as old as the associated archaeological remains. The Vogelherd hominins were recently AMS (accelerator mass spectrometry) dated to Neolithic times, around 4,000 to 5,000 years ago (Conard et al. 2004; Wild et al. 2005). An attempt to radiocarbon date a Cro-Magnon long bone failed due to lack of collagen. But a *Littorina* marine shell that had been pierced for suspension produced an AMS date of 27,680 ± 270 BP (Beta 157439), placing it within the Gravettian rather than the Aurignacian (Henry-Gambier 2004:98).

If there was an invasion of new people at the time of the Aurignacian, the question still remains whether there was hybridization between them and the resident Neanderthals, as suggested by Bräuer's (1984) "replacement with hybridization" model. Early moderns from Mladeč in the Czech Republic, recently radiocarbon dated to around 31,000 years ago, occasionally exhibit Neanderthal-like cranial features (an occipital hemi-bun, a slight supraorbital torus) (Smith 1984:175; Wild et al. 2005). But their postcranial skeletons are typically modern, with tropical limb proportions. These features could be a product of replacement with hybridized forms, or the flow of genes into Europe without large-scale population movement (assimilation). They could just as easily be due to local transition from a Neanderthal root (Smith 1984:194). Gambier (1989:208) points out that the Mladeč males show more archaic features than the females, but accepts that some interbreeding may have occurred.

The earliest Cro-Magnons are supposed to be associated with the Aurignacian industry, representing the beginning of the Upper Palaeolithic (Davies 2001; Gambier 1989; Henry-Gambier 2004). The Aurignacian includes distinctive artifact types in bone (split based bone points) and stone (strangled blades, carinated and nosed scrapers, busked burins, Dufour bladelets), animal and female figurines, and jewelry (drilled shell beads). Some of the most recent Neanderthal sites in Western Europe are associated with similar decorative objects. Assigned to the Chatelperronian, these artifacts are associated with Neanderthal skeletal remains at Arcy sur Cure and at St. Césaire, France (Hublin et al. 1996; Lévêque et al. 1993; D'Errico et al. 1998; Zilhao 2000, 2001). These cultural innovations might have been independently invented or are a product of culture contact with Cro-Magnons (Zilhao and D'Errico 1999).

THE EMERGENCE OF *HOMO SAPIENS* IN AFRICA

Two years after the first mitochondrial DNA paper, Elwyn Simons (1989:1343) concluded that "new discoveries combine to indicate that all the major steps in human evolution took place in Africa." A year earlier, Stringer and Andrews (1988a:1267) declared that the search for modern human origins was over and categorically stated that "palaeoanthropologists can ignore molecular data at their peril." While the genetic data clearly pointed to an African founder, the process of becoming modern is unclear. Whichever way you read it, the fossil evidence has been remarkably silent on this question. Even when fossils are found, their context and age remains unclear (Smith 1992b:244). Even the facts and conclusions can be disputed. For example, Grine (2000:140) states that

> the meager paleontological evidence has been viewed by a number of workers as suggesting that modern human ancestry can be traced back to an African population that is in the order of 100 thousand years ago years old . . . However, the degree to which the Late Pleistocene inhabitants of sub-Saharan Africa exhibited modern human morphology has been truly a matter of contention.

Nonetheless, it is generally concluded that between 200,000 and 100,000 years ago, the earliest modern humans appeared in Africa. Fossils from this time period exhibit traits of either *Homo heidelbergensis* or represent *Homo sapiens*; there are only minor differences between them. Examples of the latter come from Klasies River and Border Cave in South Africa, and from the Kibish Formation at Omo in southern Ethiopia, the Ndutu Beds from Olduvai, the Ngaloba Formation at Laetoli, and Lake Eyasi, all in northern Tanzania. The following sections review the fossil evidence of later human evolution in Africa.

NORTHWEST AFRICA

In North Africa, the Middle Palaeolithic began well before 200,000 years ago (maps 8.1 and 8.2; table 7.1). Assemblage variability is remarkably similar to

Table 7.1. African Middle and Upper Pleistocene hominins—A summary

Country	Homo erectus / Homo ergaster	Homo heidelbergensis	Homo sapiens
Morocco	Grotte des Littorhines, Sidi Abderrahman Thomas Quarry I Salé Kébibat Ain Marouf	Rabat Témara Jebel Irhoud?	Dar es Soltan Mugharet el Aliya El Mnasra I (Grotte des Contrebandiers) Zouhra Cave Jebel Irhoud?
Algeria	Tighenif		
Libya		Haua Fteah	
Egypt			Taramsa Hill
Sudan		Singa	
Eritrea	Buia		
Ethiopia	Konso Gardula Bouri	Bodo Omo Kibish 2 Melka Kunturé Diré Dawa?	Diré Dawa? Omo Kibish 1 and 3 Herto Aduma
Kenya	East Turkana (ER-3733, 3883) West Turkana-Nariokotome Kapthurin, Lake Baringo	Eliye Springs East Turkana (ER-3884 or Guomde, ER-999)	
Tanzania	Olduvai-OH9, others	Olduvai-Ndutu Lake Eyasi Laetoli-Ngaloba	Mumba Cave
Zambia		Kabwe	
South Africa	Swartkrans	Cave of Hearths Florisbad Elandsfontein/ Saldanha	Klasies River Die Kelders I Border Cave Hofmeyer Hoedjiespunt I Equus Cave

Source: Compiled from Bräuer 2001b:195; Klein 1999:266; and other sources)
Note: ? = uncertain whether these specimens are late *Homo heidelbergensis* or *Homo sapiens*.

that seen in the European Mousterian, and Levallois methods of core preparation are common. By the time the North African Levalloiso-Mousterian
has given way to the Aterian, the first modern humans are present (Hublin
1992:185). The date for this transition is unclear, but it was well before 40,000
years ago. Aterian lithic assemblages are Mousterian, but add a number of new
elements, notably tanged points ("pedunculates"), end scrapers, burins, and
borers. Most of the fossil humans known from the Upper Pleistocene in North
Africa are Mousterian or Aterian; there is little if any evidence of early Upper Palaeolithic archaeological sites, let alone their makers (Close 1986; Close
and Wendorf 1990). After the Aterian, there seems to be a long hiatus, where
human populations may have entirely disappeared. These regions were only
reoccupied after the last glacial maximum, with the arrival of Epipalaeolithic
people, referred to as Iberomaurusians.

The fossil record of early modern humans in northwest Africa, as elsewhere, is limited. It includes a fragmentary juvenile maxilla and a left upper
M² from the Mughraret el Aliya, discovered by Carleton Coon in 1939 (Hublin
1992:185; Débénath 2000:135). From Temara, near Rabat, one occipital fragment and a left supraorbital part of a frontal were collected in 1975 from
Upper Aterian levels (Hublin 1992:185). Nearby at el Mnasra I, or the Grotte
des Contrebandiers (Smugglers' Cave), there are archaeological levels belonging to the Neolithic, Iberomaurusian, and Aterian. One mandible was found
in 1956; it is described as very robust with large teeth, like those from Dar es
Soltane and the Grotte Zouhra (Débénath 2000:136). Renewed work in 1975
led to the discovery of more cranial fragments including an occipital, partial
parietals, and a fragment of a right frontal bone (Débénath 2000:136).

One of the most cited fossil sites is Djebel Irhoud Cave, 55 km southeast of
Safi in Morocco. This site was opened by miners in 1960 and was the subject
of research from 1961 to 1969. Associated faunal remains are described as being older than the Soltanian stage in the Moroccan coastal sequence (Hublin
2001:104). Conditions were very dry, suggesting that the levels date to MIS 6,
between 130,000 and 190,000 years ago (Smith 1993:244). An ESR (electron
spin resonance) date for the level above Irhoud 4 gave an early uptake date
of 90,000 to 125,000 and a linear uptake date between 105,000 and 190,000
(Grün and Stringer 1991; Hublin 1992:187, 2001:111).

Four specimens were recovered from Middle Palaeolithic contexts between
1961 and 1969: an adult cranium (Irhoud 1), an adult calvarium (Irhoud

2), and a child's mandible (Irhoud 3) and humerus (Irhoud 4) (Grün and Stringer 1991:185). Irhoud 1 is a nearly complete skull that was accidentally found in 1961. It is large, long and wide, with an estimated cranial capacity of 1,480 or 1,305 cc depending on calculation method (Hublin 1992:189). The low vault is an archaic trait, but the convexity of the frontal is similar to that seen in moderns. Its face is wide and low with large rectangular orbits and is no more prognathic than other moderns (Hublin 1992:189, 2001:111–112).

Irhoud 2 is an adult calvarium or skullcap, also found in 1961. Similar in form to Irhoud 1, its only Neanderthal-like features are "primitive" or pleisiomorphic ones, including its overall robusticity and flatness or platycephaly (Hublin 1992:189). Hublin (2001:112) states that its cranial bones are thinner than those of Irhoud 1 and approach the modern condition. Irhoud 3 is a mandible of an eight-year-old child, excavated in 1968 from a level 0.6 m below that of Irhoud 2. It is robust with large teeth, and has a chin and some archaic features of the posterior symphysis that are similar to mandibles from Skhūl and Qafzeh (Hublin 1992:188, 2001:112). Irhoud 4 is a juvenile humerus shaft or diaphysis found in 1969. It is robust and flattened mediolaterally (Hublin 1992:188, 2001:110). Hublin (2001:110) also mentions a fragmentary pelvis encased in breccia, which would be Irhoud 5 (Stringer and Gamble 1993:128). All four specimens have a mixture of modern and "archaic" traits. The latter have traditionally been described as similar to Neanderthals, but they can just as easily be called shared primitive traits. The former "suggest an ancestor-descendant relationship with Upper Pleistocene modern humans" (Hublin 2001:114).

From Dar es Soltane II, at least three individuals were recovered in 1975 from below an Aterian level. They include a partial skull with some of the upper face, a hemi-mandible, an adolescent mandible without the ramus, and a juvenile calvarium (Hublin 1993:119).

A 1977 salvage excavation at Zouhra Cave or El Harhoura produced a fragmentary mandible and isolated canine (Débénath 2000:136). These came from an Aterian level dated by thermoluminescence to 41,160 ± 3500 years ago (BOR 56) and 32,150 ± 4800 years ago (BOR 57) (Hublin 1992:185; Débénath 2000:136). A radiocarbon date on a *Helix* shell gives an age estimate of 25,580 ± 130 years ago (TO-2049) (Débénath 2000:136).

Most of these northwest African individuals are *Homo sapiens*, or are closer to it than to any other species. However, there is a gap between them and the

Iberomaurusians from around 18,000 years ago. They are modern humans of Mechta Afalou type, and they represent the repopulation of much of this region after the last glacial hiatus (Débénath 2000:137; Irish 2000).

This gap in North Africa between the Mousterian/Aterian and the Epipalaeolithic is only filled at Haua Fteah, a large cave on the northwest corner of Libya, in Cyrenaica (McBurney 1967). Here a long archaeological sequence extends back from recent times through to the Iberomaurusian (Eastern Oranian), the Upper Palaeolithic (Dabban), to a Levalloiso-Mousterian, ending with a Mode 4 industry (the Libyan Pre-Aurignacian). A detailed description of the archaeological sequence is given in chapter 8. Two partial mandibles were excavated from Levalloiso-Mousterian layers XXXIII and XXXII, located about 2.5 m below the earliest Upper Palaeolithic levels or 7.5 m below the surface (Tobias 1967b:338; McBurney 1967:117). Haua Fteah I, discovered in 1952, is the left ramus of a mandible, including M_2 and M_3. Trevor and Wells (1967; McBurney et al. 1953a, 1953b) estimated this individual to be between eighteen and twenty-five years old (Tobias 1967b:338). Haua Fteah II, from 1955, is also a left ascending ramus, with the M_2 and M_3 present still in crypt (unerupted). This would make the individual between twelve and seventeen years old (Trevor and Wells 1967:336; Tobias 1967b:341). When originally found, these specimens were compared to a known fossil sample, including remains from Morocco and Mount Carmel. Many had been described as "Neanderthaloids," reflecting the assumption at that time that all Middle Palaeolithic hominins belonged in this group (McBurney et al. 1953a, 1953b). Tobias (1967b:349), however, also saw similarities to sub-Saharan Africans and more recent humans: "The present study suggests that such affinities were not confined to the earliest Upper Pleistocene populations, but applied as well to later and morphologically more advanced kinds of man."

NORTHEAST AFRICA

There are no Middle Pleistocene hominins known from Egypt and Sudan (Pinhasi and Semal 2000:270). In Egypt, there are many Middle Palaeolithic archaeological sites, but not much evidence of their makers. As recently as 2000, the only Upper Pleistocene specimens from northeast Africa were Singa in Sudan and Nazlet Khater (Pinhasi and Semal 2000:271) (map 8.1). Now there is one more: the child from Taramsa Hill near the Red Sea (Vermeersch et al. 1998). The 1980 excavation at Nazlet Khater 2 hill (Boulder Hill, near

Tahta in Upper Egypt) led to the discovery of two human skeletons. One was quite fragmentary, while the other yielded more information (Thoma 1984; Vermeersch et al. 1984a:281, 1984b, 1984c; Pinhasi and Semal 2000:269). The first was a subadult male burial. According to Thoma (1984), the skull is modern, but some features in the mandible and temporal are archaic. The postcranial bones are described as robust but fully modern (Thoma 1984; Pinhasi and Semal 2000:271). The burial is associated with one bifacial axe (Vermeersch et al. 1984a:281; Gambier in Pinhasi and Semal 2000:270). At Nazlet Khater 4, a chert mining site 400 m to the southeast, a 1982 excavation yielded similar axes in an Upper Palaeolithic context (Vermeersch et al. 1984a:285). This latter site is radiocarbon dated between 35,100 and 30,360 years ago (Vermeersch et al. 1984a:285; Pinhasi and Semal 2000:270). Here Upper Palaeolithic blades were produced, as well as burins, end scrapers, and denticulates (Vermeersch et al. 1984a:285). Pinhasi and Semal (2000) conducted a morphometric study of the mandible. They conclude that it lies within the range of Middle Stone Age people and outside that of the North African specimens studied (belonging mainly to the Late Pleistocene and Holocene) (Pinhasi and Semal 2000:284).

Taramsa 1 (26°6′N, 32°42′E) is a chert mine located near Qena in Upper Egypt, 2.5 km south of the Dandara temple (Vermeersch et al. 1998:475). In Stone Age times, people dug a pit 5 m by 4 m by 1.2 m deep, which they used at two different times (Vermeersch et al. 1998:477). The skeleton of a child was placed here in a seated position. It was subsequently sealed by an undisturbed layer of extracted cobbles and then covered by another Middle Palaeolithic extraction pit (Vermeersch et al. 1998:479). Using optically stimulated luminescence and its stratigraphic position, its age is estimated to be around 55,000 years old (Vermeersch et al. 1998:483). While it is not well preserved and only beginning to be studied, it is described as anatomically modern. It is said to share some features with Iberomaurusian Mechtoids, and others with the early moderns from Skhūl and Qafzeh as well as Jebel Irhoud (Vermeersch et al. 1998:481–482).

Singa in the Sudan produced a hominin calvarium in 1924 that is described as modern or as *Homo heidelbergensis* (Bräuer 2001b:193; Stringer 2003:692). It exhibits some pathological signs, such as a growth anomaly in the parietal region (Stringer 2003:692). Using electron spin resonance, its age has been reported to be 97,000 ± 15,000 years ago (early uptake) or 160,000 ± 27,000 years ago (linear uptake) (Grün and Stringer 1991:187), and most recently has been reported as over 133,000 years old (Stringer 2002b:568).

The Middle Awash region of the Ethiopian Rift continues to produce a phenomenal fossil hominin record spanning all periods of human evolution. This includes the *Homo erectus* specimen from the Dakanihylo Member (Asfaw et al. 2002; Clark et al. 2003:748). Probably the most famous specimen in the time range discussed here is the cranium and broken parietal from a second individual discovered in 1976 at Bodo (Asfaw 1983; Clark et al. 1994:1907; Rightmire 1996). It came from a deposit composed of conglomerates and sands associated with mammal bones and Acheulian artifacts. The most recent age estimate reported is a ^{39}argon/^{40}argon date between 640,000 and 550,000 years old (Clark et al. 1994; Deino and McBrearty 2002:206; Rightmire 2001b:127). Rightmire (2001b:126) describes the skull as similar to *Homo erectus* in its massive face, projecting brow, and low constricted frontal with midline keeling, parietal angular torus, and thick vault. But it is more like *Homo heidelbergensis* in its enlarged brain (around 1300 cc), divided supraorbital torus, and other facial features (Rightmire 2001b:127). A fragmentary cranium has also been reported from the late Acheulian and Middle Stone Age site of Garba III at Melka Kunturé; little other information is available (Rightmire 1984:302). A hominin mandible was also recovered in 1933 from Middle Stone Age levels at Porc Epic Cave or Dire Dawa (Clark 1988:262). While originally classified by Vallois as "Neanderthaloid," it has since been reclassified as either *Homo heidelbergensis* or anatomically modern (Brandt 1986:58–59; Bräuer 1984:387). The archaeological context of both of these finds is reviewed in chapter 8.

Three crania have been described from the Upper Herto Member of the Bouri Formation in the Middle Awash; this unit is considered to be Late Middle Pleistocene in age (Haile-Selassie et al. 2004:1; White et al. 2003:742; map 9.1). The first, BOU-VP-16/1, is a nearly complete adult cranium, only missing the left side of the calvarium. Longer than other moderns', the skull has an estimated brain size of 1,450 cc (White et al. 2003:742). Its occipital is strongly flexed with a massive protuberance, but not a bun as in Neanderthals. It exhibits a broad face with moderate alveolar prognathism (White et al. 2003:742). This specimen is "indistinguishable from anatomically modern *Homo sapiens*" (White et al. 2003:743). The second specimen, BOU-VP-16/2, is even larger. A fragmentary adult cranium, its occipital is not as angled as the first, but both have thick vaults (White et al. 2003:742). BOU-VP-16/43 is a left parietal fragment, and BOU-VP-16/5 is a less complete juvenile cranium, representing a child of six to seven years of age. Its partial dentition includes deciduous molars, unerupted fully formed canine and premolar crowns, as well as an M^1 with wear facets (White et al. 2003:743). All of these specimens are described as morphologically intermediate between archaic and modern Africans. They were assigned to a new subspecies, *Homo sapiens idaltu* or "elder" in the Afar language and are "a population that is on the verge of anatomical modernity but not yet fully modern" (White et al. 2003:745). All three exhibit cut marks and are associated with large mammal remains as well as Acheulian and Middle Stone Age artifacts (Clark et al. 2003:750–751; Stringer 2003:692).

Most recently, five cranial specimens have been collected from surface deposits at Aduma (10°25′N, 40°31′E) and Bouri in the Middle Awash (Haile-Selassie et al. 2004:1). Surface finds associated with Middle Stone Age artifacts, they are estimated to be between 70,000 and 105,000 years old, making them the youngest hominins from this important fossil region (Haile-Selassie et al. 2004:1, 9). They include much of the cranial vault, but no facial remains or teeth. They exhibit a mosaic of modern and near-modern features and are interpreted as the logical descendants of *Homo sapiens idaltu* (Haile-Selassie et al. 2004:9).

The Omo River flows south into Lake Turkana from across the border in Ethiopia. On its west side, the Shungura Formation has yielded fragmentary hominin and numerous fossil animal remains, ranging from 4 to less than 1 million years ago. In the younger Kibish Formation, there are two crania and a partial skeleton. In 1967, Omo I was recovered partly in situ from Member 1 at locality KHS (or Kamoya's Hominid Site; 5°24.15′N, 35°55.81′E). It was originally dated to around 130,000 to 100,000 years ago, using a thorium/uranium estimate on *Etheria* mollusc shells (Butzer et al. 1969; McDougall et al. 2004:734). It consists of a rear braincase (occipital, parietals), some frontal and facial fragments, as well as a partial postcranial skeleton (Rightmire 1984:313–314; 1989:109). More fragments were recovered recently by a team who revisited the site to collect samples for ^{39}argon/^{40}argon dating (McDougall et al. 2004:734). The large, thick-boned skull is described as modern in shape; the front is less complete and exhibits a broad, flat forehead with brow ridges that are thickened medially (Stringer and Gamble 1993:129). The post-crania include part of the upper limb girdle, one forearm and hand, some vertebrae, part of the right femur, both tibiae, and the right fibula and foot; they are described as essentially modern (Day 1986:244–245; Kennedy 1984).

Omo II is a 1967 surface find from the PHS or Paul's (Abell) Hominid Site (5°24.55′N, 35°54.07′E), about 3 km to the northwest (McDougall et al. 2004:735). It was assumed to be of the same age as Omo I ((Butzer et al. 1969; Rightmire 1989:109), but both now are up to 195,000 years old (McDougall et al. 2004:736). In Member 1 of the Kibish Formation (Smith 1992b:244), the PHS site was recently revisited recently (McDougall et al. 2004; Rightmire 2001b:127; Shea et al. 2004). The skull of Omo II is more complete than Omo I, with a cranial capacity of 1,400 cc. Its braincase is long and low, with sagittal keeling and a curved occipital region, all of which would be characteristic of *Homo heidelbergensis* (Day 1986:245; Rightmire 1989:109–110). Rightmire (1989:110) concludes that "it may be too soon to identify the Omo skeletons as related unequivocally to recent humans." Omo III is composed of a glabellar and a frontoparietal fragment; the glabellar fragment is described as archaic (Day 1986:245).

EAST AFRICA

Researchers in East Africa have recovered a few similar specimens, either archaic or modern. Excavations in 1973 near Lake Ndutu at Olduvai Gorge led to the discovery of a single hominin skull, other fossil remains, and numerous artifacts (Mturi 1976; Rightmire 1983, 2001b:126; Clarke 1990). They came from a greenish sandy clay layer that belongs to the Upper Masek Beds (Rightmire 2001b:126). These are currently estimated to be between 490,000 and 780,000 years old (Deino and McBrearty 2002:206–207). As reconstructed by Ron Clarke (1990), the skull has an estimated cranial capacity of about 1,100 cc (Rightmire 1990:207, 1998a, 2001b:126), and shows a mixture of *Homo erectus* and *Homo sapiens* traits. Associated artifacts are Acheulian, but with a high percentage of spheroids and polyhedrons, cores, and flakes (Rightmire 1984:301).

The Lake Turkana basin also includes hominins dating to the Middle and Upper Pleistocene. KNM-ER 3884 or the Guomde cranium is considered to be an early modern human, although its context and age are not clear. It was recovered from Ileret close to where the ER 999 femur was found (Kelly 1996a:104). Analysis in the 1980s stressed the presence of a modern posterior vault, but with a supraorbital torus similar to archaic *Homo sapiens* (Stringer and Gamble 1993:129). Gamma ray spectrometry dates average around 272,000 years old, while uranium-series dates average 9,000 years older. ER 999 or the Guomde femur is estimated to be around 300,000 years old. It comes from a layer 9 to 11 m above the base of what was once called the Guomde Formation (now the Galana Boi Formation) (Bräuer 2001b:191; Kelly and Harris 1992:30; Kelly 1996a:104). ES-11693, a surface find of a cranium with a damaged face, comes from Eliye Springs, West Turkana (Bräuer 1989:131; Smith 1992b:244). It shows a mix of *Homo erectus* and archaic *Homo sapiens* features. The braincase is large but low, with a wide frontal. The occipital area is shaped like LH-18, or Ngaloba (Rightmire 1989).

From deposits west of Lake Baringo belonging to the Kapthurin Formation, a number of specimens have been recovered. There are two mandibles, BK 67 and BK 8518; these are considered to be archaic as they lack a mental eminence or chin (Deino and McBrearty 2002:207). Others include BK 63, a right metatarsal; BK 64, a proximal phalanx; and BK 65, an ulna (Deino and McBrearty 2002:207). For Wood, these would be classified as *Homo erectus*; for Stringer, as archaic *Homo sapiens*. McBrearty and Brooks (2000) see them as *Homo rhodesiensis*, along with Kabwe and Bodo (Deino and McBrearty 2002:207).

From Lake Eyasi to the east of Olduvai, archaeological investigations have uncovered a few hominin specimens. These include three molars excavated from the Kisese level at Mumba Cave; these are classified as archaic *Homo sapiens* (Mehlman 1989:19). At the Skull site, northeast of the lake, Kohl-Larson recovered fragmentary fossil remains of three individuals in 1935, now suggested to be over 200,000 years old. Weinert originally classified them as *Africanthropus njarasensis*, after Lake Njara, an alternate name for Lake Eyasi. But it was later discovered that this genus had already been assigned to the Florisbad skull (McBrearty 1986:56), so they became *Homo njarasensis* (Reck and Kohl-Larson 1936; White et al. 2003:745).

In the Ngaloba Beds at Laetoli, stratified above the famous footprint tuff, the LH-18 skull was excavated from a layer containing Middle Stone Age artifacts and fauna (Day et al. 1980; Smith 1992b:244; Clark 1981:177; Cohen 1996). One uranium/thorium date on an associated giraffe vertebra is estimated to be 129,000 ± 4,000 (Th-230) or 108,000 ± 30,000 years old (Pa-231) (Bräuer 1989:129; Smith 1992b:244). On geological correlation with Ndutu, it was estimated to be 120,000 ± 30,000 years old (Smith 1992b:244). Using amino acid racemization from ostrich eggshell, it is now estimated to be over 200,000 or between 100,000 and 200,000 years old (Bräuer 1989:131, 2001b:193). The skull has an estimated volume of 1,350 cc and exhibits a rounded occipital, expanded parietals, a small but continuous brow ridge, and a flattened, narrow forehead (Stringer and Gamble 1993:127; Rightmire 1989:110, 117). There is no keeling along the midline, and a canine fossa is present in the maxilla (Rightmire 1989:110, 118). It is either interpreted as transitional from archaic to modern humans (Smith 1992b:245; Rightmire 2001b:127), or as an early modern human, "though robust, fully sapient" (Clark 1981:177).

SOUTHERN AFRICA

Few fossil hominins are known from Central Africa, but this is the source of one of the most famous, Kabwe or Broken Hill, from cave deposits north of Lusaka in Zambia (Rightmire 1990:211; map 10.1). A number of bones were found by miners in 1921 and immediately labeled "Rhodesian Man," since Zambia was Northern Rhodesia at the time. Remains consisted of a cranium, one partial maxilla, one parietal, and several postcranial bones representing more than one individual (Day 1986:268; Rightmire 1990:211). Arthur Smith Woodward, classifying them as *Homo rhodesiensis*, considered them to be a Neanderthal (Bowler 1987:38; Woodward 1921, 1931). The skull exhibits a long, low cranium, massive brows and face, and a thick supraorbital torus. The frontal is flattened with slight midline keeling (Rightmire 2001b:123). Similar to Ndutu, Elandsfontein, and Bodo (Rightmire 2001b:123), Kabwe is a mixture of archaic and more modern features. The fossil hominins are associated with late Acheulian or early Middle Stone Age artifacts, and the faunal remains, including some extinct species, are estimated to be between 700,000 and 400,000 years old (Rightmire 1984:299, 2001b:127).

From southern Africa come a number of archaic and early modern human specimens (map 10.1). This is probably the region that has provided the bulk of our information about Upper Pleistocene African human evolution. From dunes near Saldanha Bay in the Western Cape comes a single cranium and fragmentary mandible, discovered by Keith Jolly and Ronald Singer in 1953. Referred to interchangeably as Elandsfontein, Hopefield, or Saldanha, the skull consists of the frontal and parietal walls and some of the occiput; both the base and the face are missing (Rightmire 2001b:126). Associated faunal material is considered to be of late Middle Pleistocene age, between 700,000 and 400,000 years old (Rightmire 2001b:127).

In 1832, a cranium and associated tooth were discovered at the mineral springs at Florisbad (Deacon 1992:178; Kuman et al. 1999:1409). The cranium consists of the frontal, parts of both parietals, and an incomplete right side of the face; it was associated with Middle Stone Age artifacts (Smith 1992b:244; Rightmire 1984:311). Rightmire (1984:311) suggests that it has a higher, broader forehead and less postorbital constriction than Kabwe, but shares with it other archaic *sapiens* features. This specimen was originally classified as *Homo helmei* (Dreyer 1935; Kuman et al. 1999:1410); this name continues to be used by some researchers (Foley and Lahr 1997; Lahr and Foley 1994, 1998, 2001; McBrearty and Brooks 2000) for a stage between *Homo heidelbergensis* and anatomically modern humans. Florisbad was dated to over 100,000 using uranium series (Smith 1992b:244), and an upper third molar tooth provides an electron spin resonance date of 259,000 ± 35,000 years ago (Bräuer 2001b:193; Klein 2001b:5). Another presumed archaic hominin is the mandible fragment from the late Acheulian layers at the Cave of Hearths in the Makapan Valley. A long archaeological sequence here ranges from the Late Acheulian through the Middle Stone Age (Mason 1962:163).

Early modern humans come from a number of South African sites. The Hoedjiespunt 1 site on Saldanha Bay in the Western Cape (33°01′45″S, 17°57′37″E) is a large fossil dune landscape, with several archaeological and palaeontological sites (Stynder et al. 2001:369). From a fossil hyena lair (the HOMS layer), researchers in 1996 recovered four hominin teeth, four to five fragments of a cranium, and two postcranial elements from one or two individuals (Parkington 1999:27). A uranium-series estimate on ostrich eggshell ranges between 130,000 and 180,000 years ago (Parkington 1999:27), while electron spin resonance, geological context, and the fauna puts the site between 300,000 and 74,000 years old (Klein 1999:399; 2001b:4). Two teeth, a left central and a left lateral mandibular incisor, come from a single subadult individual. They are described as relatively worn, but with a crown diameter similar to other Middle Pleistocene Africans, much larger than recent people (Stynder et al. 2001:369). The others are two maxillary molars, a left M^2 and a right M^3. These probably come from the same individual and are similar to other Middle Pleistocene samples (Stynder et al. 2001:369). A tibia was discovered in 1998 and is described as similar to that from Boxgrove, England (Stynder et al. 2001:379; Stringer and Trinkaus 1999). A single upper premolar and a phalanx come from a hyena den at the Sea Harvest site near Hoedjiespunt (Rightmire and Deacon 2001:542; Thackeray 1992:414). These are estimated to be between 128,000 and 40,000 years ago using radiocarbon and geological inference (Klein 1999:399, 2001b:4).

Equus Cave near Taung in the Northern Cape has produced eight isolated permanent teeth (including three molars) and one fragment of a mandible (Rightmire and Deacon 2001:542; Thackeray 1992:414). Associated with Middle Stone Age artifacts, they are variably estimated to be between 90,000 and 100,000 years old (Grine 2000:140; Klein 2001b:2; Rightmire 1989:114), or between 75,000 and over 27,000 years ago (Klein 1999:399, 2001b:4).

The most important early modern human sites in South Africa are found along the southern coast: Klasies River, Die Kelders, and Blombos Cave. The Klasies River sites (formerly referred to as Klasies River Mouth) are a series of cave openings into a cliff. Excavations by Singer and Wymer (1982) at the main site in 1967 and 1968 produced a number of variable, early modern human bones. KRM 13400 is a right mandibular body broken behind the M_2; KRM 16425 is a partial frontal with scratch marks that researchers such as Tim White think are cultural modifications (Rightmire and Deacon 1991:143, 2001:538). KRM 16651 is a left zygomatic; it is described as large relative to modern humans, but as not archaic in appearance (Rightmire and Deacon 1991:143; Bräuer and Singer 1996a, 1996b). KRM 41658 is the single largest piece of cranial vault, comprising part of the right parietal and a section of the frontal squama (Rightmire and Deacon 1991:143). Some postcranial elements are also known. The fossils are interpreted as a single, sexually dimorphic, population (Rightmire and Deacon 2001:536). Most of the early finds came from Cave 1 and cluster in front of the excavated area (Rightmire and Deacon 2001:536). More recent work by Hilary Deacon has led to more hominin discoveries.

The oldest level is the LBS or the Light Brown Sands Member. Deposition began in the last interglacial (MIS 5e), when sea level was similar to present (Rightmire and Deacon 1991:133). Two hominin maxillary fragments were recovered from these levels in cave 1A; they are estimated to be about 120,000 years old (Bräuer 2001b:193; Rightmire and Deacon 1991:133).The SAS Member is composed of interspersed layers of sands and cultural debris. Most age estimates put the SAS Member into MIS 5c. The base was ESR dated to an average of 94,000 using linear uptake and 88,000 using early uptake

(Smith 1992b:246). Many hominin remains are associated with this level. These include the 41815 mandible from the base of SAS Member in cave 1B, the most complete specimen at the site (Rightmire and Deacon 1991:135; Bräuer 2001b:194). Other finds include a first metatarsal and lumbar vertebra from Cave 1, a proximal right ulna, and several teeth (Rightmire and Deacon 1991:143). More recent discoveries include a few more teeth from shell midden deposits at the base of the SAS and a phalanx from an overlying talus deposit (Rightmire and Deacon 2001:538).

The next level is the RF Member, representing about a meter of sand in caves 1A and 2. There are Middle Stone Age artifacts but no hominin fossils. The Upper Member above it includes the Howieson's Poort archaeological horizon. Two parietal fragments and some isolated teeth have been recovered. While fragmentary, the hominin fossils from Klasies River give a minimum number of ten individuals in layers dated between 120,000 and 90,000 years old (Deacon 1992:179; Rightmire and Deacon 1991:132). They exhibit a wide range of variation. Of the five mandibles, four with the symphysis intact, only one has a chin, according to Smith (1992b:246). He interprets them as not fully modern, but close to the transition (Smith 1992b:246). However, Rightmire and Deacon describe the whole collection as robust and strongly sexually dimorphic, but basically modern (Deacon 1992:179).

Blombos Cave (34°25′S, 21°13′E) has become the most important new archaeological site for assessing issues of behavioral modernity in the South African Middle Stone Age. The stratigraphic sequence is composed of a 2,000-year-old Later Stone Age layer, then sterile sand, followed by the Stillbay and other Middle Stone Age levels. Excavations in 1997 and 1998 produced four isolated hominin teeth: a left deciduous first upper molar, a deciduous right central incisor, and right upper first and second permanent premolars (Grine et al. 2000; Rightmire and Deacon 2001:542; Grine and Henshilwood 2002:294). Further work in 1999 and 2000 led to the recovery of five more teeth: an adult right upper first or second premolar, a molar fragment, a right deciduous first molar, a left deciduous second molar, and a left deciduous central incisor, all from the maxilla (Grine and Henshilwood 2002:294). Together, these represent a minimum number of five individuals, most of whom are juveniles (Grine and Henshilwood 2002:297).

Die Kelders was first excavated by Schweizer between 1969 and 1973; thirteen hominin teeth were recovered. Later work by Marean and others produced fourteen more specimens (Grine 2000:129–30). Of these twenty-seven hominin remains, twenty-four are isolated teeth; there is also a mandible fragment and two middle hand phalanges, totally a minimum of ten individuals, all subadults (Grine 2000:129–131). They are estimated to be between 59,000 and 78,000 years old (Grine 2000:130). The teeth are larger than those in more recent African populations, but are similar to those from Klasies River, Equus, and Witkrans Caves (Grine 2000:141).

Morris and colleagues have recently reported a new age estimate for a cranium and first cervical vertebra discovered at Hofmeyer in the Eastern Cape in 1954 (Morris et al. 2005). Sediment within the braincase was recently dated through optically stimulated luminescence to $36,400 \pm 6,200$ years ago, making it one of the few specimens known from this time range in sub-Saharan Africa (Morris et al. 2005).

Border Cave near Swaziland is an important site that is often cited as proof of the presence of early modern humans during the Middle Stone Age. Here there is a 4 m sequence of alternating brown sands (BS) and white ash (WA) layers. A number of hominins have been discovered and are referred to as BC1 through BC8. BC1 is an incomplete cranial vault and possible associated postcranial remains, while BC2 is a partial mandible. Both were discovered by guano hunters between 1941 and 1942. Their provenience is unclear, but sediments adhering to the bones are similar to those from the Middle Stone Age levels (Deacon 1992:179; Bräuer 1989:128). The best estimate is that they come from deeper than the 4WA layer. If BC1 is from the 5BS, moderns could have been present as early as 170,000 years ago; if both were associated with the 4BS, they would be around 82,000 years old (Grün and Beaumont 2001:478, 480). BC3 is a partial infant skeleton excavated from the 4BS level in 1941. It is associated with a perforated *Conus bairstowi* seashell. Stratified beneath a Howieson's Poort level, BC3 is estimated to be between 70,000 and 80,000 years old (Grün and Beaumont 2001:478). BC4 is an Iron Age skeleton (Stringer and Gamble 1993:130), while BC5 is a nearly complete adult mandible discovered in 1974 in the 3WA (Howieson's Poort) layer. The most recent estimate, using electron spin resonance, is that BC 5 dates to 74,000 $\pm$ 5,000 years ago (Grün and Stringer 1991:182–183; Grün and Beaumont 2001:478; Grün et al. 2003:155). Some researchers such as Klein believe that BC3 and BC5 come from later graves that are intrusive into the Middle Stone Age layers (Bräuer 1989:128; Mitchell 2002b:3–4). More recent finds are BC6,

BC7, and BC8, discovered during removal of about a cubic meter of disturbed deposits. BC6 is a humerus, BC7 a proximal ulna, and BC8a and BC8b are two metatarsals (Grün and Beaumont 2001:477).

OUT OF AFRICA II: THE BEGINNINGS?

The earliest evidence of modern humans outside of Africa is in the Levant, the narrow coastal strip along the eastern shores of the Mediterranean. There are at least sixteen individuals known from Jebel Qafzeh and over ten from the Mugharet es Skhūl (Rightmire and Deacon 1991:155). Qafzeh was originally excavated by Neuville and Stekelis from 1932 to 1935, and then again by Vandermeersch (1981) between 1965 and 1979. Thermoluminescence dates on twenty burned flints average around 92,000 ± 5,000 years old (Valladas et al. 1988), something confirmed by electron spin resonance (Bar-Yosef 1992b:262).

Most of the Qafzeh hominins come from a terrace entrance to the cave. Upper levels are rich in fauna and contain many lithic artifacts, while the lower ones contain burials and hearths, few artifacts, and variable numbers of animal bones (Bar-Yosef 1989b:171). The archaeological sequence is Levalloiso-Mousterian, with a preference for radial preparation of cores (Bar-Yosef 1992b:262). This classical Levallois technique is most like that from Tabun layer C.

The Mugharet es Skhūl is located on Mount Carmel and also contains Vandermeersch's (1981) "Proto Cro-Magnons." Both Skhūl and Qafzeh most likely date to MIS 5e, an extremely warm phase when the Levant was an extension of Africa. While some researchers see this as the beginning of the Out of Africa II movement, it is more likely a precocious attempt that failed. As the cold returned, Neanderthals entered the Middle East, probably from further north in Eurasia, and the next modern humans found here are less than 40,000 years old. Typical Neanderthal sites are Kebara and Tabun, the latter of which provides the cultural reference sequence for much of the Middle East. At Kebara, an adult Neanderthal burial was discovered in 1983 in layer XII; two infants in layer X are also Neanderthals. The adult burial is missing the cranium as well as the right lower limb and most of the left limb. However, the hyoid and mandible are present in anatomical position, suggesting that the skull was removed in antiquity. The skeleton is of an adult male, estimated to be around 1.74 m tall, and is dated to between 61,000 and 59,000 using thermoluminescence (Bar-Yosef et al. 1992:526).

Garrod's early excavations at Tabun, using artificial horizontal layers, have made it almost impossible to determine from which level the hominins came. There are three depositional units: the lower sandy unit composed of layers G, F, and E; a middle unit of loam or loess comprising layers D and C; and an upper unit equaling layers B and the fill of chimney (Bar-Yosef 1992b:262). Layers D, C, and B are associated with Middle Palaeolithic cultural horizons. D is now estimated to be between 115,000 and 90,000 years old and C between 90,000 and 60,000 years old. Two hominins are known from Tabun—a partial female skeleton (Tabun I) and a mandible (Tabun II). Both are said to come from Tabun C level. But Neanderthals elsewhere in the Levant largely date to Tabun B, after 60,000 years ago. To make matters even more complicated, Rak (1998) has recently proposed that the Tabun people belong in the same group as Skhūl and Qafzeh.

At the onset of the Upper Palaeolithic, the number of archaeological and fossil hominin sites drops off precipitously in both the Levant and Africa. This is the reason why it is so hard to study the Middle/Upper Palaeolithic transition. In the Levant, evidence for human occupation only picks up again with the Natufian after 18,000 years ago, the last Upper Palaeolithic hunter-gatherer culture prior to the emergence of plant and animal domestication (Gilead 1991).

HOW THE FOSSIL EVIDENCE DEMONSTRATES OUR RECENT AFRICAN ORIGIN

The African record fossil hominin record can best be understood as showing a sequence extending from *Homo erectus* through *Homo heidelbergensis* to anatomically modern *Homo sapiens*. The earliest modern people are almost 200,000 years old. Since archaic and modern humans share many physical features, it is hard to draw the line to call them modern. Was the transition a gradual process of modernization (Bräuer 2001b:196), or a relatively sudden speciation event?

More transitional forms include Jebel Irhoud, Eliye Springs, Florisbad, Ngaloba, and Omo Kibish II (Smith 1992b:245). Early moderns are associated with Middle Palaeolithic or Middle Stone Age assemblages, while archaic humans are often found with late Acheulian artifacts. At the time of the proposed Out of Africa II migration, there is a paucity of fossil and archaeological evidence. In the South African Cape, there seems to be a gap in the record between these early moderns and their Later Stone Age descendants.

Sites like Klasies show no signs of occupation after 50,000 years ago while the Later Stone Age levels at Blombos and Die Kelders are only 2,000 years old. Few of the known human fossils were collected using modern methods, and their age and cultural association remain suspect. As Parkington (1999:27) reminds us, "it is sobering to think that—Klasies River Mouth aside—almost all the key human fossil specimens of Pleistocene southern Africa are without proper context." For Rightmire (2001a:233), the evidence is "frustrating." But anatomically these fossils are either modern or almost modern, and nothing contradicts the idea of an early appearance of *Homo sapiens* here (Bräuer 2001a:183; Rightmire 2001a:235). For Desmond Clark (1989:565), "the ball is now in the court of human paleontologists and archaeologists to reexamine their own data to see what sort of a bearing they have and how they might contribute to a more precise assessment of where, when, what, and how this transformation and distribution took place."

8

The Archaeological Evidence from North Africa

[The Aterians were] *a Palaeolithic people, formidably armed in comparison with its neighbours: a people who ranged southwards probably to the Niger bend, and pushed eastwards across the width of Africa to the Nile boundary, are people to have adventured beyond, one might suppose, under the same incalculable stimulus, wresting the contracting hunting grounds and watering places from weaker groups, still in thrall to an outmoded Upper Levalloiso-Mousterian tradition, or its deteriorated derivatives.* (Caton-Thompson 1946a:107)

This chapter reviews the archaeological evidence associated with the earliest modern humans in North Africa and the Sahara. The terminology used to describe North African Upper Pleistocene sites is generally based on the European Palaeolithic sequence. However, some researchers have recently expressed a preference for the three sub-Saharan Stone Ages (Hawkins and Kleindienst 2002:602; Kleindienst 2001; Garcea 2004). This may be to emphasize cultural connections with the south. This review will use both systems interchangeably, depending on the preference of the original researchers.

In many parts of North Africa, there is a long record of Late Acheulian and Middle Palaeolithic occupation. Most Middle Palaeolithic sites are older than 50,000 years and are referred to as Levallois, Mousterian, or Aterian. As elsewhere, Levallois industries are those with standardized tools produced using prepared core technology. No further shaping is done after the removal of the blank. Mousterian tools, on the other hand, are flakes struck from circular (and sometimes unipolar or bipolar) cores that are subsequently retouched into side scrapers, points, notches, and denticulates. Aterian industries are usually stratified above other Middle Palaeolithic layers, and contain distinctive foliates or leaf-shaped pieces, as well as stemmed or tanged scrapers and points. The stem or tang on the proximal end of tools is assumed to be an adaptation for hafting tools onto a shaft or handle. Tanged pieces or pedunculates are present in all regions of North Africa as far east as the Western Desert of Egypt. But they have never been found in the Nile Valley (Débénath 1994; Garcea 2004; Van Peer 1998).

While Middle Palaeolithic sites are common, Early Upper Palaeolithic ones are rare. There appears to be a hiatus in occupation extending from the late Mousterian (or Aterian) until after the last glacial maximum around 18,000 years ago. Few sites have any sign of human presence in between (Close 1986:175) when deserts expanded, and the whole region may have been uninhabitable. After this, industries are generally Mode 5 Epipalaeolithic ones since they continue into the Holocene with little obvious typological or technological change. They are dominated by backed bladelets, small blades with nearly vertical (90°) retouch running down at least one lateral edge. They may reflect the re-entry of people into the region as glacial conditions ameliorated, possibly along the Mediterranean coast, and "seem to appear out of nowhere" (Close 2002:32).

One of the few sites with an Early Upper Palaeolithic record is Haua Fteah, the famous cave in western Libya. It was first excavated by McBurney (1967) in the early 1950s. Here a Mode 4 industry, the Dabban, is stratified between a Mode 3 Levalloiso-Mousterian and a Mode 5 Epipalaeolithic assemblage, the Eastern Oranian, the local version of the Iberomaurusian (McBurney 1967). But there is also an earlier Mode 4 industry, the Libyan Pre-Aurignacian, which is stratified under a Levalloiso-Mousterian occupation layer. Sodmein Cave, located near the Red Sea coast in Egypt (Van Peer et al. 1996) may also have an early Upper Palaeolithic human presence, but this remains to be proven. There are many Mode 4 or Mode 5 industries throughout North Africa, but they are of terminal Pleistocene or Holocene age (Close 2002; Lubell 1974; Lubell et al. 1984; Lubell and Sheppard 1997; Rahmani 2004). It is therefore next to impossible to test the idea of a sudden behavioral change with the transition from Mode 3 Mousterian to Mode 4/5 Upper Palaeolithic or Epipalaeolithic technology. If this time period sees the Out of Africa II migration, it has not left much in the way of direct evidence of people, let alone dispersals.

The earliest modern humans in North Africa are associated with Middle Palaeolithic archaeological assemblages; many are close to 100,000 years old (see chapter 7). Their associated assemblages are variably classified as Mousterian, Levalloiso-Mousterian, and Aterian (Débénath 1994; Garcea 2004; Van Peer 1998), depending on their characteristic tools and the ways in which they were produced. All of these early sites fall into the Mode 3 tradition. The first true signs of change only come with the (apparently) pan-North African Aterian. It may represent some of the earliest expression of ethnic identity in material culture (Sackett 1977, 1982; Willoughby 2001a).

THE NILE VALLEY: A CORRIDOR OUT OF AFRICA?

The Nile Valley provides one of the best cultural records for the archaeology of the late Middle and Upper Pleistocene. Surprisingly, however, it provides little direct information about the timing for the hypothesized Out of Africa II migration, let alone about routes which these early people could have taken. Vermeersch (2001:103) points out that many researchers, including those like Van Peer (1998) who work on Egyptian sites, take this dispersal route for granted, even though the Levant and the Nile Valley are separated by over 2,700 km. In drier, cooler glacial periods, the Nile would also have been inhospitable (Close 1986:175). This may have forced people to move into new areas, possibly along the Red Sea or Mediterranean coasts.

The Egyptian Middle Palaeolithic can be traced back to the Late Acheulian when hand axes become associated with bifacial foliates and Nubian core production methods (Vermeersch 2001:105). Sites older than 50,000 years ago are found along the edges of the Nile Valley south of Asyut and north of the Second Cataract at Wadi Halfa (Marks 1992:240) (map 8.1). Much of what we know about the Egyptian Middle Palaeolithic comes from research done by a Belgian team composed of Pierre Vandermeersch, Philip Van Peer, and their colleagues at the Catholic University of Louvain (Van Peer 1991, 1998, 2001; Van Peer et al. 1996, 2003; Vermeersch et al. 1984a, 1984b, 1984c, 1998). They divide the period into three phases: the Early, Middle, and Late Middle Palaeolithic. Early Middle Palaeolithic sites are found in the Nile Valley before

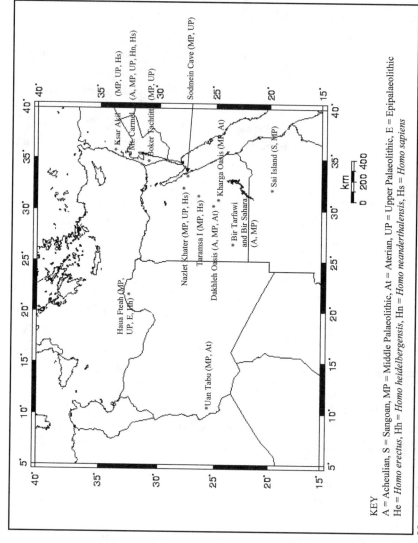

Map 8.1 Stone Age sites in Northeast Africa and the Levant

KEY

A = Acheulian, S = Sangoan, MP = Middle Palaeolithic, At = Aterian, UP = Upper Palaeolithic, E = Epipalaeolithic
He = *Homo erectus*, Hh = *Homo heidelbergensis*, Hn = *Homo neanderthalensis*, Hs = *Homo sapiens*

the last interglacial (MIS 5e) (Van Peer 1998:117). Some assemblages contain bifaces, bifacial foliates, thick Nubian scrapers, and special Levallois point production methods (Nubian 1 and 2) (figure 8.1). There are also assemblages without these diagnostic features, the non-Nubian Middle Palaeolithic (Van Peer 1998:118). In both Nubian 1 and 2, the upper surface of a Levallois core is designed to produce pointed flakes along a central ridge (Vermeersch 2001:105). Nubian 1 flint knappers make points or pointed flakes using a distal ridge created from the platform opposite to the one from which the blank is removed (Van Peer 1991:125). Nubian 2 toolmakers chose instead to strike the preparation flakes from the lateral edges (Van Peer 1998:120). Bifacial foliates and tanged pieces more characteristic of the Aterian are also present (Vermeersch 2001:105). Early Middle Palaeolithic sites are best known from surface sites in Nubia, while there are no sites of this age in Middle and Lower Egypt (Van Peer 1998:118).

Middle Middle Palaeolithic levels are stratified above Early Middle Palaeolithic ones throughout the Lower Nile Valley (Van Peer 1998:118). Van Peer divides them into two categories, the N group or Nubian Mousterian and the K group or Denticulate Mousterian. N group sites are found in northern Egypt and the Egyptian desert and use the Nubian 1 method to produce Levallois points. Occasional Nubian end scrapers, side scrapers, and foliates are

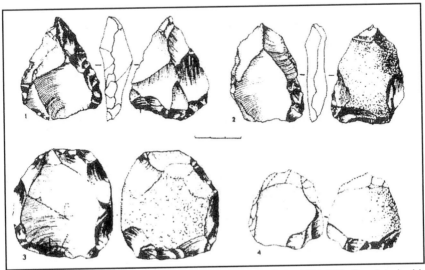

Figure 8.1 Nubian 1 and 2 production methods (Van Peer 1991:121). Reprinted with permission of Elsevier

also present, as well as denticulates. Some sites contain hand axes and there are also blades manufactured from single and opposed platform cores (Van Peer 1998:118–119; Marks 1992:243). The K group or Denticulate Mousterian is strikingly different. Nubian Levallois methods are absent, and none of the N group tool types are represented. In general, it is described as similar to the non-Nubian phase of the Early Middle Palaeolithic (Van Peer 1998:119).

The Late Middle Palaeolithic includes industries such as the Halfan of Nubia (Marks 1990; Garcea 2004:39), Safahan, Idfuan, and Khormusan, all of which are presumed to date to between 70,000 and 50,000 years ago. The Id-fuan and Halfan both combine Middle Palaeolithic technological features with Upper Palaeolithic tool types (Van Peer 1998:119; Pleurdeau 2003:44). Flakes and blades begin to be produced from single and double platform cores, while classical Levallois methods are still present (Vermeersch 2001:105). Typical sites include chert extraction localities such as Nazlet Safaha near Qena, as well as living sites near Idfu. Living sites also include burins, notches, and denticulates (Vermeersch 2001:105). Extraction sites are located next to raw material sources and contain only the early stages of tool reduction.

A good example of a chert exploitation site is Taramsa 1 (26°6′N, 32°42′E), a Nubian complex site in use throughout the Middle Palaeolithic (Van Peer 1998:117; Vermeersch et al. 1998; Wurz et al. 2005). A hill capped by cobble deposits, it is located on the left bank of the Nile opposite the modern city of Qena in Upper Egypt (Vermeersch et al. 1998:475; Van Peer 2001:48). An Early Middle Palaeolithic assemblage is characterized by hand axes, foliates, as well as by the use of Nubian point and flake production methods (Vermeersch et al. 1998:475). In the Middle Middle Palaeolithic at Taramsa 1, there are no foliates or hand axes, but Nubian production methods continue to be employed. The Late Middle Palaeolithic occupation, associated with a child burial (Vermeersch et al. 1998), is characterized by the lack of Nubian Levallois methods. Classical Levallois production continues, but now to produce blades (Vermeersch et al. 1998:475). The archaeological material from Taramsa 1 has been dated to between 49,800 ± 12,200 to 80,400 ± 19,000 BP using optically stimulated luminescence (Vermeersch et al. 1998:480–481). A recent techno-logical and typological analysis has revealed general similarities of the Taramsa Middle Palaeolithic to the MSA 1 of Klasies River (Wurz et al. 2005:1).

Khormusan sites are dated by radiocarbon to over 40,000 years ago and are considered to belong to the latest Middle Palaeolithic (Marks 1992:240–241;

Van Peer 2001:53). They contain Levallois flakes as well as denticulates and burins. Khormusan sites, such as the Arkin 5 quarry workshop, are only found in the Sudan around the Second Cataract of the Nile. Marks (1992:243) includes this site in the N group.

Van Peer (1998:120) suggests that there were two techno-complexes throughout the Middle Palaeolithic in Egypt, the Lower Nile Valley and the Nubian. Both are found in the Lower Nile Valley and neighboring deserts throughout the Middle Palaeolithic. He believes that the two may represent behavioral adaptations by separate peoples, only one of whom is native to the area (Van Peer 1998:120). Lower Nile Valley people never employed Nubian production methods, just classical Levallois ones. On the other hand, Nubian sites are defined by their reliance on Levallois prepared core methods and may be the new people (Van Peer 1998:120, 2001:48). Van Peer (1998:127) suggests that they arrived in the Lower Nile Valley from the south sometime during the latter part of the Middle Pleistocene. By the Late Middle Palaeolithic, the Nubian complex disappears from the Nile Valley, but a related culture was present elsewhere, the Aterian (Van Peer 1998:127).

By intensively studying the reduction sequences that produced Nile Valley tools, Van Peer (1998) has argued for some degree of cultural complexity in the Egyptian Middle Palaeolithic. This involves the stockpiling of raw materials and blanks away from their sources, as well as the emergence of stylistic variation in tool kits (Van Peer 1998:115, 121). He discovered that point cores are waste products, while flake cores were often transported for further reduction (Van Peer 1998:124). Toward the end of the Middle Palaeolithic, Levallois methods shifted toward the production of blades, and Upper Palaeolithic–like tools appear (Van Peer 1998:127).

With continued work and better chronology, it may be possible to test Van Peer's (1998:115, 127) idea that Northeast Africa could have been the source of a relatively sudden technological transition which produced the Upper Palaeolithic. But there is little direct evidence in the Nile Valley. Between 38,000 and 25,000 years ago, there are few or no archaeological sites. Close (1986:175) believes that there might have been people here, but their sites would have been subsequently buried by river sediments. Or the Nile was so dry that continuous human occupation would not have been possible. One possible site is the chert quarry at Nazlet Khater 4 near Qena, where bifacial tools, burins, end scrapers, denticulates, and blades are dated between 35,100 and 30,360 years ago (Van Peer 1998:129; Vermeersch et al. 1984a:285; Pinhasi and Semal 2000:270). After 25,000 BP, true Mode 4 Upper Palaeolithic sites appear in the Nile Valley, at places such as Shuwikhat (Van Peer 1998:130; Close and Wendorf 1990:49). Located south of Nazlet Khater, Shuwikhat contains classic Upper Palaeolithic blade and burin assemblages, but no backed bladelets (Close 2002:33). The first Epipalaeolithic industries appear in Upper Egypt around 21,000 years ago and belong to the Fakhurian (Lubell 1974; Close 2002:33). Elsewhere they appear by 18,000 years ago, as conditions warmed. By now, there is direct evidence of a widening economy, a broad spectrum adaptation (Flannery 1969:77) that includes wild cereals and shellfish collecting (Close 1996; Close and Wendorf 1990:49; Wendorf and Schild 1980).

There have been occasional reports of Middle Palaeolithic assemblages in the Nile Valley of neighboring Sudan (Mohamed 1992). The first systematic surveys were done here by K. J. Sanford and William J. Arkell in the 1920s and 1930s. The Aswan High Dam project of the 1960s led to the discovery of numerous Palaeolithic sites in both southern Egypt and the Sudan (Mohamed 1992:72). Mohamed (1992) conducted a survey of the Khartoum area in 1980. She identified one Middle Palaeolithic site at Wadi Seidna (16°15′30″N, 32°32′30″E) and two others at Jebel Mi'Eqil (16°16′15″N, 32°32′30″E). The first is an open-air site located 20 km north of Khartoum on the west bank of the Nile, while the latter is a butte- or flat-topped inselberg 10 km farther north (Mohamed 1992:72, 74). Surface artifacts were collected and analyzed using the Bordes (1961, 1972) method. They include Levallois flakes, retouched tools, and bifaces. Raw materials were mainly locally available silcrete and ferrocrete (Mohamed 1992:77, 82).

Recently there was rather surprising news. Station One is an open-air archaeological site located 30 km east of the Second Cataract in the Eastern Desert of northern Sudan. This site was recorded by Marks in 1964 and called site 1013. Eventually, the name was changed to reflect its location next to the first stop of the Sudanese railway traveling south from Wadi Halfa (Rose 2004b:207). Middle Palaeolithic artifacts are scattered on a single inselberg which rises 20 m above the pre-Nilotic peneplain (Rose 2004b:207). Artifact samples were collected from two separate 10 m² units and only recently analyzed by Rose (2004b:207). A total of 1,939 pieces includes 76 cores and 210 tools; the remainder is debitage (n=1,102) or debris (n=551 pieces). Rose studied all the tools, cores, and 25% of the debitage. The artifacts were mainly quartz obtained from the base of the inselberg. Even though the inselberg is capped by ferrocrete sandstone, the raw material preferred by most Nubian Middle Palaeolithic people, it was hardly used at all at Station One (Rose 2004b:207). There were a range of core forms produced, including centripetal and radial. This is a marked contrast with the uni- or bi-directional Levallois technology more characteristic of the Nubian Mousterian (Rose 2004b:209). Tools include side scrapers, notches, denticulates, small unifacial or bifacial foliate or leaf-shaped points, as well as ovates with flat, invasive retouch (Rose 2004b:209). Foliates are similar to those found in the North African Aterian, but there is no evidence of the diagnostic Aterian tanged pieces here (Rose 2004b:211). Rose (2004b:211) concludes that the tools, raw material preferences, and the distinctive cores all point to links with the East African Middle Stone Age. If so, it is possible that Station One is a unique sign of the Out of Africa II migration.

An Early to Middle Stone Age transitional sequence is also reported from Sai Island, in between the second and third cataracts of the Nile in northern Sudan (Van Peer et al. 2003:187; Rots and Van Peer 2006). Artifacts come from two stratified levels in black Nile sands at the southern foot of Jebel Adu, a 75 m high inselberg (Van Peer et al. 2003:188). The most distinctive tools are thin, bifacial foliates. Tools were manufactured from Levallois, Nubian, and discoidal cores; they are similar to Eastern Sahara ones from MIS 5 and to others belonging to the Nubian Complex (Van Peer et al. 2003:188–189). Lower levels are classified as late Acheulian and contain large, lanceolate hand axes (Van Peer et al. 2003:189). Overlying aeolian sands were dated by optically stimulated luminescence to 223,000 ± 19,000 years ago (Van Peer et al. 2003:190).

Three occupation levels belonging to the Sangoan come from gully fill above the ES sands (Van Peer et al. 2003:190). The Sangoan was originally defined for material from Sango Bay on Lake Victoria in Uganda (McBrearty 1991). It is identified by the presence of core axes, bifaces that retain a cortical pebble butt. At Sai Island, the lowest Sangoanlike level comes from a fine gravel deposit (BLG). No hand axes were recovered. There were few flake tools, but heavy duty (core) tools were common (hammerstones, grindstones, and several core axes). Flakes were struck from discoidal and globular cores (Van Peer et al. 2003:190). As for features, there is a dense ochre concentration and one sandstone slab with evidence of pecking and flaking. Some chert pebbles are covered by ochre, possibly as a result of grinding pigment (Van Peer et al. 2003:191). Middle Sangoan artifacts come from the top of the second or

TLG gravel unit, which is separated from the BLG by a thin layer of coarse sand; they include quartz core axes of Khor Abu Anga type (Van Peer et al. 2003:191). There are two slabs in a circular arrangement with a 2.5 m radius, and one area where sandstone flakes are associated with two lanceolate hand axes. This is the only example where hand axes are associated with Sangoan tools (Van Peer et al. 2003:191). A sand sample above the Middle Sangoan is optically stimulated luminescence dated to 182,000 ± 20,000 years ago (Van Peer et al. 2003:192). An Upper Sangoan is found in a half-meter thick deposit of sands and gravel lenses that represents the final infilling of the gully (Van Peer et al. 2003:192). The mixture of industries leads the researchers to talk about the transition as "an inter-stratification between Acheulean and Sangoan assemblages" (Van Peer et al. 2003:192), rather than a linear progression. A similar pattern is found in other parts of Africa, for example in the Kapthurin Formation west of Lake Baringo in central Kenya (McBrearty 2001; McBrearty et al. 1996).

THE WESTERN DESERT OF EGYPT

What is known about the Stone Age prehistory in the Western Desert of Egypt is mainly the product of research by two separate research teams. One is the Combined Prehistoric Expedition, composed of Fred Wendorf, Romuald Schild, Angela Close, and their colleagues, who have worked at a number of sites, most notably Bir Tarfawi and Bir Sahara East (Wendorf et al. 1987, 1993a, 1993b). The other is the Dakhleh Oasis Project (DOP), where, since 1977, a mainly Canadian and British team has investigated the entire range of human history from the Lower Palaeolithic up until historic times. More recently, at the request of the Supreme Council of Antiquities in Egypt (McDonald 2005), the team has also been working at the nearby Kharga Oasis (Hawkins 2001; Hawkins and Kleindienst 2002; Smith et al. 2004), a locality first investigated by Gertrude Caton-Thompson (1946a, 1952).

As in the Nile Valley, the oases of the Western Desert contain an archaeological record from the late Acheulian and the Middle Palaeolithic up until about 50,000 years ago (Marks 1992:240). Late Acheulian sites contain backed, double backed, and amygdaloidal bifaces, many with thick butts. Levallois flake technology is present, but it is generally radial, without points. Among the retouched tools, denticulates are always important (Marks 1992:241). Human occupation was intermittent and corresponds to periods of increased precipitation. After 50,000 years ago, it appears that the region was too arid; archaeological sites only reappear in the early Holocene, around 12,000 to 11,000 years ago (Wendorf et al. 1993a:1, 4, 1993b:566).

The work of the Combined Prehistoric Expedition (Wendorf et al. 1987, 1993a, 1993b) has led to the delineation of a long cultural record at two sites in the Western Desert, Bir Sahara East and Bir Tarfawi (22°55'N, 28°45'E). These are deflational basins, located about 10 km apart, approximately 350 km southwest of Kharga Oasis (Wendorf et al. 1993a:1). They represent the remains of large, permanent lakes which were filled with water at various points in the Middle and Early Upper Pleistocene (Hill 2001). Archaeological research began here in the early 1970s. The initial interpretation of the sequence saw two phases. The Lower Lacustrine Series represented the oldest human occupation; here a variety of Levallois and Mousterian tools were recovered, including denticulates, side scrapers, and Mousterian points (Wendorf et al. 1993a:3). Stratified above an unconformity at Bir Tarfawi is the Upper Lacustrine Series. It is associated with a lithic assemblage where foliates (leaf-shaped pieces) and tanged tools appear for the first time. This is believed to be the local version of the Aterian (Wendorf et al. 1993a:3, 1993b:570–571), a conclusion which has been controversial (Kleindienst 2001:5; Van Peer 1998:119).

Continuing research has led to the identification of five lake phases associated with Middle Palaeolithic occupations in each basin; these are separated by periods of aridity (Wendorf et al. 1987:55, 1993a:3, 1993b:552, 554; Van Peer 1998:117). All of the Middle Palaeolithic lake phases are older than 60,000 BP and may extend back as far as 230,000 BP (Miller 1993; Schwarcz and Morawska 1993; Schwarcz and Grün 1993b; Wendorf et al. 1993a:1, 1993b:565). Archaeological sites at Bir Tarfawi and Bir Sahara East are classified as living sites, lithic workshops, and/or butchery sites (Wendorf et al. 1987:49). At quarries, cores were extracted and initially worked. They were then taken to the lakeshore and further reduced into Levallois cores and tools. Later these were carried elsewhere for further reduction and use (Wendorf et al. 1993a:5). At secondary workshops at the lakeshore, tools are almost always denticulates (Wendorf et al. 1993a:5). These may represent places where plants were processed; a similar conclusion was reached for BT-14, where grindstones were also recovered (Wendorf et al. 1993b:571). On the other hand, in sites in the dry or drying lake beds, side scrapers and Mousterian points predominate, while flakes or finished tools were imported (Wendorf et al. 1993a:5, 1993b:571). The basic difference between assemblages lies in the relative percentage of denticulates versus side scrapers and Mousterian points (Wendorf et al. 1993b:571). There are also differences over time, as early assemblages are Mousterian or Levallois, while later ones resemble the Aterian (Wendorf et al. 1993b:570–571; Kleindienst 2001:5). Wendorf (et al. 1993a:1) emphasizes continuity and conservatism in tool types over about 100,000 years. The only key differences involve the beginnings of foliates and pedunculates; it is argued that these could have been introduced from elsewhere. Other innovations at this time include the use of ochre and grindstones (Wendorf et al. 1993b:573). Lithic raw materials such as quartzitic sandstone and rare quartz would have been locally available (Wendorf et al. 1993b:570). Faunal remains are limited in numbers and distribution. Gautier (1993:121, 143) interprets them as the product of selective hunting of small gazelles, with more opportunistic meat procurement from larger animals such as buffalo, rhinoceros, and giraffe.

The Dakhleh Oasis is located in a depression 300 to 400 m below the Libyan Plateau in the Western Desert (Hawkins 2001; Hawkins and Kleindienst 2002:603; figure 8.2). Kleindienst reports (2005) that prehistorians of the Dakhleh Oasis Project have conducted over twenty years of foot survey in the region and have established a sequence of occupations ranging from the late Middle Pleistocene through the mid-Holocene. Palaeoenvironmental evidence shows that the oasis was probably continuously habitable, even in hyper-arid times, due to the availability of artesian springs (Churcher and Kleindienst n.d.; Kleindienst et al. 2004).

The Dakhleh Oasis researchers defined a geological sequence made up of various geomorphic units, all of which contain stone which was exploited as raw material for tools. Three Pleistocene and older land surfaces are recognized. These are composed of gravels, terraced alluvial fans, or bajada remnants; the oldest is referred to as P-I, then P-II, and the youngest is P-III (Hawkins and Kleindienst 2002:603). Older Middle Stone Age localities are associated with P-II terraces, while more recent ones are found mainly on P-III and later surfaces (Hawkins and Kleindienst 2002:603–605). They refer to concentrations of artifacts as aggregates rather than sites, "cultural materials drawn from an archaeological occurrence" (Hawkins and Kleindienst 2002:605). An archaeological occurrence is described as "the minimal unit of

Figure 8.2 View of Dakhleh Oasis, Egypt, looking northwest from the rim of the Libyan Plateau, western el-Battikh Promontory, across the Escarpment face and the Piedmont to the oasis Lowland. The Libyan Plateau forms the skyline. Photographed by M. R. Kleindienst in 1987; reprinted with permission of Dr. M. R. Kleindienst

cultural evidence in its context" (Hawkins and Kleindienst 2002:605). While many Middle Stone Age sites have been located, there are no chronometric dates yet (Hawkins and Kleindienst 2002:605), so sites are dated by correlation with material from other Western Desert oases.

Five major lithic raw materials were employed in the Middle Stone Age: Tarawan chert, a second kind of chert (gray brown, in small nodules), various kinds of quartzite, ball chalcedony, and other materials of unknown provenance (Hawkins and Kleindienst 2002:607–608). Three basic cultural phases are identified. The oldest, a generalized MSA, is assigned to the Gifata and Teneida units, the former of which is similar to Caton-Thompson's Lower Levalloisian from Kharga. It is found in nine aggregates at six separate localities. Lithic workshops are found on high terraced gravel remnants of the P-II terrace; they are considered to be Middle Pleistocene or older (Hawkins and Kleindienst 2002:605). A typical Gifata site is Locality 187A, which contains Levallois, flake-blade, and other cores, Levallois flakes, blades and flaking debris, and few tools. Artifacts tend to be large, heavily abraded, and desert varnished. Most of the flakes are local Tarawan chert (Hawkins and Kleindienst 2002:605, 609). Figure 8.3 shows large Gifata Unit Levallois flakes from Local-

Figure 8.3 Large Gifata Unit Levallois flakes from Locality 187A, Sets I and II, Dakhleh Oasis, Egypt. Artifacts represent dispersed workshop occurrences utilizing local cherts from limestones capping the Libyan Plateau (cm scale). Photographed by A. Hollett in 1987; reprinted with permission of Dr. M. R. Kleindienst

ity 187A, Sets I and II. Kleindienst (2005) reports that their location, condition, and morphology place the unit in the same time period as Kharga, which was dated by uranium-series to over 220,000 ± 20,000 years ago. Artifacts represent dispersed workshop occurrences utilizing local cherts from limestones capping the Libyan Plateau (Hawkins and Kleindienst 2002; Kleindienst 2003).

Teneida Unit sites are located in the southeast palaeo-oasis, a previously wet region which is beyond the limit of the modern oasis. An example of such a site is Locality 361, a lag concentration where 2,141 artifacts were collected. It includes the latest Middle Stone Age in the Sheikh Mabruk Unit, as well as an older Middle Stone Age occurrence. Raw materials are the same Tarawan chert (from a minimum of 6 to 10 km away), along with some quartz, quartzite, and petrified wood. Imported limestone cobbles were used as soft hammers or anvils (Hawkins and Kleindienst 2002:609). Another generalized Middle Stone Age was found eroding out of the basal unit of the Pleistocene lake sediments. Aggregates include occupational debris and tools, but few cores or cortical flakes (Hawkins and Kleindienst 2002:606). These lie on the P-III surface, in an area outside of the central lowland of the oasis (Kleindienst 2001:7).

The third Middle Stone Age variant is referred to as the Dakhleh Unit of the Aterian Technocomplex (Hawkins 2001; Hawkins and Kleindienst 2002:606).

It includes tanged and/or basally thinned tools, bifacial foliates, and blades produced by predominantly Levallois methods (Hawkins and Kleindienst 2002:606). Workshops are found in gravel terraces and remnants of terraces, in and on ancient artesian spring mounds, on lagged sandstone surfaces and on Pleistocene lake sediments (Hawkins and Kleindienst 2002:606). Points from Locality 283 are illustrated in figure 8.4. Points were made on Tarawan cherts and are abraded and lightly patinated, but without desert varnish.

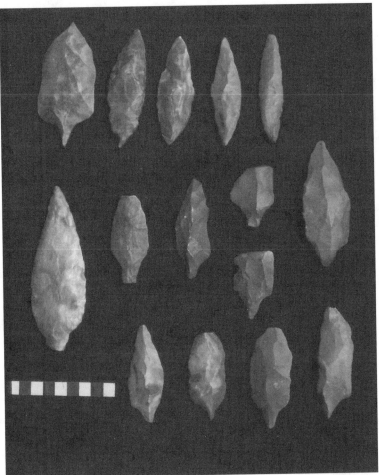

Figure 8.4 Dakhleh Unit (Aterian Complex) points from Locality 283, re-deposited and lagged on the floor of a rock tank basin in the northeastern Lowland, Dakhleh Oasis, Egypt. Points are made on Tarawan cherts, abraded and lightly patinated, but lacking desert varnish. Photographed by M. R. Kleindienst in 1991; reprinted with permission of Dr. M. R. Kleindienst

There is no direct dating at Dakhleh, but the estimated age lies between 90,000 and 40,000 years ago, when local conditions were more humid (Hawkins 2001; Hawkins and Kleindienst 2002; Kleindienst 2005).

Four workshops have been located; all contain Tarawan chert from secondary sources and very few exotic materials (Hawkins and Kleindienst 2002:610, 617). There is no evidence of Libyan Desert silica glass artifacts, a surprise since this material was commonly used elsewhere in Western Desert Aterian sites (Hawkins and Kleindienst 2002:619). Hawkins and Kleindienst (2002:620) conclude that the Aterians may not have been in regular contact with similar groups elsewhere. A fourth Middle Stone Age is referred to as the Khargan Technocomplex. Found on the surface, it is probably younger than the Aterian. A uranium-series date of 40,000 ± 10,000 years ago provides a good minimum date for the Aterian (Hawkins and Kleindienst 2002:605). All Middle Stone Age people here regularly carried Tarawan chert over 10 km, and sometimes up to 40 km, even when other raw materials were closer (Hawkins and Kleindienst 2002:621). Finished tools are found farther away from raw material sources than debitage. At some point, Tarawan chert is replaced by quartzite (Hawkins and Kleindienst 2002:622).

Research at Kharga Oasis was initiated by Caton-Thompson (1946a, 1952) in the 1930s. She identified Acheulian, Lower and Upper Levallois, Kharga Aterian, and Khargan Units (Smith et al. 2004:426), as well as Epipalaeolithic and later occupations. She also identified several Aterian variants with "equatorial antecedents" (Kleindienst 2001:4). Her Levallois assemblages (Caton-Thompson 1946b) are associated with tufas (precipitated calcium carbonate deposits representing wetter periods), while the Kharga Aterian and Khargan are found on tufa surfaces, jebel tops, or in silty pan sediments (Smith et al. 2004:426). Starting in 1998, members of the Dakhleh team began to examine the Stone Age prehistory of this neighboring oasis, becoming the Kharga Oasis Prehistoric Project or KOPP in 2001 (Smith et al. 2004:408). They used the sub-Saharan African sequence to define their sites, and they revised Caton-Thompson's cultural sequence. Lower Levallois assemblages are now referred to as belonging to an older Middle Stone Age or Refuf Unit, while her Upper Levallois is now classified as a younger Middle Stone Age.

Sites range from 250,000 to 40,000 years ago, the same period as those at Bir Sahara East and Bir Tarfawi (Hawkins and Kleindienst 2002:601; Mandel and Simmons 2001; Smith et al. 2004). Four areas with fossil spring tufas, deposits of precipitated calcium carbonates, have been studied (Smith et al. 2004:407–408, 411). Early and Middle Stone Age lithic materials are found on top of the tufas or embedded within them (Smith et al. 2004:407). The oldest and highest level is the Plateau Tufa, 10 to 15 m below the Libyan Plateau. It overlies bedrock and is possibly more than 400,000 years old. There is no sign of humans at this time (Smith et al. 2004:430). Later, there was an erosional phase which removed much of the Plateau Tufa; this occurred during a period of varying rainfall (Smith et al. 2004:430). A more humid period led to the deposition of Wadi Tufa 1, and Acheulian sites are probably both older and possibly younger than this. This was followed by a dry phase at Midauwara leading to wind-induced erosion. Humid phases documented elsewhere at Kharga and Dakhleh are absent here (Smith et al. 2004:431). A second wet phase led to the deposition of Wadi Tufa 2, sometime between 120,000 and 140,000 years ago; younger Middle Stone Age sites date to this period (Smith et al. 2004:431–432). After this time, it is dry again. Subsequent wet phases, dating to 100,000 and 50,000 years ago, are only documented at Mata'na (Smith et al. 2004:434). Middle Stone Age sites are found underneath the 100,000-year-old deposits. There are no archaeological finds associated with the 50,000-year-old event, although the Kharga researchers think that it could correspond to the Khargan Aterian or Khargan Unit (Smith et al. 2004:434).

THE RED SEA AND NORTHEAST AFRICA: COASTAL ADAPTATIONS?

Archaeologists have recently become increasingly interested in the prehistory of the lands bordering the Red Sea. This region could provide a route for hominin dispersal out of Africa, an alternative to the Nile Valley. There is some support for this from genetics (Quintana-Murci et al. 1999), as well as from the reconstruction of the past landscape of the basin. A team has recently reported attempts to core the Red Sea in order to get a sediment record of the history of sea-level changes during the last glacial, 70,000 to 25,000 years ago (Sirocko 2003:813; Siddall et al. 2003:853). This was a critical time period for the dispersal of Africans into Eurasia, and it corresponds to the loss of an archaeological signature in much of North Africa and the Sahara.

The Red Sea is an enclosed basin; its connection at the Strait of Bab el Mandeb to the south is only 18 km wide (Sirocko 2003:813). During full glacials, the amount of surface water flowing into the Red Sea was very low

(Sirocko 2003:813), so land masses might have emerged or been close to the surface. However, a study of the marine oxygen isotopes of the central Red Sea core, GHEOTUE-KL11, does not contain a record for the last glacial maximum or an early Holocene cold phase. These represent periods when the seawater was so salty that no plankton were deposited (Siddall et al. 2003:855). In the Upper Pleistocene, several periods of high and low sea level are recorded, especially from 70,000 and 40,000 years ago. These were times of abrupt climate change (Sirocko 2003:813; Siddall et al. 2003:854), in which one or more Out of Africa II migrations could have occurred.

What does the archaeological record have to say? There are only a few sites that have been identified along the Red Sea; this is probably a product of the lack of field research, rather than a true indication of population density. One of the most important sites is Sodmein Cave (26°14′27″N, 33°58′12″E). It is located 35 km northwest of Quseir in Egypt in Wadi Sodmein (Van Peer 2001:53; Moeyersons et al. 2002:837). It is one of the first sites in the Eastern Desert of Egypt to show an archaeological sequence ranging from the Middle Palaeolithic through the Neolithic (Van Peer et al. 1996:151; Mercier et al. 1999:1339; Van Peer 1998:117; Moeyersons et al. 2002). Stratigraphic units are numbered A to J from top to bottom. A to C date to the Holocene, then there is a stratigraphic hiatus between around 7,500 to 25,000 years ago (Moeyersons et al. 2002:848). D represents wetter conditions around 25,000 years ago and is associated with two Upper Palaeolithic units, labeled 1 and 2. E is assigned to a Middle Palaeolithic stage 1, F to Middle Palaeolithic 2, the F/G disconformity to Middle Palaeolithic 3, and G to Middle Palaeolithic 4; the last level is estimated to be over 45,000 years old (Moeyersons et al. 2002:842). There is another disconformity between layers I and J; the top of the J complex is thermoluminescence dated to around 115,000 years old. Both faunal and sedimentological evidence suggest that it was wetter than usual (Moeyersons et al. 2002:842, 847).

The archaeological sequence is as follows. Upper Palaeolithic level 1 consists of a few blades and cores and may just be reworked material from Upper Palaeolithic level 2 (Van Peer et al. 1996:153). Level 2 contains many blades with unprepared platforms, as well as single-direction cores. These represent true Upper Palaeolithic technology, but they are different from all early Nile Valley blade industries. Few retouched tools were recovered, and there is evidence of Levallois technology. Artifacts were also found around a hearth, charcoal from which was accelerator radiocarbon dated to 25,200 ± 500 BP (UtC-3313) (Mercier et al. 1999:1340; Van Peer et al. 1996:153, 155). The most recent Middle Palaeolithic level contains few artifacts. There are burins, some Levallois tools, and one complete and one fragmentary projectile point with basal thinning on their ventral face which resemble Emireh points from the Levant. This industry is described as transitional from the Middle to the Upper Palaeolithic, similar to that from Boker Tachtitt (Marks 1983, 1990, 1992) in southern Israel (Mercier et al. 1999:1340; Van Peer et al. 1996:153–154). Middle Palaeolithic level 2 contains blades and Levallois technology. These are radiocarbon dated to 29,950 ± 900 BP (GrN-16782) (Van Peer et al. 1996:153). The presence of tanged Levallois products has led the excavators to consider that it may represent some sort of Aterian (Mercier et al. 1999:1340). If so, it would represent the furthest east that this industry is found, and would make its absence from the Nile Valley especially striking.

Middle Palaeolithic level 3 is associated with a radiocarbon date that is over 45,000 years old (UtC-3317). It is composed of both classical Levallois technology and Nubian 1 point production, and blades are rare (Mercier et al. 1999:1340; Van Peer et al. 1996:154). Middle Palaeolithic level 4 from layer G is present in the southern part of the cave. It may actually be part of the Middle Palaeolithic level 3. Artifacts belong to the N group and include typical Nubian points and cores. One associated radiocarbon date is over 44,500 years BP (Lv-2087) (Mercier et al. 1999:1340). Included in this level is a single classic (radial) Levallois flake with a band of red ochre (Van Peer et al. 1996:154). Middle Palaeolithic level 5 belongs to some phase of MIS 5. The oldest cultural level, it is found in the northern part of the cave (Van Peer et al. 1996:154; Van Peer 2001:54). It includes three ash layers, a large hearth, and a few artifacts, along with the burned bones of various large mammals (Mercier et al. 1999:1340). Artifacts include bifaces such as those in the first two lake phases at Bir Tarfawi (Van Peer 1998:118; Van Peer et al. 1996:154). Six fragments of two large burned flint blocks gave thermoluminescence dates averaging 118,000 ± 8,000 years ago, MIS 5e or 5d (Mercier et al. 1999:1339).

The Abdur Reef Limestone site in Eritrea (Walter et al. 2000, Stringer 2000; Bruggemann et al. 2004) remains one of the few records of human occupation on the Red Sea coast itself. The site is one of several emerged coral reef terraces on the west coast of the Buri Peninsula, 609 km southeast of Massawa (Bruggemann et al. 2004:180, 191; Stringer 2000:24–25). Corals were dated by

TIMS (thermal ionization mass spectrometry) uranium-thorium dating to 125,000 ± 7,000 years ago, within MIS 5e (Bruggemann et al. 2004:179, 195; Walter et al. 2000:66–67; Stringer 2000:24). The bottom of the sequence here consists of marine, estuarine, and fluvial sediments that are ^{39}argon/^{40}argon dated between 0.90 ± 0.04 and 0.72 ± 0.01 million years ago. These were faulted, folded, and eroded prior to deposition of the Abdur Reef Limestone (Bruggemann et al. 2004:181).

The Abdur Reef Limestone is the remnant of a shallow coral reef system that existed around 125,000 years ago (Bruggemann et al. 2004:182). Afterward, the sea level rose, providing a surface for the growth of oyster beds (Walter et al. 2000:67). The site was near an ancient shoreline and laterally gives way to beach deposits, which include fossil mammal bones. Stone artifacts are found in the basal cobble zone, the lower part of the lower shell zone, and the beach deposits (Walter et al. 2000:67). The original report describes a number of bifacial tools manufactured from fine-grained volcanic rocks, as well as from chert and quartz. Flake and blade tools were mainly obsidian and, occasionally, chert and quartz. Raw material sources probably ranged between 1 and 20 km away from this site. The report also notes the presence of an older occupation in the Buri sequence, composed of obsidian tools (Walter et al. 2000:67). More recent research led to the identification of two kinds of archaeological assemblages. The first are Acheulian and include bifaces and cores that have a maximum length of 6 to 25 cm. These are manufactured on volcanic rocks (including obsidian), chert, and quartz. Artifacts are associated with the oyster beds, encrusted on the basal lag deposits or in the lower half of the overlying limestone layer. They are only present in the northernmost of three separate but related archaeological localities, and may represent tools for harvesting oysters in a near shore environment (Bruggemann et al. 2004:202). The second assemblage type includes Middle Stone Age–like flakes and blades, between 5 and 15 cm long. Mainly obsidian, with some chert and quartz, these are found in three separate localities that represent near shore and beach environments. Here they are associated with remains of marine invertebrates and large land mammals. The two may mark the coexistence of the Middle Stone Age and Acheulian, or a late transition between the two (Bruggemann et al. 2004:200–204).

Walter et al. (2000:68) state that there have been other reports of Acheulian-like tools near emerged reef terraces in the Danakil depression and Egypt, but these are not well published. They suggest that the manufacturers of the Abdur tools occupied a coastal area and made use of near-shore marine food resources, similar to the Middle Stone Age people at various sites in South Africa (Parkington 1999; Singer and Wymer 1982). This could have been a general process of accommodation to the coast at this time and might mark a fundamental change in human behavior (Walter et al. 2000:66, 68). This is intriguing, given the current emphasis on the role of omega-3 fatty acids from fish oils in regulating brain function and mental health (Horrobin 1998, 2001).

Why did the coast become attractive at this time, but not earlier? Walter et al. suggest that during a period of increased dryness in the full glacial, people migrated here from the interior, but they recognized that even the Red Sea basin might be uninhabitable (Walter et al. 2000:69). Once on the coast, increasing competition for marine resources led to the dispersal events responsible for Skhūl and Qafzeh (Walter et al. 2000:69). They conclude that it would be possible to test this idea by looking at "perhaps the entire eastern shoreline of Africa" (Walter et al. 2000:69). Finally, Buia, south of Massawa, has also yielded about 200 archaeological localities. But these are classically Acheulian, with variable numbers of large bifaces and choppers, and are assumed to date to around 1 million years ago (Martini et al. 2004).

SOMALIA AND ETHIOPIA

The earliest archaeological collections from Somalia were obtained in the 1880s. Until Desmond Clark's survey during World War II, little contextual data were available for any of them (Clark 1954:16, 41). An officer in the British Army's East African Command, Clark (1954:xxxv–xxxvi) famously had his soldiers collect archaeological material whenever the front line against the Italians changed. After the war, he employed the terminology of the First Pan-African Congress of Prehistory to create the first prehistoric sequence for Somalia (Clark 1954). Clark documented a Stone Age sequence beginning with the Acheulo-Levalloisian, through the Levalloisian, Somaliland Stillbay, and the transitional Middle to Later Stone Age or Somaliland Magosian. Three Later Stone Age phases were also defined (Clark 1954:158). The Acheulo-Levalloisian includes Acheulian sites with evidence of prepared core production; these might represent the oldest signs of human occupation of the country. The Lower Levalloisian included prepared cores, faceted flakes and flake-blades, steep-trimmed core scrapers, choppers, and a few large points (Clark 1954:172). Upper Levalloisian assemblages contained the same kinds of artifacts, but included more subrectangular and subtriangular prepared cores (relative to earlier oval and disc ones) (Clark 1954:176). There were signs of gradual technological innovation over time, and artifact sizes decrease accordingly (Clark 1954:188; Gresham and Brandt 1996:162). The Somaliland Stillbay was documented at three stratified sites: Bur Eibe (later referred to as Buur Heybe) (map 9.1), Ohole, and Jesomma. Its most notable tools are points and scrapers produced by flat percussion flaking (Clark 1954:192). The Magosian was defined in relation to Porc Epic Cave, also known as Diré Dawa (Clark 1954:203). In one of his later review papers, Clark (1993a:153) proposed that Upper Palaeolithic–like blade technology might have developed locally here from Levallois point and Nubian core technology. Clark's work inspired Steven Brandt to visit Somalia in order to restudy its prehistoric record. Brandt (1986) later reassessed Clark's Stone Age sequence for the Horn. In the 1980s, he led a survey that documented about 700 prehistoric sites along the Jubba River (Gresham and Brandt 1996:157). Based on surface samples, they defined three Middle Stone Age assemblages: a generalized, a big, and a little MSA. Their "Big MSA" includes large flakes, cores, tools, and a high percentage of shaped tools. The "Little MSA" has many small Levallois cores, flakes, and tools (Gresham and Brandt 1996:159).

Brandt (1988:40) returned to conduct excavations at Buur Heybe, a granitic inselberg in southern Somalia, in 1983 and 1985. In 1935, Grazioni excavated two trenches covering an area of about 7 m² within the Gogoshiis Qabe rock-shelter ("the place of the mat") and uncovered a Middle and Later Stone Age sequence (Clark 1954:xxxv; Brandt 1986:42, 77, 1988). One trench was dug to 3.5 m without hitting bedrock. Later on, Brandt (1988:43) opened an area of about 32 m sq; most of these contained cultural occupations about 1.2 m deep (Brandt 1988:43). The top cultural occupation is composed of brown silty sands and is of early Holocene age. Below this level is the Later Stone Age Eibian Industry, what Desmond Clark (1954:226) initially called Doian. It includes distinct pressure-flaked tools (points and trihedral rods), microliths, and scrapers, usually manufactured on non-local cherts and local quartz. Below this level is a transitional Middle/Later Stone Age industry, then an undated Middle Stone Age occupation (Brandt 1988:43).

The Ethiopian early archaeological record is much more complete, but it is also patchy. Ever since the Omo project of the 1970s which documented over 4 million years of human history (Coppens et al. 1976), a lot of attention has been paid to the Pliocene and early Pleistocene fossil hominin and Early Stone Age record. Only recently have some researchers decided that the later Pleistocene history could be just as important. Omo researchers discovered a number of fossil hominin bones in the later Kibish Formation. One, Omo II, was assigned to *Homo heidelbergensis*, while another, Omo I, appeared to represent an anatomically modern human (Rightmire 1984:313, 1989:109). Outcrops of the Kibish Formation were revisited in 2002 and 2003 by Shea et al. (2004) in order to document the distribution of Middle Stone Age sites. The KHS site where the Omo Kibish 1 hominin specimen came from was relocated; a small lithic scatter and some fauna were present. At another site, BNS, a number of stone artifacts, faunal remains, and ostrich eggshell were recorded (Shea et al. 2004; McDougall et al. 2004). The third site, AHS, has a number of Middle Stone Age levels and contains some hominin remains. All three include radial preparation of local cryptocrystalline silicas to make small artifacts (Shea et al. 2004). Surface finds in the same area include small foliate bifaces, larger lanceolate bifaces, and cordiform hand axes, but these are nearly absent from the excavated samples (Shea et al. 2004).

One of the first sites discovered in Ethiopia was Melka Kunturé; its long cultural sequence includes the Acheulian to Middle Stone Age transition (Chavaillon et al. 1979; Clark 1988:265). Located 50 km south of Addis Ababa at an altitude of 2,300 to 2,400 m, there are seven separate localities with Middle Stone Age occupations (Chavaillon et al. 1979; Clark 1988:265; Brandt 1986:49). One of them, Garba III, includes seven cultural layers. The oldest is a late Acheulian living floor, containing hand axes, cleavers, some side scrapers, and bifacial points (Clark 1988:265). The six later levels have no Acheulian bifaces, but an increasing number of side scrapers and points, mainly in obsidian (Clark 1988:265; Phillipson 1993:83). They have been described as Stillbaylike, since they include bifacial and part-bifacial points, end and side scrapers, backed blades, and other tools made from Levallois and blade cores (Brandt 1986:49).

Gademotta and Kulkuletti are found on the slope of an old volcano overlooking Lake Ziway in the Ethiopian lakes section of the rift valley (Clark 1988:239; Brandt 1986:47). Excavations in 1971 by Wendorf and Schild led to the recovery of over 47,000 stone artifacts from four Middle Stone Age locations at the former and three at the latter (Brandt 1986:49). These include bifacial and unifacial points, side and convergent scrapers, notches, denticulates, as well as tools more common in later periods: burins, end scrapers, and backed blades (Brandt 1986:49). Potassium-argon dates put the occupation between 181,000 and 149,000 years before present (Brandt 1986:49). Locally available obsidian flows were exploited for lithic raw materials (Clark 1988:258). The earliest Middle Stone Age occupation (ETH-72-8B) is found on a horizon overlying a level with small bifaces (Clark 1988:258). It is located below a volcanic tuff, potassium-argon dated to 235,000 ± 5,000 BP (Clark 1988:239; Deino and McBrearty 2002:208; McBrearty 2001:91). Retouched tools include unifacial and bifacial points as well as side scrapers (Clark 1988:258). The only real changes over time are an increasing percentage of blades, the introduction of non-Levallois blade cores, and a corresponding decrease in numbers of Levallois cores (Clark 1988:258–260; Phillipson 1993:83; Pleurdeau 2003:43).

The Middle Awash area of southern central Ethiopia has become a major focus for Plio-Pleistocene human palaeontology and archaeology (White et al. 1993, 1994). There is also evidence of occupation during the Middle and Upper Pleistocene, as marked by fossil hominin localities such as Bodo (Asfaw 1983; Clark et al. 1984; Rightmire 1996), Herto (Clark et al. 2003; White et al. 2003), and Aduma (Haile-Selassie et al. 2004). One of the first Middle Stone Age sites found in this region was Ala Kanasa. Here a small lithic assemblage and hearth were observed in stratified later Pleistocene sands and silts; they overlie silts with horizons yielding artifacts including "advanced" Acheulian bifaces (Clark, Asfaw et al. 1984; Clark 1988:260). Tools include bifacial and unifacial points, side scrapers, and a single Levallois point; most are made on fine grained non-local raw materials (Clark 1988:260).

The Upper Herto Member of the Bouri Formation yielded a number of anatomically modern human fossils, as well as Acheulian and Middle Stone Age artifacts (Clark et al. 2003:748; White et al. 2003). A sand unit at the base of the Upper Herto Member contains Acheulian bifaces (hand axes, cleavers), Levallois flakes, side scrapers, and a few blades. The assemblage is closest to Garba III at Melka Kunturé. Most tools were manufactured on basalt, while the points and blades are obsidian. Occasionally artifacts were made on cryptocrystalline silica. The age of this material is estimated to be between 160,000 ± 2,000 and 154,000 ± 7,000 years old, based on ^{39}argon/ ^{40}argon dating. Faunal remains include riverine and savanna forms (Clark et al. 2003:750).

The Stone Age prehistory of the Middle Awash has become the focus of renewed research attention (Brooks et al. 2002; White et al. 2003; Clark et al. 2003; Yellen et al. 2005). Brooks et al. (2002:A8) have conducted six field seasons in the Aduma Region, in an area of 15 km², and they have identified many Early and Middle Stone Age localities. Most are proposed to be between 90,000 and 40,000 BP (Brooks et al. 2002:A8; Yellen et al. 2005). Some recently discovered anatomically modern fossil human crania eroding from sediments stratified above the Herto Member at Aduma and Bouri are estimated to be between 79,000 and 105,000 years old. At both locations, they are directly associated with obsidian Middle Stone Age artifacts (Haile-Selassie et al. 2004:3). Artifacts include small, finely made unifacial and bifacial points, as well as microlithic Levallois and Levalloislike cores, points, and small scrapers. Their variety appears to increase over time (Brooks et al. 2002:A8–A9). Faunal remains show that river resources (hippopotamus, crocodile, and possibly fish) were important throughout the sequence; savanna animals are also present (Brooks et al. 2002:A8).

One of the first Stone Age sites investigated in Ethiopia was Porc Epic Cave. It is located around 400 km east of the capital of Addis Ababa, near the city of Dire Dawa (Pleurdeau 2003:18). Teilhard de Chardin excavated the site in 1928 and Abbé Henri Breuil and Paul Wernert followed him in 1933 (Breuil et al. 1951). They used 10 cm units and excavated to a depth of over 1.5 m. Faunal remains, stone artifacts, and a half of a hominin mandible were recovered from a massive breccia and one overlying flowstone (Pleurdeau 2003:18–19; Clark 1954:xxxv, 1988:262; Brandt 1986:50, 58–59). Desmond Clark revisited the site in 1974 and dug a 6 m² trench (Clark, Williamson et al. 1984; Clark 1988:262; Brandt 1986:50). Williamson expanded this to an area of 40 m² in 1975 and 1976 (Pleurdeau 2003:21). The lower part of the sequence was assigned to the Middle Stone Age, and its minimum age lies between 60,000 and 77,000 years old, using obsidian hydration (Clark 1988:262; Pleurdeau 2003:20–21). Eighty percent of the lithics were manufactured from local chert; others are obsidian from up to 100 km away and basalt. They include points, side scrapers, burins, borers, composite tools, and backed pieces. Clark (1988:262) concluded that there was no significant technological change over time.

Recently Pleurdeau (2003:23) examined all stone artifacts over 20 mm in length, as well as cores from two squares excavated in 1975 and 1976. Raw materials were divided into various kinds of cryptocrystalline silica (69% of the total), basalt (17%), obsidian (8%), sandstone (2%), and/or quartzite

(2%). The silicas and quartzite were from local sources, while the basalt and obsidian came from over 100 km away (Pleurdeau 2003:24–25). Retouched tools formed 17% of his assemblages. Points were most common; these are unifacial or bifacial and are similar to Stillbay ones (Pleurdeau 2003:36, 42). Others include side scrapers and notches, as well as some backed pieces (bladelets and lunates) and end scrapers (Pleurdeau 2003:36, 40). The backed pieces come from all levels at Porc Epic, except the deepest ones. It is possible that these were present during the Middle Stone Age, so it is imperative to redate the site (Pleurdeau 2003:42).

A salvage project was conducted at the future site of the Gilgel Gibe Dam in southwest Ethiopia starting in 1999. This region is 250 km southeast of Addis Ababa (Brandt et al. 2004). Over 30,000 artifacts were collected from forty sites ranging in age from the Acheulian through the Iron Age (Brandt et al. 2004). Middle and Later Stone Age sites were located along the edge of the proposed dam's reservoir. One notable open-air site was Liben Bore, which contains over 2 m of continuous occupation beginning with the Middle/Later Stone Age transition and ending with the Iron Age (Brandt et al. 2004). This continuous record led Brandt et al. (2004) to propose that Gilgel Gibe could have remained a focus for Pleistocene hominin populations of the Horn of Africa even during the driest phases of the Pleistocene.

A recent survey has uncovered a large Acheulian site west of Gondar (Todd et al. 2004). Kernet is composed of a 5 ha scatter of bifaces; test excavations showed the presence of well-preserved fauna and artifacts. In the western highlands of Ethiopia, the same group of researchers identified a series of Middle Stone Age sites along the Shinfa River, which flows through the Kolla and Voina Dega plateaus into the Blue Nile (Todd et al. 2004). Artifacts include unifacial and bifacial points, debitage, as well as faunal remains and buried hearths (Todd et al. 2004).

THE LEVANT: A POINT OF COMPARISON?

The Levant, the eastern Mediterranean coastal strip presently part of Lebanon, Palestine, and Israel, is one of the best known Palaeolithic regions (Bar-Yosef 1993, 1994). A series of deep caves have produced long cultural historical sequences ranging from the Acheulian to the end of the Pleistocene. As in North Africa, the Middle Palaeolithic was a period of dense occupation. The transition from the Middle to the Upper Palaeolithic seems to be a local process, but there is also evidence of an intrusive Aurignacian. Van Peer's research in the Nile Valley suggests that the appearance of the Nubian complex may be the initial sign of the dispersal of early modern humans (Van Peer 1998; Vermeersch 2001:105). Other researchers see no direct archaeological links at all (Marks 1990, 1992:229). It is hard to compare the two regions on account of different research traditions and site types. The Levant has many deep caves, representing occupation sites, while the Egyptian sites are mainly places for the extraction of flint nodules (Vermeersch 2001:106). Researchers working in the Levant have concentrated on the tools, while those working in Egypt study methods of tool production (Vermeersch 2001:104–105).

In the Levant, the end stages of the Acheulian are marked by the presence of a transitional industry referred to as Acheulo-Yabrudian or Mugharan (Barkal et al. 2003:977). It has three variants, one of which, the Pre-Aurignacian or Amudian, resembles the Libyan Pre-Aurignacian of Haua Fteah (Barkal et al. 2003:978; Marks 1992:230; Vishnyatsky 1994). At Tabun it is dated by thermoluminescence to between 270,000 and 330,000 years ago (Bar-Yosef and Kuhn 1999:325). A recently discovered site, Qesem Cave (32°11′N, 34°98′E), which is located 12 km east of Tel Aviv, contains 7.5 m of deposits, including a late Acheulian and the Acheulo-Yabrudian (Barkal et al. 2003:977). Electron spin resonance dates of speleothems above and below the archaeological deposits show that they are between 382,000 and 207,000 years old (Barkal et al. 2003:978).

The subsequent cultural period is referred to as the Levantine Mousterian (Bar-Yosef 1989a, 1993, 1994; Bar-Yosef and Vandermeersch 1993). Tabun is one of a series of caves in the Wadi Mughara on Mount Carmel, south of Haifa; others include el Wad and Skhūl. They were first excavated in the 1930s by a team led by Dorothy Garrod (Garrod and Bate 1937; McCown and Keith 1937). At Tabun, Garrod recognized three phases of a Levallois Mousterian, in layers B, C, and D; these were seen as developmental stages, with no overlap in time (Marks 1992:232, 236). The oldest phase, Tabun D or early Levantine Mousterian, is characterized by the production of blanks from Levallois, unipolar blade, and point cores. It is estimated to be somewhere between 120,000 to 130,000 and 180,000 to 200,000 years old (Bar-Yosef 1989a, 1989b), or possibly earlier (Rink et al. 2003:197). Tabun C is characterized by classical radial Levallois core preparation. It is used to produce typical Levallois flakes (Bar-Yosef and Kuhn 1999:325). Other artifacts are side scrapers and Mousterian points on large flat flakes (Marks 1992:232). Similar assemblages are found at Skhūl and Qafzeh, where they are associated with "proto Cro-Magnon" hominins (Bar-Yosef and Vandermeersch 1993; Vandermeersch 1981), in other words, with the bones of anatomically modern people. These are considered to belong to MIS 5e (Valladas et al. 1988; Mercier et al. 1993). Garrod's Neanderthal fossils (a partial skeleton and a separate mandible) were also said to come from layer C, yet elsewhere they are associated with Tabun B artifacts. These include blanks removed from either unipolar or bipolar Levallois cores; radial cores were also produced. Points are often short and broad, while flakes tend to be elongated, almost bladelike (Bar-Yosef 1989a, 1989b, 1992a, 1992b, Bar-Yosef and Vandermeersch 1993; Lieberman and Shea 1994; Shea 1989, 1998, 2003).

There is evidence of a local transition from Middle to Upper Palaeolithic at two sites in the Levant, K'sar Akil in Lebanon (Azoury et al. 1986; Bergman 1988) and Boker Tachtitt in the Negev (Marks 1983, 1990, 1992; Bar-Yosef and Kuhn 1999). At K'sar Akil, Levallois methods gradually evolve into true Upper Palaeolithic ones (Clark and Lindly 1989a, 1989b:970; Bar-Yosef 1989b:163). The transitional assemblages are marked by the appearance of some distinctive tools, including the chamfered blade, "a tool on which a broad transverse flake was removed from the distal end, using a platform shaped by a distal lateral direct retouch" (Gilead 1991:108). Burins and rare Emireh points are also found (Bar-Yosef 1989b:163; 1992a:197). Boker Tachtitt shows a similar process of transition from points to single platform blade technology (Marks 1983, 1990, 1992; Bar-Yosef and Kuhn 1999:328; Clark and Lindly 1989b:970; Gilead 1991:118). The transitional Emiran or Emirian Industry has been radiocarbon dated to 47,200 ± 9,050 (SMU-580), 44,930 ± 2,420 (SMU-259), and/or greater than 45,055 ± 4,100 (SMU-184) (Bar-Yosef 1992b:264). Early levels in Emiran assemblages have high percentages of the eponymous Emireh as well as Levallois points, end scrapers, and burins. The latest levels include Levallois points removed from unipolar cores (referred to as "non Levallois" technology) as well as burins and scrapers (Bar-Yosef 1989b:164).

There is no need for a new population to enter with an Upper Palaeolithic adaptation. After 40,000 years ago, the local Upper Palaeolithic or Ahmarian is interstratified with a Levantine Aurignacian. While the former is derived from the Middle Palaeolithic, the latter is a mirror image of the European industry of the same name and may have its origins in the same region (Gilead

1991:121, 129). It is only now that there is a sign of change and possibly new people. But they could easily have a European source, not an African one. While the Levant has provided a long Middle and Upper Palaeolithic sequence, it is not directly comparable to that anywhere in Africa. Despite the quality of evidence, it does not record any evidence of the hordes of people expected by the Out of Africa II model.

LIBYA: HAUA FTEAH AND OTHER SITES

While just about everywhere in North Africa has a Middle Palaeolithic presence, the Early Upper Palaeolithic is not well known from anywhere. Haua Fteah, a large natural cave on the northern coast of Cyrenaica in Libya, seems to be the only place with an Early Upper Palaeolithic record (Close 1986:175; McBurney 1967:1). Located near the foot of the Gebel el Akhdar or Green Mountain, this site was excavated by a team led by Charles McBurney (1967: xiii, 1) in 1951, 1952, and 1955. A 35 ft by 30 ft excavation was attempted, then only a portion ("deep sounding") was excavated to a total depth of 42.5 ft (approximately 13 m); even at this depth, the researchers never hit sterile deposits (McBurney 1967:5). The deep sounding levels were given spit numbers, while the upper excavation units have Roman numerals from I to XXXV as well as spit numbers (McBurney 1967) (figure 8.5). The only dates are conventional radiocarbon ones and extrapolations from them. McBurney also made use of isotope ratios in excavated shellfish in order to relatively date stratigraphic levels. Especially for the oldest levels, the dates are probably only minimal estimates of the true age of these cultural deposits.

   The lowest level is assigned to the Libyan Pre-Aurignacian and is defined by the presence of parallel-sided blades produced from prismatic cores (figure 8.6). McBurney (1967:90) argues that its focus on blade technology is greater than that in true Upper Palaeolithic contexts. This is a Mode 4 industry and has striking similarities with the Levantine Pre-Aurignacian, Amudian, or Acheulo-Yabrudian from Layer E at Tabun and from the Jabrud rock-shelter in Syria (McBurney 1967:326; Barkal et al. 2003:978; Clark 1993a:154). It was originally estimated to be between 80,000 and 65,000 years old (McBurney 1967:325). McBurney (1967:90) himself had mixed feelings about the Libyan Pre-Aurignacian. For him, it was best described as an "archaic leptolithic assemblage with virtual absence of Levalloisian traits" (McBurney 1967:325), leptolithic meaning bladelike (Laplace 1966). While the associated cores are

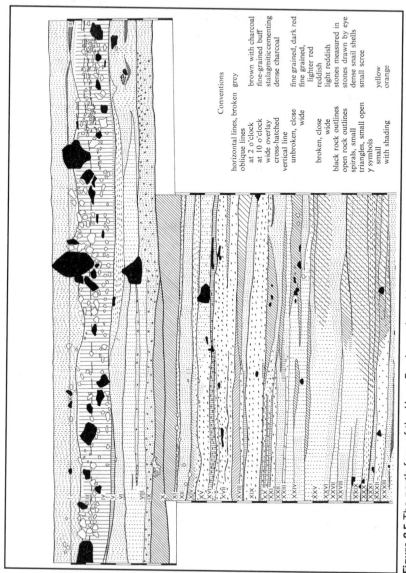

Figure 8.5 The north face of the Haua Fteah stratigraphic sequence (McBurney 1967:6). Reprinted with permission of Cambridge University Press

Conventions

horizontal lines, broken	grey
oblique lines	
at 2 o'clock	brown with charcoal
at 10 o'clock	fine-grained buff
wide overlay	stalagmitic cementing
cross-hatched	dense charcoal
vertical line	
unbroken, close	fine grained, dark red
wide	fine grained, lighter red
broken, close	reddish
wide	light reddish
black rock outlines	stones measured in
open rock outlines	stones drawn by eye
spirals, small	dense snail shells
triangles, small open	small scree
y symbols	
small	yellow
with shading	orange

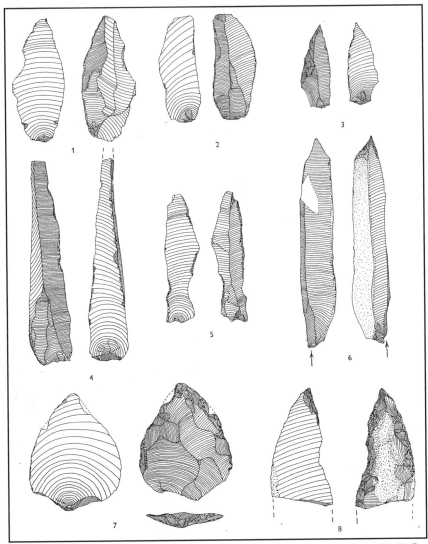

Figure 8.6 Libyan Pre-Aurignacian artifacts from Haua Fteah (McBurney 1967:79). Reprinted with permission of Cambridge University Press

prismatic, they were not manufactured using the Upper Palaeolithic punch technique nor by Levallois platform preparation (McBurney 1967:325).

The existence of an unbroken succession from Acheulian through Levalloisian to evolved Levalloisoid or Mousterian-type industries is so well established in many parts of the world that the notion of an intervening stage *prior* to the final

Middle Palaeolithic and distinguished by Upper Palaeolithic affinities comes as something of a shock. (McBurney 1967:92)

Later archaeologists have stressed its parallels with early industries in the Levant, as well as those in the South African Cape, such as Klasies River. These parallels include evidence of seafood exploitation, the presence of a precocious blade industry, reliance on hafted points, and the possible association with MIS 5e (McBurney 1967:99; Clark 1974a:190, 1993a:156; Vishnyatsky 1994).

Some secondary publications describe the presence of a Mode 3 Levalloiso-Mousterian level stratified below the Libyan Pre-Aurignacian, but this is not mentioned in McBurney's (1967) original monograph. His Levalloiso-Mousterian is found just below the top of the deep sounding level (in layer XXXV). Past temperature estimates derived from shell oxygen isotopes point to an environment similar to present, which had to be MIS 5e (McBurney 1967:106). At the time, he estimated that this meant that it was earlier than 60,000 to 55,000 years ago (McBurney 1967:326), whereas we now know that this stage belongs much further back in the past. The two partial hominin mandibles discovered here came from the final horizons of this phase (McBurney 1967:326). The lowest level is a mix of Levalloiso-Mousterian and Upper Palaeolithic elements (end scrapers and the first burins) (McBurney 1967:115). B I, the first substage of the Levalloiso-Mousterian, has a leptolithic aspect; over time this decreases and the assemblages behave more like typical Mousterian flake ones. Side scrapers remain rare, and there are almost no points (McBurney 1967:119, 326). It is interpreted as a highly specialized Levalloiso-Mousterian, possibly derived from people farther east (McBurney 1967:131). McBurney also suggests that the people of Haua Fteah could have played a role in the origin of the Aterian. This is based on the presence of some bifaces, including foliates, as well as pieces with incipient tangs (McBurney 1967:131, 326).

McBurney (1967:326) felt that the Mousterian had an Eastern Asiatic origin; the people who brought it to Haua Fteah might have become acculturated to the Pre-Aurignacian natives; over time, these innovations (or people carrying them), could have spread along the Mediterranean coast to produce the Aterian. Alternately, they could have just interacted with the Aterians already there (McBurney 1967:326). The subsequent phase B II of the Mousterian was thought to have existed in a cold period around 55,000 years ago; it is characterized by the presence of a Levalloiso-Mousterian paralleling developments in the Levant. The B III assemblage is probably Aterian, while the final phase, B IV, is characterized by a simple Levalloiso-Mousterian, without tanged elements, burins, or end scrapers. It is supposed to last until around 40,000 years ago (McBurney 1967:326), after which the true Upper Palaeolithic Dabban emerged.

The Dabban is named for the type site of Hagfet ed Dabba, located 35 mi inland and southwest of Haua Fteah. McBurney (1967:125, 168) uncovered a 6-ft-deep cultural sequence here. It is a true Mode 4 industry, with backed blades, end scrapers, and burins. He thought that its closest parallels were with the Emirian Industry of the Levant (McBurney 1967:326). In its early phase, up to half of the tools were backed blades; many of these were small and would have needed to be hafted. Chamfered blades, index fossils for the Levantine Ahmarian, made up about 5% of tools in the early phase and increase in frequency over time. In the later phase, chamfered and backed blades become less common, and scrapers and then burins increase (McBurney 1967:167).

McBurney emphasized the sudden change from the Middle to the Upper Palaeolithic evident in the Haua Fteah sequence. He could not resist a dig at his fellow Africanist archaeologists, dealing with the Middle to Later Stone Age transition south of the Sahara:

> No more complete contrast can be imagined than between this situation and, say, the shadowy transitions reported from south of the Sahara, such as the so-called "Second Intermediate Period." (McBurney 1967:135)

A more recent study of 204 retouched tools from the Dabban levels might make people think twice (Hiscock 1996). Following lead of Rolland and Dibble (1990; Dibble and Rolland 1992), Hiscock (1996:658) shows that scrapers were continually being modified into burins and vice versa. He concludes that there is no standardization of tools as expected in assemblages of this age. Or, there could be more continuity with the Middle Palaeolithic than generally thought (Hiscock 1996:664).

In Layer XV, the Dabban is succeeded by the Eastern Oranian; it appears sometime around 18,000 years ago (Garcea 2004:39; McBurney 1967:185). It is a Mode 5 industry, with large numbers of backed bladelets making up 82% to 94% of the retouched tools (Close 2002:32; McBurney 1967:185, 213; Lubell et al. 1984:155). It is the local version of the Iberomaurusian, the industry defined by Pallary in 1909 (McBurney 1967:185; Phillipson 1993:94; Close

1986:171, 174, 2002:32; Irish 2000). McBurney (1967:327) thought the Eastern Oranian represented a new population (Close 2002:33), originally from either the Maghreb or the Middle East. This is a reasonable conclusion, even at a time when population migration was the preferred explanation of culture change. In general, Haua Fteah is notable for a number of reasons. It may represent the only site in North Africa or the Sahara that was occupied by people during the last glacial maximum (Close and Wendorf 1990:47). Its precocious Libyan Pre-Aurignacian industry has parallels elsewhere and dates to a time period that might be critical for the transformation to behavioral modernity. Clearly, this site begs to be reinvestigated sometime in the near future.

More Libyan sites have been identified recently due to research by Italian archaeologists (Barich et al. 2003; Cremaschi et al. 1998; Garcea 2004). One of these is Jebel Gharbi or Jebel Nafusah in northwestern Libya. Uranium/thorium dates on calcareous crusts above and below an Aterian-bearing silt layer bracket this culture between 85,000 and 43,000 years ago (Barich et al. 2003; Garcea 2004:33). Accelerator radiocarbon dates place the Aterian layers at the recent end of this range, 43,000 to 44,000 years ago. There is also an Upper Palaeolithic industry with blades before the Iberomaurusian; it is dated to around 18,000 years ago (Garcea 2004:33, 39).

Ain Zargha or Ras el Wadi is located near the modern village of Jado (Garcea 2004:33). Here there are three cultural stratigraphic horizons. The bottom or lower unit contains Middle Palaeolithic artifacts. The upper unit is a layer of colluvial silt and loess containing an Aterian assemblage. The top unit is a calcrete, which formed at the same time as a soil containing Later Stone Age (in other words, Upper Palaeolithic or Epipalaeolithic) artifacts. It is dated to $27,310 \pm 320$ BP by conventional radiocarbon (Beta 154576) and to $30,000 \pm 9,000$ by uranium/thorium (Garcea 2004:33).

There are five Aterian sites located around a permanent spring at Ras el Wadi at the foot of the Jebel Gharbi mountain range at Shakshuk (Garcea 2004:33–34). Notches and denticulates are the most common tool types at all sites, and there are also Aterian tanged pieces (Garcea 2004:34). Levallois methods were used at all Middle Palaeolithic sites, while later Aterians switched to opposed and single-platform cores. As a result, they manufactured Upper Palaeolithic–like tools, including end scrapers, perforators, and becs (Garcea 2004:34). Test excavations at ST-03-68, a site in the Wadi Sel, produced a sequence that includes a soil with Aterian artifacts; this was radiocarbon dated to 43,500 ± 2,110 years ago (Beta 167098). It was located below a charcoal horizon with a few Later Stone Age artifacts, dated to 25,500 ± 400 years ago (Beta 167099) (Garcea 2004:34). Garcea (2004:34) is convinced that there is no direct connection between the Aterian and Later Stone Age, as there is at least 10,000 years in between the two.

The Uan Tabu rock-shelter is located in the Tadrart Acacus, farther south in central Sahara (Garcea 2004:34). Its lowest level or Unit IV is composed of five layers (numbered 21–25). A maximum of 1 m thick, it is separated from the upper three units by an unconformable erosional surface with a stone line (Garcea 2004:35). Above this is 4 to 5 cm of loose yellow sand, lying on a thin gypsum crust; it, too, marks an unconformity with the upper Holocene units (Garcea 2004:35). Layer 22 in the upper part of the Aterian deposit produced an optically stimulated luminescence date of 61,000 ± 10,000 years old (Garcea 2004:35). On typological grounds, Garcea (2004:35) suggests that there are two Aterian occupations. In the earlier one, only sandstone was used for artifact production. In the upper unit, other materials are present. Levallois flake cores, flakes, and blades are more common in the upper than the lower layer (Garcea 2004:35). In the upper unit, "unpatterned" single-platform cores are more abundant, as are side scrapers and perforators. End scrapers, burins, truncation flakes, and *hachoirs* (bifacial scrapers/small chopping tools) are only found in the uppermost layer, while the lower layers include naturally backed knives, tanged points and tools, and *hachereaux* (cleavers). However, notches and denticulates are the most common tools in both layers (Garcea 2004:35–36).

In order to determine how old the occupation at Uan Tabu is, Garcea compares it with the one from Uan Afuda. Here, there is evidence of a "more ephemeral occupation" by Middle Palaeolithic people, who supposedly had an Aterian industry (Garcea 2004:35), with thermoluminescence dates of 70,500 ± 9,500 and 73,000 ± 10,000 years old. One optically stimulated luminescence date is 69,000 ± 7,000 BP, while another from sands below the archaeological horizon is dated to 90,000 ± 10,000 BP (Garcea 2004:35). Garcea therefore concludes that the Aterian may be earlier in the Sahara than in its coastal Mediterranean heartland (Garcea 2004:36; Ferring 1975:113), described in the next section.

THE MAGHREB AND NORTHWEST AFRICA

The Maghreb, composed of the northern parts of Morocco, Algeria, and Tunisia, is divided into two biogeographic provinces (map 8.2). The inland

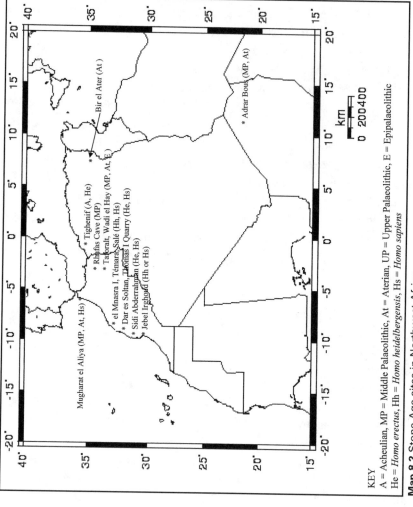

KEY

A = Acheulian, MP = Middle Palaeolithic, At = Aterian, UP = Upper Palaeolithic, E = Epipalaeolithic
He = *Homo erectus*, Hh = *Homo heidelbergensis*, Hs = *Homo sapiens*

Map 8.2 Stone Age sites in Northwest Africa

one is more open, with dry-adapted vegetation, while the coastal edge has more forest (Hublin 2001:100). The boundary between the two shifts toward the littoral during various stages of the Pleistocene, as the Sahara waxes and wanes (Hublin 2001:100). In the last ice age phase, the Atlas Mountains were glaciated; vegetation belts were over 1,000 m lower, and grassland replaced forest in many areas (Clark 1980a:547; Close and Wendorf 1990:42). During the last glacial maximum, temperatures were 3°C to 7°C cooler than present, but it is aridity that is the major controlling factor on vegetation and human occupation (Close and Wendorf 1990:42; Hublin 2001:100).

The first archaeological research in Morocco took place around Tangiers at end of the nineteenth century (Bouzouggar et al. 2002:208). It eventually led to the recognition of a series of marine terraces, each representing an ancient shore covered by dunes. The age of the terraces increases as one moves inland (Hublin 2001:100). Biberson (1961a) defined a sequence for the Quaternary. Marine stages include the Ouljian at 5 to 8 m above sea level, the Anfatian at 25 to 30 m, the Maarifian at 55 to 60 m, and the Messaoudian at 80 to 100 m (Hublin 2001:100). In between were continental deposits and cemented dunes, representing the Soltanian, Tensiftian, Amirian, Saletian, and other phases (Hublin 2001:100). Biberson (1961b) defined four pebble tool stages and many Acheulian ones in these terraces and suggested that they included a cultural sequence similar to that from Olduvai Gorge. More recent reassessments of the evidence argue convincingly that there is no clear evidence of occupation prior to the start of the Middle Pleistocene, marked here by the Amirian. This would place the earliest human presence well into the Acheulian (Raynal et al. 1995, 2001; Hublin 2001:100–102). The only good candidate for an Oldowan site in the Maghreb is Ain Hanech, the "Source du Serpent" in eastern Algeria. It was discovered in 1947 during a palaeontological survey by Camille Arambourg (1950; Arambourg and Balout 1952; Balout 1955). In recent years, the site has been restudied by Sahnouni (1998; Sahnouni and de Heinzelin 1998; Sahnouni et al. 2002, 2004; Geraads et al. 2004). While the original lithic collections mainly contain flaked limestone spheroids (Willoughby 1987), the most recent work has led to the discovery of many small flakes and retouched tools (Hublin 2001:103).

As mentioned earlier, the first Acheulian dates to around the Lower/Middle Pleistocene boundary. In Unit L of the Thomas 1 Quarry, flint and quartzite artifacts could be as old as 1 million years. They include chopping tools, polyhedrons, trihedrons, and some bifaces and cleavers. Here flakes were struck from both discoidal cores and polyhedrons (Hublin 2001:103). Rhino Cave in the Oulad Hamida 1 Quarry contains what Hublin (2001:103) calls "spectacular Acheulian assemblages" with artifacts and white rhinoceros bones. Artifacts include bifaces and rare flake tools, mainly notches and denticulates. Sidi Abderrahman was one of the first sites to be studied in detail (Hublin 2001:103). At three localities, Bear's Cave, the Sidi Abderrahman extension, and Cap Chatelier, flakes from discoidal cores are associated with some cleavers and ovate flake hand axes. At Cap Chatelier, the final Acheulian is dated to over 200,000 years ago by optically stimulated luminescence (Hublin 2001:103).

At the end of the Acheulian, there appears to have been an arid phase. Moister conditions present by 130,000 years ago are associated with widespread Mousterian or Levallois-Mousterian sites (Phillipson 1993:90). These industries are classified either as Mousterian (including Levallois variants) or Aterian. Mousterian assemblages include many side scrapers, points, denticulates, backed blades, points, backed flakes, and Levallois pieces. Aterian assemblages contain the same types of tools: but add end scrapers, burins, borers, foliates, and stemmed or tanged pieces. The tang is either unifacially or bifacially retouched; other than this, a tool might show no further modification (Caton-Thompson 1946a:90; Kleindienst 2001:4). Or tanged points might be bifacially retouched on the stem and unifacially worked on the business end, the point. "It is clear that the tang is a specialized, local invention to facilitate hafting the stone cutting/scraping parts of a tool in the most efficient manner" (Clark 1980a:547). Along with some Syrian Middle Palaeolithic points with bitumen glue or mastic (Boëda et al. 1996), this is some of the earliest evidence for composite tools.

The Aterian was defined by Reygasse (1919–1920) for assemblages from Bir-el-Ater (now Oued Djebanna) in northeast Algeria (Kleindienst 2001:4; Caton-Thompson 1946a:89). This open-air site was composed of deposits on the banks of a streambed. Here the surface deposit was around 1.3 m thick. Beneath it was about 1 m of gravel, then a layer of argillaceous sands, and beneath this, about 1 m deposit including Aterian artifacts with gravel underneath. The occupation level was described as an Aterian floor with ash and fragmentary animal bones (Caton-Thompson 1946a:100). Reygasse described an assemblage with Levallois artifacts, as well as pedunculates or tanged pieces (Caton-Thompson 1946a).

Caton-Thompson (1946a) discussed the evidence for the Aterian culture at her Huxley Memorial lecture for the Royal Anthropological Institute in 1946. She concluded that what is known about it "is distressingly limited" (Caton-Thompson 1946a:88). Defined by its distinctive tanged points, the Aterian represented "a new formidable mechanical force let loose in the African world" (Caton-Thompson 1946a:88). It had a wide distribution throughout North Africa, including the Western Desert of Egypt (at Siwa and Kharga oases). But, as is still supported, there was no sign of it in the Nile Valley or farther east (Caton-Thompson 1946a:89), except possibly at Sodmein Cave (Mercier et al. 1999:1340). In Northwest Africa, however, it was found as far south as 18° N, showing an enviable "Aterian disregard for climatic extremes" (Caton-Thompson 1946a:90). Like most of her successors, Caton-Thompson (1946a:90) stressed the continuity between the Aterian and earlier Levalloiso-Mousterian technology (Caton-Thompson 1946a:90) more characteristic of the Middle Palaeolithic. Where a stratigraphic sequence was available, the Aterian was always younger than this Levalloiso-Mousterian, but older than any Epipalaeolithic industry (Caton-Thompson 1946a:99). There was a break with the past, however, since the Aterians were the harbingers of the future Upper Palaeolithic modern.

What to do about Levallois blade technology, which was also seen in the Aterian? Is this a precocious Upper Palaeolithic development, or just an accident? Unlike many contemporary researchers such as McBurney (1967:90), Caton-Thompson thought that the concept of "blade" should never be used for the products of Levallois technology. It

> should be used exclusively for the product of blade-cores, not for the narrow or parallel-sided flakes yielded by all tortoise-core industries. For these, the term "flake-blade" seems apt. (Caton-Thompson 1946a:90, 1946b:61)

This is similar to the terminology chosen for the Middle Stone Age industries in South Africa. The issue has been reviewed by Bar-Yosef and Kuhn (1999) who document the presence of blades in many Middle (and even Lower) Palaeolithic contexts. Other archaeologists remain split about whether or not Levallois blades have the same significance as Upper Palaeolithic ones.

Most research on the Aterian has been conducted in the Maghreb and Northwest Africa. Jacques Tixier standardized a classification for its tools. He used Bordes's (1961) Lower and Middle Palaeolithic typology and added thirty new categories for tanged objects (Kleindienst 2001:5). For Tixier, the Aterian was best understood as a Mousterian of Levallois debitage, but one with a blade element. He defined it as

> un facies moustérien de debitage Levallois souvent laminaire (avec une forte proportion de talons facettées), à nombreux racloirs, à pointes relativement abondantes, avec une proportion de grattoirs (souvent en bout de lame) plus fort que dans tous les autres faciés moustériens. Une partie non négligable de son outillage (parfois jusquà 1/4) est formée de pièces présentant à leur partie proximale un pédoncule en général taillé sur les deux faces. (Tixier 1967:795; also in Kleindienst 2001:5)

Ferring (1975) includes seven main categories in the Aterian, composed of Mousterian points, side scrapers, end scrapers, burins, denticulates, bifacial foliates, and pedunculates (figure 8.7). Some researchers such as Débénath (1994) argue that the Aterian extends along the coast of Algeria and Morocco, with sites decreasing in density farther inland. But Kleindienst suggests that this might be a product of the fact that most research has been done in the Maghreb. For her, there could be a link between the Aterian and the Lupemban industry of central and West Africa, where bifaces and occasional tanged pieces are present in otherwise Middle Stone Age contexts (Kleindienst 2001:6, 9; Hawkins and Kleindienst 2002).

The Aterian could be as old as 90,000 years and as recent as 20,000 BP (Kleindienst 2001:6–7). Haua Fteah provided the first evidence that the Aterian was beyond, or close to, the radiocarbon limit, since it was dated here to 47,000 ± 3,200 years (GrN-2023) (McBurney 1967; Garcea 2004:36). This would place it within MIS 4 and as recent as MIS 2. The only thing that is known for sure is that Aterian people were long gone by the time of the height of the last glacial maximum of 18,000 years ago (Close 2002:32).

A number of Middle Palaeolithic sites have been studied in Morocco. The Mugharet El Aliya ($35°45'N, 5°56'W$) is located at Cap Ashankar, 11 km south of Tangiers (Wrinn and Rink 2003:124). It was first excavated by an amateur group between 1936 and 1938, then by two Americans (J. R. Nahon and W. A. Doolittle), and afterward by Carleton Coon and colleagues (Bouzouggar et al. 2002:208; Wrinn and Rink 2003). Eleven stratigraphic levels were identified by the original excavators, and their assemblages were recently reanalyzed (Bouzouggar et al. 2002:208). The sequence begins with recent artifacts, then

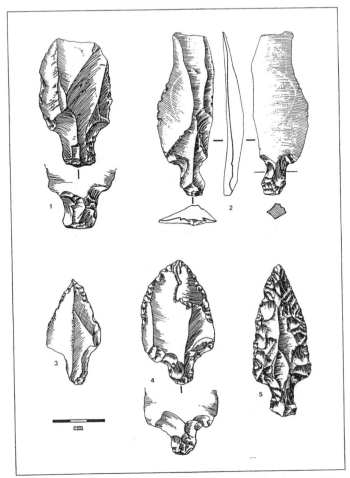

Figure 8.7 Levallois and Aterian artifacts from northwest Africa (Débénath 1994:24). Reprinted with permission of *Sahara* and Dr. André Débénath

Roman-Islamic and Neolithic ones. An Aterian occupation is present in layers 5 and 6, while layer 7 is virtually sterile. Layer 9 is considered to be Aterian or "Moustero-Levallois," but only a few artifacts were recovered (Bouzouggar et al. 2002:210, 212). Level 7 contained thirteen artifacts. The base of level 6 yielded 29 artifacts, including 2 small Levallois cores, 1 discoidal and 1 bipolar core, 15 side scrapers, 1 limace, 1 Mousterian point, and 2 large foliates (Bouzouggar et al. 2002:215). Level 6 was much richer; it contained 431 lithic artifacts: 27 cores, 216 flakes and blades, and 188 retouched tools (112 side scrapers, 5 Mousterian points, 52 foliate points, and 19 leptolithic pieces) (Bouzouggar et al. 2002:222, 236). Level 5 reportedly contained 431 artifacts, but none are available for study. Generally, the Middle Palaeolithic artifacts were made using lineal and recurrent Levallois methods, as well as bipolar blade technology (Bouzouggar et al. 2002:234, 236).

Electron spin resonance dates were obtained from ungulate teeth stored at the Peabody Museum. Early uptake ages range from 39,000 ± 4,000 to 44,000 ± 5,000 years old, while linear uptake gives dates between 47,000 ± 5,000 and 56,000 ± 5,000 years old (Garcea 2004:33). Teeth from the lower layers give an early uptake date of 62,000 ± 6,000 and a linear uptake date of 81,000 ± 9,000 years old (Wrinn and Rink 2003; Wrinn, forthcoming; Garcea 2004:33).

The site of Dar es Soltan in Morocco includes two Aterian levels; the lower one is older than 30,000 years and has many side scrapers. Both it and the upper layer have many tanged pieces along with a few foliates (Ferring 1975:117).

Taforalt Cave, or the "Grotte des Pigeons," is located in the Beni Snassen Mountains of eastern Morocco (Hublin 2001:104; Wengler 2001:76). It was first excavated in 1944 by A. Ruhlmann, who uncovered three Middle Palaeolithic assemblages, along with associated faunal remains (Wengler 2001:76). Layers D and F are Aterian, while the underlying layer H is Mousterian. In the Aterian, many Levallois blades were recovered (Ferring 1975:117). Side scrapers are more common than end scrapers, but end scrapers are frequent. There are many more bifacial foliates than pedunculates (Wengler 2001:76). The final Aterian was originally radiocarbon dated to either 30,400 or 32,600 BC (Camps 1975:182; Ferring 1975:117), and there is also an Iberomaurusian occupation here possibly as long as 22,000 years ago (Close 2002:32).

The Grotte du Rhafas in the Ouija Mountains of eastern Morocco was discovered in 1979 (Wengler 2001:76). Four and a half meters of cultural deposits have been identified in three stratigraphic units, separated by major erosional stages (Wengler 2001:76–77). The earliest belongs to the inter-Tensiftian or early Soltanian interglacial, the local equivalent to MIS 5e. In its uppermost levels, there were some Mousterian artifacts and one sub-triangular hand ax (Wengler 2001:77). The next or Soltanian 1 level contains several Mousterian horizons; two of these have evidence of living floor structures (Wengler 2001:76). The third layer includes a gradual transition from the

Mousterian to the Aterian (Wengler 2001:76; Wrinn and Rink 2003:123). The Aterian is dated by different methods to between 60,000 and 80,000 years ago (Garcea 2004:33). Above this latest level, there is evidence of a Middle Holocene Neolithic (Wengler 2001:76–77). The same raw materials are used in all Middle Palaeolithic sites (Hublin 1992:186, 2001:104; Wengler 1990, 2001:76). The most common are green quartzite, green silicified schist, and chalcedony; they come from sources no more than 30 to 40 km away from the site. Other kinds of flint and chalcedony come from about twice as far. These higher quality materials are more common in the Aterian than in the earlier Mousterian (Hawkins and Kleindienst 2002:602).

In the Wadi el Hay, there are several Stone Age sites. Station Météo 1 (at a meteorological station) has evidence of a Mousterian occupation while Station Météo 2 is Aterian (Wengler 2001:74). Another site, labeled "Sans Nom" or "Without Name" contains a Proto Aterian. These open-air sites are located about 100 m apart on the bank of the Wadi el Hay; each covers an area of between 300 and 400 m² (Wengler 2001:74). All stages of lithic reduction are represented, but the most popular is Levallois recurrent, with centripetal preparation. Most (78% to 95.8%) of the material is local Wadi el Hay chalcedony, while the few exotics were introduced as shaped cores and then were further reduced (Wengler 2001:75; Hawkins and Kleindienst 2002:602).

El Mnasra I at Temara in Morocco was once known as the Grotte des Contrebandiers or "Smugglers' Cave." It contains Neolithic, Iberomaurusian, and Aterian levels. Associated hominin finds include a mandible discovered in 1956 and cranial fragments recovered in 1975 (Débénath 2000:136; Débénath et al. 1990). Bouzouggar (1997) studied the lithic raw materials from three Aterian levels. These are composed of mainly local quartz, quartzite, chert, and gray limestone. Faunal remains are dominated by savanna species (Bouzouggar et al. 2002:239). Marine shells are also present and are abundant from the middle Aterian (24,000 to 23,000 years ago) onward (Bouzouggar et al. 2002:241). In the Aterian levels there are also four tools manufactured on rib bones (Henshilwood et al. 2001:633).

Ifri n'Ammer is a rock-shelter in the Moroccan Eastern Rif. It contains an Aterian occupation dated between 38,570 and 41,030 BP (KIA 8822) and a Mousterian one between 50,240 and 52,950 calibrated years BP (KIA 8824) (Mikdad and Eiwanger 2000; Garcea 2004:33).

One question that has resurfaced over the last few years is whether or not there were contacts between Morocco and the Iberian Peninsula. At its narrowest point, the Strait of Gibraltar is only 14 km wide; in periods of low sea level, some offshore islands would have become exposed (Barton et al. 2001:490; Garcea 2004:27, 30). Could this have led to biological or cultural contact between the people on either side? Most palaeoanthropologists see no evidence for a connection at all, since Neanderthals persist quite late in Iberia (Barton et al. 2001:490; Zilhão 2000, 2001), while Middle Palaeolithic North Africans were anatomically modern or near modern.

A related question is what happened to the people who created the Aterian. In most, if not all of North Africa, there is no sign of a human presence after the Aterian until around 18,000 years ago. Conditions were so dry and cold during the last glacial maximum that people could not survive; they either disappeared or migrated elsewhere. Roche suggests that they crossed the Strait of Gibraltar to become the Solutreans; this culture is associated with the last glacial maximum refugium in southern France and Iberia (Débénath 2000:137; Garcea 2004). There are several technological innovations associated with them, including the earliest evidence of pressure flaking (Straus 1995). The possibility of an Aterian origin was proposed as early as 1942 by Pericot y Garcia (1942) as a result of excavations at the Spanish Solutrean cave site of Parpalló. He saw a strong connection between the tanged points and foliates found in both regions (Caton-Thompson 1946a:117). Given the lack of any direct evidence, the Aterian to Solutrean relationship is about as believable as the idea that Solutreans crossed the North Atlantic at the height of the last glacial, one of the harshest periods of human existence, in order to become the American Palaeo-Indians (Bradley and Stanford 2004; Stanford and Bradley 2002; for a rebuttal, see Straus 2000). But there is an alternative model. As conditions worsened, the Aterians could have retreated south into the Sahara (Débénath 2000:137) and into Western and Central Africa. The general technological similarities between the Aterian and the Middle Stone Age Lupemban Industry could be used to support a migration or the presence of a large interaction zone between the two regions.

In order to test the idea of contact between Morocco and southwestern Europe, a British team responsible for reanalysis of the Middle Palaeolithic Neanderthal cave sites of Gibraltar (Stringer et al. 2000) began collaborating with Moroccan archaeologists. In 2001, they conducted a search for Upper

Pleistocene Moroccan coastal sites (Barton et al. 2001:490). At the limestone area of Tétouan, they studied Ghar Cahal or the "Black Cave" which is located on a ridge above a small valley overlooking the Strait of Gibraltar. Its Neolithic levels had been studied earlier, but now it was recognized that Middle and Upper Palaeolithic (Iberomaurusian) levels were also present. Farther south in the Talembote region is the Oued Laou; this is a large river system with steep-sided gorges (Barton et al. 2001:490). Another site of interest is Kehf el Hammar, where Neolithic and Iberomaurusian levels were studied previously (Barton et al. 2001:490).The British team also recorded over thirty caves, rock-shelters, and open-air sites in a nearby gorge, the Ouled Ali Mansur Valley (Barton et al. 2001:490). The Moroccan area bordering the Strait of Gibraltar is clearly worthy of renewed attention.

Farther east, there are few people in the Maghreb in the period between the Aterian and the Iberomaurusian. It is possible that large parts of North Africa were abandoned for as much as 20,000 years. Toward the end of the last glacial maximum, Mode 5 Iberomaurusian people appear, generally following the Mediterranean coast (Lubell et al. 1984:170). Their technology is microlithic, with a high percentage of backed bladelets. Partially backed, obtuse-ended forms are common. When geometric microliths are present, segments (crescents) predominate; microburins are also present in all assemblages (Lubell et al. 1984:149). An index fossil for this period is the La Mouillah point, a bladelet pointed by means of a microburin facet (Lubell et al. 1984:149).

The Iberomaurusian is present by 22,000 BP at Taforalt in Eastern Morocco, as well as at Tamar Hat in Eastern Algeria by over 20,000 BP (Close and Wendorf 1990:42; Close 2002:32). In its earliest phases, the Iberomaurusian is only present along the coast and its immediate hinterland (Close and Wendorf 1990:43); by the Pleistocene/Holocene boundary, it has expanded into the interior (Lubell et al. 1984:165; Close 2002:32–34). Iberomaurusian sites contain many cemeteries or ossuaries. These include Taforalt (where there are 183 individuals known), Afalou (n=50), and Columnata (n=114) (Lubell et al. 1984:157–158). All belong to the Mechta Afalou population, who tend to be robust, and who have had their upper central incisors removed (Close and Wendorf 1990:44; Irish 2000). They have little anatomical similarity to earlier people, except to the individual found at the Upper Palaeolithic chert mine at Nazlet Khater (Close 2002:33; Pinhasi and Semal 2000; Thoma 1984; Vermeersch et al. 1984a, 1984b, 1984c).

THE SAHARA: RICH GRASSLAND OR IMPENETRABLE DESERT?

The great desert of the Sahara had been uninhabitable for tens of thousands of years and remained so until the beginning of the Holocene. (Close 2002:33)

At various times in the Pleistocene, the Sahara could have been a barrier to human migration out of Africa. In wetter periods, it was replaced by well-watered grasslands, and it could have allowed hominin dispersals. This has been well documented for the early Holocene (Adams et al. 1997) when there were hunter/gatherer/fishers throughout what is now arid desert, part of Sutton's (1977) African aqualithic. Most of the attention of palaeoenvironmental specialists has been on the Holocene history, not earlier periods. Is there any evidence of earlier wet periods associated with the expansion of human settlement? Hublin (2001:100) discusses the evidence showing that the Sahara Desert increases and decreases in response to Milankovitch forcing. While agreeing that aridity was the main feature in the Maghreb for most of the Quaternary, it is clear that there was a time when conditions were radically different (Hublin 2001:100). The desert almost totally disappeared during MIS 3 (Rognon 1996). There is evidence of dry savanna during MIS 4 at Doukkalla II and during MIS 2 at El Haroura Cave, both in Morocco (Hublin 2001:100). MIS 5 sees numerous rainy phases (during MIS 5e, 5c, and 5a), as well as the return of the desert in stages 5b and 5d (Hublin 2001:102). Palaeontological sites show that the Sahara only became a boundary during the Middle Pleistocene; before this, the large mammal fauna has strong connections to East Africa (Hublin 2001:102). After this, Palaeoarctic or Eurasian fauna starts appearing; this could represent a movement of animals across the Strait of Gibraltar (Hublin 2001:102).

At the end of the Middle Pleistocene, during a dry period, there is some evidence of human occupation in the Sahara and Morocco. Archaeological remains can be assigned to Bordes's Mousterian of Acheulian Tradition, as they include small cordiform and triangular hand axes, some small cleavers, and Levallois flake tools (Clark 1980a:545). Middle Palaeolithic people took advantage of the increased humidity and returned to areas that had been occupied earlier during the Acheulian (Clark 1980a:545). There are more Levalloiso-Mousterian sites than Acheulian ones, as well as later Aterian occupations. Clark (1980a) identified regional variants in the Aterian, with possible ethnic markers. In the northwest there were many tanged tools, denticulates, and end scrapers. Few side scrapers are found and no bifacial lanceolate points. In the southern and eastern Sahara, unifacial tanged forms are less common. They are replaced by bifacial and tanged pieces, as well as lanceolate and leaf-shaped bifacial points. End scrapers, borers, and burins are more common than side scrapers, and there are many blades struck using Levallois and direct percussion methods (Clark 1980a:548).

There have long been reports in the central Sahara of surface scatters belonging to either the Mousterian or the Aterian (Clark 1993b:64). Adrar Bous (29°19′N, 8°57′E) remains the only site in the central or western Sahara where an Aterian is stratified over a Mousterian. It is located in an isolated massif in the northwest corner of the Ténéré Desert (Clark 1993b:49; Smith 1993:69). Clark conducted fieldwork at Adrar Bous in 1970 and discovered archaeological material ranging in age from the Late Acheulian through to the Neolithic. He collected many artifacts from surface sites and also conducted some test excavations (Clark 1993b; Hawkins and Kleindienst 2002:602). In some of the surface collections, only certain types of artifacts were kept for analysis.

The Mousterian collections include large Levallois and non-Levallois flakes and blades with minimal retouch (Clark 1980a:549, 1993b:55). They are associated with a wet phase. Local raw materials used include rhyolite, basalt, microgranite, metamorphosed vitric tuff, hornfels, and graywacke (Clark 1993b:51, 65; Hawkins and Kleindienst 2002:603). There are no tanged or bifacial points during the Mousterian, and scrapers were only lightly retouched (Clark 1993b:55).

The Aterian is associated with much drier conditions. As elsewhere, at the end of the Aterian, this area was abandoned, not to be resettled until after 12,000 years ago (Clark 1993b:51–52). Exotics, such as fine-grained green chertlike silicified vitric tuff from 280 km to the northeast, represent 7% of the unselected Mousterian assemblages and 8% of unselected Aterian ones (Clark 1993b:51; Hawkins and Kleindienst 2002:603). Clark (1993b:55) thinks that S/142/70 is a good model of an unselected Aterian assemblage. It includes a bewildering range of shaped points (tanged, bifacial, parti-bifacial, leaf-shaped, and unifacial), as well as side scrapers, end scrapers, notches, denticulates, burins, and other ("miscellaneous") tools. No faunal remains were recovered from any of the sites at Adrar Bous (Clark 1993b:55, 65).

Tillet (1985) reports on a 1976 to 1979 Stone Age survey conducted in the northern part of the Lake Chad basin. The lake basin covers an area of about

2 million square kilometers and is surrounded by massifs and plateaus (Tillet 1985:164). There is evidence of increasingly moist conditions between 40,000 and 20,000 years ago, what has been labeled the Ghazalian. It is intersected by a drier phase (the Inter-Ghazalian) between 22,000 and 29,000 years ago (Tillet 1985:166). Between 20,000 and 12,000 years ago, there is a return to dry conditions (Tillet 1985:167). In the Chad basin, there is some evidence of Levallois industries underlying Aterian occupations that may represent the Mousterian (Tillet 1985:171). At Bilma, artifacts are found within a layer of lake sediments under a lacustrine calcareous deposit; they are radiocarbon dated to 33,000 ± 2500 BP (Gif-1788) (Tillet 1985:172). The debitage is similar to that found in Aterian sites, but no tanged pieces or large foliates were recovered. There were, however, some pieces that are slightly narrowed at the base by alternate notches that could represent incipient tangs (Tillet 1985:172). Tillet also describes Seggedim, an Aterian site located next to a lake near a black quartzite outcrop, which was the major lithic raw material source. A combination of a habitation and quarry site covers approximately 3.5 ha (Tillet 1985:172).

In general, there is a substantial Upper Pleistocene archaeological record throughout North Africa and the Sahara, areas that are presently very dry. It begins with the Acheulian and includes Levalloiso-Mousterian and Aterian versions of the Middle Palaeolithic. In all but a few places, there is a hiatus in human settlement corresponding with parts of MIS 3 and 2. Almost the entire region may have been depopulated as a result of extreme aridity. The first sign of people returning dates to around 18,000 to 20,000 years ago, Mode 5 Epipalaeolithic industries that continue into the Holocene without any abrupt change. In relation to the origins of behavioral modernity and the symbolism question, there is not a lot of direct evidence. If there was a sudden change in behavior toward the end of the Middle Palaeolithic, it corresponds with the complete disappearance of people. On the other hand, the technological norms associated with the Aterian undoubtedly point to the emergence of an ethnic identity that could be expressed in material culture. It was the first true North African "culture" in the full range of its anthropological definition.

9

The Archaeological Evidence
from Sub-Saharan Africa I

*Africa has already revealed herself as the Upper Pleistocene home of a
very remarkable physical diversity of man,* sapiens *and non* sapiens,
*distributed, on the evidence of his plethora of artifacts, in densities
of tropical population unparalleled elsewhere in prehistory.* (Caton-
Thompson 1946a:112)

This and the following chapter review the archaeological evidence associ-
ated with the emergence of modern humans in Africa south of the Sahara.
Throughout this enormous region, A. J. H. Goodwin and P. Van Riet Lowe's
(Goodwin 1928a, 1928b, 1929a, 1929b, 1929c, 1929d; Goodwin and Van Riet
Lowe 1929; Volman 1984:169) Stone Age sequence is still widely used. It was
first proposed in 1929 and was made the standard at the First Pan-African
Congress on Prehistory in 1947 (Kleindienst 1962, 1967). Eventually, two
more transitional periods were added, between the Early and Middle Stone
Age (First Intermediate) and between the Middle and Later Stone Age (Second
Intermediate) (Clark 1957: resolution 6, p. xxxiii; Allsworth-Jones 1986:154).

Early Stone Age refers to the earliest signs of material culture, currently
dated to around 2.5 to 2.6 million years ago in the Middle Awash region of
Ethiopia (Semaw 2000; Semaw et al. 1997, 2003) and to 2.3 million years ago
west of Lake Turkana in northern Kenya (Kibunjia 1994; Kibunjia et al. 1992;
Roche et al. 1999). Similar sites are known from the Shungura Formation in
the Omo River basin in southern Ethiopia (Merrick 1976; Merrick and Mer-

rick 1976). The Early Stone Age is currently subdivided into the Oldowan and Acheulian. Oldowan assemblages are composed of flakes detached from pebble cores and the cores themselves. Either or both could have been functional tools (Leakey 1971; Toth and Schick 1986), but the cores seemed to exhibit much more formal variation than the flakes. Acheulian assemblages include variable numbers of bifacial hand axes, cleavers, and picks; these are manufactured on either large flakes or cores. Sometimes even a single hand ax is enough to define a site as Acheulian, as at Duinefontein near Cape Town (Klein et al. 1999; Cruz-Uribe et al. 2003; McBrearty 2001:84). Contrast this to Mary Leakey's contention that over half of the shaped tools would have to be hand axes or cleavers before an African site would belong to this Industrial Complex. However, while reviewing two papers by Stiles (1979a, 1979b), Bordes (1979:11) dryly pointed out that there was no Acheulian at Saint Acheul, the type site. Archaeologists have long been struck by the monotony of lithics; while the "same general form is attained by different means at different localities" (McBrearty 2001:84), the final products are often indistinguishable. Did Acheulian hominins share some kind of mental template, an image of what a biface had to be? Or is it just an accident, the inevitable product of bifacial reduction methods? The oldest Acheulian is around 1.6 million years old, while the youngest dates to around 200,000 years ago. For McBrearty (2001:91) and many others, the Acheulian to Middle Stone Age transition occurs when hand axes and cleavers are replaced by unifacial or bifacial points. This could be a result of a (possibly gradual) shift from hand held to hafted tools (McBrearty 2001:91; Clark 1993a: 152).

Middle Stone Age assemblages, on the other hand, are composed of points and scrapers made on flakes struck from radial, disc, or Levallois cores (Goodwin 1929c). Flakes tend to be triangular with convergent dorsal scars and faceted (prepared) striking platforms (Volman 1984:194). They are marked by the absence of Acheulian bifaces and other core tools (Mehlman 1989:5; Thackeray 1992:388), but are clearly derived from this earlier period (Clark 1988:236; 1989:570). Rightmire (1984:317) concluded that "in general, technological advances relative to the latest Acheulian do not appear to be striking." The Middle Stone Age was also thought to be a temporal stage, but its range was not well understood (Clark 1988:236). This remained a problem until the late 1980s when new chronometric dating techniques (described in chapter 4) were developed. Numerous open-air, rock-shelter, and cave sites in South Africa have been studied for almost a century. But in East Africa, the focus of archaeological attention, until recently, was on the archaeology of human origins or, alternately, on the proto-historic periods (C. Kusimba 1999; Gowlett 1990; Robertshaw 1990b, 1995). Upper Pleistocene prehistory was only of interest to a select few, until it became associated with the earliest *Homo sapiens*.

Subsequent Later Stone Age artifacts are manufactured on distinctive parallel-sided blade or bladelet cores. The bipolar technique was also employed to smash apart the ubiquitous small quartz pebbles in central and southern Africa. Retouched tools include scrapers, geometric microliths, and backed tools, with or without microburins (Ambrose 2002:10). The latter are produced when one or both ends of a bladelet are notched and removed by a single burinlike blow. Microburin technique may only start at the end of the Pleistocene as at sites like Matupi Cave in the Democratic Republic of the Congo (Van Noten 1977; Ambrose 2002:12). Ambrose (2002:10) and Sibel Barut Kusimba (1999:183) feel that the use of fine-grained exotics may have been an incentive for the adoption of microlithic technology, due to the increasing cost of obtaining appropriate stone. Or it could reflect the development of regional social networks (Ambrose 2002:10), a sign of something like the San !hxaro reciprocity exchange system (Wiessner 1977, 1982, 1983, 2002). Ambrose (2002:9) also lists other possible causes for the increasing popularity of microliths: the invention of composite tools, the development of punch blade technology, the introduction of bow and arrow hunting, increased mobility giving access to new resources, and/or the need to curate scarce, but highly prized, raw materials.

As a number of archaeologists point out, there are also many Middle Stone Age (and earlier) assemblages with some sort of blade technology (McBrearty and Brooks 2000; Tryon and McBrearty 2002:211; Bar-Yosef and Kuhn 1999). The most notable are the flake-blades of South Africa (Thackeray 2000:154). For Singer and Wymer, who excavated countless examples from the Klasies River, flake-blades are

flakes which have been struck from prismatic cores so that their sides are roughly parallel. The more elegant examples may be called blades; this term is not used in this account, however, as it would exclude too many others which, although somewhat coarser and less regular, still satisfy the above criteria. (Singer and Wymer 1982:50; also in Thackeray 2000:154)

Generally, flake-blades were produced through a faceting platform. When removed from a cylindrical or conical, they were used without any further modification. It is this Levalloislike production method that is used as the criterion for classifying elongated, parallel-sided flake-blades rather than true (prismatic) blades.

There is a continuing debate about what happened at the Middle to Later Stone Age transition. For Klein (1992, 1994, 2000, 2001a, 2001b), this is the time of the emergence of true behavioral modernity, a process that could have been quite sudden. With Later Stone Age innovations in technology and adaptation, anatomically modern Africans could compete with Eurasian archaic humans, making the Out of Africa II dispersal possible and almost inevitable. Others see the transition as the sign of a period of migration or extinction of local populations throughout much of the continent. It corresponds to a period of increasing cold and dryness, when populations suffered severe stress. It may also be the single most important cause of the reduced genetic variation seen in living human populations worldwide (see chapter 6). Testing these ideas remains difficult, since there are few places with transitional industries (Deacon and Wurz 2001:56).There is a marked hiatus in human occupation spanning the Middle to Later Stone Age transition. Since this is the period in which early *Homo sapiens* populations become behaviorally modern, it is imperative to identify places where transitional sites exist.

EAST AFRICA

A number of East African sites contain Middle Stone Age sites (map 9.1). Many of these were discovered during the search for traces of Plio-Pleistocene people, rather than through a concerted effort to examine the later periods. One region that fits this description is Koobi Fora or the east side of Lake Turkana (Isaac and Harris 1997) (figure 9.1), where palaeontological and archaeological research began in 1969 (Isaac and Isaac 1997; Coppens et al. 1976). The entire Turkana Basin is composed of outcrops of Pliocene and Pleistocene fossiliferous sediments inter-stratified with volcanic ash levels. On the east side, the archaeological record begins around 1.8 million years ago, and spans much of the same time range as that in Beds I and II at Olduvai Gorge in northern Tanzania (Leakey 1971). Initially, Koobi Fora was subdivided into numbered sampling areas; numbers 1 to 99 were allocated to Ileret, 100 to 199 to the Koobi Fora region, and 200 to 299 to the Allia Bay region (figure 9.1) (R. Leakey 1978:8).

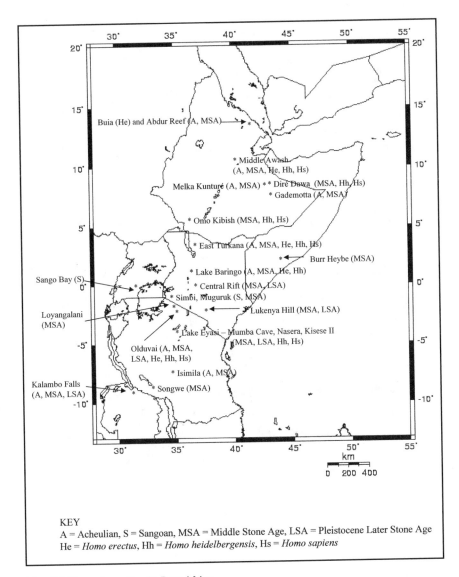

KEY
A = Acheulian, S = Sangoan, MSA = Middle Stone Age, LSA = Pleistocene Later Stone Age
He = *Homo erectus*, Hh = *Homo heidelbergensis*, Hs = *Homo sapiens*

Map 9.1 Stone Age sites in East Africa

Figure 9.1 Top: Koobi Fora or East Turkana, northern Kenya. Bottom: Allia Bay, East Turkana

Middle Stone Age fieldwork became a focus here only in the 1990s (Kelly 1996a, 1996b; Kelly and Harris 1992). Sites were discovered in three areas, all associated with the Galana Boi Formation (Kelly 1996a:88). As is traditional in Kenya and Tanzania, these sites were classified using the SASES or Standardized African Site Enumeration System (Nelson 1971). Based on the Borden (1954) system developed for Canada, SASES designations give coordinates for a rectangle with 15 min of longitude and 15 min of latitude. These are reported using capital and lowercase letters, with the first two letters referring to latitude and the second two to longitude. For example, the Songwe River Valley in southwestern Tanzania, the focus of my own fieldwork, includes SASES units IcIu and IdIu. Sites are numbered in order of discovery, so we recorded IcIu-1 through IcIu-18, and IdIu-11 through IdIu-26.

The first Middle Stone Age sites at Koobi Fora are located along an escarpment south of the Ileret police post, about 5 km away from the modern lakeshore (Kelly 1996a:85). FwJi-1 (4°2′N, 36°14′E) was recorded in 1974 when a hominin femur (KNM ER-999) was recovered; it was re-examined in 1990 (Kelly 1996a:89, 92, 1996b:48; Kelly and Harris 1992:30). Artifacts were observed eroding out of two sand horizons, labeled A and B (Kelly 1996a:94–96). A partial hominin cranium (KNM ER-3884) was discovered a few kilometers away in the 1980s (Kelly and Harris 1992:30). FwJj-2 (4°19′N, 16°13′E), in area 17, was discovered in 1991 (Kelly 1996a:107, 1996b:48). North of FwJj-1, it is associated with an outcrop about one kilometer in area. A total of 120 artifacts were recovered; all except five are surface finds. The majority of finds are unretouched flakes and flake fragments, but several "Levalloislike" cores are also reported (Kelly and Harris 1992:32). Most are chert and chalcedony, while others are lava (phonolite and/or basalt) or quartz (Kelly 1996a:111). FwJj-3 (4°19′N, 36°14′E) was recorded in 1992 (Kelly and Harris 1992:32). It is located 0.75 km southeast of FwJi-2. Here artifacts are eroding from a "distinct" horizon of colluvial origin which extends up to 20 cm below the modern ground surface (Kelly 1996a:116, 1996b:48).

The second set of Middle Stone Age occurrences come from the back slopes of the Karari Escarpment. This is inland, 23 km away from the modern lakeshore. It lies closer to the basin margin where silica raw materials are available. Sites here contain more lava than the Ileret sites but are dominated by cryptocrystalline silica (Kelly and Harris 1992:30, 32). FxJj-66 (4°4′N, 36°20′E) was found in 1990 in area 112 (Kelly 1996a:131). Here 177 lithic artifacts were collected from a 500 m long section of eroded outcrop (Kelly 1996a:116). FxJj-61 represents material collected by following a single outcrop over a distance of 1 km. A low density of artifacts, mainly flaking debris, were recovered from carbonate-rich sands and occasional silts (Kelly and Harris 1992:30; Kelly 1996a:150, 1996b:48).

A third kind of site is found along the lakeshore in area 104. GaJj-17 (4°28′N, 36°18′E) is located 15 km east of the Lake Turkana shoreline (Kelly

1996a:162). Artifacts are located in a coarse to medium sandstone deposit overlying fine-grained sands, representing an ancient beach (Kelly 1996b:48; Kelly and Harris 1992:30, 32). Generally, all lithics contain Levalloislike technology, with a preference for cryptocrystalline silica (Kelly 1996a:243). Raw materials may have been transported up to 40 km away from river channels draining Miocene volcanics at Buluk (Kelly 1996b:51). Middle Stone Age sites from Koobi Fora are generally small-density occurrences spread over variable distances. So these might be interpreted as aggregates, rather than true sites or assemblages.

For the last two decades, the Baringo Palaeoanthropological Research Project (Hill 1999, 2002) has prospected in the Tugen Hills west of Lake Baringo in central Kenya. The Tugen Hills extend about 100 km north to south along the edge of the rift valley. Fossiliferous deposits range from 16 million years ago to recent (Hill 2002:1). Archaeological work was initially carried out by a Belgian team in the 1980s (Cornelissen 1992; Cornelissen et al. 1990). Among the Middle Stone Age sites that they recorded was GnJh-17, where artifacts are associated with a paleosol (Yellen 1996:924). Since 1990, McBrearty and colleagues have recorded about thirty new fossil and archaeological sites in the Kapthurin Formation (McBrearty 1999, 2001; McBrearty et al. 1996; Tryon and McBrearty 2002:217; Deino and McBrearty 2002). Between 125 and 150 m thick, this unit dates from 700,000 to less than 200,000 years ago (Hill 2002:1; Deino and McBrearty 2002:186). The sites lie between two volcanic horizons: the K2 Pumice Tuff (which averages around 0.543 ± 0.004 million years old) and K3A, the Upper Kasurein Basalt (0.552 ± 0.015 million years old). Others underlie the Grey Tuff (0.509 ± 0.009 million years old).

In what is reconstructed as a lakeshore environment, they have recorded a number of archaeological sites including GnJh-41, GnJh-42, and GnJh-57 (Deino and McBrearty 2002:187, 207). Surface collections are described as belonging to an "informal flake industry" produced on small cobbles, while hand axes are quite rare (Deino and McBrearty 2002:207). While they date to the latter part of the Early Stone Age, they have little resemblance to a typical East African Acheulian (Deino and McBrearty 2002:185; McBrearty 2001) where hand axes litter the landscape as far as the eye can see. The catwalk site at Olorgesailie (Isaac 1977), for example, is what is traditionally considered to be the Acheulian norm.

K3, or the Middle Silts and Gravels Member, lies between the Grey Tuff and includes the Bedded Tuff (K4). K4 is found near the top of the Kapthurin Formation. It is over 15 m thick (Tryon and McBrearty 2002:220) and contains at least five archaeological sites:GnJh-63, GnJh-17, GnJh-28, GnJh-15, and GnJh-03 (Deino and McBrearty 2002:187). They belong to one or more of the Acheulian, Sangoan, Levallois, or Fauresmith (Tryon and McBrearty 2002:211). A minimum age for these occurrences is provided by two overlying pumaceous units; one is dated to 235,000 ± 2,000 years old, while the other is 284,000 ± 2,000 years old (Tryon and McBrearty 2002:211). All artifacts are made on lava, usually trachytic basalt. This most recent Acheulian is characterized by fewer cleavers, small, heavily flaked hand axes, and the first evidence of blades and Levallois technology (Tryon and McBrearty 2002:212). Levallois methods were used to make small flakes as well as preforms for bifaces (Deino and McBrearty 2002:185).

Gnjh-02 covers 2 ha and is associated with the K3 Member, 3 m below the base of K4 (Tryon and McBrearty 2002:218). Earlier researchers (Leakey et al. 1969) recovered many distinctive artifacts here, including unifacial tools on large Levallois flakes with minimal ventral trimming, blades, and both Levallois and non-Levallois debitage (Tryon and McBrearty 2002:218–219). At GnJh-03, between 20% and 30% of the cores were used to produce blades. Fully one-quarter of the excavated flakes are blades, produced by Levallois or non-Levallois production methods (McBrearty 2001:89; Deino and McBrearty 2002:185, 208; Hill 2002:5). Van Noten excavated an area of 500 m² at GnJh-15 in the 1980s; the artifacts were associated with a paleosol just below the local base of K4. McBrearty excavated an additional 100 m² area in 1997; together, 5,000 to 6,000 artifacts were recovered (Tryon and McBrearty 2002:219; McBrearty 2001:91). Only a few are retouched tools: some are small bifaces and biface fragments on cobbles. More than seventy pieces of red ochre were observed, weighing over 5 kg (Deino and McBrearty 2002:185, 208). There are also some grindstones that may have been used to process it (Tryon and McBrearty 2002:219). The artifact layer lies between deposits [39]argon/[40]argon dated between 509,000 ± 9,000 and 284,000 ± 12,000 years ago (McBrearty 2001:91).

Gnjh-63 represents an area of about 30 m². Excavated in 1997 and 1999, it yielded about 100 stone artifacts as well as faunal remains within a K4 paleosol. Artifacts include a single hand ax, cores, and one point roughout from a higher level (Tryon and McBrearty 2002:219; McBrearty 2001:91). Another site is GnJi-28 or Rorop Lingop, from 6 km north of the main Kapthurin Formation exposures. The assemblage is composed of 770 artifacts, and includes small hand axes, Levallois flakes and cores, and some informal points (Tryon and McBrearty 2002:219). The hand axes are described as grading into points or disc and radial cores and are some of the oldest ever found in Africa (McBrearty 2001:91; Tryon and McBrearty 2002:228).

The Mukogodo Hills are a series of mountains and inselbergs on the eastern rim of the Laikipia Plateau in north central Kenya. About twenty-five rock-shelter sites have been identified by a team led by Bruce Dickson (Dickson et al. 2004; Dickson and Gang 2002:1; Gang 1997; Kuehn and Dickson 1999; Pearl 2001; Pearl and Dickson 2004). Two of them, Shurmai and Kakwa Lelash, have been test excavated. Shurmai Rock-shelter (GnJm-1, 0°30′5″N, 37°12.911′E) is one of four cavities on the north side of the Shordika inselberg, at an elevation of 1,280 m (Dickson and Gang 2002:3–4). It was test excavated in 1993 and 1994 (Kuehn and Dickson 1999:67). The bottom level, Unit 1, is composed of poorly sorted rockfall (Kuehn and Dickson 1999:72). Above this is a dense Middle Stone Age level, with discoidal cores and triangular shaped points on "crude basalt" (Pearl and Dickson 2004:568; Kuehn and Dickson 1999:72). Tools include points, denticulates, gravers, and naturally backed knives. During the Later Stone Age, microlithic bladelets and small flakes are more abundant (Dickson and Gang 2002:17). Unit 2 has a IRSL (infrared stimulated luminescence) thermoluminescence date of 45,211 ± 5,356 BP, considered to be a minimal age (UWTL-202) (Kuehn and Dickson 1999:72; Pearl and Dickson 2004:568). Unit 3 is a medium thick bed of poorly sorted sand, gravel, and silt, gray in color. It contains a dense cultural accumulation with microblades and many faunal remains (Kuehn and Dickson 1999:78). This Later Stone Age level produces an uncalibrated accelerator radiocarbon date of 20,000 ± 80 BP (Beta-85593) (Dickson and Gang 2002:4; Kuehn and Dickson 1999:78–79). The overlying Unit 4 is composed of poorly sorted gravel, sand, silt, and clay and contains Neolithic and historic artifacts (Dickson and Gang 2002:6; Kuehn and Dickson 1999:79–80).

Kakwa Lelash Rockshelter (GnJm-2) is located on the top of the east face of a granitic gneiss inselberg, 5.5 km northwest of Shurmai. At an elevation of 1,230 m, the rock-shelter is 60 m long by 10 to 20 m wide (Dickson and Gang 2002:3, 6). The earliest occupation is an undated Later Stone Age, estimated to be more than 40,000 years old (Dickson and Gang 2002:6). Lithic artifacts from both sites were examined and compared (Dickson and Gang 2002:1). The most common raw materials are basalt, chert, obsidian, and quartz; the quartz and basalt are local and come from sources within 5 km of the site. The nearest obsidian source is Mount Kenya, 70 km away (Dickson and Gang 2002:9–10). There are significant raw material differences between the Middle and Later Stone Age (Dickson and Gang 2002:11). The former are almost always local, while in the latter, exotics are more abundant (Dickson and Gang 2002:13, 18).

Members of the same research team conducted a more recent survey of open-air sites in the Tol and Kipsing River valleys, focusing on their geoarchaeological context (Dickson et al. 2004; Pearl and Dickson 2004). They studied eleven alluvial stratigraphic sections and defined five distinct sedimentary units. Two of these, Peleta and Kipsing, belong to the Pleistocene and the other three belong to the Holocene (Dickson et al. 2004:156). Peleta levels include weathered basalt cores, flakes, and tools artifacts, all likely Middle Stone Age (Dickson et al. 2004:156).

In Kenya, Middle Stone Age sites have been most intensively studied in the Central Rift Valley and the Lake Victoria basin. In the former, hominins made use of the abundant obsidian outcrops. Sourcing this volcanic glass (Merrick and Brown 1984; Merrick et al. 1994) produced exchange or social networks that extend into northern Tanzania (Mehlman 1989). At Enkapune ya Muto or GtJi-12, also known as Twilight Cave, Stan Ambrose (1998b, 2001b) has excavated one of the earliest Later Stone Age industries, stratified above a Middle Stone Age level and dated to over 40,000 years ago. Ostrich eggshell beads are present here, as well as in assemblages dated to around the same period at White Paintings Rockshelter in Botswana (Robbins 1997) and possibly at Loiyangalani in the Serengeti of Tanzania (Bower 1977, 1981; Thompson et al. 2004). Enkapune ya Muto is on the Mau Escarpment west of Lake Naivasha at an elevation of 2,400 m, near many obsidian sources. In 1982 and 1987, Ambrose (1998b:377) excavated a 5.54 m deep sequence to bedrock; it includes later Holocene deposits as well as the middle of Upper Pleistocene. A series of volcanic tephras or distinctive ash zones was used for dating and cross-correlation of deposits. Here the Middle to Later Stone Age transition may have occurred before 46,000 years ago, as determined through radiocarbon dating as well as obsidian hydration (Ambrose 1998b:377–379, 388).

The Holocene sequences include the Iron Age, then the Elmenteitan Neolithic. A series of levels with Eburran lithics follow. Under the third volcanic ash or VA3 is found a dark brown gritty loam or DBL1 layer. This contains stone tools belonging to the Sakutiek Industry. Ambrose (1998b:382) describes this as a typical LSA (Later Stone Age) with thumbnail end scrapers, *outils écaillés*, and a low percentage of backed microliths. But it also contains some thin, part bifacial small knives, flattened discoids, discoidal cores, and faceted platform flakes similar to those from Middle Stone Age levels. Ambrose (1998b:388) describes this as a Later Stone Age, but with similarities to Second Intermediate transitional industries. It yields an obsidian hydration date of 18,860 years old if one assumes the temperature was similar to present, and 35,350 years old if the temperature was 5°C less than now, as might be expected during a full glacial. A radiocarbon date of 35,800 BP is also reported, but other dates are as recent as 16,300 BP (Ambrose 1998b:382, 384). These are within the same range as Mumba Höhle and Kisese II in northern Tanzania (Ambrose 1998b:388; Inskeep 1962). Among the finds are 13 finished ostrich eggshell beads, 12 preforms, and 593 eggshell fragments (Ambrose 1998b:382).

Under the dark brown loam are two gray gravel layers (GG1 and GG2) and one of orange, gravelly, loamy sand (OL), averaging 1.15 m thick. Artifacts are found in low densities and are assigned to the Nasampolai Industry. It includes large-backed blades and geometric microliths, a few *outils écaillés*, and some scrapers and burins. This is also described as Later Stone Age (Ambrose 1998b:383, 388). Some blades have traces of red ochre opposite the unmodified edge; Ambrose (1998b:383) believes that these represent traces of hafting. Deposits are dated by obsidian hydration to 24,760 years ago, if it is assumed that the temperature was like that at present. If 5°C cooler than present, the levels would be as much as 46,410 years old (Ambrose 1998b:384). The basal horizon is represented by RBL4, a dark red brown to dark brown gritty loam deposit with low densities of bone and flaked stone. These contain the Middle Stone Age Endingi Industry. Flakes have faceted platforms and radial dorsal flake scar patterns (Ambrose 1998b:384; 2002:14). *Outils écaillés* and scrapers are the dominant tools, and three backed microliths were recovered from the first two levels. Two flakes have traces of red ochre, while there is also a single ochre-stained lower grindstone. The oldest radiocarbon date is 41,400 ± 700 BP (Ambrose 1998b:384). Obsidian hydration produces a date of 17,320 years before present at a temperature like present, but could be as early as 32,458 BP if the temperature was 5°C cooler (Ambrose 1998b:384). Quartz and chert are more abundant in the Middle Stone Age than in the Later Stone Age levels. The closest quartz source was 65 km away, while the chert source remains unknown (Ambrose 2001b:34).

Ambrose conducted more recent research at other sites in the Central Rift. One of these is Marmonet Drift (GtJi-15), located in the Naivasha-Nakuru basin at an altitude of 2,040 m (Ambrose 2001b:33). Here, there are four main Middle Stone Age cultural horizons and eleven or twelve separate tephra layers in a 21-meter-thick stratigraphic sequence (Ambrose et al. 2002:A4; Ambrose 2001b:33). The three earliest cultural horizons contain radial cores and flakes with faceted platforms. The fourth includes retouched points and artifacts made on obsidian from the most distant source, up to 90 km away from the site (Ambrose et al. 2002:A4).

Nutmot or Ntuka River 3 (GvJh-11) is an open-air site on the western margin of the southern rift, 60 to 90 km away from the nearest obsidian source (Ambrose 2002:14; Ambrose et al. 2002:A4). It is associated with a 9-meter-thick stratigraphic sequence in which two distinct volcanic units can be identified. The lowest levels, strata 15 and 16, are 2.7 m thick. They contain an industry transitional between the Middle and Later Stone Age. It contains radial and blade cores, small obsidian bifacial points, blades with faceted platforms, and narrow-backed microliths (Ambrose 2002:14, 16; Ambrose et al. 2002:A4; Brooks and Robertshaw 1990:150). Since these levels are more than 5 m below a level radiocarbon dated to around 30,000 BP, Ambrose (2002:14, 16) concludes that they could be over 60,000 years old.

There are three Later Stone Age levels, in strata 8, 9, and 10, 3 to 5 m above the lower tephra. The youngest of these is accelerator radiocarbon dated at 29,975 BP (Ambrose et al. 2002:A4). There is also an amino acid racemization date of 32,000 BP (Ambrose 2002:14). The Later Stone Age is dominated by small flakes and bipolar cores; there are few blades or bladelets, and no backed tools. Obsidian was used for about 16% of this assemblage, as opposed to 64% in transitional stratum 15 (Ambrose 2002:14–15). Another site, Norikiushin, Ntuka River 4, or GvJh-12, includes a 2.5 m stratigraphic sequence. Here an archaeological industry stratified between two tephras includes large obsidian-backed geometric pieces, blades with faceted platforms, and points struck from radial cores (Ambrose et al. 2002:A4).

Prospect Farm (0°36′S, 36°11′E) is an open-air site on the north flanks of Mount Eburru at an elevation of 2,120 m. Anthony conducted excavations at two localities here in 1963 and 1964 (Merrick 1975:268). This produced a long stratigraphic sequence, over 45 ft thick, containing four Middle Stone Age phases (I is the oldest and IV the most recent) (Anthony 1978:5; Kelly 1996a:250, 257; Merrick 1975:268). There are also assemblages belonging to the Later Stone Age and subsequent Pastoral Neolithic (Ambrose 2001b:33; Kelly 1996a:257; Clark 1988:271). Raw material is local obsidian, with occasional basalt pieces (Kelly 1996a:272; Ambrose 2001b:34). Over time, exotic obsidian types increase (Ambrose 2001b:24). Ambrose interprets Phase III as the last Middle Stone Age and Phase IV as transitional to the Later Stone Age. Obsidian hydration dates suggest that Phase III is between 46,500 to 53,100 years old, while Phase IV is between 45,700 and 53,500 years old (Ambrose 1998b:379, 2002:13). The overlying Early Later Stone Age is between 21,800 and 32,500 years old (Ambrose 1998b:379). Over time, Middle Stone Age artifacts get larger (Clark 1988:271). But Anthony (1978) saw little change over time.

Prolonged Drift or GrJi-11 (0°29′S, 36°11′E) is located at an elevation of 1,820 m along the Enderit River on the floor of the Lake Nakuru basin 15 km northwest of Prospect Farm (Ambrose 2001b:33; Merrick 1975; Kelly 1996a:248–250; Clark 1988:272). The youngest Middle Stone Age levels are situated 1.4 m below a paleosol capped by volcanic ash that may date to around 35,000 years ago (Ambrose 2001b:33, 2002:15; Clark 1988:272).

Lukenya Hill is an inselberg 8 km long and about 2 km wide, rising 200 m above the surrounding Athi Plain in southern Kenya (Kusimba 2001, 2003; Merrick 1975:26). Both Middle and Later Stone Age sites have been discovered here. The Middle Stone Age sites, GvJm-22 and GvJm-16, are located on the southeast side of the hill. They were originally excavated by Gramley and colleagues, followed by Merrick (1975:22) in 1971. GvJm-16 consists of upper and lower rock-shelters (Merrick 1975:29). Merrick (1975:29, 34) defined three main geological units, labeled A, B, and C; these contain separate archaeological units each, also labeled A, B, and C. Unit A contains casual scrapers, discoidal cores, and some bifacial and unifacial points. It is interpreted as Middle Stone Age, or as transitional to the Later Stone Age. Unit B is a Later Stone Age including backed microliths, small core scrapers, convex end scrapers, and ostrich eggshell beads, while Unit C belongs to the Holocene

(Merrick 1975:34). Raw materials are local vein quartz, as well as obsidian and chert from undetermined sources (Merrick 1975:39, 47–48).

In 1993 and 1994, Sibel Barut Kusimba re-examined five Later Stone Age sites from the southeast side of Lukenya Hill: three rock overhangs, a single rock-shelter, and one open-air site (Barut 1996, 1997; S. Kusimba 1999:170, 2001, 2003:166; Merrick 1975). Two are over 20,000 years old, and the other three belong to the Holocene (S. Kusimba 1999:170). Raw materials include relatively local obsidian in small bombs 1 to 2 cm in diameter; chert, which comes from a number of specific sources; and quartz, which is found everywhere in the region (S. Kusimba 1999:174; 2003:170). Obsidian comes from Lake Naivasha, 150 km to the northwest, or from the Kedong Escarpment, 65 km to the west (S. Kusimba 2003:170).

Kusimba defined two Lukenya Hill Later Stone Age industries, the first of which could be up to 40,000 years old (S. Kusimba 2003:170). At GvJm-46, GvJm-62, and GvJm-19, there are many quartz artifacts. Most (60%) retouched tools are scrapers, while 12% are microliths (S. Kusimba 1999:174, 2003:170). Bipolar reduction is quite common, especially as cores become exhausted (S. Kusimba 1999:180). Quartz tools are expedient, while chert and obsidian seem to be curated for future use (S. Kusimba 1999:180; 2003:170). Tracing the movement of lithic materials across space, Kusimba proposes that prior to the last glacial maximum, people followed a collector pattern of moving resources from special work sites to home bases. But during the last glacial maximum, increasing dry and cool conditions made it necessary to be more mobile.

The second Later Stone Age, the Lukenya Hill 2 Industry from GvJm-16 and GvJm-22, is younger than the first, and shows similarities to the Naisiusiu assemblages from Olduvai Gorge to the south (S. Kusimba 2003:172). These assemblages contain less quartz and more exotic obsidian and chert (S. Kusimba 1999:174, 181). Microliths (crescents, oblique truncations, and curved backed blades) become more common (S. Kusimba 1999:174). Kusimba interprets the increase in exotics to increasingly mobile people with larger territories and assumes that the technological shift was an outcome of the invention of microlithic technology (S. Kusimba 1999:183).

Marean (1997) examined the mammal fauna from Lukenya Hill in order to develop models of foraging strategies in the Middle and Later Stone Age (Mabulla 1996:93). He suggests that a generalized grassland hunting adaptation was followed in both periods (Marean 1997:189). By revealing a catastrophic age profile for alcelaphines, Marean (1997:212, 217) suggests that GvJm-46 was a mass kill site in both periods. But hunting strategies could have changed during the last glacial maximum. As conditions became cooler and grasslands expanded, the numbers of animals could have decreased. At this point, tactical landscape strategies, where many people are involved in a planned hunt, might have come into use (Marean 1997:219).

The Lake Victoria basin was the focus of much early research on the Stone Age. It was here, from surface finds at Sango Bay, that Wayland defined the Sangoan Industry (Clark 1989:570; McBrearty 1988:389; O'Brien 1939). Typical artifacts (core axes, picks, and core scrapers) have affinities to the Acheulian, as well as to the Middle Stone Age (Mehlman 1989:5; Mercader 2002:118). Desmond Clark proposed that it represented the initial movement of people into the equatorial rain forest (Clark 1988:281; 1989:571). However, there is strong evidence that some of these areas were occupied by grasslands during Sangoan times (McBrearty 1988:388). Barham (2001b:78) resurrected the idea that the Sangoan represents something new. He has suggested that it "may reflect a loosening to ties to sources of standing water as a result of technological or social changes that remain as yet unknown."

More recent archaeological research has been done by McBrearty (1981, 1986, 1988, 1991, 1992, 1993) at Songhor, Simbi, and Muguruk. Songhor is located in the foothills of the Nandi Escarpment in Kisumu District in western Kenya. It is 2.5 km south of the Songhor Miocene hominoid site at an elevation of 1,380 m (McBrearty 1981:173). Middle Stone Age artifacts are eroding out of a reworked tuff exposed in a gully formed by a tributary of the Mbogo River (McBrearty 1981:174). Two test excavations in 1981 produced 420 Middle Stone Age artifacts, including six retouched tools (two Levallois points, two bifacial points, and two formal scrapers). Over half of these were lava and the rest were quartz (McBrearty 1981:178–180). In addition, 112 bone or bone fragments were collected. Most are unidentifiable, but those that can be classified are all extant large animals (McBrearty 1981:185–186).

Simbi is in the Kano River drainage, at an elevation of 1,300 m (McBrearty 1991, 1992, 1993). Here, there is a 5-meter-thick exposure with over twelve volcanic tuffs (McBrearty 1992:35). Middle Stone Age artifacts were collected from the surface and from test excavations. Most are produced in local phonolite and quartz (McBrearty 1992:35). On the surface, there were large

THE ARCHAEOLOGICAL EVIDENCE FROM SUB-SAHARAN AFRICA I

bifaces with untrimmed butts, picks flaked on a single end, and choppers, but only one pick was excavated. To the contrary, most of the assemblages are dominated by small flaking debris, not one's typical Sangoan; there is even a bipolar core reduction area (McBrearty 1992:35). Associated with the artifacts are some equid and bovid teeth in anatomical position, but without the surrounding bone. These grazers, along with soil carbonates, both point to a Sangoan associated with savanna conditions (McBrearty 1993). A tuff above the Sangoan layer was potassium-argon dated to between 40,000 and 65,000 years ago. But at the Kapthurin Formation, similar artifacts are between 240,000 and 250,000 years old (Tryon and McBrearty 2002:213).

Muguruk is a site in Ojolla Location, Nyanza Province, in western Kenya (McBrearty 1986, 1988:391). McBrearty studied this site in 1979 and 1980 for her doctoral research. She defined the Muguruk Formation using two related sequences, totaling about 12 m of deposits (McBrearty 1988:391, 395). Member 1, the deepest, is a conglomerate with occasional artifacts. Member 2, composed of 1.5 m of coarse-to-medium sand, contains artifacts belonging to the Ojolla Industry. This was originally Leakey and Owen's (1945) Lower Tumbian. McBrearty describes it as the local equivalent of the Sangoan and/ or Lupemban (McBrearty 1988:391). Most artifacts are debitage on Ombo phonolite. There are some large Sangoan core tools, as well as lanceolate points and point fragments of Lupemban flavor (McBrearty 1988:397). (The Lupemban is an industry which succeeds the Sangoan, but has much the same geographic distribution.) Member 3 in the central area of the site is composed of 2.5 m of mud-cracked gray clay and contains a few artifacts. Member 4, in the same area, represents 3 m of red clay sand; it contains Pundo Makwar artifacts, which means "red soil" in the local Luo language (McBrearty 1988:391, 401). This industry was originally classified as Levalloisian by Leakey and Owen (1945). Light duty scrapers are the most common retouched tools. There are few points and few heavy duty tools. This makes it different from the Ojollo Industry, but they both share radial core reduction (McBrearty 1988:391; Mercader and Marti 2003:78). Finally, on top of Member 4 is a black cotton soil which represents the current weathering regime; it contains Later Stone Age artifacts in quartz and quartzite (McBrearty 1988:391).

While there have been many Middle and Later Stone Age sites excavated in Kenya, Tanzania is a different story. Most of the research that has been done has been carried out in the north, while the rest of the country has hardly been studied at all. Sites of interest include the upper levels of Olduvai Gorge, as well as Mumba Höhle and Nasera Rockshelter, both in the Lake Eyasi basin (Mehlman 1979, 1987, 1989, 1991; Mabulla 1996). At Olduvai, Middle Stone Age artifacts are found in the Ndutu Beds, while the overlying Naisiusiu Beds contain Later Stone Age assemblages (Merrick 1975:325; Clark 1988:275; Hay 1976; Leakey et al. 1972; Skinner et al. 2003). The former consist of olivine basalt flakes with faceted platforms and radial or convergent dorsal scar patterns. These are associated with discoidal and Levallois cores, as well as a few retouched tools (four scrapers, one bifacial discoid, and one chopper) (Clark 1988:275; Merrick 1975:325). A Later Stone Age site was found in the Naisiusiu Beds, just north of the second fault. Louis Leakey collected lithic material from here and in 1931 used it to define the Kenyan Capsian (Skinner et al. 2003:1361). In 1969, his second wife, Mary Leakey, conducted additional excavations and recovered ostrich eggshells, tools, debitage, and *Equus burchelli* teeth (Merrick 1975:326; Skinner et al. 2003:1361). All of this is now assigned to the Lemuta Industry (Ambrose 1998b:379, 2002:13). The Naisiusiu Beds are the most recent at Olduvai, having been deposited after the gorge eroded to its present depth (Skinner et al. 2003:1361). Artifacts in obsidian and chert include backed blades and geometric microliths in various materials (Brooks and Robertshaw 1990:147). In 1999, Hay got an electron spin resonance date of about 60,000 years old from the analysis of a single tooth (Skinner et al. 2003:1362). Skinner and colleagues revisited the site in 2001 in order to acquire fossil mammal teeth for electron spin resonance dating. They discovered two separate artifact layers in two different localities, the older of which probably corresponds to Leakey's site (Skinner et al. 2003:1362). Dates were substantially older than expected, possibly shifting the Middle to Later Stone Age transition back to earlier than 59,000 to 62,000 years ago (Skinner et al. 2003:1365).

Lava and quartz artifacts have also been collected from the Ngaloba Beds at Laetoli, above the 3.75 million years old volcanic ash where Mary Leakey discovered three sets of hominin footprints (Leakey and Hay 1979). Stratified above the footprint tuff, the Middle Stone Age artifacts are associated with the LH-18 skull, assigned to *Homo heidelbergensis* (Day et al. 1980; Clark 1988:275). Three sites at Lake Eyasi (the Skull Site, Mumba Höhle, and Nasera), produced a long cultural sequence extending from Sangoan to proto-historic times (Mehlman 1979, 1987, 1989, 1991; Mabulla 1996; Brooks and Robertshaw 1990:148; Clark 1988:296). The sites were first studied in the

1930s by German palaeontologist Kohl-Larson and his wife (Reck and Kohl-Larson 1936), and then restudied in the 1970s by Mehlman. Most recently Mabulla (1996) has continued to investigate this sequence.

The Skull site is an open-air locality northeast of Lake Eyasi at an elevation of 1,021 m (Mabulla 1996:159). In 1935, Kohl-Larson found the fossil remains of three hominin individuals; these were eventually classified as archaic *Homo heidelbergensis* (Mabulla 1996:93). In 1977 and 1981, Mehlman collected a number of artifacts, including Sangoan core axes, choppers, and core scrapers (Mehlman 1989:160; Mabulla 1996:93). Mumba-Höhle is a rock-shelter located a few kilometers to the east of the Skull site; it was excavated by Kohl-Larson in 1938 and produced over 9 m of cultural deposits, ranging from the Middle Stone Age to the Iron Age (Mehlman 1989:11). Another site, Nasera, once known as Apis Rock, is found 90 km north of Mumba on the north side of the Soit Nasera inselberg (Mehlman 1989:12). In 1932, Louis Leakey (1936a:59) discovered one of the first Middle to Later Stone Age sequences in East Africa (Mehlman 1989:12). For him, "the culture becomes more virile and is characterized by the presence of very large numbers of backed blades often very well made, and by the tendency to make also many small crescent-shaped artefacts which are known as lunates" (Leakey 1936a:60). The cultural sequence derived from these three sites has become the yardstick for both the Middle and Later Stone Age in Tanzania. In order of age, from oldest to most recent, it is composed of the Njarasan, Sanzako, Kisele, Mumba, Naseran, Lemuta, and Silale industries.

The oldest cultural material is only found at the Skull site and is assigned to the Njarasan Industry, from the Sukuma for Lake Eyasi (Mehlman 1989:165). This is the local Sangoan and is estimated to be over 200,000 years old. Artifacts are made on volcanics and quartz, and include some core axes, radial cores, and large, simple-faceted flakes (Mabulla 1996:93, 165).

The Sanzako Industry is present in Bed VI-B at Mumba. It is an early Middle Stone Age with many side and notched scrapers, concave scrapers, bifacially modified pieces, and heavy duty tools (small bifaces and choppers). Points are rare; those present are described as large, broad, and irregular, and sundry scrapers make up more than half of scrapers (Mehlman 1989:103; Mabulla 1996:162). Most (95%) of the artifacts are quartz (from Lake Naivasha) (Mabulla 1996:162). Associated faunal remains represent exclusively modern species. There is a uranium-series estimated age of 131,000 years (Mabulla 1996:162).

The Kisele Industry is present in Bed VI-A at Mumba where it is estimated to be about 90,000 years old. At Nasera, it dates to about 56,000 years ago (Mabulla 1996:162). It contains many disc and part peripheral cores, with a few radial and Levallois cores, mainly in quartz (Mabulla 1996:163; Mehlman 1989:207). About 10% of the tools are bifacial and unifacial points, and convex end scrapers are the most common scrapers. At Nasera, there are retouched points, bifacially modified pieces, and a variety of scrapers (Mehlman 1989:200–201). Radial cores are common, but bipolar ones are also present. Mehlman (1989:266) suggests that there is a shift to bipolar flaking here, while at Mumba, bipolar methods are rare.

The Mumba Industry of Bed V contains large backed flakes ("knives") and blades similar to those from the South African Howieson's Poort. These include trapezes and short bifacial and unifacial points (Mehlman 1989:272; Clark 1992:204; Pleurdeau 2003:42; Mabulla 1996:163). Six radiocarbon dates on ostrich eggshell range from 23,600 to 65,700 BP (Ambrose 1998b:379). Three-quarters of the cores are bipolar, but other types are present (Mehlman 1989:272). Faunal remains include land snails, producing an *escargotière* (Mabulla 1996:163) similar to those from the early Holocene Capsian of the Maghreb (Lubell and Sheppard 1997; Lubell et al. 1984; Rahmani 2004). Sundry side and end scrapers are the most common retouched tools (Mehlman 1989:273). Over time, radial cores decrease in numbers, while platform and bipolar cores become more common (Mehlman 1989:311). In the earlier levels, large backed pieces are as frequent as retouched points. In later levels there are few points and backed tools, both large and microlithic (Mehlman 1989:311). Mehlman (1989:311) concludes that the Mumba Industry is "inconsistent with Goodwin's MSA concept" (Mehlman 1989:311).

The Naseran Industry has been estimated to be between 23,000 and 27,000 years old. A date of 33,200 BP has also been reported (Mehlman 1989:321; Ambrose 1998b:379). It includes small convex and convex end scrapers. Most of the material (97%) is quartz. The relative percentage of points to backed pieces is the reverse of that at Mumba-Höhle. Here points increase over time, and there are few backed pieces, all small (Mehlman 1989:318).

The overlying Lemuta Industry is dated between 14,800 and 21,600 years old (Ambrose 1998b:379). It is found in levels 4 and 5 at Nasera and is absent at Mumba (Mehlman 1989:368). It differs from earlier industries since radial and Levallois cores and retouched points are missing, while bifacial retouch is rare (Mehlman 1989:368). Medium sized (20 to 30 mm long) backed tools, end scrapers, and small convex scrapers are the most tools (Mabulla 1996:165). Above this is the Silale Industry, a Holocene Later Stone Age unit (Mabulla 1996:386).

Loiyangalani (HcJd-1) is an open-air Middle Stone Age site on the edge of the river of the same name in the famous Serengeti National Park in northern Tanzania (Bower 1977, 1981; Thompson et al. 2004). The site was discovered in 1977, and two localities 200 m apart were test excavated in 1979 (Bower 1977:20, 1981:53). These produced both Later and Middle Stone Age occupations. Later Stone Age tools are mainly scrapers, and backed pieces are rare. They are associated with ostrich eggshell, including at least one bead, as well as bits of ochre and many fish bones (Bower 1981:54). Bower (1977:22) classified the Middle Stone Age occupation as the Loyangalanian Industry. It includes many scrapers and borers, few points or bifaces, along with disc and Levallois cores. Quartzite is the most common material, then quartz, and a little obsidian (compared to much more in the Later Stone Age) (Bower 1981:54). More recent test excavations in 2000 and 2003 expanded on the study of both assemblages. The newer Middle Stone Age collections include a few bifacial pieces. There are also ochre "pencils," bone tools, ostrich eggshell beads, and fish bone (mainly the catfish *Clarias*) (Thompson et al. 2004).

Kisese II (Inskeep 1962) is a nearby rock painting shelter with a series of occupation horizons which possibly contain a transitional industry. The early Later Stone Age levels contain *outils écaillés* and convex scrapers, and later levels include backed microliths (Brooks and Robertshaw 1990:147). The transition from the Middle to the Later Stone Age is dated to 31,480 on charred ostrich eggshell (Ambrose 1998b:379; Mabulla 1996:91).

Some coastal Middle Stone Age sites have also been recently reported from Tanzania. A visit to the famous dinosaur site of Tendaguru, outside Lindi on the southern coast, resulted in the discovery of Middle Stone Age artifacts 2 km to the south, including hand axes, a core scraper, and flakes (Chami and Chami 2001:29).

Better known is Isimila (7.7°S, 35.8°E) (figure 9.2), an eroded gully or korongo with Acheulian artifacts, 20 km west of the city of Iringa in the southern highlands along the main highway to Zambia. It was studied in the 1950s (Cole and Kleindienst 1974; Hansen and Keller 1971; Howell 1961, 1972;

Howell et al. 1962). The original excavators described five cultural horizons or "sands." Artifacts were assigned to the Upper Acheulian and included large

Figure 9.2 Top: Isimila, southern Tanzania. Bottom: Acheulian artifacts at Isimila

tools in quartz, quartzite, and granite and small ones in quartz. A uranium-thorium date of 260,000 + 70,000–40,000 was obtained on bone (Howell et al. 1962:52; Clark 1988:239; Tryon and McBrearty 2002:213). Middle Stone Age artifacts are eroding out more than halfway up the sequence, and Later Stone Age artifacts can be seen close to the modern ground surface (personal observation). A similar record is preserved at Mgongo, a site on the outskirts of Iringa on the road to Dodoma, near the experimental farm of the new Tumaini (or "Hope") University.

Less advertised is that the Iringa region has numerous large granite boulders or koppies dotting the hills. Many contain rock-shelters with what appear to be significant archaeological deposits, including the Iron Age, Later Stone Age, and Middle Stone Age (figure 9.3). Some also contain rock paintings. I visited a number of these rock-shelters in the summer of 2005. Mlambalasi, 50 km west of Iringa, is best known as the burial site of Mkwawa, chief of the Wahehe in the late nineteenth century (1848–1898). He led the resistance to German colonialism and when finally surrounded, shot and killed himself rather than surrender (Briggs 2002:521–524). His head was then cut off and sent to an anthropology museum in Bremen, Germany, where it was in the collection until the 1950s, when it was returned to

Figure 9.3 Granite koppies at Iringa, southern Tanzania

Figure 9.4 Top: Mlambalasi rock-shelter. Bottom: Mode 3/Middle Stone Age arti-facts at Mlambalasi

his family. The family maintains a museum in Kalenga, west of the modern city of Iringa, where the skull is currently on display. The rest of Mkwawa's body is buried where he died at Mlambalasi. A large monument and plaque mark the spot, which was opened by then president Julius Nyerere on the 100th anniversary of Mkwawa's sacrifice. Some guidebooks report erroneously that the head was eventually buried with the body (Briggs 2002:523). Up the hill from the tomb is a large rock-shelter, with a dense surface accumulation of Iron Age artifacts. About a meter below the surface, flint and quartz flakes with faceted platforms are eroding out. This suggests that there is also a Middle Stone Age occupation (figure 9.4). In the summer of 2006, I returned to Iringa to initiate a survey of the Iringa rock-shelters, as well as to test excavate Mlambalasi.

In southwestern Tanzania, both Sangoan and flake-dominated Middle Stone Age sites were located during an initial survey of the Lake Rukwa rift valley in 1990 (Willoughby 1993b, 1996a, 1996b; Willoughby and Sipe 2002). Materials included cryptocrystalline silica, volcanics, quartz, and quartzite. They are remarkably different from the following Later Stone Age which is microlithic and quartz dominated. I excavated a Pleistocene and Holocene Later Stone Age sequence with no radical change in technology in July 1997 at IdIu-22, a collapsed volcanic rock-shelter near the modern village of Mapogoro. In June 2005, the first buried Middle Stone Age sequence was uncovered just a few kilometers to the north at site IcIu-18. These koppie rock-shelters are located south of a series of Plio-Pleistocene lacustrine deposits that represent one or more phases of expansion of Lake Rukwa (figure 9.5). There are also many open-air Middle and Later Stone Age localities, mainly associated with ancient terraces of the Songwe River. Similar artifacts were found in the late 1970s along the other Songwe River which flows into Lake Nyasa/Malawi (McBrearty et al. 1982, 1984).

WEST AFRICA

Modern West Africa is divided into a series of bands of vegetation that extend from east to west and are defined by latitude and precipitation. Along the coast south of 6°N, there are moist evergreen forests, where the annual rainfall ranges between 1,600 and 2,000 mm (Casey 2003:37). North of this is a semi-deciduous forest where the annual precipitation ranges between 1,200 and 1,600 mm; in this area, there is a dry season of about three months

Figure 9.5 Top: The Songwe River valley near Galula Village. Bottom: Middle Stone Age artifacts from Iclu-4

(Casey 2003:37). Between 8°N and 15°N is savanna, with 1,200 to 500 mm of annual rainfall (Casey 2003:37–38). North of this is the Sahel and then the

Sahara desert. Stone Age archaeological research has had mixed success in the forests and savannas of West Africa (map 9.2). Prehistoric artifacts are found on the surface in many areas but are usually from disturbed contexts (Holl 1997:305). While industrial terms have been borrowed from other parts of the continent, it is still debatable whether West African assemblages are comparable (Holl 1997:306; MacDonald 1997:331).

Almost twenty years ago, Allsworth-Jones (1986) wrote a summary paper about the Stone Age in Nigeria and Cameroon. Like elsewhere, early archaeological materials were found as a result of mining activities. His own archaeological survey in northern Nigeria from 1976 to 1978 led to the identification of a number of low-density Middle Stone Age surface sites (Allsworth-Jones 1986:155). He describes the material as very similar to that from North Africa (Allsworth-Jones 1986:166; Phillipson 1993:87), so it was classified using Bordes's (1961) system. Like elsewhere, there is usually a gap from the end of the Middle Stone Age until after the last glacial maximum. Within areas covered today by equatorial rain forest, there are find spots and possible Middle Stone Age sites currently being reported (Mercader and Marti 2003), but it is not clear if these areas were forested at the time of human occupation.

MacDonald (1997:332) describes assemblages from the Jos Plateau in northern Nigeria and northern Cameroon. Made on igneous rocks, they are divided into two facies: Mai Lumba and Zenabi. The former are associated with lateritic or iron-rich gravels, and about half of the flakes show prepared platforms (MacDonald 1997:332; Robert et al. 2003:164). There is a minimum radiocarbon age of 15,320 BP for this facies at Mayo Louti in Cameroon (MacDonald 1997:332). In contrast, the Zenabi facies, at sites such as Zenabi and Tibchi, is associated with a lower Levallois index. There are more side scrapers, and flakes tend to have plain striking platforms rather than faceted ones (MacDonald 1997:332; Allsworth-Jones 1986).

Birimi, on the Gambaga escarpment in the northern region of Ghana, has recently produced assemblages that are associated with the Middle Stone Age, a Holocene Later Stone Age (the Kintampo culture famous for its terracotta "cigars"), and an Iron Age smelting site (Casey 2003; Casey et al. 1997; Hawkins et al. 1996; Quickert et al. 2003:1291). In 1996, Middle Stone Age mudstone and quartz artifacts were discovered in situ 1 m below the modern surface. The artifacts also erode from below and within the Kintampo layer and include Levallois flakes and cores, disc cores, blades, bifaces, notches,

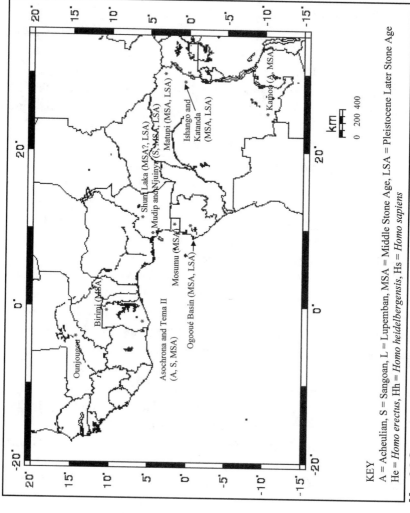

KEY

A = Acheulian, S = Sangoan, L = Lupemban, MSA = Middle Stone Age, LSA = Pleistocene Later Stone Age
He = *Homo erectus*, Hh = *Homo heidelbergensis*, Hs = *Homo sapiens*

Map 9.2 Stone Age sites in West and Central Africa

denticulates, and retouched flakes and blades, but no heavy duty (core) tools (Quickert et al. 2003:1291; Casey et al. 1997:32, 36; Hawkins et al. 1996:34). An optically stimulated luminescence date of 40,000 ± 11,800 years ago is associated with a mudstone blade with a faceted platform. At another locality, another date of 23,600 ± 2,900 years ago was obtained (Quickert et al. 2003:1295–1296). Since it is not possible to trace the Middle Stone Age horizon laterally between the two artifact occurrences, they could easily represent two separate occupations (Quickert et al. 2003:1296).

A few other Middle Stone Age sites have been reported in Ghana. Two are near the coast at Asokrochona and Tema II. At Tema II, there is a Sangoan in the balas layers of a laterite gravel; it is estimated to be between 20,000 and 25,000 years old (Quickert et al. 2003:1292). At Asokrochona, similar artifacts come from two layers overlying Acheulian deposits and underneath "Mesolithic-Neolithic" ones. They are estimated to be between 13,000 and 20,000 years old (Quickert et al. 2003:1292). Tools include scrapers, knives, notches, picks, bifaces, core axes, and choppers (MacDonald 1997:331). Above this, there is a level with increasing numbers of smaller tools and possibly Levallois flakes and cores. There are no Lupembanlike lanceolates in either assemblage, and both are assigned to an Asokrochona Industry (MacDonald 1997:331). MacDonald (1997:332) reports that the Middle Stone Age of Ghana is more like the Middle Palaeolithic of northern Africa than industries elsewhere in sub-Saharan Africa. This is partly determined from the frequency of Levallois technology. This is a conclusion that Allsworth-Jones (1986) also made for Nigeria.

One of the few places where significant Middle Palaeolithic/Middle Stone Age research has been carried out is in the Dogon country of Mali. Since 1997, a research team led by Eric Huysecom has reported Middle Palaeolithic artifacts from a series of river cuts around Ounjougou (Huysecom, Mayor et al. 2004; Huysecom, Ozainne et al. 2004; Rasse et al. 2004; Robert et al. 2003; Soriano 2003; Soriano and Rasse 2005). Some are associated with distinctive stratigraphic horizons, while others are only known from the surface. Six stratigraphic units are described. These are labeled from Unit 1 at the bottom to Unit 6 at the top (Huysecom, Mayor et al. 2004:2; Robert et al. 2003). Many contain (mainly) quartz artifacts. Unit 1 is interpreted as deposited at some time during MIS 5 and includes a few polyhedrons and spheroids (Rasse et al. 2004:335). Unit 2 yielded cores and core tools (choppers and chopping tools) at the site of Kokolo 2. These are estimated to be between 60,000 and 80,000 years old (Soriano 2003). Blade production appears around 60,000 years ago, while discoidal flaking typical of the Middle Palaeolithic only shows up between 50,000 and 55,000 years ago in Unit 3. The earliest evidence of bipolar flaking using an anvil is about 26,000 years old, and heavy scrapers are characteristic of Unit 5 (Rasse et al. 2004:338). The oldest bifacial points appear between 30,000 and 20,000 years ago in Unit 6 at Oumounaama. Then there is a hiatus until the end of the Pleistocene (Rasse et al. 2004:335; Soriano and Rasse 2005:208). At Ounjougou, there are bifacial foliates in the upper gravels; these are described as "an Aterian without tanged pieces (Robert et al. 2003:165). Generally, the Dogon assemblages are confusing, since they do not occur in any fixed or evolutionary sequence (Huysecom, Ozainne et al. 2004:293). "Levallois, discoidal and not-Levallois (laminar, bifacial foliate pieces, archaic-like) industries are alternating in the Ounjougou MSA sequence without clear evolution continuity" (Robert et al. 2003:166).

Shum Laka (5°51′37″N, 10°04′44″E, elevation of 1,750 m) is the largest of four rock-shelters in the Laka Valley 15 km southeast of Bamenda in northwest Cameroon. The Laka is a small waterfall in front of the shelter (Cornelissen 1996, 1997, 2002, 2003; Moeyersons 1997:103). The site is located along the inner wall of the Bafochu Mbu caldera and was excavated between 1991 and 1994 (Cornelissen 2003:3; Moeyersons 1997:103). There are over 3 m of archaeological deposits, which are divided into three layers—T (top), S, and P (the deepest). Layer P is a sandy layer that is present only in the center of the shelter and is estimated to be more than 30,000 years old (Cornelissen 2003:3). Layer S represents the oldest dated deposits at the entrance to the cave. Composed of sand, loam, and rockfall, radiocarbon dating suggests that it was deposited between 32,000 and 11,000 years ago (Cornelissen 2003:5; Moeyersons 1997:104). Plant macrofossils and charcoal suggest that the local vegetation was composed of montane forest, open patches, and gallery forest, making it similar to present (Moeyersons 1997:109; Cornelissen 2003:7). Faunal preservation is poor, but there is a single bone of *Hylachoerus meinertzagenia*, the giant forest hog (Cornelissen 2003:7). Layer T sits unconformably on top of these deposits in the entrance to the shelter and represents the infilling of a plunge pool from the Laka River (Moeyersons 1997:108, 111; Cornelissen 2003:8). The top of this layer dates to 9,880 BP or to 10,000 to 8,900 in calibrated years BC (Cornelissen 2003:8). Plant remains are similar to those from layer S, and charcoal throughout represents an open landscape. Artifacts were recovered from layer P, lower and upper S, and T. Vein quartz was the most common raw material, but there were also welded tuffs and basalts, chert, and some obsidian (Cornelissen 2003:8–11). All belong to the Later Stone Age, "a microlithic industry on quartz with backed implements, but without a well developed blade or radial flaking component or bipolar technique" (Cornelissen 2003:19).

Banyang-Mbo Wildlife Sanctuary in southern Cameroon contains two areas from which Stone Age artifacts have been collected (Mercader and Marti 1999b, 2003:67). At Mudip (5°15′213″N, 9°42′559″E), Mercader and Marti (2003:73) recovered 627 artifacts from a 600 m² area. Most (91%) are quartz, and only 5% are retouched tools. These include nineteen perforators, seven core scrapers, and four side scrapers, as well as some microliths (Mercader and Marti 2003:73). At Njuinye (5°95′213″N, 9°43′38″E), they collected 561 artifacts from the surface in an area covering 11,900 m². Most of these were also quartz. In road cuts, a number of artifact horizons can be observed. Layers 1 and 3 contain Early and Middle Stone Age artifacts (Mercader and Marti 2003:80) or Sangoan pieces (Cornelissen 2003:21). There is one radiocarbon date of 34,700 ± 560 BP for the base of layer 3 (Cornelissen 2002:218). Artifacts exhibit single-platform core technology, and tools include a heavy scraper, drills, denticulates, notches, and some geometrics (Cornelissen 2003:20). Later Stone Age artifacts here date to late Pleistocene (17,800 ± 180 BP) and the early Holocene (Cornelissen 2002:218).

Mosumu (1°43′37″N, 10°04′39″E) is located in Monte Alen National Park, within the Uoro Tectonic Rift of Equatorial Guinea (Mercader et al. 2002:74; Mercader and Marti 2003). Artifacts were collected from an area of about 1,000 m² which is now within the tropical forest (Mercader and Marti 1999a, 2003:65). Artifacts are described as "undiagnostic" quartz and quartzite pieces (Mercader and Marti 2003:67–68). Ten test pits were excavated from an area of 22 m² at Mosumu; the cultural deposits in these ranged from 0.5 to 6 m in depth. Eighteen accelerator radiocarbon dates were taken; fourteen of these were Holocene, two were from the Pleistocene to Holocene boundary, and two belonged to the late Pleistocene, between 20,000 and 30,000 years ago (Mercader et al. 2002:77). A 2-meter-deep stratigraphic sequence was composed of the following: gneissic bedrock, then a stone line with Middle Stone Age artifacts (layer 1). Above this was a fine-grained sediment layer which includes the Later Stone Age (layer 2) (Mercader et al. 2002:77–78). Stone lines are layers of gravel of varying thickness, which are often interpreted as indicators of aridity (Mercader et al. 2002:71, 94).

A total of 5,584 stone artifacts were recovered from the Middle Stone Age levels, and 871 from the Later Stone Age (Mercader and Marti 2003:68). Of the former, 72.1% were quartzite, 27.7% quartz, and only 0.13% flint pieces (Mercader and Marti 2003:68). The thirty-seven retouched tools included small lanceolates, core axes, large bifacial scrapers, perforators, steep-edged core scrapers, side scrapers, and small choppers (Mercader and Marti 2003:71, 78).

CENTRAL AFRICA

The Congo River, along with its basin and tributaries, extends throughout central Africa (Barham 2001a, 2001b:66). In the lowlands today, there is humid equatorial rain forest; in higher elevations, there is deciduous dry woodland (Barham 2001b:69) (map 9.2). During full glacials, forests decreased and may have only survived in small refugia. Sands from the Kalahari Desert point to periods of extreme aridity in cold periods (map 3.3). The Stone Age prehistory of Central Africa has been recently reviewed by Barham (2001b) and Cornelissen (2002).

Belgian research in the southern region of the former Belgian Congo colony led to the creation of a regional sequence. In the 1930s, Colotte conducted excavations into Kalahari sand deposits at Kalina Point, Kinshasa (Barham 2001b:66). He used this to create a regional sequence of the Kalinian (Acheulian), Djokocian (where large bifaces were replaced by flake tools), and the Ndolian (for Later Stone Age microliths) (Barham 2001b:66). In 1944, Breuil added the Lupemban as a sub-phase of the Djokocian (Breuil 1944; Barham 2001b:66). The type site is at the Lupemba stream near Tshikapa, in the Democratic Republic of the Congo, formerly Zaire (Clark 2001:37; McBrearty 1988:389). In many parts of central Africa, it follows the Sangoan, and contains similar artifacts, core axes, and other heavy duty tools. Added to these are foliate and lanceolate points (Clark 1988:244–245). The age of the Lupemban is unclear. Barham (2001b:78) suggests that it could date to MIS 7 (253,000 to 186,000 years ago) or earlier.

When examining the central African record, the most significant behavioral question is when did hominins begin to occupy the rain forest? Barham (2001b:78) has no doubts: "The existing record shows that the roots of modernity are deeply embedded in the forests of Middle Pleistocene central Africa." The mark of forest dwelling, he argues, is the appearance of the Lupemban and possibly even the earlier Acheulian (Barham 2001b, Mcbrearty and Brooks 2000). Others feel that hunter-gatherers could not make a living in these hostile environments, due to the lack of sufficient food (Mercader 2002:118, 2003a:2). What kind of evidence is there?

Mercader (2002:122) argues that the presence of many final Pleistocene Later Stone Age sites in the Congo basin means that people were living here prior to the end of the ice ages. But it is necessary to prove that the regions were forested at the time of occupation. For example, Matupi Cave is in the forest now; but when people lived there, the local environment was dominated by savanna rather than trees (Van Noten 1977:36). Mercader collected plant phytoliths from three archaeological sites in the Ituri; the oldest of these, Matangai Turi Northwest, dates to between 19,000 and 10,000 years ago. It contains some evidence of forest in the most recent levels, but the older deposits are dominated by grass (Mercader et al. 2000:102).

One of the few early sites is Kamoa (0°24′55″S, 25°9′19″E) in Shaba Province in the southern Congo. It is located at an elevation of 1,050 to 1,100 m near the Kamoa River (Cahen 1975:7). It was first identified in 1939, and Cahen (1975:14) excavated a number of test trenches here in 1969 and 1970. This produced a sequence with the Acheulian, Middle Stone Age, a Holocene Later Stone Age, and the succeeding Iron Age. Stone artifacts were produced in a variety of rocks including siliceous sandstone, quartz, and quartzite (Cahen 1975:59). Acheulian artifacts include bifaces, end scrapers, side scrapers, notches, cleavers, trihedral points, picks, rabots, knives, and spheroids. These are associated with radial, "globular," and Levallois cores (Cahen 1975:71, 145). There are also Victoria West cores and flakes for bifacial cleavers, as well as Kombewa or Janus flakes, with a bulb on both surfaces. Cahen sees it as an evolved or final Acheulian, similar to that from Kalambo Falls (Cahen 1975:145; Clark 2001:620).

Middle Palaeolithic artifacts come from a stratigraphic layer labeled Fluvial Gravels I and include narrow bifaces with more or less parallel edges, Levallois cores and flakes, and circular "Mousterian" cores (Cahen 1975:146). This would fit into the Middle Stone Age. After the Middle Palaeolithic, there is a transitional industry in an altered ochreous sand deposit; it contains small, circular Levallois cores, burins, some narrow bifacial points, as well as blade and bladelet cores (Cahen 1975:93, 149). There is also a Holocene Later Stone Age in a second, similar sand deposit (Cahen 1975:93, 150; Cornelissen 2002:220).

In review articles, Cornelissen (2002:208) and Mercader and Brooks (2001:212) both propose that there were two Stone Age variants between 40,000 and 12,000 years ago—the Lupemban and a quartz microlithic tradition. Both were present before, during, and after the last glacial maximum (Cornelissen 2002:228). The former includes heavy bifacial and light duty tools in a variety of raw materials. The quartz microlithic tradition seems to be associated with open environments, with forest nearby (Cornelissen 2002:225). Examples of sites with this kind of occupation are Matupi Cave in the Ituri, as well as open-air sites like Ishango 11 and 14 in the Semliki River valley (Cornelissen 2002:217; Mercader and Brooks 2001:202).

Ishango is open air on the beach where the Semliki River exits Lake Edward (Brooks and Robertshaw 1990:155). It includes a late Pleistocene Ishangan Industry with double and single barbed bone points, Later Stone Age lithics, and remains of fish and mammals, and it is estimated to be between 20,000 and 25,000 years old (Brooks and Smith 1987; Brooks and Robertshaw 1990:155; Yellen 1996:917–918, 1998). The pre–last glacial maximum levels are described as similar to the middle levels of Matupi Cave, 125 km to the north. Quartz pebbles were preferred materials, even when other materials were present, and they were reduced through hard hammer percussion, bipolar, and blade production methods (Mercader and Brooks 2001:204, 207).

Katanda is on the eastern bank of the Semliki River, 6 km downstream from its source in Lake Edward (Brooks et al. 1995; Yellen 1996:915; Yellen et al. 1995). It was first identified in the 1930s by Fuchs, and was investigated by Boaz (1987) and others in the 1980s (Yellen 1996:917). The archaeological remains range from a possible Oldowan at Senga 5A (Boaz 1987; Harris et al. 1987) to the Iron Age (Yellen 1996:917). The basal deposits, the Lusso beds, date to the Pliocene. Above them, Lower and Middle Pleistocene fluvial deposits are capped at Katanda by the ABS carbon paleosol which is at least 75,000 years old (Henshilwood et al. 2001:634). Above these are the Upper Pleistocene Katanda beds and, finally, the late Pleistocene and Holocene Katwe ash deposits (Yellen 1996:917). Middle Stone Age occurrences at Katanda are estimated to be around 90,000 years old (Yellen 1996:915). In three field seasons, from 1986 to 1990, three sites were excavated: Katanda 2, 9, and 16 (Yellen

1996:918). Katanda 2 is on the south side of the ravine and contains Early and Middle Stone Age components (Yellen 1996:918). Katanda 9 is an open-air Middle Stone Age located just above the ABS paleosol across the ravine from Katanda 2, while Katanda 16 is located 400 m to the north. It possibly represents a living floor (Yellen 1996:915, 918). An area of 35.2 m² was excavated and produced over 10,000 stone artifacts, along with many fish and fragmentary mammal bones (Yellen 1996:918). Mehlman studied 7,366 of the lithics, most of which (91.8%) were debitage. Slightly more than two-thirds (73.3%) were quartz and 25.0% were manufactured on local gray quartzite. A few were made on brown chert, from an unknown source (Yellen 1996:918). Most of the 257 cores were radial or part-peripheral, and tools consist of scrapers, some bifacially modified pieces and heavy duty pieces (Yellen 1996:918). There are no Stillbay or Lupemban types (Yellen 1996:918). There were seven complete or fragmentary barbed bone points and two unbarbed points; similar finds have been made at Katanda 2 and 16 (Yellen 1996:918). The associated fish remains belong to the genera *Clarius* and *Synodontis*; today these large catfish can grow to more than 30 kg in weight (Yellen 1996:918). Sediments around the bone points were originally thermoluminescence dated to 82,000 ± 8,000 years ago (Brooks et al. 1995; Yellen 1998:173). Seven additional dates were recently obtained; these cluster between 60,000 and 70,000 years old (Feathers and Migliorini 2001:961).

Matupi Cave (1°13′53″N, 29°49′23″E) is one of forty caves in the Mount Hoyo limestone massif in the Ituri, eastern Congo, 70 km west of Lake Albert (Van Noten 1977:35; Van Neer 1984:60; Brooks and Robertshaw 1990:154–155). At an elevation of 1,450 m, it documents an early appearance of the Later Stone Age (Cornelissen 2002:217, 2003:2; Phillipson 1993:85). An initial 1 m² test pit was expanded to 10 m² of excavation area in 1974; artifacts were collected from 5 cm artificial strata (Van Noten 1977:35; Van Neer 1984:60). The top was a mix of modern and Iron Age occupation. Then there were four Later Stone Age levels, with milky vein quartz and quartz crystal artifacts. The first of these extends to a depth of 65 cm and is estimated to date to between 2,000 and 12,000 BP. It contains a low density of microlithic Later Stone Age artifacts: geometric microliths, fragments of awls and bone points, ostrich eggshell beads, and ground and natural red ochre (Van Noten 1977:36). From 65 to 140 cm below datum, there is a denser Later Stone Age. It contains a few geometric microliths, a number of borers, one fragment of a decorated schist bored stone, and two drills. Red ochre is common and some of it is ground. This level is estimated to date between 12,000 and 21,000 BP (Van Noten 1977:36). The third Later Stone Age level, between 140 and 185 cm, ranges between 21,000 and 32,000 BP. It is low-density deposit that is still fully microlithic. But few geometrics were recovered; the deepest one, a small semi-circle or lunate, comes from the 170–175 cm level. Bipolar cores and *pièces ésquillés* are common in the lower half of this level, and rock crystal and hematite are present (Van Noten 1977:36). The lowest levels, from 185 to 210 cm, are estimated to date between 32,000 and over 40,700 BP (GrN-7246). The industry is "still fully microlithic from the technological point of view" (Van Noten 1977:39). Van Noten (1977:40) stresses the frequency of what he identifies as woodworking tools: notches, scrapers, and burins. While the site is now in the rain forest, all past environmental indicators point to grassland at time of occupation (Van Noten 1977:36; Van Neer 1984:69). The most recent levels document the shift to a closed habitat between 14,000 and 3,000 years ago (Cornelissen 2002:223; Van Neer 1984:69).

A number of Later Stone Age and Later Iron Age rock-shelter sites have been identified in the Ituri equatorial rain forest (Mercader et al. 2003:47; Mercader and Brooks 2001:198–199). The oldest artifacts are radiocarbon dated to over 18,800 ± 100 BP (Mercader et al. 2003:48). The Later Stone Age artifacts are almost all quartz and include small core scrapers, side scrapers, small points, perforators, and microlithic pebble tools (Mercader et al. 2003:48). Plant phytoliths include many arboreal species, raising the possibility of a final Pleistocene forest occupation (Mercader 2002:122–123; Mercader et al. 2000; Mercader 2003b). Mercader and Brooks (2001:198) compared the Ituri and Semliki sites. They concluded that "the early LSA of the African tropics is indeed represented across large regions and diverse ecological boundaries" (Mercader and Brooks 2001:198). But whether or not Acheulian or Middle Stone Age people penetrated the forest before them remains to be proven.

10

The Archaeological Evidence from Sub-Saharan Africa II

When investigation in Africa is intensified and the chronologies have been improved, then we can expect that the uncertainties prevailing today [regarding the origins of Homo sapiens*] will be considerably reduced.* (Clark 1981:187–188)

This chapter deals with the Middle and early Later Stone Age prehistoric sequence in a number of southern African countries, including Zambia, Zimbabwe, Botswana, Namibia, Lesotho, and South Africa (map 10.1). There was an early and sustained emphasis on the study of this period in South Africa (Deacon and Deacon 1999). Almost three-quarters of a century ago, Goodwin (1929a, 1929b, 1929c, 1929d) and Van Riet Lowe (1929a, 1929b; Goodwin and Van Riet Lowe 1929) defined the three Stone Ages that still provide the framework for most of sub-Saharan Africa. Spectacular South African coastal sites that have been described in the last two or three decades have had an impact on research elsewhere. These include Blombos Cave (Henshilwood et al. 2001, 2002, 2004), Klasies River (Singer and Wymer 1982; Deacon 1989, 1992, 1993, 2001; Deacon and Wurz 1997, 2001), and Die Kelders (Marean et al. 2000; Marean, Abe et al. 2000). Middle Stone Age people along this "Garden Route" of the modern Cape coast could be the first biologically and behaviorally modern people. There are also important coeval sites in neighboring regions and countries such as Rose Cottage Cave in the Free State (Wadley 1997, 2001a; Wadley et al. 1997; A. Clark 1997a, 1997b, 1999; Harper 1997), Sibudu Cave in

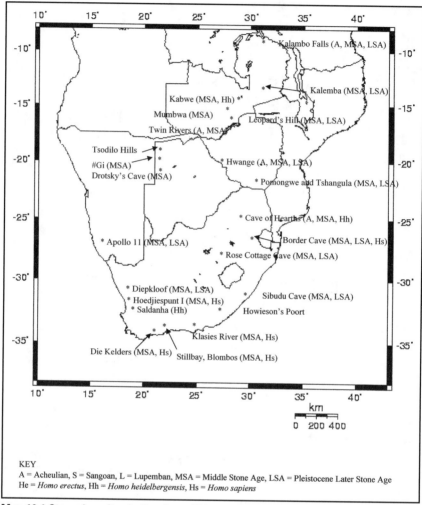

Map 10.1 Stone Age sites in Southern Africa

Kwa-Zulu Natal (Cain 2004; Villa et al. 2005; Wadley 2001b; Wadley and Jacobs 2004; Williamson 2004), and Apollo 11 in Namibia (Wendt 1976; Vogelsang 1996). Other sites of interest are Kalambo Falls in Zambia (Clark 1969, 1974b, 1980b, 2001) and White Paintings Rockshelter in the Tsodilo Hills of northwest Botswana (Murphy 1999; Robbins 1999; Robbins et al. 2000).

One of the enduring questions about the Late Pleistocene archaeological record in South Africa is the nature of distinctive Howieson's Poort Industry. Other issues are the Middle to Later Stone Age transition, whether or not there is a pre–last glacial maximum Later Stone Age, and how subsequent industries can be linked to peoples such as the San and Khoi-Khoi who lived in this region at the time of first contact with Europeans.

It is only in South Africa that the Middle Stone Age is well known. The type section for an archaeological sequence comes from a series of caves at Klasies River (formerly Klasies River Mouth) (Singer and Wymer 1982; Deacon 1989; Feathers 2002:177; Thackeray 1989, 1992; Thackeray and Kelly 1988). Excavations in 1967 and 1968 by Ronald Singer and John Wymer produced four Middle Stone Age levels, labeled Middle Stone Age I (or MSA 1) to IV or (MSA 4), with a distinctive macrolithic Mode 5 industry, the Howieson's Poort, sandwiched in the middle (Singer and Wymer 1982). Middle Stone Age artifacts contained long, thin flake-blades (blades made from prepared cores rather than prismatic ones) manufactured on local quartzite. The periods were classified on the frequencies of specific kinds of flake-blades, as well as by the presence of other tool types. This Middle Stone Age sequence was modified by Volman (1984:201–209) to a single stage after the Howieson's Poort, MSA 3 (Mitchell 2002a:81). MSA 1 assemblages include many radial and disc cores, numerous small, broad flake-blades, and a few retouched tools. In the MSA 2, tools like denticulates, points, and scrapers are more common, and the number of prepared cores also increases (Mitchell 2002a:82; Volman 1984:201–209). MSA 3 assemblages show a return to the general lithic patterns seen prior to the Howieson's Poort (Mitchell 2002:82).

In the Howieson's Poort, the dominant forms are large-backed and geometric pieces, especially crescents (also referred to as segments or lunates). They are often produced on finer grained rock rather than the quartzite used in the other Middle Stone Age levels. They are only distinguished from Later Stone Age types by their large size (Thackeray 1992:390; Ambrose and Lorenz 1990). The Howieson's Poort takes its name from the site of the same name northeast of Klasies River where this material was first excavated (Stapleton and Hewitt 1927, 1928). It was labeled a transitional industry when first reported, but its presence in between typical Middle Stone Age levels at Klasies River and many other sites such as Border Cave, Rose Cottage Cave, Apollo 11 Cave in Namibia, possibly at Die Kelders, below Middle Stone Age levels at Sehonghong and other sites in Lesotho, as well as at Montagu Cave, or above them at Nelson Bay Cave and the Cave of Hearths (Thackeray 1992:387, 396) clearly shows its proper affiliation. But it is unclear just how old the

Howieson's Poort is; various dates have been suggested, ranging from 80,000 to 40,000 BP (Thackeray 1992:403; Mitchell 2002a:81–82; Parkington 1990).

When it comes to the end of the Middle Stone Age, the coastal sites in South Africa unfortunately share the same problem seen in many other regions of Africa. There are very few places, if any, with the transition. The sites with the best record were occupied when the ocean was nearby, as can be seen by their extensive use of shellfish and other coastal resources. But in a full glacial, sea level would have significantly dropped, and people who wanted to maintain this way of life would have had to move onto the continental shelf. As a result, the transitional record would now be underwater and inaccessible.

The origin of the Later Stone Age remains problematic (Klein 2001b:7). Wadley (1993:245) argues that archaeologists are no longer certain what the period represents. Goodwin and Van Riet Lowe saw the Later Stone Age as representing "several stone industries and/or cultures that included non-lithic items, such as ostrich eggshell beads and worked bone implements, and excluded MSA stone tools, except as recycled manuports" (Wadley 1993:244).

One of the earliest Later Stone Age assemblages may come from levels 1WA and 1BS.LR at Border Cave; if so, it would date to around 39,000 BP (Wadley 1993:260). There are few formal tools or bladelets. *Pièces ésquillées* (scalar pieces) are common, implying a heavy reliance on bipolar flaking techniques, and ground bone points and ostrich eggshell beads appear for the first time (Wadley 1993:260). The Later Stone Age also appears early at White Paintings Rockshelter in the Tsodilo Hills of Botswana (Robbins 1999; Robbins et al. 2000), and this includes the first ostrich eggshell beads. In historic times, such beads formed the nucleus of the !hxaro system of reciprocal exchange between partners in different ecological zones (Wiessner 1977, 1982, 2002; Ambrose 1998b; Mitchell 1997a, 1997b; Robbins 1999).

> !Hxaro involved a roughly balanced, delayed exchange of nonfood gifts—beads, arrows, tools, clothing—that gave information about the status of an underlying relationship. Partners were said to "hold each other in their hearts" and be willing to offer various kinds of assistance when one had and the other was in need. (Wiessner 2002:421)

!Hxaro is best interpreted as a safety net in times of food stress for the Ju/'hoansi or San (Mitchell 1997b:387–388; Ambrose 1998b:388; Mitchell 1997a:343). Special items exchanged between trade partners include arrows (backed microliths, bone points) and ostrich eggshell beads (Mitchell 1997b:388). Mitchell (1997b, 2002b:8) feels that the !hxaro system, and other aspects of San culture, were present by the early Holocene or terminal Pleistocene (Ambrose 1998b:388). This issue illustrates one of the strengths and drawbacks of South Africa Later Stone Age research. Given the wealth of historic and ethnohistoric documentation of hunter-gatherers, it is a legitimate question to ask how far back in time their behavior can be traced.

The earliest Later Stone Age appears to be around 40,000 years old. The term Early Later Stone Age (ELSA) is used for microlithic assemblages older than 20,000 BP where blades are absent (Mitchell 2002a:113). They include unretouched bladelets and many heavily worked bipolar cores or outils écaillés. Other elements include scrapers; backed tools, bone tools, and ostrich eggshell beads (Mitchell 2002a:112–113). After the last glacial maximum, there is more evidence of the Later Stone Age, called the Robberg Industry. It is microlithic and includes pieces struck from bipolar and bladelet cores, dated to between 19,000 and 9,500 BP. Retouched tools are rare and include scrapers and backed bladelets. Robberg assemblages show a preference for fine-grained lithics (Deacon 1990b:178; Mitchell 1997b:368, 2002a:120; Wadley 1993:265). Around 12,000 years before present, however, they were replaced in many parts of South Africa by a non-microlithic industry based on side-struck flakes, the Oakhurst, which lasted until 8,000 BP (Wadley 1993:243). Coarse-grained lithics are more common, and bladelets are rare; there are few formal tools except for large scrapers (Deacon 1990b:178). It is eventually replaced by the Wilton, with small scrapers, backed microliths, organic tools, and ornaments, along with rock art (Deacon 1990b:178). The Wilton can be directly linked to the people who were present at the time of European contact. Janette Deacon (1990b) sees the entire Later Stone Age succession as a series of separate groups or cultures. But Parkington (1990) prefers to interpret the evidence as the outcome of shifting site use as the sea level rose at the end of the Pleistocene.

ZAMBIA

The archaeological site of Kalambo Falls (8°30′S, 31°15′E) in northeast Zambia was discovered in 1953. A team led by Desmond Clark conducted field research here from 1956 to 1966 and identified numerous Stone Age occurrences (Clark 1969, 1974b, 1980b, 2001; Schick 2001:467). But there was a significant delay in publishing the third Kalambo Falls monograph which describes most of the Early and Middle Stone Age material (Clark 2001). Nevertheless, it offers a detailed description of assemblages, as well as a culture historical reconstruction for this long-utilized location. Given that there have been significant advances in chronometric dating in the four decades since fieldwork was conducted here, all published dates must be provisional.

The Kalambo Falls archaeological sites are found at an altitude of 1,150 m along the river of the same name which flows from Ufipa Highlands in Tanzania into Lake Tanganyika (Clark 2001:3). Today this area is part of the Zambezian floral region, *miombo* woodlands with *Brachystegia* and other trees (Clark 2001:1). Artifact occurrences were eventually described as aggregates rather than sites, because they are associated with gravel or stone line deposits, so they may belong to more than one culture historical period (Clark 2001:34, 286, 623). Stone lines are layers of gravel above bedrock; they are capped by clay or sand deposits. The environmental meaning of such features remains unknown (Mercader 2003a:9). Most of the finds are composed of clusters of stone artifacts, and no quarry sites are known from this region (Clark 2001:621).

Clark identified two localities, labeling them A and B. He described a sequence including the Late Acheulian, Sangoan, a Middle Stone Age with points, the Later Stone Age, and Iron Age (Clark 1974, 2001; Mercader 2002:118). What is unique and unparalleled about Kalambo Falls is the presence of waterlogged deposits; plant preservation has been exceptional, but no bones survive (Barham 2001b:67; Clark 2001:28, 34). Plant macrofossils and pollen were originally studied by Van Zinderen Bakker; more recently, the data was reanalyzed by Taylor and his colleagues (Taylor et al. 2001). During the Acheulian occupation (pollen zone KA1), the local vegetation was similar to the present, but possibly wetter (Taylor et al. 2001:73). The Sangoan sites belong to zone KA2, and possibly date to MIS 5a and 4; at this time, it was cooler and wetter than present (Taylor et al. 2001:74). Burned logs and fruits associated with the Sangoan include forest genera (Mercader 2002:118). The third or KA3 zone is associated with a radiocarbon date of less than 27,500 ± 2,300 BP. The environment was apparently cooler than present, and there is substantial evidence of grasses (Taylor et al. 2001:74).

In order to describe the archaeological sequence, Clark used the typology and culture historical sequences approved by the 1965 Burg Wartenstein conference on the "Systematic Investigation of the African Later Tertiary and

Quaternary," subsequently published as *Background to Evolution in Africa* (Bishop and Clark 1976; Clark and Kleindienst 1974; Kleindienst 1962, 1967). Cores are divided into specialized (Levallois or prepared cores) and unspecialized. Raw materials include local quartzites, silicified mudstones (cherts), as well as some quartz, chalcedony, and pothole stones (Clark 2001:64).

The Acheulian aggregates were placed into the Bwalya Industry, which was further subdivided into two phases, the Moola (or Upper Acheulian) and the Inuga (or Final Acheulean) (Clark 2001:39). Core axes, that index fossil of the Sangoan, first appear in the Inuga Phase (Clark 2001:246). These are partially bifacial tools produced by hard hammer percussion of cobbles and blocks; their butts remain cortical (Clark 2001:246). Clark thought these were shaped for chopping rather than cutting (Roe 2001a:497). The Upper Acheulian is at least 100,000 to 200,000 years old and could be as old as 300,000 to 400,000 BP (Clark 2001:622). While bifaces (especially hand axes and cleavers) are the diagnostic elements, some assemblages have a lot of light duty tools (Clark 2001:628). These include small scrapers, modified flakes, borers, and proto-burins or wedges (Clark 2001:628–629). Clark (2001:629) also reported the recovery of rubbing and grinding stones from site B.

The Sangoan is estimated to appear between 100,000 and 190,000 years ago, based on amino acid racemization dating of wood from the underlying Acheulian layer (Tryon and McBrearty 2002:213; Barham 2001b:67). A uranium-series date on wood associated with the Sangoan originally was said to date between 65,000 and 86,000 years ago (Clark 2001:622). For Clark (2001:246), Acheulian bifaces are lighter than Sangoan core axes, but there could be a continuum of forms. Generally, he saw signs of general continuity over time from the Acheulian to the Sangoan as the environment shifted from open grasslands to closed woodlands (Roe 2001b:643). Since Sangoan sites were associated with regions that presently have high rainfall and thicker vegetation cover, Clark felt that this culture represented people moving into the forest for the first time (Clark 1988:281; 1989:571; 2001:38; McBrearty 1988:388). The distinctive core axes could have been used for woodworking or processing forest resources (Clark 2001:632). However, as mentioned in chapter 9, Sangoan tools are associated with grassland environments at sites like Simbi in western Kenya.

Sangoan and later Middle Stone Age assemblages are identified by their stratigraphic position, technology, and typology (Clark 2001:623). The local version, the Chipeta Industry, is beyond the radiocarbon limit. A uranium-series date on wood was between 50,000 and 80,000 years old (Clark 2001:38, 234). There are no lanceolates, but there are occasional core axes and other Sangoan types, along with many small scrapers and other flake tools (Clark 2001:38, 246; McBrearty 1988:388). Most Sangoan artifacts are debitage; of the tools, only about 10% are the large diagnostic types. As was the case for McBrearty's (1999, 2001; McBrearty et al. 1996) late Acheulian in the Kapthurin Formation, there seems to be a lot more assemblage variation than expected. All Acheulian types are present in the Sangoan, and vice versa (Clark 2001:629).

Barham (2001a, 2001b:65) sees the emergence of behavioral modernity in Zambia as related to "the transition to composite technology and the associated development of a new regionally distinct industry." This is the Lupemban, which can possibly be traced back to as much as 300,000 years ago. At Kalambo Falls, the Lupemban is represented by the Nakisasa and Siszya industries. In the former, core tools include axes, picks, chisels, choppers, polyhedrons, and spheroids. There are also a few hand axes, cleavers, and lanceolates, as well as large scrapers (Clark 2001:234, 632). Flake tools include small scrapers, proto-burins, becs, and pointed tools (Clark 2001:89). It is at this time that the first evidence of Levallois flake production appears; it increases in importance in the subsequent Siszya, along with other disc core reduction methods (Clark 2001:234, 623, 632). Feldspathic quartzite is the most common raw material, but chert was also used, especially to produce long, thin flakes (Clark 2001:247, 632).

Clark describes two components within the Siszya or later Lupemban phase; the older is A, the younger B. These are subdivided on degree of artifact wear, as well as artifact form and change in production methods (Clark 2001:83–84). The large cutting tools are now lanceolates rather than hand axes or cleavers. Other heavy duty tools still remain: core axes, picks, core scrapers, choppers, and polyhedrons. Light duty tools include truncated flakes and blades, trapezes, backed flakes and blades, points, small scrapers, burins, becs, borers, pointed items, and discs (Clark 2001:89). Clark emphasizes the presence of smaller, lighter, and parallel-sided tools in the Siszya, as well as large blades and triangular flakes (Clark 2001:247, 623). Raw materials are primarily chert, and secondarily chalcedony and silcrete (Clark 2001:247).

These Middle Stone Age industries are followed by the Polungu, which is described as an early Holocene Later Stone Age, as late Sisyza, or as "Second

Intermediate" (Clark 2001:10, 621–622). Two assemblage types are described, the Hillslope and Rubble components (Clark 2001:10). They include single and double platform cores, a few core axes, picks, and scrapers. Other tools include backed and truncated bladelets, short unifacial triangular points, small convex scrapers, and a few burins and proto-burins (Clark 2001:10). Clark notes the presence of small blade cores and pressure-flaked points. While both are new, they are probably directly derived from the earlier Siszya Industry (Clark 2001:624). The Stone Age sequence at Kalambo Falls ends with a Holocene Later Stone Age, the Kaposwa Industry. It is a typical central African Later Stone Age with microburins and microliths, as well as backed bladelets and flakes. There are also ground and polished stone axes and bored stones (Clark 2001:10).

Kabwe or Broken Hill is a Middle Stone Age site with remains of archaic *Homo sapiens* or *Homo heidelbergensis*. The various fossil remains were originally classified as *Homo rhodesiensis* by Woodward (1921, 1931). The site consists of two hills of dolomitic limestone; the first was originally 15 m high, but was mined away during the search for zinc and copper (Avery 2002:537; Day 1986:267). On faunal grounds, the level with the hominin remains has been estimated to be around 400,000 years old (Avery 2002:537). The Middle Stone Age artifacts were originally assigned to the Stillbay or Proto-Stillbay Industry (Day 1986:268).

Mumbwa Cave (15°01′S, 26°59′E) is located 190 km northwest of the Zambian capital of Lusaka (Avery 1996:63; Barham 1996, 2000). It was first studied in 1925 by Macrae (Barham 1996:191). An Italian group who visited the cave in 1930 described a sequence consisting of an ancient Palaeolithic layer, then 2 m of sterile deposits, then 60 cm of sediments with Mousterian artifacts. Stratified above this layer there was a Recent Stone Age deposit, and finally a layer with ceramics and iron objects that was described as Neolithic (Barham 1996:191). Desmond Clark investigated the site in 1939, and Karla Savage reassessed his results in 1973. In 1993, Barham (1996:191) excavated a test pit at the edge of the original 1930 excavation and uncovered a 6 m sequence, as well as two rock-cut, beehive-shaped enclosures against the north wall of the main cave. There was a third enclosure at a lower level with fragmentary human remains and stone tools (Barham 1996:191–192). The lithics were described as coming from above and below a sterile clay deposit. They are generally Middle Stone Age and include quartz flakes from prepared cores, radial and

Levallois cores, large scrapers, awls, spheroids, and lumps of hematite (Barham 1996:192, 1998, 2002a). In 1994, Barham conducted excavations of three additional areas. In area II, assigned to the Upper Middle Stone Age, there were hearths built with blocks of cave limestone and imported stone. These contained ash, burned bone, burned limestone, and reddened sediments (Barham 1996:193). In area I in the same level, there appeared to be the remains of a semi-circular structure with postholes (Barham 1996:195). The outline was 175 cm long and 30 to 40 cm wide and contained ash, baked sediment, lithic debitage, and bone (Barham 1996:195–197).

Twin Rivers, Zambia (15°31'S, 28°11'E), is located 24 km southwest of Lusaka (Clark and Brown 2001:305; Barham 2000, 2001b, 2002b; Barham and Smart 1996). Here there are fissures in an east-west direction that have filled with red sandy clay earth, later cemented into breccia (Clark and Brown 2001:305–306). The breccia is interstratified with, and overlain by, speleothems (Barham and Smart 1996:287). In 1953, Kenneth Oakley visited the site and identified two units: an upper brown and a lower, hard pink breccia (Clark and Brown 2001:306). The lower was tentatively assigned to the Early Stone Age, the upper to the Middle Stone Age (Clark and Brown 2001:306). Clark excavated here in 1954 and 1956, collecting Lupemban and Later Stone Age artifacts, and Barham followed in 1999, recovering 929 mainly quartz artifacts (Barham 2002b:588; Barham and Smart 1996:287; Clark and Brown 2001:316). They included unifacial and bifacial points, small bifaces from radial and multiple platform cores, and backed flakes and blades (Barham 2001b:70, 2002b:585; Brooks and Robertshaw 1990:144). Heavy duty tools include core axes, picks, bifacial lanceolates, choppers, scrapers, spheroids, and grindstones (Barham and Smart 1996:287). These Lupemban deposits were originally thought to belong to the late Pleistocene, an idea supported by conventional radiocarbon dates of greater than 33,200 BP (UCLA-707) and 22,800 ± 1,000 BP (UCLA-229). A more recent uranium-series date of 230,000 + 35,000/28,000 was obtained from a speleothem (Barham and Smart 1996:289; Cornelissen 2002:211; Clark and Brown 2001:305, 325; Deino and McBrearty 2002:208). More recent uranium estimates for the Lupemban range between 270,000 and 170,000 years ago (Barham 2001:67) or between 400,000 and 140,000 years ago (Barham 2002b:585). There is also substantial evidence of ochre processing, presumably as pigment (Barham 2001:69, 2002a).

At least five excavated site sequences have industries where microblades and/or backed pieces are stratified above Middle Stone Age layers: Kalambo Falls, Leopard's Hill Cave, Kalemba, Nsalu Cave, and Mumbwa Cave (Brooks and Robertshaw 1990:144). Levels 25 to 40 at Leopard's Hill Cave and levels H to K at Kalemba exhibit backed and geometric pieces associated with otherwise Middle Stone Age artifacts (Brooks and Robertshaw 1990:145). Phillipson (1976:vii, 119) examined a number of sites in eastern Zambia in 1966, 1970, and 1979 and identified Middle Stone Age, Later Stone Age, and Iron Age occupations. However, of the four excavated sites he describes, Pleistocene deposits were only found at Kalemba.

Kalemba (14°07′S 32°309′E) is a gneiss rockshelter located on the southeast side of the Chipwete valley. Kalemba means "the painted place"; local people refer to a whole series of hills around the site by this name (Phillipson 1976:119). Phillipson's (1976:112, 127) excavations revealed thirteen stratigraphic horizons labeled from S at the top to G, the lowest; N to G belong to the Pleistocene. A series of radiocarbon dates were obtained on charcoal or bone apatite; the oldest date is greater than 37,000 BP (originally reported as over 35,000 BC; GX-2609). However, the sequence includes reversed dates (Cornelissen 2002:220; Phillipson 1976:127). Artifacts throughout the sequence are made predominantly of crystalline and vein quartz, with the former becoming the most common during the Holocene (Cornelissen 2002:221). There were 726 retouched tools recovered. The first backed tools were found in horizon I; they increase in time to be over 97% of the retouched tools in the top two levels (Phillipson 1976:143). Over 90% of the tools in the earliest layers are scrapers, but these drop to less than 1% in level R (Phillipson 1976:143). Points are subtriangular, foliate, or ovate, and geometric pieces first appear around 26,000 years ago (Cornelissen 2002:221; Phillipson 1976:145, 1993:71).

Phillipson grouped the Kalemba assemblages into four cultural phases. The earliest is from horizon G and is greater than 37,000 years old. This level was only excavated in a limited area, due to roof fall. It is a typical Mode 3 and the tools are points and scrapers (Phillipson 1976:166, 189). The second phase is described as initially Mode 3, changing over time into a transitional industry. It is estimated to be between 27,000 and 21,000 years old and is found in horizons H to K. Retouched tools represent less than 0.2% of the flaked stone. While cores are predominantly radial, the earliest backed tools (flakes) are found here. Other tools include points (mainly sub-triangular and unifacial) and the same types of scrapers as seen earlier (Phillipson 1976:166–168, 190). The third phase, horizons K to N, is Mode 5 and dates between 17,000 and 13,000 years ago. Scrapers decrease in size and numbers over time and are replaced by backed pieces. Geometrics first appear in horizon M, mainly pointed and deep crescents (Phillipson 1976:166). Ground stone tools become more common, and there is also evidence of what Phillipson (1976:166–168) calls manufactured pigment discs and points. This industry is described as Nachikufan I (Phillipson 1976:190, 1993:71; Brooks and Robertshaw 1990:144; Miller 1969, 1971; Sampson and Southard 1973).

Earlier work by Desmond Clark at Nachikufu Cave led to the definition of a Nachikufan culture with three subdivisions (Phillipson 1976:14; Miller 1969, 1971; but see Sampson and Southard 1973). The Nachikufan began sometime at the end of the last glacial maximum; it is characterized by microlithic technology, especially bladelets. Other tools include narrow, pointed curved-backed flakes, and a number of scrapers. Bored or drilled stones are common (Phillipson 1976:14). The other two stages are Holocene and are distinguished by changes in geometric microliths (Phillipson 1976:14).

The most recent level at Kalemba Rockshelter, horizons O to S, is less than 8,000 years old. By now, artifacts are almost completely microlithic. Most of the cores are single and double platform, but bipolar cores also appear (Phillipson 1976:166). Tools represent up to 1.8% of the total flaked pieces; almost all of them are backed, with geometrics being the most common (Phillipson 1976:167). Phillipson (1976:190) names this Mode 5 industry the Makwe Industry after another site where similar material was excavated earlier. The top levels include Iron Age pottery representing some sort of contact of the Later Stone Age hunter-gatherers with Bantu farmers (Phillipson 1976:188). Phillipson (1976:193) thinks that Kalemba shows that the Later Stone Age was a local development from the earlier Middle Stone Age.

Leopard's Hill Cave is located 50 km southeast of Lusaka (Miller 1969; Phillipson 1976:199). It contains a Middle Stone Age estimated to be about 36,000 years old (Phillipson 1976:198). Above this is what Clark (1970:241) described as proto-Later Stone Age dated between 24,000 and 20,000 years ago. Artifacts are large and made of quartz. Tools include backed pieces (up to 13% of the tools are backed microliths), rare foliates, and a variety of scrapers (Cornelissen 2002:220; Phillipson 1976:199). This is described as similar to that from Kalemba K and L, but the Leopard's Hill Cave cores were shaped to remove bladelets. After this, there is a break in the cultural sequence, then a series of Nachikufan layers, the oldest of which is estimated to be 17,000 years old (Cornelissen 2002:220; Phillipson 1976:200).

Mwambacimo in the Lunsemfwa Basin has a last glacial maximum Later Stone Age level dated to around 18,080 BP (Cornelissen 2002:220). The assemblage is almost entirely quartz (96%) and microlithic. Retouched tools include backed bladelets and flakes, some segments, and other geometrics. Above this are a number of Nachikufan layers (Cornelissen 2002:221).

ZIMBABWE

Research on the later Pleistocene prehistory of Zimbabwe has been intermittent (Walker 1990). The spectacular Iron Age sites from which the country has taken its name were the focus of intense research quite early in the British colonial period and continue to be today (Pwiti 2005). The Stone Age has never had this kind of attention, but it appears that the cultural historical sequence is similar to that elsewhere in southern Africa. After the Acheulian, there is the Sangoan Industry with crude triangular picks, thick hand axes or core axes, and small flake tools. In more open country, there are light duty or flake industries, classified as the Charaman (Phillipson 1993:68). Then there is a Mode 3 Bambatan Industry. Named for Bambata Cave near Bulawayo, it was originally referred to as a Stillbay culture (Larsson 1996:201). Here, there are unifacial sub-triangular points, some bifaces, and flake scrapers (Phillipson 1993:68).

Walker (1990) conducted a number of Stone Age excavations in the 1970s (Larsson 1996:201). In a review of the evidence, he states that most research occurred in central Matabeleland, in the Matopos Hills, and around the city of Bulawayo. Over 460 LSA sites have been identified in the Matopos, and most are less than 13,000 years old. Only two of the ten excavated Later Stone Age belong to the Pleistocene (Walker 1980, 1990:208). On the other hand, about thirty Middle Stone Age sites have been identified, some from open-air contexts (Walker 1980:19, 1990:210). The lack of Middle and early Later Stone Age sites might reflect a population reduction at the height of the last glacial (Walker 1990:209–210). The adoption of microlithic technology, bows, arrows, and digging stone weights might have been a response to the cooling environment (Walker 1990:211).

Walker describes a number of sites that contribute to the debate about the nature of the Middle Stone Age. They include Nswatugi Cave (20°32′S 28°28′E), which he excavated in the 1970s. This produced a sequence 5 m in depth (Walker 1980:19). On the top, there is a thin layer with a nineteenth-century grain bin, representing the Khami Industry (Walker 1980:19). Then, there is about 1 m of ash with Pomongwe artifacts. There are two radiocarbon dates associated with this level, both within the Holocene (Walker 1980:19, 21). Microliths are present but backed tools are rare. There seems to be a shift from scrapers to backed tools over time, and bone tools are common (Walker 1980:21). Below the ash there is a sterile, thin, orange-brown layer. This is dated to 10,265 ± 90 BP (Pta 2218) and is culturally sterile (Walker 1980:21). Underneath is 4 m of probable Middle Stone Age deposits. At time of publication, these had not been analyzed; however, it was noted that backed tools are present only in the top layer. Charcoal near the top yields a date of over 41,940 years BP (Pta-1772), effectively beyond the radiocarbon limit (Walker 1980:21). Fauna represent larger bovids and equids than in later levels. The other notable feature of Nswatugi Cave is the presence of a burial at a depth of around 1.2 m below the surface, estimated to be between 9,000 and 10,000 years old. It was laid out in a contracted position, with its head to the east and its back to the wall (Walker 1980:21).

Tshangula Cave (20°28′S, 28°32′E) was originally excavated by C. K. Cooke (1963), but the results were never written up, according to Walker (1980:21). The top 2 cm belongs to the Khami Industry and includes Bambata pottery, ostrich eggshell beads, hammerstones, and anvils (Cooke 1963:134). Below this is a microlithic Later Stone Age, similar to the South African Wilton. Then there is a white ash layer, followed by a level with Magosianlike debitage. (The Magosian was once used for industries thought to be transitional between the Middle and Later Stone Age. But most "Magosian" sites have been shown to be accidental mixtures of the two periods.) Below this is a reddish earth layer with Stillbay tools. Bedrock was reached at 47 in below the ground surface (Cooke 1963:144).

Cooke (1963, 1980) identified a late Middle Stone Age which he named the Tshangula Industry. Tshangula assemblages typically contain Later Stone Age elements such as microliths, bone, and shell artifacts (Walker 1990:207). But Walker (1990:207) points out that this term has been used for anything that appears to be transitional between the Middle and Later Stone Age, such as Unit 3 at Tshangula itself.

Pomongwe Cave is a 60 by 50 ft rock-shelter in a granite koppie in the Matobo area (Cooke 1963:75; Klimowicz and Haynes 1996:126). Cooke carried out research here in 1960 and 1961 (Cooke 1963). He described twenty-seven stratigraphic layers in a deposit measuring 13 ft 5 in deep (Cooke 1963:80–82). Level 27B was the bottom. Composed of granite eroding from the bedrock, it contained no cultural materials (Cooke 1963:86). Layers 27A to 21 contain what Cooke (1963:86, 90) describes as large pseudo-tortoise cores, rough small tortoise cores, steep-sided scrapers, pebble tools, anvils, small points, stone balls, and notched scrapers. It is estimated to be between 25,000 and 30,000 years old and is described as Proto-Stillbay (Cooke 1963:147). Layers 21 to 13B are estimated to be between 10,000 and 16,000 years old and contain a Stillbay deposit (Cooke 1963:147). Layers 10 to 13A contained an unknown macrolithic phase, with microlithic debitage but no microlithic tools; it was described as Magosian. According to Cooke (1963:94), this was "a period of decadence at the termination of the Stillbay occupation" with "no semblance of a well-made MSA artifact." There were also some ostrich eggshell beads, some fragmentary bone points, and a notched bone (Cooke 1963:97). Layers 10 to 7 were described as puzzling. In a white ash deposit, there are a few cores, circular scrapers, as well as ostrich eggshell beads, awls, ornaments, and a single needle (Cooke 1963:97). A second excavation that did not reach bedrock produced a similar sequence (Cooke 1963:101–102). Raw material preference seems to change over time. The Proto-Stillbay and Stillbay are mainly vein quartz, while the Magosian level includes up to one-third cryptocrystalline silica (Cooke 1963:133). There are bone and shell artifacts in the Tshangula, Pomongwe, and Wilton (Holocene Later Stone Age) levels, including bone points, spatulate-ended bone tools, ostrich eggshell beads, and freshwater mussels. There are also two large wooden points and four smaller ones in the Wilton and Pomongwe levels (Cooke 1963, 1980:25). In the Tshangula level, there was also a single, 5 cm long, engraved, circular piece of bone flaked around the edges like a scraper (Cooke 1980:27).

Walker (1980:22) excavated the balk between Cooke's 1963 second and third trenches at the back of the cave. He uncovered a Khami Later Stone Age level, then a Tshangula deposit radiocarbon dated to 11,020 ± 60 BP (Pta-2300) and 14,860 ± 115 BP (Pta-2299) (Walker 1980:22). An early Later Stone Age, the Maleme Industry, overlies the Middle Stone Age deposit, but Walker interprets this as evidence of post-depositional disturbance (Walker 1990:208).

Shashabugwa Shelter (20°33′S, 28°33′E) is located on the base of a hill on the edge of a large open area. It also has Khami deposits in the top levels, and there was only a limited deeper excavation. Walker (1980:21–22) describes a small sample of Middle Stone Age artifacts including triangular unifacial and bifacial points; these become more common with depth. But there is no sign of backed tools. In a summary article, Walker (1980:23) concluded that Khami is the same as the Wilton in the Cape region of South Africa, while Pomongwe industries are not found in the wetter, eastern part of Zimbabwe (Walker 1980:23). The Tshangula Industry is separated from an earlier Middle Stone Age (Bambata) by rockfall at a number of sites. This may represent a cultural hiatus between 35,000 and 20,000 years ago, most likely due to late glacial cold, dry conditions (Walker 1980:23). Faunal remains in Middle Stone Age sites are dominated by large bovids, while those from the end of the Pleistocene and later are smaller (Walker 1980:23).

There have been a few places where Stone Age field research has been conducted more recently. One of these is Hwange National Park, which covers an area of 14,650 km² from 18°30′ to 19°50′S latitude, and 25°45′ to 27°40′E longitude (Klimowicz and Haynes 1996:121). Here, there are a number of pans, depressions that are seasonally filled with water (Haynes 1996:71). The northern part of the park is rugged and has shallow soils developed on karoo sandstones and mudstones. There are also Jurassic basalt, Precambrian schists, quartzites, and granite/gneiss bedrock (Klimowicz and Haynes 1996:121). Mopane woodlands and mixed woodland/grassland cover the northern hills, while the rest is deep Kalahari sands (Klimowicz and Haynes 1996:121). The earliest signs of human activity include late Acheulian hand axes, picks, scrapers, denticulates, perforators, disc cores, choppers, and spoke shaves (Klimowicz and Haynes 1996:125). These belong to what Jones calls the Bembesi culture or Fauresmith (Klimowicz and Haynes 1996:125). The Middle Stone Age begins with the Bambatan Industry, which contains thick prepared cores, some crescents, and more bifacial than unifacial points. It is estimated to be around 100,000 years old, as determined by amino acid racemization of ostrich eggshell (Klimowicz and Haynes 1996:124–125). Then there is the Tshangula Industry, with thin prepared cores, more unifacial than bifacial points, bipolar anvils, small scrapers, large crescents, and some bored stones. This is estimated to be between 30,000 and 40,000 years old. A transitional industry follows with microliths, core scrapers, bone tools, ostrich eggshell beads, ground stone, and triangular points (Klimowicz and Haynes 1996:125).

BOTSWANA

The first artifacts were recovered in Botswana in 1930 (Robbins and Murphy 1998:50), but only a few archaeologists have ever carried out more intensive research. A focus of early research was Drotsky's Cave in the Gewihaba Hills of the Western Kalahari Desert (Robbins et al. 1996). John Yellen carried out a series of test excavations here in 1969. A total of sixty-one stone artifacts were recovered from one unit, as well as ostrich eggshell, fauna, and charcoal. In three other test pits, no cultural remains were found (Robbins et al. 1996:8). A date of 12,200 ± 150 BP was obtained for a level 31 cm below the datum. This was the first in situ terminal Pleistocene material known from this region (Robbins et al. 1996:8). The artifacts are mainly silcrete debitage; there were neither microliths nor blade technology (Robbins et al. 1996:8). In 1991, Robbins and colleagues excavated a 1 m² test pit 130 cm deep and did not reach the bottom of the deposit (Robbins et al. 1996:9). A layer of charcoal 50 to 80 cm below the surface was interpreted as the main cultural layer (Robbins et al. 1996:9). A radiocarbon date of 11,240 ± 90 BP (Beta-50163) was obtained from charcoal at a depth of 50 cm below datum. The base of the charcoal layer, at 70 to 80 cm, gave a date of 12,450 ± 80 BP (Beta-47862) (Robbins et al. 1996:10).

Subsequent to this, 10 m² units were chosen for excavation. From 0 to 50 m, there was no evidence of an occupational surface. Material recovered included fifty-one stone artifacts, thirty-three of which were manufactured in the local travertine. There were only two retouched tools, a chert burin and a scraper (Robbins et al. 1996:11). The main cultural layer extends from 50 to 80 cm. It contains many artifacts, such as ostrich eggshell fragments and animal bones, especially of African bullfrogs (Robbins et al. 1996:11, 13). There were 146 pieces of debitage, 6 cores, 10 retouched pieces, 8 pieces with edge damage, and a single grindstone fragment (Robbins et al. 1996:11). While there were no backed microliths, there were many chert bladelets and four bladelet cores (Robbins et al. 1996:11). There were two ostrich eggshell beads and 197 additional shell fragments. Of the latter, fifty-three are burned, possibly from cooking (Robbins et al. 1996:11). From 80 to 130 cm, there were some lithics as well as one grindstone, but no retouched tools. Twenty ostrich eggshell fragments and two beads were also recovered (Robbins et al. 1996:12). Faunal remains represent all vertebrate classes except fish (Robbins et al. 1996:13). Associated environmental indicators point to dry conditions after 11,000 BP. Before this, the wettest period extended from 18,000 to 11,500 years BP (Robbins et al. 1996:20). Robbins (et al. 1996:21) concludes that the site was used when local conditions were becoming warmer and drier.

The Tsodilo Hills are a group of inselbergs 40 km southwest of the Okavango River, 125 km to the north of Drotsky's Cave (Robbins et al. 1996:9, 2000; Murphy 1999). The three main hills are composed of schist, quartzite, and marble; from largest to smallest, they are known as the Male, Female, and Child (Thomas et al. 2003:54; Murphy 1999:90; Robbins et al. 2000:1086). The area is famous for its cave paintings and evidence of mining for the mineral specularite (Robbins and Murphy 1998:60). There are also numerous archaeological sites dating to the Early Iron Age, as well as the Later and Middle Stone Age (Robbins et al. 2000:1086).

White Paintings Rockshelter (figure 10.1), Rhino Cave, and possibly Depression Rockshelter all contain evidence of Middle Stone Age occupation (Robbins and Murphy 1998:58; Robbins et al. 2000:1086). White Paintings Rockshelter is located at the base of Male Hill and is named for the white paintings on its walls (Robbins et al. 2000:1086). A total of 32 m² were excavated by Robbins and colleagues in 10 cm units, but only two squares extend to the full depth of 7 m. Of the eleven stratigraphic units identified, all but one represent arid conditions (Robbins et al. 2000:1090). The sequence ex-

Figure 10.1 White Paintings Rockshelter, Tsodilo Hills, Botswana

tends from the historic period until at least 100,000 years ago (Robbins et al. 2000:1085). The top 80 cm includes historic occupation, then a Later Stone Age contemporary with Early Iron Age farmers (Robbins et al. 2000:1096). Below this is the Upper Fish layer, from 80/90 cm to 130 cm below datum. It, and the Lower Fish level from 210 to 280 cm below datum, have extensive evidence of fish exploitation, notably *Clarius* and *Tilapia* (Robbins et al. 2000:1098; Thomas et al. 2003:54). Stone tools are microlithic: backed bladelets, backed points, crescents, side and end scrapers, burins, and awls (Robbins et al. 2000:1099). But non-retouched bladelets and flakes dominate. Bipolar cores are largely quartz and quartzite, while bladelet and multiple platform cores are produced on other raw materials (Robbins et al. 2000:1100).

Between 130/140 to 210 cm, there is a low-density Later Stone Age occupation with burins, awls, equal numbers of side and end scrapers, fewer backed bladelets and crescents, and the first blade cores (Robbins et al. 2000:1100). The numbers of unworked ostrich eggshells begin to increase at around 150 cm depth (Robbins et al. 2000:1100). There is a single accelerator radiocarbon date of 31,100 years BP on a broken ostrich eggshell bead at a depth between 190 and 200 cm (Robbins 1999; Robbins et al. 2000:1111). The Lower Fish level, from 210 to 280 cm, is estimated to be 48,000 years old (Robbins et al. 2000:1101). It contains an early microlithic technology with backed bladelets, crescents, backed points, notches, becs, burins, awls, and drills (Robbins et al. 2000:1101, 1103). Up to a quarter of the raw materials are non-local cryptocrystalline silica and silcrete; the rest are local quartzite (Robbins et al. 2000:1102). There are quartz and quartzite bipolar and flat bladelet cores, as well as multiplatform cores (Robbins et al. 2000:1103).

Between 300 and 410/420 cm, there is an industry which is best described as transitional between the Middle and Later Stone Age; it is estimated to be between 65,000 and 48,000 years old (Robbins et al. 2000:1103–1104; Robbins and Murphy 1998:58; Feathers 2002:193). It shows a shift from microlithic technology to the production of large blades from prepared cores. Tools include retouched blades, burins, large scrapers, notches, and awls. From 410/420 to the base of the sequence at 7 m, there are Middle Stone Age deposits (Robbins and Murphy 1998:58). These begin with the base of the lowest schist fall (Robbins et al. 2000:1105). Lithics are composed of unifacial and bifacial points, large side and end scrapers, denticulates, notches, burins, awls, and becs (Robbins et al. 2000:1105). Bladelets are also present up to a depth of 660 cm. Bipolar or multiplatform blade cores are common, and there are also some disc and prepared cores. There is one thermoluminescence date of 66,400 ± 6,500 years BP from the 500 cm level. This is similar to #Gi, an open-air Middle Stone Age site to the south, where an ostrich eggshell from the level 4 Middle Stone Age was amino acid racemization dated to between 65,000 and 85,000 BP. A thermoluminescence date of 77,000 ± 11,000 has also been reported (Robbins and Murphy 1998:58; Brooks and Robertshaw 1990:138). But final Middle Stone Age levels as recent as 28,000 years old have been reported in Rose Cottage Cave (Robbins et al. 2000:1105). White Paintings Rockshelter shows a marked change in raw materials with depth. In the Middle Stone Age, 55% of the lithics are produced on non-local chert and silcrete. In the Later Stone Age, quartz and quartzite were preferentially selected (Murphy 1999:281; Robbins et al. 2000:1105; Robbins and Murphy 1998:59).

Rhino Cave, named for the white rhino painting on its north wall, is located at the north end of Female Hill; its deposits were excavated in 1965 and 1966 (Robbins and Murphy 1998:60). Its Middle Stone Age levels include bifacial and unifacial points, large end and side scrapers, awls, denticulates, notches, and large unretouched blades. Most are made of non-local rocks, with others on local quartz crystal (Robbins and Murphy 1998:60).

Depression Cave in the Tsodilo Hills yielded 5 m of deposits. More than 90% of the lithics were manufactured using local quartz or quartzite (Robbins and Murphy 1998:61). There are no diagnostic points, and the flaking debris, including bladelet cores, makes it appear to be Later Stone Age throughout (Robbins and Murphy 1998:61). A radiocarbon date of 18,190 ± 180 BP was obtained for a level 270 to 280 cm below datum (Robbins and Murphy 1998:61; Brooks and Robertshaw 1990:138). There are still 2 m of microlithic deposits below, putting an origin of this technology of around 37,000 years old (Brooks and Robertshaw 1990:141).

NAMIBIA

Apollo 11 Cave (27°45'S, 17°6'E), on a tributary of the Orange River, remains one of the few documented Stone Age sites in Namibia (Wendt 1976; Miller et al. 1999:1541; Mitchell 1997a:343). Wendt (1976) excavated a sequence composed of a Holocene Later Stone Age, an Early Later Stone Age, and a level which appears to be transitional to the Middle Stone Age. This is followed by a Howieson's Poort and finally an older Middle Stone Age which is assigned to the Stillbay culture (Miller et al. 1999:1541; Phillipson 1993:69). Up until 1996, this was the only published stratigraphic sequence for the country (Vogelsang 1996:209). The site is exceptional for its notched bone fragments, and seven stone fragments with painted images, suggested to be dated between 27,500 and 25,500 BP (D'Errico et al. 2003:14; Henshilwood et al. 2001:633; Wadley 2001a:203; Mitchell 2002b:7; Wendt 1976 in Vogelsang 1996:210). Deacon (1990b:180) suggests that they could be Middle Stone Age or last glacial maximum. Sixty-two fragments of ostrich eggshell were submitted for amino acid racemization (Miller et al. 1999:1540). The results put the Howieson's Poort levels at 63,000 ± 6,000 and 69,000 ± 7,000 BP. The underlying Stillbay levels are at least 83,000 years old (Miller et al. 1999:1543).

    Vogelsang (1996) conducted a survey of the central region of Namibia, where sites are associated with inselbergs and dry waterholes (Vogelsang 1996:211). He defined five Middle Stone Age "complexes," all with lithics made on faceted platforms (Vogelsang 1996:209). The oldest includes pointed flakes and irregular blades, but almost no retouched tools. These are made on quartzite and calcareous mudstone (Vogelsang 1996:210). The second or Developed Middle Stone Age includes bifacial points made on cryptocrystalline silica. The same material was preferred in the Howieson's Poort for small segments or crescents (Vogelsang 1996:210). But quartzite is the more common and was used to produce "basal scrapers" and blades (Vogelsang 1996:209). The third is an Unmodified Middle Stone Age. This has almost no retouched tools, but many pointed flakes and relatively short blades. Various raw materials were used, but there is a high percentage of cryptocrystalline silica (Vogelsang 1996:209). The fourth is the Howieson's Poort. As in South Africa, it is marked by segments and convex or straight backed blades. Retouch is composed of backing and truncation (Vogelsang 1996:209). The final, or Youngest, Middle Stone Age has no standardized tool types. There are many quartz artifacts, and a few, irregular blades, and the assemblage is dominated by debitage (Vogelsang 1996:209). Generally, Vogelsang (1996:207) concludes that, except for the Howieson's Poort, there are only minor changes over time. There are ostrich eggshells associated with these deposits, but most of these have not been shaped in any way (Vogelsang 1996:210).

LESOTHO

The first archaeologist to work in Lesotho, a land-locked country sur-rounded by South Africa, was Pat Carter, who, starting in 1969, described a number of Stone Age sites including Ha Soloja and Moshebi's Shelter, in the Sehlabathebe Basin; Melikane and Sehonghong, located along tributaries of the Orange River; and Belleview, in neighboring KwaZulu-Natal (Carter and Vogel 1974; Mitchell 1992:7–8). Later Stone Age levels are present at all five sites, except for Ha Soloja, where it was removed for house construc-tion (Mitchell 1992:8). Moshebi's Shelter and Melikane both contain a sequence of a pre-Howieson's Poort Middle Stone Age, Howieson's Poort levels, and a post-Howieson's Poort Middle Stone Age (Mitchell 1992:9). This is repeated at many South African sites (Thackeray 1992). Sehonghong Rockshelter includes only the Howieson's Poort and subsequent Middle Stone Age (Mitchell 1992:9). There is an Early Later Stone Age at Melikane, which is described as "highly informal" (Mitchell 1992:9). Conventional radiocarbon dates are available for all of these sites except Moshebi's Shel-ter (Mitchell 1992:10; Carter and Vogel 1974). They show that the Middle Stone Age at Ha Soloja and Melikane is beyond the radiocarbon limit (Mitchell 1992:10).

Sehonghong is the only major rock-shelter in the region (Carter and Vogel 1974; Mitchell 1990, 1992, 1996:634, 1997a, 1997b). It contains a record from recent back to the last glacial maximum (Mitchell 1996:623). Carter identified four Middle Stone Age levels. The most recent one dates to 20,900 ± 270 or 19,860 ± 220 BP (Wadley 1993:263, 1997:443). Mitchell (1996:624) conducted fieldwork here in 1992 and produced what he calls a more complex sequence. One of Carter's Middle Stone Age levels belongs to the Later Stone Age (Clark 1997b:454). It is described as Robberg, as it shares gradual microlithization over time (Mitchell 1992:9, 15). Both industries are marked by irregular cores, bipolar technology, no Leval-lois technique, and only a few retouched tools (Clark 1997b:455–456). There is also a Middle Stone Age with large flake-blades; this is classified as MSA 3 using Volman's (1984) system (Mitchell 1996:625–626). Mitchell (1996:626) pointed to the possibility of Howieson's Poort at the base of the sequence. But if so, it could be quite recent. There are radiocarbon dates of 30,900 ± 550 (Pta-787) and 32,150 ± 770 BP for a layer 1.5 m above bedrock (Mitchell 1996:624).

SOUTH AFRICA

South Africa is divided into a number of ecological zones, including shrub lands, grasslands, and desert. This is in addition to the Cape which has a Mediterranean climate with *fynbos* shrub. Local climate ranges from subtropical in the east to extremely arid in the west (Deacon 1992:177). The archaeological record of concern here comes mainly from caves and rock-shelters, but there are some important open-air sites as well. These will be discussed by geographic location. While more attention will be paid to the Middle Stone Age sites, some Pleistocene (and more recent) Later Stone Age sites will be included for comparative purposes.

Late or Final Acheulian assemblages are known from a number of sites such as the Cave of Hearths, Wonderwerk Cave, Montagu Cave, Rooidam, and Elandsfontein (Deacon and Wurz 2001:60). Elandsfontein is located on a series of dunes (Luyt et al. 2000:399) north of Cape Town. Here fossil fauna is associated with two duricrusts. The first is a calcareous deposit and is associated with hand axes and other Acheulian artifacts. Fauna include many archaic forms, so this level is estimated to be between 700,000 and 400,000 years old (Luyt et al. 2000:399). The upper level is ferruginous and includes Middle Stone Age artifacts and more modern-looking fauna. It represents a cool period, probably less than 115,000 years old (Luyt et al. 2000:399).

Another site which contains both Acheulian and Middle Stone Age components is Florisbad. This is an open-air site near Bloemfontein composed of a series of spring vents and 7 m of associated deposits which formed above them. It was discovered in 1912 and became the type site for the Florisian land mammal age (Kuman et al. 1999:1409). More recent excavations were carried out between 1981 and 1984, and then again in the 1990s (Brink and Henderson 2001:9). A partial hominin skull and associated tooth were found in 1932 (Schwarcz 2001:51; Brink and Henderson 2001:4; Kuman et al. 1999:1409). An electron spin resonance date of 259,000 ± 35,000 BP was obtained from the tooth (Kuman et al. 1999:1410; Schwarcz 2001:51; Brink and Henderson 2001:7; Tryon and McBrearty 2002:213). Florisbad contains twelve Middle Stone Age units, eleven of which contain artifacts (Kuman et al. 1999:1414). All dates are provided by electron spin resonance. There is an early Middle Stone Age in the basal deposits that postdates the formation of the springs at 279,000 ± 47,000 years BP (Kuman et al. 1999:1409). It contains some artifacts, but no bifaces (Kuman et al. 1999:1419). There is a highly retouched Middle Stone Age level above this,

which is dated to 157,000 ± 21,000 years BP (Kuman et al. 1999:1409). Here medium side scrapers dominate, many resembling blades (Kuman et al. 1999:1414).
Above this is a Middle Stone Age occupation with few retouched tools; it is dated
to 121,000 ± 6,000 BP (Kuman et al. 1999:1409). Then there is a final Middle
Stone Age level. Of the 116 stone artifacts collected, there were 3 to 4 triangular
flakes and 10 pieces with faceted striking platforms (Kuman et al. 1999:1422).
Numerous faunal remains were introduced to the site, either by carnivores or
hominins. Brink and Henderson (2001:4) feel that the species present at Florisbad offer strong proof of hunting. They also report on two new localities in the
Modder River drainage which might contribute to this discussion. At Damvlei,
Middle Stone Age artifacts are associated with some calcretized bone fragments
on an old land surface within a shallow sequence of sandy clays (Brink and
Henderson 2001:16). At Erfkroon, there are two fossil bearing horizons, B (the
older) and A. Brink and Henderson (2001:17) interpret B as fluvial transported
fossil material of Florisian age, while A is a paleosol in sandy clays, as at Damvlei.
These sites are estimated to be around 125,000 years old.

Sites like Klasies River on the Tsitsikama Coast west of the modern city of
Port Elizabeth contain a long Middle Stone Age sequence extending from the
last interglacial (MIS 5e) until about 60,000 years ago (Deacon 1992:178; Wurz
2002:1002). Klasies River (formerly Klasies River Mouth) (34°06′S, 24°24′E)
(Deacon 1998, 2001; Deacon and Geleijnse 1988; Deacon and Shuurman
1992; Deacon and Wurz 1997, 2001; Feathers 2002; Singer and Wymer 1982;
Thackeray 1989; Wurz 1999, 2002; Wurz et al. 2005) consists of a number of
caves and rock-shelters set into Table Mountain sandstone cliffs. Excavations
at the main site (figure 10.2) in 1967 and 1968 by Singer and Wymer (1982)
resulted in the uncovering of 20 m of cultural deposits (Deacon and Wurz
2001:58; Wurz 1999). These include hearths, shell, and bone middens that are
separated by sterile sand layers (Deacon and Wurz 2001:58) (figure 10.3). Hilary Deacon excavated here from 1984 to 1989.

Klasies remains the type site for the South African Middle Stone Age (Deacon and Wurz 2001:58). Singer and Wymer (1982) defined five sub-stages;
from bottom to top, they are the Middle Stone Age 1, 2, Howieson's Poort,
and Middle Stone Age 3 and 4. MSA 1 and 2 are found in the basal light
brown sands or LBS Member. Above this is the SAS (sands-ash-shell) Member, then the RF or Rockfall Member. These both contain MSA 2 deposits. In
the Upper Member above, there are Howieson's Poort and then MSA 3 occu-

Figure 10.2 Klasies River

Figure 10.3 Sequence of hearths and shellfish, Klasies River Main Site

pations. The sequence finishes with the MSA 4 (Grün and Stringer 1991:181).
The MSA 1 contains long, thin flake-blades made on local quartzite, some of
which were retouched into points (Thackeray 1989:34–35; 2000:147) (figure
10.4). Middle Stone Age 2 assemblages included higher percentages of con-

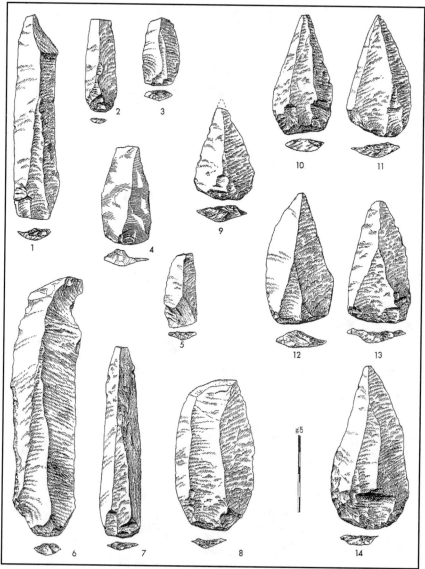

Figure 10.4 Flake-blades from the MSA 1 levels of Klasies River (Singer and Wymer
1982:59). Reprinted with permission of the University of Chicago Press

vergent blades and worked points. They are followed by the large-backed and geometric pieces (crescents or segments) characteristic of the Howieson's Poort (figure 10.5). These are often made in finer-grained materials, but

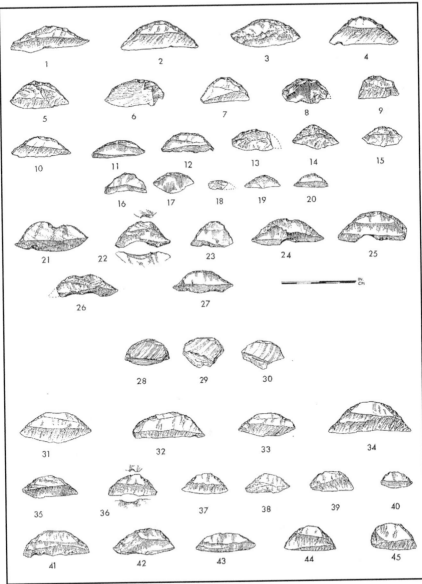

Figure 10.5 Crescents from the Howieson's Poort levels at Klasies River (Singer and Wymer 1982:96). Reprinted with permission of the University of Chicago Press

local quartzite is still present. There are also typical Middle Stone Age flake-blades, but these tend to be smaller than in other levels. The Howieson's Poort is followed by the MSA 3 and returns to the quartzite unifacial points and flake-blades with lateral retouch (or knives) characteristic of the MSA 2. The final levels, MSA 4, are defined by the presence of small, convergent, quartzite flake-blades. The MSA 3 and deeper levels were beyond the limit of radiocarbon dating (Vogel 2001:265). A number of methods have been applied to the Klasies deposits and give variable estimates of age (Feathers 2002; Feathers and Bush 2000; Grün and Stringer 1991; Vogel 2001), ranging from 120,000 to 50,000 years ago.

Nelson Bay Cave is located on the Robberg Peninsula in Plettenberg Bay, 530 km east of Cape Town (Kusimba 2003:146). Research by Inskeep in 1964 led to discovery of over 6 ft of cultural deposits (Kusimba 2003:146). These include the Holocene LSA (Wilton and Albany) and a late glacial Later Stone Age, the Robberg. Then, there is a half meter of rubble, then 2 m of Middle Stone Age deposits. Volman argues that the Middle Stone Age belonged to the Howieson's Poort, while Kusimba (2003:150) argues for a sequence of ten Middle Stone Age levels; the first seven are Howieson's Poort, and the last three are MSA 1 and 2.

Blombos Cave (34°24.857'S, 21°13.371'E) is located 300 km east of Cape Town (Henshilwood et al. 2001:634, 2002; D'Errico et al. 2001, 2005; Henshilwood and Sealy 1997; Henshilwood, Sealy et al. 2001:422). It is composed of a wave-cut cliff above the basal layer of Table Mountain sandstone (Henshilwood et al. 2001:634). It is currently around 100 m from the ocean shore and about 35 m above sea level (Jacobs et al. 2003a:600). The first excavations here were conducted in 1991; they identified a Holocene Later Stone Age, which is less than 2,000 years old (Henshilwood, Sealy et al. 2001:422; D'Errico et al. 2001:309). Work from 1992 to 2000 resulted in the discovery of three Middle Stone Age phases (BBC M1, M2, and M3) under the BBC hiatus level, about 5 to 40 cm of sterile yellow or great dune sand (Henshilwood et al. 2001:634, 637; D'Errico et al. 2001:309). The most recent Middle Stone Age level, or MSA 1, is classified as Stillbay. It contains over 400 unifacial and bifacial stone lanceolate points, as well as bone points (Henshilwood, Sealy et al. 2001:427; Henshilwood et al. 2001:634; D'Errico et al. 2001:310, 2005:6; Thackeray 2000:149,165). Twenty-eight bone tools have been recovered from this level as well as a few from deeper deposits (Henshilwood et al. 2001:631). In the

BBC M2 levels, there are over twenty worked bone tools, but few bifacial tools (Henshilwood et al. 2001:635; D'Errico et al. 2001:310). The deepest or BBC M3 level consists of a dense shell midden with typical unretouched Middle Stone Age flake-blades (Henshilwood et al. 2001:635; D'Errico et al. 2001:310).

Blombos is remarkable for a number of other features. There is over 8 kg of red ochre in this sequence, most of it in BBC M3; it was worked by scraping and grinding into pencil and crayon forms (Henshilwood et al. 2001:635–636, 668). There are also two pieces of ochre engraved with a cross-hatched pattern and one engraved bone fragment (Henshilwood et al. 2001:634–635; Henshilwood, Sealy et al. 2001; D'Errico et al. 2001:309). Forty-one perforated marine tick (*Nassarius kraussianus*) shell beds were also recovered from the Middle Stone Age levels (D'Errico et al. 2005:3, 9). Shellfish remains are abundant and seem to increase in density with depth (Henshilwood, Sealy et al. 2001:441). There are some fish bones in all three levels (Henshilwood, Sealy et al. 2001:443, 445). At various sites, Stillbay artifacts are found below Howieson's Poort ones. They are suggested to be between 65,000 and 70,000 years old (Henshilwood et al. 2001:638). The BBC hiatus sands have been dated by optically stimulated luminescence to an average of 70,100 ± 1,900 years before present; this provides a minimum age for the deeper Middle Stone Age occupation (Jacobs et al. 2003a:610).

Pinnacle Point is located in coastal quartzite sandstone cliffs at Cape St. Blaize. These are capped by calcretes and dunes (Marean et al. 2004:20). This site was identified by Goodwin in 1932 and was the basis for his Mossel Bay Industry. A 1997 cultural resource management survey identified twenty-eight archaeological sites here. Twenty-one of these have Middle Stone Age deposits, including fifteen rock-shelters or caves (Marean et al. 2004:14, 16). Marean and colleagues have conducted test excavations at four of them: Caves 9, 13A, 13B, and 13C (Marean et al. 2004). Caves 13A and 13B have produced rich MSA deposits. The 600 stone artifacts recovered include mainly unretouched flakes, blades, and points (Marean et al. 2004:46). They belong to the Mossel Bay Industry or MSA 2 (Marean et al. 2004:49). Raw materials are mainly quartzite, but quartz crystals, silcrete, and cryptocrystalline silicas are also occasionally used (Marean et al. 2004:14, 41). Along with the small sample of animal bones, one hominin parietal fragment, and a mandibular right central incisor were also recovered (Marean et al. 2004:71).

Boomplaas Cave (33°23′S, 22°11′E) is situated in the foothills of the Swart-
burg range, 75 km inland from the modern coast (Miller et al. 1999:1542).
It was excavated by Deacon in the 1970s and produced 5 m of deposits.
These include a historic and herder level, then a Later Stone Age, two levels
of Middle Stone Age, and near the bottom, a Howieson's Poort level (Vogel
2001:262; Miller et al. 1999:1542). The base of the uppermost Middle Stone
Age is dated to 34,000 BP, while the overlying Later Stone Age level dates to
21,000 BP (Vogel 2001:262). The Howieson's Poort is dated to 62,400 ± 2,000
BP (Vogel 2001:262; Feathers 2002:193).

Elands Bay Cave contains a sequence with both Middle and Later Stone
Age (Parkington 1990:216). The basal level is composed of a stony lag deposit above bedrock, and it contains Middle Stone Age artifacts. Above it is
the lower level, which includes lithics on irregular quartz chunks (Parkington 1990:216). An early Later Stone Age is dated to 20,180 BP at the top and
45,000 at the bottom. Faunal remains are rare in this level, but include teeth
and extremities of large bovids and equids, while smaller mammals and tortoises are also present (Parkington 1990:216). There appears to be a hiatus
in occupation between 14,000 and 18,000 years ago. Parkington (1990:216,
226) believes that people followed the coast onto the continental shelf as the
sea level dropped in the last glacial (Parkington 1990:216, 226). The middle
level is estimated to date between 13,500 and 8,000 years ago and marks
the postglacial return of the ocean to within 100 m of the site (Parkington
1990:216). Fauna is dominated by shellfish and marine animals, and fish
increase after 11,000 years ago, as terrestrial fauna decreases (Parkington
1990:216, 219). Quartz lithics dominate; these are smaller than earlier and
include bipolar and single-platform cores as well as unretouched bladelets
(Parkington 1990:219).

Die Kelders Cave 1 or Klipgat (34°32′S, 19°22′E) (Marean 2000; Thackeray 2000; Marean, Goldberg et al. 2000:8; Avery et al. 1997) is one of a
series of caves in the steep cliffs below the tourist village of the same name,
120 km southeast of Cape Town. It was first examined between 1969 and
1973 by Frank Schweizer, who was interested in early animal domestication,
then by Marean and his colleagues (Marean, Goldberg et al. 2000:8). The
7.5 m sequence was subdivided by Schweizer into seventeen layers (Thackeray 2000:150). Layers 16 and 17 at the bottom are composed of quartzite
beach boulders and sand and represent MIS 5e. Layers 4 through 15 are

alternating Middle Stone Age archaeological horizons (the even numbers) and sterile sands (the odd numbers). Above this is layer 3, a culturally sterile unit of yellow iron-stained sands. Layer 2 represents a Late Quaternary high sea level. Layer 1 at the top is a 1 to 1.5 m thick Later Stone Age shell midden, containing domestic sheep and pottery (Marean, Goldberg et al. 2000:16; Thackeray 2000:151; Klein and Cruz-Uribe 2000:173). Marean's group slightly revised this stratigraphic picture (Marean, Goldberg et al. 2000:22). They argue that layers 2 and 3 represent a period when the cave was filled by a large sand dune. They group layers 4 and 5 into a single unit, layer 6, and interpret it as a dense Middle Stone Age layer associated with massive chunks of roof fall (Marean, Goldberg et al. 2000:27). Eighteen of the twenty-seven hominin fossil specimens come from here and represent a minimum of four individuals. They are associated with many quartz and quartzite artifacts (Marean, Goldberg et al. 2000:30). Layer 7, which Schweizer interpreted as a sterile unit, is composed of alternating dark and light orange-brown sands with occasional artifacts. Layer 8 is associated with dark, red-brown, poorly sorted sand and contains quartz and quartzite artifacts, along with one hominin specimen. It is a human occupation or a natural accumulation of micromammals by raptors (Marean, Goldberg et al. 2000:33). Layer 9 is 5 to 10 cm of lighter and darker sand lenses. It contains some artifacts, with more silcrete than in later levels (Marean, Goldberg et al. 2000:34).

Layer 10 consists of up to 10 cm of red-brown sand with alternating light and dark lenses. The dark lenses include faunal remains and artifacts. Artifacts consist of large quartz, quartzite, and silcrete flakes. Taphonomic studies show that the small bovids here were probably accumulated by raptors, while the animals larger than 18 kg are a product of human activities. One hominin specimen was also recovered (Marean, Goldberg et al. 2000:36). Layer 11 is a non-occupation deposit, but contains some artifacts, a single hominin specimen, and many faunal remains (Marean, Goldberg et al. 2000:36). The distinctive dark layer 12 is found throughout the excavation. It contains many stone artifacts and abundant evidence of use of silcrete (Marean, Goldberg et al. 2000:38). Layer 13, another non-occupation layer, follows, and it also contains some quartz and quartzite artifacts. It is followed by occupation layer 14 which includes many stone artifacts and large mammal remains, as well as two hominin specimens (Marean, Goldberg et al. 2000:39). Most of these are isolated human teeth (Marean 2000:4). In addition to the stone artifacts and fauna, two upper grindstones stained by red ochre were recovered. There are also small red ochre nodules or patches and six worked ochre pieces (Thackeray 2000:151, 157).

The age of these deposits has been assessed using electron spin resonance and thermoluminescence (Schwarcz and Rink 2000; Feathers and Bush 2000:91). The former suggests that all these deposits accumulated within about 10,000 to 15,000 years, during MIS 4 (Marean, Goldberg et al 2000:39; Feathers and Bush 2000). Electron spin resonance dates on bovid teeth range from 64,000 to 75,000 BP, with an average 70,000 ± 4,000 BP using the early uptake model. The late uptake dates average around 88,000 ± 7, 000 BP, about 28% older. They confirm that these deposits accumulated relatively rapidly (Schwarcz and Rink 2000:123,128). These dates are intriguing, as they overlap with the Howieson's Poort Industry elsewhere (Schwarcz and Rink 2000:128). There are no signs of this kind of industry at Die Kelders 1, but there are higher percentages of silcrete at this time (Marean 2000:4; Thackeray 2000:147, 149; Feathers and Bush 2000:117).

There are also a number of sites on the west or Atlantic coast north of Cape Town. Klein and colleagues argue that terrestrial foods were less abundant here than on the south coast, since there is less precipitation, but marine resources more than compensated (Klein et al. 2004:5709). That may be why there are such extensive shell middens for both Middle and Stone Age periods. Some of these have been studied by John Parkington (1999) of the University of Cape Town. One is Hoedjiespunt 1 (33°0145′S, 17°57′37″E), located on the peninsula of the same name in Saldanha Bay (figure 10.6). It is part of a large fossil dune landscape and contains a number of archaeological and fossil sites (Stynder et al. 2001:369). The stratigraphic sequence from top to bottom is as follows: The top is composed of 2 m of calcrete. Then, there is a cemented shell midden which contains Middle Stone Age tools, ostrich eggshell fragments, ochre, marine shell (mainly *Patella*), and burned animal bones. Standard thermoluminescence as well as infrared stimulated luminescence of sediments both show that it dates between 40,000 and 20,000 BP (Stynder et al. 2001:372). Below this is a dark loamy archaeological layer with bone, as well as one with quartz Middle Stone Age artifacts. Faunal remains include marine vertebrates such as jackass penguin (*Spheniscus demersus*), Cape cormorant (*Phalacrocoras capensis*), and some

Figure 10.6 Hoedjiespunt

terrestrial invertebrates, including the angulate tortoise (*Chersina angulata*) (Stynder et al. 2001:371). This is estimated to date to 117,000 BP or MIS 5e (Stynder et al. 2001:372). Under this are two shelly sand deposits, with few marine fossils.

The nearby palaeontological site (HOMS) has a main bone-bearing layer. Grazing animals such as black wildebeest (*Connochaetes gnou*) and red hartebeest (*Alcelaphus buselaphus*) are abundant, along with carnivores such as *Canis mesomelas*, the black-headed jackal (Stynder et al. 2001:372). Hyenas are said to be the main agents of accumulation. The estimated maximum age is 550,000 years old, but since there is also Florisian or Florisbadlike fauna, it probably dates between 200,000 and 300,000 years ago (Stynder et al. 2001:372).

Parkington (1999:25) points out that there are many shell middens with Middle Stone Age occupations in the Western Cape. Most have good bone preservation, because of the calcium carbonate in the associated shellfish. Detailed studies can produce comparisons between the Holocene and Last Interglacial resource use (Parkington 1999:27). He proposes that the Middle Stone Age people left more ochre and more ostrich eggshells and ate a more limited range of marine resources and larger limpets than subsequent Later Stone Age ones (Parkington 1999:28).

Diepkloof Cave (Parkington 1999) is located in the *fynbos* zone of the Western Cape (figure 10.7). It contains both Later and Middle Stone Age levels, as well as numerous cave paintings. The Middle Stone Age artifact layers are estimated to be greater than 40,000 years old via accelerator radiocarbon dating. One thermoluminescence date of 63,000 years ago has also been reported (Parkington 1999:27). The layers include ostrich eggshell fragments with incised lines (Wadley 2001a:203; Mitchell 2002b:5).

Figure 10.7 Diepkloof Cave

Ysterfontein (32.20°S, 18.09°E) is an open-air site 70 km north-northwest of Cape Town (Halkett et al. 2003:955; Klein et al. 2004). It was discovered during construction in the 1980s, and in 2002, the University of Cape Town began excavations. This revealed a 3 to 3.5 m thick deposit of cemented sands and calcretes on a diorite platform, 7 m above the current sea level (Halket et al. 2003:955). A calcrete deposit caps the sequence about 4 m above the base; there is another calcrete midway between, with weakly cemented sands above and below the shelf (Halket et al. 2003:956). A stratigraphic study of different deposits shows that there are six sedimentary units above the calcrete and three below (Klein et al. 2004:5709). Accelerator radiocarbon dates were obtained on an ostrich eggshell; these suggest that the cultural deposits are over 30,000 years old and have a maximum possible age of 60,000 years BP (Halkett et al. 2003:957–958).

There are similar stone tools in both layers, but the upper one has more tools and a wider variety of lithic raw materials (Klein et al. 2004:5710). About half of the artifacts are silcrete; others are made of calcrete, quartz, and dio-rite. They include radial cores and flakes or flake-blades with faceted butts, or typical South African Middle Stone Age. No bone tools or ostrich eggshell ar-tifacts were found (Halkett et al. 2003:958, 961; Klein et al. 2004:5710). There are ochre fragments, including one with striations on the concave surface; these "underscore a widely recognized MSA interest in red pigment" (Halkett et al. 2003:959). There are no Howieson's Poort or Stillbay types, suggest-ing that this deposit might be too young (Halkett et al. 2003:959; Klein et al. 2004:5710). Fauna is dominated by shellfish (Halkett et al. 2003:960). There are no fish bones, but many snakes, tortoise, mammals, and birds (Halkett et al. 2003:960–961). The most common bird is the jackass penguin, suggesting that the people who accumulated this deposit lacked the technology or ability to catch flying birds (Halkett et al. 2003:961). The most abundant mammal is the Cape dune mole rat; there are also a number of bovids, all of which are characteristic of a moister, bushier environment than in historic times (Halkett et al. 2003:961).

On the Indian Ocean coast is the province of KwaZulu-Natal, which con-tains at least one major Stone Age site, Sibudu Cave. It is located on a west-southwest facing cliff above the Tongati River, 40 km north of Durban (Cain 2004; Villa et al. 2005; Wadley 2001b:1; Wadley and Jacobs 2004:145; Lombard 2004, 2005:280; Williamson 2004). The cave is 55 m long and 18 m wide (Wad-ley 2001b:2). Mazel conducted the first excavations in 1983, digging a small trench which revealed upper layers with Middle Stone Age artifacts and Later Iron Age pottery. Below 30 cm, there are only Middle Stone Age artifacts (Wad-ley 2001b:3; Wadley and Jacobs 2003:145). Two radiocarbon dates on charcoal are reported. At 20 to 30 cm, in layer MOD2, the date was 26,000 ± 420 BP (Pta-3765). However, a date of 24,200 ± 290 BP (Pta-3767) was obtained for material from layer GAA2, 79 to 88 cm below datum (Wadley 2001b:3).

Wadley and her colleagues initiated new excavations in 1998; their initial trench was 1.5 m deep. There are Iron Age deposits in the top layer; and it appears that the Iron Age people dug several large pits into the Middle Stone Age deposits (Wadley and Jacobs 2004:145). There is no Later Stone Age, but a final Middle Stone Age layer labeled MOD is present and is composed of mottled brown, fine sand with white ash, black charcoal, and orange-brown sand. It is the source of Mazel's date (Wadley and Jacobs 2004:146–147). Un-derneath is the O MOD layer which is composed of a mottled orange-brown deposit. Charcoal at a 224 cm depth produced a radiocarbon date of 34,300 ± 2000 BP (Pta-8142) (Wadley 2001b:5). Below this are numerous levels with Middle Stone Age artifacts (G MOD, RSp, YSp, BSp, BSp2, and SPCA). A 2 m² test pit was excavated down to over 2 m deep without hitting bedrock (Wadley and Jacobs 2004:145, 147).

Middle Stone Age stone artifacts are mainly hornfels and dolerite in the upper layers, but quartz increases in frequency with depth (Wadley and Jacobs 2004:149). A few cores were uncovered, including radial, blade, irregular, and multiple-platform types. Tools include unifacial and bifacial points, hollow-based points, straight and convex scrapers, scaled pieces, and notches (Wadley and Jacobs 2004:149). Some are made on thick blades, others on thick flakes (Wadley 2001b:11). The most recent Middle Stone Age layers include a few radial and other cores, as well as debitage (Wadley 2001b:11). Wadley (2001b:14) suggests that the deepest deposit may represent a very early Middle Stone Age occupation, while the one immediately above is similar to Volman's Middle Stone Age 2A. The most recent discovery is of a Howieson's Poort level below the later MSA one in square B6 (Wadley and Jacobs 2004:145, 150). This is estimated to be more than 61,000 years old (Lombard 2005:283). It contains backed tools (segments) on dolerite as well as a higher percentage of blades and more large sandstone flakes than in the more recent Sibudu Middle Stone Age (Wadley and Jacobs 2004:150).

A residue analysis of 412 Middle Stone Age artifacts was carried out. Plant residues are more common than animal ones, while ochre traces are present on many lithics (Williamson 2004:174; Wadley and Jacobs 2004:145, 150). A similar study of twenty-four post–Howieson's Poort points from Sibudu Cave revealed plant traces on the proximal and medial parts and animal traces on the distal ends. This is unequivocal proof that these points were hafted for use as hunting weapons (Lombard 2004:37). A different study concentrated on microfracture analysis, residue analysis, and use wear to determine how fifty Middle Stone Age bifacial and unifacial points were hafted (Lombard 2005:280, 283). Just over half (52%) of them had hafting indicators, composed of fractures along the lateral edges, while the proximal edges were rounded as a result of hafting wear (Lombard 2004:37, 2005:289).

Umhlatuzana rock-shelter is found 100 km to the northwest of Sibudu, and 35 km west of Durban (Wadley 2001a:211). It contains the Howieson's Poort, but no earlier Middle Stone Age occupation (Wadley 2001a:211, 2001b:15; Wadley and Jacobs 2004:150). The final Middle Stone Age deposit here is dated between 37,000 and 41,000 years BP (Clark 1997b:456).

Rose Cottage Cave (29°13′S, 27°28′E) is the most important Stone Age site known from the Free State (Wadley 1997, 2001a; A. Clark 1997a, 1997b, 1999; Harper 1997). It is located northeast of Lesotho in the Caledon River corridor (Wadley 1997:439). Excavations were conducted by Malan between 1943 and 1945, by Beaumont in 1962, and by Wadley starting in 1987 (Wadley 1997:439, 2001a:210). Wadley opened up an area of 38 m² to expose the Holocene Later Stone Age, and she excavated a smaller area into the Middle Stone Age deposits (Wadley 1997:439, 2001a:211). The extremely long sequence is 6.3 m deep, and includes pre– and post–Howieson's Poort Middle Stone Age levels, the Howieson's Poort, a final Middle Stone Age in level Ru, and Pleistocene and Holocene Later Stone Age levels (Wadley 2001b:210; A. Clark 1999:95). The basal levels contain a Middle Stone Age with many points, as well as some scrapers and knives. Within the debitage categories, flake-blades are more common than flakes, and there are also some bladelets (Wadley 1997:441). The next fifteen layers belong to the Howieson's Poort. In the following deposits, backed tools are rarer, while scrapers, points, and knives reoccur. There are also fewer flake-blades and bladelets, but more flakes (Wadley 1997:441). Above the KAR level, the Middle Stone Age rarely has retouched tools (Wadley 1997:441). In the subsequent Dc level, the next to last Middle Stone Age contains standardized, clear opaline microlithic points (Wadley 2001a:211, 2001b:15). Wadley (2001a:213) argues that the hearths change from "unstructured" to fewer, more widely spaced features. She notes that debitage, and in one case ochre, tends to cluster around hearths (Wadley 2001a:213). Dates for Sibudu have been problematic, but the final Middle Stone Age is estimated to be around 28,000 years old (A. Clark 1997a, 1997b, 1999:95–96, 1997b:449; Woodborne and Vogel 1997:476).

There is evidence of the continuity and transition from the Middle to the Later Stone Age in levels G and G2 (A. Clark 1999:95; Wadley 2001a:211). Later Stone Age production methods were used to produce *outils écaillés* and bladelets. Retouched tools are composed of knives, large side scrapers, and unifacial and bifacial points (A. Clark 1999:98; Wadley 1997:441), much more typical of the Middle Stone Age. This is not the average Later Stone Age or even Robberg and is dated to 20,600 ± 250 BP (Pta-5568) in level G (Wadley 1997:441; A. Clark 1997b:449, 1999:98). Raw materials include siltstones, sandstones, and tuffaceous rocks (Wadley 1997:442).

The oldest true Later Stone Age appears around 13,000 years ago (A. Clark 1997b:454, 1999:95–96; Wadley 1993:262). It is a Robberg with only a few retouched tools, including backed pieces, scrapers, and thin bladelets (Wadley 1997:442). Cores are single platform and *outils écaillés* are also present (Wadley 1997:442). Wadley (1997:443, 2001a:213) argues that there is strong evidence for features and activity areas in this level. The end of the sequence includes Holocene Later Stone Age levels (Wadley 1997:442).

Strathalen Cave B is located in the Eastern Cape in the foothills of the Drakensberg Mountains. It contains a Middle Stone Age deposit that is said to date to around 22,000 BP (A. Clark 1997b:456). Another site, Border Cave, is located on the western flank of the Lebombo Mountains. Its name comes from its proximity to the Swaziland border (Beaumont et al. 1978; Miller et al. 1999:1540). It is composed of 4 m of alternating brown sands (BS) and white ash (WA) layers numbered from top to bottom. The archaeological sequence includes the MSA 1, Howieson's Poort, and MSA 3, as well as a very early Later Stone Age in levels 1WA and 1BS.LR. The latter two levels have been dated at 39,000 BP and 39,000 to 30,000 BP respectively (Grün and Stringer 1991:183; Miller et al. 1999:1540; Wadley 1993:260). More recent methods have provided an average age of 38,000 BP (Bird et al. 2003:946).

A number of dating methods have been applied to the Middle Stone Age levels of Border Cave, with mixed results (Grün and Beaumont 2001). Amino acid racemization of ostrich eggshells provides dates from 45,000 ± 5,000 years ago (for the Howieson's Poort/Middle Stone Age 3 boundary) to about 75,000 ± 5,000 for the transition between the Howieson's Poort and the underlying MSA 1 (Grün and Stringer 1991:182; Miller et al. 1999:1541). Radiocarbon dates suggest that the BC 5 hominin mandible from the base of 3BS-3WA is older than 58,200 years ago. The first bladelets appear here between 56,500 and 41,600 years old (Bird et al. 2003:947).

Howieson's Poort is a small cave near Grahamstown in the Eastern Cape (Wurz 1999:38). It is located north of Klasies River, near the Wilton type site (Sampson 1974:231). It was excavated over eighty years ago by Reverend P. Stapleton, a Jesuit schoolteacher, and John Hewitt, a zoologist and director of the local museum (Stapleton and Hewitt 1927, 1928). The site was re-excavated in 1965 by Hilary and Janette Deacon (Thackeray 1992:390; Wurz 1999:38). It is a single component site with large crescents and backed pieces (Kusimba 2003:142; Wurz 1999:38). Even the original excavators recognized its similarities to the Later Stone Age (Stapleton and Hewitt 1928:407), and it was interpreted as a transitional sequence. This lasted until similar artifacts were discovered stratified between true Middle Stone Age levels at many other sites (Kusimba 2003:142; Ambrose and Lorenz 1990:3; Thackeray 1992; Volman 1984:203). It has puzzled archaeologists ever since. For Marean (2000:3), it is "incongruous mixes of archaic and more derived tool forms and technologies." For Deacon (1992:181), it is proof that Middle Stone Age South Africans were behaviorally as well as skeletally modern. Perhaps the most telling comment comes from Derek Roe (2001b:645): "The southern African MSA has produced many unexpected surprises, over the years: The Howieson's Poort was one."

Another reason the South African sites are so important is that their faunal remains have been used by Richard Klein to test his ideas about the mental and cultural capacities of Middle Stone Age hunters (Klein 1979, 2001b; Klein and Cruz-Uribe 1991, 1996). He contrasts the animals represented in these sites and concludes that Middle Stone Age hunters were less effective than (mainly Holocene) Later Stone Age people (Klein and Cruz-Uribe 1996:315). They failed to acquire dangerous terrestrial prey such as Cape buffalo (*Syncerus caffer*) as often as Later Stone Age people. Instead, they concentrated on relatively docile eland (*Taurotragus oryx*), even though buffalo was probably more abundant, as they were in historic times (Klein and Cruz-Uribe 1996:320). But Klein does admit that Middle Stone Age hunters lacked projectiles such as bows and arrows (Klein and Cruz-Uribe 1996:322), so they were unlikely to take on animals that were perfectly capable of defending themselves.

The situation is no better when marine resources are considered. Since shellfish and tortoises in Middle Stone Age contexts are quite large, Klein infers lower human population densities (Klein and Cruz-Uribe 1996:316, 2000). Middle Stone Age people used Cape fur seals (*Arctophalus pusillus*) throughout the year, unlike Later Stone Age people who scheduled coastal visits to exploit young seals washed up on shore (Klein and Cruz-Uribe 1996:317). They failed to figure out the life cycle of these animals. "The differences in bovid and seal exploitation help explain why Middle Stone Age people did not spread from Africa, even though they were anatomically more modern than their Eurasian contemporaries" (Klein and Cruz-Uribe 1996:315).

Early studies of Middle Stone Age faunas concentrated on taphonomic or site formation issues (Binford 1984). Sites like Klasies River exhibit a peculiar skeletal element distribution, what has become known as the Klasies faunal pattern (Klein 1976, 1989a, 1989b; Milo 1998:99; Bartram and Marean 1999). There are fewer large bovid upper limb elements than expected, but more heads and lower limbs. In contrast, as many upper limb elements as lower limb elements are included for small bovids (Milo 1998:101). Klein suggests that this could be the result of bias by the original excavators, or differential import or destruction of skeletal elements by carnivores or people (Bartram and Marean 1999:11; Turner 1984). Binford (1984) suggests that the Klasies River main site was a place where non-modern human scavengers, rather than true hunters, sought shelter (Deacon and Wurz 2001:59). Using butchery marks, Milo (1998) shows that lower limb elements were available to scavengers and suggests that hominins only had late access to carcasses (Milo 1998:101). Middle Stone Age people would then be marginal predators on small bovids, and even more marginal scavengers on large bovids (Milo 1998:101). But he concluded that there are signs that these people were "formidable hunters within the limits imposed by their technology" (Milo 1998:126), true people without culture!

The jury is still out on how modern South African Middle Stone Age people were. For Klein (2001b:2), the conclusion is clear. "However modern these people may have been anatomically, they were behaviorally primitive in the manner of the Neandertals" (Klein 2001b:2). For others, at least the most recent Middle Stone Age people were behaviorally indistinguishable from Later Stone Age or even recent hunter-gatherers. According to Henshilwood and colleagues, the wealth of new evidence "is turning the tide in favour of models positing behavioral modernity in Africa at a time far earlier than previously accepted" (Henshilwood et al. 2001:631). But Klein's perspective persists in the literature. As more evidence surfaces, it engenders more discussion and debate. For Klein (in Balter 2002:1223) and for many others, "the meaning of these pieces will remain debatable so long as they are unique."

11

Conclusions: What Does It Mean to Be a Modern *Homo sapiens?*

The mechanism whereby modern man spread throughout the world is, therefore, not so much in question as the sequence of events whereby this came about. (J. D. Clark 1981:187)

One might think that, if those systematics were adequate to the task at hand, the question of our origins would have been settled long ago. However, as is evident to even a casual reader of its literature, there is as much controversy now in modern human origins research as ever, and no resolution to that controversy is in sight. (G. A. Clark 2002:62)

The issue of the capacity for modern behavior or modern culture, and the evolution of cognition, will continue to play a major role in the debates on the nature of the Upper Palaeolithic revolution and the ensuing cultural changes. (Bar-Yosef 2002:383)

From the preceding chapters, it should be clear that the evidence relating to the African origins of modern humans produces more questions than answers. While there are many Upper Pleistocene archaeological sites in Africa, few date to the transition which is supposed to mark the beginnings of behavioral modernity here. It is therefore not currently possible to determine the nature of this process, let alone whether it was sudden or gradual. Haua Fteah in Libya is one of the few places with an early Upper Palaeolithic industry (McBurney 1967). In Africa south of the Sahara, there are a number of Pleistocene Later Stone Age sites, but few from the transitional period. So it is still not certain whether the evolution of the whole suite of Upper Palaeolithic traits was an

African process at all. It could have just as easily been an outcome of the initial dispersal of anatomically modern people into Eurasia. In this scenario, it is the movement of people north that precipitated the behavioral revolution.

As shown in chapter 7, the fossil record of early modern humans is slightly better. Anatomically modern humans are clearly present in Africa by 200,000 years ago. So far, the oldest skeletal remains come from a number of localities in the Kibish Formation along the Omo River in Ethiopia. In the 1960s, remains of three individuals were recovered here that have been recently re-dated to up to 195,000 years ago (McDougall et al. 2004; Shea et al. 2004). It is just a matter of time before a date prior to 200,000 years ago is announced. This would be more comforting to prehistorians, as it would suggest the transition to anatomical modernity accompanied the transition from the Acheulian into the Middle Palaeolithic/Middle Stone Age. It is an important technological boundary, one where large bifaces were replaced by a myriad of styles of hafted projectile points.

The most likely direct ancestral species for the first modern Africans, *Homo heidelbergensis*, appear to have been skeletally more like living people than later Eurasian Neanderthals. As a result, it is hard to see signs of the speciation event that produced both them and the earliest modern people. Palaeoanthropologists who have studied the fossil material firsthand differ on whether or not they see a gradual or sudden transition from what they often prefer to call "archaic" *Homo sapiens* into anatomically modern people (Bräuer 1992, 2001a, 2001b; Rightmire 1984, 1989, 1998a, 2001a). However, in the most recent version of his textbook, *The Human Career*, Klein (1999) goes in the opposite direction. He refers to all post–*Homo erectus* Africans as *Homo sapiens*.

It is still unclear what patterns and processes produced the earliest modern Africans. There is less known about why some of their descendants migrated elsewhere after only 50,000 years ago. The two Levantine sites with earlier modern humans, Skhūl and Qafzeh, are best understood as part of a limited expansion out of Africa during the extremely temperate MIS 5e sub-stage. Both African environments and African fauna appeared in the Levant at this time (Tchernov 1988; Goren-Inbar and Speth 2004). It is unlikely that such people remained in the Levant for another 60,000 years while they waited for the opportunity to disperse northward. In fact, after MIS 5e, conditions became more severe, and glacial conditions returned. It is at this point that European Neanderthals spread south to occupy the same territory. Sometime in MIS 3, early modern humans spread again from the south and entered temperate Europe. At this point, they encountered the Neanderthals, and the process of the eventual extinction of Neanderthals began. Whether or not hybridization or assimilation occurred still remains a mystery.

Models of modern human origins discussed in chapter 5 range from the extremes of complete replacement on one hand to multiregional continuity on the other. The African evidence fits both models. Under the replacement model, Africa should be the only continent to show continuity from earlier people into modern humans. Everywhere else, anatomically modern humans should appear relatively suddenly. On the other hand, multiregional models presume a continuity of populations in Eurasia, something that is not supported by either the fossil or the archaeological data. Intermediate models, such as Bräuer's (1984, 1989) replacement with hybridization and Smith's assimilation (Eswaran 2002; Eswaran et al. 2005; Smith 1982, 1984; Smith et al. 1989, 2005), suggest that both newcomers and indigenous populations had a role in later human evolution. African genes persist in high frequencies today, according to this idea, because there were always more Africans than non-Africans. The genetic data reviewed in chapter 6 points to some version of replacement. This is supported by the fossil evidence and new chronometric dates that argue for an early appearance of modern humans in Africa as well as their later coexistence with Neanderthals in Europe. But it does not definitively prove that replacement was the process that is responsible for the survival of anatomically modern people outside of Africa. The role of Upper Pleistocene Africans in the ancestry of people elsewhere ultimately remains a problem for archaeologists and palaeontologists working in Eurasia.

While the archaeological evidence from Africa is becoming clearer, questions still remain. Was there a sudden transition at the Middle to Upper Palaeolithic boundary? Will archaeological sites showing this transition ever be found? Were the impacts of the last glacial maximum so severe that group size decreased or people left previously densely populated regions completely? Can the global pattern of Upper Pleistocene human evolution be reassessed in light of the African archaeological evidence in order to give a more balanced understanding? Finally, what can African Stone Age archaeology say to contemporary Africans as well as to students of later African societies?

The research discussed in this book attempts to put Africa in its rightful place as paramount in all stages of human evolution, even that of *Homo sapi-*

ens. When added to genetic data, it reinforces the notion of our recent common ancestry and shared biocultural heritage. There are a number of points that bear repeating. Middle Palaeolithic/Middle Stone Age Africans were not people without culture. But neither were their Eurasian cousins, the Neanderthals. To the contrary, both were experimenting with new technologies and new ways of life in the ever changing environments of the Upper Pleistocene.

A lot of our ideas about what it means to be human reflect old constructions of the past. Human evolutionary studies contain a lot of ideas, but few facts to back them up. Sometimes it seems that researchers never let the facts get in the way of a good theory, and many theories are not testable anyway (Pilbeam 1980; Willoughby 2005). Landau (1991) suggests that most models have no more basis in fact that the origin myths of other societies. On the other hand, there is a need to explain ourselves and our uniqueness and its causes. Symbolism, abstract thinking, and language have all been proposed to be the products of what makes us human.

Chapter 2 reviewed the history of ideas about modern human origins. It shows that later African prehistory has always been constructed in the light of the Western European record and the achievements of Cro-Magnons. But even Upper Palaeolithic archaeologists know that this area is unusual, and probably represents a small cul-de-sac of the Palaeolithic world (Straus 1995). With new dates (chapter 4) and genetic data (chapter 6), palaeoanthropologists are forced to focus on the later Pleistocene record from Africa, rather than later events in Europe. The genetic evidence continues to grow at an astronomical rate. There are almost weekly publications about mutations in particular genes or other genetic loci that appear to be associated with something that is unique to living humans. It makes us wish that we could genetically sample some fossil hominins, to see if they have the modern version of these sequences.

This book was envisaged as a contribution to the growing debate on modern human origins. It intentionally took a multidisciplinary and interdisciplinary focus and showed the need to look at information from many allied sciences. As usual, most archaeologists and human palaeontologists are consumers of this information, rather than its creators. On the one hand, it is clear that we archaeologists need to learn more in order to have a dialogue with other scientists. On the other hand, we need to re-evaluate our own ideas and models, in order to see which represent the more likely scenarios. It is only in this way that the study of the archaeological and the palaeontological record of human evolution will become equal partners in scientific discourse.

WHAT IS BEHAVIORAL MODERNITY?

African Stone Age specialists continuously talk about behavioral modernity and how it can be seen in the archaeological record. But, as Wadley (2001a:204) writes, "cultural modernity needs to be defined in a way that focuses on behavioural issues first, and thereafter on material culture correlates." In other words, there are changes in technology and adaptation associated with the beginnings of the African Later Stone Age or Upper Palaeolithic, but it is not clear what they mean in behavioral terms. It is also possible that these innovations were shared with other kinds of hominins. In chapter 1, it was suggested that we could draw a parallel between the debates about modern human origins and Wolf's (1982, 1997) early European explorers trying to understand the place of non-Western people in their world. These people were supposed to be isolated from more "civilized" populations, yet the mere fact of first contact created connections everywhere (Wolf 1997:4). By the time anthropology was developed as a way to study these others, they were already part of the world's social and economic systems. They were not so different after all from the outsiders who first wrote about them.

In some way, we can argue that the first anatomically modern humans had, or developed, a new cultural system and a novel way of perceiving their landscape. It is reflected in the products of symbolism and ethnicity, what archaeologists identify as style. It is entirely possible that there was a gradual appearance of these new traits, both in Europe with *Homo neanderthalensis* and in Africa with *Homo sapiens* (D'Errico 2003; D'Errico et al. 2003; Gamble 1994; McBrearty and Brooks 2000). Or, it could have been a sudden transition, brought on by external environmental stresses (Ambrose 1998a, 2001a; Klein 1992, 1995) or by some yet unknown internal, sociocultural cause.

Table 11.1 reviews some of the traits used to describe innovations that are supposed to be characteristic of the Upper Palaeolithic revolution (Mellars 1991, 2002; Bar-Yosef 2002; McBrearty and Brooks 2000; Henshilwood and Marean 2003; Willoughby 2001a). As reviewed in chapter 1, these include blade and/or bladelet technology, standardized tool production, personal adornment, portable art, use of pigments such as red ochre, organic tools (bone, ivory, and antler), long distance trade, exchange and/or information networks, composite tools, the ability to express one's ethnic identity in material culture, the use of fish or shellfish, and movement into new territories. How many of these are expressed, or have their origins, in the African Middle Palaeolithic/Middle Stone Age? Here are a few examples.

Table 11.1. Selected signs of behavioral modernity—The African evidence

Signs of Behavioral Modernity	Some African Middle Palaeolithic/ Middle Stone Age Examples	Selected References
Mode 4 blade tools and/or Mode 5 microlithic technology	Libyan Pre-Aurignacian, Haua Fteah; Flake-blade technology in South African Middle Stone Age and geometrics in Howieson's Poort; blades in Kapthurin Formation, Kenya	McBurney 1967; Singer and Wymer 1982; McBrearty et al. 1996
Standardized tool production	Flake-blade technology in South African Middle Stone Age and geometrics in Howieson's Poort, South Africa Production of Levallois, non-Levallois, and Aterian projectile points	Singer and Wymer 1982; McBrearty and Brooks 2000
Personal adornment	Ostrich eggshell beads in Middle Stone Age contexts in Kenya (Enkapune ya Muto), Tanzania (Mumba Cave, possibly at Loiyangalani, Serengeti), Botswana (White Paintings Rockshelter), South Africa (Border Cave, Cave of Hearths); Drilled marine shells (Blombos Cave)	Ambrose 1998b; Thompson et al. 2004; Henshilwood et al. 2004; McBrearty and Brooks 2000; Mehlman 1989; Robbins 1999
Portable (mobiliary) art	Plaquette, Apollo 11 Cave, Namibia Incised red ochre at Blombos Cave	Henshilwood et al. 2002
Red ochre	Extensive use of red ochre in most Middle Stone Age contexts	Barham 1998
Bone/ivory/antler tools	Bone harpoons, Katanda, Congo Blombos Cave, South Africa	Brooks et al. 1995; Henshilwood et al. 2001
Long distance trade, exchange and/or information networks	Regional point styles Long distance transport of lithic raw materials	McBrearty and Brooks 2000
Composite tools	Aterian tanged pieces Howieson's Poort, South Africa	Débénath 1994; Stapleton and Hewitt 1927, 1928
Isochrestic variation and expression of ethnic identity	Regional traditions such as the Aterian in North Africa, Songwe MSA and LSA, Tanzania	McBrearty and Brooks 2000; Willoughby and Sipe 2002
Use of fish or shellfish	Eritrea (Abdur Reef)? Blombos Cave, Klasies River, other South African coastal sites	Walter et al. 2000; Singer and Wymer 1982; Thackeray 1992
Movement into new territories	Tropical rainforests of central Africa deserts—Kalahari, Sahara? The Out of Africa II dispersal	Mercader 2002, 2003a; Mercader and Marti 2003; Ferring 1975; Garcea 2004; Robbins et al. 1996, 2000
Association with anatomically modern Homo sapiens	Everywhere	Bräuer 1989, 1992; Rightmire 1984, 1989, 2001a, 2001c

There are unusual industries such as the Libyan Pre-Aurignacian industry from Haua Fteah, a Mode 4 industry sandwiched between two Levalloiso-Mousterian Mode 3 assemblages. It contains a prismatic blade technology and is stratified well below the Dabban, which represents the first true Upper Palaeolithic occupation (Close 1986:175). Blade technology is present in the Acheulian of the Kapthurin Formation in Kenya (Mcbrearty et al. 1996). Most archaeologists would say that the flake-blade technology of the South African Middle Stone Age (Singer and Wymer 1982; Thackeray 1992) would also fit into Mode 4. Stylistic similarities in the Aterian, an industry where tanged points and other retouched tools are found over a large range in North Africa and the Sahara, may represent an example of isochrestic variation (Sackett 1982), an ethnic marker. But the absence of the Aterian from the Nile Valley remains puzzling. The presence of stems or tangs on numerous stone tools is the signature feature of the Aterian (figures 8.4 and 8.7). Presumably, these were shaped to facilitate hafting the stone piece onto a handle, in order to create a composite tool (Clark 1974a:190; Débénath 1994; Ferring 1975). A similar conclusion is reached for some South African tools; "Retouch on stone artifacts in earlier Middle Stone Age assemblages strongly suggests that Middle Stone Age peoples were hafting both carefully retouched and otherwise untrimmed pieces by the early Upper Pleistocene" (Volman 1984:193–194; also Thackeray 1989:45). These flake-blades as well as points from the North African Aterian can be interpreted as exhibiting culturally significant regional variation. The different kinds of projectile points illustrated by both Clark (1993a:155) and McBrearty and Brooks (2000:498) also reflect stylistic or isochrestic patterns (Sackett 1977, 1982), what Aldhouse-Green (2001:116) calls a sign of enhanced self awareness. Some of this may have a temporal framework. Thackeray and Kelly (1988:23) argue that the changes in flake-blades form over time and "are of the kind often labeled 'stylistic' by archaeologists."

Ostrich eggshell beads are present in Middle Stone Age levels at Enkapune ya Muto, Kenya, around 39,900 BP (Ambrose 1998b), possibly at Loiyangalani in the Serengeti (Bower 1977, 1981; Thompson et al. 2004), as well as at Kisese II and Mumba Cave, all in Tanzania. They have also been reported from other sites, including White Paintings Rockshelter in the Tsodilo Hills of Botswana (Robbins 1999), and in South Africa at Border Cave, Bloomplaas, and the Cave of Hearths (D'Errico et al. 2003, 2005:5–6). D'Errico and colleagues also report a perforated *Nassarius gibbosulus* shell from the Aterian levels at Oued Djebanna in Algeria (D'Errico et al. 2005:6).

Drilled marine shells are present at Blombos Cave (D'Errico et al. 2005; Henshilwood et al. 2004). Bone harpoons dating to 80,000 years ago have been reported from Katanda, in the eastern Congo (Brooks et al. 1995). There is clear evidence of standardization of tool forms in the Howieson's Poort of South Africa, as well as in the Middle Stone Age flake-blade assemblages of South Africa. In addition, a case can be made that Levallois technology itself involves a great deal of forethought and planning. Bifacial foliate (leaf-shaped) stone points, as well as bone points, are reported from the latest Middle Stone Age (BBC M1) levels from Blombos (Henshilwood et al. 2001; D'Errico et al. 2001, 2005; Henshilwood and Sealy 1997). These are close to 75,000 years old. Blombos and many other South African Middle Stone Age sites show evidence of extensive exploitation of shellfish and other coastal resources. In addition, many archaeologists have noted the presence of red ochre (hematite) at Middle Stone Age sites, and at Blombos, there is a single piece with a series of intersecting hatch mark incisions (Henshilwood et al. 2001:634–635, 2002; Henshilwood, Sealy et al. 2001).

It is possible that Middle Stone Age people moved into new territories. This includes the rain forests of central Africa (Mercader 2002, 2003a; Mercader and Marti 2003). Some of the sites discussed in previous chapters are found in modern desert regions, such as the Sahara and Kalahari. This might represent early occupations of dry environments, but as the Quaternary Environment Network's climate simulations show (map 3.4), there were extremely wet periods when these deserts were reduced or eliminated. The Out of Africa II migration could also be interpreted as the ultimate sign of movement into new areas. In most scenarios, there was nothing stopping these people from going wherever they wished to go. Finally, most of the Middle Palaeolithic/Middle Stone Age sites in Africa are associated with anatomically modern humans, and these extend at least as far back as 200,000 years ago.

Generally, most Africanist archaeologists support the idea that, prior to the beginnings of the Upper Palaeolithic or Later Stone Age, anatomically modern people had some aspects of a modern behavioral repertoire. Regardless of this, there may have been key changes just before the Out of Africa II migration began. Bower (2005:121) feels that these need to be studied in detail, even if not from a simple trait list approach. He sees them as reflecting Palaeolithic thought, such as self-awareness, social or group life, and the emergence of the modern mind (Bower 2005:122).

WHAT IS BIOLOGICAL MODERNITY?

The African evidence for the origins of anatomically modern people was reviewed in chapter 7. It shows that while Upper Pleistocene fossils remain fragmentary and scarce, they support the idea of an in situ evolution of the skeletal structures that we presently retain. How to divide up this record remains unclear. Some wish to see a new species every time the archaeological record shifts (Mcbrearty and Brooks 2000; Foley and Lahr 1997). In this scenario, Acheulian industries are associated with *Homo erectus/Homo ergaster*, as well as with *Homo heidelbergensis*. Mode 3 technologies are associated with *Homo heidelbergensis* and early *Homo sapiens* in Africa and with Neanderthals in Western Eurasia. Palaeontologists like Bräuer (1992, 2001a, 2001b) see a gradual transition from "archaic" humans into anatomically modern ones. But McBrearty and Brooks (2000) resurrect *Homo rhodesiensis* and *Homo helmei* and see both as present prior to the emergence of anatomically modern *Homo sapiens*.

While there are different ways to divide up the fossil record, this does not significantly affect our interpretation of the African evidence. Biological modernity appeared at least by 200,000 years ago. But there is another problem. If these people were like us, why are none of them found outside Africa until after 50,000 or even 40,000 years ago? The only exception to this pattern are the "proto Cro-Magnons" of Skhūl and Qafzeh (Vandermeersch 1981), who are best interpreted as Africans whose ancestors dispersed to the Levant during an unusually warm period, MIS 5e. Earlier hominins, starting with *Homo erectus/Homo ergaster*, entered a Eurasian world where they might have faced few natural obstacles. However, African modern humans would have encountered the indigenous human groups who should have been better adapted to their native cold, northern, glacial environments. In order to survive or compete, Klein (1992) is convinced that these early modern humans had to have made the behavioral transition to modern hunter-gatherer lifeways. There could easily be another explanation. Genetic evidence points to repeated periods of stress and bottlenecks that postdate the appearance of Mitochondrial Eve. These could have been the result of catastrophic environmental change, such as the global change that is said to be the outcome of the Mount Toba eruption (Ambrose 1998a, 2003; Rampino and Ambrose 2000; Rampino and Self 1992). Or it could have been a product of regular glacial cycling (Willoughby 1993b). There is growing evidence for increased environmental extremes toward the end of the Pleistocene. The book *Climate Change in Prehistory: The End of the Reign of Chaos*, by Burroughs (2005), points this out clearly and stresses the unpredictability of Pleistocene environments versus the warm, but monotonous, conditions of the Holocene or post-glacial.

Does the archaeological picture help us understand the appearance of biological modernity? Yes, but it would then bear on the question of the end of the long Acheulian industry, rather than on key events within the Middle Stone Age. It is still possible that a simultaneous transition took place in both anatomy and behavior, as has been argued for many other stages of the Palaeolithic (Ambrose 2001a; Foley 1989; Toth and Schick 1986; Willoughby 1996c).

AFRICA IN UPPER PLEISTOCENE PREHISTORY: REASSESSING DESMOND CLARK'S "PERIPHERAL OR PARAMOUNT?"

Indeed, the researchers of the last few years have produced a large, and still growing, body of evidence strongly suggesting that, not only was it in Africa that the human race first began, but that just about every significant biological and cultural advance—at least for the first 2½ million years—took place in Africa. (Clark 1974a:175)

Desmond Clark had a significant role in the development of African Stone Age research. He conducted field research throughout the continent and was famous for his syntheses of African prehistory. In 1974, he produced such a review and analysis of data when he presented the Huxley Memorial Lecture at the Royal Anthropological Institute. Caton-Thompson (1946a) had done a similar presentation in 1946 about the Aterian, as had Hrdlička (1927) almost twenty years earlier for the Neanderthals. When re-examined, Clark's assessment is a prescient paper, foreshadowing much of the changes of perspective that would come in the 1990s. His basic conclusions are as follows. Africa was central for all stages of human evolution, not just the earliest record. This might be surprising to many of his colleagues who generally felt that "the prehistory of Europe is emphatically the prehistory of humanity" (Clark 1974a:176). Since Africa is an enormous continent, it contains a wide range of ecological zones (Clark 1974a:180). These clearly played a role in the emergence of early humans as well as the first *Homo sapiens*. It is this latter transition that needed the most revision. At the time Clark was writing, it was generally felt that Africa was "a region of cultural stagnation and genetic isolation during the Upper Palaeolithic" (Clark 1974a:187).

> Not only does the available evidence indicate that it was in that continent that those developments which gave us our humanity had their origins, but also that it now appears that some of the technological innovations of the Pleistocene and earlier Holocene were first developed there or, at least, were of equal antiquity inside as outside the continent. (Clark 1974a:193)

By this time, Clark had recognized a number of innovations in African Middle Palaeolithic/Middle Stone Age, similar to those listed in table 11.1. The Middle Stone Age was not the temporal equivalent of the European Upper Palaeolithic, but of the Middle Palaeolithic, then felt to go back to around 100,000 years ago (Clark 1974a:188). So Clark (1974a:189) was convinced that the transition to modernity in Africa occurred at the same time as in Europe.

IN EVOLUTIONARY TERMS, WHAT DOES IT MEAN TO BE A MODERN HOMO SAPIENS?

Basically, it all comes down to this fundamental question: In evolutionary terms, what does it mean to be a "modern" human? When do early hominins achieve this status and why? Modern palaeoanthropological discourse seems centered on the debates surrounding "people like us" (Ingold 1995). It is a status that only a few populations share. Having a skeletal anatomy identical to that of present people is obviously not enough. As mentioned in chapter 1, Europeans saw themselves as the first people with history. When confronted with indigenous people elsewhere, they created social models to explain the boundaries between themselves and the others. A similar process seems to underlie the study of modern human origins. Many palaeoanthropologists continue to argue that only Eurasian Upper Palaeolithic people had true culture. They seem to believe that, even if there were earlier modern humans in Africa, they only became people like us when they were confronted with new challenges in northern glacial environments. In other words, what made them human was the decision to leave Africa for elsewhere. This is what Proctor

(2003:225) called the "out of Africa, thank God" scenario. Later human evolution was, and continues to be, seen as a European process. There are many more researchers working on this problem outside of Africa rather than inside it, where our most recent common ancestors actually lived.

If this is the case, what are the future prospects for the study of recent human evolution in Africa? Sometimes it seems that researchers studying this period will never have the cachet or media attention lavished on the discoverers of fossils of our earliest ancestors. It is also hard to compete with the fabulous artistic and cultural record of Upper Palaeolithic peoples throughout Europe, especially in regions such as the Dordogne River valley in southern France. This is where later Palaeolithic research began. Right from the start, it was clear that those sites were made by people like us, no question about it. To some extent, my own research history has paralleled the beginnings of the new, emerging African paradigm. My doctoral supervisor, Dr. James Sackett of UCLA, repeatedly reminded us that "if it didn't happen in the Dordogne, it wasn't important" (Sackett, personal communication). Even if I worked on Early Stone Age material from Africa (Willoughby 1987), it had to be within the European paradigm. But as soon as I completed my doctoral program in 1985, the world of later human evolution began to be revolutionized. History repeated itself. In the 1960s, when new radiometric dates were applied to sites in Bed I at Olduvai Gorge, East Africa became the region with the longest fossil and cultural record of humanity. Starting in the late 1980s, newer chronometric dating methods showed that Africa was undoubtedly the continent in which the emergence of our own species occurred. Few students get such an opportunity to challenge their advisers and to have the chance to say that many of the things they learned were wrong. An African role in the emergence of anatomically and behaviorally modern humans was unexpected. But the new dates and molecular data show the formative role the continent had in all stages of our evolution.

On the other hand, if the geneticists wanted to pick a region and time for which there is little hard palaeoanthropological data, they could not have done a better job. This book has reviewed the archaeological and fossil evidence of the period said to be associated with the last great evolutionary transition, the beginnings of what made us truly human. But it remains an extremely limited record. Part of this is due to the history of research. There are still many regions of the continent that have never been visited by archaeologists or palaeontologists, let alone studied in detail. There is also a significant hiatus between the Middle and Later Stone Age; few transitional sites exist. This could be archaeological signs of bottlenecking and near extinction of the founder population, and it makes it difficult to test the various models of modernity. Since it is close to possible last glacial forest refugia, it is East Africa which is the most likely region to preserve such evidence (Klein 1992:12, 1999:492). My own research in southern Tanzania is an attempt to document Middle Stone Age and Pleistocene Later Stone Age sites. My goal is to document and to explain the cultural transformation that may have occurred at this time.

With the shift of attention back to our founding continent, there remains much more for both African and expatriate researchers to do. We have known for a long time that humans lack fundamental genetic differences, something which goes back to Lewontin's (1972) pioneering study. This is the party line about "race," something which is repeatedly mentioned in many introductory anthropology courses, including my own. Our diversity is due to our many different cultures, not our biology. At a time when societies and nations are becoming more and more fragmented while also being drawn together in new ways, it is important to remember our common roots. Out of Africa II was one of the first, if unintentional, examples of global colonization (Gamble 1994). While it may have led to the extinction of indigenous Eurasian populations, it also started an evolutionary process that we still carry in our genes and skeletons today. It is only by expanding the fossil and archaeological record from Africa that we will understand this process, what happened and why, and what role it continues to have in our history. Like those people who set off for the unknown around 50,000 years ago, we remain Africans "under the skin."

References

Abbate, E., A. Albianelli, A. Azzaroli, M. Benvenuti, B. Tasfarmariam, P. Bruni, N. Cipriani, et al. 1998. "A one-million-year-old *Homo* cranium from the Danakil (Afar) depression of Eritrea." *Nature* 393 (6684): 458–460.

Adams, J. M., H. Faure, and QEN members. 1997. "Review and atlas of palaeovegetation: Preliminary land ecosystem maps of the world since the last glacial maximum." Oak Ridge National Laboratory, Tennessee. http://www.esd.ornl.gov/projects/qen/adams1.html.

Agassiz, L. 1840. *Etudes sur les glaciers.* Neuchatel: Jent et Gassmann.

Ahern, J. C. M., I. Karavanic, M. Paunovic, I. Janković, and F. H. Smith. 2004. "New discoveries and interpretations of hominid fossils and artifacts from Vindija Cave, Croatia." *Journal of Human Evolution* 46 (1): 25–65.

Aitken, M. J., C. B. Stringer, and P. A. Mellars, eds. 1993. *The origin of modern humans and the impact of chronometric dating.* Princeton, NJ: Princeton University Press.

Aitken, M. J. and H. Valladas. 1992. "Luminescence dating relative to human origins." *Philosophical Transactions of the Royal Society* 337b(1280): 139–144.

Aitken, M. J. and H. Valladas. 1993. "Luminescence dating relative to human origins." In M. J. Aitken, C. B. Stringer, and P. A. Mellars, eds., *The origin of modern humans and the impact of chronometric dating.* Princeton, NJ: Princeton University Press, pp. 27–39.

Akazawa, T., K. Aoki, and O. Bar-Yosef, eds. 1998. *Neandertals and modern humans in Western Asia.* New York: Plenum Press.

Aldhouse-Green, S. 2001. "*Ex Africa semper aliquid novi*: The view from Pontnewydd." In S. Milliken and J. Cook, eds., *A very remote period indeed: Papers on the Palaeolithic presented to Derek Roe.* Oxford: Oxbow Books, pp. 114–119.

Alexander, C. A. 1872. "Man as the contemporary of the mammoth and the reindeer in Middle Europe." Annual report of the Board of Regents of the Smithsonian

Institution, showing the operations, expenditures, and condition of the institution for the year 1867. Washington, DC: Government Printing Office, pp. 335–362.

Alimen, H. 1975. "Les 'isthmes' hispano-marocain et siculo-tunisien aux temps acheuléens." *L'Anthropologie* 79:399–436.

Allen, J., J. Golson, and R. Jones, eds. 1977. *Sunda and Sahul: Prehistoric studies in Southeast Asia, Melanesia and Australia.* London: Academic Press.

Alley, R. B. 2000a. "Ice core evidence of abrupt climatic changes." *Proceedings of the National Academy of Sciences* 97 (4): 1331–1334.

Alley, R. B. 2000b. *The two mile time machine.* Princeton, NJ: Princeton University Press.

Allsworth-Jones, P. 1986. "Middle Stone Age and Middle Palaeolithic: The evidence from Nigeria and Cameroun." In G. N. Bailey and P. Callow, eds., *Stone Age prehistory.* Cambridge: Cambridge University Press, pp. 153–168.

Ambrose, S. H. 1998a. "Late Pleistocene human population bottlenecks, volcanic winter, and differentiation of modern humans." *Journal of Human Evolution* 34 (6): 623–651.

Ambrose, S. H. 1998b. "Chronology of the Later Stone Age and food production in East Africa." *Journal of Archaeological Science* 25 (4): 377–392.

Ambrose, S. H. 2001a. "Paleolithic technology and human evolution." *Science* 291 (5509): 1748–1753.

Ambrose, S. H. 2001b. "Middle and Late Stone Age settlement patterns in the Central Rift Valley, Kenya: Comparisons and contrasts." In N. Conard, ed., *Settlement dynamics of the Middle Palaeolithic and Middle Stone Age. Tübingen publications in prehistory 1.* Tübingen: Kerns Verlag, pp. 21–43.

Ambrose, S. H. 2002. "Small things remembered: Origins of early microlithic industries in sub-Saharan Africa." In R. G. Elston and S. L. Kuhn, eds., "Thinking small: Global perspectives on microlithization." *Archaeological Papers of the American Anthropological Association* 12:9–29.

Ambrose, S. H. 2003. "Did the super-eruption of Toba cause a human population bottleneck?" *Journal of Human Evolution* 45 (3): 231–237.

Ambrose, S. H., A. Deino, M. D. Kyule, I. Steele, and M. A. J. Williams. 2002. "The emergence of modern human behavior during the Late Middle Stone Age in the Kenya Rift Valley." *Journal of Human Evolution* 42 (3): A3–A4.

Ambrose, S. H. and K. Lorenz. 1990. "Social and ecological models for the MSA in Southern Africa." In P. Mellars, ed., *The emergence of modern humans.* Ithaca: Cornell University Press, pp. 3–33.

Andrews, P. A. and I. Tekkaya. 1980. "A revision of the Turkish Miocene hominoid *Sivapithecus meteai.*" *Palaeontology* 23:85–95.

Anthony, B. 1978. *The Prospect Industry—A definition.* PhD diss., Harvard University.

Arambourg, C. 1950. "Traces possibles d'une industrie primitive dans un niveau Villafranchien d'Afrique du Nord." *Bulletin de la Société Préhistorique Française* 47:348–350.

Arambourg, C. 1963. "L'*Atlanthropus mauritanicus.*" *Mémoires et Archives de l'Institut de Paléontologie Humaine* 32:37–190.

Arambourg, C. and L. Balout. 1952. "Du nouveau à l'Ain Hanech." *Bulletin de la Société d'Histoire de l'Afrique du Nord* 43:152–169.

Arambourg, C. and P. Biberson. 1956. "The fossil human remains from the Paleolithic site of Sidi Abderrahman (Morocco)." *American Journal of Physical Anthropology* 13:191–202.

Arsuaga, J. L., J. M. Bermudez de Castro, and E. Carbonell, eds. 1997. "The Sima de los Huesos hominid site." Special issue, *Journal of Human Evolution* 33 (2/3): 105–421.

Ascenzi, A., I. Biddittu, P. F. Cassoli, A. G. Segre, and E. Segre-Naldini. 1996. "A calvarium of late *Homo erectus* from Ceprano, Italy." *Journal of Human Evolution* 31 (5): 409–423.

Ascenzi, A., F. Mallegni, G. Manzi, A. G. Segre, and E. Segre-Naldini. 2000. "A re-appraisal of Ceprano calvaria affinities with *Homo erectus*, after the new reconstruction." *Journal of Human Evolution* 39 (4): 443–450.

Asfaw, B. 1983. "New hominid parietal from Bodo, Middle Awash Valley, Ethiopia." *American Journal of Physical Anthropology* 61 (3): 367–371.

Asfaw, B., W. H. Gilbert, Y. Beyene, W. K. Hart, P. R. Renne, G. WoldeGabriel, E. S. Vrba, and T. D. White. 2002. "Remains of *Homo erectus* from Bouri, Middle Awash, Ethiopia." *Nature* 416 (6878): 317–320.

Avery, D. M. 1996. "Late Quaternary environmental change at Mumbwa Caves, Zambia." In G. Pwiti and R. Soper, eds., *Aspects of African archaeology*. Harare: University of Zimbabwe Publications, pp. 63–70.

Avery, D. M. 2002. "Taphonomy of micromammals from cave deposits at Kabwe (Broken Hill) and Twin Rivers in central Zambia." *Journal of Archaeological Science* 29 (5): 537–544.

Avery, G., K. Cruz-Uribe, P. Goldberg, F. E. Grine, R. G. Klein, M. J. Lenardi, C. Marean, et al. 1997. "The 1992–1993 excavations at the Die Kelders Middle and Later Stone Age cave site, South Africa." *Journal of Field Archaeology* 24 (3): 263–291.

Azoury, I., C. Bergman, and L. Copeland. 1986. "K'sar Akil, Lebanon: A technological and typological analysis of the transitional and early Upper Palaeolithic levels of K'sar Akil and Abu Halka." *BAR International Series* 289.

Baba, H., F. Aziz, Y. Kaifu, G. Suwa, R. T. Kono, and T. Jacob. 2003. "*Homo erectus* calvarium from the Pleistocene of Java." *Science* 299 (5611): 1384–1388.

Bada, J. L. 1985. "Aspartic acid racemization ages of California PaleoIndian skeletons." *American Antiquity* 50 (3): 645–647.

Bada, J. L. and P. M. Helfman. 1975. "Amino acid racemization dating of fossil bones." *World Archaeology* 7:160–183.

Bailey, W. J. 1993. "Hominoid trichotomy: A molecular view." *Evolutionary Anthropology* 2 (3): 100–108.

Bakker, R. 1986. *The dinosaur heresies: New theories unlocking the mystery of the dinosaurs and their extinction.* New York: Morrow.

Baksi, A. K., B. Hsu, M. O. Williams, and E. Ferrar. 1992. "⁴⁰Ar/³⁹Ar dating of the Bruhnes-Matuyama geomagnetic field reversal." *Science* 256 (5055): 356–357.

Balout, L. 1955. *Préhistoire de l'Afrique du Nord.* Paris: Arts et Métiers Graphiques.

Balter, M. 2002. "What made humans modern?" *Science* 295 (5558): 1219–1225.

Balter, M. and A. Gibbons. 2002. "Were 'little people' the first to venture out of Africa?" *Science* 297 (5578): 26–27.

Bamford, M. K. and Z. Henderson. 2003. "A reassessment of the wooden fragment from Florisbad, South Africa." *Journal of Archaeological Science* 30 (6): 637–650.

Barber, B. R. 1992. "Jihad vs. McWorld." *Atlantic Monthly* 269 (3): 53–55, 58–63.

Barber, B. R. 1996. *Jihad versus mcworld: How globalism and tribalism are reshaping the world.* New York: Ballantine Books.

Barber, L. 1980. *The heyday of natural history.* Garden City, NY: Doubleday.

Barbujani, G., A. Magagni, E. Minch, and L. L. Cavalli-Sforza. 1997. "An apportionment of human DNA diversity." *Proceedings of the National Academy of Sciences* 94 (9): 4516–4519.

Barham, L. 1996. "Recent research on the Middle Stone Age at Mumbwa Caves, Central Zambia." In G. Pwiti and R. Soper, eds., *Aspects of African archaeology.* Harare: University of Zimbabwe Publications, pp. 191–200.

Barham, L. 1998. "Possible early pigment use in south-central Africa." *Current Anthropology* 39 (5): 703–710.

Barham, L. 2000. *The Middle Stone Age of Zambia, south central Africa.* Bristol: Western Academic and Specialist Press.

Barham, L. 2001a. Preface to *Human roots: Africa and Asia in the Middle Pleistocene,* by L. Barham and K. Robson-Brown, eds. Bristol: Western Academic and Specialist Press, pp. xvii–xv.

Barham, L. 2001b. "Central Africa and the emergence of regional identity in the Middle Pleistocene." In L. Barham and K. Robson-Brown, eds., *Human roots: Africa and Asia in the Middle Pleistocene.* Bristol: Western Academic and Specialist Press, pp. 65–88.

Barham, L. 2002a. "Systematic pigment use in the Middle Pleistocene of South Central Africa." *Current Anthropology* 43 (1): 181–190.

Barham, L. 2002b. "Backed tools in Middle Pleistocene central Africa and their evolutionary significance." *Journal of Human Evolution* 43 (5): 585–603.

Barham, L. and K. Robson-Brown, eds. 2001. *Human roots: Africa and Asia in the Middle Pleistocene.* Bristol: Western Academic and Specialist Press.

Barham, L. S. and P. L. Smart. 1996. "An early date for the Middle Stone Age of central Zambia." *Journal of Human Evolution* 30 (3): 287–290.

Barich, B. E., G. Bodrato, E. A. A. Garcea, C. Conati Barbaro, and C. Giraudi. 2003. "Northern Libya in the final Pleistocene: The late hunting societies of Jebel Gharbi." *Studi in onore di Lidiano Bacchielli. Quaderni di Archeologia della Libya* 18:259–265.

Barkal, R., A. Gopher, S. E. Lauritzern, and A. Frumkin. 2003. "Uranium series dates from Qesem Cave, Israel, and the end of the Lower Palaeolithic." *Nature* 423 (6943): 977–979.

Barton, R. N. E., A. Bouzouggar, and C. B. Stringer. 2001. "Bridging the gap: New fieldwork in northern Morocco." *Antiquity* 75 (289): 489–490.

Bartram, L. E. and C. W. Marean. 1999. "Explaining the 'Klasies pattern': Kua ethnoarchaeology, the Die Kelders Middle Stone Age archaeofauna, long bone fragmentation and carnivore ranging." *Journal of Archaeological Science* 26 (1): 9–29.

Barut, S. 1996. "Obsidian source use in the Later Stone Age at Lukenya Hill, Kenya." In G. Pwiti and R. Soper, eds., *Aspects of African archaeology*. Harare: University of Zimbabwe Publications, pp. 297–305.

Barut, S. 1997. Later Stone Age lithic raw material use at Lukenya Hill, Kenya. PhD diss., University of Illinois at Urbana-Champaign.

Bar-Yosef, O. 1989a. "Geochronology of the Levantine Middle Palaeolithic." In P. Mellars and C. Stringer, eds., *The human revolution*. Princeton, NJ: Princeton University Press, pp. 589–610.

Bar-Yosef, O. 1989b. "Upper Pleistocene cultural stratigraphy in Southwest Asia." In E. Trinkaus, ed., *The emergence of modern humans*. Cambridge: Cambridge University Press, pp. 154–180.

Bar-Yosef, O. 1992a. "The role of Western Asia in modern human origins." *Philosophical Transactions of the Royal Society* 337B (1280): 193–200.

Bar-Yosef, O. 1992b. "Middle Palaeolithic chronology and the transition to the Upper Palaeolithic in Southwest Asia." In G. Bräuer and F. H. Smith, eds., *Continuity or replacement*. Rotterdam: A. A. Balkema, pp. 261–272.

Bar-Yosef, O. 1993. "The role of Western Asia in modern human origins." In M. J. Aitken, C. B. Stringer, and P. A. Mellars, eds., *The origin of modern humans and the impact of chronometric dating*. Princeton, NJ: Princeton University Press, pp. 132–147.

Bar-Yosef, O. 1994. "The contributions of Southwest Asia to the study of the origin of modern humans." In M. H. Nitecki and D. V. Nitecki, eds., *Origins of anatomically modern humans*. New York: Plenum Press, pp. 23–66.

Bar-Yosef, O. 2002. "The Upper Palaeolithic revolution." *Annual Review of Anthropology* 31:363–393.

Bar-Yosef, O. and S. Kuhn. 1999. "The big deal about blades: Laminar technologies and human evolution." *American Anthropologist* 101 (2): 322–338.

Bar-Yosef, O. and B. Vandermeersch. 1993. "Modern humans in the Levant." *Scientific American* 268 (4): 94–100.

Bar-Yosef, O., B. Vandermeersch, B. Arensburg, A. Belfer-Cohen, P. Goldberg, H. Laville, L. Meignen, Y. Rak, J. D. Speth, E. Tchernov, A.-M. Tillier, and S. Weiner. 1992. "The excavations in Kebara Cave, Mt. Carmel." *Current Anthropology* 33 (5): 497–550.

Batzer, M. A., S. S. Arcot, J. W. Phinny, M. Algeria-Hartman, D. H. Kass, S. M. Milligan, C. Klimpton, et al. 1996. "Genetic variation of recent Alu insertions in human populations." *Journal of Molecular Evolution* 42 (1): 22–29.

Beaumont, P. B., H. de Villiers, and J. C. Vogel. 1978. "Modern man in sub-Saharan Africa prior to 49,000 years BP: A review and evaluation in particular reference to Border Cave." *South African Journal of Science* 74 (11): 409–419.

Beauval, C., B. Maureille, F. Lacrampe-Cuyabére, D. Serre, D. Peressinotto, J.-G. Bordes, D. Cochard, et al. 2005. "A late Neandertal femur from Les Rochers-de-Villeneuve, France." *Proceedings of the National Academy of Sciences* 102 (20): 7085–7090.

Bechky, A. 1990. *Adventuring in East Africa*. San Francisco: Sierra Club Books.

Begun, D. R. 2003. "Planet of the apes." *Scientific American* 289 (2): 74–83.

Behrensmeyer, A. K. 2006. "Climate change and human evolution." *Science* 311 (5760): 476–478.

Bergman, C. 1988. "K'sar Akil and the Upper Palaeolithic of the Levant." *Paléorient* 14 (2): 201–210.

Biberson, P. 1961a. "Le cadre paléogeographique de la préhistoire du Maroc Atlantique." *Publications de Service des Antiquités du Maroc* 16:1–235.

Biberson, P. 1961b. *Le Paléolithique inférieur du Maroc atlantique*. Publication 17. Morocco: Service des Antiquités.

Bickerton, D. 1990. *Language and species*. Chicago: University of Chicago Press.

Bickerton, D. 2002. "From protolanguage to language." In T. J. Crow, ed., "The speciation of modern *Homo sapiens*." *Proceedings of the British Academy* 106. Oxford: Oxford University Press, pp. 103–120.

Billinger, M. S. 2006. Beyond the racial paradigm: New perspectives on human biological variation. PhD diss., University of Alberta.

Bilsborough, A. and B. Wood. 1986. "The nature, origin and fate of *Homo erectus*." In B. Wood, L. Martin, and P. Andrews, eds., *Major topics in primate and human evolution*. Cambridge: Cambridge University Press, pp. 295–316.

Binford, L. R. 1973. "Interassemblage variability: The Mousterian and the functional argument." In C. Renfrew, ed., *The explanation of culture change: Models in prehistory*. London: Duckworth, pp. 227–254.

Binford, L. R. 1980. "Willow smoke and dog's tails: Hunter-gatherer settlement systems and archaeological site formation." *American Antiquity* 45 (1): 4–20.

Binford, L. R. 1984. *Faunal remains from Klasies River mouth*. New York: Academic Press.

Binford, L. R. 1985. "Human ancestors: Changing views of their behavior." *Journal of Anthropological Archaeology* 4:292–327.

Binford, L. R. 1989. "Isolating the transition to cultural adaptations: An organizational approach." In E. Trinkaus, ed., *The emergence of modern humans*. Cambridge: Cambridge University Press, pp. 18–41.

Binford, L. R. and S. R. Binford. 1966. "A preliminary analysis of functional variability in the Mousterian of Levallois facies." In J. D. Clark and F. C. Howell, eds., "Recent studies in palaeoanthropology." *American Anthropologist* 68 (2): 238–295.

Binford, S. R. and L. R. Binford. 1969. "Stone tools and human behavior." *Scientific American* 220:70–84.

Bird, M. I., L. K. Fifield, G. M. Santos, P. B. Beaumont, Y. Zhou, M. L. di Tada, and P. A. Hausladen. 2003. "Radiocarbon dating from 40 to 60 ka BP at Border Cave, South Africa." *Quaternary Science Reviews* 22 (8/9): 943–947.

Bischoff, J. L., D. D. Shamp, A. Aramburu, J. L. Arsuaga, E. Carbonell, and J. M. Bermudez de Castro. 2003. "The Sima de los Huesos hominids date to beyond U/Th equilibrium (350kyr) and perhaps to 400–500 kyr: New radiometric dates." *Journal of Archaeological Science* 30 (30): 275–280.

Bishop, W. W. 1967. "Annotated lexicon of Quaternary stratigraphical nomenclature in East Africa." In W. W. Bishop and J. D. Clark, eds., *Background to evolution in Africa*. Chicago: University of Chicago Press, pp. 375–395.

Bishop, W. W. 1969. "Pleistocene stratigraphy in Uganda." *Geological Survey of Uganda Memoir* 10.

Bishop, W. W. 1976. "Comparison of Australopithecine-bearing deposits in Eastern and Southern Africa—A new look at a sixteen year old problem." *Annals of the South African Museum* 71:225–237.

Bishop, W. W., ed. 1978. *Geological background to fossil man: Recent research in the Gregory Rift Valley, East Africa*. Edinburgh: Scottish Academy Press.

Bishop, W. W. and J. D. Clark, eds. 1967. *Background to evolution in Africa*. Chicago: University of Chicago Press.

Bishop, W. W. and M. Posnansky. 1960. "Pleistocene environments and early man in Uganda." *Uganda Journal* 24:44–61.

Boas, F. 1940. *Race, language and culture*. New York: Macmillan.

Boaz, N. 1987. *Evolution of environments and Hominidae in the African Western Rift Valley*. Martinsville, VA: Virginia Museum of Natural History.

Bobe, R., and A. K. Behrensmeyer. 2004. "The expansion of grassland ecosystems in Africa in relation to mammalian evolution and the origin of the genus *Homo*." *Palaeogeography, Palaeoclimatology, Palaeoecology* 207 (3/4): 399–420.

Boëda, E. 1994. Le *Concept Levallois: Variabilité des Méthodes*. Monographies du CRA 9. Paris: Editions de Centre National de Recherches Scientifiques.

Boëda, E., J. Connan, D. Dessort, S. Muhesen, N. Mercier, H. Valladas, and N. Tisnerat. 1996. "Bitumen as a hafting material on Middle Palaeolithic artifacts." *Nature* 380 (6572): 336–338.

Bolus, M. and N. J. Conard. 2001. "The late Middle Palaeolithic and earliest Upper Palaeolithic in Central Europe and their relevance for the out of Africa hypothesis." *Quaternary International* 75 (1): 29–40.

Boquet-Appel, J.-P. and P. Y. Demars. 2000. "Neanderthal contraction and modern human colonization of Europe." *Antiquity* 74 (285): 544–552.

Bonnefille, R. and F. Chalie. 2000. "Pollen-inferred precipitation time-series from equatorial mountains, Africa, the last 40,000 years BP." *Global and Planetary Change* 26 (1–3): 25–50.

Borden, C. E. 1954. "A uniform site designation scheme for Canada." *Anthropology in British Columbia* 4:44–48.

Bordes, F. 1961. *Typologie du Paléolithique Ancien et Moyen*. Bordeaux: Delmas.

Bordes, F. 1972. *A tale of two caves*. New York: Harper & Row.

Bordes, F. 1973. "On the chronology and contemporaneity of different Palaeolithic cultures in France." In C. Renfrew, ed., *The explanation of culture change: Models in prehistory.* London: Duckworth, pp. 217–226.

Bordes, F. 1979. "Comment on D. Stiles, 'Palaeolithic culture and culture change: Experiments in theory and method.'" *Current Anthropology* 20 (1): 10–11.

Bordes, F. 1981. "Vingt-cinq ans après: Le complexe moustérien revisité." *Bulletin de la Société Préhistorique Française* 78:77–87.

Bordes, F., ed. 1971. *The origin of* Homo sapiens. Paris: UNESCO.

Bordes, F. and D. de Sonneville-Bordes. 1970. "The significance of variability in Palaeolithic assemblages." *World Archaeology* 2:61–73.

Boucher de Perthes, J. 1847. *Antiquités Celtiques et Antédiluviennes. Mémoire sur l'industrie primitive et les arts à leur origin.* Vol. 1. Paris: Treuttel and Wurtz.

Boucher de Perthes, J. 1857. *Antiquités Celtiques et Antédiluviennes. Mémoire sur l'industrie primitive et les arts à leur origine.* Vol. 2. Paris: Treuttel and Wurtz.

Boucher de Perthes, J. 1864. *Antiquités Celtiques et Antédiluviennes. Mémoire sur l'industrie primitive et les arts à leur origine.* Vol. 3. Paris: Jung-Treuttel.

Boule, M. 1911–1913. "L'homme fossile de La Chapelle-aux-Saints." *Annals de Paléontologie* 6, 7, and 8.

Bouzouggar, A. 1997. "Economie des matières premières et du débitage dans la sequence Atérienne de la grotte d'el Msnara I (Ancienne grotte des Contrebandiers—Maroc)." *Préhistoire Anthropologie Méditerranéennes* 6:35–51.

Bouzouggar, A., J. K. Kozlowski, and M. Otte. 2002. "Etude des ensembles lithiques atériens de la grotte d'El Aliya à Tanger." *L'Anthropologie* 106 (2): 207–248.

Bowen, D. 1978. *Quaternary geology.* Oxford: Pergamon Press.

Bower, J. R. F. 1977. "Preliminary report of a study of prehistoric cultures of the Serengeti National Park." *Nyame Akuma* 11:20–27.

Bower, J. R. F. 1981. "Excavations at a Middle Stone Age site, Serengeti National Park, Tanzania." *Nyame Akuma* 18:53–55.

Bower, J. R. F. 2005. "On 'modern behavior' and the evolution of human intelligence." *Current Anthropology* 46 (1): 121–122.

Bowler, J. M., H. Johnston, J. M. Olley, J. R. Prescott, R. G. Roberts, W. Shawcross, and N. A. Spooner. 2003. "New ages for human occupation and climatic change at Lake Mungo, Australia." *Nature* 421 (6925): 837–840.

Bowler, P. J. 1987. *Theories of human evolution: A century of debate 1844–1944.* Oxford: Basil Blackwell.

Bowler, P. J. 1989. *The invention of progress: The Victorians and the past.* Oxford: Basil Blackwell.

Brace, C. L. 1964. "The fate of the 'classic' Neandertals: A consideration of hominid catastrophism." *Current Anthropology* 5 (1): 3–34.

Brace, C. L. 1967. *The stages of human evolution: Human and cultural origins.* Englewood Cliffs, NJ: Prentice Hall.

Brace, C. L. 1995. "Biocultural interaction and the mechanism of mosaic evolution in the emergence of 'modern' morphology." *American Anthropologist* 97 (4): 711–721.

Brace, C. L. 2005. *"Race" is a four letter word.* Oxford: Oxford University Press.

Bradley, B. and D. Stanford. 2004. "The North Atlantic ice-edge corridor: A possible Palaeolithic route to the New World." *World Archaeology* 36 (4): 459–478.

Bradley, R. S. 1985. *Quaternary Paleoclimatology: Methods of Paleoclimatic reconstruction.* Boston: Allen and Unwin.

Brain, C. K., ed. 1993. *Swartkrans: A cave's chronicle of early man.* Transvaal Museum Monograph 9. Pretoria, South Africa: Transvaal Museum.

Brandt, S. A. 1986. "The Upper Pleistocene and early Holocene prehistory of the Horn of Africa." *African Archaeological Review* 4:41–82.

Brandt, S. A. 1988. "Early Holocene mortuary practices and hunter/gatherer adaptations in Southern Somalia." *World Archaeology* 20 (1): 40–56.

Brandt, S., J. Kinahan, A. Desse, E. Fisher, T. Hagos, A. Negash, and H. Said. 2004. "The Pleistocene archaeology of Southwestern Ethiopia: A dam approximation." *Abstracts of the Paleoanthropology Society Meeting, Montreal, Quebec.* http://www.paleoanthro.org.

Bräuer, G. 1984. "A craniological approach to the origin of anatomically modern *Homo sapiens* in Africa and implications for the appearance of modern Europeans." In F. H. Smith and F. Spencer, eds., *The origins of modern humans.* New York: Alan R. Liss, pp. 327–410.

Bräuer, G. 1989. "The evolution of modern humans: A comparison of the African and non-African evidence." In P. Mellars and C. Stringer, eds., *The human revolution.* Princeton, NJ: Princeton University Press, pp. 123–154.

Bräuer, G. 1992. "Africa's place in the evolution of *Homo sapiens.*" In G. Bräuer and F. H. Smith, eds., *Continuity or replacement.* Rotterdam: A. A. Balkema, pp. 83–98.

Bräuer, G. 2001a. "The 'out of Africa' model and the question of regional continuity." In P. V. Tobias, M. A. Raath, J. Moggi-Cecchi, and G. A. Doyle, eds., *Humanity from African naissance to coming millennia.* Florence: Firenze University Press, pp. 183–189.

Bräuer, G. 2001b. "The KNM-ER 3884 hominid and the emergence of modern anatomy in Africa." In P. V. Tobias, M. A. Raath, J. Moggi-Cecchi, and G. A. Doyle, eds., *Humanity from African naissance to coming millennia.* Florence: Firenze University Press, pp. 191–197.

Bräuer, G. and R. Singer. 1996a. "The Klasies zygomatic bone: Archaic or modern?" *Journal of Human Evolution* 30 (2): 161–165.

Bräuer, G. and R. Singer. 1996b. "Not outside the modern range." *Journal of Human Evolution* 30 (2): 173–174.

Bräuer, G. and F. H. Smith, eds. 1992. *Continuity or replacement: Controversies in Homo sapiens evolution.* The Hague: A. A. Balkema.

Breuil, H. 1944. "Le Paléolithique au Congo Belge d'après les recherches du Docteur Cabu." *Transactions of the Royal Society of South Africa* 30 (II): 143–167.

Breuil, H., P. Teilhard de Chardin, and P. Wernert. 1951. "Le Paléolithique du Harrar." *L'Anthropologie* 55:219–230.

Briggs, P. 2002. *Tanzania with Zanzibar, Pemba and Mafia.* 4th ed. Chalfont St. Peter, UK: Bradt Travel Guides.

Brink, J. S. and Z. L. Henderson. 2001. "A high-resolution last interglacial Middle Stone Age horizon at Florisbad in the context of other open-air occurrences in the central interior of southern Africa: An interim statement." In N. Conard, ed., *Settlement dynamics of the Middle Palaeolithic and Middle Stone Age. Tübingen publications in prehistory 1*. Tübingen: Kerns Verlag, pp. 1–20.

Broberg, G. 1975. *Homo sapiens L. studien: Carl von Linné naturuppfattning och människolära*. Uppsala: Almquist and Wiksell.

Broecker, W. S. 1987. "Unpleasant surprises in the Greenhouse." *Nature* 328 (6126): 123–126.

Broecker, W. S. 2000. "Converging paths leading to the role of the oceans in climate change." *Annual Review of Energy and the Environment* 25:1–19.

Broecker, W. S. and G. H. Denton. 1990. "What drives glacial cycles?" *Scientific American* 262 (1): 48–56.

Brook, E. J. 2005. "Tiny bubbles tell all." *Science* 310 (5752): 1285–1287.

Brooks, A. S., P. E. Hare, J. E. Kokis, G. H. Miller, R. D. Ernst, and F. Wendorf. 1990. "Dating Pleistocene archaeological sites by protein diagenesis in ostrich eggshells." *Science* 248 (4951): 60–64.

Brooks, A. S., D. M. Helgren, J. S. Cramer, A. Franklin, W. Hornyak, J. M. Keating, R. G. Klein, et al. 1995. "Dating and context of three Middle Stone Age sites with bone points in the Upper Semliki Valley, Zaire." *Science* 268 (5210): 548–553.

Brooks, A. S. and P. Robertshaw. 1990. "The glacial maximum in tropical Africa: 22,000–12,000 BP." In C. Gamble and O. Soffer, eds., *The world at 18,000 BP: Low latitudes*. Vol 2. London: Unwin Hyman, pp. 121–169.

Brooks, A. S. and C. C. Smith. 1987. "Ishango revisited: New age determinations and cultural interpretations." *African Archaeological Review* 5:65–78.

Brooks, A. S., J. E. Yellen, M. Tappen, and D. M. Helgren. 2002. "Middle Stone Age adaptations at Aduma, Middle Awash Region, Ethiopia." *Journal of Human Evolution* 42 (3): A8–A9.

Brooks, K., C. A. Scholz, J. W. King, J. Peck, J. T. Overpeck, J. M. Russell, and P. Y. O. Amoako. 2005. "Late-Quaternary lowstands of Lake Bosumtwi, Ghana: Evidence from high-resolution seismic-reflection and sediment-core data." *Palaeogeography, Palaeoclimatology, Palaeoecology* 216 (3/4): 235–249.

Broom, R. and J. T. Robinson. 1949. "A new type of fossil man." *Nature* 164:322–323.

Brose, D. and M. H. Wolpoff. 1971. "Early Upper Paleolithic man and late Middle Paleolithic tools." *American Anthropologist* 73 (5): 1156–1194.

Brown, P., T. Sutikna, M. J. Morwood, R. P. Soejano, Jatmiko, E. W. Saptomo, and R. A. Due. 2004. "A new small-bodied hominin from the Late Pleistocene of Flores, Indonesia." *Nature* 431 (7012): 1055–1061.

Brown, R. A. and G. J. Armelagos. 2001. "Apportionment of racial diversity: A review." *Evolutionary Anthropology* 10 (1): 34–40.

Bruggemann, J. H., R. T. Buffler, M. M. M. Guillaume, R. C. Walter, R. von Cosel, B. N. Ghebretensae, and S. M. Berhe. 2004. "Stratigraphy, palaeoenvironments and model for the deposition of the Abdur Reef Limestone: Context for an important archaeological site from the last interglacial on the Red Sea coast of Eritrea." *Palaeogeography, Palaeoclimatology, Palaeoecology* 203 (3–4): 179–206.

Brunet, M. 2001. "Chadian australopithecines: Biochronology and environmental context." In P. V. Tobias, M. A. Raath, J. Moggi-Cecchi, and G. A. Doyle, eds., *Humanity from African naissance to coming millennia*. Florence: Firenze University Press, pp. 103–106.

Brunet, M., A. Beauvillain, Y. Coppens, E. Heintz, A. H. E. Moutaye, and D. Pilbeam. 1995. "The first australopithecine 2,500 km west of the Rift Valley (Chad)." *Nature* 378 (6554): 273–275.

Brunet, M., A. Beauvillain, Y. Coppens, E. Heintz, A. H. E. Moutaye, and D. Pilbeam.1996. "*Australopithecus bahrelghazali*, une nouvelle espèce d'Hominidé ancien de la région de Koro Toro (Tchad)." *Comptes Rendus de l'Academie des Sciences, Paris* 324:341–345.

Brunet, M., F. Guy, D. Pilbeam, D. E. Lieberman, A. Lilius, H. T. Mackaye, M. S. Ponce de Leon, C. E. Zollikofer, and P. Vignaud. 2005. "New material of the earliest hominid from the Upper Miocene of Chad." *Nature* 434 (7034): 752–755.

Brunet, M., F. Guy, D. Pilbeam, H. T. Mackaye, A. Likius, D. Ahounta, A. Beauvillain, et al. 2002. "A new hominid from the Upper Miocene of Chad, Central Africa." *Nature* 418 (6894): 145–151.

Bunn, H. T. 1991. "A taphonomic perspective on the archaeology of human origins." *Annual Review of Anthropology* 20:433–467.

Burkitt, M. C. 1928. *South Africa's past in stone and paint*. Cambridge: Cambridge University Press.

Burroughs, W. J. 2005. *Climate change in prehistory: The end of the reign of chaos*. Cambridge: Cambridge University Press.

Butzer, K. W. 1971. *Environment and archaeology*. Chicago: Aldine.

Butzer, K. W. 1975. "Geological and ecological perspectives on the Middle Pleistocene." In K. W. Butzer and G. Ll. Isaac, eds., *After the Australopithecines: Stratigraphy, ecology and culture change in the Middle Pleistocene*. The Hague: Mouton, pp. 857–875.

Butzer, K. W. 1976. "Pleistocene climates." *Geoscience and Man* 13:27–43.

Butzer, K. W., F. H. Brown, and D. L. Thurber. 1969. "Horizontal sediments of the lower Omo Valley: The Kibish Formation." *Quaternaria* 11:15–29.

Butzer, K. W. and G. Ll. Isaac, eds. 1975. *After the Australopithecines: Stratigraphy, ecology and culture change in the Middle Pleistocene*. The Hague: Mouton.

Butzer, K. W., G. Isaac, J. Richardson, and C. Washbourn-Kamau. 1972. "Radiocarbon dating of East African lake levels." *Science* 197 (4027): 1069–1076.

Cahen, D. 1975. Le site archéologique de la Kamoa (Région du Shaba, République du Zaïre) de l'âge de la pierre ancien à l'âge du fer. *Annales Sciences Humaines* 84. Tervuren: Musée Royal de l'Afrique Centrale.

Cain, C. R. 2004. "Notches, flaked and ground bone artefacts from Middle Stone Age and Iron Age layers of Sibudu Cave, KwaZulu-Natal, South Africa." *South African Journal of Science* 100 (3/4): 195–197.

Calvin, W. H. 1998. "The great climate flip-flop." *Atlantic Monthly* 281 (1): 47–64.

Calvin, W. H. 2002. *A brain for all seasons: Human evolution and abrupt climate change.* Chicago: University of Chicago Press.

Camerini, J. R., ed. 2002. *The Alfred Russel Wallace reader—A selection of writings from the field.* Baltimore: Johns Hopkins University Press.

Camps, G. 1975. "The prehistoric cultures of North Africa: Radiocarbon chronology." In F. Wendorf and A. E. Marks, eds., *Problems in prehistory: North Africa and the Levant.* Dallas: Southern Methodist University Press, pp. 181–192.

Cane, M. A. and P. Molnar. 2001. "Closing of the Indonesian seaway as a precursor to east African aridification around 3–4 million years ago." *Nature* 411 (6834): 157–162.

Cann, R. L. 1987. "In search of Eve." *Science* Sept./Oct: 30–37.

Cann, R. L. 1988. "DNA and human origins." *Annual Review of Anthropology* 17:127–143.

Cann, R. L. 1992. "A mitochondrial perspective on replacement or continuity in human evolution." In G. Bräuer and F. H. Smith, eds., *Continuity or replacement.* Rotterdam: A. A. Balkema, pp. 65–73.

Cann, R. L. 2001. "Genetic clues to dispersal in human populations: Retracing the past from the present." *Science* 291 (5509): 1742–1748.

Cann, R. L. 2002. "Tangled genetic roots." *Nature* 416 (6876): 32–33.

Cann, R. L., O. Rickards, and J. K. Lum. 1994. "Mitochondrial DNA and human evolution: Our one lucky mother." In M. H. Nitecki and D. V. Nitecki, eds., *Origins of anatomically modern humans.* New York: Plenum Press, pp. 135–148.

Cann, R. L., M. Stoneking, and A. C. Wilson. 1987. "Mitochondrial DNA and human evolution." *Nature* 325 (6099): 31–36.

Caramelli, D., C. Laluez-Fox, C. Vernesi, M. Lari, A. Casoli, F. Mallegni, B. Chiarelli, et al. 2003. "Evidence for a genetic discontinuity between Neandertals and 24,000 year old anatomically modern humans." *Proceedings of the National Academy of Sciences* 100 (11): 6493–6597.

Carbonell, R., J. M. Bermudez de Castro, J. L. Arsuaga, J. C. Diez, A. Rosas, G. Cuenca-Bescos, R. Sala, M. Mosquera, and X. P. Rodriguez. 1995. "Lower Pleistocene hominids and artifacts from Atapuerca-TD6 (Spain)." *Science* 269 (5225): 826–830.

Carroll, S. B. 2003. "Genetics and the making of *Homo sapiens.*" *Nature* 422 (6934): 849–857.

Carter, P. L. and J. C. Vogel. 1974. "The dating of industrial assemblages from stratified sites in eastern Lesotho." *Man*, n.s., 9 (4): 557–570.

Cartmill, M. 1993. *A view to a death in the morning: Hunting and nature through history.* Cambridge: Harvard University Press.

Cartmill, M. 2001. "Taxonomic revolutions and the animal-human boundary." In R. Corbey and W. Roebroeks, eds., *Studying human origins: Disciplinary history and epistemology.* Amsterdam: Amsterdam University Press, pp. 97–106.

Casey, J. 2003. "The archaeology of West Africa from the Pleistocene to the Mid Holocene." In J. Mercader, ed., *Under the canopy—The archaeology of tropical rain forests.* New Brunswick: Rutgers University Press, pp. 35–63.

Casey, J., R. Sawatzky, D. I. Godfrey-Smith, N. Quickert, A. C. D'Andrea, M. Wollstonecroft, and A. Hawkins. 1997. "Report of excavations at the Birimi site in Northern Ghana." *Nyame Akuma* 48:32–38.

Caton-Thompson, G. 1946a. "The Aterian industry: Its place and significance in the Palaeolithic world." The Huxley Memorial Lecture for 1946. *Journal of the Royal Anthropological Institute* 76 (2): 87–130.

Caton-Thompson, G. 1946b. "The Levalloisian industries of Egypt." *Proceedings of the Prehistoric Society* 12:57–120.

Caton-Thompson, G. 1952. *Kharga Oasis in prehistory.* London: University of London.

Cavalli-Sforza, L. L. and M. W. Feldman. 2003. "The application of molecular genetic approaches to the study of human evolution." *Nature Genetics.* Suppl. no. 33:266–275.

Cavalli-Sforza, L. L., P. Menozzi, and A. Piazza. 1993. "Demic expansions and human evolution." *Science* 259 (5095): 639–646.

Cavalli-Sforza, L. L., P. Menozzi, and A. Piazza. 1994. *The history and geography of human genes.* Princeton, NJ: Princeton University Press.

Cavalli-Sforza, L. L. and J. D. Watson, eds. 1997. Abstracts of papers presented at the 1997 meeting on human evolution. Cold Spring Harbor: Cold Spring Harbor Laboratory.

Cavalli-Sforza, L., A. C. Wilson, C. R. Cantor, R. M. Cook-Deegan, and M. C. King. 1991. "Call for a worldwide survey of human genetic diversity: A vanishing opportunity for the human genome project." *Genomics* 11 (2): 490–491.

Chami, F. A. and R. Chami. 2001. "Narosura pottery from the southern coast of Tanzania: First incontrovertible coastal Later Stone Age pottery." *Nyame Akuma* 56:29–35.

Chase, P. G. 1991. "Symbols and Palaeolithic artifacts: Style, standardization and the imposition of arbitrary form." *Journal of Anthropological Archaeology* 10 (3): 193–214.

Chase, P. G. 2001. "'Symbolism is two different phenomena': Implications for archaeology and palaeontology." In P. V. Tobias, M. A. Raath, J. Moggi-Cecchi, and G. A. Doyle, eds., *Humanity from African naissance to coming millennia.* Florence: Firenze University Press, pp. 199–212.

Chase, R., and H. L. Dibble. 1987. "Middle Palaeolithic symbolism: A review of current evidence and interpretations." *Journal of Anthropological Archaeology* 6 (3): 263–296.

Chavaillon, J., N. Chavaillon, F. Hours, and M. Piperno. 1979. "From the Oldowan to the Middle Stone Age at Melka-Kunturé (Ethiopia): Understanding cultural changes." *Quaternaria* 21:87–114.

Chazan, M. 1995a. "The language hypothesis for the Middle-to-Upper Paleolithic transition: An examination based on a multiregional lithic analysis." *Current Anthropology* 36 (5): 749–768.

Chazan, M. 1995b. "The meaning of *Homo sapiens.*" In R. Corbey and B. Theunissen, eds., *Ape, man, ape man: Changing views since 1600.* Leiden: Department of Prehistory, Leiden University, pp. 229–240.

Chazan, M. 1997. "Redefining Levallois." *Journal of Human Evolution* 33 (6): 719–735.

Chen, Yu-sheng, A. Torroni, L. Excoffier, A. S. Santachiara-Benerecetti, and D. C. Wallace. 1995. "Analysis of mtDNA variation in African populations reveals the most ancient of all human continent-specific haplogroups." *American Journal of Human Genetics* 57 (1): 133–149.

Chen, Yu-sheng, A. Olckers, T. G. Schurr, A. M. Kogelnik, K. Huoponen, and D. C. Wallace. 2000. "MtDNA variation in the South African Kung and Khwe and their genetic relationships to other African populations." *American Journal of Human Genetics* 66 (4): 1362–1383.

Childe, V. G. 1981. "Valedictory." In S. Green, ed., *Prehistorian: A biography of V. Gordon Childe.* Bradford-on-Avon: Moonraker Press, pp. 166–175. (Orig. pub. 1957.)

Churcher, C. S. and M. R. Kleindienst. n.d. "Great lakes in the Dakhleh Oasis: Mid-Pleistocene freshwater lakes in the Dakhleh Oasis depressions, Western Desert, Egypt." In A. J. Mills, ed., *The Oasis papers IV: Proceedings of the fourth international conference of the Dakhleh Oasis project.* Oxford: Oxbow Books.

Churchill, S. E. 1998. "Cold adaptation, heterochrony, and Neandertals." *Evolutionary Anthropology* 7 (2): 46–60.

Clague, J. 2005. "Status of the Quaternary." *Quaternary Science Reviews* 24 (23/24): 2424–2425.

Clark, A. M. B. 1997a. "The MSA/LSA transition in Southern Africa: New technological evidence from Rose Cottage Cave." *South African Archaeological Bulletin* 52:113–121.

Clark, A. M. B. 1997b. "The final Middle Stone Age at Rose Cottage Cave: A distinct industry in the Basutolian ecozone." *South African Journal of Science* 93:449–458.

Clark, A. M. B. 1999. "Late Pleistocene technology in Rose Cottage Cave: A search for modern behavior in an MSA context." *African Archaeological Review* 16 (2): 93–119.

Clark, G. A. 1989. "Alternative models of Pleistocene biocultural evolution." *Antiquity* 63:153–161.

Clark, G. A. 1999. "Highly visible, curiously intangible." *Science* 283 (5410): 2029–2032.

Clark, G. A. 2002. "Neandertal archaeology—Implications for our origins." *American Anthropologist* 104 (1): 50–67.

Clark, G. A. and J. M. Lindly. 1989a. "The case for continuity: Observations on the biocultural transition in Europe and Western Asia." In P. Mellars and C. Stringer, eds., *The human revolution.* Princeton, NJ: Princeton University Press, pp. 626–676.

Clark, G. A. and J. M. Lindly. 1989b. "Modern human origins in the Levant and Western Asia." *American Anthropologist* 91 (4): 962–985.

Clark, G. A. and C. M. Willermet, eds. 1997. *Conceptual issues in modern human origins research.* Hawthorne: Aldine de Gruyter.

Clark, J. D. 1954. *The prehistoric cultures of the Horn of Africa: An analysis of the Stone Age cultural and climatic succession in the Somalilands and eastern parts of Abyssinia.* Cambridge: Cambridge University Press.

Clark, J. D. 1957. "Resolutions." In J. D. Clark, ed., *Third Pan-African congress on prehistory, Livingstone, 1955.* London: Chatto and Windus, pp. xxxi–xxxiv.

Clark, J. D., ed. 1969. *Kalambo Falls prehistoric site I.* Cambridge: Cambridge University Press.

Clark, J. D. 1970. *The prehistory of Africa.* London: Thames and Hudson.

Clark, J. D. 1974a. "Africa in prehistory: Peripheral or paramount?" The Huxley Memorial Lecture for 1974. *Man,* n.s., 10 (2): 175–198.

Clark, J. D., ed. 1974b. *Kalambo Falls prehistoric site II.* Cambridge: Cambridge University Press.

Clark, J. D. 1980a. "Human populations and cultural adaptations in the Sahara and Nile during prehistoric times." In M. Williams and H. Faure, eds., *The Sahara and the Nile.* Rotterdam: Balkema, pp. 527–582.

Clark, J. D. 1980b. "Raw material and African lithic technology." *Man and Environment* 4:44–55.

Clark, J. D. 1981. "'New men, strange faces, other minds': An archaeologist's perspective on recent discoveries relating to the origins and spread of modern man." *Proceedings of the British Academy* 67:163–192.

Clark, J. D. 1988. "The Middle Stone Age of East Africa and the beginnings of regional identity." *Journal of World Prehistory* 2 (3): 235–305.

Clark, J. D. 1989. "The origins and spread of modern humans: A broad perspective on the African evidence." In P. Mellars and C. Stringer, eds., *The human revolution.* Princeton, NJ: Princeton University Press, pp. 565–588.

Clark, J. D. 1992. "African and Asian perspectives on the origins of modern humans." *Philosophical Transactions of the Royal Society* 337B (1280): 201–215.

Clark, J. D. 1993a. "African and Asian perspectives on the origins of modern humans." In M. J. Aitken, C. B. Stringer, and P. A. Mellars, eds., *The origin of modern humans and the impact of chronometric dating.* Princeton, NJ: Princeton University Press, pp. 148–178.

Clark, J. D. 1993b. "The Aterian of the Central Sahara." In L. Krzyzaniak, M. Kobusiewicz, and J. Alexander, eds., *Environmental change and human culture in the Nile Basin and Northern Africa until the second millennium BC.* Poznan: Poznan Archaeological Museum, pp. 49–67.

Clark, J. D. 2001. *Kalambo Falls prehistoric site III. The earlier cultures: Middle and Earlier Stone Age.* Cambridge: Cambridge University Press.

Clark, J. D., B. Asfaw, G. Assefa, J. W. K. Harris, H. Kurashina, R. C. Walter, T. D. White, and M. A. J. Williams. 1984. "Palaeoanthropological discoveries in the Middle Awash Valley, Ethiopia." *Nature* 307:423–428.

Clark, J. D., T. Beyene, G. WoldeGabriel, W. K. Hart, P. R. Renne, H. Gilbert, A. Defleur, et al. 2003. "Stratigraphic, chronological and behavioural contexts of Pleistocene *Homo sapiens* from Middle Awash, Ethiopia." *Nature* 423 (6941): 747–752.

Clark, J. D., J. de Heinzelin, K. D. Schick, W. K. Hart, T. D. White, G. WoldeGabriel, R. C. Walter, et al. 1994. "African *Homo erectus*: Old radiometric ages and young Oldowan assemblages in the Middle Awash Valley, Ethiopia." *Science* 264:1907–1910.

Clark, J. D. and K. S. Brown. 2001. "The Twin Rivers Kopje, Zambia: Stratigraphy, fauna and artefact assemblages from the 1954 and 1956 excavations." *Journal of Archaeological Science* 28 (3): 305–330.

Clark, J. D. and M. R. Kleindienst. 1974. "The Stone Age cultural sequence: Terminology, typology and raw material." In J. D. Clark, ed., *Kalambo Falls prehistoric site II.* Cambridge: Cambridge University Press, pp. 71–106.

Clark, J. D., K. D. Williamson, J. W. Michels, and C. A. Marean. 1984. "A Middle Stone Age occupation at Porc Epic Cave, Dire Dawa (east-central Ethiopia)." *African Archaeological Review* 2:37–71.

Clark, J. G. D. 1977. *World prehistory.* 3rd ed. Cambridge: Cambridge University Press.

Clarke, R. J. 1977. "A juvenile cranium and some adult teeth of early *Homo* from Swartkrans, Transvaal." *South African Journal of Science* 73:46–49.

Clarke, R. J. 1990. "The Ndutu cranium and the origin of *Homo sapiens*." *Journal of Human Evolution* 19:699–736.

Clifford, J. and G. Marcus, eds. 1986. *Writing culture: The poetics and politics of ethnography.* Berkeley: University of California Press.

Close, A. E. 1986. "The place of the Haua Fteah in the Late Palaeolithic of North Africa." In G. N. Bailey and P. Callow, eds., *Stone Age prehistory.* Cambridge: Cambridge University Press, pp. 169–180.

Close, A. E. 1996. "Plus ça change: The Pleistocene-Holocene transition in Northeast Africa." In L. Straus, B. V. Eriksen, J. M. Erlandson, and D. R. Yesner, eds., *Humans at the end of the Ice Age: The archaeology of the Pleistocene-Holocene transition.* New York: Plenum Press, pp. 43–60.

Close, A. E. 2002. "Backed bladelets are a foreign country." In R. G. Elston and S. L. Kuhn, eds., "Thinking small: Global perspectives on microlithization." *Archaeological Papers of the American Anthropological Association* 12:31–44.

Close, A. E. and F. Wendorf. 1990. "North Africa at 18,000 BP." In C. Gamble and O. Soffer, eds., *The world at 18,000 BP: Low latitudes.* Vol 2. London: Unwin Hyman, pp. 41–57.

Cohen, P. 1996. "Fitting a face to Ngaloba." *Journal of Human Evolution* 30 (4): 373–379.

Cole, G. H. and M. R. Kleindienst. 1974. "Further reflections on the Isimila Acheulian." *Quaternary Research* 4:346–355.

Cole, S. 1954. *The prehistory of East Africa.* Harmondsworth: Penguin.

Cole, S. 1975. *Leakey's luck: The life of Louis Seymour Bazett Leakey, 1903–1972.* London: Collins.

Conard, N. J. and M. Bolus. 2003. "Radiocarbon dating the appearance of modern humans and timing of cultural innovations in Europe: New results and new challenges." *Journal of Human Evolution* 44 (3): 331–371.

Conard, N., P. M. Grootes, and F. H. Smith. 2004. "Unexpectedly recent dates for human remains from Vogelherd." *Nature* 430 (6996): 198–201.

Conroy, G. C. 1997. *Reconstructing human origins: A modern synthesis.* New York: Norton.

Cook, A. B. 1903. "Les galets peints de Mas d'Azil." *L'Anthropologie* 14:655–660.

Cooke, C. K. 1963. "Report on excavations at Pomongwe and Thangula Caves, Matopo Hills, Southern Rhodesia." *South African Archaeological Bulletin* 18 (71): 73–151.

Cooke, C. K. 1980. "Wooden and bone artifacts: Pomongwe Cave, Matobo District, Zimbabwe." *South African Archaeological Bulletin* 35 (131): 25–29.

Cooke, H. B. S. 1957. "The problem of Quaternary glacio-pluvial correlation in East and Southern Africa." In J. D. Clark, ed., *Proceedings of the third Pan-African congress of prehistory, Livingstone, 1955.* London: Chatto and Windus, pp. 51–55.

Cooke, H. B. S. 1958. "Observations relating to Quaternary environments in East and Southern Africa." *Geological Society of South Africa*, annexure to vol. 60.

Cooke, H. B. S. 1967. "The Pleistocene sequence in South Africa and problems of correlation." In W. W. Bishop and J. D. Clark, eds., *Background to evolution in Africa.* Chicago: University of Chicago Press, pp. 175–184.

Cooke, H. B. S. and V. J. Maglio. 1971. "Plio-Pleistocene stratigraphy in East Africa in relation to proboscidean and suid evolution." In W. W. Bishop and J. A. Miller, eds., *Calibration of Hominoid evolution.* Edinburgh: Scottish Academic Press, pp. 303–329.

Coolidge, F. L. and T. Wynn. 2001. "Executive functions of the frontal lobes and the evolutionary ascendancy of *Homo sapiens.*" *Cambridge Archaeological Journal* 11 (2): 255–260.

Coolidge, F. L. and T. Wynn. 2005. "Working memory, its executive functions, and the emergence of modern thinking." *Cambridge Archaeological Journal* 15 (1): 5–26.

Coon, C. S. 1962. *The origin of races.* New York: Knopf.

Coppens, Y. 1994. "East side story: The origin of humankind." *Scientific American* 270 (5): 88–95.

Coppens, Y., F. C. Howell, G. Ll. Isaac, and R. E. F. Leakey, eds. 1976. *Earliest man and environments in the Lake Rudolf Basin.* Chicago: University of Chicago Press.

Corbey, R. 2005. *The metaphysics of apes: Negotiating the ape-human boundary.* Cambridge: Cambridge University Press.

Corbey, R. and W. Roebroeks. 2001a. "Does disciplinary history matter? An introduction." In R. Corbey and W. Roebroeks, eds., *Studying human origins: Disciplinary history and epistemology.* Amsterdam: Amsterdam University Press, pp. 1–8.

Corbey, R. and W. Roebroeks, eds. 2001b. *Studying human origins: Disciplinary history and epistemology.* Amsterdam: Amsterdam University Press.

Cormack, J. L. 1999. "Setting their sights/sites on Uganda: Walter William Bishop and Edward James Wayland." In P. Andrews and P. Banham, eds., *Late Cenozoic environments and Hominid evolution: A tribute to Bill Bishop.* London: Geological Society, pp. 7–13.

Cornelissen, E. 1992. *Site GnJh-17 and its implications for the archaeology of the middle Kapthurin Formation, Baringo, Kenya.* Annales, Sciences Humaines 133. Tervuren:

Musée Royale de l'Afrique Centrale.

Cornelissen, E. 1996. "Shum Laka (Cameroon): Late Pleistocene and early Holocene deposits." In G. Pwiti and R. Soper, eds., *Aspects of African prehistory*. Harare: University of Zimbabwe Press, pp. 257–263.

Cornelissen, E. 1997. "Central African transitional cultures." In J. O. Vogel, ed., *Encyclopedia of precolonial Africa*. Walnut Creek: AltaMira Press, pp. 312–320.

Cornelissen, E. 2002. "Human response to changing environments in Central Africa between 40,000 and 12,000 BP." *Journal of World Prehistory* 16 (3): 197–235.

Cornelissen, E. 2003. "On microlithic quartz industries at the end of the Pleistocene in Central Africa: The evidence from Shum Laka (NW Cameroon)." *African Archaeological Review* 20 (1): 1–24.

Cornelissen, E., A. Boven, A. Davi, J. Hus, K. Ju Yong, E. Keppens, E. Langohr, et al. 1990. "The Kapthurin Formation revisited." *African Archaeological Review* 8:23–76.

Cremaschi, M., S. di Lernia, and E. A. A. Garcea. 1998. "Some insights on the Aterian in the Libyan Sahara: Chronology, environment, and archaeology." *African Archaeological Review* 15 (4): 261–286.

Crichton, M. 1990. *Jurassic park: A novel*. New York: Knopf.

Croll, J. 1867. "On the eccentricity of the earth's orbit, and its physical relations to the glacial epoch." *Philosophical Magazine* 33:119–131.

Croll, J. 1875. *Climate and time in their geological relations: A theory of secular changes of the earth's climate*. London: Daldy, Isbister.

Crow, T. J. 2000. "Schizophrenia is the price that *Homo sapiens* pays for language: A resolution of the central paradox in the origin of the species." *Brain Research Review* 31:118–129.

Crow, T. J., ed. 2002. *The speciation of modern* Homo sapiens. *Proceedings of the British Academy 106*. Oxford: Oxford University Press, pp. 31–47.

Crowley, T. J. 2002. "Cycles, cycles everywhere." *Science* 295 (5559): 1473–1474.

Cruciani, F., P. Santolamazza, Peidong Shen, C. Macaulay, P. Moral, A. Olckers, D. Modiano, et al. 2002. "A back migration from Asia to sub-Saharan Africa supported by high-resolution analysis of human Y-chromosome haplotypes." *American Journal of Human Genetics* 70 (5): 1197–1214.

Cruz-Uribe, K., R. G. Klein, G. Avery, M. Avery, D. Halkett, T. Hart, R. G. Milo, C. G. Sampson, and T. P. Volman. 2003. "Excavation of buried Late Acheulean (Mid-Quaternary) land surfaces at Duinefontein 2, Western Cape Province, South Africa." *Journal of Archaeological Science* 30 (5): 559–575.

Currie, P. 2004. "Muscling in on hominid evolution." *Nature* 428 (6981): 373–374.

Curtis, G., R. Lewin, and C. C. Swisher III. 2000. *Java man: How two geologists changed the history of human evolution*. New York: Scribner.

Daniel, G. 1943. *The three ages: An essay on archaeological method*. Cambridge: Cambridge University Press.

Daniel, G. 1975. *A hundred and fifty years of archaeology*. London: Duckworth.

Dart, R. 1925. "*Australopithecus africanus*: The man-ape of South Africa." *Nature* 115:195–199.

Dart, R. 1953. "The predatory transition from ape to man." *International Anthropological and Linguistic Review* 1:201–219.

Dart, R. 1957. *The osteodontokeratic culture of Australopithecus prometheus.* Transvaal Museum Memoir 10.

Darwin, C. R. 1859. *The origin of species by means of natural selection, or, the preservation of favoured races in the struggle for existence.* London: John Murray.

Darwin, C. R. 1871. *The descent of man and selection in relation to sex.* London: John Murray.

Darwin, C. R. 1909. *The foundations of the origin of species: Two essays written in 1842 and 1844.* Ed. F. Darwin. Cambridge: Cambridge University Press.

Darwin, C. R. n.d. *The origin of species and the descent of man.* New York: Modern Library. (Orig. pub. 1859 and 1871.)

Davies, W. 2001. "A very model of a modern human industry: New perspectives on the origins and spread of the Aurignacian in Europe." *Proceedings of the Prehistoric Society* 67:195–217.

Day, M. H. 1986. *Guide to fossil man.* 4th ed. Chicago: University of Chicago Press.

Day, M. H. and P. H. Banham. 1999. "Bill Bishop: A retrospective appreciation and bibliography." In P. Andrews and P. Banham, eds., *Late Cenozoic environments and hominid evolution: A tribute to Bill Bishop.* London: Geological Society, pp. 1–4.

Day, M. H., M. D. Leakey, and C. Magori. 1980. "A new hominid fossil skull (L. H. 18) from the Ngaloba Beds, Laetoli, northern Tanzania." *Nature* 284:55–56.

Day, M. H. and C. B. Stringer. 1982. "A reconsideration of the Omo Kibish remains and the *erectus-sapiens* transition." In M. A. de Lumley, ed., *L'Homo erectus et la place de l'homme de Tautavel parmi les hominides fossiles.* Nice: Centre National de Recherches Scientifiques, pp. 814–846.

Deacon, H. J. 1989. "Late Pleistocene palaeoecology and archaeology in the Southern Cape, South Africa." In P. Mellars and C. Stringer, eds., *The human revolution.* Princeton, NJ: Princeton University Press, pp. 547–564.

Deacon, H. J. 1992. "Southern Africa and modern human origins." *Philosophical Transactions of the Royal Society* 337B (1280): 177–183.

Deacon, H. J. 1993. "Southern Africa and modern human origins." In M. J. Aitken, C. B. Stringer, and P. A. Mellars, eds., *The origin of modern humans and the impact of chronometric dating.* Princeton, NJ: Princeton University Press, pp. 104–117.

Deacon, H. J. 1998. "Elandsfontein and Klasies River revisited." In N. M. Ashton, F. Healy, and P. B. Pettitt, eds., *Stone Age archaeology: Essays in honour of John Wymer.* Oxford: Oxbow Books, pp. 23–28.

Deacon, H. J. 2001. "Modern human emergence: An African archaeological perspective." In P. V. Tobias, M. A. Raath, J. Moggi-Cecchi, and G. A. Doyle, eds., *Humanity from African naissance to coming millennia.* Florence: Firenze University Press, pp. 213–222.

Deacon, H. J. and J. Deacon. 1999. *Human beginnings in South Africa: Uncovering the secrets of the Stone Age.* Walnut Creek: AltaMira Press.

Deacon, H. J. and V. B. Geleijnse. 1988. "The stratigraphy and sedimentology of the main site sequence, Klasies River, South Africa." *South African Archaeological Bulletin* 43:5–14.

Deacon, H. J. and R. Shuurman. 1992. "The origins of modern people: The evidence from Klasies River." In G. Bräuer and F. H. Smith, eds., *Continuity or replacement*. Rotterdam: A. A. Balkema, pp. 121–129.

Deacon, H. J. and S. Wurz. 1997. "Klasies River main site, Cave 2: A Howieson's Poort occurrence." In G. Pwiti and R. Soper, eds., *Aspects of African archaeology*. Harare: University of Zimbabwe Publications, pp. 213–218.

Deacon, H. J. and S. Wurz. 2001. "Middle Pleistocene populations of Southern Africa and the emergence of modern behaviour." In L. Barham and K. Robson-Brown, eds., *Human roots: Africa and Asia in the Middle Pleistocene*. Bristol: Western Academic and Specialist Press, pp. 55–63.

Deacon, J. 1990a. "Weaving the fabric of Stone Age research in Southern Africa." In P. Robertshaw, ed., *A history of African archaeology*. London: James Currey, pp. 39–58.

Deacon, J. 1990b. "Changes in the archaeological record in South Africa at 18,000 BP." In C. Gamble and O. Soffer, eds., *The world at 18,000 BP: Low latitudes*. Vol 2. London: Unwin Hyman, pp. 170–188.

Deacon, T. W. 1997. *The symbolic species: The coevoluton of language and the brain*. New York: Norton.

Débénath, A. 1994. "L'Atérien du nord d'Afrique et du Sahara." *Sahara* 6:21–30.

Débénath, A. 2000. "Le peuplement préhistorique du Maroc: Données récentes et problèmes." *L'Anthropologie* 104 (1): 131–145.

Débénath, A., J. P. Raynal, J. Roche, J. P. Texier, and D. Freembach. 1990. "Stratigraphie, habitat, typologie et devenir de l'atérien marocain: Données récentes." *Comptes-Rendus de l'Academie des Sciences* 294:1247–1250.

Deino, A. and S. McBrearty. 2002. "^{40}Ar/^{39}Ar dating of the Kapthurin Formation, Baringo, Kenya." *Journal of Human Evolution* 42 (1/2): 185–210.

deMenocal, P. B. 1995. "Plio-Pleistocene African climate." *Science* 270 (5233): 53–59.

deMenocal, P. B. 2004. "African climate change and faunal evolution during the Pliocene-Pleistocene." *Earth and Planetary Science Letters* 220 (1/2): 3–24.

deMenocal, P. B., W. F. Ruddiman, and E. M. Pokras. 1993. "Influences of high and low latitude processes on African terrestrial climate: Pleistocene eolian records from equatorial Atlantic drilling program site 663." *Paleooceanography* 8 (2): 209–242.

Dennell, R. 2001. "From Sangiran to Olduvai 1937–1960: The quest for 'centres' of hominid origins in Asia and Africa." In R. Corbey and W. Roebroeks, eds., *Studying human origins: Disciplinary history and epistemology*. Amsterdam: Amsterdam University Press, pp. 45–66.

Dennell, R. 2003. "Dispersal and colonisation, long and short chronologies: How continuous is the Early Pleistocene record for hominids outside East Africa?" *Journal of Human Evolution* 45 (6): 421–440.

Dennell, R. and W. Roebroeks. 1996. "The earliest colonization of Europe: The short chronology revisited." *Antiquity* 70 (269): 535–542.

D'Errico, F. 2003. "The invisible frontier: A multiple species model for the origin of behavioral modernity." *Evolutionary Anthropology* 12 (4): 188–202.

D'Errico, F. and M. F. S. Goni. 2003. "Neandertal extinction and the millennial time scale climatic variability of OIS 3." *Quaternary Science Reviews* 22 (8/9): 769–788.

D'Errico, F., C. Henshilwood, G. Lawson, M. Vanhaeren, A.-M. Tillier, M. Soressi, F. Bresson, et al. 2003. "Archaeological evidence for the emergence of language, symbolism, and music—An alternative multidisciplinary perspective." *Journal of World Prehistory* 17 (1): 1–70.

D'Errico, F., C. Henshilwood, M. Vanhaeren, and K. van Niekerk. 2005. "*Nassarius kraussianus* shell beads from Blombos Cave: Evidence for symbolic behaviour in the Middle Stone Age." *Journal of Human Evolution* 48 (1): 3–24.

D'Errico, F., C. Henshilwood, and P. Nilsson. 2001. "An engraved bone fragment from c. 70,000 year-old Middle Stone Age levels at Blombos Cave, South Africa: Implications for the origin of symbolism and language." *Antiquity* 75 (288): 309–318.

D'Errico, F., J. Zilhão, M. Julien, D. Baffier, and J. Pelegrin. 1998. "Neanderthal acculturation in Europe: A critical review of the evidence and its interpretation." *Current Anthropology* 39:S1–S44.

Diamond, J. 1997. *Guns, germs and steel: The fates of human societies.* New York: Norton.

Dibble, H. L. and O. Bar-Yosef, eds. 1995. *The definition and interpretation of Levallois technology.* Madison: Prehistory Press.

Dibble, H. L. and P. Mellars, eds. 1992. *The middle Palaeolithic: Adaptation, behavior and variability.* Philadelphia: University Museum Monograph, 72.

Dibble, H. L. and N. Rolland. 1992. "On assemblage variability in the Middle Palaeolithic of Western Europe: History, perspectives, and a new synthesis." In H. L. Dibble and P. Mellars, eds., *The Middle Palaeolithic: Adaptation, behavior and variability.* University Museum Monograph, 72:1–28.

Dickson, D. B. and G. Y. Gang. 2002. "Evidence of the emergence of 'modern' behavior in the Middle and Later Stone Age lithic assemblages at Shurmai rockshelter (GmJm-1) and Kakwa Lelash rockshelter (GnJm-2) in the Mukogodo Hills of north-central Kenya." *African Archaeological Review* 19 (1): 1–26.

Dickson, D. B., F. B. Pearl, G.-Y. Gang, S. Kahinju, and S. Wandibba. 2004. "Site reconnaissance in the Kipsing and Tol River watersheds of Central Kenya: Implications for Middle and Later Stone Age land-use patterns. *African Archaeological Review* 21 (3): 152–191.

Dinesen, I. (K. Blixen). 1937. *Den afrikanske farm.* Copenhagen: Gyldendal.

Dinesen, I. (K. Blixen).1938. *Out of Africa.* London: Putnam.

Ding, Y.-C., H.-C. Chi, D. L. Grady, A, Morishima, J. R. Kidd, K. K. Kidd, P. Flodman, et al. 2002. "Evidence of positive selection acting at the human dopamine receptor D4 gene locus." *Proceedings of the National Academy of Sciences* 99 (1): 309–314.

Ditchfield, P., J. Hicks, T. Plummer, L. C. Bishop, and R. Potts. 1999. "Current research on the Late Pliocene and Pleistocene deposits north of the Homas Mountain, Southwestern Kenya." *Journal of Human Evolution* 36 (2): 123–150.

Donald, M. 1991. *Origin of the modern mind: Three stages in the evolution of culture and cognition.* Cambridge: Harvard University Press.

Dorus, S., E. J. Vallender, P. D. Evans, J. R. Anderson, S. L. Gilbert, M. Mahowald, G. J. Wyckoff, C. M., Malcom, and B. T. Lahn. 2004. "Accelerated evolution of nervous system genes in the origins of *Homo sapiens.*" *Cell* 119 (7): 1027–1040.

Dreyer, T. F. 1935. "A human skull from Florisbad, Orange Free State, with a note on the endocranial cast by C. U. Ariens Kappers." *Proceedings of the Koninklijke Akademie van Wetenschappen te Amsterdam* 38:3–12.

Duarte, C., J. Mauricio, P. B. Pettitt, R. Souto, E. Trinkaus, H. van der Plicht, and J. Zilhão. 1999. "The early Upper Palaeolithic human skeleton from the Abrigo do Lagar Velho (Portugal) and modern human emergence in Iberia." *Proceedings of the National Academy of Sciences* 96 (13): 7604–7609.

Dubois, E. 1894. *Pithecanthropus erectus, eine menschenaehnliche Ubergangsform aus Java.* Batavia: Landesdruckerei.

Duggen, S., K. Hoernie, P. van den Bogaard, L. Ripka, and J. P. Morgan. 2003. "Deep roots of the Messinian salinity crisis." *Nature* 422 (6932): 602–606.

Dupont, L. M., S. Jahns, F. Marret, and Shi Ning. 2000. "Vegetation changes in equatorial West Africa: Time-slices for the last 150 ka." *Palaeogeography, Palaeoclimatology, Palaeoecology* 155 (1/2): 95–122.

Du Toit, A. 1947. "Palaeolithic environments in Kenya and the Union—A contrast." *South African Archaeological Bulletin* 2:28–40.

Editors of *Life.* 1961. *The emergence of man.* New York: Time.

Emiliani, C. 1955. "Pleistocene temperatures." *Journal of Geology* 63:538–578.

Enard, W., P. Khaitovich, J. Klose, S. Zollner, F. Heissig, P. Givalisco, K. Nieselt-Struwe, et al. 2002a. "Intra- and interspecific variation in primate gene expression patterns." *Science* 296 (5566): 340–343.

Enard, W., M. Przeworski, S. E. Fisher, C. S. L. Lai, V. Wiebe, T. Kitano, A. P. Monaco, and S. Pääbo. 2002b. "Molecular evolution of FOXP2, a gene involved in speech and language." *Nature* 418 (6900): 869–872.

EPICA (European Project for Ice Coring in Antarctic) Community Members. 2004. "Eight glacial-interglacial cycles from an Antarctic ice core." *Nature* 429 (6992): 623–628.

Eswaran, V. 2002. "A diffusion wave out of Africa: The mechanism of the modern human revolution?" *Current Anthropology* 43 (5): 749–774.

Eswaran, V., H. Harpending, and A. R. Rogers. 2005. "Genomics refutes an exclusively African origin of humans." *Journal of Human Evolution* 49 (1): 1–18.

Evans, P. D., S. L. Gilbert, N. Mekel-Bobrov, E. J. Vallender, J. R. Anderson, L. M. Vaez-Azizi, S. A. Tishkoff, R. R. Hudson, and B. T. Lahn. 2005. "Microcephalin, a gene regulating brain size, continues to evolve adaptively in humans." *Science* 309 (5741): 1717–1720.

Falk, D. 1992. *Braindance: New discoveries about human origins and brain evolution.* New York: Henry Holt.

Falk, D. 2004. *Braindance: New discoveries about human origins and brain evolution.* Rev. ed. Gainesville: University Press of Florida.

Falush, D., T. Wirth, B. Linz, J. K. Pritchard, M. Stephens, M. Kidd, M. J. Blaser, et al. 2003. "Traces of human migrations in *Helicobacter pylori* populations." *Science* 299 (5612): 1582–1585.

Feathers, J. K. 1996. "Luminescence dating and modern human origins." *Evolutionary Anthropology* 5 (1): 25–36.

Feathers, J. K. 2002. "Luminescence dating in less than ideal conditions: Case studies from Klasies River Main site and Duinefontein, South Africa." *Journal of Archaeological Science* 29 (2): 177–194.

Feathers, J. K. and D. A. Bush. 2000. "Luminescence dating of Middle Stone Age deposits at Die Kelders." *Journal of Human Evolution* 38 (1): 91–119.

Feathers, J. K. and E. Migliorini. 2001. "Luminescence dating at Katanda—A reassessment." *Quaternary Science Reviews* 20 (5–9): 961–966.

Feinberg, H. M. and J. B. Solodow. 2002. "Out of Africa." *Journal of African History* 43 (2): 255–261.

Feldman, M. W., R. C. Lewontin, and M.-C. King. 2003. "A genetic melting pot." *Nature* 424 (6947): 374.

Ferring, C. R. 1975. "The Aterian in North African prehistory." In F. Wendorf and A. E. Marks, eds., *Problems in prehistory: North Africa and the Levant.* Dallas: Southern Methodist University Press, pp. 113–126.

Flannery, K. V. 1969. "Origins and ecological effects of early domestication in Iran and the Near East." In P. J. Ucko and G. W. Dimbleby, eds., *The domestication and exploitation of plants and animals.* London: Duckworth, pp. 73–100.

Flint, R. F. 1959a. "On the basis of Pleistocene correlation in East Africa." *Geological Magazine* 96:265–284.

Flint, R. F. 1959b. "Pleistocene climates in Eastern and Southern Africa." *Bulletin of the Geological Society of America* 70:343–374.

Flint, R. F. 1967. "Introduction to stratigraphical considerations." In W. W. Bishop and J. D. Clark, eds., *Background to evolution in Africa.* Chicago: University of Chicago Press, pp. 187–189.

Flint, R. F. 1971. *Glacial and Quaternary geology.* New York: Wiley.

Foley, R. 1987a. *Another unique species: Patterns in evolutionary ecology.* New York: Wiley.

Foley, R. 1987b. "Hominid species and stone tool assemblages: How are they related?" *Antiquity* 61 (233): 380–392.

Foley, R. 1989. "The ecological conditions of speciation: A comparative approach to the origins of anatomically-modern humans." In P. Mellars and C. Stringer, eds., *The human revolution.* Princeton, NJ: Princeton University Press, pp. 298–318.

Foley, R. and M. M. Lahr. 1997. "Mode 3 technologies and the evolution of modern humans." *Cambridge Archaeological Journal* 7 (1): 3–36.

Forster, P. 2004. "Ice ages and the mitochondrial DNA chronology of human dispersals: A review." *Philosophical Transactions of the Royal Society* 359B (1442): 255–264.

Forster, P. and S. Matsumara. 2005. "Did early humans go north or south?" *Science* 308 (5724): 965–966.

Frayer, D. W., M. H. Wolpoff, A. G. Thorne, F. H. Smith, and G. Pope. 1993. "Theories of modern human origins: The palaeontological test." *American Anthropologist* 95 (1): 14–50.

Frere, J. 1800. "Account of flint weapons discovered at Hoxne in Suffolk." *Archaeologia* 13:204–205.

Fuller, M., C. J. Laj, and E. Herrero-Bervera. 1996. "The reversal of the earth's magnetic field." *American Scientist* 84 (6): 552–561.

Gabunia, L. and A. Vekua. 1995. "A Plio-Pleistocene hominid from Dmanisi, East Georgia, Caucasus." *Nature* 373 (6514): 509–512.

Gabunia, L., S. Anton, D. Lordkipanidze, A. Vekua, A. Justus, and C. C. Swisher III. 2001. "Dmanisi and dispersal." *Evolutionary Anthropology* 10 (5): 158–170.

Gabunia, L., A. Vekua, D. Lordkipanidze, C. C. Swisher III, R. Ferring, A. Justus, M. Nioradze, et al. 2000. "Earliest Pleistocene hominid cranial remains from Dmanisi, Republic of Georgia: Taxonomy, geological setting, and age." *Science* 288 (5468): 1019–1025.

Gagneux, P., C. Wills, U. Gerlof, D. Tautz, P. A. Morin, C. Boesch, B. Fruth, G. Hohmann, O. A. Ryder, and D. S. Woodruff. 1999. "Mitochondrial sequences show diverse evolutionary histories of African hominoids." *Proceedings of the National Academy of Sciences* 96 (9): 5077–5082.

Gambier, D. 1989. "Fossil hominids from the early Upper Palaeolithic (Aurignacian) of France." In P. Mellars and C. Stringer, eds., *The human revolution*. Princeton, NJ: Princeton University Press, pp. 194–211.

Gamble, C. 1986. *The Palaeolithic settlement of Europe*. Cambridge: Cambridge University Press.

Gamble, C. 1994. *Timewalkers: The prehistory of global colonization*. Cambridge: Harvard University Press.

Gamble, C. 1999. *The Palaeolithic societies of Europe*. Cambridge: Cambridge University Press.

Gang, G.-Young. 1997. Comparative analysis of lithic materials recovered from Shurmai (GnJm-1) and Kakwa Lelash (GnJm-2) Rockshelters, Kenya. PhD diss., Texas A and M University.

Garcea, E. A. A. 2004. "Crossing deserts and avoiding seas: Aterian North African–European relations." *Journal of Anthropological Research* 60 (1): 27–53.

Gargett, R. 1989. "Grave shortcomings: The evidence for Neandertal burial." *Current Anthropology* 30 (2): 157–190.

Gargett, R. 1999. "Middle Palaeolithic burial is not a dead issue: The view from Qafzeh, Saint-Césaire, Kebara, Amud and Dederiyeh." *Journal of Human Evolution* 37 (1): 27–90.

Garrod, D. A. E. and D. M. A. Bate. 1937. *The Stone Age of Mount Carmel 1: Excavations at the Wady-el-Mughara.* Oxford: Clarendon Press.

Gasse, F. 2000. "Hydrological changes in the African tropics since the last glacial maximum." *Quaternary Science Reviews* 19 (1–5): 189–211.

Gathorne-Hardy, F. J. and W. E. H. Harcourt-Smith. 2003. "The super-eruption of Toba, did it cause a human bottleneck?" *Journal of Human Evolution* 45 (3): 227–230.

Gautier, A. 1993. "The Middle Paleolithic archaeofauna from Bir Tarfawi (Western Desert, Egypt)." In F. Wendorf, R. Schild, A. E. Close, et al., *Egypt during the last interglacial: The Middle Paleolithic of Bir Tarfawi and Bir Sahara East.* New York: Plenum Press, pp. 121–143.

Geological Survey of Tanganyika. 1959. *Annual Report.* Part 1. Dar es Salaam: Government Printer.

Geraads, D., F. Amni, and J.-J. Hublin. 1992. "Le gisement pléistocène moyen d'Ain Maarouf près de El Hajeb, Maroc. Présence d'un hominidé." *Comptes Rendus de l'Academie des Sciences* 314:319–323.

Geraads, D., J.-J. Hublin, J. J. Jaeger, H. Tong, S. Sen, and P. Tourbeau. 1986. "The Pleistocene hominid site of Ternifine, Algeria: New results on the environment, age and human industries." *Quaternary Research* 25:380–386.

Geraads, D., J. P. Raynal, and V. Eisenmann. 2004. "The earliest occupation of North Africa: A reply to Sahnouni et al. (2002)." *Journal of Human Evolution* 46 (6): 751–761.

Gilead, I. 1991. "The Upper Palaeolithic period in the Levant." *Journal of World Prehistory* 5:105–154.

Glatzmaier, G. A., R. S. Coe, L. Hongre, and P. H. Roberts. 1999. "The role of the earth's mantle in controlling the frequency of geomagnetic reversals." *Nature* 401 (6756): 885–890.

Glatzmaier, G. A. and P. Olson. 2005. "Probing the geodynamo." *Scientific American* 292 (4): 50–57.

Goodman, A. 1995. "The problematics of race in contemporary biological anthropology." In N. Boaz and L. Wolfe, eds., *Biological anthropology: The state of the science.* Bend, IN: International Institute for Human Evolutionary Research, pp. 215–239.

Goodman, M. 1962. "Evolution of the immunologic species specificity of human serum proteins." *Human Biology* 33:104–150.

Goodman, M. 1963. "Man's place in the phylogeny of the primates as reflected in serum proteins." In S. L. Washburn, ed., *Classification and human evolution.* Chicago: Aldine, pp, 204–224.

Goodman, M. 1996. "Epilogue: A personal account of the origins of a new paradigm." *Molecular Phylogenetics and Evolution* 5 (1): 269–385.

Goodwin, A. J. H. 1928a. "An introduction to the Middle Stone Age in South Africa." *South African Journal of Science* 25:410–418.

Goodwin, A. J. H. 1928b. "Sir Langham Dale's collection of stone implements." *South African Journal of Science* 25:419–426.

Goodwin, A. J. H. 1929a. "The Earlier Stone Age in South Africa II: The Stellenbosch industry." In A. J. H. Goodwin and C. Van Riet Lowe, "The Stone Age cultures of South Africa." *Annals of the South African Museum* 27:9–51.

Goodwin, A. J. H. 1929b. "The Earlier Stone Age in South Africa III: The Victoria West industry." In A. J. H. Goodwin and C. Van Riet Lowe, "The Stone Age cultures of South Africa." *Annals of the South African Museum* 27:53–69.

Goodwin, A. J. H. 1929c. "The Earlier Stone Age in South Africa IV: The Fauresmith industry." In A. J. H. Goodwin and C. Van Riet Lowe, "The Stone Age cultures of South Africa." *Annals of the South African Museum* 27:71–94.

Goodwin, A. J. H. 1929d. "The Middle Stone Age." In A. J. H. Goodwin and C. Van Riet Lowe, "The Stone Age cultures of South Africa." *Annals of the South African Museum* 27:95–145.

Goodwin, A. J. H. and C. Van Riet Lowe. 1929. "The Earlier Stone Age in South Africa I: An introductory survey of the geographical and archaeological conditions in South Africa." In "The Stone Age cultures of South Africa." *Annals of the South African Museum* 27:1–7.

Goren-Inbar, N. and J. D. Speth, eds., 2004. *Human paleoecology in the Levantine corridor.* Oxford: Oxbow Books.

Goren-Inbar, N. and I. Saragusti. 1996. "An Acheulian biface assemblage from Gesher Benot Ya aqov, Israel: Indications of African affinities." *Journal of Field Archaeology* 23 (1): 15–30.

Goucher, C. 1981. "Iron is iron 'til it is rust: Trade and ecology in the demise of West African iron-smelting." *Journal of African History* 22 (2): 179–189.

Gould, S. J. 1981. *The mismeasure of man.* New York: Norton.

Gould, S. J. 1987. *Time's arrow, time's cycle.* Cambridge: Harvard University Press.

Gowlett, J. 1990. "Archaeological studies of human origins and early prehistory in Africa." In P. Robertshaw, ed., *A history of African archaeology.* London: James Currey, pp. 13–38.

Graslund, B. 1987. *The birth of prehistoric chronology.* Cambridge: Cambridge University Press.

Gravina, B., P. Mellars, and C. B. Ramsey. 2005. "Radiocarbon dating of interstratified Neanderthal and early modern human occupations at the Chatelperronian type-site." *Nature* 438 (7064): 51–56.

Grayson, D. K. 1983. *The establishment of human antiquity.* New York: Academic Press.

Gregory, J. W. 1896. *The great rift valley.* London: John Murray.

Gresham, T. and S. Brandt. 1996. "Variability in the MSA of the Horn of Africa." In G. Pwiti and R. Soper, eds., *Aspects of African archaeology.* Harare: University of Zimbabwe Publications, pp. 157–163.

Grine, F. 2000. "Middle Stone Age human fossils from Die Kelders Cave 1, Western Cape Province, South Africa." *Journal of Human Evolution* 38 (1): 129–145.

Grine, F. and C. Henshilwood. 2002. "Additional human remains from Blombos Cave, South Africa (1999–2000 excavations)." *Journal of Human Evolution* 42 (3): 293–302.

Grine, F. E., C. S. Henshilwood, and J. C. Sealy. 2000. "Human remains from Blombos Cave, South Africa (1997–1998 excavations)." *Journal of Human Evolution* 38 (6): 755–765.

Grine, F., R. Klein, and T. Volman. 1991. "Dating, archaeology and human fossils from the Middle Stone Age levels of Die Kelders, South Africa." *Journal of Human Evolution* 21 (5): 363–395.

Groves, C. P. 1989. *A theory of human and primate evolution.* Oxford: Oxford University Press.

Groves, C. P. and V. Mazak. 1975. "An approach to the taxonomy of the Hominidae: Gracile Villafranchian hominids of Africa." *Casopis pro Mineralogii e Geologii* 20:225–247.

Gruber, J. W. 1965. "Brixham Cave and the antiquity of man." In M. E. Spiro, ed., *Context and meaning in cultural anthropology.* New York: Free Press, pp. 373–402.

Grün, R. 1993. "Electron spin resonance dating in palaeoanthropology." *Evolutionary Anthropology* 2 (5): 172–181.

Grün, R. and P. B. Beaumont. 2001. "Border Cave revisited: A revised ESR chronology." *Journal of Human Evolution* 40 (6): 467–482.

Grün, R., P. B. Beaumont, P. V. Tobias, and S. Eggins. 2003. "On the age of Border Cave 5 human mandible." *Journal of Human Evolution* 45 (2): 155–167.

Grün, R., and C. B. Stringer. 1991. "Electron spin resonance dating and the evolution of modern humans." *Archaeometry* 33 (2): 153–199.

Haeckel, E. 1892. *The history of creation.* 4th ed. English. London: Kegan Paul, Trench, Trubner and Company. (Orig. pub. 1868.)

Hagelberg, E. 1996. "Mitochondrial DNA in ancient and modern humans." In A. J. Boyce and C. G. N. Mascie-Taylor, eds., *Molecular biology and human diversity.* Cambridge: Cambridge University Press, pp. 1–11.

Haidle, M. N. 2000. "Ignorant relatives or thinking siblings? A discussion of the 'cognitive revolution' at around 40,000 BP." In J. Orschiedt and G.-C. Weniger, eds., *Neanderthals and modern humans—Discussing the transition.* Mettmann, Germany: Neanderthal Museum, pp. 275–286.

Haile-Selassie, Y. 2001. "Late Miocene hominids from the Middle Awash, Ethiopia." *Nature* 412 (6843): 178–181.

Haile-Selassie, Y., B. Asfaw, and T. D. White. 2004. "Hominid cranial remains from Upper Pleistocene deposits at Aduma, Middle Awash, Ethiopia." *American Journal of Physical Anthropology* 123 (1): 1–10.

Halkett, D., T. Hart, R. Yates, T. P. Volman, J. E. Parkington, J. Orton, R. G. Klein, K. Cruz-Uribe, and G. Avery. 2003. "First excavation of intact Middle Stone Age layers at Ysterfontein, Western Cape Province, South Africa: Implications for Middle Stone Age ecology." *Journal of Archaeological Science* 30 (8): 955–971.

Hallam, A. 1989. *Great geological controversies.* 2nd ed. Oxford: Oxford University Press.

Hamilton, A. C. 1976. "The significance of patterns of distribution shown by forest plants and animals in tropical Africa for the reconstruction of Upper Pleistocene palaeo-environments: A review." *Palaeoecology of Africa* 9:63–97.

Hamilton, A. C. 1982. *Environmental history of East Africa: A study of the Quaternary*. London: Academic Press.

Hammer, M. F. 1995. "A recent common ancestry for human Y chromosomes." *Nature* 378 (6555): 376–378.

Hammer, M. F., T. Karafet, A. J. Redd, H. Jarjanazi, S. Santachiara-Benerecetti, H. Soodyall, and S. L. Zegura. 2001. "Hierarchical patterns of global human Y chromosome diversity." *Molecular Biology and Evolution* 18:1189–1203.

Hammer, M. F., A. B. Spurdle, T. Karafet, M. R. Bonner, E. T. Wood, A. Novelletto, P. Malaspina, et al. 1997. "The geographic distribution of human Y chromosome variation." *Genetics* 145 (3): 787–805.

Hammer, M. F. and S. L. Zegura. 1996. "The role of the Y chromosome in human evolutionary studies." *Evolutionary Anthropology* 5 (4): 116–134.

Hammer, M. F. and S. L. Zegura. 2002. "The human Y chromosome haplogroup tree: Nomenclature and phylogeography of its major divisions." *Annual Review of Anthropology* 31:303–321.

Hansen, C. L. and C. M. Keller. 1971. "Environment and activity patterning at Isimila Korongo, Iringa District, Tanzania: A preliminary report." *American Anthropologist* 73 (5): 1201–1211.

Harpending, H. C., M. A. Batzer, M. Gurven, L. B. Jorde, A. R. Rogers, and S. T. Sherry. 1998. "Genetic traces of ancient demography." *Proceedings of the National Academy of Sciences* 95 (4): 1961–1967.

Harpending, H., J. Relethford, and S. T. Sherry. 1996. "Methods and models for understanding human diversity." In A. J. Boyce and C. G. N. Mascie-Taylor, eds., *Molecular biology and human diversity*. Cambridge: Cambridge University Press, pp. 283–299.

Harpending, H., S. T. Sherry, A. R. Rogers, and M. Stoneking. 1993. "The genetic structure of ancient human populations." *Current Anthropology* 34 (4): 483–496.

Harper, P. T. N. 1997. "The MSA sequences at Rose Cottage Cave: A search for continuity and discontinuity." *South African Journal of Science* 93 (10): 470–475.

Harris, J. M. and T. D. White. 1979. "Evolution of the Plio-Pleistocene Suidae." *Transactions of the American Philosophical Society* 69 (2).

Harris, J. W. K., P. G. Williamson, J. Verniers, M. J. Tappen, K. Stewart, D. Helgren, J. de Heinzelin, N. T. Boaz, and R. V. Bellomo. 1987. "Late Pliocene hominid occupation in Central Africa: The setting, context and character of the Senga 5A site, Zaire." *Journal of Human Evolution* 16 (7/8): 701–728.

Harris, M. 1968. *The rise of anthropological theory: A history of theories of culture*. New York: Thomas Y. Crowell.

Hawkins, A. 2001. Getting a handle on tangs: Defining the Dakhleh Unit of the Aterian Technocomplex. A study in surface archaeology from Dakhleh Oasis, Western Desert, Egypt. PhD diss., University of Toronto.

Hawkins, A., J. Casey, D. Godfrey-Smith, and A. C. D'Andrea. 1996. "A Middle Stone Age component at the Birimi site, Northern Region, Ghana." *Nyame Akuma* 46:34–36.

Hawkins, A. L. and M. R. Kleindienst. 2002. "Lithic raw material usages during the Middle Stone Age at Dakhleh Oasis, Egypt." *Geoarchaeology* 17 (6): 601–624.

Hawks, J. and M. H. Wolpoff. 2003. "Sixty years of modern human origins in the American Anthropological Association." *American Anthropologist* 105 (1): 89–100.

Hay, R. L. 1976. *Geology of the Olduvai Gorge.* Berkeley: University of California Press.

Hay, R. L. 1980. "The KBS tuff controversy may be ended." *Nature* 284 (5755): 401.

Hay, R. L. 1990. "Olduvai Gorge: A case history in the interpretation of hominid palaeoenvironments in East Africa." *Geological Society of America Special Paper* 242: 23–37.

Hayden, B. 1993. "The cultural capacities of Neandertals: A review and re-evaluation." *Journal of Human Evolution* 24 (2):113–146.

Haynes, G. 1996. "Quaternary climates and environmental changes in Hwange National Park, Zimbabwe." In G. Pwiti and R. Soper, eds., *Aspects of African archaeology.* Harare: University of Zimbabwe Publications, pp. 71–81.

Hays, J. D., J. Imbrie, and N. J. Shackleton. 1976. "Variations in the earth's orbit: Pacemaker of the ice ages." *Science* 194 (4270): 1121–1132.

Hedges, S. B. 2000. "A start for population genomics." *Nature* 408 (6813): 652–653.

Hedges, S. B., S. Kumar, K. Tamura, and M. Stoneking. 1992. "Human origins and analysis of mitochondrial DNA." *Science* 255 (5045): 737–739.

Heizmann, E. P. J. and D. R. Begun. 2001. "The oldest Eurasian hominoid." *Journal of Human Evolution* 41 (5): 463–481.

Hennig, W. 1966. *Phylogenetic systematics.* Urbana: University of Illinois Press.

Henry-Gambier, D. 2004. "Les fossiles de Cro-Magnon (Les Eyzies-de-Tayac, Dordogne): Nouvelles données sur leur position chronologique et leur attribution culturelle." *Bulletins et Mémoires de la Société d'Anthropologique de Paris,* n.s., 14:89–112.

Henshilwood, C. S., F. D'Errico, M. Vanhaeren, K. van Niekerk, and Z. Jacobs. 2004. "Middle Stone Age shell beads from South Africa." *Science* 304 (5669): 404.

Henshilwood, C. S., F. D'Errico, C. W. Marean, R. G. Milo, and R. Yates. 2001. "An early bone tool industry from the Middle Stone Age at Blombos Cave, South Africa: Implications for the origins of modern human behavior, symbolism and language." *Journal of Human Evolution* 41 (6): 631–768.

Henshilwood, C. S., F. D'Errico, R. Yates, Z. Jacobs, C. Triboli, G. A. T. Duller, N. Mercier, et al. 2002. "Emergence of modern human behavior: Middle Stone Age engravings from South Africa." *Science* 295 (5558): 1278–1280.

Henshilwood, C. S. and C. W. Marean. 2003. "The origin of modern human behavior." *Current Anthropology* 44 (5): 627–651.

Henshilwood, C. and J. Sealy. 1997. "Bone artefacts from the Middle Stone Age at Blombos Cave, Southern Cape, South Africa." *Current Anthropology* 38 (5): 890–895.

Henshilwood, C., J. Sealy, R. Yates, K. Cruz-Uribe, P. Goldberg, F. E. Grine, R. G. Klein, C. Poggenpoel, K. van Niekerk, and I. Watts. 2001. "Blombos Cave, Southern Cape,

South Africa: Preliminary report on the 1992–1999 excavations of the Middle Stone Age." *Journal of Archaeological Science* 28 (4): 421–448.

Hewitt, G. 2000. "The genetic legacy of the Quaternary ice ages." *Nature* 405 (6789): 907–913.

Hewitt, J. 1921. "On several implements and ornaments from Strandlooper sites in the Eastern Province." *South African Journal of Science* 18:454–467.

Hewitt, J. and R. P. Stapleton. 1925. "On some remarkable stone implements in the Albany Museum." *South African Journal of Natural History* 5:23–28.

Hill, A. 1999. "The Baringo Basin, Kenya: from Bill Bishop to BPRP." In P. Andrews and P. Banham, eds., *Late Cenozoic environments and Hominid evolution: A tribute to Bill Bishop*. London: Geological Society, pp. 85–97.

Hill, A. 2002. "Palaeoanthropological research in the Tugen Hills, Kenya." *Journal of Human Evolution* 42 (1/2): 1–10.

Hill, C. L. 2001. "Geologic contexts of the Acheulian (Middle Pleistocene) in the Eastern Sahara." *Geoarchaeology* 16 (1): 65–94.

Hiscock, P. 1996. "Transformations of Upper Palaeolithic implements in the Dabban industry from Haua Fteah." *Antiquity* 70 (269): 657–664.

Hoffman, K. A. 1988. "Ancient geomagnetic reversals: Clues to the geodynamo." *Scientific American* 258 (5): 76–83.

Holl, A. 1997. "Western Africa: The prehistoric sequence." In J. O. Vogel, ed., *Encyclopedia of precolonial Africa*. Walnut Creek: AltaMira Press, pp. 305–312.

Horan, R. D., E. Bulte, and J. F. Shogren. 2005. "How trade saved humanity from biological exclusion: An economic theory of Neanderthal extinction." *Journal of Economic Behaviour and Organization* 58 (1): 1–29.

Horrobin, D. 1998. "Schizophrenia: The illness that made us human." *Medical Hypotheses* 50:269–288.

Horrobin, D. 2001. *The madness of Adam and Eve: How schizophrenia shaped humanity*. London: Corgi Books.

Hoss, M. 2000. "Neanderthal population genetics." *Nature* 404 (6777): 453–454.

Howell, F. C. 1952. "Pleistocene glacial ecology and the evolution of 'classic Neandertal' man." *Southwestern Journal of Anthropology* 8:377–410.

Howell, F. C. 1957. "The evolutionary significance of variation and varieties of 'Neanderthal' man." *Quarterly Review of Biology* 32:330–347.

Howell, F. C. 1961. "Isimila—A Palaeolithic site in Africa." *Scientific American* 205 (4): 118–129.

Howell, F. C. 1972. "Uranium-series dating of bone from the Isimila prehistoric site, Tanzania." *Nature* 237 (5349): 51–52.

Howell, F. C., G. H. Cole, and M. R. Kleindienst. 1962. "Isimila—An Acheulean occupation site in the Iringa Highlands, Southern Highlands Province, Tanganyika." In G. Mortelmans and J. Nenquin, eds., "Actes du IVe Congrès Panafricain de Préhistoire et de l'Etude du Quaternaire." *Annales de Musée Royal de l'Afrique Centrale, Tervuren* 40:43–80.

Howells, W. W. 1942. "Fossil man and the origin of races." *American Anthropologist* 44 (2): 182–193.

Howells, W. W. 1967. *Mankind in the making.* Garden City, NY: Doubleday.

Howells, W. W. 1973. "Cranial variation in man: A study by multivariate analysis of patterns of difference among recent human populations." *Papers of the Peabody Museum of Archaeology and Ethnology* 67.

Howells, W. W. 1976. "Explaining modern man: Evolutionists versus migrationists." *Journal of Human Evolution* 5 (5): 477–495.

Howells, W. W. 1993. "Explaining modern man: Evolutionists versus migrationists." In R. Ciochon and J. Fleagle, eds., *The human evolution sourcebook.* Englewood Cliffs, N.J.: Prentice Hall, pp. 628–637. (Orig. pub. 1976.)

Hrdlička, A. 1927. "The Neanderthal phase of man." The Huxley Memorial Lecture for 1927. *Journal of the Royal Anthropological Institute* 57:249–274.

Hsu, K. J. 1983. *The Mediterranean was a desert: A voyage of the Glomar Challenger.* Princeton, NJ: Princeton University Press.

Hublin, J.-J. 1985. "Human fossils from the North African Middle Pleistocene and the origins of *Homo sapiens*." In E. Delson, ed., *Ancestors: The hard evidence.* New York: Alan R. Liss, pp. 282–288.

Hublin, J.-J. 1992. "Recent human evolution in northwestern Africa." *Philosophical Transactions of the Royal Society* 337B (1280): 185–191.

Hublin, J.-J. 1993. "Recent human evolution in northwestern Africa." In M. J. Aitken, C. B. Stringer, and P. A. Mellars, eds., *The origin of modern humans and the impact of chronometric dating.* Princeton, NJ: Princeton University Press, pp. 118–131.

Hublin, J.-J. 2001. "Northwestern African Middle Pleistocene hominids and their bearing on the emergence of *Homo sapiens*." In L. Barham and K. Robson-Brown, eds., *Human roots: Africa and Asia in the Middle Pleistocene.* Bristol: Western Academic and Specialist Press, pp. 99–121.

Hublin, J.-J., F. Spoor, M. Braun, F. Zonneveld, and S. Condemi. 1996. "A late Neanderthal associated with Upper Palaeolithic artefacts." *Nature* 381 (6579): 224–226.

Hulot, G., C. Eymin, B. Langlais, M. Mandea, and N. Olsen. 2002. "Small-scale structure of the geodynamo inferred from Oerstad and Magsat satellite data." *Nature* 418 (6881): 620–623.

Hutton, J. 1795. *Theory of the Earth with proofs and illustrations.* Edinburgh: William Creech.

Huxley, J. 1942. *Evolution: The modern synthesis.* London: G. Allen and Unwin.

Huxley, T. H. 1959. *Man's place in nature.* Ann Arbor: University of Michigan Press. (Orig. pub. 1863.)

Huysecom, E., A. Mayor, S. Ozainne, M. Rasse, K. Schaer, and S. Soriano. 2004. "Oungoujou: Plus de 100,000 ans d'histoire en Pays Dogon (Mali)." *Archéologie Suisse* 27 (3): 2–13.

Huysecom, E., S. Ozainne, L. Cissé, H. Doutrelepont, A. Gallay, D. Konaté, A. Mayor, et al. 2004. "Du Paléolithique ancient a nos jours: La sequence archéologique et paléoenvironnementale du gisement d'Ounjougou (Pays Dogon, Mali)." In S. Sanogo and T. Togola, eds., *Acts of the 11th Congress of the Pan African association for prehistory and related fields, Bamako, Mali, 2001*. Bamako: Institut des Sciences Humaines, pp. 289–327.

Imbrie, J. and K. P. Imbrie. 1979. *Ice Ages: Solving the mystery*. Short Hills: Enslow.

Ingman, M., H. Kaessmann, S. Pääbo, and U. Gyllenstein. 2000. "Mitochondrial genome variation and the African origin of modern humans." *Nature* 408 (6813): 708–713.

Ingold, T. 1994. "Tool-using, toolmaking and the evolution of language." In D. Quiatt and J. Itani, eds., *Hominid culture in primate perspective*. Niwot: University Press of Colorado, pp. 279–314.

Ingold, T. 1995. "People like us—The concept of the anatomically modern human." In R. Corbey and B. Theunissen, eds., *Ape, man, ape man: Changing views since 1600*. Leiden: Department of Prehistory, Leiden University, pp. 241–262.

Ingold, T. 2002. "Between evolution and history: Biology, culture, and the myth of human origins." In M. Wheeler, J. Ziman, and M. Boden, eds., *The evolution of cultural entities. Proceedings of the British Academy 112*. Oxford: Oxford University Press, pp. 43–66.

Inskeep, R. 1962. "The age of the Kondoa rock paintings in the light of recent excavations at Kisese II rock shelter." In G. Mortelmans and J. Nenquin, eds., "Actes du IVe Congrès Panafricain de Préhistoire et de l'Etude du Quaternaire." *Annales de Musée Royal de l'Afrique Centrale, Tervuren* 40:249–256.

Insoll, T. 2003. *The archaeology of Islam in sub-Saharan Africa*. Cambridge: Cambridge University Press.

International Human Genome Sequencing Consortium. 2001. "Initial sequencing and analysis of the human genome." *Nature* 409 (6822): 860–921.

International Human Genome Sequencing Consortium. 2004. "Finishing the euchromatic sequence of the human genome." *Nature* 431 (7011): 931–945.

Irish, J. D. 2000. "The Iberomaurusian enigma: North African progenitor or dead end?" *Journal of Human Evolution* 39 (4): 393–410.

Isaac, G. Ll. 1975. "Sorting out the muddle in the middle: An anthropologist's post-conference appraisal." In K. W. Butzer and G. Ll. Isaac, eds., *After the Australopithecines: Stratigraphy, ecology and culture change in the Middle Pleistocene*. The Hague: Mouton, pp. 875–887.

Isaac, G. Ll. 1977. *Olorgesailie: Archeological studies of a Middle Pleistocene lake basin in Kenya*. Chicago: University of Chicago Press.

Isaac, G. Ll. 1978a. "Food sharing and human evolution: Archaeological evidence from the Plio-Pleistocene of East Africa." *Journal of Anthropological Research* 34:311–325.

Isaac, G. Ll. 1978b. "The food-sharing behavior of protohuman hominids." *Scientific American* 238 (4): 90–108.

Isaac, G. Ll. and B. Isaac, eds. 1997. *Koobi Fora research project 5: Plio-Pleistocene archaeology*. Oxford: Clarendon Press.

Isaac, G. Ll. and J. W. K. Harris. 1997. "The Stone artefact assemblages: A comparative study." In G. Ll. Isaac and B. Isaac, eds., *Koobi Fora research project 5: Plio-Pleistocene archaeology.* Oxford: Clarendon Press, pp. 262–362.

Jacobs, Z., G. A. T. Duller, and A. G. Wintle. 2003a. "Optical dating of dune sand from Blombos Cave, South Africa I: Multiple grain data." *Journal of Human Evolution* 44 (5): 599–612.

Jacobs, Z., A. G. Wintle, and G. A. T. Duller. 2003b. "Optical dating of dune sand from Blombos Cave, South Africa II: Single grain data." *Journal of Human Evolution* 44 (5): 613–625.

Jahns, S., M. Huls, and M. Sarnthein. 1998. "Vegetation and climate history of west equatorial Africa based on a marine pollen record off Liberia (site GIK 16776) covering the last 400,000 years." *Review of Palaeobotany and Palynology* 102 (3/4): 277–288.

Janković, I. 2005. "Neandertals . . . 150 years later." *Collegium Antropologicum* 28. Suppl. no. 2:379–401.

Jegalian, K. and B. T. Lahn. 2001. "Why the Y is so weird." *Scientific American* 284 (2): 56–61.

Jenkins, A. C. 1978. *The naturalists: Pioneers of natural history.* New York: Mayflower Books.

Jia Lanpo and Huang Weiwen. 1990. *The story of Peking man.* Beijing: Foreign Languages Press.

Johanson, D. C. and T. D. White. 1979. "A systematic assessment of early African hominids." *Science* 203 (4378): 321–330.

Johanson, D. C., T. D. White, and Y. Coppens. 1978. "A new species of the genus *Australopithecus* (Primates: Hominidae) from the Pliocene of Eastern Africa." *Kirtlandia* 28:1–14.

Johnsen, S. J., D. Dahl-Jensen, N. Gundestrut, J. P. Steffensen, H. B. Clausen, H. Miller, V. Masson-Delmotte, A. F. Sveinbjornsdottir, and J. White. 2001. "Oxygen isotope and palaeotemperature records from six Greenland ice-core stations: Camp Century, Dye-3, GRIP, GISP2, Renland and North GRIP." *Journal of Quaternary Science* 16 (4): 299–307.

Johnson, T. C., E. T. Brown, J. McManus, S. Barry, P. Barker, and F. Gasse. 2002. "A high resolution paleoclimate record spanning the last 25,000 years in southern East Africa." *Science* 296 (5565): 113–114, 131–132.

Johnson, T. C., A. C. Cohen, K. Kelts, J. T. Lehman, D. A. Livingstone, M. R. Talbot, and R. F. Weiss. 1993. "IDEAL: An international decade for the East African lakes: Science and implementation plan." *PAGES workshop report series* 93-2.

Jolly, D., D. Taylor, R. Marchant, A. Hamilton, R. Bonnefille, F. Bucher, and G. Riollet. 1997. "Vegetation dynamics in central Africa since 18,000 years BP: Pollen records from the interlacustrine highlands of Burundi, Rwanda and Western Uganda." *Journal of Biogeography* 24 (4): 495–512.

Jones, R. 1999. "Dating the human colonization of Australia: Radiocarbon and luminescence revolutions." In J. Coles, R. Bewley, and P. Mellars, eds., "World prehistory." *Proceedings of the British Academy* 99:37–65.

Jones, J. S. and S. Rouhani. 1986. "How small was the bottleneck?" *Nature* 319 (6053): 449–450.

Jurmain, R., H. Nelson, L. Kilgore, and W. Trevanthan. 1997. *Introduction to physical anthropology*. 7th ed. Belmont: West/Wadsworth.

Kaessmann, H., F. Heißig, A. von Haeseler, and S. Pääbo. 1999. "DNA sequence variation in a region of low recombination on the human X chromosome." *Nature Genetics* 22:78–81.

Kaessmann, H., V. Wiebe, and S. Pääbo. 1999. "Extensive nuclear DNA sequence diversity among chimpanzees." *Science* 286 (5442): 1159–1162.

Kaufman, D. 1999. *Archaeological perspectives on the origins of modern humans: A view from the Levant*. Westport: Bergin and Garvey.

Ke, Y., B. Su, X. Song, D. Lu, L. Chen, H. Li, C. Qi, et al. 2001. "African origin of modern humans in East Asia: A tale of 12,000 Y chromosomes." *Science* 292 (5519): 1151–1153.

Kelly, A. J. 1996a. Intra-regional and inter-regional variability in the East Turkana (Kenya) and Kenyan Middle Stone Age. PhD diss., Rutgers University.

Kelly, A. J. 1996b. "Recently recovered Middle Stone Age assemblages from East Turkana, northern Kenya: Their implications for understanding technological adaptations during the Late Pleistocene." In C. C. Magori, C. B. Saanane, and F. Schrenck, eds., "Four million years of hominid evolution in Africa." *Kaupia/Darmstäder Beiträge zur Naturgeschichte* 6:47–55.

Kelly, A. J. and J. W. K. Harris. 1992. "Recent findings of Middle Stone Age material from East Turkana." *Nyame Akuma* 38:29–34.

Kennedy, G. E. 1984. "The emergence of *Homo sapiens*: The postcranial evidence." *Man* 19:94–110.

Kennedy, G. E. 1992. "The evolution of *Homo sapiens* as indicated by features of the postcranium." In G. Bräuer and F. H. Smith, eds., *Continuity or replacement*. Rotterdam: A. A. Balkema, pp. 209–218.

Kent, P. 1978. "Historical background—Early exploration in the East African Rift—The Gregory Rift Valley." In W. W. Bishop, ed., *Geological background to fossil man*. Edinburgh: Scottish Academic Press, pp. 1–4.

Keyser, A. W., C. G. Menter, J. Moggi-Cecchi, T. R. Pickring, and L. R. Berger. 2000. "Drimolen: A new hominid-bearing site in Gauteng, South Africa." *South African Journal of Science* 94 (6): 193–197.

Kibunjia, M. 1994. "Pliocene archaeological occurrences in the Lake Turkana basin." *Journal of Human Evolution* 27 (1/2/3): 159–171.

Kibunjia, M., H. Roche, F. Brown, and R. Leakey. 1992. "Pliocene and Pleistocene archaeological sites west of Lake Turkana, Kenya." *Journal of Human Evolution* 23 (5): 431–438.

Kidder, J. H., R. L. Jantz, and F. H. Smith. 1992. "Defining modern humans: A multivariate approach." In G. Bräuer and F. H. Smith, eds., *Continuity or replacement*. Rotterdam: A. A. Balkema, pp. 157–177.

Kimura, M. 1983. *The neutral theory of molecular evolution*. Cambridge: Cambridge

University Press.

Kittler, R., M. Kayser, and M. Stoneking. 2003. "Molecular evolution of *Pediculus humanus* and the origin of clothing." *Current Biology* 13 (16): 1414–1417.

Klein, R. G. 1970. "Problems in the study of the Middle Stone Age of South Africa." *South African Archaeological Bulletin* 25 (3/4): 127–135.

Klein, R. G. 1976. "The mammalian fauna of the Klasies River Mouth sites, Cape Province, South Africa." *South African Archaeological Bulletin* 31:75–98.

Klein, R. G. 1979. "Stone Age exploitation of animals in Southern Africa." *American Scientist* 67 (2): 151–160.

Klein, R. G. 1989a. "Biological and behavioural perspectives on modern human origins in southern Africa." In P. Mellars and C. Stringer, eds., *The human revolution.* Princeton, NJ: Princeton University Press, pp. 529–546.

Klein, R. G. 1989b. "Why does skeletal part representation differ between smaller and larger bovids at Klasies River Mouth and other archaeological sites?" *Journal of Archaeological Science* 6:363–381.

Klein, R. G. 1992. "The archaeology of modern human origins." *Evolutionary Anthropology* 1 (1): 5–14.

Klein, R. G. 1994. "The problem of modern human origins." In M. H. Nitecki and D.V. Nitecki, eds., *Origins of anatomically modern humans.* New York: Plenum Press, pp. 3–21.

Klein, R. G. 1995. "Anatomy, behavior and modern human origins." *Journal of World Prehistory* 9 (2): 167–198.

Klein, R. G. 1998. "Why anatomically modern people did not disperse from Africa 100,000 years ago." In T. Akazawa, K. Aoki, and O. Bar-Yosef, eds., *Neandertals and modern humans in Western Asia.* New York: Plenum Press, pp. 509–521.

Klein, R. G. 1999. *The human career.* 2nd ed. Chicago: University of Chicago Press.

Klein, R. G. 2000. "Archaeology and the evolution of human behavior." *Evolutionary Anthropology* 9 (1): 17–36.

Klein, R. G. 2001a. "Fully modern humans." In G. W. Feinman and T. D. Price, eds., *Archaeology at the millennium: A source book.* New York: Kluwer, pp. 109–135.

Klein, R. G. 2001b. "Southern Africa and modern human origins." *Journal of Anthropological Research* 57 (1): 1–16.

Klein, R. G. 2003. "Whither the Neanderthals?" *Science* 299 (5612): 1525–1527.

Klein, R. G., G. Avery, K. Cruz-Uribe, D. Halkett, T. Hart, R. G. Milo, and T. P. Volman. 1999. "Duinefontein 2: An Acheulean site in the Western Cape Province of South Africa." *Journal of Human Evolution* 37 (2): 153–190.

Klein, R. G., G. Avery, K. Cruz-Uribe, D. Halkett, J. E. Parkington, T. Steele, T. P. Volman, and R. Yates. 2004. "The Ysterfontein 1 Middle Stone Age site, South Africa, and early human exploitation of coastal resources." *Proceedings of the National Academy of Sciences* 101 (16): 5708–5715.

Klein, R. G. and K. Cruz-Uribe. 1991. "The bovids from Elandsfontein, South Africa, and their implications for the age, palaeoenvironment, and origins of the site." *African Archaeological Review* 9:21–79.

Klein, R. G. and K. Cruz-Uribe. 1996. "Exploitation of large bovids and seals at Middle and Later Stone Age sites in South Africa." *Journal of Human Evolution* 31 (4): 315–334.

Klein, R. G. and K. Cruz-Uribe. 2000. "Middle and Later Stone Age large mammal and tortoise remains from Die Kelders Cave 1, Western Cape Province, South Africa." *Journal of Human Evolution* 38 (1): 169–195.

Kleindienst, M. R. 1962. "Components of the East African Acheulian assemblage: An analytical approach." In G. Mortelmans and J. Nenquin, eds., "Actes du IVe Congrès Panafricain de Préhistoire et de l'Etude du Quaternaire." *Annales de Musée Royal de l'Afrique Centrale, Tervuren* 40:81–111.

Kleindienst, M. R. 1967. "Questions of terminology in regard to the study of Stone Age industries in eastern Africa: 'Culture stratigraphic units.'" In W. W. Bishop and J. D. Clark, eds., *Background to evolution in Africa.* Chicago: University of Chicago Press, pp. 821–859.

Kleindienst, M. R. 2001. "What is the Aterian? The view from Dakhleh Oasis and the Western Desert, Egypt." In C. A. Marlow and A. J. Mills, eds., *The Oasis papers 1: The proceedings of the first conference of the Dakhleh Oasis project.* Oxford: Oxbow Books, pp. 1–14.

Kleindienst, M. R. 2003. "Strategies for studying Pleistocene archaeology based upon surface evidence: First characterization of an older Middle Stone Age unit, Dakhleh Oasis, Egypt." In G. E. Bowen and C. A. Hope, eds., *The Oasis papers 3: Proceedings of the third international conference of the Dakhleh Oasis project. Dakhleh Oasis project monograph 14.* Oxford: Oxbow Books, pp. 1–42.

Kleindienst, M. R. 2005. Personal communication.

Kleindienst, M. R., C. S. Churcher, J. R. Smith, and H. P. Schwarcz. 2004. "Mid- to Late Pleistocene palaeolakes in the Dakhleh Oasis, Western Desert, Egypt." Paper presented at the annual meeting of the Geological Society of America, Denver, Colorado. *Abstracts with Programs* 36 (5): 122.

Klimowicz, J. and G. Haynes. 1996. "The Stone Age archaeology of Hwange National Park, Zimbabwe." In G. Pwiti and R. Soper, eds., *Aspects of African archaeology.* Harare: University of Zimbabwe Publications, pp. 121–128.

Knight, A. 2003. "The phylogenetic relationship of Neandertal and modern human mitochondrial DNAs based on informative nucleotide sites." *Journal of Human Evolution* 44 (5): 627–632.

Knight, A., M. A. Batzer, M. Stoneking, H. K. Tiwari, W. D. Scheer, R. J. Herrera, and P. L. Deininger. 1996. "DNA sequences of Alu elements indicate a recent replacement of the human autosomal genetic component." *Proceedings of the National Academy of Sciences* 93 (9): 4360–4364.

Kordos, L. and D. R. Begun. 2002. "Rudabanya: A late Miocene subtropical swamp deposit with evidence of the origin of the African apes and humans." *Evolutionary Anthropology* 11 (2): 45–57.

Kramer, A. 1993. "Human taxonomic diversity in the Pleistocene: Does *Homo erectus* represent multiple hominid species?" *American Journal of Physical Anthropology* 91 (2): 161–171.

Krijgsman, W., F. J. Hilgen, I. Raffi, J. Sierro, and D. S. Wilson. 1999. "Chronology, causes and progression of the Messinian salinity crisis." *Nature* 400 (6745): 652–655.

Krings, M., C. Capelli, F. Tschentscher, H. Geisert, S. Meyer, A. von Haeseler, K. Grosschmidt, G. Possnert, M. Paunovic, and S. Pääbo. 2000. "A view of Neandertal genetic diversity." *Nature Genetics* 26 (2): 144–146.

Krings, M., H. Giesert, R. W. Schmitz, H. Krainitski, and S. Pääbo. 1999. "DNA sequences of the mitochondrial hypervariable region II from the Neandertal type specimen." *Proceedings of the National Academy of Sciences* 96 (10): 5581–5585.

Krings, M., A. Stone, R. W. Schmitz, H. Krainitzki, M. Stoneking, and S. Pääbo. 1997. "Neandertal DNA sequences and the origin of modern humans." *Cell* 90 (1): 19–30.

Krings, M., A.-H. Salem, K. Bauer, H. Geisert, A. K. Malek, L. Chaix, D. Wilsby, et al. 1999. "MtDNA analysis of Nile River Valley populations: A genetic corridor or a barrier to migration?" *American Journal of Human Genetics* 64 (4): 1166–1176.

Kuehn, D. D. and D. B. Dickson. 1999. "Stratigraphy and noncultural site formation at the Shurmai rockshelter (GnJm1) in the Mukogodo Hills of north-central Kenya." *Geoarchaeology* 14 (1): 63–85.

Kukla, G. J., M. L. Bender, J.-L. De Beaulieu, G. Bond, W. S. Broecker, P. Cleveringa, J. E. Gavin, et al. 2002. "Last interglacial climates." *Quaternary Research* 58 (1): 2–13.

Kuman, K., M. Inbar, and R. J. Clarke. 1999. "Palaeoenvironments and cultural sequence of the Florisbad Middle Stone Age hominid site, South Africa." *Journal of Archaeological Science* 26:1409–1425.

Kusimba, C. 1999. *The rise and fall of Swahili states.* Walnut Creek: AltaMira Press.

Kusimba, S. B. 1999. "Hunter-gatherer land use patterns in Later Stone Age East Africa." *Journal of Anthropological Archaeology* 18 (2): 165–200.

Kusimba, S. B. 2001. "The early Later Stone Age in East Africa: Excavations and lithic assemblages from Lukenya Hill." *African Archaeological Review* 18 (2): 77–123.

Kusimba, S. B. 2003. *African foragers: Environment, technology, interactions.* Walnut Creek: AltaMira Press.

Kusimba, S. B. 2005. "What is a hunter-gatherer? Variation in the archaeological record of Eastern and Southern Africa." *Journal of Archaeological Research* 13 (4): 337–366.

Lahr, M. M. 1996. *The evolution of modern human diversity: A study of cranial variation.* Cambridge: Cambridge University Press.

Lahr, M. M. and R. Foley. 1994. "Multiple dispersals and modern human origins." *Evolutionary Anthropology* 3 (2): 48–60.

Lahr, M. M. and R. Foley. 1998. "Towards a theory of modern human origins: Geography, demography and diversity in recent human evolution." *Yearbook of Physical Anthropology* 41:137–176.

Lahr, M. M. and R. Foley. 2001. "Mode 3, *Homo helmei* and the pattern of human evolution in the Middle Pleistocene." In L. Barham and K. Robson-Brown, eds., *Human roots: Africa and Asia in the Middle Pleistocene.* Bristol: Western Academic and Specialist Press, pp. 23–39.

Lahr, M. M. and R. Foley. 2004. "Human evolution writ small." *Nature* 431 (7012): 1043–1044.

Lai, C. S. L., S. E. Fisher, J. A. Hurst, F. Vargha-Khadem, and A. P. Monaco. 2001. "A forkhead-domain gene is mutated in a severe speech and language disorder." *Nature* 413 (6855): 519–523.

Laitman, J. 1984. "The anatomy of human speech." *Natural History* 93 (8): 20–27.

Laitman, J. 1985. "Evolution of the hominid upper respiratory tract: The fossil evidence." In P. V. Tobias, V. Strong, and H. White, eds., *Hominid evolution: Past, present and future.* New York: Alan R. Liss, pp. 281–286.

Laitman, J. T., J. S. Reidenberg, P. J. Gannon, B. Johannson, K. Landahl, and P. Liberman. 1990. "The Kebara hyoid: What can it tell us about the evolution of the hominid vocal tract?" *American Journal of Physical Anthropology* 81:254.

Lamphere, M. A. 2000. "Comparison of conventional K-Ar and ^{40}Ar/^{39}Ar dating of young mafic volcanic rocks." *Quaternary Research* 53 (3): 294–301.

Landau, M. 1991. *Narratives of human evolution.* New Haven: Yale University Press.

Langlands, B. W. 1967. "The published works of E. J. Wayland." *Uganda Journal* 31:33–42.

Laplace, G. 1966. "Recherches sur l'origine et l'évolution des complexes leptolithiques." Ecole française de Rome. *Mélanges d'archéologie et d'histoire. Suppléments* 4. Paris: E. de Boccard.

Larsson, L. 1996. "The Middle Stone Age of Zimbabwe: Some aspects of former research and future aims." In G. Pwiti and R. Soper, eds., *Aspects of African archaeology.* Harare: University of Zimbabwe Publications, pp. 201–206.

Lartet, E. and H. Christy. 1865–1875. *Reliquiae Aquitanicae, being contributions to the archaeology and palaeontology of Perigord and the adjoining provinces of Southern France.* London: Williams and Norgate.

Laville, H., J.-P. Rigaud, and J. R. Sackett. 1980. *Rock shelters of the Perigord: Geological stratigraphy and archaeological succession.* New York: Academic Press.

Leakey, L. S. B. 1931. *The Stone Age cultures of the Kenya Colony.* Cambridge: Cambridge University Press.

Leakey, L. S. B. 1932. "The Oldoway human skeleton." *Nature* 129:721–722.

Leakey, L. S. B. 1936a. *Stone Age Africa: An outline of prehistory of Africa.* London: Oxford University Press.

Leakey, L. S. B. 1936b. "Fossil human remains from Kanam and Kanjera, Kenya Colony." *Nature* 138:643.

Leakey, L. S. B. 1951. *Olduvai Gorge: A report on the evolution of the hand-axe culture in Beds I-IV.* Cambridge: Cambridge University Press.

Leakey, L. S. B. 1952. "The Olorgesailie prehistoric site." In L. S. B. Leakey and S. Cole, eds., *Proceedings of the Pan-African congress of prehistory, Nairobi, 1947.* New York: Philosophical Library, p. 209.

Leakey, L. S. B. 1953. *Adam's ancestors.* London: Methuen.

Leakey, L. S. B. 1955. "The climatic sequence of the Pleistocene in East Africa." In L. Balout, ed., *Actes du Congrès Panafricain de Préhistoire II, Alger, 1952.* Paris: Arts et

Métiers Graphiques, pp. 293–294.

Leakey, L. S. B. 1959. "A new fossil skull from Olduvai." *Nature* 201:967–970.

Leakey, L. S. B. 1967. *Olduvai Gorge 1951–1961.* Cambridge: Cambridge University Press.

Leakey, L. S. B. 1974. *By the evidence: Memoirs, 1932–1951.* New York: Harcourt Brace Jovanovich.

Leakey, L. S. B., J. F. Evernden, and G. H. Curtis. 1961. "Age of Bed I, Olduvai Gorge, Tanganyika." *Nature* 191:478–479.

Leakey, L. S. B. and W. E. Owen. 1945. "A contribution to the study of the Tumbian culture in East Africa." *Coryndon Memorial Museum Occasional Paper 1.* Nairobi: Coryndon Museum.

Leakey, L. S. B. and J. D. Solomon. 1929. "East African archaeology." *Nature* 124:9.

Leakey, L. S. B., P. V. Tobias, and J. R. Napier. 1964. "A new species of the genus *Homo* from Olduvai Gorge." *Nature* 202:7–9.

Leakey, M. D. 1971. *Olduvai Gorge III: Excavations in Beds I and II 1960–1963.* Cambridge: Cambridge University Press.

Leakey, M. D. 1975. "Cultural patterns in the Olduvai sequence." In K. W. Butzer and G. Ll. Isaac, eds., *After the Australopithecines: Stratigraphy, ecology and culture change in the Middle Pleistocene.* The Hague: Mouton, pp. 477–493.

Leakey, M. D. 1994. *Olduvai Gorge V: Excavations in Beds III, IV, and the Masek Beds 1968–1971.* Cambridge: Cambridge University Press.

Leakey, M. D. and J. M. Harris. 1987. *Laetoli: A Pliocene site in Northern Tanzania.* Oxford: Oxford University Press.

Leakey, M. D. and R. L. Hay. 1979. "Pliocene footprints in the Laetolil Beds at Laetoli, northern Tanzania." *Nature* 278 (5702): 317–323.

Leakey, M. D., R. L. Hay, G. H. Curtis, R. E. Drake, M. K. Jackes, and T. D. White. 1976. "Fossil hominids from the Laetolil Beds." *Nature* 262 (5568): 460–466.

Leakey, M. D., R. L. Hay, D. L. Thurber, R. Protsch, and R. Berger. 1972. "Stratigraphy, archaeology, and age of the Ndutu and Naisiusiu Beds, Olduvai Gorge, Tanzania." *World Archaeology* 3 (3): 328–341.

Leakey, M. D., P. V. Tobias, J. E. Martyn, and R. E. F. Leakey. 1969. "An Acheulian industry with prepared core technique and the discovery of a contemporary hominid mandible at Lake Baringo, Kenya." *Proceedings of the Prehistoric Society* 3:48–76.

Leakey, M. E., C. S. Feibel, I. McDougall, and A. Walker. 1995. "New 4 million year old hominid species from Kanapoi and Allia Bay, Kenya." *Nature* 376 (6541): 565–571.

Leakey, M. E., F. Spoor, F. H. Brown, P. N. Gathogo, C. Kiarle, L. N. Leakey, and I. McDougall. 2001. "New hominin genus from eastern Africa shows diverse Middle Pliocene lineages." *Nature* 410 (6827): 433–440.

Leakey, R. E. F. 1978. Introduction to *The fossil hominids and an introduction to their context, 1968–1974 of Koobi Fora research project.* Vol 1. by M. G. Leakey and R. E. F. Leakey, eds. Oxford: Clarendon Press, pp. 1–13.

Le Gros Clark, W. E. 1947. "Observations on the anatomy of the fossil Australopithecinae." *Journal of Anatomy* (London) 81:300–303.

Lévêque, F., A. M. Backer, and M. Guilbaud, eds. 1993. *Context of a late Neandertal: Implications of multidisciplinary research for the transition to Upper Palaeolithic adaptations at St. Césaire, Charente-Maritime, France. Monographs in World Archaeology* 16. Madison: Prehistory Press.

Lewin, R. 1987. *Bones of contention.* New York: Simon and Schuster.

Lewin, R. 1993. *The origin of modern humans.* New York: W. H. Freeman.

Lewontin, R. 1972. "The apportionment of human diversity." *Evolutionary Biology* 6:381–398.

Lieberman, D. 1995. "Testing hypotheses about recent human evolution from skulls: Integrating morphology, function, development, and phylogeny." *Current Anthropology* 36 (2): 159–197.

Lieberman, D. 1998. "Sphenoid shortening and the evolution of modern human cranial shape." *Nature* 393 (6681): 158–162.

Lieberman, D. E., B. M. McBratney, and G. Krovitz. 2002. "The evolution and development of cranial form in *Homo sapiens*." *Proceedings of the National Academy of Sciences* 99 (3): 1134–1139.

Lieberman, D. E. and J. Shea. 1994. "Behavioral differences between archaic and modern humans in the Levantine Mousterian." *American Anthropologist* 96 (2): 300–332.

Lieberman, P. 1989. "The origins of some aspects of human language and cognition." In P. Mellars and C. Stringer, eds., *The human revolution.* Princeton, NJ: Princeton University Press, pp. 391–414.

Lieberman, P. 1991. *Uniquely human: The evolution of speech, thought and selfless behavior.* Cambridge: Harvard University Press.

Lieberman, P. 1998. *Eve spoke: Human language and human evolution.* New York: Norton.

Lieberman, P., J. T. Laitman, J. S. Reidenberg, and P. J. Gannon. 1992. "Anatomy, physiology, acoustics and perception of speech: Essential elements in analysis of the evolution of human speech." *Journal of Human Evolution* 23 (6): 447–467.

Lindly, J. M. and G. A. Clark. 1990. "Symbolism and modern human origins." *Current Anthropology* 31 (3): 233–261.

Linnaeus, C. 1758. *Systema Naturae per Naturae Regna Tria, Secundum Classes, Ordines, Genera, Species cum Characteribus, Differentiis Synonymis, Locis.* 10th ed. Stockholm: Laurentii Sylvii.

Livingstone, D. A. 1975. "Late Quaternary climatic change in Africa." *Annual Review of Ecology and Systematics* 6:249–280.

Livingstone, F. 1964. "On the nonexistence of human races." In A. Montagu, ed., *Concept of race.* New York: Free Press, pp. 46–60.

Lombard, M. 2004. "Distribution patterns of organic residues on Middle Stone Age points from Sibudu Cave, Kwazulu-Natal, South Africa." *South African Archaeological Bulletin* 59 (180): 37–44.

Lombard, M. 2005. "Evidence of hunting and hafting during the Middle Stone Age at Sibudu Cave, Kwa-Zulu-Natal, South Africa: A multianalytical approach." *Journal of*

Human Evolution 48 (3): 279–300.

Lovejoy, O. 1981. "The origin of man." *Science* 211 (4480): 341–350.

Lubell, D. 1974. "The Fakhurian: A Late Paleolithic industry from Upper Egypt." *Papers of the Geological Society of Egypt* 58. Cairo: Geological Society of Egypt.

Lubell, D. and P. Sheppard. 1997. "Northern African advanced foragers." In J. O. Vogel, ed., *Encyclopedia of precolonial Africa*. Walnut Creek: AltaMira Press, pp. 325–330.

Lubell, D., P. Sheppard, and M. Jackes. 1984. "Continuity in the Epipalaeolithic of Northern Africa with emphasis on the Maghreb." *Advances in World Prehistory* 3:143–191.

Lubbock, J. 1865. *Pre-historic times: As illustrated by ancient remains, and the manner and customs of modern savages.* London: Williams and Norgate.

Lubbock, J. 1969. *Prehistoric times: As illustrated by ancient remains, and the manner and customs of modern savages.* Reprint of 7th ed. (1913). Oosterhout: Anthropological Publications. (Orig. pub. 1865.)

Lucotte, G. 1989. "Evidence for the paternal ancestry of modern humans: Evidence from a Y-chromosome specific sequence polymorphic DNA probe." In P. Mellars and C. Stringer, eds., *The human revolution*. Princeton, NJ: Princeton University Press, pp. 39–46.

Lucotte, G. 1992. "African pygmies have the more ancestral gene pool when studied for Y-chromosome DNA haplotypes." In G. Bräuer and F. H. Smith, eds., *Continuity or replacement*. Rotterdam: A. A. Balkema, pp. 75–81.

Luyt, J., J. A. Lee-Thorp, and G. Avery. 2000. "New light on Middle Pleistocene west coast environments from Elandsfontein, Western Cape Province, South Africa." *South African Journal of Science* 96 (7): 399–403.

Lyell, C. 1830–1833. *Principles of geology, being an attempt to explain the former changes of the earth's surface by reference to causes now in operation.* 3 vols. London: John Murray.

Mabulla, A. Z. P. 1996. Middle and Later Stone Age land-use and lithic technology in the Eyasi Basin, Tanzania. PhD diss., University of Florida.

Macaulay, V., C. Hill, A. Achilli, C. Rengo, D. Clarke, W. Meehan, J. Blackburn, et al. 2005. "Single, rapid coastal settlement of Asia revealed by analysis of complete mitochondrial genomes." *Science* 308 (5724): 1034–1036.

Macchiarelli, R., L. Bondioli, M. Chech, A. Coppa, I. Fiore, R. Russom, F. Vecchi, Y. Libsekal, and L. Rook. 2004. "The Late Early Pleistocene human remains from Buia, Danakil Depression, Eritrea." *Revista Italiana di Paleontologia e Stratigrafia*. Suppl. no. 110:133–144.

MacDonald, K. 1997. "Western African and southern Saharan advanced foragers." In J. O. Vogel, ed., *Encyclopedia of precolonial Africa*. Walnut Creek: AltaMira Press, pp. 330–334.

Macdougall, D. 2004. *Frozen Earth: The once and future story of ice ages.* Berkeley: University of California Press.

Malan, B. D. 1957. "The term 'Middle Stone Age.'" In J. D. Clark, ed., *Proceedings of the third Pan-African congress on prehistory, Livingstone.* London: Chatto and Windus, pp. 223–227.

Malthus, T. 1798. *An essay on the principle of population, as it affects the future improvement of society.* London: J. Johnson.

Mandel, R. D. and A. H. Simmons. 2001. "Prehistoric occupation of Late Quaternary landscapes near Kharga Oasis, Western Desert of Egypt." *Geoarchaeology* 16 (1): 95–117.

Manzi, G., F. Mallegni, and A. Ascenzi. 2001. "A cranium for the earliest Europeans: Phylogenetic position of the hominid from Ceprano, Italy." *Proceedings of the National Academy of Sciences* 98 (17): 10011–10016.

Manzi, G., E. Bruner, and P. Passarello. 2003. "The one-million-year old *Homo* cranium from Bouri (Ethiopia): A reconsideration of its *H. erectus* affinities." *Journal of Human Evolution* 44 (6): 731–736.

Marcus, G. F. and S. E. Fisher. 2003. "FOXP2 in focus: What can genes tell us about speech and language?" *Trends in Cognitive Sciences* 7 (6): 257–262.

Marean, C. W. 1997. "Hunter-gatherer foraging strategies in tropical grasslands: Model building and testing in the East African Middle and Later Stone Age." *Journal of Anthropological Archaeology* 16 (3): 189–225.

Marean, C. W. 2000. "The Middle Stone Age at Die Kelders Cave 1, South Africa." *Journal of Human Evolution* 38 (1): 3–5.

Marean, C. W., Y. Abe, C. J. Frey, and R. C. Randall. 2000. "Zooarchaeological and taphonomic analysis of the Die Kelders Cave 1 layers 10 and 11 Middle Stone Age larger mammal fauna." *Journal of Human Evolution* 38 (1): 197–233.

Marean, C. W. and Z. Assefa. 2005. "The Middle and Upper Pleistocene African record for the biological and behavioral origins of modern humans." In A. Stahl, ed., *African archaeology: A critical introduction.* Oxford: Blackwell, pp. 93–129.

Marean, C. W., P. Goldberg, G. Avery, F. E. Grine, and R. G. Klein. 2000. "Middle Stone Age stratigraphy and excavations at Die Kelders Cave 1 (Western Cape Province, South Africa): The 1992, 1993 and 1995 field seasons." *Journal of Human Evolution* 38 (1): 7–42.

Marean, C. W., P. J. Nilssen, K. Brown, A. Jerardino, and D. Stynder. 2004. "Paleoanthropological investigations of Middle Stone Age sites at Pinnacle Point, Mossel Bay (South Africa): Archaeology and hominid remains from the 2000 field season." *Paleoanthropology* (July): 14–83. http://www.paleoanthro.org.

Marks, A. E. 1983. "The Middle to Upper Paleolithic transition in the Levant." *Advances in World Archaeology* 2:51–98.

Marks, A. E. 1990. "The Middle and Upper Palaeolithic in the Near East and the Nile Valley: The problem of cultural transformation." In P. Mellars, ed., *The emergence of modern humans: An archaeological perspective.* Ithaca: Cornell University Press, pp. 56–80.

Marks, A. E. 1992. "Upper Pleistocene archaeology and the origins of modern man." In T. Akazawa, K. Aoki, and T. Kimura, eds., *The evolution and dispersal of modern humans in Asia.* Tokyo: Hokusen-sha, pp. 229–251.

Marks, A. E., J. Phillips, H. Crew, and C. R. Ferring. 1971. "Prehistoric sites near En-Avdat in the Negev." *Israel Exploration Journal* 21:13–24.

Marks, A. E. and P. W. Volkman. 1983. "Changing core reduction strategies: A technological shift from the Middle to the Upper Palaeolithic in the southern Levant." In E. Trinkaus, ed., "The Mousterian legacy." *BAR International Series* 164:13–33.

Marks, J. M. 1995. *Human biodiversity*. New York: Aldine de Gruyter.

Marks, J. M. 2002. *What it means to be 98% chimpanzee: Apes, people and their genes.* Berkeley: University of California Press.

Marotzke, J. 2000. "Abrupt climate change and thermohaline circulation: Mechanisms and predictability." *Proceedings of the National Academy of Sciences* 97 (4): 1347–1350.

Martini, F., Y. Libsekal, O. Filippi, A. Ghebre/her, H. Kashay, A. Kiros, G. Martino, et al. 2004. "Characterization of lithic complexes from Buia Dandiero Basin, Danakil Depression, Eritrea." *Revista Italiana di Paleontologia e Stratigrafia.* Suppl. no. 110: 99–132.

Mason, R. J. 1962. *Prehistory of the Transvaal.* Johannesburg: Witwatersrand University Press.

Mayr, E. 1942. *Systematics and the origin of species.* New York: Columbia University Press.

McBrearty, S. 1981. "Songhor: A Middle Stone Age site in Western Kenya." *Quaternaria* 23:171–190.

McBrearty, S. 1986. The archaeology of the Muguruk site, Western Kenya. PhD diss., University of Illinois at Urbana-Champaign.

McBrearty, S. 1988. "The Sangoan-Lupemban and MSA sequences at the Muguruk site, Western Kenya." *World Archaeology* 19 (3): 388–420.

McBrearty, S. 1991. "Recent research in Western Kenya and its implications for the status of the Sangoan industry." In J. D. Clark, ed., *Cultural beginnings.* Bonn: Dr. Rudolf Habelt GMBH, pp. 159–176.

McBrearty, S. 1992. "Sangoan technology and habitat at Simbi." *Nyame Akuma* 38:34–40.

McBrearty, S. 1993. "Reconstructing the environmental conditions surrounding the appearance of modern humans in East Africa." In R. Jamieson, S. Abonyi, and N. Mirau, eds., *Culture and environment: A fragile coexistence.* Calgary: Chacmool Archaeological Association, pp. 145–154.

McBrearty, S. 1999. "The archaeology of the Kapthurin Formation." In P. Andrews and P. Banham, eds., *Late Cenozoic environments and Hominid evolution: A tribute to Bill Bishop.* London: Geological Society, pp. 143–156.

McBrearty, S. 2001. "The Middle Pleistocene of East Africa." In L. Barham and K. Robson-Brown, eds., *Human roots: Africa and Asia in the Middle Pleistocene.* Bristol: Western Academic and Specialist Press, pp. 81–98.

McBrearty, S., L. Bishop, and J. Kingston. 1996. "Variability in traces of Middle Pleistocene hominid behavior in the Kapthurin Formation, Baringo, Kenya." *Journal of Human Evolution* 30 (6): 563–580.

McBrearty, S. and A. S. Brooks. 2000. "The revolution that wasn't: A new interpretation of the origin of modern human behavior." *Journal of Human Evolution* 39 (5): 453–563.

McBrearty, S., S. A. C. Waane, and T. Wynn. 1982. "Mbeya Region archaeological survey." *Tanzania Notes and Records* 88/89:15–32.

McBrearty, S., T. Wynn, and S. A. C. Waane. 1984. "Archaeological survey in Mbeya Region, Southern Tanzania." *Azania* 19:128–132.

McBurney, C. B. M. 1967. *The Haua Fteah (Cyrenaica) and the Stone Age of the southeast Mediterranean.* Cambridge: Cambridge University Press.

McBurney, C. B. M., J. C. Trevor, and L. H. Wells. 1953a. "A fossil human mandible from a Levalloiso-Mousterian horizon in Cyrenaica." *Nature* 172:889–892.

McBurney, C. B. M., J. C. Trevor, and L. H. Wells. 1953b. "The Haua Fteah fossil jaw." *Journal of the Royal Anthropological Institute* 83:71.

McCown, T. D. and A. Keith. 1937. *The Stone Age of Mount Carmel 2: The fossil human remains from the Levalloiso-Mousterian.* Oxford: Clarendon Press.

McDermott, F., R. Grün, C. B. Stringer, and C. J. Hawkesworth. 1993. "Mass spectrometric Uranium-series dates for Israeli Neanderthal/early modern hominid sites." *Nature* 363 (6426): 252–255.

McDermott, F., C. Stringer, R. Grün, C. T. Williams, V. K. Din, and C .J. Hawkesworth. 1996. "New Late-Pleistocene uranium-thorium and ESR dates for the Singa hominid (Sudan)." *Journal of Human Evolution* 31 (6): 507–516.

McDonald, M. M. A. 2005. Personal communication.

McDougall, I., F. H. Brown, and J. G. Fleagle. 2004. "Stratigraphic placement and age of modern humans from Kibish, Ethiopia." *Nature* 433 (7027): 733–736.

McManus, J. F. 2004. "A great grand-daddy of ice cores." *Nature* 429 (6992): 611–612.

Mehlman, M. J. 1979. "Mumba-Höhle revisited: The relevance of a forgotten excavation to some current issues in East African prehistory." *World Archaeology* 11:80–94.

Mehlman, M. J. 1987. "Provenience, age and associations of archaic *Homo sapiens* crania from Lake Eyasi, Tanzania." *Journal of Archaeological Science* 14 (2): 133–162.

Mehlman, M. J. 1989. *Later Quaternary archaeological sequences in Northern Tanzania.* PhD diss., University of Illinois, Urbana.

Mehlman, M. J. 1991. "Context for the emergence of modern man in eastern Africa: Some new Tanzanian evidence." In J. D. Clark, ed., *Cultural beginnings.* Bonn: Dr. Rudolf Habelt GMBH, pp. 177–196.

Mekel-Bobrov, N., S. L. Gilbert, P. D. Evans, E. J. Vallender, J. R. Anderson, R. R. Hudson, S. A. Tishkoff, and B. T. Lahn. 2005. "Ongoing adaptive evolution of ASPM, a brain size determinant in *Homo sapiens.*" *Science* 309 (5741): 1720–1722.

Mellars, P. 1973. "The character of the Middle-Upper Palaeolithic transition in south-western France." In C. Renfrew, ed., *The explanation of culture change: Models in prehistory.* London: Duckworth, pp. 255–276.

Mellars, P. 1989. "Technological changes across the Middle-Upper Palaeolithic transition: Economic, social and cognitive perspectives." In P. Mellars and C.

Stringer, eds., *The human revolution*. Princeton, NJ: Princeton University Press, pp. 338–365.

Mellars, P. 1991. "Cognitive changes and the emergence of modern humans." *Cambridge Archaeological Journal* 1 (1): 63–76.

Mellars, P. 1993. "Archaeology and the population-dispersal hypothesis of modern human origins in Europe." In M. J. Aitken, C. B. Stringer, and P. A. Mellars, eds., *The origin of modern humans and the impact of chronometric dating*. Princeton, NJ: Princeton University Press, pp. 196–216.

Mellars, P. 1996. *The Neanderthal legacy: An archaeological perspective from Western Europe*. Princeton, NJ: Princeton University Press.

Mellars, P. 2002. "Archaeology and the origins of modern humans: European and African perspectives." In T. J. Crow, ed., *The speciation of modern Homo sapiens. Proceedings of the British Academy* 106. Oxford: Oxford University Press, pp. 31–47.

Mellars, P. 2004. "Neanderthals and the modern human colonization of Europe." *Nature* 432 (7016): 461–465.

Mellars, P. 2005. "The impossible coincidence. A single-species model for the origins of modern human behavior in Europe." *Evolutionary Anthropology* 14 (1): 12–27.

Mellars, P. 2006. "A new radiocarbon revolution and the dispersal of modern humans in Eurasia." *Nature* 439 (7079): 931–935.

Mellars, P., ed. 1990. *The emergence of modern humans: An archaeological perspective*. Ithaca: Cornell University Press.

Mellars, P. A., M. J. Aitken, and C. B. Stringer. 1993. "Outlining the problem." In *The origin of modern humans and the impact of chronometric dating*. Princeton, NJ: Princeton University Press, pp. 3–11.

Mellars, P. and C. B. Stringer, eds. 1989. *The human revolution: Behavioural and biological perspectives on the origins of modern humans*. Princeton, NJ: Princeton University Press.

Mercader, J. 2002. "Forest people: The role of African rainforests in human evolution and dispersal." *Evolutionary Anthropology* 11 (3): 117–124.

Mercader, J. 2003a. "Introduction—The Paleolithic settlement of rain forests." In J. Mercader, ed., *Under the canopy: The archaeology of tropical rain forests*. New Brunswick: Rutgers University Press, pp. 1–31.

Mercader, J. 2003b. "Foragers of the Congo—The early settlement of the Ituri forest." In J. Mercader, ed., *Under the canopy: The archaeology of tropical rain forests*. New Brunswick: Rutgers University Press, pp. 93–116.

Mercader, J. and A. Brooks. 2001. "Across forests and savannas: Later Stone Age assemblages from Ituri and Semliki, Democratic Republic of Congo." *Journal of Anthropological Research* 57 (2): 197–217.

Mercader, J. and R. Marti. 1999a. "Middle Stone Age site in the tropical forests of Equatorial Guinea." *Nyame Akuma* 51:14–24.

Mercader, J. and R. Marti.1999b. "Archaeology in the tropical forest of Banyang-Mbo, SW Cameroon." *Nyame Akuma* 52:17–24.

Mercader, J. and R. Marti. 2003. "The Middle Stone Age occupation of Atlantic central Africa—New evidence from Equatorial Guinea and Cameroon." In J. Mercader, ed., *Under the canopy: The archaeology of tropical rain forests.* New Brunswick: Rutgers University Press, pp. 64–92.

Mercader, J., R. Marti, I. J. Gonzalez, A. Sanchez, and P. Garcia. 2003. "Archaeological site formation in rain forests: Insights from the Ituri Rock Shelters, Congo." *Journal of Archaeological Science* 30 (1): 45–65.

Mercader, J., R. Marti, J. L. Martinez, and A. Brooks. 2002. "The nature of 'stone-lines' in the African Quaternary record: Archaeological resolution at the rainforest site of Mosumu, Equatorial Guinea." *Quaternary International* 89 (1): 71–96.

Mercader, J., F. Runge, L. Vrydaghs, H. Doutrepont, C. E. N. Ewango, and J. Juan-Tressera. 2000. "Phytoliths from archaeological sites in the tropical forest of Ituri, Democratic Republic of Congo." *Quaternary Research* 54 (1): 102–112.

Mercier, N., J. Valladas, O. Bar-Yosef, B. Vandermeersch, C. Stringer, and J. L. Joron. 1993. "Thermoluminescence date for the Mousterian burial site of es-Skhūl, Mt. Carmel." *Journal of Archaeological Science* 20 (2): 169–174.

Mercier, N., H. Valladas, L. Froget, J. L. Joron, P. M. Vermeersch, Pm. Van Peer, and J. Moeyersons. 1999. "Thermoluminescence dating of a Middle Palaeolithic occupation at Sodmein Cave, Red Sea Mountains (Egypt)." *Journal of Archaeological Science* 26 (11): 1339–1345.

Merrick, H. V. 1975. Change in Later Pleistocene lithic industries in Eastern Africa. PhD diss., University of California at Berkeley.

Merrick, H. V. 1976. "Recent archaeological research in the Plio-Pleistocene deposits of the Lower Omo Valley, Southwestern Ethiopia." In G. Ll. Isaac and E. McCown, eds., *Human origins.* Menlo Park: W. A. Benjamin, pp. 461–481.

Merrick, H. V. and F. H. Brown. 1984. "Obsidian sources and patterns of source utilization in Kenya and northern Tanzania: Some initial findings." *African Archaeological Review* 2:129–152.

Merrick, H. V., F. H. Brown, and W. P. Nash. 1994. "Use and movement of obsidian in the Early and Middle Stone Ages of Kenya and northern Tanzania." In S. T. Childs, ed., "Society, culture and technology in Africa." *MASCA* Suppl. no. 11:29–44.

Merrick, H. V. and J. P. S. Merrick. 1976. "Archaeological occurrences of earlier Pleistocene age, from the Shungura Formation." In Y. Coppens, F. C. Howell, G. Ll. Isaac, and R. E. F. Leakey, eds., *Earliest man and environments in the Lake Rudolf Basin.* Chicago: University of Chicago Press, pp. 574–584.

Mikdad, A. and J. Eiwanger. 2000. "Recherches préhistoriques et protohistoriques dans le Rif oriental (Maroc): Rapport préliminaire." *Beiträge zue Allgemeinen und Vergleichenden Archäologie* 20:109–167.

Milankovitch, M. 1920. *Théorie mathématique des phénomènes thermiques produits per la radiation solaire.* Paris: Gauthier-Villars.

Milankovitch, M. 1941. *Kanon der Erdbestrahlung und seine Andwendung auf das Eiszeitenproblem.* Royal Serbian Academy Special Publication 133:1–633.

Milankovitch, M. 1969. *Canon of insolation and the Ice-Age problem.* Jerusalem: Israel Program for Scientfic Translations.

Miller, G. H. 1993. "Chronology of hominid occupation at Bir Tarfawi and Bir Sahara East based on the epimerization of isoleucine in ostrich eggshells." In F. Wendorf, R. Schild, A. E. Close, et al., *Egypt during the last interglacial: The Middle Paleolithic of Bir Tarfawi and Bir Sahara East.* New York: Plenum Press, pp. 241–251.

Miller, G. H., P. B. Beaumont, H. J. Deacon, A. S. Brooks, P. E. Hare, and A. J. T. Jull. 1999. "Earliest modern humans in southern Africa dated by isoleucine epimerization in ostrich eggshell." *Quaternary Science Reviews* 18 (13): 1537–1548.

Miller, G. H., P. B. Beaumont, A. J. T. Jull, and B. Johnson. 1993. "Pleistocene geochronology and palaeothermometry from protein diagenesis in ostrich eggshells: Implications for the evolution of modern humans." In M. J. Aitken, C. B. Stringer, and P. A. Mellars, *The origin of modern humans and the impact of chronometric dating.* Princeton, NJ: Princeton University Press, pp. 49–68.

Miller, S. F. 1969. The Nachikufan industries of the Later Stone Age in Zambia. PhD diss., University of California, Berkeley.

Miller, S. F. 1971. "The age of Nachikufan industries in Zambia." *South African Archaeological Bulletin* 26 (103/104): 143–146.

Milo, R. G. 1998. "Evidence for hominid predation at Klasies River Mouth, South Africa, and its implications for the behaviour of early modern humans." *Journal of Archaeological Science* 25 (2): 99–133.

Milo, R. and D. Quiatt. 1993. "Glottogenesis and anatomically modern *Homo sapiens*: The evidence for and implications of the late origin of vocal language." *Current Anthropology* 34 (5): 569–598.

Milo, R. and D. Quiatt. 1994. "Language in the Middle and Late Stone Ages: Glottogenesis in anatomically modern *Homo sapiens*." In D. Quiatt and J. Itani, eds., *Hominid culture in primate perspective.* Niwot: University Press of Colorado, pp. 321–339.

Mitchell, P. J. 1990. "A palaeoecological model for archaeological site distribution in southern Africa during the Upper Pleniglacial and Late Glacial." In C. Gamble and O. Soffer, eds., *The world at 18,000 BP: Low latitudes.* Vol. 2. London: Unwin Hyman, pp. 189–205.

Mitchell, P. J. 1992. "Archaeological research in Lesotho: A review of 120 years." *African Archaeological Review* 10:3–34.

Mitchell, P. J. 1996. "Late Quaternary landscape at Sehonghong, Lesotho highlands, southern Africa." *Antiquity* 70 (269): 623–638.

Mitchell, P. J. 1997a. "Southern African advanced foragers." In J. O. Vogel, ed., *Encyclopedia of precolonial Africa.* Walnut Creek: AltaMira Press, pp. 341–346.

Mitchell, P. J. 1997b. "Holocene Later Stone Age hunter-gatherers south of the Limpopo River, ca. 10,000–2000 BP." *Journal of World Prehistory* 11 (4): 339–424.

Mitchell, P. J. 2002a. *The archaeology of Southern Africa.* Cambridge: Cambridge University Press.

Mitchell, P. J. 2002b. "Hunter-gatherer archaeology in southern Africa: Recent research, future trends." *Before Farming* 1 (3): 1–18. http://www.waspress.co.uk/journals/beforefarming.

Mitchell, P. J., R. Yates, and J. Parkington. 1996. "Africa at the transition." In L. Straus, B. Eriksen, J. Erlandson, and D. Yesner, eds., *Humans at the end of the Ice Age: The archaeology of the Pleistocene-Holocene boundary.* New York: Plenum Press, pp. 15–41.

Moeyersons, J. 1997. "Geomorphological processes and their palaeoenvironmental significance at the Shum Laka cave (Bamenda, western Cameroon)." *Palaeogeography, Palaeoclimatology, Palaeoecology* 133 (1/2): 103–116.

Moeyersons, J., P. M. Vermeersch, and P. Van Peer. 2002. "Dry cave deposits and their palaeoenvironmental significance during the last 115 ka, Sodmein Cave, Red Sea Mountains, Egypt." *Quaternary Science Reviews* 21 (7): 837–851.

Mohamed, A. A. B. 1992. "Three Middle Palaeolithic assemblages from central Sudan: A comparative study." In J. Sterner and N. David, eds., *An African commitment: Papers in honour of P. L. Shinnie.* Calgary: University of Calgary Press, pp. 71–84.

Moore, P. D. 1998. "Did forests survive the cold in a hotspot?" *Nature* 391 (6663): 124–125.

Morgan, L. H. 1877. *Ancient society.* New York: Holt.

Morell, V. 1995. *Ancestral passions: The Leakey family and the quest for humankind's beginnings.* New York: Simon and Schuster.

Morley, C. K., S. M. Cunningham, R. M. Harper, and W. A. Wescott. 1992. "Geology and geophysics of the Rukwa Rift, East Africa." *Tectonics* 11 (1): 69–81.

Morris, A. G., I. Ribot, and F. E. Grine. 2005. "A nearly complete human cranium from the MSA/LSA transition in Southern Africa." Paper presented at the 12th Congress of the Pan African Archaeological Association for Prehistory and Related Studies, Gaborone, Botswana.

Morwood, M. J., F. Aziz, Nasruddin, D. R. Hobbs, P. O'Sullivan, and A. Raza. 1999. "Archaeological and palaeontological research in central Flores, east Indonesia: results of fieldwork 1997–1998." *Antiquity* 73 (280): 273–286.

Morwood, M. J., P. Brown, Jatmiko, T. Sutikna, E. W. Saptomo, K. E. Westaway, R. A. Due, et al. 2005. "Further evidence for small-bodied hominins from the Late Pleistocene of Flores, Indonesia." *Nature* 437 (7061): 1012–1017.

Morwood, M. J., P. B. O'Sullivan, F. Aziz, and A. Raza. 1998. "Fission-track ages of stone tools and fossils on the east Indonesian island of Flores." *Nature* 392 (6672): 173–176.

Morwood, M. J., R. P. Soejano, R. G. Roberts, T. Sutikna, C. S. M. Turney, K. E. Westaway, W. J. Rink, et al. 2004. "Archaeology and age of a new hominin from Flores in eastern Indonesia." *Nature* 431 (7012): 1087–1091.

Mountain, J. L., A. A. Lin, A. M. Bowcock, and L. L. Cavalli-Sforza. 1993. "Evolution of modern humans: Evidence from nuclear DNA polymorphisms." In M. J. Aitken, C. B. Stringer, and P. A. Mellars, eds., *The origin of modern humans and the impact of chronometric dating.* Princeton, NJ: Princeton University Press, pp. 69–83.

Movius, H. L. 1944. "The Lower Palaeolithic cultures of Southern and Eastern Asia." *Transactions of the American Philosophical Society* 38 (4): 329–420.

Mturi, A. A. 1976. "New hominid from Lake Ndutu, Tanzania." *Nature* 262: 484–485.

Murdock, G. P. 1959. *Africa: Its peoples and their culture history.* New York: McGraw Hill.

Murphy, M. L. 1999. Changing human behavior: The contribution of the White Paintings Rock Shelter to an understanding of changing lithic reduction, raw material exchange, and hunter-gatherer mobility in the interior regions of southern Africa during the Middle and early Late Stone Age. PhD diss., Michigan State University.

Murrill, R. I. 1981. *Petralona Man.* Springfield: Charles C. Thomas.

Nelson, C. 1971. "A standardized site enumeration system for the continent of Africa." *Bulletin of the Pan African Committee on Nomenclature and Terminology* 4:6–12.

Nitecki, M. H. and D. V. Nitecki, eds. 1994. *Origins of anatomically modern humans.* New York: Plenum Press.

Noble, W. and I. Davidson. 1996. *Human evolution, language and mind.* Cambridge: Cambridge University Press.

Oakley, K. 1970. "Analytical methods of dating bones." In D. Brothwell and E. Higgs, eds., *Science in archaeology.* New York: Praeger, pp. 24–34.

O'Brian, P. 1980. *The fortune of war.* London: Fontana/Collins.

O'Brien, T. P. 1939. *The prehistory of Uganda protectorate.* Cambridge: Cambridge University Press.

O'Rourke, D., M. G. Hayes, and S. W. Carlyle. 2000. "Ancient DNA studies in physical anthropology." *Annual Review of Anthropology* 29:217–242.

Olson, P. 2002. "The disappearing dipole." *Nature* 418 (6881): 591–594.

Omoto, K. and P. V. Tobias, eds. 1998. *The origins and past of modern humans.* Singapore: World Scientific.

Orscheidt, J. and G.-C. Weniger, eds. 2001. *Neanderthals and modern humans: Discussing the transition. Central and Eastern Europe from 50,000 to 30,000 BP.* Mettmann: Neanderthal Museum.

Ovchinnikov, I. G., A. Gotherstrom, F. P. Romanova, V. M. Kharitonov, K. Liden, and W. Goodwin. 2000. "Molecular analysis of Neanderthal DNA from the northern Caucasus." *Nature* 404 (6777): 490–493.

Pääbo, S. 2003. "The mosaic that is our genome." *Nature* 421 (6921): 409–412.

Pakenham, T. 1991. *The scramble for Africa, 1876–1912.* New York: Random House.

Parkington, J. 1990. "A view from the south: Southern Africa before, during, and after the Last Glacial Maximum." In C. Gamble and O. Soffer, eds., *The world at 18,000 BP: Low latitudes.* Vol 2. London: Unwin Hyman, pp. 214–228.

Parkington, J. 1999. "Western Cape landscapes." In J. Coles, R. Bewley, and P. Mellars, eds., "World prehistory: Studies in memory of Grahame Clark." *Proceedings of the National Academy* 99:25–35.

Partridge, T. C. 1997. "Cainozoic environmental change in Southern Africa, with special emphasis on the last 200,000 years." *Progress in Physical Geography* 21 (1): 3–22.

Partridge, T. C., P. B. deMenocal, S. A. Lorentz, M. J. Paiker, and J. C. Vogel. 1997. "Orbital forcing of climate over South Africa: A 200,000 year rainfall record from the Pretoria Saltpan." *Quaternary Science Reviews* 16:1125–1133.

Pearl, F. B. 2001. Late Pleistocene archaeological and geoarchaeological investigations in the Mukogodo Hills and Ewaso Ng'iro Plains of central Kenya. PhD diss., Texas A and M University.

Pearl, F. B. and D. B. Dickson. 2004. "Geoarchaeology and prehistory of the Kipsing and Tol River watersheds in the Mukogodo Hills region of Central Kenya." *Geoarchaeology* 19 (6): 565–582.

Pearson, O. M. 2000a. "Activity, climate, and postcranial robusticity: Implications for modern human origins and scenarios of adaptive change." *Current Anthropology* 41 (4): 569–607.

Pearson, O. M. 2000b. "Postcranial remains and the origin of modern humans." *Evolutionary Anthropology* 9 (6): 229–247.

Pearson, O. M. 2004. "Has the combination of genetic and fossil evidence solved the riddle of modern human origins?" *Evolutionary Anthropology* 13 (4): 145–159.

Penck, A., and E. Brückner. 1909. *Die Alpen im Eiszeitalter.* Vols 1–3. Leipzig: Tauchnitz.

Pericot y Garcia, L. 1942. *La Cueva del Parpalló (Gandia): Excavaciones del Servicio de investigación prehistórica de la excma.* Madrid.

Pfeiffer, J. E. 1982. *The creative explosion.* New York: Harper & Row.

Phillipson, D. R. 1976. *Prehistory of Eastern Zambia.* Nairobi: British Institute in Eastern Africa.

Phillipson, D. R. 1993. *African archaeology.* 2nd ed. Cambridge: Cambridge University Press.

Pickford, M. and B. Senut. 2001. "The geological and faunal context of Late Miocene hominid remains from Lukeino, Kenya." *Comptes rendus de l'academie de Paris: Sciences de la terre et des planètes* 332:145–152.

Piggott, S. 1976. *Ruins in a landscape.* Edinburgh: Edinburgh University Press.

Piggott, S. 1981. "Vast perennial memorials." In J. D. Evans, B. W. Cunliffe, and C. Renfrew, eds., *Antiquity and man: Essays in honour of Glyn Daniel.* London: Thames and Hudson, pp. 19–25.

Pilbeam, D. R. 1980. "Major trends in human evolution." In L. K. Konigsson, ed., *Current argument on early man.* Oxford: Pergamon Press, pp. 261–285.

Pilbeam, D. R. 1982. "New hominoid skull material from the Miocene of Pakistan." *Nature* 295:232–234.

Pilbeam, D. R. 1986. "Hominoid evolution and hominoid origins." *American Anthropologist* 88 (2): 295–312.

Pillans, B. and T. Naish. 2004. "Defining the Quaternary." *Quaternary Science Reviews* 23 (23/24): 2271–2282.

Pinhasi, R. and R. Semal. 2000. "The position of the Nazlet Khater specimen among prehistoric and modern African and Levantine populations." *Journal of Human Evolution* 39 (3): 269–288.

Pleurdeau, D. 2003. "Le Middle Stone Age de la grotte de Porc-Epic (Dire Dawa, Ethiopie)." *L'Anthropologie* 107 (1): 15–48.

Plummer, T., L. C. Bishop, P. Ditchfield, and J. Hicks. 1999. "Research on Late Pliocene Oldowan sites at Kanjera South, Kenya." *Journal of Human Evolution* 36 (2): 151–170.

Poirier, F. 1977. *Fossil evidence: The human evolutionary journey.* 2nd ed. St. Louis: C. V. Mosby.

Porat, N., M. Chazan, H. Schwarcz, and L. K. Horwitz. 2002. "Timing of the Lower to Middle Paleolithic boundary: New dates from the Levant." *Journal of Human Evolution* 43 (1): 107–122.

Posnansky, M. 1967. "Wayland as an archaeologist." *Uganda Journal* 31:9–12.

Posnansky, M. 1970. "African prehistory and geographical determinism." In K. C. Edwards, R. H. Osborne, F. A. Barnes, and J. C. Doomkamp, eds., *Geographical essays in honour of Professor K. C. Edwards.* Nottingham: Department of Geography, University of Nottingham, pp. 215–223.

Potts, R. 1998. "Environmental hypotheses of hominin evolution." *Yearbook of Physical Anthropology* 41:93–136.

Potts, R. 2001. "Mid Pleistocene environmental change and human evolution." In L. Barham and K. Robson-Brown, eds., *Human roots: Africa and Asia in the Middle Pleistocene.* Bristol: Western Academic and Specialist Press, pp. 5–21.

Potts, R., A. K. Behrensmeyer, A. Deino, P. Ditchfield, and J. Clark. 2004. "Small Mid-Pleistocene hominin associated with East African Acheulean technology." *Science* 305 (5680): 75–79.

Proctor, R. N. 2003. "Three roots of human recency: Molecular anthropology, the refigured Acheulean and the UNESCO response to Auschwitz." *Current Anthropology* 41 (2): 213–239.

Pwiti, G. 2005. "Southern Africa and the East African coast." In A. Stahl, ed., *African archaeology: A critical introduction.* Oxford: Blackwell, pp. 378–391.

Quickert, N. A., D. I. Godfrey-Smith, and J. L. Casey. 2003. "Optical and thermoluminescence dating of Middle Stone Age and Kintampo bearing sediments at Birimi, a multi-component archaeological site in Ghana." *Quaternary Science Reviews* 22 (10–13): 1291–1297.

Quintana-Murci, L., O. Semino, H.-J. Bandelt, G. Pasarino, K. McElreavey, and A. S. Santachiara-Benerecetti. 1999. "Genetic evidence of an early exit of *Homo sapiens sapiens* from Africa through eastern Africa." *Nature Genetics* 23 (4): 437–441.

Rahmani, N. 2004. "Technological and cultural change among the last hunter-gatherers of the Maghreb: The Capsian (10,000–6,000 BP)." *Journal of World Prehistory* 18 (1): 57–105.

Rak, Y. 1990. "On the differences between two pelvises of Mousterian context from the Qafzeh and Kebara Caves, Israel." *American Journal of Physical Anthropology* 81 (3): 323–332.

Rak, Y. 1998. "Does any Mousterian cave present evidence of two hominid species?" In T. Akazawa, K. Aoki, and O. Bar-Yosef, eds., *Neandertals and modern humans in*

West Asia. New York: Plenum Press.

Ramachandran, S., O. Deshpande, C. C. Roseman, N. A. Rosenberg, M. W. Feldman, and L. L. Cavalli-Sforza. 2005. "Support from the relationship of genetic and geographic distance in human populations for a serial founder effect originating in Africa." *Proceedings of the National Academy of Sciences* 102 (44): 15942–15947.

Rampino, M. R. and S. H. Ambrose. 2000. "Volcanic winter in the Garden of Eden: The Toba supereruption and the Late Pleistocene human populations crash." In F. W. McCoy and G. Heiken, eds., *Volcanic hazards and disasters in human antiquity.* Special Publication 345. Boulder: Geological Society of America, pp. 71–82.

Rampino, M. R. and S. Self. 1992. "Volcanic winter and accelerated glaciation following the Toba super-eruption." *Nature* 359 (6390): 50–52.

Rasse, M., S. Soriano, C. Tribolo, S. Stokes, and E. Huseycom. 2004. "La sequence pléistocène supérieur d'Ounjougou (Pays Dogon, Afrique de l'Ouest): Évolution géomorphologique, enregistrements sédimentaires et changements culturels." *Quaternaire* 15 (4): 329–341.

Raynal, J.-P., F. Z. S. Alaoui, D. Geraads, L. Magoga, and A. Mohi. 2001. "The earliest occupation of North Africa: The Moroccan perspective." *Quaternary International* 75 (1): 65–75.

Raynal, J.-P., L. Magoga, F. Z. Sbihi-Alaoui, and D. Geraads. 1995. "The earliest occupation of Atlantic Morocco: The Casablanca evidence." In W. Roebroeks and T. Van Kolfschoten, eds., *The earliest occupation of Europe.* Leiden: University of Leiden Press, pp. 255–262.

Reck, H. and L. Kohl-Larson. 1936. "Erster Uberbuch über die jungdiluvialen Tier- und Menschfunde Dr. Kohl-Larson's in nordöstlichen Teil des Njarasa—Grabens (Ostafrika)." *Geologische Rundschau* 27:401–441.

Reed, D. L., V. S. Smith, S. L. Hammond, A. R. Rogers, and D. H. Clayton. 2004. "Genetic analysis of lice supports direct contact between modern and archaic humans." *Public Library of Science Biology* 2 (11): e340.

Relethford, J. H. 1994. "Craniometric variation among modern human populations." *American Journal of Physical Anthropology* 95 (1): 53–62.

Relethford, J. H. 2001. *Genetics and the search for modern human origins.* New York: Wiley-Liss.

Relethford, J. H. 2002. "Apportionment of global human genetic diversity based on craniometrics and skin color." *American Journal of Physical Anthropology* 118 (4): 393–398.

Relethford, J. H. and H. Harpending. 1994. "Craniometric variation, genetic theory, and modern human origins." *American Journal of Physical Anthropology* 95 (3): 249–270.

Renfrew, C. 1973. *Before civilization: The radiocarbon revolution and prehistoric Europe.* London: Jonathan Cape.

Renfrew, C. and P. Bahn. 2000. *Archaeology: Theories, methods, and practice.* 3rd ed. London: Thames and Hudson.

Renne, P. R., W. D. Sharp, A. L. Deino, G. Orsi, and L. Civetta. 1997. "^{40}Ar/^{39}Ar dating into this historical realm: Calibration against Pliny the Younger." *Science* 277 (5330): 1279–1280.

Reygasse, M. 1919–1920. "Etudes de Palethnologie Maghrébine (Nouvelle série)." *Rec. de Notes et Mémoires de la Société Archeologique de Constantine* 53.

Rightmire, G. P. 1983. "The Lake Ndutu cranium and early *Homo sapiens* in Africa." *American Journal of Physical Anthropology* 61:245–254.

Rightmire, G. P. 1984. "*Homo sapiens* in sub-Saharan Africa." In F. H. Smith and F. Spencer, eds., *The origins of modern humans.* New York: Alan R. Liss, pp. 295–325.

Rightmire, G. P. 1989. "Middle Stone Age humans from Eastern and Southern Africa." In P. Mellars and C. Stringer, eds., *The human revolution.* Princeton, NJ: Princeton University Press, pp. 109–122.

Rightmire, G. P. 1990. *The evolution of Homo erectus: Comparative anatomical studies of an extinct human species.* Cambridge: Cambridge University Press.

Rightmire, G. P. 1996. "The human cranium from Bodo, Ethiopia: Evidence for speciation in the Middle Pleistocene?" *Journal of Human Evolution* 31 (1): 21–39.

Rightmire, G. P. 1998a. "The first anatomically advanced humans from South Africa and the Levant." In K. Omoto and P. V. Tobias, eds., *The origins and past of modern humans.* Singapore: World Scientific, pp. 126–138.

Rightmire, G. P. 1998b. "Human evolution in the Middle Pleistocene: The role of *Homo heidelbergensis.*" *Evolutionary Anthropology* 6:218–227.

Rightmire, G. P. 2001a. "Diversity in the earliest modern populations from South Africa, Northern Africa and Southwest Asia." In P. V. Tobias, M. A. Raath, J. Moggi-Cecchi, and G. A. Doyle, eds., *Humanity from African naissance to coming millennia.* Florence: Firenze University Press, pp. 231–236.

Rightmire, G. P. 2001b. "Comparison of Middle Pleistocene hominids from Africa and Asia." In L. Barham and K. Robson-Brown, eds., *Human roots: Africa and Asia in the Middle Pleistocene.* Bristol: Western Academic and Specialist Press, pp. 123–134.

Rightmire, G. P. 2001c. "Patterns of hominid evolution and dispersal in the Middle Pleistocene." *Quaternary International* 75 (1): 77–84.

Rightmire, G. P. and H. Deacon. 1991. "Comparative studies of late Pleistocene human remains from Klasies River Mouth, South Africa." *Journal of Human Evolution* 20 (2): 131–156.

Rightmire, G. P. and H. Deacon. 2001. "New human teeth from Middle Stone Age deposits at Klasies River, South Africa." *Journal of Human Evolution* 41 (6): 535–544.

Rink, W. J., D. Richter, H. P. Schwarcz, A. E. Marks, K. Monigal, and D. Kaufman. 2003. "Age of the Middle Palaeolithic site of Rosh Ein Mor, Central Negev, Israel: Implications for the age range of the early Levantine Mousterian of the Levantine corridor." *Journal of Archaeological Science* 30 (2): 195–204.

Robbins, L. R. 1997. "Eastern African advanced foragers." In J. O. Vogel, ed., *Encyclopedia of precolonial Africa.* Walnut Creek: AltaMira Press, pp. 335–341.

Robbins, L. R. 1999. "Direct dating of ostrich eggshell in the Kalahari." *Nyame Akuma* 52:11–16.

Robbins, L. and M. L. Murphy. 1998. "The Early and Middle Stone Age." In P. Lane, A. Reid, and A. Segobye, eds., *Ditswa Mmung—The archaeology of Botswana.* Gaborone: Botswana Society and Pula Press, pp. 50–64.

Robbins, L. R., M. L. Murphy, G. A. Brook, A. H. Ivester, A. C. Campbell, R. G. Klein, R. G. Milo, K. M. Stewart, W. S. Downey, and N. J. Stevens. 2000. "Archaeology, palaeoenvironment, and chronology of the Tsodilo Hills White Paintings Rock Shelter, Northwest Kalahari Desert, Botswana." *Journal of Archaeological Science* 27 (11): 1085–1113.

Robbins, L., M. L. Murphy, N. J. Stevens, G. A. Brook, A. H. Ivester, K. A. Haberyan, R. G. Klein, et al. 1996. "Paleoenvironment and archaeology of Drotsky's Cave: Western Kalahari Desert, Botswana." *Journal of Archaeological Science* 23 (1): 7–22.

Robert, A., S. Soriano, M. Rasse, S. Stokes, and E. Huysecom. 2003. "First chrono-cultural reference framework for the West African Paleolithic: New data from Ounjougou, Dogon Country, Mali." *Journal of African Archaeology* 1 (2): 151–169.

Roberts, M. B., C. B. Stringer, and S. A. Parfitt. 1994. "A hominid tibia from Middle Pleistocene sediments at Boxgrove, UK." *Nature* 369 (6478): 311–313.

Roberts, N. 1984. "Pleistocene environments in time and space." In R. Foley, ed., *Hominid evolution and community ecology.* London: Academic Press, pp. 25–53.

Robertshaw, P. 1990a. "A history of African archaeology: An introduction." In *A history of African archaeology.* London: James Currey, pp. 3–12.

Robertshaw, P. 1990b. "The development of archaeology in East Africa." In *A history of African archaeology.* London: James Currey, pp. 78–94.

Robertshaw, P. 1995. "The last 200,000 years (or thereabouts) in Eastern Africa: Recent archaeological reports." *Journal of Archaeological Research* 3 (1): 55–86.

Robinson, J. T. 1953. "*Telanthropus* and its phylogenetic significance." *American Journal of Physical Anthropology* 11:445–501.

Robinson, R. E. and J. Gallagher. 1961. *Africa and the Victorians: The climax of imperialism in the dark continent.* New York: St. Martin's.

Roche, H., A. Delangse, J.-P. Brugal, C. Feibel, M. Kibunjia, V. Mourre, and P. J. Texier. 1999. "Early hominid stone tool production and technical skill 2.34 MYR ago in West Turkana, Kenya." *Nature* 399 (6731): 57–60.

Roe, D. 1994. "A metrical analysis of selected sets of handaxes and cleavers from Olduvai Gorge." In M. D. Leakey with D. Roe, eds., *Olduvai Gorge 5: Excavations in Beds III, IV, and the Masek Beds, 1968–1971.* Cambridge: Cambridge University Press, pp. 146–234.

Roe, D. 2001a. "The Kalambo Falls large cutting tools: A comparative metrical and statistical analysis." In J. D. Clark, ed., *Kalambo Falls prehistoric site III. The earlier cultures: Middle and Earlier Stone Age.* Cambridge: Cambridge University Press, pp. 492–599.

387387387387387387387387387387387387387387387387387387387387387387387387
387387387387387387387387387387387387387387387387387387387387387387387387
387387387387387387387387387387387387387387387387387387387387387387387387
387387387387387387387387387387387387387387387387387387387387387387387387

Roe, D. 2001b. "A view of the Kalambo Falls Early and Middle Stone Age assemblages in the context of the Old World Palaeolithic." In J. D. Clark, ed., *Kalambo Falls prehistoric site III. The earlier cultures: Middle and Earlier Stone Age*. Cambridge: Cambridge University Press, pp. 636–647.

Roebroeks, W. 2001. "Hominid behaviour and the earliest occupation of Europe: An exploration." *Journal of Human Evolution* 41 (5): 437–461.

Roebroeks, W. and R. Corbey. 2001. "Biases and double standards in palaeoanthropology." In *Studying human origins: Disciplinary history and epistemology*. Amsterdam: Amsterdam University Press, pp. 67–76.

Roebroeks, W. and T. van Kolfschoten. 1994. "The earliest occupation of Europe: A short chronology." *Antiquity* 68 (260): 489–503.

Roebroeks, W. and T. van Kolfschoten, eds. 1996. *The earliest occupation of Europe*. Leiden: University of Leiden.

Rogers, A. R. and H. Harpending. 1992. "Population growth makes waves in the distribution of pairwise genetic differences." *Molecular Biology and Evolution* 9:552–569.

Rognon, P. 1996. "Climatic change in the African desert between 130,000 and 10,000 bp." *Comptes rendus de l'Academie des Sciences* 323:549–561.

Rolland, N. 1998. "The Lower Palaeolithic settlement of Eurasia with special reference to Europe." In M. D. Petraglia and R. Korisettar, eds., *Early human behaviour in global context*. London: Routledge, pp. 187–230.

Rolland, N. 2001. "The initial peopling of Eurasia and the early occupation of Europe in its Afro-Asian context: Major issues and current perspectives." In S. Milliken and J. Cook, eds., *A very remote period indeed*. Oxford: Oxbow Books, pp. 78–94.

Rolland, N. and H. Dibble. 1990. "A new synthesis of Middle Palaeolithic variability." *American Antiquity* 55 (3): 480–499.

Rose, J. I. 2004a. "The question of Upper Pleistocene connections between East Africa and South Arabia." *Current Anthropology* 45 (4): 551–555.

Rose, J. I. 2004b. "New evidence for the expansion of an Upper Pleistocene population out of East Africa." *Cambridge Archaeological Journal* 14 (2): 205–216.

Rots, V. and P. Van Peer. 2006. "Early evidence of complexity in lithic economy: Core-axe production, hafting and use in Late Middle Pleistocene site 8-B-11, Sai Island (Sudan)." *Journal of Archaeological Science* 33 (3): 360–371.

Rudwick, M. J. S. 1976. *The meaning of fossils: Episodes in the history of palaeontology*. 2nd ed. Chicago: University of Chicago Press.

Ruse, M. 1979. *The Darwinian revolution: Science red in tooth and claw*. Chicago: University of Chicago Press.

Ruvolo, M. 1996. "A new approach to studying modern human origins: Hypothesis testing with coalescence time distributions." *Molecular Phylogenetics and Evolution* 5 (1): 202–219.

Ruvolo, M. 1997. "Genetic diversity in hominoid primates." *Annual Review of Anthropology* 26:515–540.

Sackett, J. R. 1977. "The meaning of style in archaeology: A general model." *American Antiquity* 42:369–380.

Sackett, J. R. 1981. "From de Mortillet to Bordes: A century of French Palaeolithic research." In G. Daniel, ed., *Towards a history of archaeology*. London: Thames and Hudson, pp. 85–99.

Sackett, J. R. 1982. "Approaches to style in lithic archaeology." *Journal of Anthropological Archaeology* 1 (1): 59–112.

Sackett, J. R. 2000. "Human antiquity and the Old Stone Age: The nineteenth century background to paleoanthropology." *Evolutionary Anthropology* 9 (1): 37–49.

Sahnouni, M. 1998. "The Lower Palaeolithic of the Maghreb: Excavations and analyses at Ain Hanech, Algeria." *BAR International Series* 689/*Cambridge Monographs in African Archaeology* 42.

Sahnouni, M. and J. de Heinzelin. 1998. "The site of Ain Hanech revisited: New investigations at this Lower Pleistocene site in northern Algeria." *Journal of Archaeological Science* 25 (11): 1083–1100.

Sahnouni, M., D. Hadjouis, J. van der Made, A. Derradji, A. Canals, M. Medig, H. Belahrech, Z. Harichane, and M. Rabhi. 2002. "Further research at the Oldowan site of Ain Hanech, North-eastern Algeria." *Journal of Human Evolution* 43 (6): 925–937.

Sahnouni, M., D. Hadjouis, J. van der Made, A. Derradji, A. Canals, M. Medig, H. Belahrech, Z. Harichane, and M. Rabhi. 2004. "On the earliest human occupation in North Africa: A response to Geraads et al." *Journal of Human Evolution* 46 (6): 763–775.

Sampson, C. G. 1974. *The Stone Age archaeology of Southern Africa*. New York: Academic Press.

Sampson, C. G. and M. D. Southard. 1973. "Variability and change in the Nachikufan industry of Zambia." *South African Archaeological Bulletin* 28 (111–112): 78–89.

Sarich, V. M. 1985. "A molecular approach to the question of human origins." In R. L. Ciochon and J. G. Fleagle, eds., *Primate evolution and human origins*. Menlo Park: Benjamin/Cummings, pp. 314–322. (Orig. pub. 1971.)

Sarich, V. M. and A. C. Wilson. 1967. "Immunological time scale for human evolution." *Science* 158:1200–1203.

Schepartz, L. A. 1993. "Language and modern human origins." *Yearbook of Physical Anthropology* 36:91–126.

Schick, K. D. 2001. "An examination of Kalambo Falls Acheulean site B5 from a geoarchaeological point of view." In J. D. Clark, ed., *Kalambo Falls prehistoric site III. The earlier cultures: Middle and Earlier Stone Age*. Cambridge: Cambridge University Press, pp. 463–480.

Schlanger, N. 2003. "The Burkitt affair revisited. Colonial implications and identity politics in early South African prehistoric research." *Archaeological Dialogues* 10 (1): 5–26.

Schmerling, P. C. 1833–1834. *Recherches sur les Ossements Fossils découvertes dans les Cavernes de la Province de Liège*. 2 Vols. Liège: Collardin.

Schmitz, R. W., D. Serre, G. Bonani, S. Faine, F. Hillgruber, H. Krainitzki, S. Pääbo, and F. H. Smith. 2002. "The Neanderthal type site revisited: Interdisciplinary investigations of skeletal remains from the Neander Valley, Germany." *Proceedings of the National Academy of Sciences* 99 (20): 13342–13347.

Schoetensack, O. 1908. *Der Unterkiefer des Homo heidelbergensis aus den Sanden von Mauer bei Heidelberg.* Leipzig: Wilhelm Engelmann.

Schrire, C., J. Deacon, M. Hall, and D. Lewis-Williams. 1986. "Burkitt's milestone." *Antiquity* 60:123–131.

Schwarcz, H. P. 1992. "Uranium-series dating in paleoanthropology." *Evolutionary Anthropology* 1 (2): 56–62.

Schwarcz, H. P. 1993. "Uranium-series dating and the origin of modern man." In M. J. Aitken, C. B. Stringer, and P. A. Mellars, eds., *The origin of modern humans and the impact of chronometric dating.* Princeton, NJ: Princeton University Press, pp. 12–26.

Schwarcz, H. P. 2001. "Chronometric dating of the Middle Pleistocene." In L. Barham and K. Robson-Brown, eds., *Human roots: Africa and Asia in the Middle Pleistocene.* Bristol: Western Academic and Specialist Press, pp. 41–53.

Schwarcz, H. P., W. M. Buhay, R. Grün, H. Valladas, E. Tchernov, O. Bar-Yosef, and B. Vandermeersch. 1989. "ESR dating of the Neandertal site, Kebara Cave, Israel." *Journal of Archaeological Science* 16:653–659.

Schwarcz, H. P. and R. Grün. 1992. "Electron spin resonance (ESR) dating of the origin of modern man." *Philosophical Transactions of the Royal Society* 337B (1280): 145–148.

Schwarcz, H. P. and R. Grün. 1993a. "Electron spin resonance (ESR) dating of the origin of modern man." In M. J. Aitken, C. B. Stringer, and P. A. Mellars, eds., *The origin of modern humans and the impact of chronometric dating.* Princeton, NJ: Princeton University Press, pp. 40–48.

Schwarcz, H. P. and R. Grün. 1993b. "Electron spin resonance dating of tooth enamel from Bir Tarfawi." In F. Wendorf, R. Schild, A. E. Close, et al., *Egypt during the last interglacial: The Middle Paleolithic of Bir Tarfawi and Bir Sahara East.* New York: Plenum Press, pp. 234–237.

Schwarcz, H. P., R. Grün, B. Vandermeersch, O. Bar-Yosef, H. Valladas, and E. Tchernov. 1988. "ESR dates for the hominid burial site of Qafzeh in Israel." *Journal of Human Evolution* 17:733–737.

Schwarcz, H. P. and L. Morawska. 1993. "Uranium-series dating of carbonates from Bir Tarfawi and Bir Sahara East." In F. Wendorf, R. Schild, A. E. Close, et al., *Egypt during the last interglacial: The Middle Paleolithic of Bir Tarfawi and Bir Sahara East.* New York: Plenum Press, pp. 205–217.

Schwarcz, H. P. and J. Rink. 2000. "Electron spin resonance dating of the Die Kelders Cave 1 site, South Africa." *Journal of Human Evolution* 38 (1): 121–128.

Schwarcz, H. P. and J. Rink. 2001. "Skinflint dating." *Quaternary Science Reviews* 20 (5/9): 1047–1050.

Schwartz, J. H. 2004. "Getting to know *Homo erectus.*" *Science* 305 (5680): 53–54.

Semaw, S. 2000. "The world's oldest stone artefacts from Gona, Ethiopia: Their implications for understanding stone technology and patterns of human evolution between 2.6–1.5 million years ago." *Journal of Archaeological Science* 27 (12): 1197–1214.

Semaw, S., P. Renne, J. W. K. Harris, C. S. Feibel, R. L. Bernor, N. Fesseha, and K. Mowbray. 1997. "2.5 million-year-old stone tools from Gona, Ethiopia." *Nature* 385 (6614): 333–336.

Semaw, S., M. J. Rogers, J. Quade, P. R. Renne, R. F. Butler, M. Dominguez-Rodrigo, D. Stout, W. S. Hart, T. Pickering, and S. W. Simpson. 2003. "2.6-million-year-old stone tools and associated bones from OGS-6 and OGS-7, Gona, Afar, Ethiopia." *Journal of Human Evolution* 45 (2): 169–177.

Semino, O., A. S. Santachiara-Benerecetti, F. Falaschi, L. L. Cavalli-Sforza, and P. A. Underhill. 2002. "Ethiopians and Khoisan share the deepest clades of the human Y-chromosome phylogeny." *American Journal of Human Genetics* 70 (1): 165–168.

Senut, B., M. Pickford, D. Gommery, P. Mein, K. Chepboi, and Y. Coppens. 2001. "First hominid from the Miocene (Lukeino Formation, Kenya)." *Comptes rendus de l'academie de Paris: Sciences de la terre et des planètes* 332:137–144.

Serre, D., A. Langaney, M. Chech, M. Teschler-Nicola, M. Paunovic, P. Mennecler, M. Hofreiter, G. Possnert, and S. Pääbo. 2004. "No evidence of Neandertal mtDNA contribution to early modern humans." *Public Library of Science Biology* 2 (3): 313–317.

Servant, J. 2001. "The 100,000 year cycle of deglaciation during the last 450,000 years: A new interpretation of oceanic and ice core data." *Global and Planetary Change* 29 (1/2): 121–133.

Seyfert, C. K. and L. A. Sirkin. 1973. *Earth history and plate tectonics: An introduction to historical geology.* New York: Harper & Row.

Shackleton, N. J. 2000. "The 100,000 year ice age cycle identified and found to lag temperature, carbon dioxide and orbital eccentricity." *Science* 289 (5486): 1897–1902.

Shackleton, N. J., M. Chapman, M. F. Sanchez-Goñi, D. Pailler, and Y. Lancelot. 2002. "The classic marine isotope stage 5e." *Quaternary Research* 58 (1): 14–16.

Shea, J. 1989. "A functional study of the lithic industries associated with hominid fossils in the Kebara and Qafzeh caves, Israel." In P. Mellars and C. Stringer, eds., *The human revolution.* Princeton, NJ: Princeton University Press, pp. 611–625.

Shea, J. 1998. "Neandertal and early modern human behavioural variability: Regional scale approach to lithic evidence for hunting in the Levantine Mousterian." *Current Anthropology* 39:S45–S79.

Shea, J. 2003. "Neandertals, competition and the origin of modern human behavior in the Levant." *Evolutionary Anthropology* 12 (4): 173–187.

Shea, J. 2006. "The origins of lithic projectile point technology: Evidence from Africa, the Levant and Europe." *Journal of Archaeological Science* 33 (6): 823–846.

Shea, J., J. G. Fleagle, F. Brown, Z. Assefa, C. Feibel, I. McDougall, L. Bender, and A. Jagich. 2004. "Archaeology of the Kibish Formation, lower Omo Valley, Ethiopia."

Abstracts of the Paleoanthropology Society Meeting, Montreal, Quebec. http://www. paleoanthro.org.

Shen Guanjun, The-Lung Ku, Hai Cheng, R. L. Edwards, Zhenxin Yuan, and Qian Wang. 2001. "High-precision U-series dating of locality 1 at Zhoukoudian, China." *Journal of Human Evolution* 41 (6): 679–688.

Shen, P., F. Wang, P. A. Underhill, W.-H. Yang, A. Roxas, R. Sung, A. A. Lin, et al. 2000. "Population genetic implications from sequence variation in four Y chromosome genes." *Proceedings of the National Academy of Sciences* 97 (13): 7354–7359.

Shepherd, N. 2002. "The politics of archaeology in Africa." *Annual Review of Anthropology* 31:189–209.

Shepherd, N. 2003. "The modest violet. Response to 'The Burkitt affair revisited.'" *Archaeological Dialogues* 10 (1): 33–39.

Sherratt, A. 1997. "Climatic cycles and behavioural revolutions: The emergence of modern humans and the beginning of farming." *Antiquity* 71 (272): 271–287.

Shipman, P. 2001. *The man who found the missing link: Eugene Dubois and his lifelong quest to prove Darwin right.* New York: Simon and Schuster.

Sibley, C. G. and J. Ahlquist. 1984. "The phylogeny of the hominoid primates as indicated by DNA-DNA hybridization." *Journal of Molecular Evolution* 20:2–15.

Siddall, M., E. J. Rohling, A. Almogi-Labin, Ch. Hemleben, B. Mesichne, I. Schmelzer, and D. A. Smeed. 2003. "Sea-level fluctuations during the last glacial cycle." *Nature* 423 (6942): 853–858.

Siegenthaler, U., T. F. Stocker, E. Monnin, D. Lüthi, J. Schwander, B. Stauffer, D. Raynaud, et al. 2005. "Stable carbon cycle-climate relationship during the Late Pleistocene." *Science* 310 (5752): 1313–1317.

Sigmon, B. A. and J. S. Cybulski, eds. 1981. Homo erectus: *Papers in honor of Davidson Black.* Toronto: University of Toronto Press.

Simons, E. L. 1989. "Human origins." *Science* 245 (4924): 1343–1350.

Simons, E. L. and D. R. Pilbeam. 1965. "Preliminary revision of the Dryopithecinae (Pongidae, Anthropoidea)." *Folia Primatologia* 3:81–152.

Simpson, G. G. 1944. *Tempo and mode in evolution.* New York: Columbia University Press.

Singer, R. and J. Wymer. 1968. "Archaeological investigations at the Saldanha skull site in South Africa." *South African Archaeological Bulletin* 25:63–74.

Singer, R. and J. Wymer. 1982. *The Middle Stone Age at Klasies River Mouth in South Africa.* Chicago: University of Chicago Press.

Sirocko, F. 2003. "Ups and downs in the Red Sea." *Nature* 423 (6942): 813–814.

Skinner, A. R., R. L. Hay, F. Masao, and B. A. B. Blackwell. 2003. "Dating the Naisiusiu Beds, Olduvai Gorge, by electron spin resonance." *Quaternary Science Reviews* 22 (10–13): 1361–1366.

Smith, A. B. 1993. "Terminal Palaeolithic industries of Sahara: A discussion of new data." In L. Krzyzaniak, M. Kobusiewicz, and J. Alexander, eds., *Environmental change and human culture in the Nile Basin and Northern Africa until the second millennium BC.* Poznan: Poznan Archaeological Museum, pp. 69–75.

Smith, F. H. 1982. "Upper Pleistocene hominid evolution in south-central Europe: A review of the evidence and analysis of trends." *Current Anthropology* 23 (6): 667–686.

Smith, F. H. 1984. "Fossil hominids from the Upper Pleistocene of Central Europe and the origin of modern Europeans." In F. H. Smith and F. Spencer, eds., *The origins of modern humans*. New York: Alan R. Liss, pp. 137–209.

Smith, F. H. 1991. "The Neandertals: Evolutionary dead ends or ancestors of modern people?" *Journal of Anthropological Research* 47 (2): 219–238.

Smith, F. H. 1992a. "The role of continuity in modern human origins." In G. Bräuer and F. Smith, eds., *Continuity or replacement*. Rotterdam: A. A. Balkema, pp. 145–156.

Smith, F. H. 1992b. "Models and realities in modern human origins: The African fossil evidence." *Philosophical Transactions of the Royal Society* 337B (1280): 243–250.

Smith, F. H. 1993. "Models and realities in modern human origins: The African fossil evidence." In M. J. Aitken, C. B. Stringer, and P. A. Mellars, eds., *The origin of modern humans and the impact of chronometric dating*. Princeton, NJ: Princeton University Press, pp. 234–248.

Smith, F. H., A. T. Chamberlain, M. S. Riley, A. Cooper, C. B. Stringer, M. J. Collins, I. Ovchinnikov, et al. 2001. "Not just old but old and cold." *Nature* 410 (6830): 771–772.

Smith, F. H., I. Janković, and I. Karavanic. 2005. "The assimilation model, modern human origins in Europe, and the extinction of Neandertals." *Quaternary International* 137 (1): 7–19.

Smith, F. H., A. B. Falsetti, and S. M. Donnelly. 1989. "Modern human origins." *Yearbook of Physical Anthropology* 32:35–68.

Smith, F. H. and F. Spencer, eds. 1984. *The origins of modern humans: A world survey of the fossil evidence*. New York: Alan R. Liss.

Smith, F. H., E. Trinkaus, P. B. Pettitt, I. Karavanic, and M. Paunovic. 1999. "Direct radiocarbon dates for Vindija G1 and Velika Pecina Late Pleistocene hominid remains." *Proceedings of the National Academy of Sciences* 96 (22): 12281–12286.

Smith, J. R., R. Giegengack, H. P. Schwarcz, M. M. A. McDonald, M. R. Kleindienst, A. L. Hawkins, and C. S. Churcher. 2004. "A reconstruction of Quaternary pluvial environments and human occupations using stratigraphy and geochronology of fossil-spring tufas, Kharga Oasis, Egypt." *Geoarchaeology* 19 (5): 407–439.

Solecki, R. 1971. *Shanidar: The first flower people*. New York: Knopf.

Solomon, J. D. 1939. "The Pleistocene succession in Uganda." In T. P. O'Brien, *The prehistory of Uganda protectorate*. Cambridge: Cambridge University Press, pp. 15–50.

Sonneville-Bordes, D. de. 1963. "Upper Palaeolithic cultures of Western Europe." *Science* 142 (3590): 347–355.

Sonneville-Bordes, D. de. 1974/1975. "Les listes-types: Observations de méthode." *Quaternaria* 18:9–43.

Sonneville-Bordes, D. de. 1975. *L'âge de la pierre*. 4th ed. Paris: Presses Universitaires. (Orig. pub. 1961.)

Sonneville-Bordes, D. de, and J. Perrot. 1953–1956. "Essai d'adaptation des méthodes statistiques au Paléolithique supérieur." *Bulletin de la Société Préhistorique Française* 50:323–333, 51 (7): 327–335, 52 (1/2): 76–79, 54 (7/8): 408–412, 54 (9): 547–559.

Soriano, S. 2003. "Quand archaïque n'est pas ancien! Etudes de cas dans le Paléolithique du Pays dogon (Ounjougou, Mali)." *Annales de la Donation Fyssen* 18:79–92.

Soriano, S. and M. Rasse. 2005. "Avant les Dogon: le site d'Ounjougou (Mali)." *Archéologies. Vingt ans de recherches françaises dans le monde*. Paris: Maisonneuve et Larose, ADPF, ERC, pp. 206–208.

Spahni, R., J. Chappellaz, T. F. Stocker, L. Loulergue, G. Hausammann, K. Kawamura, J. Flückiger, J. Schwander, D. Raynaud, V. Masson-Delmotte, and J. Jouzel. 2005. "Atmospheric methane and nitrous oxide of the Late Pleistocene from Antarctic ice cores." *Science* 310 (5752): 1317–1321.

Spencer, F. H. 1984. "The Neandertals and their evolutionary significance: A brief historical survey." In F. H. Smith and F. Spencer, eds., *The origins of modern humans*. New York: Alan R. Liss, pp. 1–49.

Spencer, F. H. 1990a. *Piltdown: A scientific forgery*. London: Oxford University Press.

Spencer, F. H. 1990b. *The Piltdown papers, 1908–1955: The correspondence and other documents relating to the Piltdown forgery*. London: Oxford University Press.

Speth, J. 2004. "News flash: Negative evidence convicts Neanderthals of gross mental incompetence." *World Archaeology* 34 (4): 519–526.

Spratt, B. G. 2003. "Stomachs out of Africa." *Science* 299 (5612): 1528–1529.

Stanford, D. and B. Bradley. 2002. "Ocean trails and prairie paths? Thoughts about Clovis origins." In N. J. Jablonski, ed., "The first Americans: The Pleistocene colonization of the New World." *Memoirs of the California Academy of Sciences* 27, pp. 255–271.

Stanley, S. M. 1992. "An ecological theory for the origin of *Homo*." *Paleobiology* 18 (3): 237–257.

Stanley, S. M. 1995. "Climatic forcing and the origin of the human genus." In *Effects of past global change on life*. Washington, DC: National Academy Press, pp. 233–243.

Stanley, S. M. 1996. *Children of the Ice Age*. New York: Harmony Books.

Stapleton, R. P. and J. Hewitt. 1927. "Stone implements from a rock-shelter at Howieson's Poort near Grahamstown." *South African Journal of Science* 24:574–587.

Stapleton, R. P. and J. Hewitt. 1928. "Stone implements from a rock-shelter at Howieson's Poort near Grahamstown." *South African Journal of Science* 25:399–409.

Stedman, H. H., B. W. Kozyak, A. Nelson, D. M. Thesler, L. T. Su, D. W. Low, C. R. Bridges, J. B. Schrager, N. Minugh-Purvis, and M. A. Mitchell. 2004. "Myosin gene mutation correlates with anatomical changes in the human lineage." *Nature* 428 (6981): 415–418.

Stein, L. D. 2004. "End of the beginning." *Nature* 431 (7011): 915–916.

Stiles, D. A. 1979a. "Palaeolithic culture and culture change: Experiments in theory and method." *Current Anthropology* 20 (1): 1–21.

Stiles, D. A. 1979b. "Early Acheulian and developed Oldowan." *Current Anthropology* 20 (1):126–129.

Stoczkowski, W. 2002. *Explaining human origins: Myth, imagination and conjecture.* Cambridge: Cambridge University Press.

Stocking, G. 1987. *Victorian anthropology.* New York: Free Press.

Stoneking, M. 1993. "DNA and recent human evolution." *Evolutionary Anthropology* 2 (2): 60–73.

Stoneking, M. 1994. "In defense of 'Eve': A response to Templeton's critique." *American Anthropologist* 96 (1): 131–141.

Stoneking, M. and R. L. Cann. 1989. "African origin of human mitochondrial DNA." In P. Mellars and C. Stringer, eds., *The human revolution.* Princeton, NJ: Princeton University Press, pp. 17–30.

Stoneking, M., S. T. Sherry, A. J. Redd, and L. Vigilant. 1993. "New approaches to dating suggest a recent age for the human mtDNA ancestor." In M. J. Aitken, C. B. Stringer, and P. A. Mellars, eds., *The origin of modern humans and the impact of chronometric dating.* Princeton, NJ: Princeton University Press, pp. 84–103.

Strachan, T. and A. P. Read. 1996. *Human molecular genetics.* Oxford: Bios Scientific.

Straus, L. G. 1995. "The Upper Palaeolithic of Europe: An overview." *Evolutionary Anthropology* 4 (1): 4–16.

Straus, L. G. 2000. "Solutrean settlement of North America? A review of reality." *American Antiquity* 65 (2): 219–226.

Straus, L. 2001. "Africa and Iberia in the Pleistocene." *Quaternary International* 75 (1): 91–102.

Straus, L. G. 2005. "On the demise of the Neandertals." *Quaternary International* 137 (1): 1–5.

Straus Jr., W. and A. J. E. Cave. 1957. "Pathology and posture of Neanderthal man." *Quarterly Review of Biology* 32 (4): 348–363.

Stringer, C. B. 1989a. "Documenting the origin of modern humans." In E. Trinkaus, ed., *The emergence of modern humans.* Cambridge: Cambridge University Press, pp. 97–141.

Stringer, C. B. 1989b. "The origin of early modern humans: A comparison of the European and non-European evidence." In P. Mellars and C. Stringer, eds., *The human revolution.* Princeton, NJ: Princeton University Press, pp. 232–244.

Stringer, C. B. 1990. "The emergence of modern humans." *Scientific American* 263 (6): 98–104.

Stringer, C. B. 1992. "Replacement, continuity and the origin of *Homo sapiens.*" In G. Bräuer and F. H. Smith, eds., *Continuity or replacement.* Rotterdam: A. A. Balkema, pp. 9–24.

Stringer, C. B. 1993a. "Reconstructing recent human evolution." In M. J. Aitken, C. B. Stringer, and P. A. Mellars, eds., *The origin of modern humans and the impact of chronometric dating.* Princeton, NJ: Princeton University Press, pp. 179–195.

Stringer, C. B. 1993b. "New views on modern human origins." In T. Rasmussen, ed., *The origin and evolution of humans and humanness*. Boston: Jones and Bartlett, pp. 75–94.

Stringer, C. B. 1994. "Out of Africa—A personal history." In M. H. Nitecki and D. V. Nitecki, eds., *Origins of anatomically modern humans*. New York: Plenum Press, pp. 149–174.

Stringer, C. B. 2000. "Coasting out of Africa." *Nature* 405 (6782): 24–26.

Stringer, C. B. 2002a. "The morphology and behavioural origins of modern humans." In T. J. Crow, ed., *The speciation of modern* Homo sapiens. *Proceedings of the British Academy*. Vol 106. Oxford: Oxford University Press, pp. 23–30.

Stringer, C. B. 2002b. "Modern human origins: Progress and prospects." *Philosophical Transactions of the Royal Society of London* 357 (1420)B: 563–579.

Stringer, C. B. 2003. "Out of Ethiopia." *Nature* 423 (6941): 692–694.

Stringer, C. B. and P. Andrews. 1988a. "Genetic and fossil evidence for the origin of modern humans." *Science* 239 (4845): 1263–1268.

Stringer, C. B. and P. Andrews. 1988b. "Modern human origins." *Science* 241 (4867): 773–774.

Stringer, C. B., R. N. E. Barton, and J. C. Finlayson, eds. 2000. *Neanderthals on the edge: Papers from a conference marking the 150th anniversary of the Forbes Quarry discovery, Gibraltar*. Oxford: Oxbow Books.

Stringer, C. B. and C. Gamble. 1993. *In search of the Neanderthals: Solving the puzzle of human origins*. London: Thames and Hudson.

Stringer, C. B., R. Grün, H. P. Schwarcz, and P. Goldberg. 1989. "ESR dates for the hominid burial site of es Skhūl in Israel." *Nature* 338 (6218): 756–758.

Stringer, C. B., J.-J. Hublin, and B. Vandermeersch. 1984. "The origin of anatomically modern humans in Western Europe." In F. H. Smith and F. Spencer, eds., *The origins of modern humans: A world survey of the fossil evidence*. New York: Alan R. Liss, pp. 51–135.

Stringer, C. B. and R. McKie. 1996. *African exodus: The origins of modern humanity*. London: Jonathan Cape.

Stringer, C. B. and E. Trinkaus. 1999. "The human tibia from Boxgrove." In M. B. Roberts and S. A. Parfitt, eds., *Boxgrove: A Middle Pleistocene hominid site at Eartham Quarry, Boxgrove, West Sussex*. London: English Heritage, pp. 420–422.

Stumpf, M. and D. B. Goldstein. 2001. "Genealogical and evolutionary inference with the human Y chromosome." *Science* 291 (5509): 1738–1742.

Stynder, D. D., J. Moggi-Cecchi, and L. R. Berger. 2001. "Human mandibular incisors from the late Middle Pleistocene locality of Hoedjiespunt 1, South Africa." *Journal of Human Evolution* 41 (5): 369–383.

Suc, J.-P., A. Bertini, S. A. G. Leroy, and D. Suballyova. 1997. "Towards lowering of the Pliocene/Pleistocene boundary to the Gauss/Matuyama Reversal." *Quaternary International* 40:37–42.

Sutton, J. E. G. 1977. "The African aqualithic." *Antiquity* 51:25–34.

Swisher III, C. C., G. H. Curtis, T. Jacob, A. G. Getty, A. Suprijo, and Widiasmoro. 1994. "Age of the earliest known hominids in Java, Indonesia." *Science* 263 (45150): 1118–1121.

Talbot, M. R. and T. Johannessen. 1992. "A high resolution palaeoclimatic record for the last 2,500 years in tropical West Africa from the carbon and nitrogen isotopic composition of lacustrine organic matter." *Earth and Planetary Science Letters* 110:23–37.

Talbot, M. R., D. A. Livingstone, P. G. Palmer, J. Maley, J. M. Melack, G. Delibrias, and S. Gulliksen. 1984. "Preliminary results from sediment cores from Lake Bosumtwi, Ghana." *Palaeoecology of Africa* 16:173–192.

Tattersall, I. 1995. *The fossil trail: How we know what we think we know about human evolution.* New York: Oxford University Press.

Tattersall, I. 2002. *The monkey in the mirror.* New York: Harcourt.

Taylor, D. M., R. Marchant, and A. C. Hamilton. 2001. "A reanalysis and interpretation of palynological data from the Kalambo Falls prehistoric site." In J. D. Clark, ed., *Kalambo Falls prehistoric site III. The earlier cultures: Middle and Earlier Stone Age.* Cambridge: Cambridge University Press, pp. 66–81.

Taylor, R. E. 1997. "Radiocarbon dating." In R. E. Taylor and M. J. Aitken, eds., *Chronometric dating in archaeology.* New York: Plenum Press, pp. 63–96.

Taylor, R. E., L. A. Payen, C. A. Prior, P. J. Slota Jr., R. Gillespie, J. A. J. Gowlett, R. E. B. Hedges, et al. 1985. "Major revisions in the Pleistocene age assessments for North American human skeletons by 14C accelerator mass spectrometry: None older than 11,000 ^{14}C years BP" *American Antiquity* 50 (1): 136–140.

Tchernov, E. 1988. "Biochronology of the Middle Palaeolithic and dispersal events of hominids in the Levant." *L'Homme de Neandertal* 2:153–168.

Templeton, A. R. 1992. "Human origins and analysis of mitochondrial DNA sequences." *Science* 255 (5045): 737.

Templeton, A. R. 1993. "The Eve hypothesis: A genetic critique." *American Anthropologist* 95 (1): 51–72.

Templeton, A. R. 1994. "'Eve' hypothesis compatibility versus hypothesis testing." *American Anthropologist* 96 (1): 141–147.

Templeton, A. R. 2002. "Out of Africa again and again." *Nature* 416 (6876): 45–51.

Terrell, J. 2001. "Ethnolinguistic groups, language boundaries and culture history: A sociolinguistic model." In J. Terrell, ed., *Archaeology, language and history: Essays on culture and ethnicity.* Westport: Bergin and Garvey, pp. 199–221.

Thackeray, A. I. 1989. "Changing fashions in the Middle Stone Age: The stone artefact sequence from Klasies River main site, South Africa." *African Archaeological Review* 7:33–57.

Thackeray, A. I. 1992. "The Middle Stone Age south of the Limpopo River." *Journal of World Prehistory* 6 (4): 385–440.

Thackeray, A. I. 2000. "Middle Stone Age artifacts from the 1993 and 1995 excavations of Die Kelders Cave 1, South Africa." *Journal of Human Evolution* 38 (1): 147–168.

Thackeray, A. I. and A. J. Kelly. 1988. "Technological and typological analysis of Middle Stone Age assemblages antecedent to the Howieson's Poort at Klasies River main site." *South African Archaeological Bulletin* 43 (147): 15–26.

Thackeray, J. F. 2002. "Palaeoenvironmental change and re-assessment of the age of Late Pleistocene deposits at Die Kelders cave, South Africa." *Journal of Human Evolution* 43 (5): 749–754.

Thangaraj, K. G. Chaubey, T. Kivisild, A. G. Reddy, V. K. Singh, A. A. Rasalkar, and L. Singh. 2005. "Reconstructing the origin of Andaman Islanders." *Science* 308 (5724): 996.

Theunissen, B.1989. *Eugene Dubois and the ape-man from Java*. Dordrecht: Kluwer Academic.

Thoma, A. 1984. "Morphology and affinities of the Nazlet Khater man." *Journal of Human Evolution* 13 (3): 287–296.

Thomas, D. S. G., G. Brook, P. Shaw, M. Bateman, K. Haberyan, C. Appleton, D. Nash, S. McLaren, and F. Davies. 2003. "Late Pleistocene wetting and drying in the NW Kalahari: An integrated study from the Tsodilo Hills, Botswana." *Quaternary International* 104 (1): 53–67.

Thomas, M. F. 2000. "Late Quaternary environmental changes and the alluvial record in humid tropical environments." *Quaternary International* 72 (1): 23–36.

Thomas, N. 2003. *Cook: The extraordinary voyages of Captain James Cook*. Toronto: Viking Canada.

Thompson, J. C., J. R. F. Bower, E. C. Fisher, Z. A. P. Mabulla, C. W. Marean, K. Stewart, and C. F. Vondra. 2004. "Loiyangalani: Behavioral and taphonomic aspects of a Middle Stone Age site in the Serengeti Plain, Tanzania." *Abstracts of the Paleoanthropology Society Meeting, Montreal, Quebec.* http://www .paleoanthro.org.

Thomsen, C. J. 1836. *Ledetraadt til nordisk Oldkyndighed.* Copenhagen, pp. 27–90.

Thomson, R., J. K. Pritchard, P. Shen, P. J. Oefner, and M. W. Feldman. 2000. "Recent common ancestry of human Y chromosomes: Evidence from DNA sequence data." *Proceedings of the National Academy of Sciences* 97 (13): 7360–7365.

Thorne, A. and M. Wolpoff. 1981. "Regional continuity in Australasian Pleistocene hominid evolution." *American Journal of Physical Anthropology* 55:337–348.

Thorne, A. G. and M. H. Wolpoff. 1992. "The multiregional evolution of humans." *Scientific American* 266 (4): 76–83.

Tillet, T. 1985. "The Palaeolithic and its environment in the northern part of the Chad Basin." *African Archaeological Review* 3:163–177.

Tishkoff, S. A., E. Dietzsch, W. Speed, A. J. Pakstis, J. R. Kidd, K. Cheung, B. Bonne-Tamir, et al. 1996. "Global patterns of linkage disequilibrium at the CD4 locus and modern human origins." *Science* 271 (5254): 1380–1387.

Tixier, J. 1963. *Typologie de l'Epipaléolithique du Maghreb.* Paris: Arts et Métiers Graphiques.

Tixier, J. 1967. "Procédés d'analyse et questions de terminologie concernant l'étude des ensembles industriels du Paléolithique recent et de l'Epipaléolithique dans l'Afrique du Nord-Ouest." In W. W. Bishop and J. D. Clark, eds., *Background to evolution in Africa*. Chicago: University of Chicago Press, pp. 771–820.

Tobias, P. V. 1962. "A re-examination of the Kanam mandible." In G. Mortelmans and J. Nenquin, eds., *Actes du IVe Congrès Pan-Africain de Préhistoire et de l'étude du Quaternaire*. Tervuren: Musée Royal de l'Afrique Centrale 1:341–360.

Tobias, P. V. 1967a. *Olduvai Gorge 2: The cranium of* Australopithecus (Zinjanthropus) *boisei*. Cambridge: Cambridge University Press.

Tobias, P. V. 1967b. "The hominid skeletal remains of Haua Fteah." In C. B. M. McBurney, ed., *The Haua Fteah (Cyrenaica) and the Stone Age of the southeast Mediterranean*. Cambridge: Cambridge University Press, pp. 338–352.

Tobias, P. V. 1984. *Dart, Taung and the "missing link": An essay on the life and work of Emeritus Professor Raymond Dart*. Johannesburg: Witwatersrand University Press.

Todd, L. C., J. Kappelman, and M. Glantz. 2004. "Glimpses into the Paleolithic archaeology of northwestern Ethiopia." *Abstracts of the Paleoanthropology Society Meeting, Montreal, Quebec*. http://www.paleoanthro.org.

Toth, N. 1982. The stone technologies of early homnids at Koobi Fora, Kenya: An experimental approach. PhD diss., University of California, Berkeley.

Toth, N. and K. Schick. 1986. "The first million years: The archaeology of protohuman culture." *Advances in Archaeological Method and Theory* 9:1–96.

Trauth, M. H., M. A. Maslin, A. Deino, and M. R. Strecker. 2005. "Late Cenozoic moisture history of East Africa." *Science* 309 (5743): 2051–2053.

Trevor, J. C. and L. H. Wells. 1967. "Preliminary report on the second mandibular fragment from Haua Fteah, Cyrenaica." In C. B. M. McBurney, ed., *The Haua Fteah (Cyrenaica) and the Stone Age of the southeast Mediterranean*. Cambridge: Cambridge University Press, pp. 336–337.

Trigger, B. G. 1984. "Alternative archaeologies: Nationalist, colonialist, imperialist." *Man*, n.s., 19 (3): 355–370.

Trigger, B. G. 1989. *A history of archaeological thought*. Cambridge: Cambridge University Press.

Trinkaus, E. 1983. *The Shanidar Neandertals*. New York: Academic Press.

Trinkaus, E. 1984. "Neanderthal pubic morphology and gestation length." *Current Anthropology* 25:509–514.

Trinkaus, E. 1993. "Femoral neck-shaft angles of the Qafzeh-Skhūl early modern humans and activity levels among immature Near Eastern Middle Palaeolithic hominids." *Journal of Human Evolution* 25 (5): 393–416.

Trinkaus, E., ed. 1983. "The Mousterian legacy: Human biocultural change in the Upper Pleistocene." *BAR International Series* 164.

Trinkaus, E., ed. 1989. *The emergence of modern humans: Biocultural adaptations in the Later Pleistocene*. Cambridge: Cambridge University Press.

Trinkaus, E. and P. Shipman. 1993. *The Neandertals—Changing the image of mankind*. New York: Knopf.

Tryon, C. 2002. "Middle Pleistocene sites from the 'southern' Kapthurin Formation of Kenya." *Nyame Akuma* 57:6–13.

Tryon, C. and S. McBrearty. 2002. "Tephrostratigraphy and the Acheulean to Middle Stone Age transition in the Kapthurin Formation." *Journal of Human Evolution* 42 (1/2): 211–235.

Turner, A. 1984. "Hominids and fellow travelers: Human migration into high latitudes as part of a large mammal community." In R. Foley, ed., *Hominid evolution and community ecology.* London: Academic Press, pp. 193–217.

Turner, A. 1989. "Sample selection, schlepp effects and scavenging: The implications of partial recovery for interpretations of the terrestrial mammal assemblage from Klasies River Mouth." *Journal of Archaeological Science* 16:1–11.

Tylor, E. B. 1871. *Primitive culture.* London: John Murray.

Underhill, P. A., G. Passarino, A. A. Lin, P. Shen, M. M. Lahr, R. A. Foley, P. J. Oefner, and L. L. Cavalli-Sforza. 2001. "The phylogeography of Y chromosome binary haplotypes and the origins of modern human populations." *Annals of Human Genetics* 65 (1): 43–62.

Underhill, P. A., P. Shen, A. A. Lin, Li Jin, G. Passarino, W. H. Yang, E. Kauffman, et al. 2000. "Y chromosome sequence variation and the history of human populations." *Nature Genetics* 26 (3): 358–361.

Valladas, H., J.-L. Joron, G. Valladas, B. Arensburg, O. Bar-Yosef, A. Belfer-Cohen, P. Goldberg, et al. 1987. "Thermoluminescence dates for the Neanderthal burial site at Kebara in Israel." *Nature* 330 (6144): 159–160.

Valladas, H., N. Mercier, L. Froget, E. Hovers, J.-L. Joron, W. H. Kimbel, and Y. Rak. 1999. "TL dates for the Neanderthal site of the Amud Cave, Israel." *Journal of Archaeological Science* 26 (3): 259–268.

Valladas, H., J. L. Reyss, J.-L. Joron, G. Valladas, O. Bar-Yosef, and B. Vandermeersch. 1988. "Thermoluminescence dating of Mousterian 'Proto-Cro-Magnon' remains from Israel and the origin of modern man." *Nature* 331 (6157): 614–616.

Van Andel, T. H. and W. Davies, eds. 2003. *Neanderthals and modern humans in the European landscape during the last glaciation.* Cambridge: McDonald Institute for Archaeological Research.

Vandermeersch, B. 1981. *Les hommes fossiles de Qafzeh.* Paris: Editions du CNRS.

Vandermeersch, B. 1989. "The evolution of modern humans: Recent evidence from Southwest Asia." In P. Mellars and C. Stringer, eds., *The human revolution.* Princeton, NJ: Princeton University Press, pp. 155–164.

Van Neer, W. 1984. "Faunal remains from Matupi Cave, an Iron Age and Late Stone Age site in northeastern Zaire." *Mededelingen van de Koninklije Academie voor Wetenschappen, Lettern en Schone Kunsten van België* 46 (2): 59–76.

Van Noten, F. 1977. "Excavations at Matupi Cave." *Antiquity* 51 (201): 35–40.

Van Peer, P. 1991. "Interassemblage variability and Levallois style: The case of the Northern African Middle Palaeolithic." *Journal of Anthropological Archaeology* 10 (2): 107–151.

Van Peer, P. 1992. *The Levallois reduction strategy.* Madison: Prehistory Press.

Van Peer, P. 1998. "The Nile corridor and the out-of-Africa model: An examination of the archaeological record." *Current Anthropology* 39:S115–S140.

Van Peer, P. 2001. "The Nubian complex settlement system in northeast Africa." In N. Conard, ed., *Settlement dynamics of the Middle Palaeolithic and Middle Stone Age. Tübingen Publications in Prehistory* 1. Tübingen: Kerns Verlag, pp. 45–63.

Van Peer, P., R. Fullager, S. Stokes, R. M. Bailey, J. Moeyersons, F. Steenhoudt, A. Geerts, T. Vanderbeken, M. de Dapper, and F. Geus. 2003. "The Early to Middle Stone Age transition and the emergence of modern human behaviour at site 8-B-11, Sai Island, Sudan." *Journal of Human Evolution* 45 (2): 187–193.

Van Peer, P., P. M. Vermeersch, J. Moeyersons, and W. Van Neer. 1996. "Palaeolithic sequence at Sodmein Cave, Red Sea Mountains, Egypt." In G. Pwiti and R. Soper, eds., *Aspects of African archaeology.* Harare: University of Zimbabwe Publications, pp. 149–156.

Van Riet Lowe, C. 1929a. "The Later Stone Age—Introduction." In A. J. H. Goodwin and C. Van Riet Lowe, "The Stone Age cultures of South Africa." *Annals of the South African Museum* 27:147–150.

Van Riet Lowe, C. 1929b. "The Smithfield industry in the Orange Free State." In A. J. H. Goodwin and C. Van Riet Lowe, "The Stone Age cultures of South Africa." *Annals of the South African Museum* 27:151–206.

Van Riet Lowe, C. 1952. "The Pleistocene geology and prehistory of Uganda," part II: Prehistory. *Geological Survey of Uganda Memoir* 6.

Van Riper, A. B. 1993. *Men among the mammoths: Victorian science and the discovery of human prehistory.* Chicago: University of Chicago Press.

Vargha-Khadem, F., D. G. Gadian, A. Copp, and M. Mishkin. 2005. "FOXP2 and the neuroanatomy of speech and language." *Nature Reviews Neuroscience* 6 (2): 131–138.

Vekua, A., D. Lordkipanidze, G. P. Rightmire, J. Agusti, R. Ferring, G. Maisuradze, A. Mouskhelishvili, et al. 2002. "A new skull of early *Homo* from Dmanisi, Georgia." *Science* 297 (5578): 85–99.

Venter, J. C. et al. 2001. "The sequence of the human genome." *Science* 291 (5507): 1304–1351.

Verheyen, E., W. Salzburger, J. Snoeks, and A. Meyer. 2003. "Origin of the superflock of cichlid fishes from Lake Victoria, East Africa." *Science* 300 (5617): 325–329.

Vermeersch, P. M. 2001. "'Out of Africa' from an Egyptian point of view." *Quaternary International* 75 (1): 103–112.

Vermeersch, P. M., G. Gijselings, and E. Paulissen. 1984a. "Discovery of the Nazlet Khater Man, Upper Egypt." *Journal of Human Evolution* 13 (3): 281–286.

Vermeersch, P. M., E. Paulissen, G. Gijselings, M. Otte, A. Thoma, P. Van Peer, and R. Lauwers. 1984b. "33,000 year old mining site and related *Homo* in the Egyptian Nile Valley." *Nature* 309:342–344.

Vermeersch, P. M., E. Paulissen, G. Gijselings, M. Otte, A. Thoma, and C. Charlier. 1984c. "Une minière de silex et un squelette du paléolithique supérieur ancien à Nazlet Khater, Haute Egypt." *L'Anthropologie* 88:231–244.

Vermeersch, P. M., E. Paulissen, S. Stokes, C. Charlier, P. Van Peer, C. Stringer, and W. Lindsay. 1998. "A Middle Palaeolithic burial of a modern human at Taramsa Hill,

Egypt." *Antiquity* 72 (277): 475–484.

Vigilant, L., M. Stoneking, H. Harpending, C. Hawkes, and A. C. Wilson. 1991. "African populations and the evolution of human mitochondrial DNA." *Science* 253 (5027): 1503–1507.

Vignaud, P., P. Duringer, H. T. Mackaye, A. Likius, C. Blondel, J.-R. Boisserie, L. de Bonis, et al. 2002. "Geology and palaeontology of the Upper Miocene Toros-Menalla hominid locality, Chad." *Nature* 418 (6894): 152–155.

Villa, P., A. Delagnes, and L. Wadley. 2005. "A late Middle Stone Age artifact assemblage from Sibudu (Kwa-Zulu-Natal): Comparisons with the European Middle Palaeolithic." *Journal of Archaeological Science* 32 (3): 399–422.

Vishnyatsky, L. B. 1994. "'Running ahead of time' in the development of Palaeolithic industries." *Antiquity* 68 (258): 134–140.

Vogel, J. C. 2001. "Radiometric dates for the Middle Stone Age in South Africa." In P. V. Tobias, M. A. Raath, J. Moggi-Cecchi, and G. A. Doyle, eds., *Humanity from African naissance to coming millennia.* Florence: Firenze University Press, pp. 261–268.

Vogel, J. C. and P. B. Beaumont. 1972. "Revised radiocarbon chronology for the Stone Age in South Africa." *Nature* 237:50–51.

Vogelsang, R. 1996. "The Middle Stone Age in Southwestern Namibia." In G. Pwiti and R. Soper, eds., *Aspects of African archaeology.* Harare: University of Zimbabwe Publications, pp. 207–211.

Voight, B. F., S. Kudaravalli, Xiaoquan Wen, and J. K. Protchard. 2006. "A map of recent positive selection in the human genome." *Public Library of Science Biology* 4 (3): e72.

Volman, T. P. 1984. "Early prehistory of southern Africa." In R. G. Klein, ed., *Southern African prehistory and Paleoenvironments.* Rotterdam: Balkema, pp. 169–220.

Vrba, E. S. 1993. "The pulse that produced us." *Natural History* 102 (5): 47–51.

Vrba, E. S. 1995. "On the connection between paleoclimate and evolution." In E. S. Vrba, H. Denton, T. C. Partridge, and L. H. Burckle, eds., *Paleoclimate and evolution, with special emphasis on human origins.* New Haven: Yale University Press, pp. 24–45.

Vrba, E. S., G. H. Denton, T. C. Partridge, and L. H. Burckle, eds. 1995. *Paleoclimate and evolution, with special emphasis on human origins.* New Haven: Yale University Press.

Wadley, L. 1993. "The Pleistocene Later Stone Age south of the Limpopo River." *Journal of World Prehistory* 7 (3): 243–296.

Wadley, L. 1997. "Rose Cottage Cave: Archaeological work 1987 to 1997." *South African Journal of Science* 93:439–444.

Wadley, L. 2000. "The early Holocene layers of Rose Cottage Cave, Eastern Free State: Technology, spatial patterns and environment." *South African Archaeological Bulletin* 60 (171): 18–31.

Wadley, L. 2001a. "What is cultural modernity? A general view and a South African perspective from Rose Cottage Cave." *Cambridge Archaeological Journal* 11 (2): 201–221.

Wadley, L. 2001b. "Preliminary report on excavations at Sibudu Cave, KwaZulu-Natal." *Southern African Humanities* 13:1–17.

Wadley, L., D. M. Avery, A. M. B. Clark, B. S. Williamson, C. R. Thorpe, P. T. N. Harper, S. Woodborne, J. C. Vogel, and J. Binneman. 1997. "Excavations at Rose Cottage Cave." *South African Journal of Science* 93 (10): 439–482.

Wadley, L. and Z. Jacobs. 2004. "Sibudu Cave, Kwa-Zulu-Natal: Background to the excavations of Middle Stone Age and Iron Age occupations." *South African Journal of Science* 100 (3/4): 145–151.

Wainscoat, J. S., A. V. S. Hill, A. L. Boyce, J. Flint, M. Hernandez, S. L. Thein, J. M. Old, et al. 1986. "Evolutionary relationships of human populations from an analysis of nuclear DNA polymorphisms." *Nature* 319 (6053): 491–493.

Wainscoat, J. S., A. V. S. Hill, S. L. Thein, J. Flint, J. C. Chapman, D. J. Weatherall, J. B. Clegg, and D. R. Higgs. 1989. "Geographical distribution of alpha- and beta-globin gene cluster polymorphisms." In P. Mellars and C. Stringer, eds., *The human revolution.* Princeton, NJ: Princeton University Press, pp. 31–38.

Walker, A. and R. E. F. Leakey, eds. 1993. *The Nariokotome* Homo erectus *skeleton.* Cambridge: Harvard University Press.

Walker, A., M. R. Zimmerman, and R. E. F. Leakey. 1982. "A possible case of hypervitaminosis A in *Homo erectus.*" *Nature* 296 (5854): 248–250.

Walker, G. 2004. "Frozen time." *Nature* 429 (6992): 596–597.

Walker, N. J. 1980. "Later Stone Age research in the Matopos." *South African Archaeological Bulletin* 35 (131): 19–24.

Walker, N. J. 1990. "Zimbabwe at 18,000 BP." In C. Gamble and O. Soffer, eds., *The world at 18,000 BP: Low latitudes.* Vol 2. London: Unwin Hyman, pp. 206–213.

Wallace, A. R. 1865. "On the varieties of man in the Malay Archipelago." *Transactions of the Ethnological Society of London,* n.s., 3:209–212.

Walter, R. C., R. T. Buffler, J. H. Bruggemann, M. M. M. Guillaume, S. M. Berhe, B. Negassi, Y. Libsekel, et al. 2000. "Early human occupation of the Red Sea Coast of Eritrea during the last interglacial." *Nature* 405 (6782): 65–69.

Ward, R. and C. B. Stringer. 1997. "A molecular handle on the Neanderthals." *Nature* 388 (6639): 225–226.

Watson, E., K. Bauer, R. Aman, G. Weiss, A. von Haeseler, and S. Pääbo. 1996. "Mitochondrial DNA sequence diversity in Africa." *American Journal of Human Genetics* 59 (2): 437–444.

Watson, E., P. Foster, M. Richards, and H.-J. Bandelt. 1997. "Mitochondrial footprints of human expansions in Africa." *American Journal of Human Genetics* 61 (3): 691–704.

Watson, J. D. and F. H. C. Crick. 1953. "A structure for Deoxyribose Nucleic Acid." *Nature* 171:737–738.

Wayland, E. J. 1934. "Rifts, rivers, rains and early man in Uganda." *Journal of the Royal Anthropological Institute* 64:333–352.

Weaver, T. D. and C. C. Roseman. 2005. "Ancient DNA, late Neandertal survival, and modern-human-Neandertal genetic admixture." *Current Anthropology* 46 (4): 677–683.

Weidenreich, F. 1937. "The relation of *Sinanthropus pekinensis* to *Pithecanthropus, Javanthropus,* and Rhodesian man." *Journal of the Royal Anthropological Institute* 67:51–65.

Weidenreich, F. 1943. "The 'Neanderthal Man' and the ancestors of '*Homo sapiens.*'" *American Anthropologist* 45 (1): 39–48.

Weidenreich, F. 1947. "Facts and speculations concerning the origin of *Homo sapiens.*" *American Anthropologist* 49 (2): 187–203.

Weiner, J. S. 1955. *The Piltdown forgery.* London: Oxford University Press.

Wells, S. 2002. *The journey of man: A genetic odyssey.* Princeton, NJ: Princeton University Press.

Wells, R. S., N. Yuldasheva, R. Ruzibakiev, P. A. Underhill, I. Evseeva, J. Blue-Smith, Li Jin, et al. 2001. "The Eurasian heartland: A continental perspective on Y-chromosome diversity." *Proceedings of the National Academy of Sciences* 98 (18): 10244–10249.

Wendorf, F. and R. Schild. 1980. *Loaves and fishes: The prehistory of Wadi Kubbaniya.* Dallas: Institute for the Study of Earth and Man, Southern Methodist University.

Wendorf, F., A. Close, and R. Schild. 1987. "Recent work on the Middle Palaeolithic of the Eastern Sahara." *African Archaeological Review* 5:49–62.

Wendorf, F., R. Schild, and A. E. Close. 1993a. Introduction to *Egypt during the last interglacial: The Middle Paleolithic of Bir Tarfawi and Bir Sahara East,* by F. Wendorf, R. Schild, A. E. Close, et al. New York: Plenum Press, pp. 1–7.

Wendorf, F., R. Schild, and A. E. Close. 1993b. "Summary and conclusions." In F. Wendorf, R. Schild, A. E. Close, et al., *Egypt during the last interglacial: The Middle Paleolithic of Bir Tarfawi and Bir Sahara East.* New York: Plenum Press, pp. 552–573.

Wendt, W. E. 1976. "'Art mobilier' from the Apollo XI Cave, South West Africa: Africa's oldest dated works of art." *South African Archaeological Bulletin* 31:5–11.

Wengler, L. 1990. "Economie des matières premiéres et territoire dans le Moustérien et l'Atérien maghrébins: Exemples du Maroc orientale." *L'Anthropologie* 94 (2): 335–360.

Wengler, L. 2001. "Settlements during the Middle Palaeolithic of the Maghreb." In N. Conard, ed., *Settlement dynamics of the Middle Palaeolithic and Middle Stone Age. Tübingen Publications in Prehistory* 1. Tübingen: Kerns Verlag, pp. 65–89.

White, J. W. C. 2004. "Do I hear a million?" *Science* 304 (5677): 1609–1610.

White, M. J. 2000. "The Clactonian question: On the interpretation of core-and-flake assemblages in the British Lower Palaeolithic." *Journal of World Prehistory* 14 (1): 1–63.

White, T. D., B. Asfaw, D. DeGusta, H. Gilbert, G. D. Richards, G. Suwa, and F. C. Howell. 2003. "Pleistocene *Homo sapiens* from Middle Awash, Ethiopia." *Nature* 423 (6941): 742–747.

White, T. D., G. Suwa, and B. Asfaw. 1994. "*Australopithecus ramidus*: A new species of early hominid from Aramis, Ethiopia." *Nature* 371 (6495): 306–312.

White, T. D., G. Suwa, W. K. Hart, R. C. Walter, G. WoldeGabriel, J. de Heinzelin, J. D. Clark, B. Asfaw, and E. Vrba. 1993. "New discoveries of *Australopithecus* at Maka in Ethiopia." *Nature* 366 (6452): 261–265.

Wiessner, P. 1977. !Hxaro: A regional system of reciprocity for reducing risk among the !Kung San. PhD diss., University of Michigan.

Wiessner, P. 1982. "Risk, reciprocity and social influences on !Kung San economies." In E. Leacock and R. B. Lee, eds., *Politics and history in band societies*. Cambridge: Cambridge University Press, pp. 61–84.

Wiessner, P. 1983. "Style and social information in Kalahari San projectile points." *American Antiquity* 48 (2): 253–276.

Wiessner, P. 2002. "Hunting, healing and !*hxaro* exchange: A long-term perspective on !Kung (Ju/'hoansi) large game hunting." *Evolution and Human Behavior* 23 (6): 407–436.

Wild, E. M., M. Teschler-Nicola, W. Kutschera, P. Steier, E. Trinkaus, and W. Wanek. 2005. "Direct dating of Early Upper Palaeolithic human remains from Mladeč." *Nature* 435 (7040): 332–335.

Wilkins, L. 1979. *"Know thyself" in Greek and Latin literature*. New York: Garland.

Willerslev, E., and A. Cooper. 2005. "Ancient DNA." *Proceedings of the Royal Society Series* B 272 (1558): 3–16.

Williamson, B. S. 2004. "Middle Stone Age tool function from residue analysis at Sibudu Cave." *South African Journal of Science* 100 (3/40): 174–178.

Willoughby, P. R. 1976. An analysis of early postglacial European prehistory. MA thesis, University of Alberta.

Willoughby, P. R. 1987. "Spheroids and battered stones in the African Early and Middle Stone Age." *Cambridge Monographs in African Archaeology* 17/BAR *International Series* 321.

Willoughby, P. R. 1991. "Human origins and the sexual division of labour: An archaeological perspective." In D. Walde and N. D. Willows, eds., *The archaeology of gender*. Calgary: Chacmool Archaeological Association, pp. 284–291.

Willoughby, P. R. 1993a. "The Middle Stone Age and modern human origins." *African Archaeological Review* 11:3–20.

Willoughby, P. R. 1993b. "Culture, environment and the emergence of *Homo sapiens* in East Africa." In R. Jamieson, S. Abonyi, and N. Mirau, eds., *Culture and environment: A fragile coexistence*. Calgary: Chacmool Archaeological Association, pp. 135–143.

Willoughby, P. R. 1994. "The origin and dispersal of modern humans." In A. Herring and L. Chan, eds., *Strength in diversity: A reader in physical anthropology*. Toronto: Canadian Scholar's Press, pp. 235–258.

Willoughby, P. R. 1996a. "The Middle Stone Age in Southwestern Tanzania." In C. C. Magori, C. B. Saanane, and F. Schrenck, eds., "Four million years of hominid evolution in Africa." *Kaupia/Darmstäder Beiträge zur Naturgeschichte* 6:57–69.

Willoughby, P. R. 1996b. "Middle Stone Age technology and adaptation in Southwestern Tanzania." In G. Pwiti and R. Soper, eds., *Aspects of African archaeology*. Harare: University of Zimbabwe Publications, pp. 177–189.

Willoughby, P. R. 1996c. "The meaning of the Acheulean-Middle Stone Age transition in Africa." In D. A. Meyer, P. C. Dawson, and D. T. Hanna, eds, *Debating complexity*:

Proceedings of the 26th annual Chacmool conference, 1993. Calgary: Chacmool Archaeological Association, pp. 202–211.

Willoughby, P. R. 2000. "Archaeologists, palaeoanthropologists and the people without culture." In M. Boyd, J. C. Erwin, and M. Hendrikson, eds., *The entangled past: Integrating history and archaeology.* Calgary: Chacmool Archaeological Association, pp. 281–291.

Willoughby, P. R. 2001a. "Recognizing ethnic identity in the Upper Pleistocene: The case of the African Middle Stone Age/Middle Palaeolithic." In J. Terrell, ed., *Archaeology, language and history: Essays on culture and ethnicity.* Westport: Bergin and Garvey, pp. 125–152.

Willoughby, P. R. 2001b. "Middle and Later Stone Age technology from the Lake Rukwa Rift, Southwestern Tanzania." *South African Archaeological Bulletin* 56 (174/175): 34–45.

Willoughby, P. R. 2005. "Palaeoanthropology and the evolutionary place of humans in nature." *International Journal of Comparative Psychology* 18 (1): 60–90.

Willoughby, P. R. Forthcoming. "How much of early human evolution was a response to catastrophe?" In *Apocalypse then: Proceedings of the 35th annual Chacmool conference.* Calgary: University of Calgary Press.

Willoughby, P. R. and C. Sipe. 2002. "Stone age prehistory of the Songwe River Valley, Lake Rukwa basin, Southwestern Tanzania." *African Archaeological Review* 19 (4): 203–221.

Wilson, A. C. and R. L. Cann. 1992. "The recent African genesis of humans." *Scientific American* 266 (4): 68–73.

Wilson, A. C., R. L. Cann, S. M. Carr, M. George, U. B. Gyllenstsen, K. M. Kelm-Bychowski, R. G. Higuchi, et al. 1985. "Mitochondrial DNA and two perspectives on evolutionary genetics." *Biological Journal of the Linnean Society* 26:375–400.

Wilson, A. C., M. Stoneking, and R. L. Cann. 1991. "Ancestral geographic states and the peril of parsimony." *Systematic Zoology* 40 (3):363–365.

Wintle, A. G. 1996. "Archaeologically-relevant dating techniques for the next century: Small, hot and identified by acronyms." *Journal of Archaeological Science* 23 (1): 123–138.

WoldeGabriel, G., Y. Haile-Selassie, P. R. Renne, W. K. Hart, S. H. Ambrose, B. Asfaw, G. Heiken, and T. White. 2001. "Geology and palaeontology of the Late Miocene Middle Awash Valley, Afar Rift, Ethiopia." *Nature* 412 (6843): 175–178.

Wolf, E. 1982. *Europe and the people without history.* Berkeley: University of California Press.

Wolf, E. 1997. *Europe and the people without history.* 2nd ed. Berkeley: University of California Press.

Wolpoff, M. H. 1989a. "Multiregional evolution: The fossil alternative to Eden." In P. Mellars and C. Stringer, eds., *The human revolution.* Princeton, NJ: Princeton University Press, pp. 62–108.

Wolpoff, M. H. 1989b. "The place of the Neandertals in human evolution." In E. Trinkaus, ed., *The emergence of modern humans.* Cambridge: Cambridge University Press, pp. 97–141.

Wolpoff, M. H. 1992. "Theories of modern human origins." In G. Bräuer and F. H. Smith, eds., *Continuity or replacement.* Rotterdam: A. A. Balkema, pp. 25–63.

Wolpoff, M. H. and R. Caspari. 1996. "The modernity mess." *Journal of Human Evolution* 30 (2): 167–172.

Wolpoff, M. H. and R. Caspari. 1997. *Race and human evolution: A fatal attraction.* New York: Simon and Schuster.

Wolpoff, M. H., J. Hawks, and R. Caspari. 2000. "Multiregional, not multiple origins." *American Journal of Physical Anthropology* 112 (1): 129–136.

Wolpoff, M. H., B. Mannheim, A. Mann, J. Hawks, R. Caspari, K. R. Rosenberg, D. W. Frayer, G. W. Gill, and G. Clark. 2004. "Why *not* the Neandertals?" *World Archaeology* 34 (4): 527–546.

Wolpoff, M. H., J. N. Spuhler, F. H. Smith, J. Radovcic, G. Pope, D. W. Frayer, R. Eckhardt, and G. Clark. 1988. "Modern human origins." *Science* 241 (4867): 772–773.

Wolpoff, M. H. and A. G. Thorne. 1991. "The case against Eve." *New Scientist* 130 (1774): 37–41.

Wolpoff, M. H., A. G. Thorne, F. H. Smith, D. W. Frayer, and G. G. Pope. 1994. "Multiregional evolution: A world-wide source for modern human populations." In M. H. Nitecki and D. V. Nitecki, eds., *Origins of anatomically modern humans.* New York: Plenum Press, pp. 175–199.

Wong, K. 2005. "The morning of the modern mind." *Scientific American* 292 (6): 86–95.

Wood, B. 1991. *Koobi Fora research project 4: Hominid cranial remains.* Oxford: Clarendon Press.

Wood, B. 1992. "Origin and evolution of the genus *Homo.*" *Nature* 355 (6363): 783–790.

Wood, B. and M. Collard. 1999. "The human genus." *Science* 284 (5411): 65–71.

Wood, B. and M. Collard. 2001. "The meaning of *Homo.*" *Ludus Vitalis* IX (15): 63–74.

Woodborne, S. and J. C. Vogel. 1997. "Luminescence dating at Rose Cottage Cave: A progress report." *South African Journal of Science* 93 (10): 476–478.

Woodward, A. S. 1921. "A new cave man from Rhodesia, South Africa." *Nature* 108:371–372.

Woodward, A. S. 1931. "On the Broken Hill skull." *Illustrated London News* 159:682–685.

Wright, J. D. 2001. "The Indonesian valve." *Nature* 411 (6834): 142–143.

Wrinn, P. J. Forthcoming. "Reanalysis of the Pleistocene archaeofauna from Mugharet el 'Aliya, Tangier, Morocco: Implications for the Aterian." In R. Miller, ed., *Actes du XIVième Congrès de l'Union Internationale des Sciences Préhistoriques et Protohistoriques, Liège, 2001.*

Wrinn, P. J. and W. J. Rink. 2003. "ESR dating of tooth enamel from Aterian levels at Mugharet el 'Aliya (Tangier, Morocco)." *Journal of Archaeological Science* 30 (1): 123–133.

Wu Rukang. 1985. "New Chinese *Homo erectus* and recent work at Zhoukoudian." In E. Delson, ed., *Ancestors: The hard evidence.* New York: Alan R. Liss, pp. 245–248.

Wurz, S. 1999. "The Howieson's Poort backed artefacts from Klasies River: An argument for symbolic behavior." *South African Archaeological Bulletin* 54 (169): 38–50.

Wurz, S. 2002. "Variability in the Middle Stone Age lithic sequence 115,000–60,000 years ago at Klasies River, South Africa." *Journal of Archaeological Science* 29 (9): 1001–1015.

Wurz, S., P. Van Peer, N. le Rouz, S. Gardner, and H. J. Deacon. 2005. "Continental patterns in stone tools: A technological and biplot-based comparison of early Late Pleistocene assemblages from Northern and Southern Africa." *African Archaeological Review* 22 (1): 1–24.

Wynn, T. and F. L. Coolidge. 2004. "The expert Neandertal mind." *Journal of Human Evolution* 46 (4): 467–487.

Yellen, J. E. 1996. "Behavioural and taphonomic patterning at Katanda 9: A Middle Stone Age site, Kivu Province, Zaire." *Journal of Archaeological Science* 23 (6): 915–932.

Yellen, J. E. 1998. "Barbed bone points: Tradition and continuity in Saharan and sub-Saharan Africa." *African Archaeological Review* 15:173–198.

Yellen, J. E., A. S. Brooks, E. Cornelissen, M. J. Mehlman, and K. Stewart. 1995. "A Middle Stone Age worked bone industry from Katanda, Upper Semliki Valley, Zaire." *Science* 268 (5210): 553–556.

Yellen, J., A. Brooks, D. Helgren, M. Tappen, S. Ambrose, R. Bonnefille, J. Feathers, et al. 2005. "The Archaeology of Aduma Middle Stone Age Sites in the Awash Valley, Ethiopia." *Paleoanthropology* 3:25–100. http://www.paleoanthro.org.

Young, D. 1992. *The discovery of evolution.* Cambridge: Cambridge University Press.

Zilhão, J. 2000. "Fate of the Neandertals." *Archaeology* 53 (4): 24–31.

Zilhão, J. 2001. Anatomically archaic, behaviourally modern: The last Neanderthals and their destiny. 23rd Kroon-Voordracht lecture, Amsterdam's Archeologisch Centrum van de Universiteit van Amsterdam.

Zilhão, J. and F. D'Errico. 1999. "The chronology and taphonomy of the earliest Aurignacian and its implications for the understanding of Neandertal extinction." *Journal of World Prehistory* 13 (1): 1–69.

Zischler, H., H. Geisert, A. von Haeseler, and S. Pääbo. 1995. "A nuclear 'fossil' of the mitochondrial D-loop and the origin of modern humans." *Nature* 378 (5556): 489–492.

Zollikofer, C. E., M. S. Ponce de Leon, D. E. Lieberman, F. Guy, D. Pilbeam, A. Likius, H. T. Mackay, P. Vignaud, and M. Brunet. 2005. "Virtual cranial reconstruction of *Sahelanthropus tchadensis.*" *Nature* 434 (7034): 755–759.

Zubrow, E. 1989. "The demographic modeling of Neanderthal extinction." In P. Mellars and C. Stringer, eds., *The human revolution.* Princeton, NJ: Princeton University Press, pp. 212–231.

Index

About the Author

Pamela R. Willoughby is associate professor of anthropology at the University of Alberta in Edmonton, Alberta, Canada. She was born in Kingston, Ontario, Canada, and received a BA (honors) degree from Trent University in 1974, an MA from the University of Alberta in 1976, and a PhD from UCLA in 1985, all in anthropology. Willoughby is a Palaeolithic archaeologist and palaeoanthropologist and is a specialist on African Stone Age prehistory. Her other academic interests focus on lithic analysis, the history of archaeological thought, African prehistory, and the study of human evolution.

During her career, Willoughby has participated in archaeological field projects in Canada and many parts of Africa. Since 1989, she has carried out field research in southern Tanzania, specifically in the Mbeya and Iringa regions. This involves documenting archaeological sites of all periods ranging from the Acheulian through the Iron Age into the historic period. Her research began just as geneticists and geochronologists began to stress the role of Africa in the emergence of anatomically modern humans. As a result, the focus of Willoughby's fieldwork soon became the Middle and Later Stone Age and the transition between the two. This is said to be associated with the appearance of the first truly modern people and is the focus of this book.

Since 1994, Willoughby has been editor of *Nyame Akuma*, the official biannual field research bulletin of the Society of Africanist Archaeologists. From 2001 to 2003, she was also a distinguished lecturer for Sigma Xi, the Scientific Research Society, and had the opportunity to introduce a number of general science audiences to current debates on issues of early human evolution and modern human origins.